Undocumented Windows™

ANDREW SCHULMAN
DAVID MAXEY
MATT PIETREK

Series Editor:

Andrew Schulman

Addison-Wesley Publishing Company

Reading, Massachusetts Menlo Park, California
New York Don Mills, Ontario Wokingham, England
Amsterdam Bonn Sydney Singapore Tokyo Madrid
San Juan Paris Seoul Milan Mexico City Taipei

Many of the designations used by manufacturers and sellers to distinguish their products are claimed as trademarks. Where those designations appear in this book and Addison-Wesley was aware of the trademark claim, the designations have been printed in initial capital letters.

The author and publisher have taken care in preparation of this book, but make no expressed or implied warranty of any kind and assume no responsibility for errors or omissions. No liability is assumed for incidental or consequential damages in connection with or arising out of the use of the information or programs contained herein.

Library of Congress Cataloging-in-Publication Data

Schulman, Andrew.
    Undocumented Windows : a programmer's guide to reserved Microsoft Windows API functions / by Andrew Schulman, David Maxey, and Matt Pietrek.
        p.   cm.
    Includes index.
    ISBN 0-201-60834-0
    1. Windows (Computer programs) 2. Microsoft Windows (Computer program) I. Maxey, David. II. Pietrek, Matt. III. Title.
QA76.76.W56S38 1992
005.4'3--dc20   92-14831
                                                                   CIP

Series Editor: Andrew Schulman
Managing Editor: Amorette Pedersen
Production Editor: Andrew Williams
Line drawings: Jennifer Noble
Set in 10.5-point ITC Galliard by Benchmark Productions

3 4 5 6-ARM-96959493
Third printing, December 1993

Thanks to Phar Lap for providing the foundation on which we based the graphics.

CONTENTS

CHAPTER 5 KERNEL: Windows System Services 189

CHAPTER 6 USER: Microsoft Windows User Interface 399

PREFACE

Welcome to the exciting world of Windows internals!

Most Windows programming books, even the good ones, have a certain predictability: you know in advance what topics are going to be covered and what the code will look like. Open the book to a random page, and you'll find calls to TextOut(), BeginPaint(), and other familiar Windows functions.

We feel confident that, if nothing else, the contents of this book will surprise most Windows programmers. Open the book to a random page, and the chances are good that you will find something you've never seen before. The topics covered—walking task lists, disassembling Windows functions, treating HWNDs as pointers, seeing what interrupts WinExec generates, shifting atom handles right by 2, and so on—are important aspects of Windows programming, but have been neglected in most treatments of the subject. Furthermore, even the "look" of our code is different: you see main() instead of WinMain(), printf() instead of TextOut(), and tiny functions that handle a single message, instead of massive fourteen-page switch statements.

Why Undocumented Windows?

We might as well tell you that, at first, at least one of us did not want to do this book. For sure, we wanted to do a book on Windows programming. We had just finished the book *Undocumented DOS*, and were looking forward to working for a change with a nice, clean, documented interface: the Windows API.

What happened was that, almost immediately, we stumbled into the problem of undocumented Windows. At work, one of the authors needed to look at some commercial Windows programs, and kept running into calls to functions that weren't documented in the Windows Software Development Kit (SDK), the Device Driver Kit (DDK), or even in Microsoft's "Open Tools" material. Mainstream Windows programs were calling functions like GlobalMasterHandle(), GetHeapSpaces(), and SetInternalWindowPos(), that just weren't documented anywhere. Weird!

Well, not so weird. The experience of working on *Undocumented DOS* didn't leave us completely unprepared for the possibility that Windows too, despite the relative newness of its first usable version (3.0, May 1990), would already have "insider" knowledge and undocumented functions.

We also began to see a lot of scattered notes about undocumented Windows flying around networks like CompuServe and Usenet. As with undocumented DOS, the randomness of these notes was bothersome. For example, someone would see that some Microsoft program was calling InitTask(). Hmm, InitTask() isn't in WINDOWS.H! Aha, they would say, here's the "smoking gun": proof that Microsoft uses undocumented functions and that the FTC ought to do something about it. A few messages later, it would turn out that InitTask() is part of the startup code used by every Windows program in existence. Anyhow, it quickly became clear that it would be good to systematize all of this, and turn out a standard document on undocumented Windows.

Almost two years later, here it is. *Undocumented Windows* is about as complete as possible for the *core* of Windows: KERNEL, USER, and GDI. This book systematically covers undocumented functions, data structures, and messages in Windows 3.0 and 3.1, retail and debug versions, in Standard and Enhanced mode. In addition, we cover various undocumented aspects of documented functions and messages, such as the true meaning of InSendMessage()'s return value, or the wParam for WM_NCPAINT.

In other words, it took an entire book just to cover KERNEL, USER, and GDI. There is another entire low-level area, some of it undocumented and some of it just very obscurely documented, that includes DPMI, virtual device drivers (VxDs), the Virtual Machine Manager (VMM), INT 2Fh and other software-interrupt services provided by Windows, device drivers, the Windows DOS extenders, file formats, WinDebug, Windows' interactions with TSRs and memory managers, the SmartDrive interfaces, and so on, that requires an entire separate book. (Yes, we're working on it! We're thinking of calling it *Dirty Windows*.)

Most of the work on this book was done during the two-year reign of Windows 3.0 (some might call this period Life Under the UAE). Some of the functions that were undocumented in 3.0 become documented in 3.1. "Became"? Actually, this happened because of mounting pressure on Microsoft to document some of the key functions that many commercial developers were using anyhow. That some of these functions have been documented in 3.1 underlines, rather than undermines, the usefulness of this material: if, as the record shows, some of the most useful undocumented functions are eventually going to be documented by Microsoft, you might as well use them *now*. Think of it as a way to get a two-year jump on your more stodgy competition.

What's In This Book?

If you're looking at someone else's copy of this book, hopefully it will simply fall open to "the good parts." If not, here are some of the parts we're most pleased with:

- How to be a "drag and drop" server in 3.1 *and* *3.0* (See DragObject() in chapter 6.)
- Where are the five famous DCs? (See DCE in chapter 6.)
- How are atoms managed? (See Atom Table in chapter 5.)
- How do all the different Windows handles (tasks, instances, modules, PSP/PDB, task queues) relate? And, given one type of handle, how do I derive another? (See the introduction to chapter 5.)
- What does an HWND point to? (See WND in chapter 6.)
- What does an HDC point to? (See DC in chapter 8.)
- What are those [compatibility] flags in Windows 3.1? (See GetAppCompat-Flags() in chapter 5.)
- What exactly is the "free system resources" problem, and how did USER's local heaps change from Windows 3.0 to 3.1? (See the introduction to chapter 6).
- Where do messages go? (See the Task Queue in chapter 5, and the System Message Queue in chapter 6.)
- What does WinExec() return? (See chapter 5.)

Actually, there's a lot more than this, but this list provides some idea of the questions that this book answers.

What Handles Point To

Of course, some of these undocumented functions, messages, and data structures can—if used in accordance with the safety and hygiene tips in chapter 1—be incorporated into Windows programs. Beyond this, however, really what we hope this book provides is *understanding*.

In the sense we mean it, "understanding" almost seems like a dirty word in Windows programming circles. The phrase "you can use a handle without knowing what it points to" is repeated so often, it has become the mantra of Windows programming. Like any mantra, it is best repeated without thinking too carefully about its implications.

In this book, we tell you what handles point to. For example, an HTASK, such as GetWindowTask() returns and EnumTaskWindows() expects, is the segment (selector) portion of a far pointer to the Task Database. Can you use an HTASK without knowing what a Task Database is? Absolutely. Usually you *should* use an HTASK without worrying about what it actually points to. But in some cases, knowing how Windows' internal data structures really look can yield crucial techniques. As an example, check out HANDLES.H and HANDLES.C in the introduction to chapter 5.

More important, while "knowing and forgetting" is a good educational technique, "not knowing" isn't. Knowing what a Task Database is, and then choosing to forget this when working with an HTASK, is completely different from the being utterly *clueless* about what an HTASK is.

At its extreme, the whole "you can use a handle without knowing what it points to" abstraction encourages a state of deliberate cluelessness. This works okay in the short run, but it also has the danger of producing programmers who program without understanding, capable only of cautiously cut-and-pasting code fragments from Petzold's book and the SDK examples. This is the Windows-specific version of what one recent engineering textbook describes as "programmers who lack a clear understanding of how or why their programs make real things happen." Abstractions and interfaces are a crucial engineering discipline, but:

> The abstractions work sufficiently well now that our curricula (and, for that matter, our job descriptions) accommodate specialists whose understanding of computer systems is cripplingly incomplete. We confer computer science degrees on theorists who may be helpless when programming is required, on hardware designers to whom the high-level structure of the system to which they contribute is a mystery, and on programmers who lack a clear understanding of how or why their programs make real things happen. Often what passes for technical breadth takes the form of multiple specialties: Students exhibit pockets of local facility, unable to connect them into an effective understanding of the system as a whole. Such people can and do perform useful functions, but their potential for creativity is limited by their acceptance of the boundaries of their specialties. They shy from the challenge to venture beyond familiar approaches, to reshape problems, to develop new interfaces and revise existing ones; they accept the mysterious rather than unveiling it, over-sensitized to their own limitations. They are, in effect, imprisoned by the abstractions they have been taught.
>
> Outstanding students, in contrast, somehow develop a perspective that illuminates the interfaces between technologies, rather than the technologies themselves, as the most important structural elements of their discipline. They view the interfaces with respect but not reverence; they examine both sides of an abstraction, treating it as an object of study rather than a boundary between the known and the intractably mystical (Stephen A. Ward and Robert H. Halstead, Jr., *Computation Structures*, Cambridge MA: MIT Press, 1990).

Sound familiar? If Windows programmers are to go beyond the state of fearful cut-and-pasting, of using massive switch statements because that's what the SDK examples do, and of blindly following by rote all the other nasty and unnecessary practices put forward in the SDK, it will be helpful if they examine what's on the other sound of the boundary between a HANDLE on the one hand, and a real, live data structure on the other.

Doesn't this go against the whole notion of encapsulation, black boxes, and "information hiding"? These are absolutely crucial tried-and-true engineering principles, yet they seem to dictate that everything be done on a "need to know" basis; it would follow, then, that system internals, such as we present them in this book, are one type of thing you should definitely not need to know, maybe even that it's bad to know them.

It's absolutely true that encapsulation, black boxes, and information hiding are good things. None of us could get anything done if *nothing* was hidden from us, if *everything* was documented. (Jorge Luis Borges has a beautiful story, "Funes the Memorious," on this very theme.) In many ways, we wish the designers of the Windows API had done *more* to hide what goes on in the internals of Windows. For example, why should programmers have to mess with MakeProcInstance()? This could, and should, have been hidden from us! Much of the mechanics of Windows could have been hidden behind higher-level programming interfaces. As the WINIO library presented in chapter 4 shows, one can present programmers with a simple, familiar interface like printf( ), and still have it internally "do the right thing."

But, as with everything else, there is a price paid for hiding system internals. Jeff Duntemann, in an article on "The Tragedy of the Black Box" (*Dr. Dobb's Journal*, December 1991) has noted what the price is: "my lack of understanding of the hidden parts of the system cripples my understanding of those parts of the system that I can see." As Jeff points out, this is particularly true when the "black box" isn't complete, and you have to tinker with the system.

At times, even Microsoft itself seems to understand that the idea of programming on a "need to know" basis doesn't work. For example, the Windows SDK includes the source code for the default window procedure, DefWindowProc( ). With this code, you can see what default handling Windows provides for different messages. As a consequence, the default window procedure is one of the few really well-understood parts of the Windows API. As another example, the DDK includes source code for many of the drivers that come with Windows; even just browsing through this code gives you a much better feel for what Windows does.

Anyone who has ever traced through a Windows API routine in CVW or Soft-ICE/Windows will know what we're talking about here. One aim of this book is simply to provide a lot more information on what Windows looks like "inside," and (especially in chapters 1-4) to provide guidance on how to go about exploring its internals on your own. Programmers necessarily construct mental models of the systems they work on; needless to say, it helps if this model actually reflects reality in some way.

What's on the Disk?

As with *Undocumented DOS*, the disk accompanying this book is not just a carbon copy of the source code that appears in the book. Of course, all the sample programs from the KERNEL, USER, and GDI chapters are here, but there are also many ready-to-run utilities. For example:

- MAPWIN (chapter 2) displays the names of Windows API functions called by a program or DLL, and the names of functions provided by DLLs.

- EXEUTIL (chapter 2) shows what *undocumented* Windows API functions a program or DLL uses.
- RESDUMP (chapter 3) displays an textual representation of the resources (dialog boxes, menus, string tables, accelerator tables, and so on) in a Windows program or DLL.
- CALLFUNC (chapter 4) is a Windows interpreter that provides instant access to Windows API calls: to try out a function call, you can just type it in, without having to write or compile a program.
- SNOOP (chapter 4) is a message "spy" that focuses on undocumented messages and on the behavior of the Windows built-in window procedures.
- WISPY (I Spy for Windows; chapter 4) is a protected-mode interrupt interceptor that logs the interrupts in a window.
- ATOMWALK (chapter 5) displays every atom in every atom table on the system.
- WINMOD and WINTASK (chapter 5) provide detailed information about modules and tasks.
- USERWALK (chapter 6) and GDIWALK (chapter 8) provide detailed information about USER's and GDI's local heaps, and of USER and GDI objects such as WNDs and DCs.
- CORONER (chapter 10) is a postmortem analyzer, similar to Dr. Watson and WinSpector.

For reasons of space, some of these utilities do not come with source code. However, there is enough depth to some of these programs that you will be able to use them for quite some time, without worrying about source. By time you do want the source, our forthcoming book on building Windows tools, *The DOS Programmer's Guide to Windows*, will hopefully be out. We're really not practicing "information hiding" here; we just ran out of room!

Most of these utilities are written using the WINIO library, which also comes on the accompanying disk, as .LIB files for Borland C++ and Microsoft C/C++.

There are several general-purpose header files, such as HANDLES.H (with HANDLES.C, for KERNEL data structures), USEROBJ.H, and GDIOBJ.H.

Who Are You?
You will get more out of this book if you know the C programming language than if you don't. All the source code is compatible with Borland C++ 3.0 and 3.1, and with Microsoft C 6.0 and Microsoft C/C++ 7.0. On the other hand, almost everything here is applicable to other languages, including Turbo Pascal for Windows (TPW) and Visual Basic (VB). The bibliography recommends several books that you can use to bridge the gap between, say, our C-centric explanation of GetHeapSpaces() in *Undocumented Windows* and what you would have to do to call GetHeapSpaces() in TPW or VB.

Obviously, it will also aid your understanding of this book if you are familiar with the *documented* Windows API. It would be difficult to fully appreciate

GlobalMasterHandle(), for example, if you've never used GlobalAlloc(). On the other hand, DOS programmers with only a smattering of Windows experience may find that, seen from the angle of *Undocumented Windows*, Windows programming is a little more interesting, and more open and accessible, than they first suspected. If you liked mucking around in undocumented DOS, you're going to love Windows, because Windows is a much bigger mess than plain-vanilla DOS ever was.

For Windows "power users" who do not consider themselves programmers, there are a few parts of this book that might prove interesting. For example, check out the discussion of [compatibility] flags in chapter 5's section on GetAppCompatFlags(), or the dissection of Task Manager in chapter 3. Several of the utilities on disk should be useful to someone who likes to go Easter Egging in Windows.

What Versions of Windows?

As noted earlier, our goal here is to cover KERNEL, USER, and GDI in Windows 3.0, 3.1, retail and debug versions, in Standard and Enhanced mode.

In other words: *no real mode*! This book simply assumes that Windows 3.0 real mode doesn't exist. Certainly, it ought never to have existed. Unlike many other Windows programming books that are revisions of earlier books written during the bad old days of Windows 2.x, this is an entirely new book and is not carrying around any baggage from real mode. The assumption throughout is that Windows is a protected-mode DOS extender. If, for whatever reason, you feel that Windows 3.0 real mode is important, you are not going to be happy with us. Nor is there much here on Windows versions prior to 3.0.

On the other hand, we think that version 3.0 is still quite important. Just because 3.1 is out doesn't mean that 3.0 has fallen off the face of the earth. Remember, it was almost two years from the release of 3.0 to the release of 3.1; there are a lot of copies of 3.0 out there, still in use. Compatibility with 3.0 Standard and Enhanced modes is important. In some cases, we show how to implement a new 3.1 feature on top of 3.0.

Looking to the future, how about Win32 and NT (New Technology)? It's important to separate the two: the Win32 API is the future of Windows programming, yet NT seems as if it will be a niche product (how many of your customers have been clamoring for C2-level security and the ability to run on RISC processors?). One future product that seems like a winner is Win32s, Microsoft's planned "subset" of Win32 that will run right on top of Windows 3.1. The Win32 API is mentioned in various places throughout this book. In some cases, functions and messages that were undocumented in 3.x are documented in Win32. At the same time, even some documented features of Windows, such as the selector-manipulation functions, will not be supported in Win32. In particular, it seems that ToolHelp will not be part of Win32.

Speaking of ToolHelp, it is a crucial part of this book. With ToolHelp, Microsoft has opened up Windows a little to provide an interface to Windows 3.0 and 3.1 internals. ToolHelp does not provide access to the actual data structures used by Windows, but to a (largely read-only) layer above them. For example, a ToolHelp TASKENTRY structure is not identical to a Task Database, and changing fields in a TASKENTRY will not alter the behavior of any tasks. But in many cases, ToolHelp does the job, and should be used wherever possible instead of the actual undocumented data structures. Chapter 10 of this book is devoted to ToolHelp, and is far more extensive than the chapter on ToolHelp that Microsoft provides in the 3.1 SDK *Programmer's Reference.*

There is no contradiction between using ToolHelp and using undocumented Windows: in fact, they can work quite well together in the same program. There are many examples throughout the book of using ToolHelp, and then dropping down to undocumented Windows (the actual data structures) when the layering ToolHelp provides is not adequate.

How Did We Find This Stuff Out?

Something almost everyone asks us is, "How did you find this stuff out?" Chapters 1 through 4 of this book are really an extended answer to that question. To start with, Microsoft doesn't do very much to hide undocumented functions. The new executable (NE) format used by Windows is almost designed to expose the names of undocumented functions. We started reverse engineering using the tools Microsoft provides, such as EXEHDR and CodeView for Windows (CVW). We gradually built better tools for exploring Windows, many of which are on the accompanying disk. Other tools we built became a new product, Windows Source, available from V Communications. When Nu-Mega's Soft-ICE/Windows came out, we greedily pounced on that. Finally, we built several disassemblers of our own which we found very handy, but which are not yet quite ready for prime time.

Beta versions of the Windows 3.1 SDK came with debug versions of Windows with complete CV debug symbol tables; coupled with a disassembler such as Windows Source that can use CV symbol tables, this helped tremendously. Unfortunately, these complete symbol tables were stripped down in the final release of the 3.1 SDK.

In addition to reverse engineering, we also tried to find as much information as we could in sources like old Windows 2.x documentation, header files that come with the DDK, and the Win32 API.

Acknowledgments

But really, the way we found out much of what's in this book, was with a lot of help from our friends. The following were especially helpful in helping us over the rough spots:

Len Berk, John "Knuckles" Benfatto (Phar Lap), Paul Bonneau (Windows/DOS Developer's Journal), Ralf Brown, Ron Burk (Windows/DOS Developer's Journal), Geoff Chappell, Bob Chiverton, Alan Cobb, Thuan-Tit Ewe (Metaware), Michael Geary, Frank Grossman (Nu-Mega Technologies), Brad Kingsbury (Symantec), David Lection, Bill Lewis (Qualitas), Ron Mann (Praxsys), Mike Maurice, Darren Miclette (IBM WIN-OS/2), Robert Moote (Phar Lap), Duncan Murdoch, Dan Norton, Andrew Pargeter, Jeroen Pluimers, Jeff Richter, Art Rothstein, Enrique Salem (Symantec), Brett Salter (Periscope), Michael Shiels, Richard Smith (Phar Lap), Victor

Stone (Borland), Phil Taylor (Borland), Frank Van Gilluwe (V Communications), and Jonathan Zuck.

Also, there are a surprisingly large number of people who, for one reason or another, prefer to remain anonymous. All we can say is, thanks!

Our literary agent, Claudette Moore, got this book started.

The staff at Benchmark Productions and Addison-Wesley, especially Andrew Williams, Amy Pedersen, Jennifer Noble, Chris Williams, and Abby Cooper, made sure this book got out.

This book could not have been produced without the CompuServe Information Service. Practically all work on this book occurred over CompuServe. However, there's no need to formally express our indebtedness to CIS, because our monthly credit-card bills already reflect this.

Andrew Schulman: During the long period that I was working on *Undocumented Windows*, my employers at Phar Lap Software showed unusual forbearance and support. Considering how much this book cut into my work, Richard Smith, John "Knuckles" Benfatto, and Robert Moote were absurdly understanding and supportive. My coworkers, particularly Rob Adams, Andre Sant'Anna, Diego Escobar, Karl Kinsella, Maria Vetrano, and Alan Convis, helped with this book in various ways.

Trudy Neuhaus and Neil Rubenking at *PC Magazine* helped immensely with a two-part series on undocumented Windows that, much transformed, eventually became chapter 1. Trudy has put up with intolerable delays in other articles because of this book. Thanks!

Gretchen Bilson at *Microsoft Systems Journal* and Jon Erickson at *Dr. Dobb's Journal* were also incredibly understanding about delays caused by this book.

Above all, I want to thank Ray Valdes, Ray Duncan, Claudette Moore, Pete Olympia, Randy Wallin, Jon Udell, and Tony Rizzo, for providing opportunities and encouragement over the years.

Especially during the last few months of working on this project, my son Matthew and my wife Amanda Claiborne put up with me in various ways. Thanks ! In spite of obstacles put in her way by this book, Amanda has won a Mellon Fellowship at Brandeis. Matthew's fifth birthday is approaching, and he is nearing completion on his initiation into the Teenage Mutant Ninja Turtles. Cowabunga, dude!

David Maxey: I particularly want to acknowledge the contribution of my family, for being so tolerant of the empty place at the dinner table, and especially of my wife, who stood in for me in my role as a normally functioning human being.

Matt Pietrek: I would like to thank my wife, April, and my "boys," Gunther and Theodore, for letting me work the many nights and weekends that this book required. I would also like to extend thanks to my coworkers, especially E.S., E.B, and P.E. [The editor feels obligated to point out that the said "boys" are in fact two dachshunds.]

Andrew Schulman (CIS 76320,302; andrew@pharlap.com)
David Maxey (CIS 70401,3057)
Matt Pietrek (CIS 76117,1720)
June 1992

CHAPTER ■ 1

This Was Not Supposed to Happen

A key goal of Microsoft Windows is to be more orderly than MS-DOS. DOS is a "house of cards," with memory-resident (TSR) programs, device drivers, disk caches, memory managers, DOS extenders, networks, and multitasking environments (such as Windows itself) all competing for control of your machine. From the software developer's perspective, Windows often looks a lot saner. It provides a wide-ranging and seemingly all-inclusive collection of services—such as protected mode, multitasking, dynamic linking, window management, and graphics—that plain-vanilla DOS doesn't offer. Often, Windows lets developers concentrate on making a program do what it is supposed to do rather than on the underhanded shenanigans—including the use of undocumented system functions—that are necessary to create a great DOS application.

For example, since Windows 3.x runs applications in protected mode, you no longer need to worry about expanded memory, overlays, or other methods for shoehorning software into 640K. As with any other protected-mode DOS extender (which is largely what Windows is), the 640K limit is gone, and along with it a whole class of DOS programming problems.

Another example is TSR (terminate and stay resident) programming. To write a robust TSR, you must use undocumented DOS functions; you simply have no choice. But in the multitasking Windows environment, all applications are *automatically* memory-resident, so the problem of writing TSRs disappears. (This holds for Windows applications only; if you want to write DOS TSRs that behave properly under Windows, you actually have an *additional* set of worries.) Furthermore, dynamic linking in Windows largely (though not entirely) eliminates the need for programs to hook interrupts to provide services to other programs.

The most visible contrast between Windows orderliness and DOS messiness is in graphics programming. DOS doesn't provide services for doing graphical or even full-screen character-mode programs such as a spreadsheet, word processor, or CAD programs. The ROM BIOS video services that do exist are too slow. Consequently, most major PC commercial applications write directly to video memory, program the video controller, and generally perform various low-level, exotic dances with the video hardware. Windows, on the other hand, makes these sorts of tricks unnecessary—and, in fact, pretty much forbids them—by providing a relatively device-independent collection of graphics functions, with moderately acceptable performance, that Windows applications politely call.

The idea of "undocumented Windows," then, is really somewhat alarming. Using undocumented functions is *exactly* the sort of problem Windows was supposed to solve! Making use of functions that Microsoft has implemented but not documented fits in perfectly with the free-wheeling style of DOS, but it seems to contradict the entire spirit and purpose of Windows. By providing an API much more extensive and capable than DOS's, Windows is supposed to make such low-level tricks unnecessary.

In much the same way that high-level programming languages are supposed to shield programmers from having to know assembly language or understand microprocessor architecture, the Windows API is supposed to shield programmers from low-level tricks. This intent is a little amusing, because the Windows API itself is so low-level that it is notorious for requiring eighty lines of code to spell "hello world!" on the display. But these eighty lines of code *are* in fact quite high level in that they should work on any machine that can run Windows, including machines that are not fully PC-compatible, such as Japanese NEC computers.

That high-level coding is one of the key principles of Windows is spelled out nicely in the text of a Microsoft invitation to a Windows hardware-engineering conference:

> Why focus on Windows PCs?
> Because Microsoft Windows creates the opportunity for PC hardware vendors to innovate freely when designing new systems and subsystems. Windows, unlike the MS-DOS standard that preceded it, leaves open the door to engineering innovation by shielding the software writer from any need to write directly to the hardware. Any personal computer capable of running Windows smoothly can support all of the software written to the Windows application programming interface (API). As a result, the engineering focus has shifted. In the new Windows world, it's hardware innovation and performance that count, not hardware conformance. ("Windows Hardware Engineering Conference," 1-3 March 1992, Advance Invitation).

Wouldn't it be great if Windows could really shift the engineering focus? By writing only to the documented Windows API, we could let Windows move us to radically improved platforms. Intel wouldn't be happy about it, perhaps, but if everyone played by the rules and wrote to the documented Windows API, Microsoft might even be able to move us, our code, and our customers to advanced RISC architectures and away from the ugly world of segments, IBM compatibility, MS-DOS compatibility, and all the other boring little issues that loom so large today.

In other words, one of the key ideas behind Windows is that developers should write to the Windows API and to that alone (note that this API does at present include at least some INT 21h DOS calls). Unless you're writing a Windows device driver, you don't do any low-level coding. You certainly don't make any undocumented Windows calls or rely on knowledge about internal Windows data structures. That would just be resurrecting the evils of MS-DOS!

But how likely a scenario is this? How many commercial Windows applications can really "play by the rules" and still be marketable, with decent performance and with the features users expect? The idea that the Windows API can totally replace low-level coding seems, unfortunately, no more reasonable than the idea that C++ can totally replace assembly language—in other words, not very reasonable at all.

Actually, the idea that Windows shields programmers from low-level complexity is a bit of a sham. Most Windows programmers would probably agree that you *must* be intimately familiar with the Intel machine architecture (particularly the stack) to be a really good Windows applications developer; in DOS you can get away without such knowledge for a fairly long time. One programmer reports that it was not until he started doing Windows that he ever had occasion to use assembly language or to examine his compiler's startup code. Portable? High level? Huh?

What we will see in this chapter is that key commercial Windows applications, including Microsoft's own, use undocumented API calls. In some cases, these calls have since been documented by Microsoft, though only *after* developers went ahead and used them anyway, without Microsoft's blessing. In other words, real-world use of the Windows API has driven the documentation, rather than the other way around. Writing only to the documented Windows API sounds great, but it has failed in the real world.

What went wrong with the lovely notion of Windows programming without tricks, without low-level, nonportable code, without undocumented shenanigans? What went wrong, mostly, is that Windows succeeded. By winning the operating-system wars Windows is now paying the price of success: large numbers of programmers are banging on the system, and they need to make it do all sorts of things for which it was probably never intended.

The use of undocumented features, in other words, is the inevitable price of success. MS-DOS paid this price, and now Windows will. Interestingly, Windows too is now being called a "house of cards."

While solving many old problems, Windows has introduced a number of new problems. If you think about it, this is hardly surprising: to provide so much more functionality, the Windows API had to be that much "richer" than that of character-mode DOS; that richness, of course, introduces much more complexity and, hence, a number of entirely new programming problems.

For example, while Windows applications run in protected mode and can therefore enjoy multi-megabytes of memory, real-mode DOS has not gone away and probably won't go away anytime soon. Some Windows programs need access to device drivers, TSRs, network drivers, absolute memory locations, or even undocumented DOS functions and data structures. The Windows API, extensive though it is, fails to provide adequate functionality for communicating with real mode from a protected-mode Windows application. There are plenty of *undocumented* Windows functions, however, that do provide this needed functionality.

Another example: Instead of the asynchronous interrupts that many DOS applications have to worry about, events in Windows arrive in the form of properly behaved messages. This is a benefit to nonpreemptive multitasking; in fact, the requirement that a Windows application explicitly *ask* for its next message is what makes Windows multitasking nonpreemptive. Rather than hook INT 8 to get timer events, for instance, a Windows application uses the documented SetTimer() API call to politely ask for timer messages. Even such timer messages arrive synchronously only when the application asks for them by calling the GetMessage() function. But, well regulated though it may be, it is not the behavior that some applications need from a timer—or from other message sources, for that matter. Often an application needs to know about something as soon as it happens, even if it's in the middle of doing something else. Again, one solution is to use undocumented Windows API functions (in this case, the system-timer functions provided by SYSTEM).

In Windows 3.1, Microsoft has rightly made a big fuss over "drag and drop." It's a great feature. It was also provided in Windows 3.0 but used undocumented messages, data structures, and functions that only File Manager knew about. In 3.1, Microsoft documented an entirely new drag-and-drop protocol, but it still has not documented the original drag-and-drop protocol, which persists in 3.1, and which allows for the creation of both drag-and-drop clients and *servers*. Microsoft has not officially documented how to be a drag-and-drop *server*, and the publication of an excellent *Microsoft Systems Journal* article on that subject ("Drop Everything," by Jeff Richter) faced opposition from within the company. Chapters 6 and 7 of this book contain extensive discussions of how to be a drag-and-drop client or server in Windows 3.1 or 3.0.

We've been discussing new problems raised by Windows 3.0, but not every situation where a programmer might use an undocumented Windows function is entirely new. For example, just as DOS support for writing debuggers was until recently completely undocumented and is still incorrectly documented by Microsoft, existing Windows debuggers, such as Turbo Debugger for Windows (TDW), Multiscope, and Microsoft's own CodeView for Windows (CVW), all rely heavily on undocumented functions. With its "Open Tools" strategy (discussed later in this chapter) and its new ToolHelp library, Microsoft is making a genuine effort to document some of the key Windows interfaces needed to write debuggers and other Windows development tools. However, Windows debuggers, "spy" programs, memory browsers, and the like will probably continue to use undocumented Windows functions for some time.

For better or worse, Windows commercial application programming has a lot of the chaos and unruliness that one associates with DOS programming. This is not terribly surprising, considering that Windows is incredibly complex, and considering that, for the foreseeable future, it is an extension to, and not a replacement for, good old MS-DOS. The widespread use of undocumented functions in Windows applications is not a deplorable fall from grace either, but a healthy sign of vitality. Developers are *stretching* the system's capabilities. As the economist Joseph Schumpeter noted in a somewhat different context, "If the system was perfect, it wouldn't work." Bless this mess!

Backdoor Programming

Undocumented Windows API functions, messages, and data structures are just one part of the Windows programming netherworld. Other parts of this netherworld include

- The DOS Protected Mode Interface (DPMI)
- The Windows Device Driver Kit (DDK), in particular Enhanced mode Virtual Device Drivers (VxDs, or .386 files)
- The "Open Tools" materials provided by Microsoft to Independent Software Vendors (ISVs)
- The ToolHelp dynamic link library (made available in Windows 3.1 but also backward-compatible with Windows 3.0)

Windows is much more than simply the functions described in the WINDOWS.H header file that comes with the SDK and with SDK replacements such as Borland C++. WINDOWS.H does not come close to defining the extent of the Windows programming universe.

The interfaces listed above are of much wider interest than one might at first suspect. For example, the Microsoft Windows Device Driver Kit (DDK) should interest not just those few who are writing Windows device drivers. The DDK is the only place that Microsoft documents the INT 2Fh interface that Windows provides to applications running in the Enhanced mode DOS box. Because it is provided to the legions of DOS applications, this INT 2Fh interface is potentially of much wider interest than the Windows API itself, which is only directly accessible to Windows applications, not to DOS applications running under Windows.

Likewise, Enhanced mode "virtual device drivers" or VxDs (.386 files) are often really not device drivers at all. VxDs are the most powerful Windows applications one can write. Any time something looks impossible in Windows, it's often *trivial* to do from a tiny VxD. Some programmers even regard VxDs and the DDK as the "real" Windows API, and the higher-level functions documented in the SDK as mere window dressing, so to speak. VxDs may also be important in DOS 6.0.

Dynamic Linking Aids Snooping

So how does one go about finding undocumented Windows functions? Ironically, by using the very feature that makes Windows services better regulated, better documented, and quite simply less ad hoc than DOS services: *dynamic linking*. Whereas the MS-DOS API uses interrupt vectors (whose ultimate expression is the TSR), the Windows API uses dynamic linking (whose ultimate expression is the DLL, or dynamic link library).

Windows is not, as is frequently believed, made up of components such as Program Manager, Control Panel, and Task Manager. These are no more part of Windows than

COMMAND.COM is truly part of DOS; replacements such as the Norton Desktop for Windows (NDW) show, and even a cursory examination of the SHELL= statement in the SYSTEM.INI configuration file reveals, that these various managers are all dispensable.

Instead, Windows is made up of DLLs (dynamic link libraries). Three DLLs provide the core of the Windows API. In the earlier, unsuccessful real-mode versions of Windows, these three DLLs were spliced together into one file, but in version 3.0 and higher they are separate entities. They are

- KERNEL (system services—memory management, task management, dynamic links, etc., with three different versions of this module: KERNEL.EXE for the absurd Windows Real mode that disappeared in Windows 3.1, KRNL286.EXE for 286 machines or Standard mode, and KRNL386.EXE for 386 and higher processors)
- GDI (Graphical Device Interface services: works with a DISPLAY device driver such as VGA.DRV to display text, rectangles, etc.)
- USER (user interface services: creating windows, sending messages, etc.)

Of course, there are many other DLLs whose exported functions make up the Windows API. Some of these, such as WIN87EM.DLL, COMMDLG.DLL, and TOOLHELP.DLL, even have DLL filename extensions. Others, such as SYSTEM.DRV and KEYBOARD.DRV, are Windows device drivers; device drivers in Windows are simply DLLs under another name. In Windows 3.1 and in the Multimedia Extensions for Windows, the Control Panel is extensible via *.CPL files; these too are nothing more than DLLs. Even Windows *.FON font files are also just DLLs that export discardable, shareable, read-only data (resources) rather than code. Thus, aside from the one very confusing fact that this single type of file goes under such an assortment of different guises (EXE, DLL, DRV, CPL, FON, and so on), Windows is made up of DLLs.

An important aside: A "module" in Windows is not quite the same as a DLL. For example, we saw that the three DLLs, KERNEL.EXE, KRNL286.EXE, and KRNL386.EXE, are three different implementations of the Windows KERNEL module. Likewise, V7VGA.DRV and VGAMONO.DRV are two different implementations of the Windows DISPLAY module. The possible distinction between a DLL's or DRV's file name ("VGA.DRV") and its module name ("DISPLAY") is one of the underpinnings of Windows device-independence.

Even Windows programs (such as WINWORD.EXE or PROGMAN.EXE) are very similar to DLLs because both DLLs and Windows executables use the same "segmented-executable" file format that is a superset of the .EXE format used under DOS. Libraries (DLLs) *export* functions, and programs *import* these functions: that's what dynamic linking is. Windows programs are similar to DLLs in that, in addition to importing functions, they also export functions, which are "callbacks" to be used by Windows itself. In effect, Windows treats programs as though they were libraries. This upside-down quality causes Windows, a library of functions, to treat your program as though it, too, were a library, making this one of the most confusing aspects of Windows programming. Similarly, DLLs *import* functions too, using the services of other DLLs.

Given that the components of Windows itself (such as USER.EXE) and Windows programs (such as MYPROG.EXE) look almost the same, it is not surprising that an application can also provide its own DLLs that appear indistinguishable from the DLLs that come "built in" to Windows. Another way of saying this is that the built-in ones aren't all that built-in—aside from their special knowledge of undocumented functions and data structures, that is.

We will see in a few minutes (and chapter 2 of this book shows this in even more detail) that we can find, by mere inspection, the name of every function that a DLL exports. We can then see if a prototype for this function appears in WINDOWS.H. This gives us a rough idea of what's undocumented. More important, we can also find the name of every function that a Windows program imports. By then comparing this list against the list of documented functions, we can determine which programs use undocumented functions and thereby come up with a rough idea of which ones are important and genuinely useful.

The structure of segmented executable files makes it trivial, and almost enjoyable, to do this sort of exploration. Actual disassembly of code becomes important at a much later stage than it would in DOS. In other words, precisely because Windows is so much more orderly about the way that services are provided and used than plain-vanilla DOS ever was, it is very easy for us to see that maybe the Windows world isn't quite so orderly and well-regulated, after all.

Inside NDW

To reiterate, because of the way Windows works, Windows .EXE files are more structured than DOS .EXE (not to mention .COM) files. Windows dynamic linking makes it easy to see what API calls a Windows application might use, without running the program or even disassembling it.

Let's take as an example the Norton Desktop for Windows (NDW). Peter Norton first become a household name through his book, *Inside the IBM PC.* It's fitting then that we go "inside" NDW. The first release of NDW had some odd behavior and took too long to load, but NDW is easily the coolest collection of Windows utilities available; it is a must-have replacement for Window's own Program Manager, at least in Windows 3.0 (the File Manager in 3.1 definitely gives NDW a run for its money).

NDW is a collection of programs, such as NDW.EXE itself, SIW.EXE (System Information for Windows), SLEEPER.EXE (screen saver), NDDW.EXE (Norton Disk Doctor), and so on, plus several dynamic link libraries, such as NWIN.DLL, NDWDLL.DLL, and NDLL.DLL. Commercial Windows applications often use not only the KERNEL, GDI, and USER DLLs that come bundled with Windows, but also their own DLLs.

Of the many executable files that come with NDW, let's arbitrarily select one to examine in detail: NBWIN.EXE (Norton Backup for Windows). NBWIN.EXE, like all Windows programs, DLLs, and device drivers, is in Microsoft's segmented-executable (or "new executable," or simply NE) file format.

Microsoft C comes with a utility, EXEHDR, to inspect NE files; similarly Borland C++ comes with TDUMP. If we use TDUMP to examine NBWIN.EXE, we find, in the middle of many other details about the file, a list of the "modules" (DLLs and device drivers) whose services NBWIN directly uses:

```
C:\BORLANDC\BIN>tdump \ndw\nbwin.exe
...
Module Reference Table
  Module  1: NDWDLL
  Module  2: NDLL
  Module  3: NBWRES
  Module  4: NBWFD
  Module  5: NWIN
  Module  6: KERNEL
  Module  7: GDI
  Module  8: USER
  Module  9: KEYBOARD
```

TDUMP and EXEHDR can also tell us exactly which Windows API functions NBWIN (or any other Windows program, DLL, or device driver) uses. If you stop to think about it, such snooping capabilities are simply amazing. In MS-DOS, it is comparatively difficult to learn which software interrupts and functions a program uses; here, by seeing which Windows API functions a program uses (or at least which ones it references, which is not quite the same thing), we can do a high-level disassembly, without disassembling one line of code.

Unfortunately, the form in which TDUMP and EXEHDR present this material is not terribly useful. You wouldn't know it at first, but the following output from EXEHDR shows some of the Windows API functions used by NBWIN:

```
C:\BIN>exehdr /v \ndw\nbwin.exe
...
    PTR     0333   imp KERNEL.169
    PTR     010b   imp GDI.35
    PTR     0013   imp KERNEL.47
    PTR     00a8   imp USER.33
    PTR     017d   imp KERNEL.51
    PTR     009b   imp USER.36
    PTR     01e2   imp KERNEL.52
    PTR     02b0   imp USER.420
    PTR     00e4   imp GDI.45
    PTR     0089   imp USER.39
    PTR     0133   imp USER.40
```

In the module.ordinal format—such as KERNEL.169, USER.33, or GDI.35—the ordinal number is simply an identifier for a function exported by a given DLL. Windows functions almost always have names, which appear in DLLs as NULL-terminated

ASCII (ASCIIZ) strings such as "GETFREESPACE" or "STRETCHBLT," but programs or other DLLs that use these services generally reference them with the shorter module.ordinal form. Unfortunately, TDUMP and EXEHDR only show this short form, leaving it up to us to figure out what KERNEL.169 or GDI.35 is.

When running a utility such as TDUMP or EXEHDR on a Windows program like NBWIN.EXE, the program dumps out raw data that can be made useful by finding the ASCIIZ names that correspond to each module.ordinal import reference. We find these simply by running TDUMP or EXEHDR again, but this time on the DLLs that *export* the functions that the program *imports*.

For example, we can see in the EXEHDR output above that one section of NBWIN.EXE uses some functions from the Windows USER module. If we now examine USER.EXE with the EXEHDR utility, we see a list of every function that USER exports (unfortunately, it is not sorted in any way):

```
C:\BIN>exehdr \windows\system\user.exe
...
Library:        USER
Description:    Microsoft Windows User Interface
...
Exports:
ord seg offset name
465  14 03c6   DRAGDETECT exported, shared data
404   8 0296   GETCLASSINFO exported, shared data
175  12 0999   LOADBITMAP exported, shared data
 88  24 22e4   ENDDIALOG exported, shared data
500   1 558e   FARCALLNETDRIVER exported, shared data
272   1 1ac5   ISZOOMED exported, shared data
168   3 20bd   SETCARETBLINKTIME exported, shared data
147  38 015a   SETCLIPBOARDVIEWER exported, shared data
...
 40   1 59cc   ENDPAINT exported, shared data
...
```

In all, about 400 functions are listed in USER.EXE alone. Not surprisingly, if we examine this list, we will see plenty of functions that, from their names alone, sound useful, but that are not listed in the Windows *Programmer's Reference* or in the WINDOWS.H header file. These are usually, but not always, undocumented functions.

Let's not approach undocumented Windows from this angle, however. Rather than embark on an Easter egg hunt, trying to find every function exported from a DLL that doesn't happen to be listed in the *Programmer's Reference* or in WINDOWS.H, we can instead approach undocumented Windows from the perspective of existing commercial Windows applications that *use* undocumented functions. Otherwise, the search for undocumented functions can become more like collecting baseball cards and less like software engineering.

Examining the EXEHDR NBWIN output again, we can see that, for example, NBWIN imports USER.40. Looking next at the last line of the EXEHDR USER list of exports, we can see that ordinal #40 in the USER module corresponds to the function

ENDPAINT. Thus, we now know that EndPaint() is one of the Windows API functions called by NBWIN. This is hardly surprising, because it is almost impossible to produce any screen output in Windows without calling this documented function. But we could carry out this same import/export process for *every* module.ordinal referenced by NBWIN, or any other Windows program or executable, and produce a complete picture of the Windows services it uses. That is more interesting.

In fact, the picture that emerges is *extremely* interesting, but to do it this way would also be extremely boring. This is just the sort of work that a computer is good for! What we really need is a utility that prints out a list of all the Windows API functions that a program uses, silently doing all the work of matching up module.ordinal imports in one file with ASCIIZ name exports from another.

This utility is MAPWIN (provided on the accompanying disk), written by Richard Smith, president of Phar Lap Software. We could have saved ourselves a lot of work and simply used MAPWIN to begin with, instead of messing with EXEHDR and TDUMP. But it is informative to step through once "by hand," so to speak, the process that MAPWIN carries out automatically, so you can see where its results come from. For more details on MAPWIN, see chapter 2.

If we examine NBWIN.EXE with MAPWIN, we get a list of the Windows API calls, both documented and undocumented, that NBWIN makes. A portion of the output is shown below:

```
C:\BIN>mapwin @win30.imp \ndw\nbwin.exe
...
GETPROFILESTRING (KERNEL.58)
GETPROP (USER.25)
GETSELECTORBASE (KERNEL.186)
GETSTOCKOBJECT (GDI.87)
GETSUBMENU (USER.159)
GETSYSCOLOR (USER.180)
GETSYSTEMMENU (USER.156)
GETSYSTEMMETRICS (USER.179)
GETTEMPFILENAME (KERNEL.97)
GETTEXTEXTENT (GDI.91)
GETTEXTMETRICS (GDI.93)
GETTICKCOUNT (USER.13)
GETVERSION (KERNEL.3)
GETWINDOW (USER.262)
GETWINDOWLONG (USER.135)
GETWINDOWRECT (USER.32)
GETWINDOWTEXT (USER.36)
GETWINDOWWORD (USER.133)
GETWINFLAGS (KERNEL.132)
GLOBALADDATOM (USER.268)
GLOBALALLOC (KERNEL.15)
GLOBALCOMPACT (KERNEL.25)
GLOBALDOSALLOC (KERNEL.184)
GLOBALDOSFREE (KERNEL.185)
GLOBALFREE (KERNEL.17)
GLOBALHANDLE (KERNEL.21)
GLOBALLOCK (KERNEL.18)
```

```
GLOBALNOTIFY (KERNEL.154)
GLOBALREALLOC (KERNEL.16)
GLOBALUNLOCK (KERNEL.19)
GRAYSTRING (USER.185)
INFLATERECT (USER.78)
INITAPP (USER.5)
INITTASK (KERNEL.91)
INVALIDATERECT (USER.125)
INVERTRECT (USER.82)
ISDIALOGMESSAGE (USER.90)
...
```

In all, MAPWIN lists 238 different functions referenced by NBWIN.EXE. As is typical for Windows applications, a little over half the different functions used are in the USER (window manager) module, about a quarter are in the KERNEL (system services) module, and the remaining functions belong to other modules such as GDI (graphics) and KEYBOARD. NBWIN also uses some functions from the DLLs that come with the Norton Desktop.

Naturally, some functions used by NBWIN are also used by nearly every other Windows application in existence. Functions such as RegisterClass(), CreateWindow(), GetMessage(), and DefWindowProc(), for example, are essentially "boilerplate," part of the standard litany for creating a Windows application, and are called by 95% of all Windows programs (the other 5% can be extremely useful Windows utilities, however).

What we're interested in seeing are what *undocumented* features of Windows NBWIN might be using. We need to filter out every "standard" call made by NBWIN, that is, every function that appears either in the WINDOWS.H header file or in the Microsoft Windows *Programmer's Reference* or the *Guide to Programming*. (The *Guide to Programming* documents several important items intended to be used only in assembly language and therefore not included in the *Programmer's Reference*.) This topic is addressed in more detail in chapter 2 of this book. For now, we can simply say that if the documented calls are somehow filtered out, we're eventually left with seven items, referenced by Norton Backup for Windows but listed nowhere in the Windows 3.0 SDK manuals or header files. They are

__0040h (KERNEL.193)

GETHEAPSPACES (KERNEL.138)

GETSELECTORBASE (KERNEL.186)

INITAPP (USER.5)

INITTASK (KERNEL.91)

SETSELECTORBASE (KERNEL.187)

WAITEVENT (KERNEL.30)

It seems, then, that we have finally arrived at our subject: here are Windows API calls made by a major Windows application, produced by a firm known for producing robust, high-quality software, and not found anywhere in the Windows 3.0 SDK.

Open Tools: No Longer Undocumented Windows

Actually, we're not quite there yet. We first need to deal with the three functions Init-App(), InitTask(), and WaitEvent(). These sound interesting; what strange thing could NBWIN be doing?

Nothing very strange at all. Whenever you run MAPWIN, you will see these same three functions, for they are part of the standard Windows startup code, called from any and every Windows application in existence!

When writing Windows applications in C or C++, your program's perceived start of execution is at the WinMain() function, rather than at the standard main() function used everywhere else in the C world. This use of WinMain() rather than main() is totally unnecessary and should be regarded as a design flaw of the Windows API. Be that as it may, WinMain() is called with four arguments:

```
int PASCAL WinMain(HANDLE hInstance, HANDLE hPrevInstance,
    LPSTR lpszCmdLine, int nCmdShow)
```

Note the deliberate use of passive voice—"is called"—above. *Who* calls WinMain? WinMain() is not the true entry point for your program. Instead, the initial entry point is indicated, just as under plain-vanilla DOS, with an END statement in an assembly-language module. It is the startup code, provided with your compiler's run-time library, that provides this END statement and that sets things up for, and calls, WinMain(). On entry to a Windows program (DLLs operate differently), the CPU registers hold the following values:

BX   Stack size
CX   Heap size
DI   Instance handle (hIntance)
SI   Previous instance (hPrevInstance)
ES   Program segment prefix (PSP)

The question is, what happens between here and WinMain()? What happens is that the startup code provided by the compiler's run-time library calls InitTask(), WaitEvent(), and InitApp(). Although the Windows 3.0 SDK does not contain source-code for the startup module, Borland C++ does; if you have Borland C++, you can learn all about Windows startup by reading the nicely commented file \BORLANDC\EXAMPLES\STARTUP\C0W.ASM. (Microsoft C/C++ 7.0 includes startup source too.)

Even though the details of these three calls are probably of interest to only those working on a compiler with Windows support or to someone who has worked on implementing custom versions of the KERNEL and USER modules, the politics behind these three little function calls are rather interesting.

Until Windows 3.1, InitTask(), WaitEvent(), and InitApp() really were not documented anywhere in the Windows SDK. Thus, for years, every single Windows application contained three undocumented calls. This is bizarre because the SDK is really not part of Windows itself, and therefore it ought to have no more privileged a position than any other application or third-party development tool.

By not documenting these calls needed to take a Windows application from startup to WinMain(), and thereby allow it to actually *run* under Windows (talk about a crucial feature!), Microsoft's SDK for years had a near monopoly on the Windows development-tools market. This was particularly annoying because, other than this startup code, the SDK didn't bring much to the party. The Windows API functions are often referred to in third-party books as "Kit routines" or "SDK functions," but, as we've already noted, Windows dynamic linking means that these functions are actually part of the DLLs contained in every retail copy of Windows that someone buys off the shelf at Egghead; they are definitely *not* part of the SDK. The SDK, in other words, provides remarkably little other than the "secret sauce" of making a Windows program jump through the necessary hoops before it gets to WinMain().

Eventually someone at Microsoft must have figured out that although Microsoft makes some money from the SDK, the company as a whole does much better by sales of Windows itself. Therefore, it is in the interests of Microsoft to have excellent Windows development tools available, even if they compete with its own SDK and with its own C compiler.

The end result is what Microsoft calls the "Open Tools Strategy," an attempt to "level the playing field" in Windows development tools by making key pieces of previously undocumented information available to tools vendors, including direct competitors with Microsoft C and the SDK, such as Borland and Zortech/Symantec. An enormous three-ring binder of this material is available to "independent software vendors" (ISVs) by sending Internet mail to isv@microsoft.com. Much of this material has also been made available in the Windows 3.1 SDK, as articles in the "Overviews" manual.

The Open Tools binder provides information on the following previously undocumented topics:

- Windows Application Startup (how to call WinMain(): the InitApp(), InitTask(), and WaitEvent() functions)
- Windows Prologs and Epilogs (initialization of the DS register for callback functions)
- Windows 80x87 Floating Point Emulator (WIN87EM.DLL and OS fixups)
- Self-Loading Windows Applications (the PatchCodeHandle() function used by some versions of Microsoft Word for Windows and Microsoft Excel; see the description of PatchCodeHandle() in chapter 5 of this book).
- Creating Windows Hosted Debuggers (documents functions such as DirectedYield() and SetEventHook())
- Resource Formats within Executable Files (however, what about resource formats outside executable files, in the .RES files produced by the resource compiler?)
- Executable File Format (most of this has already been documented in OS/2 1.x, which uses the same segmented-executable NE file format as Windows)

- Object Module Format for Windows (in particular, IMPDEF and EXPDEF records, which form the link between an application's call to, for example, GetVersion() on the one hand, and module.ordinal pairs such as KERNEL.3 on the other; these .OBJ records are also documented in yet another obscure but useful Microsoft offering, the Microsoft C *Developer's Toolkit Reference.*)
- Library and Import Library Formats (structure of a Windows import library as produced by the IMPLIB utility)

Open Tools also helps underline the point that WINDOWS.H and the SDK do not define the full extent of the Windows universe. As another example of the same point—that there's much more to Windows than what's in WINDOWS.H and the SDK—it should also be noted that some Windows API functions that seem undocumented are actually described in the Windows Device Driver Kit (DDK).

There is a tendency among those exploring undocumented Windows to jump to the conclusion that anything not in WINDOWS.H is therefore undocumented, and there is a sentiment among Windows programmers that WINDOWS.H, Petzold, and the *Programmer's Reference* neatly encompass all of the Windows API. Those interested in undocumented Windows should also become familiar with lesser-known but important documented aspects of Windows such as the DDK, DPMI, and Open Tools.

Finally, Undocumented Windows

Returning to NBWIN, we are now left with four genuinely undocumented items. Two of these are now documented in the 3.1 SDK, but they were not documented when NBWIN was built, and they are still not documented for 3.0 (which hasn't disappeared, remember). The only reason they eventually *were* documented is that programs like NBWIN were using them anyhow, documentation or no documentation:

__0040h (KERNEL.193)
GetHeapSpaces (KERNEL.138)
GetSelectorBase (KERNEL.186)
SetSelectorBase (KERNEL.187)

Four items may not seem like a lot, but remember that we're looking at a single program. As we'll see later on, key Windows applications, including Microsoft's own applications, use many additional undocumented Windows API functions.

The Saga of Free System Resources
Let's look at the GetHeapSpaces() function (KERNEL.138) first, because it relates to one of the more visible and confusing aspects of Windows performance, stability, and capacity: System Resources, that is, the percentage of free system resources shown

(along with the amount of free memory) in the Program Manager About... box. This number is important to end users of Windows because it determines—almost more than the amount of free memory—the number of applications that can reasonably be run at the same time. All Norton Desktop for Windows applications, including NBWIN, show the free system resources percentage in their About... boxes.

Where does this information come from? And what does it really mean?

Like the 3.0 Program Manager, NDW computes the percentage of free system resources on the basis of the undocumented GetHeapSpaces() function:

```
extern DWORD FAR PASCAL GetHeapSpaces(HANDLE hModule);
```

The window manager (USER) and the Graphical Device Interface (GDI) are just modules in Windows. Like any other Windows DLL or application, they have default local heaps, whose size is at most 64K bytes, and from which memory can be allocated with the documented LocalAlloc() function. What makes USER and GDI special is that these modules are used by all other modules in the system: every window or menu an application creates looks to USER like just another LocalAlloc() from a local heap; every device context (DC) handle, brush, pen, region, font, or bitmap an application creates looks to GDI like just another LocalAlloc() from a local heap.

The implications of this in Windows 3.0 are rather frightening, and in Windows 3.1 they are still somewhat alarming. In 3.0, because all Windows applications share a single 64K heap in USER and a single 64K heap in GDI, the amount of memory remaining in these two heaps might be more important than the amount of total system memory. Even with the megabytes of memory available in protected mode, the number of applications that could be run simultaneously—and their stability—is still constrained by these two 64K barriers. In Windows 3.1, USER and GDI have multiple local heaps, thereby partially relieving the free system resources problem. Menus were a particular problem and were moved out of USER's default local heap. However, as the USERWALK and GDIWALK programs in chapters 6 and 8 show, there is still a definite upper limit on how many windows, menus, DCs, pens, brushes, and so on can be created at one time.

Why do USER and GDI use LocalAlloc() to allocate system resources for other applications? Why not call GlobalAlloc() and thereby remove any 64K limit? Because it is more efficient for USER and GDI to address resources with two-byte near pointers than with the four-byte far pointers that would be necessary for objects created via GlobalAlloc(). The designers of Windows made a time vs. space trade-off.

The free system resources percentage, then, is simply the percentage of USER's heaps that remains free or the percentage of GDI's heaps that remains free, whichever one is smaller. Given a module handle, the undocumented GetHeapSpaces() function returns an unsigned long (DWORD) that contains in its high word the total number of bytes in the module's default local heap, and in its low word the number of *free* bytes. As shown on the following page, it is up to the application that calls GetHeapSpaces() to compute percentages and pick the one that's smaller:

```
/* undocumented Windows call: KERNEL.138 */
extern DWORD FAR PASCAL GetHeapSpaces(WORD hModule);

void heap_info(char *module, WORD *pfree, WORD *ptotal, WORD *ppercent)
{
    DWORD info = GetHeapSpaces(GetModuleHandle(module));
    *pfree = LOWORD(info);
    *ptotal = HIWORD(info);
    *ppercent = (WORD) (((DWORD) *pfree) * 100L) / ((DWORD) *ptotal));
}

// ...
WORD user_free, user_total, user_percent;
WORD gdi_free, gdi_total, gdi_percent;
WORD total_free;

heap_info("USER", &user_free, &user_total, &user_percent);
heap_info("GDI",  &gdi_free,  &gdi_total, &gdi_percent);
total_free = min(user_percent, gdi_percent);
```

Note that GetHeapSpaces() is passed an arbitrary module handle, such as those returned from the documented GetModuleHandle() function. Two points are important here. First, all we need to get this information is the ASCIIZ name (such as "USER" or "GDI") of a module. Windows makes extensive use of strings rather than magic numbers, making it a far more accessible and open system than plain-vanilla DOS. Second, note that GetHeapSpaces() is passed an *arbitrary* module handle and is not limited to use with GDI and USER. (On the other hand, the call GetHeapSpaces (GetModuleHandle("KERNEL")) makes no sense because KERNEL has no local heap.)

Accessing Undocumented Functions

Often, all that is necessary to use GetHeapSpaces() is a function prototype like the one shown above. WINDOWS.H does not contain prototypes for undocumented functions (this is pretty much what makes them undocumented!), so you need to supply one yourself, as illustrated in the code above.

Import libraries such as LIBW.LIB in Microsoft C and IMPORT.LIB in Borland C++ usually contain the necessary IMPDEF records, even for undocumented functions. However, if the linker complains about an "unresolved external" or "undefined symbol" when you try to call an undocumented function, the import library you are using does *not* contain the necessary IMPDEF record. For example, some undocumented functions have been yanked from the Windows 3.1 SDK version of LIBW.LIB, even when the functions still exist in 3.1 itself.

If you get an "unresolved external" or "undefined symbol" error from the linker when trying to use an undocumented function, there are a couple of different solutions:

continued

continued

First you can use the IMPLIB utility to create your own import library, you can use Windows run-time dynamic linking to access the function, or you can use the *import* statement in a linker .DEF file. We'll discuss the first two here.

The IMPLIB utility (included with the Microsoft Windows SDK, but also provided with most third-party Windows development tools, such as Borland C++) takes in a DLL (actually, any segmented executable with exports) and produces a corresponding .LIB file that you can then link into your program. (The .LIB file, of course, doesn't contain any code, just IMPDEF records for each function exported from the DLL.) For example

```
implib kernel.lib \win31\system\krnl386.exe
```

The second way to access undocumented functions when you run into an "unresolved external" or "undefined symbol" error is to use run-time dynamic linking. The usual form of dynamic linking in Windows is actually not all that dynamic: it occurs when Windows loads a program into memory. In contrast, to get a callable pointer to a function in a DLL with run-time dynamic linking, a program need only know the ASCIIZ name of the DLL and of the item it wants to access; it passes the module name to a function such as LoadLibrary() or GetModuleHandle(), and the function name to GetProcAddress(). Thus, rather than rely on the presence of IMPDEF records in a .LIB file, you can entirely bypass the .LIB file and link to the function via GetProcAddress(). For example

```
DWORD (FAR PASCAL *GetHeapSpaces) (WORD hModule);
WORD kernel;
DWORD user_info;

kernel = GetModuleHandle("KERNEL");
GetHeapSpaces = GetProcAddress(kernel, "GETHEAPSPACES");
user_info = GetHeapSpaces(GetModuleHandle("USER"));
```

Notice that we're using GetModuleHandle() for two different purposes here: once to get a module handle to KERNEL that we can use with GetProcAddress(), to get a function pointer to GetHeapSpaces(), and a second time to get a module handle to USER that we pass to GetHeapSpaces() itself.

If you are familiar with traditional K&R C, you may wonder how we can call GetHeapSpaces() without having to explicitly reference the function pointer and call (*GetHeapSpaces)(). The answer is simply that in ANSI C, which all Windows-capable C compilers support, and in C++, (*pfunc)() and pfunc() are equivalent; this is handy when using GetProcAddress().

At the end of this chapter, we will see that GetProcAddress() is useful not only for accessing an undocumented function that is missing from an import library, but also for *safe* use of the undocumented function, to ensure that it really exists in the version of Windows your program is running under. ■

The *implementation* of GetHeapSpaces() in KERNEL itself relies on another undocumented function, LocalCountFree(), which returns the number of free bytes in a local heap. GetHeapSpaces() then uses the documented GlobalSize() function to get the total size of the heap. See chapter 5 for details.

It is obviously a problem for something as visible to end users as the free system resources percentage to rely on an undocumented function. Microsoft decided not to document the GetHeapSpaces() function but instead to provide what seemed like equivalent functionality. TOOLHELP.DLL, included with Windows 3.1, contains the function, SystemHeapInfo(), that provides the same information. ToolHelp does not come with Windows 3.0 but *will* work on top of it (this is a nice demonstration, by the way, of the power of dynamic linking). An addendum to the SDK license agreement permits developers to redistribute ToolHelp and certain other DLLs along with their applications, so it seems as if The Free System Resources Problem has been solved: Call the documented SystemHeapInfo() function rather than the undocumented GetHeapSpaces() function, and ship TOOLHELP.DLL along with your application.

So why would someone continue using GetHeapSpaces() rather than go with TOOLHELP? Aside from a desire not to change code that already "works," the problem is that, quite reasonably, few companies want to ship a DLL along with their product just to show one silly number in their About... boxes. In particular, once you start shipping a system DLL such as TOOLHELP, your Install program needs to worry about "registration" issues: what if the user already has TOOLHELP in a later version than the one you ship? With DLLs, you can get into a number of nasty "versionitis" issues (this is a nice demonstration, by the way, of the *downside* to dynamic linking).

Eventually, Microsoft settled on the following method: use the undocumented (but hereby quasi-sanctioned) GetHeapSpaces() function in Windows 3.0; use a new, documented function, GetFreeSystemResources(), in Windows 3.1 and higher. An application uses the documented GetVersion() function to determine which version of Windows it is running under. Given the differences from one version of Windows to the next, GetVersion() is crucial whenever you are working with undocumented functions. This is illustrated in the following short example program, FREERES.C:

```
/* FREERES.C */

#include "windows.h"

// handy function from Petzold, Programming Windows
void OkMsgBox(char *szCaption, char *szFormat, ...)
{
    char szBuffer[256] ;
    char *pArguments ;

    pArguments = (char *) &szFormat + sizeof szFormat ;
    wvsprintf(szBuffer, szFormat, pArguments) ; // changed from vsprintf
    MessageBox(NULL, szBuffer, szCaption, MB_OK) ;
}
```

```
#define GET_PROC(modname, funcname) \
    GetProcAddress(GetModuleHandle(modname), funcname)

void heap_info(char *module, WORD *pfree, WORD *ptotal, WORD *ppercent)
{
    static DWORD (FAR PASCAL *GetHeapSpaces)(WORD hModule) = 0;
    DWORD info;

    if (! GetHeapSpaces)      // one-time initialization
        if (! (GetHeapSpaces = GET_PROC("KERNEL", "GETHEAPSPACES")))
            OkMsgBox("Error", "Can't find GetHeapSpaces\n");

    /* In ANSI C and C++, pfunc(x) is identical to (*pfunc)(x) */
    info = GetHeapSpaces(GetModuleHandle(module));
    *pfree = LOWORD(info);
    *ptotal = HIWORD(info);
    *ppercent = (WORD) ((((DWORD) *pfree) * 100L) / ((DWORD) *ptotal));
}

int PASCAL WinMain(HANDLE hInstance, HANDLE hPrevInstance,
    LPSTR lpszCmdLine, int nCmdShow)
{
    WORD vers = GetVersion();

    if ((LOBYTE(vers) == 3) && (HIBYTE(vers) == 0)) // 3.0
    {
        WORD user_free, user_total, user_percent;
        WORD gdi_free, gdi_total, gdi_percent;

        heap_info("USER", &user_free, &user_total, &user_percent);
        heap_info("GDI", &gdi_free,  &gdi_total, &gdi_percent);

        OkMsgBox("System Resources",
            "USER heap: %u bytes free out of %u (%u%% free)\n"
            "GDI heap: %u bytes free out of %u (%u%% free)\n"
            "Free system resources: %u%%\n",
                user_free, user_total, user_percent,
                gdi_free, gdi_total, gdi_percent,
                min(user_percent, gdi_percent));
    }
    else    // 3.1+
    {
      WORD FAR PASCAL (*GetFreeSystemResources)(WORD id) =
            GET_PROC("USER", "GETFREESYSTEMRESOURCES");
        if (! GetFreeSystemResources)
            OkMsgBox("Error", "Can't find GetFreeSystemResources\n");
        else
            OkMsgBox("System Resources",
                "USER heap: %u%% free\n"
                "GDI heap: %u%% free\n"
                "Free system resources: %u%%\n",
                    GetFreeSystemResources(2),      // USER
                    GetFreeSystemResources(1),      // GDI
                    GetFreeSystemResources(0));     // total
    }
    return 0;
}
```

Even though GetHeapSpaces() persists in 3.1, the GetVersion() check is important. USER and GDI in Windows 3.1 have *multiple* local heaps; GetHeapSpaces() only checks a module's single *default* local heap. Often, GetHeapSpaces() will return a "reasonable" number in 3.1, but GetFreeSysytemResource() is still the correct function to use. In many situations, GetVersion() will be quite important when you want to use undocumented functions safely. In addition, FREERES.C also shows how GetProcAddress() can be used to link to undocumented functions.

Of course, undocumented functions are also accessible from languages other than C. For example, there are several BASIC environments for Windows, including the WordBasic macro language in Microsoft Word for Windows, Microsoft Visual Basic, and Realizer, that use run-time dynamic linking to provide access to the Windows API. In WordBasic and Visual Basic, the DECLARE statement is used to access API functions (both documented and undocumented). For example:

```
Declare Function GetVersion Lib "kernel" () As Integer
Declare Function GetHeapSpaces Lib "kernel" (hModule as integer) As Long
```

Both WordBasic and Visual Basic perform only *signed* arithmetic, so it is difficult, in this example, to extract the correct LOWORD and HIWORD portions of the four-byte value returned from GetHeapSpaces(). It seems rather typical of BASIC that, while it can easily do things that in C are very difficult, it does with great difficulty things (like unsigned arithmetic) that in C are trivial. At any rate, Visual Basic maven Jonathan Zuck came up with the following implementation of GetFreeResources()(see Robert Arnson et al., *Visual Basic How-To*):

```
Declare Function GetModuleHandle Lib "Kernel" (ByVal ModName$)
Declare Function GetHeapSpaces& Lib "Kernel" (ByVal hModule)

Function GetFreeResources (ModuleName$)
    rInfo& = GetHeapSpaces&(GetModuleHandle(ModuleName$))
    Totalr& = HiWord&(rInfo&)
    FreeR& = LoWord(rInfo&)
    GetFreeResources = FreeR& * 100 \ Totalr&
End Function

Function HiWord& (LongInt&)
    Temp& = LongInt& \ &H10000
    If Temp& < 0 Then Temp& = Temp& + &H10000
    HiWord& = Temp&
End Function

Function LoWord& (LongInt&)
    Temp& = LongInt& Mod &H10000
    If Temp& < 0 Then Temp& = Temp& + &H10000
    LoWord& = Temp&
End Function

Sub Form_Paint ()
    UserFree = GetFreeResources("User")
```

```
    GDIFree = GetFreeResources("GDI")
    User.Caption = "User: " + Str$(UserFree) + "%"
    GDI.Caption = "GDI:  " + Str$(GDIFree) + "%"
End Sub
```

This example doesn't make the call to GetVersion(), or the call to the documented GetFreeSystemResources() function in 3.1, but these could easily be translated from C into BASIC. For further details on making Windows API calls from Visual Basic, see Jonathan Zuck's *Visual Basic Techniques and Utilities*. For extensive coverage of Windows API calls from both Visual Basic and WordBasic, see Woody Leonhard's book, *Windows 3.1 Programming for Mere Mortals*.

To make a long story short, something as ridiculously simple as showing the user the free system resources percentage turns out to not be so simple after all.

The Problem with Protected Mode

Let's now look at the other three undocumented items used by NBWIN:

- __0040h (KERNEL.193)
- GETSELECTORBASE (KERNEL.186)
- SETSELECTORBASE (KERNEL.187)

All three are related to the fact that Windows applications now run in protected mode. NBWIN—like most good Windows applications—runs *only* in protected mode. The idea that "good" Windows applications should be able to run in real mode was a piece of foolishness put forward in the Microsoft Windows *Guide to Programming*; thankfully, real mode is gone in Windows 3.1. Protected mode means that applications are no longer constrained by the 640K limitations of MS-DOS; NBWIN, for example, can use multi-megabytes of memory to efficiently read and backup a large number of files.

However, like any other improvement, protected mode also has a downside. Although less restrictive about the amount of memory it provides, protected mode is, as its name implies, more restrictive ("protected") about everything else. This trade-off is well worth making, but the result is that some real-mode code simply will no longer work in protected mode.

In particular, if a Windows application needs to access absolute memory locations (for instance, 522h), it can no longer do so by creating pointers out of thin air (such as 0000:0522). In real mode, pointer 0000:0522 addresses absolute memory location 522h (this equivalence between pointers and absolute memory locations is the reason it's called real mode). This equivalence doesn't hold in protected mode.

Let's say that, for some reason, you need to access absolute memory location 522h. In a real-mode program, you might do the following (yes, it is much better to use the INT 1Eh vector to get the address of the Disk Parameter Table, normally stored at 522h, but we just need an example here):

```
xor bx, bx
mov es, bx          ; es := 0
mov ax, es:[0522h]
```

Or, in C, one might use the following code:

```
#ifndef MK_FP
#define MK_FP(s,o) \
    ((void far *) (((unsigned long) (s) << 16) | (o)))
#endif

unsigned char far *fp = MK_FP(0, 0x522);
unsigned char some_byte = *fp;
```

This same code, inside a protected-mode Windows application, will cause an Unrecoverable Application Error (UAE). The problem is that the application has dereferenced a pointer that is invalid because the application merely manufactured the segment (selector) value itself; even worse, the selector happens to be zero, which in protected mode always creates a NULL pointer.

To make such code work in *any* protected-mode environment, including Windows, you need a facility that creates protected-mode addresses that "map" real-mode addresses. To do this, first allocate a selector and then set its "base address" to the absolute memory location you want to access and its "limit" (last valid byte offset) to the size you need. It's easiest to put all this inside a function whose job is to map in real-mode far pointers, such as the following imaginary map_real() function:

```
void far *map_real(void far *rmode_ptr, unsigned long nbytes)
{
    WORD sel;

    // allocate a selector
    if ((sel = get_a_selector(READWRITE_DATA)) == 0)
        return 0;   // error: no available selectors

    // set its absolute base address; base=(seg*16)+ofs
    set_selector_base(sel,
        (((DWORD) FP_SEG(rmode_ptr)) << 4) + FP_OFF(rmode_ptr));

    // set its limit; limit=last legal offset (size-1)
    set_selector_limit(sel, nbytes - 1);

    return MK_FP(sel, 0);
}
```

To use this map_real() function, a program needs to pass in the real-mode far pointer and the number of bytes it wants to access. The function returns a protected-mode pointer that should be used instead of the original real-mode pointer. A program can call map_real() during initialization and use the pointer throughout its execution. Sometime before terminating, though, the program should free the allocated selector; Windows will not automatically free it when a program exits:

```
unsigned char far *fp = map_real(0x500, 0x22 + some_length);
unsigned char some_byte = fp[0x22];
// ...
free_selector(FP.SEG (fp));
```

To turn map_real() into genuine code, we only need to locate the Windows functions that allocate, set the base and limit of, and free selectors. A selector can be allocated in Windows using the documented AllocSelector() function and freed sometime later using FreeSelector(). But how do you set its base and limit? There are numerous ways to do this in Windows, but none of them are documented by Microsoft in Windows 3.0.

The most complete solution to the problem of accessing real-mode data structures from a protected-mode Windows application is to use the INT 31h services of the DOS Protected-Mode Interface (DPMI); Windows 3.0 and 3.1 provide DPMI version 0.9 services (DPMI 1.0 currently leads a purely Platonic existence as an unimplemented specification.)

For example, to set the base and limit of an already allocated selector with DPMI, you could use the Set Segment Base Address (INT 31h AX=7) and Set Segment Limit (INT 31h AX=8) functions. To be precise, these set the base and limit of the segment *descriptor* that corresponds to a selector; such segment descriptors are located in the protected-mode Local Descriptor Table (LDT).

However, Microsoft barely documents the fact that INT 31h DPMI services are available under Windows and, in any case, approves only a small handful of them for use in Windows programs. The two DPMI functions noted above are *not* on the approved list. According to a Microsoft Developer's Note, "Windows INT 21H and NetBIOS Support for DPMI," only seven DPMI functions, all related to calling real-mode code, can be used in Windows applications. Other than these, says Microsoft, "No DPMI functions are required for Windows applications since the Kernel provides functions for allocating memory, manipulating descriptors, and locking memory."

In a sense, this is true: the Windows kernel does provide functions for manipulating descriptors (that is, setting and getting their base address and limit). Prototypes for these functions are

```
void FAR PASCAL SetSelectorBase(WORD sel, DWORD base);
void FAR PASCAL SetSelectorLimit(WORD sel, DWORD limit);
DWORD FAR PASCAL GetSelectorBase(WORD sel);
DWORD FAR PASCAL GetSelectorLimit(WORD sel);
```

The only problem is that these functions are undocumented in Windows 3.0. Thus, we're stuck with using DPMI INT 31h functions that Intel documents but that

Microsoft doesn't sanction, or with using Windows 3.0 functions that Microsoft doesn't document, or with artificially restricting the program to run only in Windows 3.1 (where the functions are, as we'll see later, finally documented). What's a programmer to do?

DPMI is certainly not the easiest solution. DPMI programming is sufficiently difficult, or at least unfamiliar, that even many experienced Windows programmers would rather use undocumented functions than use the DPMI interface. In any case, embedding calls such as INT 31h AX=7 in your application goes against the spirit of Windows programming, when there are genuine Windows functions such as SetSelectorBase() seemingly just waiting to be used. Finally, because Windows does at least provide AllocSelector(), it makes sense to stick with Windows, rather than allocating the selector with the Windows API calls and then manipulating it with INT 31h calls. (Note that none of these selector-manipulation calls, documented or undocumented, are likely to be available to 32-bit programs running under Windows NT.)

As shown below, we can use the undocumented SetSelectorBase/Limit calls to implement our map_real() function. Note that the documented AllocSelector() function takes an already existing selector to be used as a model for the new selector. Because we want a normal data selector, we can just pass the program's DS as the parameter to AllocSelector():

```
void far *map_real(void far *rmode_ptr, unsigned long nbytes)
{
    unsigned long base, limit;
    unsigned short sel;

    _asm mov sel, ds
    // sel starts off as copy of our DS: read/write data
    if ((sel = AllocSelector(sel)) == 0)
        return 0;

    base = (((DWORD) FP_SEG(rmode_ptr) << 4) + FP_OFF(rmode_ptr);
    limit = nbytes - 1;

    SetSelectorBase(sel, base);
    SetSelectorLimit(sel, limit);

    return MK_FP(sel, 0);
}
```

We started discussing map_real() because NBWIN uses the SetSelectorBase() function. Even if we don't know exactly how it uses SetSelectorBase(), NBWIN is obviously just the sort of application that needs to access real-mode data structures. Structures such as the BIOS data area, the floppy disk parameter table, the fixed disk parameter table, and so on are likely locations that a backup program would be interested in.

On the other hand, Windows does provide a set of hard-wired selectors to access popular absolute memory locations such as A0000h, B8000h (yes, there are Windows applications, such as CodeView for Windows and Turbo Debugger for Windows, that do direct screen writes), and F0000h. These selectors, which have names such as __A000H, __B800H, and __F000H, are documented in the Microsoft Windows *Guide to Programming*, though not in WINDOWS.H or in the Windows *Programmer's Reference*. These are not functions; they are global variables exported by the KERNEL module.

One of the hard-wired selectors used by NBWIN, __0040H, is not documented even in the *Guide to Programming*. As its name implies, this selector maps the BIOS data area at absolute memory location 400h. __0040H is somewhat redundant because there is yet another selector, __0000H, also undocumented, that maps the entire 64K of memory starting at absolute location zero.

To best illustrate how these selectors can often be used as an alternative to something like the map_real() function, we first need to see how to access the selectors from a C program. Because these are variables, accessing them is a little trickier than simply declaring them, as we did with undocumented Windows functions.

Two different techniques can be used to access the Windows selectors from C. First, you can use a piece of code such as the following, which uses one of the Windows selectors (__F000H) to read the machine's model value at absolute memory location FFFFEh (for example, most 386-based AT-style clones have a model value of FCh):

```
extern WORD _near _F000H;
WORD __F000H = (WORD) (&_F000H);
unsigned char far *fp = MK_FP(__F000H, 0);
unsigned char model = fp[0xFFFE];
```

Second, you can use run-time dynamic linking. When linking to variables rather than functions, we still use GetProcAddress(); the LOWORD() macro extracts the relevant portion:

```
#define GET_SEL(name) \
    ((WORD) (LOWORD(GetProcAddress(GetModuleHandle("KERNEL"), name))))

// ...
WORD __F000H = GET_SEL("__F000H");
unsigned char far *fp = MK_FP(__F000H, 0);
unsigned char model = fp[0xFFFE];
```

Using the undocumented __0000H selector to access the first 64K of memory works in the same way. The following gives a protected-mode program access to the disk parameter table at location 522h:

```
WORD __0000H = GET_SEL("__0000H");
DISK_PARAM far *tbl = MK_FP(__0000H, 0x522);
```

Since the Windows selectors can be used in an MK_FP() macro, we see that these selectors can be used instead of the segment value that would be used in real mode (for example, __F000H instead of 0xF000). Likewise, they can often be used instead of the map_real() function we just built.

Given the existence of these hard-wired selectors and the fact that they can be called from a C program, why would anyone use the Set/GetSelectorBase/Limit functions? First of all, a program may not know what addresses it needs access to until run time. Second, the Windows selectors, even if we include the incredibly useful but undocumented __0000H selector, leave a large area of memory that's inaccessible: 01000h to A0000h, plus all of extended memory (that is, absolute locations over one megabyte). To access anything in this area (a buffer located within a real-mode TSR, for example), you would need something like our map_real() function, which uses SetSelectorBase/Limit.

On the other hand, there's a real reason to stay away from the Get/Set-SelectorBase/Limit functions, at least in Windows 3.0: their implementation makes these functions potentially very dangerous. No matter what selector value you actually pass in, the 3.0 KERNEL automatically assumes that the selector is in the LDT; there is no validity checking and no provision for the possibility that you may have (probably mistakenly) passed in a GDT selector such as 40h. The 3.0 KERNEL does *not* use DPMI to implement these calls; instead, it directly smacks the LDT. In Windows 3.1, however, some of these functions have been reimplemented in a safer fashion, using the underlying DPMI calls. (See chapter 5 for details.)

Further Inside the Norton Desktop

We have been examining the undocumented calls made by Norton Backup for Windows, which is just one program in the Norton Desktop for Windows. If we do the same thing for every program and DLL that comes with NDW, we get a fairly complete picture of all the undocumented functions and variables it uses. It is merely "fairly complete" because Windows also allows a program to link in functions *while it's running*, via GetProcAddress(); any program that imports this function may use additional (possibly undocumented) functions whose names won't turn up in the MAPWIN output. To find such calls, we would need to disassemble the program with a tool such as Sourcer, or set breakpoints on the undocumented functions we're interested in, with Soft-ICE/Windows.

In any case, MAPWIN turns up NDW's use of undocumented services:

__0000H
__0040H

GetHeapSpaces (kernel.138)	SetDeskWallpaper (user.285)
GetInternalWindowPos (user.460)	SetInternalWindowPos (user.461)
GetSelectorBase (kernel.186)	SetSelectorBase (kernel.187)
GlobalMasterHandle (kernel.28)	SetSelectorLimit (kernel.189)

We already discussed __0000H, __0040H, GetHeapSpaces, and the Get/Set-SelectorBase/Limit family; later on, we will discuss some differences in the *implementation* of these functions between Windows versions 3.0 and 3.1. Let's discuss the other undocumented functions now.

Get/SetInternalWindowPos are two undocumented USER functions that can be used to get and set the restored size and position of a window, to get and set the show state, and to get the "park point" when a window is not iconized. For example, let's say you need to know where a window will be restored, but it is currently iconized:

```
RECT rcRestore;
POINT ptPark;
GetInternalWindowPos(hWnd, &rcRestore, &ptPark);
```

Similarly, if you need to *set* where a window will be restored, but it is currently iconic, you can use SetInternalWindowPos:

```
RECT rcNewRestorePosition;
// ...
SetInternalWindowPos(hwnd, SW_SHOWMINIMIZED,
    &rcNewRestorePosition, NULL);
```

In Windows 3.1, documented functions, GetWindowPlacement() and SetWindowPlacement(), provide this same functionality. Of course, these will not work in Windows 3.0, but the undocumented Get/SetInternalWindowPos() functions will continue to work in Windows 3.1. If your program *only* works in 3.1 and higher you need to use Get/SetInternal WindowPos.

GlobalMasterHandle() is used by SIW to produce its Windows Memory Display; the function returns a selector to the "master" block of the Windows global heap, which is a linked list. Using selectors kept in this master block, you can walk through all Windows memory blocks and, for example, count how much memory is being used by an application. Not surprisingly, GlobalMasterHandle() is used by most applications that display Windows memory, including Heapwalk from the Microsoft Windows SDK and hDC's Memory Viewer.

However, GlobalMasterHandle() is no longer necessary. Documented functions and data structures in Microsoft's TOOLHELP.DLL, which is available with the 3.1 SDK but which also works under Windows 3.0, can now be used in applications that display Windows memory. On the other hand, because it does not require an additional DLL, use of GlobalMasterHandle() is unfortunately likely to persist until Windows 3.1 is more prevalent than version 3.0.

SetDeskWallPaper(), an undocumented USER function, is used as part of the WallPaper() function in the NDW batch language; this batch language (designed by Morrie Wilson), is also part of the products BatchWorks, WinBatch, and Command-Post. As its name implies, the function provides programmatic access to the Windows desktop "wallpaper"; for example:

```
extern BOOL FAR PASCAL SetDeskWallPaper(LPSTR lpszBmpFilename);

if (SetDeskWallPaper(argv[1]))
    InvalidateRect(GetDesktopWindow(), NULL, TRUE);
```

Note that this function does not automatically repaint the Windows desktop; for that, you must call InvalidateRect(). In addition, this call does not save your wallpaper setting in WIN.INI; for that, you would also want to call WriteProfileString().

NDW uses several other slick tricks besides undocumented Windows functions. For example, NDW is also a heavy user of the DPMI interface, making DPMI INT 31h calls to generate real-mode INT 13h (BIOS disk services) calls. The Soft-ICE/Windows BPINT (breakpoint on interrupt) command can be used to find which INT 31h calls a Windows program makes.

The conclusion from all this? A key Windows application makes heavy use of undocumented Windows, particularly functions in KERNEL and USER. This makes sense, considering what NDW does, and considering that it aims to replace programs that many users mistakenly think of as built-in to Windows. It's important to note, on the other hand, that there are many Windows applications, just as slick in their own way as NDW, that use *no* undocumented Windows functions.

Microsoft's Use of Undocumented Windows

Where we find particularly extensive use of undocumented Windows functions is, of course, in Microsoft's own software: not surprisingly, in "shell software," such as Program Manager and in some of the debugging utilities included with the Windows SDK, but also in Microsoft's commercial applications, such as Microsoft Excel, and in its language products, such as Visual Basic (VB) and Quick C for Windows (QC/W). Of course, the main place that undocumented Windows is used is internally, by the Windows DLLs themselves.

Let's first look at "shell software"—those applications that come with Windows, and which many users confuse with Windows itself, but which are replaceable by alternate shells. Such software includes Program Manager (PROGMAN.EXE), Task Manager (TASKMAN.EXE), File Manager (WINFILE.EXE), and the old MS-DOS Executive (MSDOS.EXE). These seemingly integral parts of Windows are replaceable using the shell= statement, and in Windows 3.1 the taskman.exe= statement, in SYSTEM.INI. On the following page is the "census" of undocumented API calls revealed by running MAPWIN on the shell software from Windows 3.0 and 3.1 (where no pathname is provided, the undocumented function is used by both the Windows 3.0 and 3.1 versions of the program):

CalcChildScroll (user.462)
PROGMAN.EXE

CascadeChildWindows (user.198)
TASKMAN.EXE

ControlPanelInfo (user.273)
\WIN30\CONTROL.EXE

CreateCursorIconIndirect (user.408)
\WIN30\PROGMAN.EXE
\WIN31\SYSTEM\SHELL.DLL

DeletePathname (kernel.76)
PRINTMAN.EXE

DirectResAlloc (kernel.168)
PROGMAN.EXE
\WIN31\SYSTEM\SHELL.DLL
WINHELP.EXE

DragObject (user.464)
PROGMAN.EXE
WINFILE.EXE

DumpIcon (user.459)
PROGMAN.EXE
\WIN31\SYSTEM\SHELL.DLL

FileCdr (kernel.130)
WINFILE.EXE

GetCurPid (kernel.157)
\WIN30\PROGMAN.EXE
\WIN31\SYSTEM\SHELL.DLL
WINFILE.EXE
MSDOS.EXE
\WIN30\PIFEDIT.EXE

GetLastDiskChange (kernel.98)
MSDOS.EXE

GetSpoolJob (gdi.245)
CONTROL.EXE
PRINTMAN.EXE

GlobalMasterHandle (kernel.28)
MSDOS.EXE

IsWinOldApTask (kernel.158)
TASKMAN.EXE

LoadIconHandler (user.456)
\WIN30\PROGMAN.EXE
\WIN31\SYSTEM\SHELL.DLL
WINHELP.EXE

LongPtrAdd (kernel.180)
WINFILE.EXE

__ROMBIOS (kernel.173)
WINFILE.EXE

ScrollChildren (user.463)
\WIN30\PROGMAN.EXE

SetDeskPattern (user.279)
CONTROL.EXE

SetDeskWallpaper (user.285)
\WIN30\CONTROL.EXE

SetGridGranularity (user.284)
\WIN30\CONTROL.EXE

SetInternalWindowPos (user.461)
PROGMAN.EXE
\WIN31\WINFILE.EXE

GetHeapSpaces (kernel.138)
\WIN30\PROGMAN.EXE
\WIN31\SYSTEM\SHELL.DLL
\WIN30\WINFILE.EXE
MSDOS.EXE

SwitchToThisWindow (user.172)
TASKMAN.EXE

SystemParametersInfo (user.483)
\WIN31\PROGMAN.EXE

GetIconID (user.455)
\WIN30\PROGMAN.EXE
\WIN31\SYSTEM\SHELL.DLL

TileChildWindows (user.199)
TASKMAN.EXE

GetInternalWindowPos (user.460)
PROGMAN.EXE
\WIN31\WINFILE.EXE

That such programs require undocumented Windows clearly presents a problem for those writing alternate shells. We are already familiar with some of these functions, such as Get/SetInternalWindowPos, from our examination of NDW. Many of the other functions are used by PROGMAN.EXE in Windows 3.0 but not in 3.1. In 3.1, these functions—including CreateCursorIconIndirect(), DirectResAlloc(), DumpIcon(), GetIconID(), and LoadIconHandler()—are instead used by SHELL.DLL, which in turn is used by PROGMAN.EXE.

Moving the use of these undocumented calls out of PROGMAN.EXE and into SHELL.DLL was a good move in Windows 3.1. It means that alternates to Program Manager have a better chance of duplicating its functionality. However, it is not clear to what extent the API provided by SHELL.DLL will be documented. Microsoft's SHELLAPI.H marks several functions; ShellAbout(), DuplicateIcon(), and Extract-AssociatedIcon()—as "internal." These functions are used by the 3.1 version of Program Manager. It is not clear whether non-Microsoft shells will still be at a disadvantage, required to use functions that Microsoft regards as internal.

Because there are more intriguing-sounding functions listed than we could possibly have room to explore here, let's instead focus on a single program, the Task Manager (TASKMAN.EXE). TASKMAN is a particularly nice example, not only because it makes many undocumented calls, but because these calls *directly* relate to the program's visible operation. Click the "Cascade" button in Task Manager, and it calls CascadeChildWindows(); click the "Tile" button, and it calls TileChildWindows(); the "Switch To" button corresponds to the SwitchToThisWindow() call. Finally, a rather annoying feature of the "End Task" button is that it can't be used to shut down a DOS box; a glance at an assembly listing for TASKMAN shows that the code for "End Task" calls the undocumented IsWinOldApTask() function to determine whether a given task is a DOS box.

Aside from the way that its overt user-interface directly relates to the undocumented functions it uses, another nice thing about TASKMAN is that it is a very small program (3K) that, when disassembled with V Communications' Sourcer, produces a very clean, understandable TASKMAN.LST or TASKMAN.ASM. It turns out that Task Manager is hardly more than a facade for some undocumented Windows functions. C function prototypes and explanatory material for these functions are as follows:

```
/*
    Determine if a task belongs to the Windows WINOLDAP module,
    i.e., if it is a DOS ("old") application. The task handle
    parameter can be created from a window handle, using the
    documented GetWindowTask() function. Thus, an IsDOSBox()
    function can easily be synthesized.
*/
BOOL FAR PASCAL IsWinOldApTask(HANDLE hTask);

#define IsDOSBox(hwnd)    IsWinOldApTask(GetWindowTask(hwnd))

/*
    Performs the equivalent of a Task Manager "Switch To". The
    tRestore parameter determines whether an iconic window is
    restored, or switched to but left iconic.
*/
void FAR PASCAL SwitchToThisWindow(HWND hWnd, BOOL tRestore);

/*
    Rearranges the child windows of a specific parent into a
    cascaded formation. The Task Manager "Cascade" operation
    is equivalent to CascadeChildWindows(GetDesktopWindow()).
    MDI windows such as Program Manager must be handled differently,
    by sending a WM_MDICASCADE message, since MDI children are not
    direct descendents.
*/
void FAR PASCAL CascadeChildWindows(HWND hParent, ...);

/*
    Rearranges the child windows of a specified parent into an
    old-style (Windows 1.x) tiled formation. See comment for
    CascadeChildWindows() above for further notes.
*/
void FAR PASCAL TileChildWindows(HWND hParent, ...);

/* following only for 3.0--see below */
#define TileDesktop()   TileChildWindows(GetDesktopWindow())
```

By combining these undocumented functions with several documented functions, you can synthesize a number of additional useful functions, such as IsDOSWindow() and TileDesktop(). This last function puts the retro look and feel of Windows 1.x only a function call away and can be run when using Windows in the presence of lawyers from Apple.

Handling Extra Parameters In 3.1

In Windows 3.1, both CascadeChildWindows() and TileChildWindows() take an extra parameter that is not present in the Windows 3.0 version of these functions:

```
#if (WINVER >= 0x030a)
void FAR PASCAL CascadeChildWindows(HWND hParent, WORD wStyle);
void FAR PASCAL TileChildWindows(HWND hParent, WORD wStyle);
#endif
```

For TileChildWindows, the wStyle parameter is one of the Windows 3.1 WINDOWS.H values MDITILE_VERTICAL, MDITILE_HORIZONTAL, or MDITILE_SKIPDISABLED; for CascadeChildWindows, only the MDITILE_SKIPDISABLED option is used.

Because these functions, like almost all other Windows API functions, use the Pascal calling convention, you *must* call them with the correct number of arguments or your program may suffer a protection violation. In Windows 3.0, you cannot simply pass in the extra argument as an unused "dummy" value, as you could with a function that used the C (cdecl) calling convention.

The function prototypes shown earlier for these functions deal with this discrepancy by using ANSI C ... syntax to turn off checking after the first argument. To *call* the function, you must still use the correct number of arguments. For example:

```
void TileDesktop(void)
{
    extern WORD wVers;
    if (wVers == 0x0003)    // 3.0
        TileChildWindows(GetDesktopWindow());
    else if (wVers == 0x0a03)    // 3.1
        TileChildWindows(GetDesktopWindow(), MDITILE_VERT);
}
```

Another way to handle undocumented functions whose number or size of arguments differ from one Windows version to the next is to provide different function prototypes for each Windows version. For example:

```
void FAR PASCAL CascadeCW30(HWND hParent);
void FAR PASCAL CascadeCW31(HWND hParent, WORD wStyle);
```

In other words, CascadeCW30() and CascadeCW31() are aliases for the CascadeChildWindows() function. However, this begs the question of how to link this alias to the actual CascadeChildWindows function in the 3.0 or 3.1 version of USER.DLL. By using the function's module name and ordinal number, it's easy to perform this linkage in a Windows .DEF file. For example:

c o n t i n u e d

continued

```
IMPORTS
    CASCADECW30=USER.198    ; 3.0 CascadeChildWindows
    CASCADECW31=USER.198    ; 3.1 CascadeChildWindows
    TILECW30=USER.199       ; 3.0 TileChildWindows
    TILECW31=USER.199       ; 3.1 TileChildWindows
```

Another way, of course, is not to bother with the .DEF file at all and to instead use our old friend GetProcAddress():

```
extern void FAR PASCAL (*CascadeCW30)(HWND hParent);
extern void FAR PASCAL (*CascadeCW31)(HWND hParent, WORD wStyle);

// ...
HANDLE hUser=GetModule Handle ("USER");
CascadeCW30 = GetProcAddress(hUser, "CASCADECHILDWINDOWS");
CascadeCW31 = GetProcAddress(hUser, "CASCADECHILDWINDOWS");

// ...
extern WORD wVers;
extern HWND hwndDesktop;
    if (wVers == 0x0003)
CascadeCW30(hwndDesktop)
    else if (wVers == 0x0a03)
CascadeCW31(hwndDesktop, MDI_TILESKIPDISABLED);
```

Remember that ANSI C and C++ allow us to call through a function pointer like CascadeCW31 using either (*CascadeCW31)() or CascadeCW31(); the two are equivalent.

If you are using a programming language such as Visual Basic, Turbo Pascal, or WordBasic, it is a lot easier to create such alias functions than it is in C or C++. These other languages all provide ways to provide names of your own choosing for imported functions. Obviously, this capability should be used sparingly if you want other Windows programmers to be able to read your code!

In Turbo Pascal for Windows (TPW), you could handle CascadeCW30() and CascadeCW31() in the following way; you make the linkage to Cascade-ChildWindows() by specifying the function's module name and ordinal number:

```
uses WinProcs, WinTypes;

procedure CascadeCW30(hParent: Word); far;
    external 'USER' index 198;
procedure CascadeCW31(hParent, wStyle: Word); far;
    external 'USER' index 198;
```

continued

continued

In Visual Basic and WordBasic, the DECLARE statement has an optional ALIAS clause that is ready-made for handling the vagaries of undocumented functions. For example, in WordBasic:

```
Declare Sub CascadeCW30 Lib "User" Alias "CascadeChildWindows" \
    (hParent as integer)
Declare Sub CascadeCW31 Lib "User" Alias "CascadeChildWindows" \
    (hParent as integer, wStyle as integer)
```

(The Visual Basic declaration would say "hParent byVal" and "wStyle byVal".)

Because this "function" has no return value, it can be declared as a SUB rather than as a FUNCTION. This means that it can be called in a very natural, BASIC-looking way. The following is excerpted from Jonathan Zuck's TASKMGR, an improved clone of the Windows Task Manager written in Visual Basic:

```
'Handle a click in the Cascade command button
Sub Cascade_Click ()
    Select Case WinVer
        Case 300
            CascadeCW30 DesktopWnd
        Case 310
            CascadeCW31 DesktopWnd, MDI_TILESKIPDISABLED
    End Select
End Sub ■
```

Undocumented Debugging

Besides Microsoft's replaceable shell programs for Windows, software in the Microsoft Windows SDK also uses undocumented functions. It's important to note that some of these programs—including SPY, SHAKER, and SDKPAINT—use *no* undocumented functions. But the software listed below does show that yet another feature of Windows that developers tend to take for granted—the ability to debug—is based on undocumented foundations. This is particularly reminiscent of the situation in DOS, where for years the key "load but don't execute" function used by debuggers, such as DEBUG, SymDeb, and CodeView, was "reserved" by Microsoft:

AllocSelectorArray (kernel.206)
WINMEM32.DLL

GetSelectorBase (kernel.186)
WINMEM32.DLL
WINDEBUG.DLL

DirectedYield (kernel.150)
WINDEBUG.DLL
TOOLHELP.DLL

GlobalHandleNoRIP (kernel.159)
HEAPWALK.EXE
WINDEBUG.DLL

GlobalMasterHandle (kernel.28)
HEAPWALK.EXE
WINDEBUG.DLL
TOOLHELP.DLL

IsTaskLocked (kernel.122)
WINDEBUG.DLL

LockCurrentTask (kernel.33)
WINDEBUG.DLL

OpenPathname (kernel.75)
HEAPWALK.EXE

RegisterPtrace (kernel.202)
WINDEBUG.DLL
TOOLHELP.DLL

SelectorAccessRights (kernel.196)
WINMEM32.DLL

SetEventHook (user.321)
CVW.EXE (CodeView for Windows)

SetSelectorBase (kernel.187)
HEAPWALK.EXE
WINMEM32.DLL
WINDEBUG.DLL

SetSelectorLimit (kernel.189)
HEAPWALK.EXE
WINMEM32.DLL

WinDebug (WINDEBUG.1)
CVW.EXE (via GetProcAddress)

Not only does the Windows debugging library, WINDEBUG.DLL, use a number of undocumented functions, but even the interface it provides is undocumented! This interface, the WinDebug() function, is used by all available Windows debuggers, including CodeView for Windows (CVW), Turbo Debugger for Windows (TDW), and Multiscope. Use of WinDebug() usually does not show up in MAPWIN output because debuggers link to it at run-time via the amazing GetProcAddress() function.

WinDebug() is a hacked 32-bit version of the poorly documented DosPTrace() function from OS/2 1.x, which, in turn, is based on the ptrace() function in Unix. Like DosPTrace(), WinDebug() takes commands such as Go, Single-Step, Write Registers, Read Registers, Write Memory, and Read Memory. It returns to its caller either when the command completes or when some interesting event such as a breakpoint, protection fault, or DLL load occurs. These commands and notifications appear in a large structure whose address is passed to WinDebug(), as shown in the following somewhat contrived code fragment:

```
void FAR PASCAL WinDebug(WINDEBUG_BUF far *wdbgBuf);
// ...
WINDEBUG_BUF wdbgBuf;
WORD cs, ds;
wdbgBuf.Cmd = DBG_C_ReadReg;
WinDebug(&wdbgBuf);
cs = wdbgBuf.Client_CS;
ds = wdbgBuf.Client_DS;
```

Returning to the list of undocumented functions used by SDK software, notice that WINDEBUG.DLL imports both the IsTaskLocked() and LockCurrentTask() functions. Task locking prevents other Windows tasks from getting message input; its use by WinDebug() explains the rather annoying behavior of CVW and TDW, from which—unlike practically all other Windows applications—you cannot switch away.

Alternatives to WinDebug() are available. For one thing, the KERNEL Register-Ptrace() function allows a Windows "notification" function to be installed. Windows calls the notification function when it's about to do something interesting, like load or terminate a task, load a DLL, and so on. (Unfortunately, only one such notification function can be installed at any given time.) Other debug interfaces could be built on top of this.

Even better, Microsoft's ToolHelp API, which, as noted earlier, is available starting with the Windows 3.1 SDK, but which will also work under Windows 3.0, provides documented functions for registering handlers: InterruptRegister(), which can be used to install a handler for such exceptions as general-protection (GP) faults and even "bad" page faults, and NotifyRegister(), which can be used to catch the same events as handled by RegisterPtrace(). These are explained in more detail in chapter 10 of this book.

Clearly, Microsoft wants to move developers away from using the undocumented WinDebug() interface and toward writing Windows-hosted debuggers with TOOLHELP.DLL and some quasi-documented functions in the Open Tools materials. In other words, Microsoft isn't documenting the important WinDebug() function because it wants to see it go away. This, in fact, is *often* why Microsoft doesn't document seemingly crucial functions. WinDebug() is simply *not* going to disappear overnight (it was renamed to CVWIN.DLL and TDWIN.DLL for Windows 3.1), so it's important that developers have documentation for it; on the other hand, ToolHelp (though a lower-level interface than WinDebug) certainly is preferable in most cases, and it would be nice to see more use of ToolHelp and less use of those undocumented functions that it supplants. ToolHelp doesn't solve all the Windows problems that otherwise require undocumented functions, but it's an important step in the right direction. At the same time, another important Windows debugging interface, INT 41h, remains undocumented.

Microsoft Commercial Applications and Language Products

Probably no one objects to Microsoft's use of undocumented functions in its Windows debugging utilities. After all, debuggers are more like system software—pieces of the operating system—and less like application software. (Except that, in the crazy PC marketplace, an obscure piece of software like a debugger can become a mass-market commodity, sold in tens of thousands of copies, and hence stops being a piece of system software and becomes a piece of application software.)

But what of Microsoft's application software, such its excellent word processor, Word for Windows (which was used to write much of this book), and its Excel spreadsheet for Windows? Isn't it just downright unfair if Microsoft applications use undocumented Windows and DOS functions? We'll address this issue of fairness in a few minutes, but first let's find out how extensive this use of undocumented functions actually is.

Certainly, it is not difficult to see that the Excel spreadsheet uses undocumented Windows functions. We only need to examine EXCEL.EXE and EXCELDE.EXE with the same utility that we've been using to examine other Windows executable and libraries. The undocumented functions revealed include the following:

\EXCEL\EXCEL.EXE

EndMenu (user.187)	InquireSystem (SYSTEM.1)
FillWindow (user.324)	KillSystemTimer (user.182; called Bear182 in 3.1)
Get80x87SaveSize (SYSTEM.7)	LocalNotify (kernel.14)
GetControlBrush (user.326)	PatchCodeHandle (kernel.110)
GetPhysicalFontHandle (gdi.352)	SetSystemTimer (user.11; called Bear11 in 3.1)
GetTimerResolution (user.14)	

\EXCEL\EXCELDE.EXE

FillWindow (user.324)	GetControlBrush (user.326)

Some of these references are located inside a large table of function pointers in EXCEL.EXE, so it is difficult to tell exactly how Excel uses them. The calls GetTimerResolution(), SetSystemTimer(), and KillSystemTimer() are particularly intriguing, as these calls do not seem obviously related to the operation of Excel. As noted in chapter 6 of this book, SetSystemTimer() can allocate a Windows timer even when the documented SetTimer() function reports that one isn't available. (Note that SetSystemTimer() in USER is quite different from CreateSystemTimer() in SYSTEM, described in chapter 9.)

To see if these functions are *really* called by Excel, we can set breakpoints on them with Soft-ICE/Windows (Soft-ICE has symbolic information for all functions exported from KERNEL, USER, and GDI, even if they're undocumented). The result is that *all* of the functions listed above are indeed called while Excel is running. Some of them are also called constantly even when Excel isn't running, and so must also be used by parts of Windows itself, but the Soft Ice CSIP range qualifier lets us restrict the breakpoint to calls coming from Excel.

In any case, while it is clear that Excel really *does* use all this undocumented stuff, it is far less clear *why*. EndMenu(), for example, can be used to take down a menu when required by a more pressing event; FillWindow() simply paints a window using a given HBRUSH; GetControlBrush() retrieves an HBRUSH used for a given control. Maybe it's even all just old code that is no longer needed.

The PatchCodeHandle() function used by Excel is another can of worms. As explained in the Windows 3.1 SDK documentation, Windows permits "self-loading"

Windows applications. Normally this is done to work around a limitation of the WinExec() loader. Part of the process of writing your own Windows loader involves calling PatchCodeHandle() to create the standard Windows prologs and epilogs.

This ability to write self-loading Windows executable files invites programmers to come up with their own executable file formats. So long as certain minimal criteria are met, you could devise a new executable-file format that, for example, decompressed itself on the fly, as it was loading. Although this ability opens up a wide range of interesting possibilities for Windows software, it also means that we may see the current consistent use of the segmented-executable NE format degenerate into a kind of "file format of the week" confusion, interfering with the use of standard tools.

The first suggestion that this could happen is the executable file for version 1.x of Microsoft Word for Windows (WINWORD.EXE). Trying to run any standard segmented-executable tools on WINWORD.EXE reveals a call to PatchCodeHandle(), followed by a completely nonstandard file format. Microsoft's own EXEHDR utility knows enough about this format to issue a warning about "compressed relocation records." In short, version 1.x of WINWORD.EXE uses its own home-brew compressed executable format; unfortunately we can't examine it with any of our utilities. This is probably the only time we have encountered anything that made it difficult to examine a Windows application.

WinWord 2.0 no longer uses PatchCodeHandle() and compressed relocation records. Therefore, it is trivial to see that WINWORD.EXE does, in fact, use two undocumented Windows functions. Furthermore, the Draw, Graph, and Dialog Editor utilities that come with WinWord 2.0 (MSDRAW also comes with Microsoft Works for Windows) also use undocumented functions:

WINWORD.EXE (2.0)
EndMenu (user.187)
LoadCursorIconHandler (user.336)

MSGRAPH\GRAPH.EXE
EndMenu (user.187)
Get80X87SaveSize (SYSTEM.7)
GetHeapSpaces (kernel.138)
InquireSysten (SYSTEM.1)
LocalNotify (kernel.14)

MSDRAW\MSDRAW.EXE
InquireSystem (SYSTEM.1)
KillSystemTimer, Bear182 (user.182)
SetSystemTimer, Bear11 (user.11)

MACRODE.EXE (Dialog Editor)
LocalNotify (kernel.14)
InquireSystem (SYSTEM.1)
FillWindow (user.324)
GetControlBrush (user.326)

It's hard to know what to make of this. The undocumented functions imported from USER—EndMenu(), LoadCursorIconHandler(), FillWindow(), and GetControlBrush()—are probably serving a genuine purpose. But if, for example, you read the description of InquireSystem() in chapter 8 of this book, it's hard to see how it would be of much use to Draw, Graph, and the Dialog Editor: there are documented ways to get the same information. The LocalNotify() function was documented in Windows

2.x, but it serves little purpose in protected-mode Windows where there's much more memory to work with (perhaps this is just old code). Then again, the USER Set/KillSystemTimer functions could be working some real magic for these Microsoft applications, magic that has been declared off-limits for non-Microsoft developers.

How about Microsoft's language products for Windows, Visual Basic and Quick C for Windows? These really are applications, not systems software; at least, they are marketed that way. These too use a few undocumented functions:

\VB\VB.EXE	\QCWIN\BIN\QCWIN.EXE
EndMenu (user.187)	DirectedYield (kernel.150)
PrestoChangoSelector (kernel.177)	GetTaskQueue (kernel.35)

It is hard to decide whether the PrestoChangoSelector() function really is undocumented. In the Windows 3.0 *Programmer's Reference*, a more sedate-sounding function, ChangeSelector(), was documented but was not exported from any Windows DLL or made available in the standard import libraries. However, PrestoChangoSelector() was available instead, though this silly name was not documented in 3.0. PrestoChangoSelector(), or ChangeSelector() if you prefer, is used to implement self-modifying code or executable data in protected-mode Windows. The function works by twiddling a single bit in a descriptor table.

How can the same function turn a code selector into a data selector or a data selector into a code selector? All that is required is to twiddle (XOR) a single bit in a protected-mode descriptor. In fact, if we use Soft-ICE or Sourcer to look at the source code for the Windows 3.0 implementation of PrestoChangoSelector(), it's easy to see why the function was given this name. As seen here, the code *does* work a sort of magic:

```
; from KRNL386 3.0
PRESTOCHANGOSELECTOR proc far
    ENTER
    SAVE ds, si, di
    mov ds,cs:WIN_LDT
    mov es,cs:WIN_LDT
    mov si, wSourceSelector    ; [bp+8]
    mov di, wDestSelector      ; [bp+6]
    and si,0FFF8h              ; turn selector into LDT offset
    and di,0FFF8h              ; ditto
    mov ax,di
    mov cx,4
    cld
    rep movsw                  ; copy the 8-byte descriptor
    xor byte ptr [di-3],8      ; PRESTOCHANGO: toggle the code/data bit
    MOV es, 0                  ; push 0 / pop es
    or  al,5
    RESTORE di, si, ds
    LEAVE 4
PRESTOCHANGOSELECTOR endp
```

Like other functions in the 3.0 kernel, PrestoChangoSelector() magically ANDs a selector with 0FFF8h to turn it into the corresponding descriptor's offset in the protected-mode Local Descriptor Table (LDT). Unfortunately, this code is extremely unsafe, as it makes the unwarranted assumption that any selector belongs to the LDT; passing in a bad value will instantly corrupt the Windows LDT. This problem has been corrected in Windows 3.1, where the code more sedately uses DPMI INT 31h calls to manipulate the descriptor table:

```
; KRNL386 3.1
PRESTOCHANGOSELECTOR proc far
    ; ...
    DPMICALL GET_DESC, [bp+8]         ; INT 31h AX=000Bh
    xor byte ptr [bp-3], 8            ; PRESTOCHANGO: code <==> data
    DPMICALL SET_DESC, [bp+6]         ; INT 31h AX=000Ch
    ; ...
PRESTOCHANGOSELECTOR endp
```

As a threaded-code interpreter, it makes sense that VB would call PrestoChango-Selector(). This function is always used either to write self-modifying code or to have executable data. For example, the Windows DISPLAY driver's BITBLT module calls PrestoChangoSelector() to compile bitblts on the fly. (See the sample source code in the Windows Device Driver Kit, for example \display\4plane\bitblt\bitblt.asm.)

Quick C for Windows' use of the undocumented functions also makes sense. DirectedYield() and GetTaskQueue() (you can read more about these in chapter 5 on KERNEL) both help the QCW integrated environment orchestrate the task-switching between itself and a user's C program.

The "Chinese Wall" and FTC's Investigation of Microsoft

Given the use of undocumented Windows functions by Microsoft applications, it seems important to note that Microsoft is under investigation from the U.S. Federal Trade Commission (FTC), which will determine whether Microsoft's role as a provider of operating-system software also gives it an unfair advantage in the applications-software business.

In fact, the use of undocumented Windows functions by Microsoft applications such as Excel is probably no more nefarious than the use of undocumented Windows functions by Norton/Symantec, Borland, or any other company whose software must make Windows jump through hoops. Nonetheless, using these functions but not documenting them certainly gives the appearance of an unfair advantage over Microsoft's competitors. For this reason, Microsoft employees from time to time *deny* that any Windows application from Microsoft uses undocumented functions.

For example, Mike Maples, then head of the applications division at Microsoft, was asked by *InfoWorld* (30 December 1991) whether there wasn't supposed to be a "Chinese Wall" between the applications division and the systems-software division at Microsoft. Maples said that there was, in fact, no such wall, but,

The bigger issue would be, if we were using secrets or undocumented things, and we very consciously avoid that. A long time ago, when Windows was barely being strapped together, there were cases where things were added to make [the application division's] life easier, but they were added for other apps developers too. But right now, to my knowledge, there isn't a single undocumented thing in Windows that is used by a Microsoft application.

To this, the interviewer responded, "Yet this issue was evidently in the Federal Trade Commission's mind after they did the first round of interviews with third parties, then expanded their probe of Microsoft."

The issue of whether there is—or should be—a "Chinese Wall" between applications and operating systems at Microsoft is frequently brought up in coverage of the FTC investigation, and it is often viewed as related to the use of undocumented DOS and Windows functions by Microsoft end-user applications. For example, *PC Week* (20 May 1991) explained the term "Chinese Wall" this way: "Does Microsoft leverage control over the information flow between its operating-systems and applications groups to hobble competitors?"

However, consider whether the term "Chinese Wall" may mean something entirely different, at least to the FTC: not whether Microsoft applications take unfair advantage of undocumented goodies in DOS and Windows, but whether the applications group at Microsoft has unfair access to knowledge of *changes* that the Microsoft operating-systems group is planning. For example, while Microsoft was telling the world at large to develop applications for OS/2, its applications group may have had inside knowledge that led it instead to develop for Windows.

From what we've seen of Microsoft, though, there often seems to be very little communication between the operating-systems group and the other parts of the company—*too little* communication, in fact. For example, for all of Microsoft's talk of how NT represents the future of operating systems, Microsoft's languages group has been dragging its feet on developing the 32-bit compilers, linkers, and debuggers that are needed to give NT any hope of succeeding. Sometimes there seems to be *too much* of a wall at Microsoft.

Their use of undocumented functions shows that Microsoft applications developers obviously have access to information on Windows internals. But is this really such an unfair advantage? Any owner of this book now also has access to this information. More important, as chapters 2, 3, and 4 of this book show, anyone with a few simple tools can delve into the depths of undocumented Windows. Microsoft has made essentially no effort to keep you from finding out about these functions on your own. The Windows license agreement, of course, has a standard "no disassembly" clause, but Microsoft's own tools, such as CodeView for Windows (CVW) and EXEHDR, make it almost impossible *not* to see disassembled pieces of Windows. The point is merely that Microsoft really can't be found to have unfair access when anyone with copies of CVW and EXEHDR has essentially the same access.

The Geary Incident

That one can understand Windows internals, without access to the Windows source code, is particularly important because of a dispute involving Microsoft and the brilliant Windows programmer, Michael Geary. On the other hand, this incident also tends to contradict what we just said about Microsoft's lack of an unfair advantage, because Microsoft attorneys came after Geary for discussing undocumented Windows.

Microsoft's harassment of Geary is described in a letter by Carole Patton to *PC Week* (3 June 1991), from which the following details are taken:

On 31 October (Halloween) 1991, Adobe CEO John Warnock received a letter from Microsoft regarding Michael Geary; Geary worked on the Adobe Type Manager (ATM) and was at the time doing other projects for Adobe. Microsoft's letter accuses Geary of revealing Microsoft trade secrets: "Microsoft first learned of this unauthorized disclosure through a recent CompuServe E-mail in which Geary describes how he modifies a specific GDI entry point in Windows 3.0 in order to accommodate ATM for Windows. According to the Microsoft development team, such a modification could only have been done by someone with an intimate knowledge of the internals of Windows 3.0."

This makes it sound almost as if "an intimate knowledge of the internals of Windows 3.0" is in itself a bad thing to have. The Microsoft letter goes on to claim that Geary had gained this forbidden knowledge while working for Cooper Software, which developed much of Visual Basic. (So it really makes sense to complain to Adobe about it, right?) Since "reverse engineering" is legal, Microsoft could only go after Geary by claiming that he *didn't* reverse engineer, but instead had worked with the actual GDI source code.

What deep, dark secret had Geary revealed? As you can see from the following transcript excerpted from CompuServe, Geary, by way of discussing how ATM works, ends up describing some of the implementation details of Microsoft's CreateDC() function in GDI. It is this description of CreateDC() that Microsoft's lawyers maintained was derived from an illicit peek at the source code.

Before reading any further, think for a minute about how CreateDC() might be implemented. The function takes the name of a DISPLAY driver, plus some other parameters, and returns a handle to a display context. Somehow it has to get from a driver on disk to a display context in memory. A display driver is just a DLL with a certain set of required entry points, which are defined in the Windows DDK. Creating a display context from a driver means loading the driver and calling some of these functions. How do you think CreateDC() does this?

Okay, here's the famous CompuServe exchange, from October 1990. To put the conversation in context, recall that this was before the announcement of Windows 3.1 with TrueType:

```
#:0617 S9/Windows Developers
   04-Oct-90  11:55:29
Sb: #Adobe Fonts, How Done?
Fm: Alan Cobb
```

To: Michael Geary

The Adobe Type Manager apparently is out now. Is it set up in such a way that it transparently can be added to Windows? That is, you just install it and magically all your applications start to have less jagged screen images? Does the Windows font system allow this to be done simply? (probably not :-)

#:50774 S9/Windows Developers
   04-Oct-90 23:07:02
Sb: #50617-Adobe Fonts, How Done?
Fm: Michael Geary
To: Alan Cobb

That's right, Alan, ATM installs into Windows and existing applications work transparently with it. There is no device driver involved: ATM essentially sits between GDI and the existing device drivers.

How it works: When GDI asks any driver to realize a font (this happens when you do a SelectObject on an HFONT), ATM looks at the font parameters and sees if it has a font to match. If so, ATM returns a font structure to GDI that we mark as being our own. (This is not a raster font; GDI actually thinks it is a device vector font.) Otherwise, we pass the call on through to the driver so it or GDI can realize the font.

Then, when the driver receives an ExtTextOut call, we grab that and see if the font is one of ours. If not, we pass it through to the driver. If it is ours, ATM than rastorizes the characters from the font outlines and puts them into a memory monochrome bitmap. We then call the driver's BitBlt function to do the actual output. Depending on the size of the text string, this can be one BitBlt call per character, or else I'll merge the characters into one memory bitmap and BitBlt the whole thing. (The latter is faster, so we do that wherever possible.)

Oh--we also intercept the EnumDFonts call so we can add the Adobe fonts to the normal list of fonts. There are several other calls we intercept and tweak as well, such as the Control function. (That's known as Escape at the application level.)

I lied. There is one driver involved. ATM actually installs itself as a SYSTEM driver, of all things. It is a system driver that does nothing special with the calls made into it, just passing them all through to the original SYSTEM.DRV. The reason it's done this way is this is a reasonably convenient way to get our code loaded in early enough in the boot process.

Was it easy? Not at all... :-)

#:50918 S9/Windows Developers
    05-Oct-90 12:08:27
Sb: #50774-Adobe Fonts, How Done?
Fm: Alan Cobb
To: Michael Geary

> There is no device driver involved; ATM essentially sits
> between GDI and the existing device drivers.

> when the driver receives an ExtTextOut call, we grab that

> we also intercept the EnumDFonts call

How do you initially set up those interceptions? There is no standard provision in Windows for this, is there? Do you have to do some weird searching and repointing of addresses? Enquiring minds want to know :-).

#:1222 S9/Windows Developers
    06-Oct-90 15:15:41
Sb: #50918-#Adobe Fonts, How Done?
Fm: Michael Geary
To: Alan Cobb

Alan, it's a little on the nasty side, I'm afraid. Whenever anyone calls CreateDC, that function calls LoadLibrary to load in the .DRV file and then does a series of GetProcAddress calls to pick up the driver entry points. Right after GDI is loaded into memory, my code searches through the CreateDC function to find those two function calls, and it patches them to point to some routines of mine. My LoadLibrary intercept goes ahead and calls the original LoadLibrary and also allocates an extra data segment where I keep information about the device. This segment

```
has both a normal data selector and a CS alias. The GetProc-
Address intercept calls the original GetProcAddress function
and then looks to see if it is one of the driver routines that
I want to intercept. If not, it just returns the original
address. If it is an entry we intercept, I save the original
driver function address in my context segment and then return
the address of a little stub entry that's also in the context
segment. Then, when GDI calls that driver entry, it goes
through my code.
```

That's it! Essentially, Geary disclosed little more about Windows internals than the fact that CreateDC() calls the run-time dynamic linking functions LoadLibrary() and GetProcAddress(). If you've been doing Windows programming for any time at all, this description of CreateDC() probably occurred to you during our earlier thought-experiment. Geary is easily one of a small handful of really brilliant Windows programmers on the planet, but the revelation about how CreateDC() is implemented is hardly rocket science, and requires little more than a few minutes' reflection, not an illicit peek at the GDI source code. If someone on the Microsoft development team told Microsoft's lawyers that the inner workings of CreateDC() could only be understood by someone with inside knowledge of GDI, then quite frankly, someone at Microsoft wasn't thinking very clearly.

As a curious denoument to the Geary incident, you might note that in Windows 3.1, CreateDC() has been reimplemented. It now looks like this:

```
CreateDC:
    jmp somewhere_else
    callf LoadLibrary
    callf GetProcAddress
    callf FreeLibrary
```

In other words, CreateDC() has in 3.1 specific knowldge of ATM's need to patch GDI.

Geary was soon vindicated by Cooper Software, which informed Microsoft that, while Cooper did have access to some Windows source code, it did *not* have the code for GDI, which is what Geary had discussed on CompuServe.

In a follow-up letter, a Microsoft attorney told Adobe it was all right to retain Geary, but concluded, "I trust, however, that all parties involved will continue to be vigilant in preventing the possibility of improper use of proprietary information, including undocumented internals."

It is possible that these threatening letters to Adobe, about an incident that occurred while Geary was working for Cooper Software, are merely a sideshow in the larger battles between Microsoft and Adobe. But by threatening a competitor for discussing undocumented Windows, when Microsoft's own applications use these functions, Microsoft certainly makes us think twice that maybe its applications *do* after all have an unfair advantage. Certainly, if Microsoft wants to combat the very widely held belief that its use of undocumented functions is unfair, it needs either to stop using them or to document them. It also needs to publicly apologize to Michael Geary.

Inside Windows

Having discussed the way undocumented functions are used in Microsoft's shell programs, SDK utilities, applications, and "quick" language products, we finally turn to what is really the reason d'etre for undocumented Windows: its use internally by the Windows DLLs themselves. Each Windows DLL, DRV, and so on uses functions from the other components of Windows, and some of these functions, naturally, are undocumented. It is completely legitimate for Microsoft not to document its internal functions! It's also legitimate for us to try to figure out what's going on.

For example, the GDI (graphics device interface) module in Windows imports functions from KERNEL; GDI makes no use of services, whether documented or undocumented, from the USER (windowing) module. The undocumented functions that Windows 3.0 GDI explicitly imports from KERNEL are shown below; Windows 3.1 is somewhat different, also using our old friend, Get/SetSelectorBase.

\WIN30\SYSTEM\GDI.EXE

DeletePathname (kernel.76)	LocalHeapSize (kernel.162)
GetCurPID (kernel.157)	LongPtrAdd (kernel.180)
GetExeVersion (kernel.105)	NoHookDOSCall (kernel.101)
LocalCountFree (kernel.161)	PrestoChangoSelector (kernel.177)

Of course, this list of undocumented functions hardly gives us a well-rounded view of how GDI and KERNEL interrelate. By walking relocation information in an NE executable, it's easy to write programs (such as EXEUTIL -IMPORTS in chapter 2 of this book) that show *how many* calls are generated to a function, whether documented or undocumented; in this case, we would see that GDI relies on KERNEL for—not surprisingly—global memory allocation, locking, and (somewhat surprisingly in 3.1, where it shouldn't be necessary) unlocking. It should also be noted that GDI uses a number of *unnamed* functions provided by KERNEL (this is possible because imports occur by module.ordinal). Because we're stressing undocumented functions that we can use in our own programs, we've down-played such *unnamed* DLL functions. Still, it's important to know they exist.

The Windows USER module depends on both KERNEL and GDI, and almost all the device drivers that are part of Windows: SYSTEM, KEYBOARD, MOUSE, DISPLAY, SOUND, and COMM. The following list shows the truly enormous number of undocumented functions used by USER in Windows 3.0. Here, we really move into Windows internals:

\WIN30\SYSTEM\USER.EXE

CallProcInstance (kernel.53)

CreateUserBitmap (gdi.407)

CreateUserDiscardableBitmap (gdi.409)

Death (gdi.121)

DeleteAboveLineFonts (gdi.186)

DirectResAlloc (kernel.168)

EMSCopy (kernel.160)

ExitKernel (kernel.2)

FastWindowFrame (gdi.400)

FinalGDIInit (gdi.405)

GDIInit2 (gdi.403)

GDIMoveBitmap (gdi.401)

GDIRealizePalette (gdi.362)

GDISelectPalette (gdi.361)

GetClipRgn (gdi.173)

GetCurLogFont (gdi.411)

GetCurPID (kernel.157)

GetDCState (gdi.179)

GetExePtr (kernel.133)

GetExeVersion (kernel.105)

GetExpWinVer (kernel.167)

GetTaskDS (kernel.155)

GetTaskQueue (kernel.35)

GetTaskQueueDS (kernel.118)

GetTaskQueueES (kernel.119)

GlobalHandleNoRIP (kernel.159)

InquireVisRgn (gdi.131)

IntersectVisRect (gdi.98)

IsDCCurrentPalette (gdi.412)

IsDCDirty (gdi.169)

IsValidMetaFile (gdi.410)

IsWinOldApTask (kernel.158)

LocalCountFree (kernel.161)

LocalHeapSize (kernel.162)

LockCurrentTask (kernel.33)

OldYield (kernel.117)

PostEvent (kernel.31)

RealizeDefaultPalette (gdi.365)

RestoreVisRgn (gdi.130)

Resurrection (gdi.122)

SaveVisRgn (gdi.129)

SelectVisRgn (gdi.105)

SetDCOrg (gdi.117)

SetDCState (gdi.180)

SetDCStatus (gdi.170)

SetPriority (kernel.32)

SetTaskQueue (kernel.34)

SetTaskSignalProc (kernel.38)

ShrinkGDIHeap (gdi.354)

There's another avenue for exploring the USER module. C *source code* for two important parts of the USER module is included with the Windows SDK: \samples\defprocs\defwnd.c contains the source for the DefWindowProc() function, and \samples\defprocs\defdlg.c contains the code for DefDlgProc(). This code provides a rare inside peek at the actual source for Windows. For example, the author of DefWindowProc() has no apparent hesitation at writing a single function that's 550 (!) lines long but is embarrassed enough about using a goto statement that the label ICantBelieveIUsedAGoToStatement appears in the code. It also helps us disassemble other parts of USER and helps remind us that some of the chief users for undocumented functions exported from a DLL will be other parts of that same DLL. For example, defwnd.c shows that the undocumented EndMenu() function exported from USER is used by the DefWindowProc() function in USER. Though such internal calls are not displayed by MAPWIN, they are displayed by EXEUTIL -UNDOC in chapter 2 of this book.

We have made a rather shallow and cursory examination of the undocumented functions used by GDI and USER. What about KERNEL?

As its name implies, the kernel is supposed to sit at the center of an operating system. And sure enough, running MAPWIN on KRNL286.EXE or KRNL386.EXE turns up *no* modules that KERNEL itself depends on and no functions that it calls in any other DLL. However, the GetProcAddress() function is part of KERNEL, and KERNEL itself uses this function, particularly its initialization code (the Windows BOOTSTRAP function). KERNEL loads the other Windows modules by calling functions they export. These functions, both documented and undocumented, are shown below, to give some idea of how KERNEL actually touches numerous other parts of Windows:

MessageBox (user.1)	StringFunc (user.470)
DisableOEMLayer (user.4)	UserPaintDisable (display.500)
ExitWindows (user.7)	Disable (mouse.3)
SetSystemTimer (user.11)	Inquire (keyboard.1)
GetFocus (user.23)	Disable (keyboard.3)
IsWindow (user.47)	AnsiToOEM (keyboard.5)
PostMessage (user.110)	OEMToAnsi (keyboard.6)
GetWindowTask (user.224)	EnableKbSysReq (keyboard.136)
SignalProc (user.314)	InquireSystem (system.1)
SysErrorBox (user.320)	CreateSystemTimer (system.2)
UserYield (user.332)	DisableSystemTimers (system.5)
IsUserIdle (user.333)	Get80x87SaveState (system.7)
FinalUserInit (user.400)	

The calls to such USER functions as PostMessage() and IsWindow() indicate that KERNEL "knows about" windows and messages. This point is somewhat depressing because it means that the Windows KERNEL is not such a kernel after all. When attempting to draw a diagram of how the different Windows modules interrelate, it is impossible to draw a directed graph. Instead, as we'll see in chapter 2, the result looks more like a drunken spider's web. It gets even worse if one takes into account DOSX.EXE in Standard mode and WIN386.EXE and assorted .386 files in Enhanced mode. The architecture of Windows is baroque. But this is also probably why it works.

Why Aren't They Documented?

By now, we can see a certain pattern. Some Windows API names keep coming up again and again; clearly these functions and selectors have proven useful to serious

Windows developers. We might even attempt a sort of "top twenty hit parade" of undocumented calls (actually, there are more than twenty):

__0000H	IsWinOldApTask
__0040H	KillSystemTimer
CascadeChildWindows	LoadIconHandler
DirectResAlloc	PrestoChangoSelector
DumpIcon	RegisterPtrace
EndMenu	SetDeskWallpaper
GetHeapSpaces	SetInternalWindowPos
GetInternalWindowPos	SetSelectorBase
GetSelectorBase	SetSelectorLimit
GetSelectorLimit	SetSystemTimer
GetSpoolJob	TileChildWindows
GlobalHandleNoRIP	WinDebug
GlobalMasterHandle	

In one sense, it is foolish to ask why Microsoft Windows has undocumented functions. *Any* system of such complexity has no choice but to contain many functions that aren't described to outsiders. After all, "information hiding" is at the very foundation of modern software design. In fact, given how difficult Windows programming can be, one might well complain that Windows doesn't hide *more* of its functions. We don't much care, say, that the Death() and Resurrection() functions exported by GDI and imported by USER are undocumented—these are clearly "private" and probably of little use to us. It's a good thing that Microsoft hides such details from us; otherwise, Windows programming would be even harder than it already is.

But since many of the functions we've been discussing are clearly so useful—and, in some cases, crucial—for Windows programmers, we need to ask why *these* really useful functions are undocumented.

If you spend a few hours examining disassembled listings for some of these undocumented functions, you'll have little question why Microsoft doesn't document them! Although the documented interfaces are admittedly not models of order, the undocumented functions uncovered here are a mess. Clearly, they were thrown together at various points during the evolution of Windows as *ad hoc fixes* to problems. These problems are very real, which is the reason the functions exist in the first place and the reason outsiders often need to know about them. But the solutions are far from perfect.

Consequently, Microsoft often declines to document these functions because it wants to come up with a better, less ad hoc solution and document *that*. For example, rather than document the embarrassingly messy WinDebug() function, Microsoft instead worked on providing equivalent functionality as part of the documented ToolHelp interface. Unfortunately, when Microsoft refuses to document a function because it is working on a better one, this doesn't help the poor programmer who needs a solution *today*. That poor programmer might even work at Microsoft.

In addition to messy implementations (like Get/SetSelectorBase/Limit in Windows 3.0) or screwy interfaces (like the InquireSystem() function in SYSTEM.DRV), sometimes these undocumented functions have embarrassing, juvenile, or facetious names that would need to be changed in any published API. Examples include WinOldAppHackOMatic(), TabTheTextOutForWimps() (any programmer who calls the documented TabbedText Out() function must, we guess, be a wimp), FixBogusPublisherMetafile() (that wouldn't be Ventura Publisher, would it?), and the Death()/Resurrection() functions.

Besides the desire to provide nice functions, rather than document the existing messy ones, another typical sentiment at Microsoft is that documenting these for-internal-consumption-only interfaces will hold back future changes. As one Microsoft employee once put it, all Microsoft employees are "two releases ahead of reality" and put far more emphasis on unreleased and hypothetical versions of Windows than on whichever one exists today. In a company whose primary product sometimes seems to be change itself, documenting system internals is definitely not attractive.

Another reason for failing to document these functions is simply a mistaken notion that very few Windows programmers need to know about them. For example, Microsoft has consistently failed to see the need that many, many applications would have for accessing real-mode DOS from protected-mode Windows. Consequently, the key Windows services for doing just that have been, as we saw earlier, undocumented.

With all this talk of Microsoft's unwillingness to divulge information on undocumented functions, it should be noted that many individual Microsoft employees, when you can reach them via uunet, for example, are often very open and willing to provide information if you sound as though you really need it to do your work and are not simply Easter egging.

More important, Microsoft has a history of eventually documenting undocumented functions, if enough people use them and if enough people scream that they need to be documented. For example, the first edition (1988) of Charles Petzold's classic *Programming Windows* contained a section on "Undocumented File I/O Functions"; Microsoft documented these functions in Windows 3.0. Similarly, Tim Paterson and Steve Flenniken in *Dr. Dobb's Journal* in early 1990 (just before the release of Windows 3.0, the first useful version of Windows) described the undocumented Windows memory-management function DefineHandleTable(); this too then became documented in Windows 3.0, though not very well, perhaps because the function's importance was limited to real mode.

Another "lesson from history" is that useful undocumented functions tend to be cleaned up, rather than dropped. We saw this earlier in the case of PrestoChangoSelector(). Another good example is the Get/SetSelectorBase/Limit family, whose implementation in Windows 3.0 is positively dangerous, but which in 3.1 has been given a more robust implementation, relying on DPMI services rather than blindly banging on the LDT.

In fact, as this chapter was being written, several of the functions discussed here became documented in Windows 3.1. For example, the Get/SetSelector Base/Limit family now has prototypes in the Windows 3.1 SDK version of WINDOWS.H. This is less helpful than one would at first think because the enormous number of copies of Windows 3.0 sold means that most Windows software will need to continue to work with 3.0 as well as with 3.1. It would have been a lot more useful to document the functions in Windows 3.0 as well as in 3.1. Windows 3.1 is a vast improvement over 3.0, and it would be terrific if everyone upgrades (especially because this will contribute to the withering away of real mode), but given that almost two years went by between the release of Windows 3.0 (May 1990) and the release of Windows 3.1 (April 1992), it may take a very long time for 3.1 to replace 3.0.

The fact remains that some of the most useful undocumented functions in 3.0 became documented in 3.1. This raises an interesting question for those who maintain that it is just plain wrong to use undocumented functions: How wrong was it, really, to use these functions in Windows 3.0 if they were destined to become cleaned up and documented in Windows 3.1?

Fear, Loathing, and Portability

Let's discuss this question in more detail: how *safe* is it to use undocumented functions? This question is directly related to how yesterday's undocumented Windows functions can become tomorrow's documented functions; if the most useful undocumented functions are destined to be documented—and if, in fact, by using them, you (in an odd kind of marketplace democracy) help *make* Microsoft document them—then clearly they are safe to use.

This is a somewhat flippant answer to a truly serious question. Many programmers feel that it is dangerous to use undocumented functions. For example, Peter Norton and Paul Yao's book, *Peter Norton's Windows 3.0 Power Programming Techniques*, states, "It has been our experience that 'undocumented goodies' are interesting to look at, but dangerous to include in software that is intended for general distribution."

This statement, from a book with Peter Norton's name on the cover, is somewhat amusing in light of what we have seen of the Norton Desktop for Windows own almost flagrant use of undocumented functions. That pretty much sums up the situation with undocumented function, though: lots of shrinkwrap commercial software, quite definitely intended for general distribution, uses these functions because the authors *had no choice*, yet the same authors might say this practice is dangerous.

In what way is it unsafe to use undocumented functions? It's important to pin this down. Undocumented functions, of course, are *not* unsafe in the sense that they will work one million times and then, on the million and first call, reformat a user's hard disk. Instead, there are two ways in which undocumented functions are less safe than documented functions:

- There may be boundary conditions or odd circumstances in which the functions don't behave as advertised. This is a major reason, in fact, why they're *not* advertised! A good example is the failure of the call GetSelector-Base(__0040H) *in Windows 3.0.*
- The function may change, or be removed entirely, in some future version of Windows. This is usually what is meant when people call using undocumented functions unsafe. Because the function is undocumented, Microsoft is under no obligation to continue providing it.

So the problem with using undocumented functions is very real, but also somewhat limited: it mostly concerns *future* versions of Windows. Given that it took Microsoft almost two years to move from Windows 3.0 to version 3.1, any software that uses undocumented features should have plenty of time in which to settle down and get comfortable.

Then there are those who argue that using undocumented functions is just plain "bad engineering." We put this phrase in quotes because, for some reason, this is precisely the phrase that keeps coming up in conversations on this topic. But the idea that using undocumented functions is just "bad engineering" is based on a misunderstanding of how software engineering (or any engineering, really) works in the real world: it's full of such compromises.

Finally, there is a feeling—certainly within Microsoft, and to some extent outside it—that using undocumented functions is bad because it will hold back Microsoft's ability to make sweeping changes to the system. In the words of one participant in a USENET (comp.windows.ms.programmer) conversation on undocumented Windows, "Windows isn't DOS: it's pretty capable. Once people start getting clever with undocumented stuff in mass-market products, these calls that were intended for internal use get carved in stone. To fix any flaws or make any substantial changes, the old, unofficial calls have to be retained while new calls are added. The complexity of the system increases and everybody suffers. Play with them all you want, but PLEASE just keep it to that!"

This is a weird argument, because it assumes that Microsoft is a better judge of what belongs in the Windows API, of what should be "carved in stone," than are the actual developers of mass-market products. Sure, once developers of mass-market products start getting clever with undocumented functions, then these functions will have to be preserved in future versions, and maybe even documented. What's so bad about that? Shouldn't the actual requirements of real, live products at least in part determine what goes into the API? How is it that Microsoft somehow knows better than applications developers themselves what belongs in the future Windows API?

In other words, the point that use of undocumented functions and internals may tie Microsoft's hands is almost exactly correct. Anyone who bemoans such constraints shouldn't be in the operating-systems business in the first place. In fact, Microsoft's history shows that it is, when push comes to shove, quite adept at making its operating systems compatible with the way that mass-market products twist, reshape, and yes, occassionally misuse, its APIs. For a good example of this, see the GetApp-CompatFlags() function, described in chapter 5.

Rather than tell developers to "play" with undocumented functions, but not to actually use them, it makes far more sense to tell them *not* to play, and to use them only when absolutely necessary. Before using an undocumented function, message, or data structure, carefully check to make sure there isn't some documented function, or perhaps even awkward combination of documented functions, that will work just as well for you. In other words, using undocumented Windows is okay, but only if you have *no choice*: if you have really been responsible, looked for alternatives, and found that there really were none.

Using undocumented Windows, just for the apparent sheer joy of using an undocumented function, or because you failed to look carefully enough for documented functions that do the same thing, does unnecessarily increase the complexity of Windows. In a multitasking environment like Windows, it is particularly important for applications to try to play by the rules. Because several Windows applications can be running at the same time, Windows is really the sum total of all the key commercial applications written for it. Strange things could be happening to your program, not because of anything that it does or even that the core Windows DLLs do, but because of something out of the ordinary that, say, WinWord or Excel or PageMaker—an application—is doing. That's multitasking for you: a total testing nightmare. Any tricks your program uses might affect other programs. Use this power only for good! In particular, never use it out of sheer laziness.

As a good example of how tricks in one program can cause grief for other programs, consider the fact that, whenever one of your users runs Microsoft Word for Windows, the Reschedule() function in KERNEL doesn't get an opportunity to make DOS INT 28h idle calls. If you have a DOS TSR that depends on these calls, or if you wanted to write a Windows program that hooked INT 28h to do idle-time processing (power management? autosave?), you would be out of luck. And WinWord isn't even using an undocumented call here; it's just using PeekMessage() in a certain way. So much for the notion of Microsoft omnipotence. (So much for the notion that the WinWord developers talk to the Windows developers! Where's a decent monopoly when you need one?)

For a good example of totally unnecessary hackery, you need look no further than Windows itself. Disassembly of Windows reveals a high degree of "play": amazing assembly-language hacks used for no apparent reason other than the sheer joy of writing weird code. Jumping into *the middle* of an instruction is a particular favorite. When Microsoft's developers themselves play by very few rules, sometimes violating the standards of good programming taste for no good reason at all, is it right to complain when Windows developers outside Microsoft break the rules when absolutely necessary?

Ultimately, one has to trust the Windows software market. We trust developers not to use undocumented functions just because they are there (the "Mount Everest" approach to undocumented Windows). What will get used in commercial applications are, in general, truly useful and necessary features of undocumented Windows. And, if history is any indication, these most useful undocumented functions will eventually become documented, rather than dropped. If you really need it, you might as well use it now.

Do applications ever *unnecessarily* use undocumented functions and data-structure internals? Unfortunately, yes. An informed source tells us:

"Knowing this internal information (especially the layout of internal data structures) is really great for debugging and general understanding of what's going on. However, using it irresponsibly in a shipping application causes everyone grief in the form of decreased performance and time to market for system improvements. This kind of hackey makes the system much harder to evolve.

"There are two notorious cases of this in 3.1:

"1) Microsoft tried to reduce the size of the window instance by two additional bytes, but some applications were using the hiword of the extend style to store application information.

"2) Microsoft tried to make a performance improvement in the GDI BitBlt call by rearranging some fields in the DC and bitmap structures, but were unable to do so because applications depended on this structure.

"Perhaps most aggravating was that in both cases there were documented ways to achieve the goals of these applications!"

With the availability of TOOLHELP, the point about only using undocumented features when absolutely necessary is particularly important. As chapter 10 shows in more detail, in many cases ToolHelp provides the functionality that once required an undocumented function, or knowledge of the layout of an internal data structure. Use ToolHelp wherever possible. It's true that ToolHelp provides only a partial, distorted, read-only view of the Windows internals, but for many, many applications this partial view is perfectly adequate. Remember too that ToolHelp works in Windows 3.0, and can be redistributed along with your application for those users who do not have 3.1.

On the other hand, we know of many developers who want to use undocumented Windows calls, even when ToolHelp would work for them, because they don't want the apparent hassle of redistributing this DLL along with their application. At one point there were several different versions of ToolHelp in circulation, and applications that worked with one version would not work with another. In one case, Borland C++ shipped with a version of ToolHelp that used different ordinal numbers than the version shipped with Windows 3.1. This caused no end of grief. But as more and more users switch to 3.1, this should cease to be a problem. If you can, *use TOOLHELP!*

And even if ToolHelp does not supply a totally complete picture of Windows internals to meet your needs, you can *still* use it. As several examples in this book show, ToolHelp and undocumented functions work well together. You can use ToolHelp to do your basic heap walking, for example, and then switch over to using an undocumented function or data structure for those areas that ToolHelp does not cover. Good examples of this are the TASKWLK2 program in chapter 4, the ATOMWALK program in chapter 5 (see Atom Table), the USERWALK program in chapter 6, and the GDIWALK program in chapter 8. All these programs use ToolHelp to locate items in the Windows global heap, and then use knowledge of undocumented internals to present a more detailed view of these items.

In other words, just because an undocumented function or data structure is used in one part of a program does not obligate the use of undocumented features throughout the program. Most programs that use undocumented features will probably do so in very limited ways, in just one small part of the program, perhaps in just one small subroutine, to perform some magic that is otherwise impossible. We have seen programs that do absolutely everything "by the book," with no undocumented features except for a single call to, say, IsWinOldApTask(). That one little call makes all the difference.

To turn the same point around, just because you're using ToolHelp does not mean you are limited to TOOLHELP. We have seen Windows browsers that show only what ToolHelp itself shows; in other words, these browsers are just some user-interface slapped on top of TOOLHELP. If ToolHelp doesn't reveal the presence of Task Queues, then neither do these browsers. This seems like a shame. Where ToolHelp fears to tread, use undocumented Windows.

What About NT?

The future Windows NT ("New Technology") is causing much excitement right now and curiosity about whether Windows applications with undocumented calls will run under NT. However, it is more realistic to note that NT will require eight megabytes of memory and to ask whether many customers (i.e., people who call you on the phone, credit card in hand) will be able to, or want to, run NT itself. In its first version at least, NT is apparently intended more to put a stake in the ground than to be something that the masses of PC power users will need to rush out and buy.

On the other hand, the 32-bit NT API *is* very exciting, and we hope some home will be found for it, with reasonable memory requirements, on top of good old MS-DOS. So it's definitely important to be aware of what Microsoft is saying will happen to the Windows API under NT. The primary change for undocumented Windows is that *all* selector-manipulation functions, both documented and undocumented, will be dropped from the 32-bit Windows API; certain resource-handling functions will be dropped because executables in NT (which use the new Portable Executable 'PE' file format) are accessed as memory-mapped files.

At the same time, some undocumented functions persist in NT. For example, the NT version of USER.EXE includes functions such as CascadeChildWindows, Calc-ChildScroll, DragObject, GetInternalWindowPos, SetInternalWindowPos, SwitchTo-ThisWindow, and TileChildWindows, all of which are undocumented in 16-bit Windows.

Interestingly, some WM_ messages that are present but undocumented in 16-bit Windows have been documented in Win32. As chapter 7 explains in more detail, such messages include WM_GETHOTKEY, the WM_OTHERWINDOWXXX messages, and WM_PAINTICON.

Microsoft is saying that existing 16-bit Windows applications will run unmodified, out of the box, under NT, and that the APIs unavailable to 32-bit NT applications will "always be available to a 16-bit application running in Windows NT" (*Microsoft Systems Journal*, November-December 1991). Given the extensive use of undocumented Windows by applications such as NDW, Microsoft will probably need to provide the undocumented APIs for 16-bit Windows applications running under NT.

A good question, then, is what facilities, if any, Microsoft will provide for *mixing*, that is, calling 16-bit API functions from 32-bit Windows code. In the past, Microsoft has underestimated the need for such mixing, failing to anticipate, for example, the pressing need that many developers would have for calling real-mode code from their protected-mode Windows applications. Perhaps facilities for mixing 16- and 32-bit code will be part of an NT device driver layer. In any case, a Win32 "client" application could always use SendMessage() or PostMessage() to deliver a WM_ message request of some sort to a Win16 "server" application, asking it to make whatever calls the Win32 application itself was not allowed to make.

Interestingly, Microsoft's habit of undocumenting large pieces of functionality persists in NT: the entire low-level NT API contained in NTDLL.DLL won't be documented, apparently because Microsoft wants to discourage programmers from writing directly to the NT API; they should instead be writing to the Win32 API. Given that many of the functions in NTDLL.DLL appear to provide functionality not available through the documented interface (even in the lowest documented level, which is BASE.DLL), this may be wishful thinking. It all depends on how successful NT is. If NT is not widely used, then there will, in fact, be little incentive for developers to extend it in unforeseen ways.

In other words, Microsoft's desire to keep programmers away from the undocumented NTDLL APIs will probably succeed only if NT itself fails to gain more than a tiny percentage of the PC operating-systems market. You can have complete control over an operating system, or the operating system can gain many users and have many applications developed for it, but you can't have both at the same time.

Safe Use of Undocumented Functions

Using undocumented functions certainly isn't safe all by itself. In general, these functions should be used in a somewhat different way than you would use a function described in the SDK or prototyped in WINDOWS.H. Even though both documented and undocumented functions have the same source—the DLLs that make up Windows—the undocumented functions really *are* different: they could be removed or altered in some fundamental way, in the next release of Windows. Therefore, you should *check* that the function exists before you call it.

How can you check that a Windows function exists? By using one of Windows key features, run-time dynamic linking. The GetProc() function, shown below, can be used to get the callable address of a Windows API function:

```
FARPROC GetProc(char *szFunction, char *szModule, int nOrdinal)
{
    HANDLE hModule;
    FARPROC lpfnByName;
    FARPROC lpfnByOrd;

    if (! (hModule = GetModuleHandle(szModule)))
        if (! (hModule = LoadLibrary(szModule)))
            return 0;
    if (! (lpfnByName = GetProcAddress(hModule, szFunction)))
        return 0;
    if (! (lpfnByOrd = GetProcAddress(hModule, nOrdinal)))
        return 0;
    if (lpfnByName != lpfnByOrd)
        return 0;
    /* still here */
    return lpfnByName;
}

/* sample use */
DWORD FAR PASCAL (*GetSelectorBase)(WORD sel);
if (! (GetSelectorBase = GetProc("GETSELECTORBASE", "KERNEL", 186)))
    fail("Windows has changed! Please downgrade to an old version!");
// ...
foo = GetSelectorBase(bar);  // in ANSI C, same as (*GetSelectorBase)(bar)
```

GetProc() is extremely paranoid and overly conservative and will return zero if anything is fishy. Before using an undocumented function, you should declare a pointer to it, complete with prototype, and then call GetProc(); you will need to know both the function's name and its module.ordinal, as shown in the example above. The GetProc() function can easily be adapted to languages other than C, such as Turbo Pascal.

Another benefit to GetProc() is that it bypasses the import-library mechanism so that it makes no difference whether the function is provided in an import library. Interestingly, this also means that calls to undocumented functions made this way won't show up in a report from MAPWIN or a similar utility, only the call to GetProcAddress() will.

As noted earlier, you should also make sure to use the Windows GetVersion() function when an undocumented call has known differences from one version of Windows to another.

CHAPTER 2

Examining Windows Executables

There is a building in Paris, the Centre Pompidou (also known as the Beaubourg), whose "insides"—plumbing, wiring, skeletal structure, and so on—seem to be on the outside, the inner workings of the building revealed, or at least seemingly revealed, for all to see.

That, of course, is just the sort of edifice we're trying to construct in this book: Windows turned inside out, with its internal features, its undocumented functions and data structures, plainly visible. An obvious question then is *how* one goes about uncovering Windows' insides, how one finds undocumented functions and data structures, how one figures out what undocumented WM_ messages do, and so on.

The next three chapters present the scaffolding used during the construction of this book. We could have removed this scaffolding, just showing you the completed structure: here are the undocumented functions and data structures, here's where they are used, here's how to use them, the end. But to reveal some of Windows' inner workings only to conceal our own would substitute one form of mystery for another.

There need be no mystery here because finding undocumented Windows functions and data structures is really quite easy. What we will see is that these undocumented features are really not very well hidden at all.

In fact, Windows is somewhat like that building in Paris. Chapter 1 already noted that, by providing dynamic linking, Windows also provides special opportunities for snooping around inside the system. The Windows executable file format includes large amounts of symbolic information that the Windows kernel needs for its own purposes, but that also can be used by anyone curious about how Windows works.

This symbolic information is contained in every shrink-wrapped retail copy of Windows or of a Windows application. Every Windows DLL contains the ASCII *name* (this is what we mean by symbolic information) of every API function that it provides, whether that function is documented or undocumented. Talk about information at your fingertips! Likewise, every Windows executable contains an explicit reference to the Windows API functions it calls; these references let us look up the function's name back in the appropriate DLL. Since Windows applications (somewhat unfortunately) often seem to consist of little more than Windows API calls strung together in different ways, one can—once the standard "boilerplate" functions used by nearly every Windows application are filtered out—tell a lot about an application from the API functions that it calls.

One way to reveal Windows' insides is, of course, to disassemble it: take KRNL386.EXE, for example, submit it to a disassembler, and then pore over the resulting KRNL386.ASM or KRNL386.LST file. We will indeed take a close look at Windows disassembly in chapter 3, but the point about all the information in Windows executables is that we can discover a lot about undocumented Windows before we disassemble even one file.

This chapter will examine all this in more detail, presenting a series of utilities to examine the files that make up Windows. Because we're just examining files, the tools don't need to be Windows applications, and Windows doesn't even need to be running. (Though some of them would make excellent Windows applications if worked over by someone with a good user-interface design sense.) In other words, this is a static analysis of the Windows executable files. The same goes for Windows disassembly in chapter 3. In chapter 4, we present a *dynamic* analysis; consequently, the tools built there must be run with Windows and generally must be Windows applications.

What can we find out about Windows, without necessarily running Windows, just by looking at its files? As it turns out, a lot. We've noted that given any Windows program, we can find the names of the Windows API functions it relies on, that is, what it *imports*. Given a dynamic link library (DLL), we can find the names of the functions it provides, that is, what it *exports*. Given both imports and exports, we can build up a picture of how the various pieces of Windows relate to each other: the Windows economy, as it were.

Let's look at a Windows program. Because it's small (3K bytes), the Windows Task Manager (TASKMAN.EXE) is a good choice. This program needs to be small because (unless you reconfigure Windows) it gets loaded from disk and run every time you press Ctrl-Esc. Because of its small size, and because it relies heavily on undocumented functions, we're going to use TASKMAN as a running example throughout this chapter, looking at these mere 3K bytes from many different angles. The following page shows what TASKMAN looks like to a user of Windows.

We can see that Task Manager is really just a dialog box, with a list box, static text, and a number of buttons. It is quite similar in this way to Charles Petzold's famous HEXCALC program, which consists of nothing but a dialog box. Petzold derides his own HEXCALC as "perhaps the epitome of lazy programming"—by using CreateDialog() rather than CreateWindow(), the program avoids most of the malarkey usually associated with Windows programming—but this has become an increasingly important model for Windows utilities; for example, Visual Basic programs also use this technique.

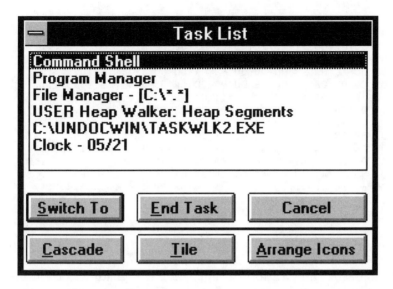

Because Task Manager is a program, it corresponds to a file somewhere, and it can be examined at this level:

```
C:\BIN>dir \win31\taskman

Volume in drive C is STACKER
Directory of C:\WIN31

TASKMAN  EXE       3744 03-10-92   3:10a
      1 file(s)          3744 bytes
                     11654784 bytes free
```

And, because it is a file, you can examine Task Manager at the lowest possible level by dumping out its bytes. Using any hex-dump utility, here is what TASKMAN.EXE looks like from the inside:

```
C:\BIN>dump \windows\taskman.exe
0000 | 4D 5A A2 00 03 00 00 00 20 00 00 00 FF FF 07 00 | MZ...... .......
0010 | 00 01 65 40 00 00 00 00 40 00 00 00 01 00 00 00 | ..e@....@.......
0020 | 00 00 00 00 00 00 00 00 00 00 00 00 00 00 00 00 | ................
0030 | 00 00 00 00 00 00 00 00 00 00 00 00 00 04 00 00 | ................
... lots of zeros ...
01f0 | 00 00 00 00 00 00 00 00 00 00 00 00 00 00 00 00 | ................
0200 | E8 53 00 54 68 69 73 20 70 72 6F 67 72 61 6D 20 | .S.This program
0210 | 72 65 71 75 69 72 65 73 20 4D 69 63 72 6F 73 6F | requires Microso
0220 | 66 74 20 57 69 6E 64 6F 77 73 2E 0D 0A 24 20 20 | ft Windows...$
0230 | 20 20 20 20 20 20 20 20 20 20 20 20 20 20 20 20 |
0240 | 20 20 20 20 20 20 20 20 20 20 20 20 20 20 20 20 |
0250 | 20 20 20 20 20 20 5A 0E 1F B4 09 CD 21 B8 01 4C |       Z.....!..L
0260 | CD 21 00 00 00 00 00 00 00 00 00 00 00 00 00 00 | .!..............
0270 | 00 00 00 00 00 00 00 00 00 00 00 00 00 00 00 00 | ................
```

```
lots of zeros ....
03f0 | 00 00 00 00 00 00 00 00 00 00 00 00 00 00 00 00 | ................
0400 | 4E 45 05 14 A9 00 09 00 99 A3 EC E3 02 03 02 00 | NE..............
0410 | 00 02 00 0C B9 04 01 00 00 00 02 00 02 00 02 00 | ................
0420 | 1C 00 40 00 50 00 7C 00 98 00 9C 00 B2 04 00 00 | ..@.P.|.........
0430 | 01 00 04 00 00 00 02 08 4E 00 7E 00 00 00 0A 03 | ........N.......
0440 | 50 00 19 05 50 1D 19 05 B4 00 50 00 51 0C 50 00 | P...P.....P.Q.P.
0450 | 04 00 05 80 01 00 00 00 00 00 BA 00 0E 00 70 1C | ..............p.
0460 | 0A 80 00 00 00 00 10 80 01 00 00 00 00 00 CC 00 | ................
0470 | 1E 00 30 0C 01 80 00 00 00 00 00 07 54 41 53 | ..0.........TAS
0480 | 4B 4D 41 4E 00 00 0E 54 41 53 4B 4D 41 4E 44 4C | KMAN...TASKMANDL
0490 | 47 50 52 4F 43 01 00 00 01 00 08 00 00 06 4B 45 | GPROC.........KE
04a0 | 52 4E 45 4C 04 55 53 45 52 01 FF 01 CD 3F 01 7B | RNEL.USER....?.{
04b0 | 00 00 18 57 69 6E 64 6F 77 73 20 54 61 73 6B 20 | ...Windows Task
04c0 | 4D 61 6E 61 67 65 72 20 33 2E 31 00 00 00 00 00 | Manager 3.1.....
.... etc. ....
```

This hex dump shows TASKMAN.EXE's executable headers. Though Windows runs on top of MS-DOS, it uses a different executable file format from DOS. The DOS EXE file format, known as the MZ format (after the MZ signature, the initials of Microsoft's Mark Zbikowski, in the first two bytes of .EXE files), does not contain enough information for an advanced protected-mode, dynamic-linking, multitasking environment such as Windows. Windows instead uses a new executable file format (with an NE signature) that contains much more symbolic information than the MZ format does.

In the hex dump of TASKMAN you can see both the MZ and NE signatures: every Windows application begins with a standard DOS executable MZ program, followed by a new-executable (NE) header. The NE format is a *superset* of the MZ format. The MZ program, or stub, is just a program that runs if the executable is invoked under DOS. This program is usually called STUB.EXE or WINSTUB.EXE, but it can be any arbitrary DOS program of any size. For example, Excel contains a DOS stub that,when Windows is not running, *starts* Windows and Excel with an INT 21h EXEC of "win.com excel.exe." For another example, see the description of KERNEL's stub (KERNSTUB) in the introduction to chapter 5.

In the hex dump of TASKMAN, you also can see several strings that look useful, or at least interesting. But hex dumping the file's bytes presents a view that is generally too low-level. We need a utility that knows something about the NE data structure and can use it to present the information in a more structured way. Both Microsoft C (including Microsoft C/C++ 7.0) and Borland C++ come with utilities that can let us look at Windows executables in this way. Microsoft's is called EXEHDR; Borland's is called TDUMP. For example, here is part of EXEHDR's view of Task Manager:

```
C:\MSC7\BIN>exehdr /v \win31\taskman.exe
Microsoft (R) EXE File Header Utility Version 3.00
Copyright (C) Microsoft Corp 1985-1992. All rights reserved.
... some boring details omitted ...

Module                  TASKMAN
Description:            Windows Task Manager 3.1
```

```
Operating system:              Microsoft Windows - version 3.10
Data:                          NONSHARED
Initial CS:IP:                 seg   1 offset 04b9
Initial SS:SP:                 seg   2 offset 0000
Extra stack allocation:        0c00 bytes
DGROUP:                        seg   2
Linker version:                5.20
32-bit Checksum:               e3eca399
Segment Table:                 00000440 length 0010 (16)
Resource Table:                00000450 length 002c (44)
Resident Names Table:          0000047c length 001c (28)
Module Reference Table:        00000498 length 0004 (4)
Imported Names Table:          0000049c length 000d (13)
Entry Table:                   000004a9 length 0009 (9)
Non-resident Names Table:      000004b2 length 001c (28)
Movable entry points:          1
Segment sector size:           16
Heap allocation:               0200 bytes
Application type:              WINDOWAPI
Other module flags:
no. type address  file   mem    flags
  1 CODE 00000500 00519  00519  EXECUTEREAD, PRELOAD, NONCONFORMING, NOIOPL,
                                 relocs, (movable), (discardable),
(nonshared)
  2 DATA 00000b40 00050  00050  READWRITE, NONSHARED, PRELOAD, NOEXPANDDOWN,
                                 NOIOPL, (movable), (nondiscardable)
Exports:
ord seg offset name
1   1    007b     TASKMANDLGPROC exported

1      type       offset       target
       BASE       0441         seg   1 offset 0000
       PTR        04f0         imp   USER.5
       PTR        01a5         imp   USER.262
       PTR        0058         imp   USER.135
       PTR        0302         imp   KERNEL.158
       PTR        04e7         imp   KERNEL.30
       ... more boring details omitted ...
       PTR        0353         imp   USER.106
       PTR        00d3         imp   USER.110
       PTR        0028         imp   USER.111
       34 relocations
```

The strings that appeared earlier in the hex dump show up here, too, but this time in a structured way. Files are just data structures on a disk, and if you know the data structure you obviously can do a better job of displaying the file than if you just dump bytes, aimlessly look for strings and so on. In this case, the data structure is the new-executable (NE) file format, which is described in the Windows 3.1 Software Development Kit (SDK) *Programmer's Reference, Volume 4: Resources*, chapters 6 and 7. (EXEHDR itself is documented in the Microsoft C/C++ 7.0 *Environment and Tools* manual, chapter 17.)

From EXEHDR's output, we can see that TASKMAN.EXE exports one function, TaskManDlgProc(). This confirms our suspicion that the Task Manager is really just a dialog box. The table that EXEHDR labels "Exports" is a synthesis of three tables found in NE files: the Entry Table, the Resident Name Table, and the Nonresident Name Table. Borland's TDUMP, incidentally, presents the three tables as they are in the file.

At the very end of the EXEHDR output, we can see that Task Manager uses a number of Windows API functions from the USER and KERNEL dynamic link libraries (this section of the EXEHDR output should really be labeled "Relocations" or "Imports"). Once again, this information is a synthesis of information from the actual, lower-level tables found in the NE file: the Segment Table, the Relocation Table for each segment, the Imported Names Table, and the Module Reference Table.

Unfortunately, it's rather difficult to tell *which* Windows API functions TASK-MAN uses, because both EXEHDR and TDUMP simply present the API functions' ordinal numbers (such as USER.262) rather than their names. An API function's ordinal number is simply its position in the entry table of the module that exports it.

As noted in chapter 1, we could now run EXEHDR again, this time on USER.EXE and KRNL386.EXE, look at their "Exports" sections, and match everything up, finding, for example, that USER.262 is actually GetWindow(). But once we know we *can* do this, there really is no point in actually doing it; it's just the sort of thing a program would be good at.

Unfortunately, it's not something that EXEHDR is good at. This deficiency of EXEHDR has spawned a small industry of improved executable-header utilities. Only rarely have their authors resisted the temptation to give these super-EXEHDR utilities names such as SEX or SEXYHDR.

Using MAPWIN

Our first utility, Phar Lap Software's MAPWIN, is a super-EXEHDR utility that makes it easy to see what API functions a Windows program, dynamic-link library (DLL), or device driver uses (imports), and what functions a program, DLL, or driver provides (exports). Phar Lap uses this utility to determine what API functions need to be implemented to run a program under its 286|DOS-Extender environment, which uses the same NE executable file format as Windows. You can use MAPWIN, provided on the accompanying disk, to snoop around inside Windows and uncover useful, undocumented API functions.

MAPWIN is a character-mode program that runs under DOS, the DOS box in Windows, or (for what it's worth) in OS/2 1.x. To use MAPWIN, simply point it at a Windows executable file. The output can be redirected to a file. For example

```
C:\BIN>mapwin \windows\taskman.exe > taskman.log

C:\BIN>mapwin \windows\system\user.exe > user.log

C:\BIN>mapwin \windows\system\system.drv > system.log
```

MAPWIN will produce a list of the executable's exports and another list of its imports, plus some other information. For example, here's what the Windows Task Manager looks like at this level:

```
C:\BIN>mapwin \win31\taskman.exe
MAPWIN: 4.0 -- Copyright (C) 1986-91 Phar Lap Software, Inc.

Dump of the .EXE file -- \win31\taskman.exe

Header information
Target operating system................Windows
Initial CS:IP.........................#0001:04B9
Initial SS:SP.........................#0002:0000
Initial DS............................#0002
Initial heap size.....................512 bytes (0x0200)
Initial stack size....................3072 bytes (0x0000)
Automatic data segment................Multiple

DLLs called by this program
KERNEL
USER


Exported entry points
TASKMANDLGPROC (taskman.1)

Imported references
__WINFLAGS (KERNEL.178)                GETWINDOWTEXT (USER.36)
ARRANGEICONICWINDOWS (USER.170)        INITAPP (USER.5)
CASCADECHILDWINDOWS (USER.198)         INITTASK (KERNEL.91)
DIALOGBOX (USER.87)                    ISWINDOW (USER.47)
DOS3CALL (KERNEL.102)                  ISWINDOWVISIBLE (USER.49)
ENDDIALOG (USER.88)                    ISWINOLDAPTASK (KERNEL.158)
FREEPROCINSTANCE (KERNEL.52)           MAKEPROCINSTANCE (KERNEL.51)
GETDESKTOPWINDOW (USER.286)            MESSAGEBEEP (USER.104)
GETDLGITEM (USER.91)                   MOVEWINDOW (USER.56)
GETKEYSTATE (USER.106)                 POSTMESSAGE (USER.110)
GETLASTACTIVEPOPUP (USER.287)          SENDMESSAGE (USER.111)
GETPROCADDRESS (KERNEL.50)             SETWINDOWPOS (USER.232)
GETSYSTEMMETRICS (USER.179)            SHOWWINDOW (USER.42)
GETWINDOW (USER.262)                   SWITCHTOTHISWINDOW (USER.172)
GETWINDOWLONG (USER.135)               TILECHILDWINDOWS (USER.199)
GETWINDOWRECT (USER.32)                WAITEVENT (KERNEL.30)
GETWINDOWTASK (USER.224)
```

The "DLLs called by this program" section shows that TASKMAN depends on KERNEL and USER; that there are no GDI calls is interesting. You do need to be somewhat cautious, though, in how you interpret this information. If TASKMAN contained calls to LoadLibrary(), LoadModule(), GetModuleHandle(), or GetSystemMetrics(SM_PENWINDOWS), then it could be linking to additional DLLs at run time.

The "Imported references" section tells us the specific functions that a program or a DLL uses. For our purposes, this is a lot more useful than what EXEHDR shows. For example, we can clearly see that our supposition about Task Manager was probably correct: it imports DialogBox(), but not CreateWindow().

Our idea was only probably correct, though, because we can also see that TASK-MAN imports GetProcAddress(). This function, part of Windows' support for run-time dynamic linking (that's right, linking while the program is running), means that

TASKMAN could be importing something else, without it showing up in the MAPWIN display: maybe even CreateWindow(). (In fact, disassembly of TASKMAN with Windows Source (see below) reveals that GetProcAddress() is being used as part of support for Pen Windows.)

Of course, the "Imported references" section is also where we find what undocumented functions, if any, are being used. As already noted, TASKMAN relies heavily on undocumented functions; MAPWIN lists the following:

```
CASCADECHILDWINDOWS (USER.198)
ISWINOLDAPTASK (KERNEL.158)
SWITCHTOTHISWINDOW (USER.172)
TILECHILDWINDOWS (USER.199)
```

The "Exported entry points" section of MAPWIN's output shows the other side of the import/export equation. In TASKMAN, this display isn't particularly interesting because TASKMAN is a program, not a library, and contains only one export. An export is a function (or data item) provided to other programs; the purpose of a library is generally to provide exports. It may seem odd, then, that TASKMAN contains *any* exports; after all, it's not a library. In Windows, however, programs have callbacks, functions that Windows calls. The key ones are window procedures (WndProcs), dialog procedures (DlgProcs), and enumeration procedures (EnumProcs); TASKMAN exports TaskManDlgProc. There are several crucial differences between programs and DLLs (the main one is that DLLs never get turned into tasks), but when examining NE files, the main difference is that DLLs generally export more functions than programs and that these functions are more general-purpose.

We can get a better illustration of the MAPWIN "Exported entry points" section by examining a DLL or DRV. For example, here's a small portion of the MAPWIN output for USER.EXE (which, despite its .EXE extension, is a DLL):

```
C:\BIN>mapwin \windows\system\user.exe
MAPWIN: 4.0 -- Copyright (C) 1986-91 Phar Lap Software, Inc.

Dump of the .DLL file -- \windows\system\user.exe
... details omitted ...

DLLs called by this program
   SYSTEM
   KEYBOARD
   MOUSE
   DISPLAY
   SOUND
   COMM
   KERNEL
   GDI

Exported entry points
   ... details omitted ...          HIDECARET (user.166)
   DELETEMENU (user.413)            EXITWINDOWS (user.7)
```

```
GETMENUITEMID (user.264)              MESSAGEBOX (user.1)
SETWC2 (user.319)                     ISTWOBYTECHARPREFIX (user.51)
CASCADECHILDWINDOWS (user.198)        GETINPUTSTATE (user.335)
GETASYNCKEYSTATE (user.249)           CREATECURSORICONINDIRECT (user.408)
RELEASEDC (user.68)                   CREATECARET (user.163)
ANSINEXT (user.472)                   SCROLLDC (user.221)
CLEARCOMMBREAK (user.211)             TILECHILDWINDOWS (user.199)
POSTQUITMESSAGE (user.6)              GETSYSTEMMETRICS (user.179)
```

Here you can see the names of many Windows API functions (forced to upper-case, because this is what LINK does with the names of functions that use the Pascal calling convention). You also can see the names of two of the undocumented functions that TASKMAN imports: CascadeChildWindows() and TileChildWindows().

When a Windows program such as TASKMAN imports these functions, it actually does so "by ordinal." The source code undoubtedly references these functions by name, but when compiled and then linked with an import library such as LIBW.LIB or IMPORTS.LIB, an IMPDEF record for USER.198 and USER.199 is placed in the executable file. (IMPDEF and EXPDEF are explained in chapters 10 and 11 of the Windows 3.1 SDK *Programmer's Reference, Volume 4: Resources*.) That's why EXEHDR and TDUMP simply print out the module name and ordinal number for the function being called; the actual function name isn't contained in the calling executable, and getting it would require going somewhere else, to the called executable.

So where does MAPWIN get the names of imported functions?

MAPWIN assigns names to imports based on a table that matches module.ordinal pairs such as USER.198 with ASCII function names such as CASCADECHILD-WINDOWS. This table is built right into MAPWIN.

Fortunately, this table can be overridden because MAPWIN does not "know" about all Windows 3.0 DLLs and device drivers; nor does it know about vendor-specific DLLs that come with many Windows applications; nor does it know about any new functions provided by Windows 3.1. The table is overridden by specifying an "import file" on the command line (you must give an exact path). For example:

```
C:\BIN>mapwin @\undocwin\winfunc.imp \windows\taskman.exe
```

An import files contains one or more lines such as the following:

```
IMPORT GETTABBEDTEXTEXTENT=USER.197
IMPORT CASCADECHILDWINDOWS=USER.198
IMPORT TILECHILDWINDOWS=USER.199
IMPORT OPENCOMM=USER.200
```

The accompanying disk comes with the file WINFUNC.IMP, which includes all exports from the following modules, for Windows 3.0 and 3.1:

```
COMM.DRV (Communications driver)
COMMDLG.DLL (Common dialogs)
```

```
DDEML.DLL (DDE Manager library)
FINSTALL.DLL (Font installer)
GDI.EXE (Graphics Device Interface)
HPPCL.DRV (HP LaserJet)
KEYBOARD.DRV (Keyboard device driver)
KRNL386.EXE (KERNEL)
LANMAN.DRV (LAN Manager API)
LZEXPAND.DLL (file decompression)
MIDIMAP.DRV (Multimedia MIDI Mapper)
MMSOUND.DRV (Multimedia Sound driver)
MMSYSTEM.DLL (Multimedia)
MOUSE.DRV (Mouse device driver)
NETAPI20.DLL (Lan Manager API)
NETWARE.DRV (Novell NetWare driver)
OLECLI.DLL (OLE Client)
OLESVR.DLL (OLE Server)
PENWIN.DLL (Pen Windows)
SHELL.DLL (Support for shell programs like PROGMAN)
SOUND.DRV (Sound device driver)
SUPERVGA.DRV (DISPLAY)
SYSTEM.DRV (Floating point, system timers, disk drives)
TOOLHELP.DLL (Debugger and tool helper)
UNIDRV.DLL (Universal Printer Driver Library)
USER.EXE (Windows User Interface)
V7VGA.3GR (GRABBER)
VER.DLL (Version-stamping library)
WIN87EM.DLL (Math Coprocessor/Emulator Library)
WINDEBUG.DLL (Ptrace for Windows)
WINMEM32.DLL (32-bit memory manager)
WINOA386.MOD (WINOLDAP; support for DOS apps)
WINNLS.DLL (Kanji Windows National Language Support)
KKLIB.DLL (Kanji Windows)
MSKANJI.EXE (Kanji Windows)
GAIJILIB.DLL (Kanji Windows)
WIFEMAN.DLL (Kanji Windows Intelligent Font Environment Manager)
```

In all, WINFUNC.IMP lists over 1600 functions.

In addition to WINFUNC.IMP, you can create your own *.IMP files by using the MAPWIN -IMPMAKE switch. For example:

```
C:\BIN>for %f in (\bigapp\*.dll) do mapwin -impmake %f >> winfunc.imp
```

You can specify multiple *.IMP files on the MAPWIN command line, like so:

```
C:\BIN>mapwin @winfunc.imp @phoo.imp @bar.imp \baz\zar\quux.exe
```

MAPWIN is extracted from a far more extensive Phar Lap utility, MAPEXE, that, in addition to these Windows NE files, also handles OS/2 1.x NE files, Windows LE files (linear executables, such as *.386 virtual device drivers), the W3 format used by WIN386.EXE, Win32/NT portable executables (PE files), and OS/2 2.0 LX files. MAPWIN handles only Windows NE files. The TDUMP utility included with Borland C++ works with LE files; the LEDUMP and W3MAP utilities provided with Windows Source (see chapter 3) work with both LE and W3 files.

Windows Module Dependencies

The "DLLs called by this program" section of MAPWIN's output, which is just a display of the Module Reference Table in an NE file, is surprisingly useful for anyone who wants to get a picture of how the different pieces of Windows fit together. For example, we've seen that TASKMAN depends on (calls functions in) KERNEL and USER, and that USER depends on KERNEL, GDI, MOUSE, and so on. If you run MAPWIN on all the executables that come with Windows, you can use the results to try to put together a dependency graph of Windows modules. For example:

PROGMAN	**KERNEL**	**SYSTEM**
KERNEL	[no DLLs used]	KERNEL
GDI	**GDI**	**MOUSE**
USER	KERNEL	SYSTEM
KEYBOARD	**USER**	KERNEL
SHELL	SYSTEM	**DISPLAY** (e.g., VGADRV)
SHELL	KEYBOARD	KEYBOARD
	MOUSE	KERNEL
	DISPLAY	**SOUND**
	SOUND	KERNEL
	COMM	**COMM**
	KERNEL	SYSTEM
	GDI	KERNEL
	KEYBOARD	
	KERNEL	
	SHELL	
	KERNEL	
	GDI	
	USER	
	KEYBOARD	

In other words, one might conclude the following:

- KERNEL, being the kernel, depends on nobody (but see the next page!).
- USER, being the topmost portion of Windows (PROGMAN, the Windows Program Manager, isn't part of Windows at all; it's just an application), depends on almost everything else: KERNEL, GDI, and a host of device drivers (SYSTEM, KEYBOARD, MOUSE, DISPLAY, SOUND, COMM).
- GDI depends only on KERNEL (but see the following information!).

continued

continued

Unfortunately, these results need to be taken along with a large dose of caution. First, even though the Module Reference Table displayed by MAPWIN indicates that KERNEL is a self-contained kernel, disassembly of KERNEL reveals that it is in fact *heavily* dependent on other modules! As already noted in chapter 1, KERNEL uses internal versions of its own GetModuleHandle() and GetProcAddress() functions to dynamically link to functions in USER, SYSTEM, KEYBOARD, MOUSE, and DISPLAY. Some kernel!

Second, we know that GDI *must* communicate with a DISPLAY device driver in some way, yet this fact is not reflected in the results shown above. Once again, the explanation is run-time dynamic linking: the CreateDC() function (actually, the InternalCreateDC() function, described in the chapter on GDI) uses LoadLibrary() and GetProcAddress() to link to the DISPLAY driver whose name is passed as its first parameter. (By the way, it was for revealing this rather obvious fact about CreateDC() that Microsoft's lawyers went after Michael Geary.)

Anyway, our attempts at drawing a directed graph of Windows modules ends up producing something that looks more like a spider's web.

Figure 2-1 shows how a dynamic-linking, multitasking, device-independent graphical windowed operating environment is constructed on top of MS-DOS.

Figure 2-1: Architecture of Windows Real Mode.

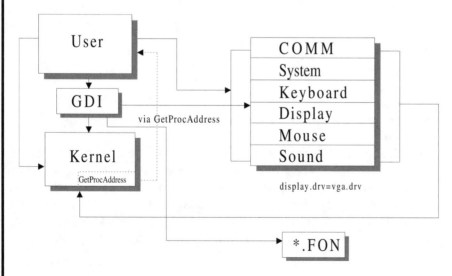

continued

continued

However, this picture is also misleading: this is really the architecture of Windows real mode. The problem with this picture is that with all these modules loaded like this on top of real-mode DOS, there's no room in which to run any applications.

Thus, we need to revise the diagram for Windows Standard mode and Enhanced mode. In Standard mode, the whole USER-GDI-KERNEL-DISPLAY-etc. mess sits on top of a 16-bit DOS extender and DPMI server in DOSX.EXE:

In Figure 2-2, Windows components are stuck on top of DOSX.EXE (DOS extender) and, in Windows 3.1, the Task Swappers DSWAP.EXE and WSWAP.EXE. Most of Windows is swapped out to disk to run an "old app" (DOS application).

Figure 2-2: Architecture of Windows Standard Mode.

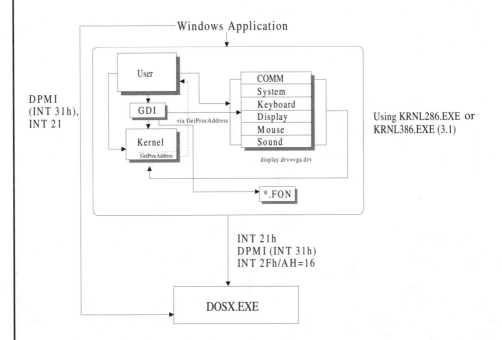

In Enhanced mode, it all rests on top of the Virtual Machine Manager (VMM), 32-bit virtual device drivers (VxDs), 32-bit DOS extender, and DPMI server collected into WIN386.EXE.

continued

continued

In Figure 2-3, Windows components are stuck on top of WIN386.EXE, which contains a DPMI server, 32-bit DOS extender, Virtual Machine Manager (VMM), and Virtual Device Drivers (VxDs).

Figure 2-3: Architecture of Windows Enhanced Mode.

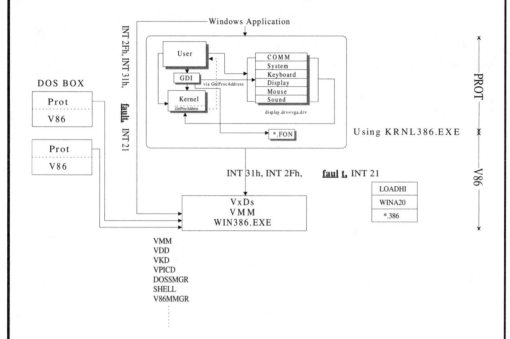

The upper portion of Windows 3.x, KERNEL in particular, communicates with the lower portions via interrupts and exceptions: DOS INT 21h calls, DOS Protected-Mode Interface (DPMI) INT 31h calls, INT 2Fh calls, deliberately generated faults, and so on.

It's certainly true that MAPWIN, or any other program that examines the Module Reference Table in NE files, could not tell us about this aspect of Windows. It also couldn't help with any calls made via run-time dynamic linking. But it did get us thinking about how Windows is put together, and it did provide most of the pieces. The fact that it isn't 100% accurate is just an indication of how important interrupts, exceptions, and run-time dynamic linking are to Windows internals. ∎

Using EXEDUMP

The nice thing about MAPWIN is that it presents a high-level view of a Windows executable; "high-level" is another way of saying that it suppresses details. There are many things about a Windows executable that MAPWIN does *not* show you; this is what makes it useful.

Unfortunately, sometimes we really need detailed information. It won't be clear until a little later *why*, but sometimes we need to know where a program's CODE and DATA segments are located in the file, where (segment:offset address) each of its exports is, where each of its imports is used, and so on.

Our next utility, EXEDUMP, presents just this sort of low-level view of a Windows (or OS/2 1.x) executable (EXE, DLL, DRV, etc.). It shows the entry table (exports), relocation table (imports), segment table, selected useful fields from the NE header, plus selected CodeView information, if present. For example, here is EXEDUMP's view of the Windows 3.1 Task Manager:

```
C:\BIN>exedump \win31\taskman.exe
name \win31\taskman.exe
program
target WINDOWS 3.10
80286 instructions
dgroup 2
start_csip 1:04b9
description "Windows Task Manager 3.1"
modname TASKMAN

begin entry
    1    007b     1     TASKMANDLGPROC

begin segtab
    1    500 0519     CODE      USE16
    2    b40 0050     DATA      USE16

begin modref
    KERNEL
    USER

begin reloc
    1    04b9     [e] start
    1    0441     [s] 1 0000      SEG
    1    04f0     [m] USER 5      PTR
    1    01a5     [m] USER 262    PTR
    1    01c6     [m] USER 262    PTR
    1    0200     [m] USER 262    PTR
    1    0058     [m] USER 135    PTR
    1    02cd     [m] USER 135    PTR
    1    031e     [m] USER 135    PTR
    1    0302     [m] KERNEL 158  PTR
    1    04e7     [m] KERNEL 30   PTR
    ... you get the idea ...
    1    0212     [m] USER 111    PTR
    1    0291     [m] USER 111    PTR
    1    029b     [m] USER 111    PTR
```

This is quite similar to what Microsoft's EXEHDR utility shows, except that it appears in a form that's more convenient for parsing by other programs (namely, EXEUTIL; see the discussion later in this chapter). Also, it does a number of things EXEHDR does not do, which we'll get to later.

First, EXEDUMP presents some header information:

- Executable type: "program" (application) or "library" (DLL or DRV).
- The target operating system: Windows or OS/2. For Windows, the target version (3.00 or 3.10) is also shown; the intended version of an executable depends on the linker used to create it.
- The Logical Segment Number (LSN) for the default data segment (DGROUP). Utilities that dump Windows executables use LSNs, which are shown in decimal (not hex), and which start with 1 (not 0).
- The entry point (starting CS:IP) for the program or library. This is *not* the same as WinMain() or LibMain(); it is the address (in LSN:offset form) of the first instruction to be executed when KERNEL loads the file; it generally corresponds to the compiler's startup code, which in turn calls WinMain() or LibMain(). (See chapter 1 and the discussion of InitTask() in chapter 5.)
- The module name and description string for the executable. These are not actually in the NE header (the description string is the first entry in the Non-resident Names Table, and the module name is the first entry in the Resident Names Table), but the header is a good place to display them.

Module Name != File Name

We've been throwing around this term "module" without explaining it. What does it mean that TASKMAN references the KERNEL module? It means that there exists an NE file that contains the string "KERNEL" as entry 0 in its Resident Names Table, and that, somewhere in TASKMAN's Relocation Tables (see the next page), there is at least one import of a function or variable that this KERNEL module exports.

But note: this KERNEL module is not necessary called KERNEL.DLL or KERNEL.EXE. Because all NE files contain their own module name (contrast this with a DOS .EXE program, which doesn't necessarily know its own name), this opens up an interesting and important possibility: the module name and file name do not need to match. You can have multiple files, all answering to the same module name. This is just the case with KERNEL: in Windows 3.0, KERNEL.EXE, KRNL286.EXE, and KRNL386.EXE are all versions of the KERNEL module.

In fact, this possible discrepancy between module name and file name is a basis for Windows device drivers: you can have a thousand different files, with names such as VGAMONO.DRV, V7VGA.DRV, and even CGA.DRV, but all with same module name, "DISPLAY", and all with same basic set of entry points. You specify the one you want with a DISPLAY.DRV= statement in the Windows SYSTEM.INI file. Same interface, different implementation: voilà! Device independence. Some might even call it object-oriented. ■

- If the executable contains its own loader, EXEDUMP displays the string "Self-loading." (See the description of PatchCodeHandle() in chapter 5 for more information on self-loading Windows applications.)
- If the default data segment (DGROUP) does not contain a valid NULL segment block, EXEDUMP displays the string "No NULL segment." (See the description of "Instance Data" in chapter 5 for more information on the NULL segment block found at offset 0 in a Windows program's default data segment.)

After the initial header information, EXEDUMP displays several tables. Each starts with a line such as "begin entry," "begin segtab," "begin CodeView," or "begin reloc." Below, we've extracted a sample of the output to help explain each table.

Entry Table

```
begin entry
    1   007b    1    TASKMANDLGPROC
```

The entry table lists every export (entry point), named and unnamed, from a Windows DLL or program. For each export, EXEDUMP shows the logical segment number (in decimal), the offset within the segment (in hex), the ordinal number of the export, and the name (if available) of the export. In the example above, in other words, entry #1 (TASKMAN.1), named TaskManDlgProc, is located at 1:007B.

In a DLL, EXEDUMP may show hundreds of exports, perhaps corresponding to Windows API functions. For example, here's part of the display from EXEDUMP \WIN31\SYSTEM\SHELL.DLL:

```
begin entry
    2   15cc    1    REGOPENKEY
    2   15fa    2    REGCREATEKEY
    2   1670    3    REGCLOSEKEY
    2   1628    4    REGDELETEKEY
    ... details omitted ...
    5   0000    38   FINDENVIRONMENTSTRING
   10   026e    39   INTERNALEXTRACTICON
    4   0550    100  HERETHARBETYGARS
    8   010e    101  FINDEXEDLGPROC
    4   128c    102  REGISTERSHELLHOOK
    4   11ca    103  SHELLHOOKPROC
    2   0000    104
    1   0077    105
    ... details omitted ...
   12   0000    127
   12   0016    128
```

For example, there is an unnamed export (function or variable), SHELL.128, at offset 16h in logical segment #12. Likewise, the 3.1 RegOpenKey() function (SHELL.1) lives at offset 15CCh in segment #2 of this version of SHELL.DLL.

When a program that calls RegOpenKey( ) dynamically links to this function, the address it gets will have an offset of 15CCh and a segment of whatever protected-mode selector corresponds to segment #2 in SHELL. The correspondence between logical segment numbers in the file and protected-mode selectors in memory is kept in the in-memory Segment Table, described in chapter 5's description of the Module Database. The Module Database is the in-memory version of the NE format.

Segment Table

```
begin segtab
    1    500 0519     CODE     USE16
    2    b40 0050     DATA     USE16
```

The segment table (segtab) lists every segment in the executable. For each segment, EXEDUMP shows the logical segment number (in decimal), the file offset for the segment (in hex), the number of bytes in the segment (again in hex), whether it is CODE or DATA, and whether it is USE16 or USE32 (through you're unlikely to find any USE32 segments in an NE file).

The existence of a segment table in NE executables represents a key difference from DOS (MZ) executables: in Windows, segments are genuine, discrete units in the file. Though many Windows DLLs do store data in their code segments, there is at least a notion of separate code and data segments. In fact, NE executables are sometimes also called segmented executables, and the Microsoft linker that produces them is called the Segmented-Executable Linker.

In our example, the first segment in TASKMAN.EXE is CODE, 519h bytes long, located at offset 500h in the file. The second segment is its single, default DATA segment (DGROUP), 50h bytes long, located at offset 0B40h in the file. Note that these offsets are from the start of the entire file, *not* from the beginning of its NE component. The use of file rather than NE offsets makes this table dependent on the size of the DOS stub program; any "rebind" utility that manipulates the DOS stub in an NE executable has to adjust all the file offsets in this table (aargh!).

Module-Reference Table

```
begin modref
    KERNEL
    USER
```

The next EXEDUMP section displays the module-reference (modref) table and is identical to the "DLLs called by this program" list shown by MAPWIN.

CodeView Symbols The next table, not present in TASKMAN.EXE, is an optional table of CodeView (CV) symbols. For example:

```
begin CodeView
    2    0000     001a     libentry.obj (MODULE)
    2    001a     090c     init.obj (MODULE)
    1    0000     00db     time.obj (MODULE)
```

```
8    0000    04ed    joy.obj (MODULE)
9    0006            rsrvptrs (USHORT)
9    000c            pStackMin (USHORT)
9    000e            pStackBot (USHORT)
2    0014            WEP (TYP 03CCh)
9    000a            pStackTop (USHORT)
9    0006            pLocalHeap (USHORT)
9    0008            pAtomTable (USHORT)
0    0001            __acrtused (TYP ABS)
8    00d2            joyReleaseCapture
... and so on ...
```

As usual, the first number is a logical segment (in decimal), and the next number is an offset within the segment (in hex). If the CodeView symbol describes an .OBJ or source module, indicated by "(MODULE)", the next number is the offset (hex) for the last byte in the module. In the example above, JOY.OBJ is located at 8:0000 through 8:04ED. For symbols other than module names, EXEDUMP shows the symbol name, followed by its type, if available. In the example above, USHORT pLocalHeap is located at 9:0006. Names are shown only for simple types; nonprimitive types are indicated with a TYP number.

In the example shown (from a debug version of MMSYSTEM.DLL), the joyReleaseCapture() function lives at 8:00D2. Because this is an export from MMSYSTEM (documented in the *Multimedia Programmer's Reference*), the EXEDUMP entry-table display would show the same information. The CodeView information is useful if it provides names for internal (nonexported) functions and variables.

EXEDUMP only shows public CodeView symbols; other information such as local variables and type information is not handled. (Borland's TDUMP displays all CodeView information.)

CodeView information is important because some releases of the debug version of Windows (included with the Windows SDK) come with very complete CodeView information that EXEDUMP can pass along to a disassembler. Unfortunately, in most releases of the debug version of Windows, all the symbols for internal (nonexported and/or undocumented) functions and variables are replaced with strings of spaces. EXEDUMP normally suppresses these mangled CodeView symbols; if you want EXEDUMP to show these blanks (it's a sad sight), use the -CVBLANKS command-line option:

```
C:\BIN>exedump -cvblanks \windev.31\debug\krnl386.exe
```

The CodeView symbol format (through Microsoft C 6.0) is documented in the *Microsoft C Developer's Toolkit Reference* (Microsoft Part No. 18161). The completely different CV format used by Microsoft C/C++ 7.0 is documented as part of Open Tools (see chapter 1).

EXEDUMP does not handle Turbo Debugger symbols, but Borland's TDUMP does display these symbols, of course. The TD symbol-table format is documented in the *Borland Languages Open Architecture Handbook* (Borland Part No. 14MN-RCH01-10).

Relocation Table

```
begin reloc
    1    04b9    [e] start
    1    0441    [s] 1 0000      SEG
    1    04f0    [m] USER 5      PTR
    1    01a5    [m] USER 262    PTR
    1    01c6    [m] USER 262    PTR
    1    0200    [m] USER 262    PTR
```

Each segment in a Windows executable is optionally followed by a relocation table. Relocations are places that need to be "fixed up" (patched) before the program can run. EXEDUMP groups all the relocation tables into one and adds a few more items that aren't really relocations, but that are convenient to place here anyway.

An executable's Windows API calls, plus any other DLL calls it makes, are all *dynamic links* that can't be resolved until the program is loaded into memory. Because all far calls need to be fixed up, Windows API calls are reflected in the relocation table; this is where we learn the full details of an executable's imports. In a large program or library, this table will be thousands of lines long. Although essential when studying imports (the functions called), it is useless when studying exports (the functions provided), so the table can be suppressed with the EXEDUMP -NORELOC switch.

For each relocation item, EXEDUMP indicates the logical segment number (in decimal), the offset within the segment (in hex), the relocation type, and additional information, which depends upon the type. The types are

[i]   Import by name: module name and function name (not ordinal) provided
[m]   Import by ordinal: module name and ordinal provided
[n]   Internal reference to item exported from this module
[s]   Fix up to segment:offset elsewhere in this module
[e]   Program entry point—always named "start." It is not a relocation entry, but it appears in this table anyhow.
[g]   General Protection (GP) fault handler from __GP list. This is not a relocation, but it appears in this table anyhow. (See the description of __GP in chapter 5.)

Relocations are further qualified with "PTR," "SEG," and "OFF," which indicate if an entire four-byte far pointer is to be fixed up or whether just the two-byte segment or offset is.

In the example above, "1 0441 [s] 1 0000 SEG" indicates that, at 1:0441, there are two bytes (SEG) that need to be patched with the address of segment 1. For example, there might at 1:0440 be an instruction such as "PUSH SEG Some-Handler": the PUSH opcode occupies one byte, and the two bytes to be fixed up would immediately follow at 1:0441:

```
1:0440   68 XX XX        push XXXX
1:0443   ; ...
```

Note that although the instruction starts at 1:0440, the relocation starts one byte in, at 1:0441. Only the operand needs modification, not the instruction itself.

More interesting for the study of undocumented Windows is a line such as "1 01A5 [m] USER 262 PTR": this indicates that, at 1:01A5, four bytes (PTR) need to be patched with the address of the USER.262 function. In other words, "USER 262 PTR" is the source, and "1 01A5" is the target. For example:

```
1:01A2 6A 00            push 0
1:01A4 9A XX XX XX XX   call far ptr XXXX
1:01A9 ; ...
```

When KERNEL loads this executable into memory, it will smack the four bytes at 1:01A5 with a far function pointer to USER.262. If you run EXE-DUMP -NORELOC \WIN31\SYSTEM\USER.EXE, you will see that this happens to be GetWindow(). When loading TASKMAN, KERNEL would get the address of GetWindow() from USER's Module Database.

Although needed to implement dynamic linking, these relocations also serve the secondary purpose of giving us an easy way to see which API functions an executable references. There's a lot of useful information in these initially rather unhelpful-looking lines. Essentially, the MAPWIN program shown earlier merely collects all these relocations together, throws out any duplicates, produces the name for each module.ordinal, and sorts the list alphabetically.

The TASKMAN example includes several references to USER.262, all in the same segment. Every relocation with the same source, and the same target segment, is chained together in a linked list. The relocation table merely contains the head of the chain; the rest of the linked list threads its way through the segment. EXEHDR merely shows the head of the chain; EXEDUMP shows the entire chain. Getting the entire relocation chain is important for disassembling and for seeing how often (or rather, from how many places) a particular API function is used (see EXEUTIL -UNDOC and -IMPORTS, below).

Producing .DAT Files with EXEDUMP -EXPORTS

In addition to producing listings like the one we've just examined, EXEDUMP can also produce a simple list of an executable's exports. The EXEDUMP -EXPORTS option serves the same purpose as the MAPWIN -IMPMAKE option, but it produces output in a different form, for use by EXEUTIL and by Windows Source. For example

```
C:\BIN>exedump -exports \win31\system\user.exe > \undocwin\user.dat

C:\BIN>type \undocwin\user.dat
;
; \win31\system\user.exe
; "Microsoft Windows User Interface"
```

```
;
USER . 1      MESSAGEBOX
USER . 2      OLDEXITWINDOWS
USER . 3      ENABLEOEMLAYER
USER . 4      DISABLEOEMLAYER
USER . 5      INITAPP
USER . 6      POSTQUITMESSAGE
USER . 7      EXITWINDOWS
USER . 8      WEP
USER . 10     SETTIMER
USER . 11     BEAR11
USER . 12     KILLTIMER
USER . 13     GETTICKCOUNT
USER . 14     GETTIMERRESOLUTION
USER . 15     GETCURRENTTIME
... about 400 lines omitted ...
```

If run on something other than a valid NE file, EXEDUMP -EXPORTS produces no output at all. Thus, you can generate an omnibus listing of all Windows API functions on your system with something like the following:

```
C:\BIN>for %f in (\win31\system\*.*) do exedump -exports %f >> winfunc.dat
```

The resulting file should contain about 1,000 functions in Windows 3.0 and about 1,700 in Windows 3.1.

Quickie Examinations with EXEDUMP -MAGIC and -DESC

If EXEDUMP is run on an executable file that is not in the NE format, it will print out a message such as "Use LEDUMP to examine this file" (for LE linear executables; LEDUMP is a program that comes with Windows Source); or "sorry, this is an OS/2 2.0 linear executable, not a segmented executable" (for LX files). This message is sometimes useful all by itself; EXEDUMP -MAGIC can be used to examine an executable file's "magic" (its two-byte signature):

```
MZ -- "old" DOS executable (initials of Mark Zbikowski)
NE -- new executable (Windows or OS/2 1.x)
LE -- linear executable (Windows VxD)
LX -- linear executable (OS/2 2.x)
W3 -- WIN386 collection of linear executables
PE -- portable executable (Win32/NT)
```

The EXEDUMP -DESC option prints out nothing more than an NE executable's name and description string. By collecting these, you can get a picture of many of the files that Windows uses on your hard disk:

```
C:\BIN>for %f in (\win31\*.*) do exedump -desc %f >> win_desc.log

C:\BIN>for %f in (\win31\system\*.*) do exedump -desc %f >> win_desc.log
```

```
C:\BIN>type win_desc.log
\win31\system\COMM.DRV
Windows Communications Driver

\win31\system\COMMDLG.DLL
Common Windows Dialogs, Ver. 3.10

\win31\system\CPWIN386.CPL
Windows 386 Enhanced Control Panel

\win31\system\DDEML.DLL
DDE Manager Library

\win31\system\DRIVERS.CPL
Multimedia Control Panel Drivers Applet

\win31\system\FINSTALL.DLL
Font Installer

\win31\system\GDI.EXE
Microsoft Windows Graphics Device Interface
... etc. ...
```

EXEDUMP -DESC currently handles only NE files. Obviously, this utility would be a lot more useful if it could deduce something about every single file in your Windows subdirectories, not just the NE files. However, it's a start.

EXEUTIL

EXEDUMP isn't terribly interesting or useful all by itself, but the boring-looking information it provides can be used as the foundation for many different interesting Windows-snooping utilities. We've collected a number of these into a single program, EXEUTIL. EXEUTIL runs EXEDUMP on a specified NE executable, reads in the output from EXEDUMP, and then uses it to do something useful:

EXEUTIL -FINDUNDOC	Compares an NE executable's exports with a C .H #include file to find exports of likely undocumented functions.
EXEUTIL -UNDOC	Displays all imports of undocumented functions.
EXEUTIL -IMPORTS	Displays all of an executable's imports and gives a rough indication of the most important (or at least most frequently used) ones.
EXEUTIL -DIFF	Displays the entry-point differences between two versions of an NE executable.
EXEUTIL -DUPES	Displays multiple entry points that share the same code.

Ideally, these might have been packaged as five separate .EXE files. However, they have all been written using the AWK programming language, and the AWK compiler we're using (the excellent Thompson AWK, formerly PolyAWK, from Thompson

Automation) currently produces rather large .EXE files, so a single large executable with five command-line switches seemed like a better choice than five large executables.

In every other respect, AWK turned out to be an excellent choice for writing utilities such as these. Once we have the output from EXEDUMP, finding undocumented functions is essentially an exercise in text manipulation; this is exactly what AWK, a C-like pattern-matching language from AT&T Bell Laboratories, is designed to do. (For more information, see *The AWK Programming Language* by Alfred Aho, Brian Kernighan, and Peter Weinberger.)

Finding Undocumented Functions with EXEUTIL -FINDUNDOC

Earlier, when we looked at the MAPWIN-generated list of TASKMAN's Windows API calls, the reader may have wondered how we knew which functions were undocumented. Obviously, we can go through each function listed by MAPWIN, look for the function in WINDOWS.H, look for the function in the Windows SDK *Programmer's Reference*, maybe if we're really enterprising look in the Windows Device Driver Kit (DDK), and if we don't find the function listed anywhere, decide that it's undocumented. Then we can go and carry out the same technique for the next function, and the next. In other words, bogo-search:

```
for each function that the executable imports
    if the function isn't in WINDOWS.H, SDK, or DDK
        it's undocumented
```

A far better algorithm is to move all the searching of WINDOWS.H, the SDK, and the DDK "out of the loop," as it were, and create a master list of undocumented functions:

```
/* one-time initialization */
if UNDOCWIN.DAT doesn't exist
    for each DLL and DRV in the \windows\system subdirectory
        for each export from the DLL or DRV
            if the function isn't in WINDOWS.H, SDK, or DDK
                put it in UNDOCWIN.DAT

for each function that the executable imports
    if the function IS in UNDOCWIN.DAT
        it's undocumented
```

EXEUTIL -FINDUNDOC carries out the first part of this process, or at least as much of it as can be automated. EXEUTIL -UNDOC (see next page) carries out the second part.

EXEUTIL -FINDUNDOC (from now on, we'll just say FINDUNDOC) compares the exports from a DLL with the function prototypes in a C .H #include file (the DLL and the #include file should correspond to the same version of Windows). In the following example, FINDUNDOC locates the functions exported from USER.EXE, but not prototyped in WINDOWS.H:

```
C:\BIN>exeutil -findundoc \win31\system\user.exe \win31\windev\windows.h
;
; Functions in \win31\system\user.exe but not in \win31\windev\windows.h:
; Microsoft Windows User Interface
;
USER . 2      OLDEXITWINDOWS
USER . 3      ENABLEOEMLAYER
USER . 4      DISABLEOEMLAYER
USER . 5      INITAPP
USER . 8      WEP
USER . 11     BEAR11
USER . 51     BEAR51
USER . 86     BEAR86
USER . 172    SWITCHTOTHISWINDOW
USER . 182    BEAR182
USER . 187    ENDMENU
USER . 198    CASCADECHILDWINDOWS
USER . 199    TILECHILDWINDOWS
USER . 216    USERSEEUSERDO
USER . 217    LOOKUPMENUHANDLE
USER . 273    CONTROLPANELINFO
... etc.: see USER chapter for list ...
USER . 480    GETUSERLOCALOBJTYPE
USER . 481    HARDWARE_EVENT
USER . 484    __GP
USER . 499    WNETERRORTEXT
USER . 501    WNETOPENJOB
USER . 502    WNETCLOSEJOB
USER . 503    WNETABORTJOB
... many other WNET* functions ...
```

The above list (if you include the parts we omitted for brevity) represents a reasonable approximation of the undocumented functions in USER. By a completely mechanical process, we found EndMenu(), SwitchToThisWindow(), Cascade/ Tile-Child Windows(), UserSeeUserDo(), and other gems discussed in chapter 6 on USER.

FINDUNDOC sometimes decides that a function is undocumented when in fact it's documented. (It's sort of like one's coworker who every week thinks he's found a bug in the compiler.) FINDUNDOC simply compares a DLL's exports with the contents of the .H file you've passed in, and in Windows not everything that is documented winds up in an .H file.

For example, the FINDUNDOC output from USER shown above indicates all WNET* functions as undocumented. Many Windows programmers also seem to think they're undocumented, so FINDUNDOC is in good company. These functions *are* documented, in the Windows DDK, and have a corresponding WINNET.H file. Likewise, the InitApp() function is part of the standard Windows startup code; it was documented as part of Open Tools (see chapter 1).

Normally, one would run FINDUNDOC on every EXE, DLL, and DRV in the \WINDOWS\SYSTEM subdirectory and concatenate all the results to one omnibus file such as UNDOCWIN.DAT. To keep things simple here, we'll concentrate on USER.

After producing UNDOCWIN.DAT, we can edit it by hand to remove any functions that, for one reason or another, we don't consider to be undocumented. The utilities that use UNDOCWIN.DAT (such as EXEUTIL -UNDOC; see below) skip over any line that contains a semicolon, so we can decorate the file with comments rather than delete lines; this makes UNDOCWIN.DAT a good record not only of the undocumented areas of the Windows API, but also of its semi-documented or poorly documented fringes. For example:

```
USER . 2     OLDEXITWINDOWS
USER . 3     ENABLEOEMLAYER
USER . 4     DISABLEOEMLAYER
USER . 5     INITAPP                        ;; startup
USER . 8     WEP                            ;; windows exit procedure
USER . 11    BEAR11                         SetSystemTimer
USER . 51    BEAR51                         IsTwoByteCharPrefix
USER . 86    BEAR86                         IconSize
USER . 172   SWITCHTOTHISWINDOW
USER . 182   BEAR182                        KillSystemTimer
USER . 187   ENDMENU
... etc. ....
USER . 480   GETUSERLOCALOBJTYPE
USER . 481   HARDWARE_EVENT
USER . 484   __GP
USER . 499   WNETERRORTEXT                  WINNET.H "internal"
USER . 501   WNETOPENJOB                    ;; DDK
USER . 502   WNETCLOSEJOB                   ;; DDK
USER . 503   WNETABORTJOB                   ;; DDK
... etc. ...
```

The items that should be commented-out in UNDOCWIN.DAT include anything documented in the DDK or Open Tools, plus any WndProcs or WEPs (Windows exit procedures). On the other hand, functions such as the Get/SetSelectorBase/Limit family, which are documented in 3.1, but which were undocumented in 3.0, can be added back in.

In addition to looking up functions in WINDOWS.H, remember that in the Windows 3.1 SDK there are a large number of important auxiliary #include files, such as OLE.H, DDE.H, SHELLAPI.H, TOOLHELP.H, and so on. These can be used to check for undocumented functions in their corresponding DLLs. For example, we can verify that every named export from TOOLHELP.DLL is documented in TOOLHELP.H (WEP is just a Windows exit procedure):

```
C:\BIN>exeutil -findundoc \win31\system\toolhelp.dll
\win31\windev\toolhelp.h
;
; Functions in \win31\system\toolhelp.dll but not in \win31\windev\toolhelp.h:
```

```
; TOOLHELP - Debug/Tool Helper Library
;
TOOLHELP . 1      WEP
```

While usually used with an .H file, FINDUNDOC can actually compare the exports from a DLL with *any* readable text file. This allows decoded on-line help files to be used as input. For example, Microsoft QuickHelp files can be converted to straight text, using the Microsoft C HELPMAKE utility's /DU (decode helpfile unformatted, text only) switch:

```
C:\BIN>helpmake /DU \win31\windev\api31.hlp > \undocwin\api31.txt

C:\BIN>exeutil -findundoc \win31\system\user.dll \undocwin\api31.txt
```

Similarly, the table of contents from WinHelp files can be copied to the Windows clipboard and then pasted into a text file in Notepad, to be fed to FINDUNDOC.

When we're done, the resulting UNDOCWIN.BAT lists about 550 functions. About 400 of them are actually undocumented, with roughly 80 functions in KER-NEL, 60 in USER, and 60 in GDI.

Finding Calls to Undocumented Functions with EXEUTIL -UNDOC

Once we have a useful UNDOCWIN.DAT, we can systematically go about finding programs, DLLs, and drivers that use undocumented Windows API calls.

EXEUTIL -UNDOC compares all of an NE executable's imports against the master list of undocumented functions in UNDOCWIN.DAT. For example, here's the Windows 3.1 Task Manager again:

```
C:\BIN>exeutil -undoc \win31\taskman.exe
\WIN31\TASKMAN.EXE undocumented imports:
    ISWINOLDAPTASK (KERNEL.158)
    SWITCHTOTHISWINDOW (USER.172)
    CASCADECHILDWINDOWS (USER.198)
    TILECHILDWINDOWS (USER.199)
    Uses run-time dynamic linking (GetProcAddress)
```

TASKMAN uses undocumented functions from USER. In turn, USER itself not only exports these and other undocumented functions, but also uses undocumented functions, from GDI and KERNEL:

```
C:\BIN>exeutil -undoc \win31\system\user.exe
\WIN31\SYSTEM\USER.EXE undocumented imports:
    INTERSECTVISRECT (GDI.98)
    SELECTVISRGN (GDI.105)
    SETDCORG (GDI.117)
    DEATH (GDI.121)
    RESURRECTION (GDI.122)
    SAVEVISRGN (GDI.129)
    RESTOREVISRGN (GDI.130)
```

```
INQUIREVISRGN (GDI.131)
GETCLIPRGN (GDI.173)
GETDCSTATE (GDI.179)
SETDCSTATE (GDI.180)
SETDCHOOK (GDI.190)
SETHOOKFLAGS (GDI.192)
SHRINKGDIHEAP (GDI.354)
... about 40 lines omitted ...
```

The GDI module, in turn, not only exports these and other undocumented functions, but also imports undocumented functions from KERNEL. All of these modules internally make use of their own undocumented functions, too. The end result is a network (or is it nest?) of undocumented function calls.

In many ways, this is the most valuable information you can get about undocumented Windows. EXEUTIL -UNDOC shows, as nothing else can, what undocumented functions are truly useful. Only rarely do Windows executables use an undocumented function where a documented one, or a combination of undocumented ones, could have done the trick. Some of the undocumented calls that USER makes into GDI, or that GDI makes in KERNEL, might conceivably only be useful for components of Windows itself. But in the case of a straightforward utility such as TASKMAN, IsWinOldApTask(), SwitchToThisWindow(), CascadeChildWindows(), and TileChildWindows() are genuinely useful functions that ought to be part of the Windows programmer's arsenal. (See chapter 6 for more details about these functions.)

In addition to printing the names of any undocumented functions, EXEUTILUNDOC also prints a warning if the specified executable contains a reference to the GetProcAddress() function, for reasons that should be clear from the discussions of run-time dynamic linking earlier in this chapter.

If the specified executable contains more than 10 separate calls (that is, calls from 10 or more different segment:offset locations) to an undocumented function, EXEUTIL -UNDOC also prints the *number* of calls. For example, the following provides some indication of the undocumented functionality that USER depends on from KERNEL and GDI:

```
C:\BIN>exeutil -undoc \win31\system\user.dll
    ... just showing a few selected lines ...
    MAKEOBJECTPRIVATE (GDI.463) -- 34 references
    GETTASKQUEUEES (KERNEL.119) -- 11 references
    GETEXPWINVER (KERNEL.167) -- 24 references
    HANDLEPARAMERROR (KERNEL.327) -- 25 references
```

By themselves, these kind of statistics are fairly bogus. However, coupled with knowledge of the actual code, they serve as useful reminders. As an example, take the GetTaskQueueES() calls that USER makes: the Task Queue data structure, described in the KERNEL chapter, is really shared between KERNEL and USER. USER calls GetTaskQueueES() so that it can place WM_ messages in a task's queue. It does this in more than 10 different places, so GetTaskQueueES() is an important means of communication between USER and KERNEL.

EXEUTIL -UNDOC also tries to catch any *internal* references to undocumented functions. For example, USER.EXE exports the undocumented function EndMenu(). If you look at the source code for DefWindowProc() provided with the Windows SDK in the file DEFWND.C, you'll note that DefWindowProc(), which resides in USER, calls EndMenu(), which also resides in USER. EXEUTIL -UNDOC tries to ferret out such cases:

```
C:\BIN>exedump -undoc \win30\system\user.exe
    ... just showing internal references ...
    ENDMENU (USER.187) -- INTERNAL
    SETSYSTEMMENU (USER.280) -- INTERNAL
    GETCONTROLBRUSH (USER.326) -- INTERNAL -- 11 references
    LOADCURSORICONHANDLER (USER.336) -- INTERNAL -- 12 references
    LOADDIBCURSORHANDLER (USER.356) -- INTERNAL
    LOADDIBICONHANDLER (USER.357) -- INTERNAL
    DRAGDETECT (USER.465) -- INTERNAL
```

The above list was produced using the Windows 3.0 version of USER.EXE. Newer versions of the Microsoft linker optimize relocations of internal references to exported functions; as a consequence, this sort of information about internal references does not show up as often in 3.1 executables. Losing this information is a small price to pay, especially since we can still find it by going in and disassembling the executable.

If you run EXEUTIL -UNDOC on as many Windows programs and libraries as you can get your hands on, and if you concatenate the redirected output to a single file, you will begin to build a database of important undocumented Windows calls, much as we did in chapter 1 of this book. For example, running EXEUTIL -UNDOC on the Windows 3.1 Program Manager, File Manager, SDK Heapwalk, SHELL.DLL, TOOLHELP.DLL, and WinOldAp module yields this list:

```
\WIN31\PROGMAN.EXE undocumented imports:
    ISROMMODULE (KERNEL.323)
    SHELLABOUT (SHELL.22)
    EXTRACTASSOCIATEDICON (SHELL.36)
    DOENVIRONMENTSUBST (SHELL.37) -- 21 references
    INTERNALEXTRACTICON (SHELL.39)
    REGISTERSHELLHOOK (SHELL.102)
    GETINTERNALICONHEADER (USER.372)
    DUMPICON (USER.459)
    CALCCHILDSCROLL (USER.462)
    DRAGOBJECT (USER.464)
    uses run-time dynamic linking (GetProcAddress)

\WIN31\WINFILE.EXE undocumented imports:
    FILECDR (KERNEL.130)
    LONGPTRADD (KERNEL.180)
    SHELLABOUT (SHELL.22)
```

```
    FINDENVIRONMENTSTRING (SHELL.38)
    DRAGOBJECT (USER.464)
    WNETERRORTEXT (USER.499)
    uses run-time dynamic linking (GetProcAddress)

\WIN31\SYSTEM\SHELL.DLL undocumented imports:
    GETCURPID (KERNEL.157)
    DIRECTRESALLOC (KERNEL.168)
    GETICONID (USER.455)
    LOADICONHANDLER (USER.456)
    uses run-time dynamic linking (GetProcAddress)
    WCI (SHELL.32) -- INTERNAL
    HERETHARBETYGARS (SHELL.100) -- INTERNAL
    SHELLHOOKPROC (SHELL.103) -- INTERNAL

\WIN31\WINDEV\HEAPWALK.EXE undocumented imports:
    GLOBALHANDLENORIP (KERNEL.159)
    SHELLABOUT (SHELL.22)

\WIN31\SYSTEM\TOOLHELP.DLL undocumented imports:
    GLOBALMASTERHANDLE (KERNEL.28)
    REGISTERPTRACE (KERNEL.202)
    uses run-time dynamic linking (GetProcAddress)

\WIN31\SYSTEM\WINOA386.MOD undocumented imports:
    SETOBJECTOWNER (GDI.461)
    DOENVIRONMENTSUBST (SHELL.37)
    REGISTERSHELLHOOK (SHELL.102)
    SWITCHTOTHISWINDOW (USER.172)
    GETNEXTQUEUEWINDOW (USER.274)
    WINOLDAPPHACKOMATIC (USER.322)
```

Naturally, we can continue this way, listing not only the undocumented calls that various Windows modules rely on from USER and GDI, for example, but also listing the undocumented calls from KERNEL that USER and GDI themselves, in turn, rely on. When we're done, we end up with a rather large list that is undoubtedly interesting but also of questionable usefulness. The list can be made useful by turning it around (we wrote a 10-line throwaway AWK program for this): instead of showing the undocumented calls that each executable makes, the transformed list shows the executables that call each function:

```
CALCCHILDSCROLL (USER.462)
    \WIN31\PROGMAN.EXE
DIRECTRESALLOC (KERNEL.168)
    \WIN31\SYSTEM\SHELL.DLL
DOENVIRONMENTSUBST (SHELL.37)
    \WIN31\PROGMAN.EXE
    \WIN31\SYSTEM\WINOA386.MOD
DRAGOBJECT (USER.464)
    \WIN31\PROGMAN.EXE
    \WIN31\WINFILE.EXE
DUMPICON (USER.459)
```

```
    \WIN31\PROGMAN.EXE
EXTRACTASSOCIATEDICON (SHELL.36)
    \WIN31\PROGMAN.EXE
FILECDR (KERNEL.130)
    \WIN31\WINFILE.EXE
... etc. ...
```

It's worth reminding ourselves here that we have yet to disassemble these Windows executables. Merely by inspecting NE executables with MAPWIN, EXEDUMP, and EXEUTIL, we're gaining some genuinely useful knowledge about undocumented Windows.

Finding Calls to API Functions with EXEUTIL -IMPORTS

Our next EXEUTIL option, -IMPORTS, is just a generalization of -UNDOC. Instead of using UNDOCWIN.DAT, it uses the file WINFUNC.DAT, produced earlier with EXEDUMP -EXPORTS. It lists all imports, whether documented or undocumented. Like -UNDOC, it warns about GetProcAddress() and shows internal references (a DLL calls to its own exported functions) and counts frequently called functions.

TASKMAN is too small a program to be interesting here, because with small programs EXEUTIL -IMPORTS will produce essentially the same results as MAPWIN. If we examine a larger executable, EXEUTIL -IMPORTS gives us a crude idea of the API functions on which it heavily depends. For example

```
C:\BIN>exeutil -imports \win31\system\gdi.exe | grep references
\WIN31\SYSTEM\GDI.EXE imported references:
    LOCALALLOC (KERNEL.5) -- 18 references
    LOCALREALLOC (KERNEL.6) -- 13 references
    LOCALFREE (KERNEL.7) -- 28 references
    GLOBALALLOC (KERNEL.15) -- 46 references
    GLOBALREALLOC (KERNEL.16) -- 33 references
    GLOBALFREE (KERNEL.17) -- 90 references
    GLOBALLOCK (KERNEL.18) -- 171 references
    GLOBALUNLOCK (KERNEL.19) -- 218 references
    GLOBALSIZE (KERNEL.20) -- 19 references
    GETPROCADDRESS (KERNEL.50) -- 20 references
    GETPROFILESTRING (KERNEL.58) -- 12 references
    OPENFILE (KERNEL.74) -- 14 references
    _LCLOSE (KERNEL.81) -- 24 references
    _LREAD (KERNEL.82) -- 13 references
    SETERRORMODE (KERNEL.107) -- 16 references
    __AHSHIFT (KERNEL.113) -- 21 references
    __AHINCR (KERNEL.114) -- 50 references
    K327 (KERNEL.327) -- 21 references
```

As usual, we can't rely too heavily on such statistics. But look at the number of separate calls that this Windows 3.1 version of GDI.EXE makes to the GlobalUnlock() and GlobalLock() calls, and then compare it with the number of times GlobalAlloc() and GlobalFree() are called. From this, it looks as if GDI is still carrying around some dead weight from the days of real-mode Windows. In protected mode, it is a waste of time to unlock and relock objects. Yet the preceeding certainly seems to indicate that this is what GDI is doing.

Closer examination of 3.1 GDI confirms that, indeed, it does temporarily lock objects, manipulate them, and then unlock them; this really is a waste of time in protected mode. By pointing out when executables contain a large number of references to an API function, EXEUTIL -IMPORTS helps find anomalies such as these.

Finding DLL Changes with EXEUTIL -DIFF

When Windows 3.1 came out, the first thing that the authors of this book desperately wanted to know was: How did undocumented functions change between 3.0 and 3.1? What undocumented functions in 3.0 were dropped in 3.1? Which undocumented functions in 3.1 were new?

EXEUTIL -DIFF displays any entry-point differences between two versions of a Windows executable. For example

```
C:\BIN>exeutil -diff \win30\system\user.exe \win31\system\user.exe
Entry point differences:
            \windows\system\user.exe   \win31\system\user.exe
117 GETTASKFROMHWND
281 SNAPWINDOW
302 STATICWNDPROC
303 BUTTONWNDPROC
304 SBWNDPROC
305 DESKTOPWNDPROC
307 LBOXCTLWNDPROC
310 CONTSCROLL
311 CARETBLINKPROC
312 SENDMESSAGE2
313 POSTMESSAGE2
315 XCSTODS
... etc. ...
            \win31\system\user.exe   \windows\system\user.exe
8   WEP
11  BEAR11                           SETSYSTEMTIMER
51  BEAR51                           ISTWOBYTECHARPREFIX
86  BEAR86                           ICONSIZE
182 BEAR182                          KILLSYSTEMTIMER
184 QUERYSENDMESSAGE
216 USERSEEUSERDO
226 LOCKINPUT
231 GETSYSTEMDEBUGSTATE
245 ENABLECOMMNOTIFICATION
246 EXITWINDOWSEXEC
247 GETCURSOR
248 GETOPENCLIPBOARDWINDOW
251 SENDDRIVERMESSAGE
... etc. ...
```

From this you can see, for example, that the undocumented SnapWindow() and XCStoDS() functions in 3.0 USER are no long exported in 3.1 that what was called SetSystemTimer() in 3.0 is called BEAR11() in 3.1 and that the undocumented function UserSeeUserDo() is new to 3.1.

You can also see that the documented functions GetSystemDebugState(), SendDriverMessage(), and so on are present in 3.1, but not in 3.0. Of course, you could also turn to the Windows SDK *Programmer's Reference* to find this out. But when the 3.1 SDK states that a function is new to 3.1, sometimes the truth is that the function was also present in 3.0, but was not documented.

When Microsoft documents a previously undocumented Windows or DOS function, it generally does so by claiming that the function is *new* to whatever version under which they first decided to document it. (The reader is referred to the writings of George Orwell for further commentary on this practice.) The KERNEL Get/SetSelectorBase/Limit functions fall into this category. EXEUTIL -DIFF knows that, at this level, there is no difference between Get/SetSelectorBase/Limit in 3.0 and 3.1. When functions that were present but undocumented in one version become documented in the next version, it makes one wonder how unsafe it could have been to use these in the first place. In fact, Microsoft generally documents such functions because programmers have already been using them without its blessing.

Here's another use for EXEUTIL -DIFF: you may have Windows 2.1 disks, possibly sitting, unopened, in their original package (before 3.0, many copies of Windows were shipped, but few were used). If so, it's instructive to use EXEUTIL -DIFF to compare KERNEL, USER, and GDI for 2.1 and 3.0. It gives a good sense of how the core set of industry-standard boilerplate functions, the ones used by nearly all Windows applications, has remained remarkably stable. Windows has been under construction for nearly 10 years; one of the reasons for Windows' success now is that it is a *mature* product, with a mature API.

In some cases, this mature API includes undocumented functions. Nobody cares about pre-3.0 versions of Windows any more, but the persistence of some undocumented functions from 2.1 (or earlier) to 3.0 to 3.1 indicates that these in particular are likely to remain stable. For example, the VisRgn functions in GDI, such as OffsetVisRgn() and SelectVisRgn() (described in chapter 8), are present, though undocumented, in 2.1, 3.0, and 3.1. Other examples are the Set/GetTaskQueue functions in KERNEL and the Enable/DisableOEMLayer functions in USER. Such persistent functions are what *don't* show up when you run EXEUTIL -DIFF.

Some of the differences between 2.1 and 3.0 that EXEUTIL -DIFF reveals are important. For example

```
C:\BIN>exeutil -diff \win21\system\kernel.exe \win30\system\krnl386.exe
Entry point differences:
        \undocwin\win21\kernel.exe   \windows\system\krnl386.exe
39   SETTASKSWITCHPROC
40   SETTASKINTERCHANGE
43   ISSCREENGRAB
44   BUILDPDB
```

```
            \windows\system\krnl386.exe  \undocwin\win21\kernel.exe
77   RESERVED1                            ANSINEXT
78   RESERVED2                            ANSIPREV
79   RESERVED3                            ANSIUPPER
80   RESERVED4                            ANSILOWER
87   RESERVED5                            LSTRCMP
108  SWITCHSTACKTO                        STO
109  SWITCHSTACKBACK                      SBACK
126  MEMORYFREED
... etc. ...
```

This was how we found that the undocumented ReservedX functions in KERNEL are nothing more than place holders for the AnsiXXX functions, which in 3.0 were moved to USER. It is also revealing that only four undocumented functions in 2.1 KERNEL (SetTaskSwitchProc, SetTaskInterchange, IsScreenGrab, and BuildBPB) were removed in 3.0. Likewise, only a few were removed in USER and GDI.

Seen from the perspective of EXEUTIL -DIFF, the changes from Windows 3.0 to 3.1 are far greater than those from 2.1 to 3.0. The big change in 3.0 was the introduction of a protected-mode DOS extender, which was the only thing that could turn the nice Windows architecture into a genuinely-useful product. But because protected-mode Windows was implemented by gluing what were in many ways the old 2.1 executables on top of a DOS extender, this momentous change is not visible when we look only at DLLs.

Finding Function Equivalences with EXEUTIL -DUPES

Our final EXEUTIL option, -DUPES, does nothing more that locate multiple entry points in a Windows executable that point to the same block of code. For example

```
C:\BIN>exeutil -dupes \win30\system\user.exe
Multiple entry points for same segment:offset:
    1   1b5b      133 GETWINDOWWORD
    1   1b5b      135 GETWINDOWLONG

    1   1b5e      129 GETCLASSWORD
    1   1b5e      131 GETCLASSLONG

    1   1bf5      278 GETDESKTOPHWND
    1   1bf5      286 GETDESKTOPWINDOW

    1   6ed8       13 GETTICKCOUNT
    1   6ed8       15 GETCURRENTTIME
```

Knowing that the undocumented GetDesktopHwnd() and GetTickCount() functions are just aliases for documented functions is nice, because that's two undocumented functions we don't need to explore further.

More interesting, though, is the apparent equivalence of GetWindowWord() with GetWindowLong(), and of GetClassWord() with GetClassLong(). GetWindowWord() retrieves a two-byte word value from a specified offset in a window structure;

GetWindowLong() retrieves a four-byte long value; the GetClassWord/Long functions do the same with a window-class structure.

How can the same piece of code retrieve both a two-byte word and a four-byte long? The answer is very simple: the function always retrieves a four-byte long. In 16-bit code on the PC, four-byte values are by convention returned in the DX:AX register pair; two-byte values are returned in AX. Callers of GetWindowWord() or GetClassWord() simply ignore the value in DX.

(Having mentioned the DX:AX four-byte return value and AX two-byte return value convention for Windows functions, this seems like as good a place as any to mention the other register-usage convention for Windows functions: according to the SDK *Guide to Programming*, Windows functions are allowed to destroy any register other than DI, SI, BP, and DS.)

In Windows 3.1, EXEUTIL -DUPES is less able to uncover function equivalences. In 3.1, the entry points for most documented API functions in KERNEL, USER, and GDI have been moved into LAYER modules. The entry point in LAYER does parameter validation and then jumps to the genuine, internal routine whose name is inaccessible to EXEUTIL -DUPES.

If you look carefully at the addresses displayed by EXEUTIL -DUPES for the GetWindow/ClassWord/Long functions, you'll notice something even stranger than the equivalence of getting words and longs: the address of GetWindowWord/Long (1:1B5B) is *only three bytes* away from the address of GetClassWord/Long (1:1B5E). It seems as if GetClassWord/Long would be coming right in the middle of GetWindowWord/Long. In fact, it does. Not only that, it comes right in the middle *of an instruction*:

```
GETWINDOWWORD:
GETWINDOWLONG:
1:1b5b   31 C9        XOR CX,CX
1:1b5d   A9 B1 80     TEST    AX,80B1

GETCLASSWORD:
GETCLASSLONG:
1:1b5e   B1 80        MOV CL,80

GETWC2:
; ...
1:1b70                MOV AX,[BX]
1:1b72                MOV DX,[BX+2]
1:1b75                RET
```

That's right, if you call GetWindowWord/Long, the bytes at 1:1B5E are used as part of a (NOP) TEST AX,80B1 instruction, but if you call GetClassWord/Long, you jump right into the middle of this instruction and use the bytes as a MOV CL, 80 instruction, before falling into GETWC2 (see chapter 6). The apparent intent here was to save callers of GetWindowWord/Long from having to execute a JMP.

The next time you read or listen to a lecture from a Microsoft representative on how one should never use undocumented functions or tricks, even if you think you need to, it might be useful to remember that the code for Windows is *filled* with *unnecessary* tricks. There's an even worse example of such onanistic coding practices in the Windows API functions that retrieve values from a display context (DC); see chapter 8 on GDI chapter for all the gory details.

In any case, EXEUTIL -DUPES is useful for alerting us to possible oddness like this; it would be a lot harder to find if we were just wading through disassembly listings. The oddness in turn helps to demystify the Windows API a little, reminding us that, behind the inscrutable face sometimes worn by the SDK *Programmer's Reference*, there is just code, written by programmers.

CHAPTER ■ 3

Disassembling Windows

The reader may recall the cute robot Number 5's line, "No disassemble," from the movie *Short Circuit* a few years ago. For someone exploring the internals of an operating system, "no disassemble" really is good advice—but only up to a point. In the previous chapter, we saw that the symbolic information contained in Windows NE executables lets us discover a lot about undocumented Windows, without having to disassemble and examine any actual code. However, the knowledge we've gained about undocumented Windows in this way is partial, and in some places downright misleading.

For example, we've seen that because Windows provides run-time dynamic linking via the GetProcAddress() function, a Windows executable can access another executable without anything more than a reference to GetProcAddress() showing up in the NE header. For this reason, examination of its executable header will not show us how GDI communicates with the DISPLAY module. Only examination of the actual code for the CreateDC() function will show that.

Furthermore, by looking only at function exports and imports, we're missing out on key pieces of the Windows action, such as sending, posting, and receiving of WM_ messages, the use of software interrupts, access to fields in internal data structures, and use of resources such as menus and dialog boxes. With the exception of resources (which we'll get to later in this chapter), none of this shows up in the NE header: you have to look at the code.

In addition, while this book focuses entirely on the core of the Windows API—KERNEL, USER, and GDI—there is a lot more to Windows, particularly Enhanced mode Windows, than that. There are really three different Windows APIs; a good Windows programmer should be familiar with all three:

- The 16-bit far call/stack-based API provided by DLLs, containing functions such as CreateWindow() and GlobalAlloc(), which are documented in the SDK or in the *Device Driver Adaptation Guide* of the Windows Device Driver Kit (DDK), or which are undocumented.

- A 32-bit register/INT 20h-based API provided by, and for, virtual device drivers (VxDs), containing functions such as Get_Cur_VM_Handle and VKD_Force_Keys, which are documented in the *Virtual Device Adaptation Guide* of the DDK.

- An interrupt-based API, including the DOS Protected-Mode Interface (DPMI 0.9; INT 31h), the Virtual DMA Services (VDS; INT 4Bh), a large collection of INT 2Fh calls, plus, of course, protected-mode DOS (INT 21h) services. For example, DPMI includes functions such as "Set Processor Exception Handler Vector" and "Call Real Mode Procedure With Far Return Frame."

We need to disassemble Windows, including not only the NE files we've been examining, but also linear executable (LE) files used by VxDs; the WIN386.EXE file, which uses a W3 format to hold a large collection of VxDs; and DOS programs such as DOSX.EXE and the DOS stubs of KERNEL and WIN386.

Of course, the nice symbolic information in NE files, used by programs such as MAPWIN and EXEUTIL and demonstrated in chapter 2, can be put to excellent use by a Windows disassembler. A Windows disassembler should take all the information in an NE header and use it as though it were a debug symbol table. With the NE executable format, effectively every program comes with a symbol table, whether the program was compiled for debugging or not. (In fact, one of the authors has written a program that can input a Windows executable and output a Turbo Debugger .TDS file. This is a nice illustration of how Windows programs contain debug-like symbolic information.)

The disassembler we use should ideally "know" about Windows: when it sees a call to USER.262, it should automatically provide the name GetWindow; when it sees a DOS or DPMI call, it should provide the function's name; when a VxD makes an INT 20h call, it should automatically provide the name of the VxD service being used.

Unfortunately, one thing that Windows disassemblers currently *won't* do is handle blocks of "pcode", such as Microsoft C/C++ 7.0 optionally generates. Some Microsoft programs, such as Excel and WinWord, contain blocks of pcode. Similarly, the current generation of Windows disassemblers will not usefully disassemble Visual Basic (VB) programs, which contain BASIC code in USERDATA resources, rather than Intel instructions in CODE segments. Finally, none currently handle Win32/NT portable-executable (PE) files.

In this chapter, we will look at disassembling Windows, showing in particular how to turn the raw data of a disassembled listing into something understandable and useful. We will examine, and edit, disassembled listings for parts of TASKMAN and KERNEL.

But where does the disassembled listing come from in the first place? There are several ways to take a Windows executable and turn it into an assembly-language .LST or .ASM file. While working on this book, one of the tools we built turned into Windows Source, which is a preprocessor for V Communications' Sourcer disassembler. Together with Sourcer, Windows Source can produce commented assembly-language listings for Windows executables, DLLs, drivers, and 32-bit VxDs (including the ones built into WIN386.EXE, in particular the Virtual Machine Manager).

Windows Source

V Communications' Sourcer disassembler can be driven by text files that provide information about the program under analysis. These Sourcer definition files can be created by hand or by a program. WINP, the main program for Windows Source, transforms the output from EXEDUMP (which is also included with Windows Source) into a Sourcer definition file. For VxDs, Windows Source uses two programs, LEDUMP and W3MAP, to input an LE or W3 file and output a Sourcer definition file. The definition file is fed to Sourcer, along with the original program, to produce a .LST or .ASM file.

When used with Windows Source, Sourcer:

- Labels all *exports* from a Windows executable, DLL, or device driver
- Identifies, by name, all *imported* function calls, including all Windows API calls
- Includes CodeView symbols, such as those found in the debugging version of Windows
- Labels the program's or DLL's main entry point and automatically identifies WinMain
- Automatically identifies information such as variables in the NULL segment, general-protection fault handlers in a __GP block, and APPLOADER functions in a self-loading Windows application
- Includes the RESDUMP utility, for matching up "magic numbers" in the disassembled listing with menu and control IDs, string table numbers, and other resources
- In a VxD, identifies by name the VxD's API entry points, its Device Descriptor Block (DDB), Control procedure, Service table, plus any virtual-8086 or protected-mode API procedures
- Identifies by name all VxD services that a VxD calls
- Makes available for assembly the many VxDs embedded within the Enhanced mode WIN386 file; in particular, it allows the Virtual Machine Manager (VMM) to be disassembled
- Automatically provides comments for all DOS and DOS Protected-Mode Interface (DPMI) calls made in a Windows program.

Windows Source and Sourcer are available from V Communications (San Jose; 408-296-4224). ■

Another Windows disassembler is WinToAsm, written by Stan Mitchell and available from Eclectic Software (Milpitas, CA). Even though this chapter will focus on using Windows Source, some of the discussion is also applicable to WinToAsm.

Finally, as explained below in the "Masochist's Guide to Windows Disassembly," you can also use a non-Windows debugger such as Microsoft's SYMDEB to disassemble Windows. In fact, it's important to note that Microsoft provides all the tools necessary for Windows disassembly: SYMDEB, EXEHDR, and CodeView for Windows (CVW). The tools discussed in this chapter simply make it much easier.

A Masochist's Guide To Disassembly

If you're feeling masochistic, you can use Microsoft's SYMDEB debugger to disassemble the individual segments in Windows executables. A program such as Microsoft's EXEHDR, Borland's TDUMP, or our own EXEDUMP (chapter 2), is also needed to tell you where the CODE segments are in the file; you then feed this information to SYMDEB. Using our running example of the Windows 3.1 TASK-MAN.EXE, we find a single CODE segment, 519h bytes long, at offset 500h in the file. For example, Microsoft's EXEHDR displays this segment table:

```
C:\DISASM>exehdr \win31\taskman.exe
......
no. type address  file  mem   flags
  1 CODE 00000500 00519 00519 PRELOAD, (movable), (discardable)
  2 DATA 00000b40 00050 00050 PRELOAD, (movable)
```

You need to tell SYMDEB to disassemble this many bytes, at this location in the file. You also want to tell SYMDEB to start offsets at 0, not at 100h as it would otherwise do. There are a number of ways to do this, but the simplest, least-masochistic technique comes from Alan Cobb's *Reverse Engineering Windows and OS/2 Software*.

First, copy TASKMAN.EXE to a file with a .BIN extension:

```
C:\DISASM>copy \win31\taskman.exe taskman.bin
```

Next, make up a SYMDEB response file:

```
C:\DISASM>copy con taskman.rsp
r cs
cs+60
u 0 519
q
```

This tells SYMDEB to add 60h to the current value of the CS register, then unassemble 519h bytes, then quit. Why tell SYMDEB to change the value of CS? Because we want it to start disassembling from somewhere other than the start of the .BIN file. Why add 60h? Because we want SYMDEB to start disassembling at

continued

continued

offset 500h, and we want the offsets to start not with 100h, but with 0. In other words, given the file offset of a CODE segment in an NE file, you must tell SYMDEB to increment CS by (100h + seg_offset) / 10h.

Finally, run SYMDEB with the /X switch, to suppress its [more] display:

```
C:\DISASM>symdeb /X taskman.bin < taskman.rsp > taskman.asm
```

By the way, it's also possible to use Microsoft's even more primitive debugger, DEBUG, which comes with DOS itself. However, the DEBUG command doesn't understand expressions such as cs+60, so you would have to do the math yourself. Furthermore, DEBUG doesn't understand anything more sophisticated than the 8088 instruction set, so most Windows programs, which contain 80286 instructions such as PUSH immediate, will come out garbled.

Anyhow, we now have a TASKMAN.ASM. Let's look at part of the file:

```
2400:019F FF760E         PUSH    [BP+0E]
2400:01A2 6A00           PUSH    00
2400:01A4 9AC6010000     CALL    0000:01C6
2400:01A9 8946FC         MOV     [BP-04],AX
2400:01AC 8BF0           MOV     SI,AX
```

To use any of this, you need to apply the relocation table by hand; as noted in chapter 2, code segments are generally followed by relocation tables. In the instruction starting at 1:01A4 (2400:01A4 above), we see a far call. The 0000:01C6 target for the call is clearly not a valid address, so this part of the instruction (one byte in, at 1:01A5) needs to be fixed up.

Examining the EXEDUMP display of the TASKMAN relocation table, we see "1 01a5 [m] USER 262 PTR"; this means that the four bytes (PTR) at 1:01A5 need to be patched with the address for USER.262. But before you can apply this change to the above disassembly, you first have to note down the current contents of the relocation at 1:01A5: the number it contains, 01C6h, is the next item in the relocation chain for USER.262 in this segment:

```
2400:019F FF760E         PUSH    [BP+0E]
2400:01A2 6A00           PUSH    00
2400:01A4 9AC6010000     CALL    USER.262    ; contained 0000:01C6
2400:01A9 8946FC         MOV     [BP-04],AX
2400:01AC 8BF0           MOV     SI,AX
; ...
2400:01C0 743A           JZ  01FC
2400:01C2 56             PUSH    SI
2400:01C3 6A04           PUSH    04
2400:01C5 9A00020000     CALL    USER.262    ; contained 0000:0200
; ...
```

continued

continued

Since USER.262 is GetWindow(), and since GetWindow() is documented, we can turn this into the following, using the documentation for GetWindow() to relabel the parameters and return values used by the program:

```
2400:019F FF760E          PUSH    hWnd            ; [BP+0E]
2400:01A2 6A00            PUSH    GW_HWNDFIRST    ; 00
2400:01A4 9AC6010000      CALL    GetWindow       ; USER.262
2400:01A9 8946FC          MOV     hFirstWnd, AX   ; [BP-04]
2400:01AC 8BF0            MOV     SI,AX
; ...
2400:01C0 743A            JZ 01FC
2400:01C2 56              PUSH    hFirstWnd       ; SI
2400:01C3 6A04            PUSH    GW_OWNER        ; 04
2400:01C5 9A00020000      CALL    GetWindow
; ...
```

In other words, all you need to disassemble Windows is SYMDEB, EXEDUMP—, and a huge amount of patience. Rather than go through all this hassle, you're better off getting a genuine Windows disassembler. But the example does at least show the relationship between the addresses displayed by EXEHDR or EXEDUMP and the actual code in the file.

As one more example, let's say that, while waiting for your copy of a real Windows disassembler to arrive in the mail, you desperately need to examine the CascadeChildWindows() function in USER. First, you need to run EXEHDR, TDUMP, or EXEDUMP to find out where the function lives in USER; you find that CascadeChildWindows (USER.198) is in logical segment 15, at offset 0875h:

```
C:\DISASM>exehdr \win31\system\user.exe
......
198     15      0875    CASCADECHILDWINDOWS
```

Now you need to know where segment 15 is located within the file; once again, EXEHDR, TDUMP, or EXEDUMP show that this CODE segment is at offset 21F80h in the file, and is 1B5Ch bytes long:

```
C:\DISASM>exehdr \win31\system\user.exe
......
15  CODE    00021F80        01B5C
```

Armed with this information, you can construct a SYMDEB response file to disassemble segment 15. You take the file offset for the segment, 21F80h, add 100h to it, knock the bottom digit (which had better be 0 for any of this to work) off the result, and then tell SYMDEB to increment CS by the result:

continued

continued

```
C:\DISASM>copy con user15.rsp
r cs
cs+2208
u 0 1b5c
q

C:\DISASM>copy \win31\system\user.exe user.bin

C:\DISASM>symdeb /X user.bin < user15.rsp > user15.asm

C:\DISASM>del user.bin
```

And to locate the code for CascadeChildWindows(), you just look at offset 875h in the USER15.ASM file:

```
45A8:0875 C8140000        ENTER   0014,00
45A8:0879 57              PUSH    DI
45A8:087A 56              PUSH    SI
45A8:087B 1E              PUSH    DS
......
45A8:08B1 FF7402          PUSH    [SI+02]
45A8:08B4 6A01            PUSH    01
45A8:08B6 9A6F08E308      CALL    08E3:086F
45A8:08BB 8946FC          MOV     [BP-04],AX
45A8:08BE 57              PUSH    DI
45A8:08BF 9AB5002C09      CALL    092C:00B5
45A8:08C4 8946F6          MOV     [BP-0A],AX
......
45A8:0914 FF76F6          PUSH    [BP-0A]
45A8:0917 56              PUSH    SI
45A8:0918 6A00            PUSH    00
45A8:091A FF76EC          PUSH    [BP-14]
45A8:091D FF76EE          PUSH    [BP-12]
45A8:0920 FF76F0          PUSH    [BP-10]
45A8:0923 FF76F2          PUSH    [BP-0E]
45A8:0926 FF76FE          PUSH    [BP-02]
45A8:0929 9A14014A09      CALL    094A:0114
45A8:092E 8946F6          MOV     [BP-0A],AX
......
```

Interesting, isn't it? CascadeChildWindows() calls BeginDeferWindowPos(), runs a DefWindowPos() loop to line up the windows, and then calls EndDefer WindowPos() to show the changes all at once.

Oh, you don't see that in the above listing? The problem isn't that some lines have been omitted, because the omitted lines look just like the lines that were included. The problem is simply that you need a real Windows disassembler if you expect to get much out of looking at code like this.

continued

continued

At any rate, if you persist in using SYMDEB, you may find that the file you want to examine is too big for SYMDEB, even though you could only disassemble one segment at a time for it anyway. If this happens, you can use the EXTRACT utility on the accompanying disk. This in fact is just how we started working on this book. One of the first utilities we threw together was EXTRACT; it still comes in handy.

EXTRACT takes a portion of an existing file, and copies it to a new file. The portion is specified on the EXTRACT command line, along with the names of the old and new files. For example, you could lift the code segment (519h bytes at offset 500h in the file) out of TASKMAN.EXE, and pass it to SYMDEB:

```
C:\BIN>extract \win31\taskman.exe 0x500 0x519 seg1.bin

C:\BIN>symdeb seg1.bin
-r cs
:CS 7229
:cs+10
-u 0
```

EXTRACT expects its arguments in a particular (peculiar?) order:

```
argv[1] = source file name
argv[2] = long offset, in decimal or hexadecimal
          or, if preceded by a dash, then indicates offset from end
argv[3] = size, in decimal or hexadecimal
          or, if preceded by a dash, then indicates end of a range
          or, -stop indicates the remainder of the file
argv[4] = destination file name
```

Just to clarify some of EXTRACT's more exotic options, the following copies the last eight bytes of \PHOO\BAR.EXE into CVSIG.TMP:

```
C:\BIN>extract \phoo\bar.exe -8 -stop cvsig.tmp
```

and the following extracts the bytes from offsets B40h through B90h:

```
C:\BIN>extract \phoo\bar.exe 0xb40 -0xb90 quux.bin ■
```

Actually there's one more way to get a source listings for a Windows module: forget about disassembly and acquire the actual source code! Depending on what you're interested in, you may be able to get source code. As already noted, the Windows DDK is an incredible resource for anyone interested in Windows internals. It comes with disk upon disk of source code for many (though by no means all) of the

16-bit device drivers and 32-bit device drivers that come with Windows; the 3.1 DDK also comes with several header files (particularly WINKERN.INC, TDB.INC, and a special "internal" DDK version of WINDOWS.H) that may answer questions you have. In addition to the DDK, the Windows SDK comes with C source code for the DefWindowProc() and DefDlgProc() functions. Finally, both Borland C++ and Microsoft C/C++ 7.0 come with source code for their Windows startup routines.

Assuming you can't get source code, though, it's now time to use a disassembler. If you have questions about the legal implications of disassembly, we recommend Raymond T. Nimmer's *The Law of Computer Technology*, chapter 3 (Trade Secrets and Confidentiality), particularly the discussions at 3.05[2][b] (Sale of a Product: Reverse Engineering) and 3.07 (End Users: Reverse Engineering). Alan Cobb's *Reverse Engineering Windows and OS/2 Software* also contains a good discussion of these issues.

At some point, every Windows programmer should look at the code for Windows, if only to get some idea of what's on the other end of the line when they call a Windows API function. It's true that the whole "black box," "encapsulation" principle of modern programming is based on the idea that you needn't, and perhaps even *shouldn't*, understand what is going on internally when you call a library or operating-system function: you only need to understand its inputs, outputs, and side effects. How or why it produces these externally visible effects is supposed to be of no concern (this is a behavioralist as opposed to a Freudian approach to programming). But it has recently become widely recognized that the black-box approach has a serious downside: by teaching that an understanding of *how* something achieves its effect is irrelevant as long as you know the proper incantation, programmers end up mystified, treating interfaces (such as the Windows API) not with respect, but with reverence and even fear.

So Windows programmers should look at least once at the code for Windows. Unless you work at Microsoft, or otherwise have access to the original .C and .ASM files of Windows source code, this means disassembling Windows.

Disassembling TASKMAN

As an example of disassembling Windows, let's look, as we did in chapter 2, at the Task Manager program. TASKMAN is an excellent program with which to experiment because its internals relate in a fairly direct way to its visible operation, and because its small size (3K bytes) results in a small, easily-grasped listing. Furthermore, from running EXEUTIL -UNDOC on TASKMAN in chapter 2, we already know that TASKMAN relies on several undocumented functions:

```
C:\BIN>exeutil -undoc \win31\taskman.exe
\WIN31\TASKMAN.EXE undocumented imports:
    ISWINOLDAPTASK (KERNEL.158)
    SWITCHTOTHISWINDOW (USER.172)
    CASCADECHILDWINDOWS (USER.198)
    TILECHILDWINDOWS (USER.199)
    Uses run-time dynamic linking (GetProcAddress)
```

As an added bonus, by disassembling TASKMAN we will find some undocumented features in its operation.

The Startup Code Let's start by looking at TASKMAN's startup code. This generally isn't necessary with Windows Source because the only real reason to look at startup code is to help locate WinMain(), and Windows Source automatically finds and labels WinMain() for you. Both Borland and Microsoft provide the startup in source-code form, so there generally isn't any other reason to bother with a disassembled listing of it. However, if the disassembler you're using doesn't automatically label WinMain(), then you will need to look at the startup code to find where WinMain() is being called. In any case, it's a good way to get started with our examination of TASKMAN. Here's how Windows Source shows the startup code for the Windows 3.1 version of TASKMAN:

```
C:\SOURCER>winp \windows\taskman.exe

C:\SOURCER>sr taskman.wdf

C:\SOURCER>\dos\edit taskman.lst

      start:
1.04B9        xor bp,bp
1.04BB        push     bp
1.04BC        call     far ptr INITTASK
1.04C1        or  ax,ax
1.04C3        jz  short loc_0060
1.04C5        add cx,100h
1.04C9        jc  short loc_0060
1.04CB        mov data_0009,cx    ; (2.0030=0)
1.04CF        mov data_0010,si    ; (2.0032=0)
1.04D3        mov data_0011,di    ; (2.0034=0)
1.04D7        mov data_0012,bx    ; (2.0036=0)
1.04DB        mov data_0013,es    ; (2.0038=4B5Ah)
1.04DF        mov data_0014,dx    ; (2.003A=0)
1.04E3        xor ax,ax
1.04E5        push     ax
1.04E6        call     far ptr WAITEVENT
1.04EB        push     data_0011   ; (2.0034=0)
1.04EF        call     far ptr INITAPP
1.04F4        or  ax,ax
1.04F6        jz  short loc_0060
1.04F8        push     data_0011   ; (2.0034=0)
1.04FC        push     data_0010   ; (2.0032=0)
1.0500        push     data_0013   ; (2.0038=4B5Ah)
1.0504        push     data_0012   ; (2.0036=0)
1.0508        push     data_0014   ; (2.003A=0)
1.050C        call     WinMain     ; (03AE)
1.050F        push     ax
1.0510        call     sub_0003    ; (04A3)
1.0513        loc_0060:                ; xref 1.04C3, 04C9, 04F6
1.0513        mov al,0FFh
1.0515        push     ax
1.0516        call     sub_0003    ; (04A3)
```

This is similar to the standard startup code that you will find in nearly every Windows program. It calls three almost-undocumented functions: InitTask(), WaitEvent(), and InitApp(). These are described in the KERNEL and USER chapters of this book, and also in the Windows 3.1 SDK *Programmer's Reference, Volume 1: Overview*, chapter 22 (Windows Application Startup).

If we want to see how initially unhelpful-looking disassembled listings can be massaged to make them more useful and understandable, though, this is a good example. Look at the series of MOVs shortly after the call to InitTask():

```
1.04CB        mov data_0009,cx      ; (2.0030=0)
1.04CF        mov data_0010,si      ; (2.0032=0)
1.04D3        mov data_0011,di      ; (2.0034=0)
1.04D7        mov data_0012,bx      ; (2.0036=0)
1.04DB        mov data_0013,es      ; (2.0038=4B5Ah)
1.04DF        mov data_0014,dx      ; (2.003A=0)
```

With another disassembler, the data items might come out not as data_00XX but as ds:[00XX] or even D00XX. In any case, let's pretend that we didn't already know what InitTask() does. How would we figure out what these data_00XX items are and, therefore, what the CX, SI, DI, etc., registers hold on return from InitTask()?

We need to see where else the data_00XX items are used in the program. This is typical of working with disassembled listings: to find out what one block of code means, you often need to look first at some other block of code. In this example, most of the data_00XX variables are used again, a few lines down:

```
1.04F8        push     data_0011    ; (2.0034=0)
1.04FC        push     data_0010    ; (2.0032=0)
1.0500        push     data_0013    ; (2.0038=4B5Ah)
1.0504        push     data_0012    ; (2.0036=0)
1.0508        push     data_0014    ; (2.003A=0)
1.050C        call     WinMain      ; (03AE)
```

Five words are being pushed on the stack as parameters to WinMain(). If only we knew what those parameters were, we could provide better names than data_00XX. But we *do* know what those parameters are! WinMain(), the function being called here, always looks like:

```
int PASCAL WinMain(WORD hInstance, WORD hPrevInstance,
    LPSTR lpCmdLine, int nCmdShow);
```

In the Pascal calling convention, which is used extensively in Windows (it produces smaller code than the more flexible cdecl calling convention), arguments are pushed on the stack in the same order as they appear in a function declaration. Thus, in our example data_0011 must be hInstance, data_0010 must be hPrevInstance, data_0013:data0012 must be lpCmdLine, and data_0014 must be nCmdShow.

What makes this important is that we can now go and replace *every* occurrence of data_0011 by a more useful name such as hInstance, every occurrence of data_0010 by hPrevInstance, and so on. This will clarify not just this section of the listing, but every section of the listing that refers to these variables. Such global substitutions of useful names for placeholder names or addresses is key when working with a disassembled listing. After applying these changes to the fragment shown earlier, we end up with something more understandable:

```
; ...
1.04CB      mov data_0009,cx          ; (2.0030=0)
1.04CF      mov hPrevInstance,si      ; (2.0032=0)
1.04D3      mov hInstance,di          ; (2.0034=0)
1.04D7      mov lpCmdLine,bx          ; (2.0036=0)
1.04DB      mov lpCmdLine+2,es        ; (2.0038=4B5Ah)
1.04DF      mov nCmdShow,dx           ; (2.003A=0)
1.04E3      xor ax,ax
1.04E5      push    ax
1.04E6      call    far ptr WAITEVENT
1.04EB      push    hInstance         ; (2.0034=0)
1.04EF      call    far ptr INITAPP
1.04F4      or  ax,ax
1.04F6      jz  short loc_0060
1.04F8      push    hInstance         ; (2.0034=0)
1.04FC      push    hPrevInstance     ; (2.0032=0)
1.0500      push    lpCmdLine+2       ; (2.0038=4B5Ah)
1.0504      push    lpCmdLine         ; (2.0036=0)
1.0508      push    nCmdShow          ; (2.003A=0)
1.050C      call    WinMain           ; (03AE)
; ...
```

Thus, if we didn't already know what InitTask() returns in various registers, we could find out by working backward from the parameters to WinMain(). Conversely, if we were using a disassembler that didn't locate and label WinMain() for us, we could use the InitTask() return values to label the parameters pushed on the stack to this function (which might be labeled sub_0002 or something similarly useless), and realize that it had to be WinMain().

WinMain It was useful to look at the startup code because it illustrated the general principle of trying to substitute useful names such as hPrevInstance for useless labels such as data_0010. But, generally, the first place we'll look when examining a Windows program is WinMain(). Here is how Sourcer presents the code for WinMain() in the Windows 3.1 TASKMAN:

```
        WinMain       proc      near
1.03AE        push    bp
1.03AF        mov bp,sp
1.03B1        sub sp,12h
1.03B4        push    di
1.03B5        push    si
1.03B6        sub di,di
1.03B8        cmp [bp+0Ah],di
1.03BB        je  short loc_0047
```

```
1.03BD         sub ax,ax
1.03BF         jmp loc_0057                    ; (048E)
1.03C2  loc_0047:                              ;   xref 1.03BB
1.03C2         les si,dword ptr [bp+6]
1.03C5         cmp byte ptr es:[si],0
1.03C9         je  short loc_0053
1.03CB         mov [bp-0Eh],di
1.03CE         jmp short loc_0049              ; (03EE)
1.03D0  loc_0048:                              ;   xref 1.03F2
1.03D0         cmp byte ptr es:[si],20h        ; ' '
1.03D4         je  short loc_0050
1.03D6         mov ax,0Ah
1.03D9         imul    data_0005               ; (2.0010=0)
1.03DD         mov data_0005,ax                ; (2.0010=0)
1.03E0         mov bx,si
1.03E2         inc si
1.03E3         mov al,es:[bx]
1.03E6         cbw
1.03E7         sub ax,30h
1.03EA         add data_0005,ax                ; (2.0010=0)
1.03EE  loc_0049:                              ;   xref 1.03CE
1.03EE         cmp byte ptr es:[si],0
1.03F2         jne loc_0048
1.03F4  loc_0050:                              ;   xref 1.03D4
1.03F4         cmp byte ptr es:[si],0
1.03F8         je  short loc_0052
1.03FA         inc si
1.03FB         jmp short loc_0052              ; (0415)
1.03FD  loc_0051:                              ;   xref 1.0419
1.03FD         mov ax,0Ah
1.0400         imul    data_0006               ; (2.0012=0)
1.0404         mov data_0006,ax                ; (2.0012=0)
1.0407         mov bx,si
1.0409         inc si
1.040A         mov al,es:[bx]
1.040D         cbw
1.040E         sub ax,30h
1.0411         add data_0006,ax                ; (2.0012=0)
1.0415  loc_0052:                              ;   xref 1.03F8, 03FB
1.0415         cmp byte ptr es:[si],0
1.0419         jne loc_0051
1.041B         mov di,[bp-0Eh]
1.041E  loc_0053:                              ;   xref 1.03C9
1.041E         push    29h
1.0420         call    far ptr GETSYSTEMMETRICS
1.0425         push    ax
1.0426         push    ds
1.0427         push    16h
1.042A         call    far ptr GETPROCADDRESS
1.042F         mov [bp-0Ch],ax
1.0432         mov [bp-0Ah],dx
1.0435         or  dx,ax
1.0437         jz  short loc_0054
1.0439         push    1
1.043B         push    1
```

```
1.043D        call      dword ptr [bp-0Ch]      ;*1 entry
1.0440  loc_0054:                               ;  xref 1.0437
1.0440        push      4AF6h
1.0443        push      7Bh
1.0446        push      word ptr [bp+0Ch]
1.0449        call      far ptr MAKEPROCINSTANCE
1.044E        mov si,ax
1.0450        mov [bp-6],dx
1.0453        or   dx,ax
1.0455        jz   short loc_0055
1.0457        push      word ptr [bp+0Ch]
1.045A        push      0
1.045C        push      0Ah
1.045E        push      0
1.0460        mov ax,[bp-6]
1.0463        push      ax
1.0464        push      si
1.0465        mov [bp-12h],si
1.0468        mov [bp-10h],ax
1.046B        call      far ptr DIALOGBOX
1.0470        mov di,ax
1.0472        push      word ptr [bp-10h]
1.0475        push      word ptr [bp-12h]
1.0478        call      far ptr FREEPROCINSTANCE
1.047D  loc_0055:                               ;  xref 1.0455
1.047D        mov ax,[bp-0Ah]
1.0480        or   ax,[bp-0Ch]
1.0483        jz   short loc_0056
1.0485        push      1
1.0487        push      0
1.0489        call      dword ptr [bp-0Ch]      ;*1 entry
1.048C  loc_0056:                               ;  xref 1.0483
1.048C        mov ax,di
1.048E  loc_0057:                               ;  xref 1.03BF
1.048E        pop si
1.048F        pop di
1.0490        mov sp,bp
1.0492        pop bp
1.0493        retn      0Ah
      WinMain       endp
```

In the Pascal calling convention, the callee is responsible for clearing its arguments off the stack; this explains the RETN 0Ah return. In this particular case, WinMain() is being invoked with a NEAR call. As we saw in the startup code, with the Pascal calling convention, arguments are pushed in "forward" order. Thus, from the perspective of the called function, the last argument always has the *lowest* positive offset from BP (BP+6 in a FAR CALL, and BP+4 in a NEAR call, assuming the standard PUSH BP / MOV BP,SP function prologue; function parameters have positive offsets from BP, local variables have negative offsets from BP). In the case of WinMain in a small-model program like TASKMAN:

```
int PASCAL WinMain(HANDLE hInstance, HANDLE hPrevInstance,
    LPSTR lpCmdLine, int nCmdShow);
nCmdShow       = word ptr [bp+4]
lpCmdLine      = dword ptr [bp+6]
hPrevInstance  = word ptr [bp+0Ah]
hInstance      = word ptr [bp+0Ch]
```

We can now rewrite WinMain like so:

```
    WinMain       proc      near
    ; ...
1.03B6        sub di,di
1.03B8        cmp hPrevInstance,di          ; [bp+0Ah]
1.03BB        je  short loc_0047
1.03BD        sub ax,ax
1.03BF        jmp loc_0057                  ; (048E)
1.03C2  loc_0047:                          ;   xref 1.03BB
1.03C2        les si,dword ptr lpCmdLine    ; [bp+6]
1.03C5        cmp byte ptr es:[si],0
    ; ... etc. ...
    WinMain       endp
```

We can now see, for example, that WinMain() checks if hPrevInstance is zero (sub di, di); if it isn't, it immediately exits (jmp loc_0057).

Notice that TASKMAN appears to be inspecting its command line. The Windows documentation doesn't say anything about command-line arguments to TASKMAN, so this could be interesting. If you look in the WinMain() code shown earlier, around the label loc_0048 you will see that TASKMAN appears to be looking for a space (20h), getting a character from the command line, multiplying it by 10 (0Ah), subtracting the character '0' (30h), and doing other things that seem to indicate that it's looking for one or more *numbers*.

Rather than delve further into the code, it next makes sense to *run* TASKMAN, feeding it different numbers on the command line and seeing what it does. (It's surprising how few engineers think of actually going in and *running* a program before spending much time looking at its code.) Normally, TASKMAN runs when you type Ctrl-Esc in Windows, but TASKMAN is just a regular program that can be run, with a command line, like any Windows program.

Indeed, running "TASKMAN 1" behaves differently from just running "TASKMAN": it positions the Task List in the upper-left corner of the screen instead of in the middle. "TASKMAN 666 666" seems to position it in the lower-right corner. Basically, the arguments seem to represent an (x,y) position for TASKMAN to override its default position in the middle of the screen.

This is no big deal, of course. If we wanted extra TASKMAN features that much, it probably would take us, as software engineers, less time to write our own version of TASKMAN than to figure out what hidden "goodies" or "secrets" the existing one contains. But trying to figure out this undocumented feature will serve as an excellent example of reading and clarifying disassembled Windows listings.

Looking back at the code around loc_0048 and loc_0051, we can see that the variables data_0005 and data_0006 are being manipulated. What are these for? The answer is *not* to stare good and hard at this code until it makes sense, but to leave this area and see how the variables are used elsewhere in the program. Maybe the code somewhere else will be easier to understand.

In fact, if we search for data_0005 and data_0006 (or however the disassembler we're using represents these variables at ds:[10h] and ds:[12h]), we find them used as arguments to a Windows API function:

```
1.018B      mov data_0006,ax          ; (2.0012=0)
1.018E      push    word ptr [bp+0Eh]
1.0191      push    data_0005         ; (2.0010=0)
1.0195      push    ax
1.0196      push    si
1.0197      push    di
1.0198      push    0
1.019A      call    far ptr MOVEWINDOW
```

This shows us *immediately* what data_0006 and data_0005 are. MoveWindows() is a documented function, whose prototype appears in the SDK *Programmer's Reference:*

```
void FAR PASCAL MoveWindow(HWND hwnd, int nLeft, int nTop, int nWidth,
    int nHeight, BOOL fRepaint);
```

```
1.018B      mov data_0006,ax
1.018E      push    word ptr [bp+0Eh]    ; hwnd
1.0191      push    data_0005            ; nLeft
1.0195      push    ax                   ; nTop
1.0196      push    si                   ; nWidth
1.0197      push    di                   ; nHeight
1.0198      push    0                    ; fRepaint
1.019A      call    far ptr MOVEWINDOW
```

In other words, data_0005 has to be nLeft, and data_0006 (whose contents have been set from AX) has to be nTop. You could now do a global search and replace, changing every data_0005 in the program (not just the one here) to nLeft, and every data_0006 to nTop.

A lot of Windows disassembly is this easy: all Windows programs seem to do is call API functions, most of these functions are documented (either in the SDK or in this book), and you can use the documentation to label all arguments to the function. You then percolate these labels upward to other, possibly quite distant parts of the program.

In the case of nLeft née data_0005, and nTop née data_0006, suddenly the code in WinMain() makes more sense:

```
1.03C2  loc_0047:
1.03C2      les si,dword ptr lpCmdLine
1.03C5      cmp byte ptr es:[si],0       ; if no cmdline...
```

```
1.03C9        je  short loc_0053          ; go elsewhere
1.03CB        mov [bp-0Eh],di
1.03CE        jmp short loc_0049
1.03D0   loc_0048:
1.03D0        cmp byte ptr es:[si],20h     ; if space (20h)...
1.03D4        je  short loc_0050           ; go elsewhere
1.03D6        mov ax,0Ah
1.03D9        imul   nLeft                 ; nLeft *= 10
1.03DD        mov nLeft,ax
1.03E0        mov bx,si
1.03E2        inc si
1.03E3        mov al,es:[bx]
1.03E6        cbw                          ; ax = char
1.03E7        sub ax,30h                   ; ax -= '0' (char->number)
1.03EA        add nLeft,ax                 ; nLeft += number
1.03EE   loc_0049:
1.03EE        cmp byte ptr es:[si],0       ; if not at end of string
1.03F2        jne loc_0048                 ; get next character
; ... etc. ...
```

In essence, TASKMAN is performing the following operation here:

```
static int nLeft, nTop;
// ...
if (*lpCmdLine != 0)
    sscanf(lpCmdLine, "%u %u, &nLeft, &nTop);
```

Should you want 3.1 TASKMAN to appear in the upper-left of your screen, you could place the following line in the [boot] section of SYSTEM.INI:

```
taskman.exe=taskman.exe 1 1
```

In addition, double-clicking anywhere on the Windows desktop, at least in 3.1, will bring up TASKMAN, with the (x,y) coordinates for the double-click passed to TASK-MAN on its command line. The WM_SYSCOMMAND handler in USER is responsible for invoking TASKMAN via WinExec() whenever you press Ctrl-Esc or double-click on the desktop.

What else is going on in WinMain()? Let's look at the following block of code:

```
1.041E        push    29h
1.0420        call    far ptr GETSYSTEMMETRICS
1.0425        push    ax
1.0426        push    ds
1.0427        push    16h
1.042A        call    far ptr GETPROCADDRESS
1.042F        mov     [bp-0Ch],ax
1.0432        mov     [bp-0Ah],dx
1.0435        or      dx,ax
1.0437        jz      short loc_0054
1.0439        push    1
1.043B        push    1
1.043D        call    dword ptr [bp-0Ch]  ;*1 entry
```

The lines push 29h/call far ptr GETSYSTEMMETRICS, of course, are simply the assembly-language form of GetSystemMetrics(0x29). To understand this, we can grep in WINDOWS.H for SM_ (system metrics) and see what 0x29 is; it turns out to be SM_PENWINDOWS. Thus, we now have GetSystemMetrics(SM_PENWINDOWS). The 3.1 SDK documentation says that this returns a handle to the Pen Windows DLL, if Pen Windows is installed. As noted earlier, 16-bit return values always appear in the AX register.

Next, we can see AX—which must be either 0 or a Pen Windows module handle— on the stack along with ds:16h. Looking in the data segment at offset 16h, we see

```
2.0016      db  'RegisterPenApp', 0
```

Thus, here is what we have so far:

```
GetProcAddress(
    GetSystemMetrics(SM_PENWINDOWS),
    "RegisterPenApp")
```

GetProcAddress() returns a four-byte far function pointer (or NULL) in DX:AX. In the excerpt from WinMain, we can see this being moved into the DWORD at [bp-0Ch] (this is 16-bit code, so moving this 32-bit value, of course, requires two operations).

Clearly, it would be nice to know what the DWORD at [bp-0Ch] is. But actually, we already *do* know: it's a copy of the return value from GetProcAddress-(GetSystemMetrics(SM_PENWINDOWS), "RegisterPenApp"). In other words, it's a far pointer to the RegisterPenApp() function, or NULL if Pen Windows is not installed. We can now replace all references to [bp-0Ch] in this function with references to something like fpRegisterPenApp. Thus:

```
FARPROC fpRegisterPenApp;
fpRegisterPenApp = GetProcAddress(
    GetSystemMetrics(SM_PENWINDOWS),
    "RegisterPenApp");
```

Next, we see OR DX, AX being used to test the GetProcAddress() return value for NULL. If non-NULL, the code twice pushes 1 on the stack (note the use of "PUSH immediate" here; Windows applications only run on 80286 or higher processors, so there is no need to first place the value in a register and then push that register), and then calls through the fpRegisterPenApp function pointer:

```
1.0435      or   dx,ax
1.0437      jz   short loc_0054
1.0439      push   1
1.043B      push   1
1.043D      call   dword ptr fpRegisterPenApp
```

To understand this, we need to look in the Pen Windows SDK documentation and in PENWIN.H:

```
#define RPA_DEFAULT     1

void FAR PASCAL RegisterPenApp(UINT wFlags, BOOL fRegister);
```

Simply by looking up API calls in the Windows documentation, we can turn the whole block of assembly-language code into this:

```
void (FAR PASCAL *RegisterPenApp)(UINT, BOOL);
RegisterPenApp = GetProcAddress(
    GetSystemMetrics(SM_PENWINDOWS),
    "RegisterPenApp");
if (RegisterPenApp != 0)
    (*RegisterPenApp)(RPA_DEFAULT, TRUE);
```

We can continue in this way with all of WinMain(). When we're done, the 100 lines of assembly language for WinMain() boil down to the following 35 lines of C code:

```
// nLeft, nTop used in calls to MoveWindow() in TaskManDlgProc()
static WORD nLeft = 0, nTop = 0;

BOOL FAR PASCAL TaskManDlgProc(HWND hWndDlg, UINT msg, WPARAM wParam,
    LPARAM lParam);

int PASCAL WinMain(HANDLE hInstance, HANDLE hPrevInstance,
    LPSTR lpCmdLine, int nCmdShow)
{
    void (FAR PASCAL *RegisterPenApp)(UINT, BOOL);
    FARPROC fpDlgProc;

    if (hPrevInstance != 0)
        return 0;

    if (*lpCmdLine != 0)
        _fsscanf(lpCmdLine, "%u %u, &nLeft, &nTop); // pseudocode

    RegisterPenApp = GetProcAddress(GetSystemMetrics(SM_PENWINDOWS),
        "RegisterPenApp");

    if (RegisterPenApp != 0)
        (*RegisterPenApp)(RPA_DEFAULT, TRUE);

    if (fpDlgProc = MakeProcInstance(TaskManDlgProc, hInstance))
    {
        DialogBox(hInstance, MAKEINTRESOURCE(10), 0, fpDlgProc);
        FreeProcInstance(fpDlgProc);
    }

    if (RegisterPenApp != 0)
```

```
            (*RegisterPenApp)(RPA_DEFAULT, FALSE);

    return 0;
}
```

Examining WndProcs and DialogProcs

After you've found WinMain(), the next places to inspect are the program's window procedures and dialog procedures. (We're talking about Windows programs here; DLLs and device drivers need to be tackled from a different angle, discussed later in this chapter.) These WndProcs and DialogProcs are "callback" procedures; they're *exported* from Windows executables, almost as if the program were a DLL, so that Windows can call them. And because they are exported, these crucial procedures have *names* (almost always useful) that are accessible to any decent Windows disassembler. In TASKMAN.LST, for example, Sourcer clearly identifies TASKMANDLGPROC:

```
;
;           TASKMANDLGPROC
;

TASKMANDLGPROC   proc        far
; ...
TASKMANDLGPROC   endp
```

It works out well that the WndProcs and DialogProcs show up so nicely in the Sourcer listing because, as we know from Windows programming, these subroutines are "where the action is" in event-driven Windows applications, or at least where the action begins. Furthermore, we know that these subroutines will most likely be little more than (possibly very large) message-handling switch/case statements. From any Windows programming book, we can see that this usually looks something like this:

```
long FAR PASCAL _export WndProc(HWND hWnd, WORD message,
    WORD wParam, LONG lParam)
{
    // ...
    switch (message)
    {
        case WM_CREATE:
            // ... handle WM_CREATE message
            break;
        case WM_COMMAND:
            // ... handle WM_COMMAND message
            break;
        default:
            return DefWindowProc(hwnd, message, wParam, lParam);
    }
}
```

Actually, there's no rule that states that a Windows WndProc or DialogProc *has* to look like this; it's just that they almost always do. One could easily eliminate the switch/case statement by instead using a table (WM_USER in size) of function pointers.

Unfortunately, few Windows programs use this technique, so we're going to be stuck looking at big switch/case statements in assembly language.

Here's how the parameters to the WndProc or DialogProc will appear in the assembly-language listing (after the function prologue):

```
Long FAR PASCAL _export WndOrDialogProc(HWND hWnd, WORD message,
    WORD wParam, LONG lParam);
lParam  = dword ptr [bp+6]
wParam  = word ptr [bp+0Ah]
message = word ptr [bp+0Ch]
hWnd or hWndDlg = word ptr [bp+0Eh]
```

With this knowledge, we can replace an otherwise meaningless [bp+0Ch] with a label such as "message," a [bp+0Eh] with a "hwnd" or "hwndDlg," and so on, in *any* DialogProc and WndProc in *any* Windows program. The fixed, almost boilerplate nature of Windows programming greatly simplifies disassembly. For example, here's part of TaskManDlgProc():

```
TASKMANDLGPROC proc far
    ; ...
    mov si, hWndDlg ; [bp+0Eh]
    push    si
    push    64h
    call    far ptr GETDLGITEM
    mov di,ax
    mov ax, message ; [bp+0Ch]
    sub ax,1Ch
    jz  short loc_0005
    sub ax,0F4h
    jz  short loc_0009
    dec ax
    jnz short loc_0003
    jmp loc_0019
loc_0003:
    sub ax,353h
    jnz short loc_0004
    jmp loc_0042
loc_0004:
    jmp loc_0029
loc_0005:
    cmp word ptr wParam, 0  ; [bp+0Ah]
    je short loc_0006
    jmp loc_0029
    ; ...
TASKMANDLGPROC endp
```

The problem, of course, is what to make of all these magic numbers: 64h, 1Ch, 0F4h, and so on. How are we going to figure out what these mean?

Decoding Magic Numbers When examined via disassembled listings, Windows programs tend to contain a lot of "magic numbers." Of course, the actual source code, if we had access to it, would probably *not* contain raw, naked numbers. Instead, it would #include <windows.h>, #define numeric constants for the various resources (menus, strings, dialog controls, etc.) that it uses, and so on. Given a disassembled listing, it should be possible to turn a lot of these seemingly senseless numbers back into something understandable.

Let's start with the number 1Ch in TaskManDlgProc():

```
mov ax, message             ; [bp+0Ch]
sub ax, 1Ch
jz short loc_0005
```

If AX holds the message parameter to TaskManDlgProc(), then the value 1Ch must be a Windows WM_ message number. Looking in WINDOWS.H, we find that 0x1C is WM_ACTIVATEAPP. TaskManDlgProc() is subtracting this value from AX and then jumping somewhere if the result is 0. In other words

```
message -= WM_ACTIVATEAPP;
if (message == 0)
    goto ON_ACTIVATEAPP;
```

This is an odd way in which to test whether (message == WM_ACTIVATEAPP). If the test fails, and we don't take the jump to ON_ACTIVATEAPP, the message number has had 1Ch subtracted from it. This value has to be added back in to decode the next set of instructions:

```
sub ax,0F4h             ; 0x1C + 0xF4 = 0x110 = WM_INITDIALOG
jz  short loc_0009      ; must be ON_INITDIALOG
dec ax                  ; 0x110 + 1 = 0x111 = WM_COMMAND
jnz short loc_0003
jmp loc_0019            ; must be ON_COMMAND
```

Fortunately, most WndProcs and DialogProcs you examine will contain straightforward tests, rather than testing via subtraction. It all depends on how the C switch(message) { case WM_WHATEVER: } construct has been rendered into assembly language by the compiler. Some compilers will even generate jump tables rather than nests of tests and jumps. TASKMAN itself appears to have been written in assembler, accounting for its small size.

In any case, a WndProc or DialogProc generally contains a collection of handlers for different messages. In the case of TaskManDlgProc(), we can see that it's handling WM_ACTIVATEAPP, WM_INITDIALOG, and WM_COMMAND. By itself, this information is rather boring. However, it tells us what's happening elsewhere in the function: loc_0005 must be handling WM_ACTIVEAPP messages (so we've called it ON_ACTIVATEAPP), loc_0009 must be handling WM_INITDIALOG, and loc_0019 must be handling WM_COMMAND messages.

This same basic technique—find where the [bp+0Ch] "message" parameter to the WndProc or DialogProc is being tested, and from that identify the locations that handle various messages—can be used in any Windows program. Because handling messages is mostly what Windows applications do, once we know where the message handling is, we pretty much can have our way with the disassembled listing.

Here's what TaskManDlgProc( ) looks like now:

```
TASKMANDLGPROC proc far
    ; ...
DISPATCH_ON_MSG:
    mov ax, msg               ; [bp+0Ch]
    sub ax, WM_ACTIVATEAPP    ; 1Ch
    jz short ON_ACTIVATEAPP
    sub ax, 0F4h              ; 0x1C + 0xF4 = 0x110 = WM_INITDIALOG
    jz short ON_INITDIALOG
    dec ax                    ; 0x110 + 1 = 0x111 = WM_COMMAND
    jnz short DEFAULT         ; some other message
    jmp ON_COMMAND
DEFAULT:
    sub ax, 353h              ; 0x111 + 0x353 = 0x464 = WM_USER+0x64
    jnz short ON_PRIVATEMSG   ; some private message
    jmp loc_0042
ON_PRIVATEMSG:
    jmp loc_0029
ON_ACTIVATEAPP:
    ;; code to handle WM_ACTIVATEAPP
    cmp word ptr wParam, 0    ; [bp+0Ah]
    ; ...
ON_INITDIALOG:
    ;; code to handle WM_INITDIALOG
    ; ...
ON_COMMAND:
    ;; *** code to handle WM_COMMAND ***
    mov ax, wParam            ; [bp+0Ah]
    cmp ax, 68h               ; HUH??  WHAT'S THIS?!
    jne short loc_0020
    jmp loc_0040
    ; ....
TASKMANDLGPROC endp
```

This is starting to look pretty reasonable. In particular, once we know where WM_COMMAND is being handled, we're well on the way to understanding what the application does.

WM_COMMAND is so important for understanding an application's behavior because the handler for WM_COMMAND is where it deals with user commands such as menu selections and dialog push-button clicks, in other words, a lot of what makes an application unique. If you click on "Cascade" in Task Manager, for instance, it comes in as a WM_COMMAND; the same occurs if you click on "Tile" or "Switch To" or "End Task."

An application can tell *which* command a user has given it by looking in the wParam parameter to the WM_COMMAND message. This is what we started to see at the end of the TaskManDlgProc() excerpt on the previous page:

```
ON_COMMAND:
    ;; *** Since we're handling WM_COMMAND, wParam is idItem,
    ;; *** a control or menu item identifier
    mov ax, wParam        ; [bp+0Ah]
    cmp ax, 68h           ; must be ID number for a dialog control
    jne short loc_0020
    jmp loc_0040
loc_0020:
    jbe short loc_0021
    jmp loc_0045
loc_0021:
    dec al                ; 1
    jz short loc_0025     ; if (wParam==1) goto loc_0025
    dec al                ; 1 + 1 = 2
    jnz short loc_0022
    jmp loc_0043          ; if (wParam==2) goto loc_0043
loc_0022:
    sub al, 62h           ; already subtracted 2; 0x62 + 2 = 0x64
    jz short loc_0028
    dec al                ; 0x64 + 1 = 0x65
    jz short loc_0030
    sub al, 1             ; 0x65 + 1 = 0x66
    jnc short loc_0023
    jmp loc_0045
loc_0023:
    sub al, 1             ; 0x66 + 1 = 0x67
    ja short loc_0024
    jmp loc_0036
    ; ...
```

It's clear that wParam is being compared (in an admittedly odd way again, via subtraction) to values 1, 2, 65h, 66h, 67h. What is going on?

The values 1 and 2 are standard dialog button IDs:

```
#define IDOK        1
#define IDCANCEL    2
```

Thus:

```
dec al                  ; 1 = IDOK
jz short ON_OK          ; loc_0025
dec al                  ; 1 + 1 = 2 = IDCANCEL
jnz short loc_0022      ; not IDOK or IDCANCEL
jmp ON_CANCEL           ; loc_0043
```

The numbers 65h, 66h, etc., are specific to Task Manager, however; we're not going to find them in WINDOWS.H. But what hope then do we have of recovering the names of the commands to which these magic numbers correspond? Unless we happen to have a debug version of the program, hasn't all this information been thrown away in compiling and linking, irretrievably lost?

One of the notable things about Windows is that remarkably *little* information is thrown away. In the case of these magic numbers, which seem to correspond in some way to the different Task Manager push-buttons, it's pretty obvious that there *must* be some way of having applications tell Windows what wParam they want sent when one of their buttons is clicked or when one of their menu items is selected.

Applications almost always provide Windows with this information in their *resources*. (It's also possible to define menus and dialog controls dynamically, on the fly, but few applications take advantage of this.) These resources are part of the NE executable and are available for our inspection like any other part of the file.

This inspection of the resources in an .EXE file is carried out by the RESDUMP utility, included with Windows Source, and also provided on the disk accompanying this book. For example

```
C:\BIN>resdump \windows\taskman.exe
DIALOG 10 (OAh), "Task List"
    LISTBOX 100 (64h), ""
    DEFPUSHBUTTON 1 (01h), "&Switch To"
    PUSHBUTTON 101 (65h), "&End Task"
    PUSHBUTTON 2 (02h), "Cancel"
    STATIC 99 (63h), ""
    PUSHBUTTON 102 (66h), "&Cascade"
    PUSHBUTTON 103 (67h), "&Tile"
    PUSHBUTTON 104 (68h), "&Arrange Icons"
```

Using Resdump

RESDUMP displays information about resources in a Windows executable (EXE, DLL, DRV, etc.). Detailed information is provided for dialog boxes, controls, menus, string tables, accelerator tables, and version-information resources. RESDUMP is required for many disassembly tasks because strings, menus, dialog controls, etc., won't show up in the main disassembled listing but are needed to make sense of it.

Resources are presented in a style that is similar, but not identical, to the way they would be specified in a resource-compiler .RC file. Because menu items and control IDs may show up as either decimal or hexadecimal "magic numbers" in a disassembly listing, RESDUMP presents these numbers both ways. For example

```
C:\BIN>resdump \win31\clock.exe
; ... some details omitted ...
MENU 65515 (FFEBh)
    POPUP "&Settings"
        END
```

continued

```
continued

        1 (01h) "&Analog"
        2 (02h) "&Digital"
        0 (00h) ""
        3 (03h) "Set &Font..."
        0 (00h) ""
        6 (06h) "&No Title"
        0 (00h) ""
        7 (07h) "&Seconds"
        8 (08h) "Da&te"
        0 (00h) ""
        4 (04h) "A&bout Clock..."
        END

DIALOG 100 (64h), "Font"
    STATIC          1088 (440h), "&Font:"
    ; ...
    DEFPUSHBUTTON   1 (01h), "OK"
    PUSHBUTTON      2 (02h), "Cancel"
    GROUPBOX        1073 (431h), "Sample"
    STATIC          1093 (445h), ""
    STATIC          1092 (444h), "AaBbYyZz"

STRINGTABLE 1 (01h)
    2 (02h) "Clock"
    4 (04h) "data"
    6 (06h) "Not enough timing resources for Clock. Close other
applications and try again."
    8 (08h) "arial"
    9 (09h) "Always on &Top"
    ; ... etc. ...
```

   RESDUMP accepts two command-line options: -verbose will also show the (x,y) screen location for controls, and -hex will produce a hex-dump for each resource. RESDUMP is designed for Windows programs; it cannot be used for OS/2-style resources. ∎

It is now apparent what the numbers 64h, 65h, etc. mean. If we were writing Task Manager ourselves and using the conventional way of identifying pieces of the dialog box, we would write something like this:

```
#define IDD_SWITCHTO        IDOK
#define IDD_TASKLIST        0x64
#define IDD_ENDTASK         0x65
#define IDD_CASCADE         0x66
#define IDD_TILE            0x67
#define IDD_ARRANGEICONS    0x68
```

The last excerpt of code we examined now makes a lot more sense:

```
ON_COMMAND:
    ;; *** Since we're handling WM_COMMAND, wParam is idItem,
    ;; *** a control or menu item identifier
    mov ax, wParam              ; [bp+0Ah]
    cmp ax, 68h                 ; must be ID number for a dialog control
    ; ...
    dec al                      ; 1 = IDOK = IDD_SWITCHTO
    jz short ON_SWITCHTO        ; loc_0025
    dec al                      ; 1 + 1 = 2 = IDCANCEL
    jnz short loc_0022          ; not IDOK or IDCANCEL
    jmp ON_CANCEL               ; loc_0043
loc_0022:
    sub al, 62h                 ; 0x62 + 2 = 0x64 = IDD_TASKLIST
    jz short ON_TASKLIST        ; loc_0028
    dec al                      ; 0x64 + 1 = 0x65 = IDD_ENDTASK
    jz short ON_ENDTASK         ; loc_0030
    sub al, 1                   ; 0x65 + 1 = 0x66 = IDD_CASCADE
    jnc short loc_0023
    jmp loc_0045
loc_0023:
    sub al, 1                   ; 0x66 + 1 = 0x67 = IDD_TILE
    ja short loc_0024
    jmp ON_TILE_OR_CASCADE      ; loc_0036
    ; ...
```

In this way, we have identified loc_0036 as the place where TASKMAN's "Cascade" and "Tile" buttons are handled; we have renamed it ON_TILE_OR_CAS-CADE. Let's examine the code there to ensure that this makes sense:

```
ON_TILE_OR_CASCADE:                     ; loc_0036
    push hwndDlg                        ; si
    push 0
    call far ptr SHOWWINDOW
    call far ptr GETDESKTOPWINDOW
    mov di, ax                          ; hDesktopWnd
    cmp word ptr wParam, 66h            ; IDD_CASCADE
    jne short ON_TILE                   ; loc_0037
    push di                             ; hDesktopWnd
    push 0
    call far ptr CASCADECHILDWINDOWS
    jmp short loc_0041
ON_TILE:
    push di
    push 10h
    call far ptr GETKEYSTATE
    cmp ax, 8000h
    jb short loc_0038
    mov ax, 1                           ; 1 = MDITILE_HORIZONTAL
    jmp short loc_0039
loc_0038:
    sub ax, ax                          ; 0 = MDITILE_VERTICAL
```

```
loc_0039:
    push ax
    call far ptr TILECHILDWINDOWS
    jmp short loc_0041
```

It makes a lot of sense. We have found that the "Cascade" button in Tile Manager, after jumping through a lot of switch/case hoops, finally ends up calling the undocumented Windows API function, CascadeChildWindows( ); similarly, the "Tile" button ends up calling TileChildWindows( ). For more information on these functions, see their descriptions in chapter 6.

TASKMAN Techniques

One thing jumps out at us from the disassembled listing of ON_TILE: the call to GetKeyState( ). Because the Windows *User's Guide* says nothing about holding down a "state" (shift, etc.) key while selecting a button, this sounds like another undocumented "goodie" in TASKMAN. Indeed, if you try out the 3.1 TASKMAN, you will see that clicking on the Tile button arranges all the windows on the desktop side by side, but if you hold down the Shift key while clicking on the Tile button, the windows are arranged in a stacked formation.

To summarize, when the 3.1 TASKMAN Tile button is selected, the code that runs in response looks like this:

```
Tile:
    ShowWindow(hWndDlg, SW_HIDE);    // hide TASKMAN
    hDesktopWnd = GetDesktopWindow();
    if (GetKeyState(VK_SHIFT) == 0x8000)
        TileChildWindows(hDesktopWnd, MDITILE_HORIZONTAL);
    else
        TileChildWindows(hDesktopWnd, MDITITLE_VERTICAL);
```

As explained in the USER chapter, TileChildWindows( ) in 3.0 has only one parameter (the HWND). Thus, the GetKeyState( ) check does not appear in the 3.0 version of TASKMAN.

Similarly, the Cascade button in 3.1 TASKMAN runs the following code:

```
Cascade:
    ShowWindow(hWndDlg, SW_HIDE);    // hide TASKMAN
    CascadeChildWindows(GetDesktopWindow(), 0);
```

We can proceed through each TASKMAN option like this, rendering the assembly-language listing into more concise C. We can learn some interesting Windows programming techniques this way.

The first field to examine in TASKMAN is the Task List itself: how is the "Task List" list box filled with the names of each running application? What the list box clearly shows is a title bar for each visible top-level window, and the title bar is undoubtedly supplied with a call to GetWindowText( ). But how does TASKMAN enumerate all the top-level windows?

We should have asked ourselves this in chapter 2, when we were using utilities such as MAPWIN and EXEDUMP to examine TASKMAN, because while the program exports TASKMANDLGPROC, it does not export an enumeration procedure. Windows programs typically iterate through all windows by calling EnumWindows(). This function is passed a pointer to an application-supplied enumeration function, which must be exported. Because something like TASKMANENUMPROC isn't showing up in its list of exported functions, TASKMAN must not be calling EnumWindows(). What's it calling then? Quite simply, TASKMAN uses a GetWindow() loop to fill the "Task List" list box:

```
Task List:
    listbox = GetDlgItem(hwndDlg, IDD_TASKLIST);
    hwnd = GetWindow(hwndDlg, GW_HWNDFIRST);
    while (hwnd)
    {
        if ((hwnd != hwndDlg) &&                  // excludes self from list
            IsWindowVisible(hwnd) &&
            GetWindow(hwnd, GW_OWNER))
        {
            char buf[0x50];
            GetWindowText(hwnd, buf, 0x50);  // get titlebar
            SendMessage(listbox, LB_SETITEMDATA,
                SendMessage(listbox, LB_ADDSTRING, 0, buf),
                hwnd);  // store HWND as data to go with titlebar string
        }
        hwnd = GetWindow(hwnd, GW_HWNDNEXT);
    }
    SendMessage(lb, LB_SETCURSEL, 0, 0);       // select first item
```

The "End Task" button in TASKMAN just sends a WM_CLOSE message to the selected window, but only if it's not a DOS box. TASKMAN uses the undocumented IsWinOldApTask() function, in combination with the documented GetWindowTask() function, to determine if a given HWND corresponds to a DOS box:

```
End Task:
    // ... boring details omitted ...
    if (IsWinOldApTask(GetWindowTask(hwndTarget)))
        MaybeSwitchToSelectedWindow(hwndTarget);
    if (IsWindow(hwndTarget) &&
        (! (GetWindowLong(hwndTarget, GWL_STYLE) & WS_DISABLED)))
    {
        PostMessage(hwndTarget, WM_CLOSE, 0, 0);
    }
```

The "Arrange Icons" button simply runs the documented ArrangeIconic-Windows() function:

```
Arrange Icons:
    ShowWindow(hWndDlg, SW_HIDE);
    ArrangeIconicWindows(GetDesktopWindow());
```

The "Switch To" button in TASKMAN is also interesting. Like "Tile" and "Cascade," it's really just a user-interface covering for an undocumented Windows API function, in this case SwitchToThisWindow(). Let's walk through the process of deciphering an unlabeled Windows disassembly listing, turning it into labeled C code. Here's the code generated by Sourcer for a subroutine within TASKMAN, called from the IDD_SWITCHTO handling code in TaskManDlgProc():

```
     sub_0002:
1.0010          push    bp
1.0011          mov bp,sp
1.0013          push    di
1.0014          push    si
1.0015          push    word ptr [bp+4]
1.0018          push    41Ah
1.001B          push    word ptr [bp+4]
1.001E          push    409h
1.0021          push    0
1.0023          push    0
1.0025          push    0
1.0027          call    far ptr SENDMESSAGE
1.002C          push    ax
1.002D          push    0
1.002F          push    0
1.0031          call    far ptr SENDMESSAGE
1.0036          mov di,ax
1.0038          push    di
1.0039          call    far ptr ISWINDOW
1.003E          or  ax,ax
1.0040          jz  short loc_0001
1.0042          push    di
1.0043          call    far ptr GETLASTACTIVEPOPUP
1.0048          mov si,ax
1.004A          push    si
1.004B          call    far ptr ISWINDOW
1.0050          or  ax,ax
1.0052          jz  short loc_0001
1.0054          push    si
1.0055          push    0FFF0h
1.0057          call    far ptr GETWINDOWLONG
1.005C          test    dx,800h
1.0060          jnz short loc_0001
1.0062          push    si
1.0063          push    1
1.0065          call    far ptr SWITCHTOTHISWINDOW
1.006A          jmp short loc_0002      ; (0073)
1.006C  loc_0001:                       ;   xref 1.0040, 0052, 0060
1.006C          push    0
1.006E          call    far ptr MESSAGEBEEP
1.0073  loc_0002:                       ;   xref 1.006A
1.0073          pop si
1.0074          pop di
1.0075          mov sp,bp
1.0077          pop bp
1.0078          retn    2
```

The RETN 2 at the end tells us that this is a near Pascal function that expects one WORD parameter, which appears as [bp+4] at the top of the code. Because [bp+4] is being used as the first parameter to SendMessage(), it must be an HWND of some sort. Finally, we don't see anything being moved into AX or DX near the end of the function, so it looks as if this function has no return value:

```
void near pascal some_func(HWND hwnd)
```

The function starts off with two nested calls to SendMessage(), using the message numbers 41Ah and 409h. Because these numbers are greater than 400h, they must be WM_USER+XX values. Windows controls such as edit boxes, list boxes, and combo boxes all use WM_USER+XX notification codes. However, the only appropriate control in TASKMAN is the list box, so we can just look at the list of LB_XXX codes in WINDOWS.H. Converting hexadecimal to decimal, 1Ah is 26, so 41Ah is WM_USER+26, or LB_GETITEMDATA. Similarly, 409h is WM_USER+9, which in the case of a list box means LB_GETCURSEL. We can look up LB_GETITEMDATA and LB_GETCURSEL in the Windows *Programmer's Reference.* Earlier, we saw that TASKMAN uses LB_SETITEMDATA to store each window title's associated HWND. LB_GETITEMDATA will retrieve this hwnd:

```
hwnd = SendMessage(listbox, LB_GETITEMDATA,
    SendMessage(listbox, LB_GETCURSEL, 0, 0), 0);
```

Notice that now we're calling the parameter to some_func() a listbox, and the return value from LB_GETITEMDATA is an HWND.

How do we know it's an hwnd? We can see the LB_GETITEMDATA return value (in DI) immediately being passed to IsWindow():

```
; IsWindow(hwnd = SendMessage(...));
call far ptr SENDMESSAGE
mov di, ax
push di
call far ptr ISWINDOW
```

Next, the hwnd is passed to GetLastActivePopup(), and the HWND that GetLast ActivePopup() returns is then checked with IsWindow():

```
; IsWindow(hwndPopup = GetLastActivePopup(hwnd));
push di     ; hWnd
call far ptr GETLASTACTIVEPOPUP
mov si, ax
push si     ; hwndPopup
call far ptr ISWINDOW
```

Next, hwndPopup (in SI) is passed to GetWindowLong(). Here, it's time to look at WINDOWS.H to figure out what 0FFF0h and 800h are supposed to mean:

```
; GetWindowLong(hwndPopup, GWL_STYLE) & WS_DISABLED
push si          ; hwndPopup
push GWL_STYLE   ; 0FFF0h = -16
call far ptr GETWINDOWLONG
test dx, 800h    ; DX:AX = 800:0000 = WS_DISABLED
```

Finally, as the whole point of this exercise, assuming the window passes all its tests, its last active popup is switched to:

```
; SwitchToThisWindow(hwndPopup, TRUE)
push si          ; hwndPopup
push 1
call far SwitchToThisWindow
```

It's here that all our questions start: because SwitchToThisWindow() is not documented, we don't know the purpose of its second parameter, apparently a BOOL. More important, we can't really tell why SwitchToThisWindow() is being used, when SetActiveWindow(), SetFocus(), or BringWindowToTop() might do the trick. And why is the last active popup, not the window, being switched to?

For now, though, we're done: our function will switch to the window selected in the Task List if the window meets all the function's many preconditions:

```
void MaybeSwitchToSelectedWindow(HWND listbox)
{
    HWND hwnd, hwndPopup;

    // first figure out which window was selected in Task List
    if (IsWindow(hwnd = SendMessage(listbox, LB_GETITEMDATA,
        SendMessage(listbox, LB_GETCURSEL, 0, 0), 0)))
    {
        if (IsWindow(hwndPopup = GetLastActivePopup(hwnd)))
        {
            if (! (GetWindowLong(hwndPopup, GWL_STYLE) & WS_DISABLED))
            {
                SwitchToThisWindow(hwndPopup, TRUE);
                return;
            }
        }
    }

    /* still here -- error */
    MessageBeep(0);
}
```

Examining API Functions and Data Structures

Now that we have a good idea of what TASKMAN does (it sure took a long time to understand those 3K bytes of code!), it might be interesting to peer around the other side of the curtain. We've seen that TASKMAN calls an assortment of undocumented functions; we can now see how those undocumented functions are implemented and, at the same time, get a feel for how disassembly of DLLs differs from disassembly of programs.

Let's start with the IsWinOldApTask() function in KERNEL. You can use Sourcer, or another Windows disassembler, to get a listing of one of the KERNEL modules (KRNL286.EXE or KRNL386.EXE), just as you can get a listing of a program like TASKMAN.EXE. Because it's the most commonly used, we'll disassemble KRNL386.EXE.

The key difference between disassembling a DLL and disassembling a program is that the DLL will generally contain a larger number of smaller functions and that these functions will have exported *names* that are all available to a Windows disassembler.

Of course, we can figure out what IsWinOldApTask() does from its name alone: obviously, it takes an HTASK (a task handle, such as that returned from GetCurrentTask() or GetWindowTask()) and returns a BOOL indicating whether the specified task is an "old ap," (i.e., a DOS program running under Windows). But let's see how the function works:

```
      ISWINOLDAPTASK  proc      far
1.7309          call    sub_0016
1.730C          mov es,es:data_0643      ; (4.0060=0)
1.7311          mov ax,es:data_0033e     ; (0000:0048=0F841h)
1.7315          and ax,1
1.7318          retf    2
      ISWINOLDAPTASK  endp
```

In addition to Sourcer, which will make five passes over the code to try to link everything up, separate code from data, and do many other incredibly useful but somewhat time-consuming tasks, you might find it helpful to use a simpler disassembler such as the one built into NuMega's Soft-ICE/Windows:

```
:u iswinoldaptask
KERNEL!ISWINOLDAPTASK
0117:00007309   CALL    7247
0117:0000730C   MOV     ES,ES:[0060]
0117:00007311   MOV     AX,ES:[0048]
0117:00007315   AND     AX,0001
0117:00007318   RETF    0002
KERNEL!ISTASK
; ...
```

Let's start by looking at the subroutine that IsWinOldApTask() calls. Sourcer gives it a label, sub_0016. So what's sub_0016?

```
     sub_0016:
1.7247          mov bx,sp
1.7249          mov ax,ss:[bx+6]
1.724D  loc_1101:                          ; xref 1.7245
1.724D          or  ax,ax
1.724F          jnz short loc_1102
1.7251          mov es,word ptr cs:MYCSDS  ; (1.0030=0)
1.7256          mov ax,es:data_0077e       ; (0000:0248=0)
```

```
1.725A   loc_1102:                          ;   xref 1.724F
1.725A        mov es,ax
1.725C        retn
```

We can see that sub_0016 has the same parameter as IsWinOldApTask(). Thus, AX is a probably an HTASK. It looks as if sub_0016 checks if the HTASK is 0; if it's not, it moves the HTASK into ES; if it is 0, it moves the value of es:data_0077e into ES. Great, so what is es:data_0077e, which appears to be ds:[248h]? (The name MYCSDS showed up here because the version of KRNL386.EXE happened to have some useful CodeView symbols.)

Actually, we didn't have to go looking for es:data_0077e because in reality, by the time we looked at IsWinOldApTask(), we had already replaced the label data_0077e with a more useful one. The first thing we did with KRNL386.LST was look for small functions, any small functions. We figured that if we could understand those, it might help clarify other parts of the code. For example, one place we looked was the small documented function, GetCurrentTask():

```
   GETCURRENTTASK   proc      far
1.78F8        push     es
1.78F9        mov      es,word ptr cs:MYCSDS   ; (1.0030=0)
1.78FE        mov      ax,es:data_0077e        ; (0000:0248=0)
1.7902        mov      dx,es:data_0076e        ; (0000:0246=0)
1.7907        pop es
1.7908        retf
   GETCURRENTTASK   endp
```

Here, we knew that whatever GetCurrentTask() is returning in AX, it *must* be the current task. Thus, es:data_0077e (DS:[248h]) is some sort of global variable, holding the current task. As soon as we saw this, we did a massive global search-and-replace through the entire one-megabyte KRNL386.LST file, replacing all occurrences of data_0077e with the new name, CURR_TASK.

It's worth noting that GetCurrentTask() has an additional, undocumented return value in DX, which you can see in the code above. As explained in chapter 5, this value is the head of KERNEL's linked list of tasks. We did another global search-and-replace, taking all data_0076e and replacing them with FIRST_TASK.

Suddenly, the entire KRNL386.LST file was starting to make a lot more sense. One piece of code that made more sense was sub_0016:

```
   sub_0016:
; ...
1.7251        mov      es,word ptr cs:MYCSDS
1.7256        mov      ax,es:CURR_TASK         ; (ds:[248h])
1.725A   loc_1102:
1.725A        mov      es,ax
1.725C        retn
```

In fact, it's now fairly clear that this function moves a task handle into ES; if the passed-in task handle is 0, then sub_0016 uses the current task:

```
GetTaskIntoES proc near          ; was sub_0016
    mov bx, sp
    mov ax, ss:[bx+6]            ; HTASK
    or ax, ax
    jnz short not_zero
    ; HTASK is 0
    mov es, word ptr cs:MYCSDS   ; DS stored in code seg
    mov ax, es:CURR_TASK         ; ds:[248h]
not_zero:
    mov es, ax
    retn
GetTaskIntoES endp
```

This is no big deal by itself, but we can now replace all calls to sub_0016() with calls to GetTaskIntoES(). This should again improve the entire listing. In fact, it does; here's a function whose understandability is a good bit improved by knowing that it starts off by getting a task handle into ES:

```
        GETTASKQUEUE    proc    far
1.7268          call    GetTaskIntoES  ; sub_0016
1.726B          mov ax,es:data_0631    ; (4.0020=5744h)
1.726F          retf    2
        GETTASKQUEUE    endp
```

We thus know that, in the second line of the function, ES contains a task handle. We wouldn't have known that without figuring out the true purpose of sub_0016. But if ES contains a task handle, and if this function returns a task queue, then we know that at offset 20h of a task there's a handle to a task queue. We might not even know what these different structures are, and these offsets might differ in various versions of KERNEL, but continuing in this way will help clarify the code. (In fact, the presence of a task-queue handle at offset 20h in the task structure is quite reliable.)

Another function we looked at was GetCurrentPDB() (PDB is the weird term in Windows for what is everywhere else called the Program Segment Prefix, or PSP). Again, we already know what this function does (it's documented), but we figured that it probably was a small function that did little more than move the contents of some global variable into AX:

```
        GETCURRENTPDB   proc    far
        ; ...
3.0450          mov ds,CURR_TASK       ; (4.0248=0)
3.0454          mov ax,ds:data_0038e   ; (0000:0060=9938h)
3.0457          pop ds
3.0458          retf
        GETCURRENTPDB   endp
```

Even better! It turned out not to be a global variable, but a field within the task structure. The code for GetCurrentPDB() gets CURR_TASK into DS, then moves DS:[60h] into AX. So, offset 60h in the task structure contains a PDB. But that's a good old PSP! Because it's not a global, we need to be a little more careful in our search and replace, but we can replace many ds:[60h] or ds:data_0038e references with ds:[PSP].

With all this activity elsewhere in the file, let's look again at IsWinOldApTask() and see how our global search-and-replaces have affected it:

```
ISWINOLDAPTASK  proc      far
    call GetTaskIntoES
    mov es, es:[PSP]
    mov ax, es:data_0033e    ; psp[48h]
    and ax, 1
    retf 2
ISWINOLDAPTASK  endp
```

This is a big improvement. In fact, we now know what IsWinOldApTask() does: it first takes the task you pass in and turns it into a PSP. If you pass in 0, it gets the PSP out of the current task. From the PSP, it then examines the WORD at offset 48h and returns the bottom bit. (This undocumented field in the PSP is set by the WINOLDAP module.)

By itself, this is no big deal. But along the way, we found an undocumented aspect to GetCurrentTask() (one that let us easily walk the task list; see the KERNEL chapter) and located two fields in the task structure: the TASK_QUEUE at offset 20h, and the PSP at offset 60h. To find other fields in the task structure, or any other structure, we just continue in this same manner, examining the return value of small functions and doing global search-and-replaces.

For example, we can find another field by looking at this 3.1 function:

```
        ISTASK          proc      far
1.731B          mov bx,sp
1.731D          mov ax,ss:[bx+4]
1.7321          or  ax,ax
1.7323          jz  short loc_1107
1.7325          lsl bx,ax
1.7328          jnz short loc_1107
1.732A          cmp bx,0FCh
1.732E          jl  short loc_1107
1.7330          mov es,ax
1.7332          cmp word ptr es:data_0490e,4454h    ; (4558:00FA=0FFFFh)
1.7339          jne short loc_1107
1.733B          jmp short loc_ret_1108  ; (733F)
1.733D  loc_1107:                    ; xref 1.7323, 7328, 732E, 7339
1.733D          xor ax,ax
1.733F  loc_ret_1108:                     ; xref 1.733B
1.733F          retf    2
        ISTASK          endp
```

IsTask() is a documented 3.1 function that determines if an arbitrary WORD is a valid task handle. The code uses the Intel LSL (Load Selector Limit) instruction to ensure that the segment to which the given handle corresponds is at least 0FCh bytes in length. It then looks at offset 0FAh in the segment, hoping to find the value 4454h. Numbers such as this are usually signatures of some kind: here, 44h is D and 54h is T, so 4454h is TD (no, not Turbo Debugger: Task Database!). We now have another field for our Task Database structure: the WORD at offset 0FAh must be 4454h, the TD signature.

There isn't an IsTask() function exported in Windows 3.0 (not even an undocumented one), but we now know how to write one, assuming that is, that the Task Database has the same structure in 3.0 as we've been finding in 3.1.

In fact, it does. Too much relies on this structure for it to change much. In fact, after disassembling all this, we stumbled across a Microsoft header file for the Task Database, TDB.INC (it is included with the Windows 3.1 DDK), and found the comment "Don't you dare change anything in here or raor [Rao Remala, one of the Windows developers] will kill you; OLE depends on this (3/25/91)." A comforting thought!

Having examined IsWinOldApTask() in KERNEL, let's next look at GetWindowTask() in USER. As you may recall, it was this function that, given an HWND, provided TASKMAN with the task handle it needed for IsWinOldApTask().

Again, we can look at this function using either a Windows disassembler, such as Sourcer, or a debugger, such as Soft-ICE/Windows:

```
GetWindowTask proc far
    ; ... param validation ...
    jmp IGetWindowTask
GetWindowTask endp

IGetWindowTask:
    ;... get USER local heap into DS...
    xor ax, ax
    mov bx, [bp+6]   ; hwnd
    mov es, [bx+18]
    mov ax, es:[2]
```

It looks as if GetWindowTask() (IGetWindowTask(), actually) is working with two different structures: at offset 2 in one structure, there is what obviously must be a task handle. Obviously, because it's the return value from GetWindowTask(), which returns a task handle. At offset 18h in what must be a WND structure (the passed-in HWND is being treated as an offset into USER's local heap), we have a handle to this first structure.

What is this first structure, a handle to which is stored at offset 18h in the WND structure, and which in turn contains at offset 2 a TASK handle? Whatever it is, it forms some sort of link between a WND and a TASK, and so would be useful to figure out.

Frankly, here it just pays to *guess* that this is a Task Queue structure and then see how far you get with this. True, there's little in KERNEL that shows a link from a Task Queue back to a Task Database. Generally you want to go in the other direction, to get from a Task Database to a Task Queue; as we saw with GetTaskQueue() above, the Task structure *does* contain, at offset 20h, a handle to its corresponding Task Queue.

But why would there be a "back" pointer, in offset 2 of the Task Queue, back to its corresponding Task Database? KERNEL wouldn't have much of a use for this, but USER would. The Task Queue, a KERNEL data structure, is where USER posts WM_ messages. While USER depends on the Task Queue structure, it only rarely needs a Task handle. Thus, keeping a Task Queue handle in the WND structure, and a Task Database handle in the Task Queue, makes a lot of sense.

You can watch this look-up happen with Soft-ICE/Windows. As we'll be explaining in more detail in the next chapter, Soft-ICE/W uses the built-in debug facilities of the 80386 to implement real-time memory-access breakpoints. (ICE stands for in-circuit emulator, and Soft-ICE is like a software in-circuit emulator.) Once you have some Task Queue handle, you can set a memory-access breakpoint (BPM) on offset 2 in the structure and see if, and how, it gets called. Soft-ICE/W provides a TASK command to view the task list; this list includes each task's Task Queue structure:

```
:task
TaskName   SS:SP       StackTop   StackBot   StackLow   TaskDB  hQueue   Events
DRWATSON   12D7:2A92   3B34       1BCA       2324       12FF    12E7     0000
WINFILE    17B7:3716   377C       1012       2498       07FF    06B7     0000
WINOLDAP   1477:1D5A   1E82       0B18       15D8       14B7    149F     0000
TASKMAN    1167:13A2   144E       00E4       0E60       11BF    1187     0000
SH         134F:3BCC   3C54       28EA       34A4       1377    135F     0001
CALLFUNC*  11AF:2BFC   2DB6       1A4C       24D4       121F    11B7     0001
```

For example, we can instruct Soft-ICE/W to break on any (read or write) access to offset 2 in WINFILE's Task Queue structure:

```
:bpm 06b7:2 rw
```

Sure enough, the breakpoint was triggered almost immediately from code in USER's segment 1, near InSendMessage():

```
push word ptr es:[2]
call PostEvent
```

And a second later:

```
push word ptr es:[2]
call WaitEvent
```

PostEvent() is undocumented, but WaitEvent() is partially documented by Microsoft in its description of Windows startup code (3.1. SDK *Programmer's Reference, Volume 1: Overview*, chapter 22). While Microsoft's documentation does not suggest anything like the use shown here (see the KERNEL chapter in this book for a proper explanation of WaitEvent() and PostEvent()), it does at least say that WaitEvent() expects a TASK handle. Thus, we are confirmed in our suspicion that offset 2 in the Task Queue structure is a Task Database handle.

How do we know it's a Task Queue structure, though? We know because the code that calls WaitEvent() is preceded by a few lines with a call to the undocumented KERNEL function, GetTaskQueueES(), the purpose of which is fairly clear from its name, and whose implementation in KERNEL clears up any remaining doubts:

```
GetTaskQueueES proc far
    mov es, cs:MYCSDS          ; ds:[30h]
    mov es, es:CURR_TASK       ; ds:[0228h]
    mov es, es:TASK_QUEUE      ; task:[20h]
GetTaskQueueES endp
```

The Soft-ICE/W breakpoint also found that the SendMessage2() and Reply-Message() functions in USER both use offset 2 of the Task Queue to get a TASK handle to pass to SetPriority(), apparently to make sure that the message recipient's task gets scheduled.

We now have a good understanding of the seemingly simple call, IsWinOld-ApTask(GetWindowTask(hwnd)):

```
GetWindowTask(HWND):
    from HWND, get WND (just treat HWND as offset into USER local heap)
    from WND offset 18h, get handle to TASK_QUEUE structure
    from TASK_QUEUE offset 2, get handle to TASK_DB structure

IsWinOldApTask(HTASK):
    from TASK_DB offset 60h, get selector to PSP (PDB)
    from PDB offset 48h, get flags
    return flags AND 1
```

Note how knowing these structures gives us a link from a window handle to a task queue to a task database to a PSP. If we needed it, for example, we could now write a GetWindowPSP() function, even though no such function exists in Window. It would just be a matter of packaging up the structure access:

```
#define PSP_FROM_HTASK(hTask) \
    *((WORD far *) MK_FP(hTask, 0x60))

#define PSP_FROM_HWND(hWnd) \
    PSP_FROM_HTASK(GetWindowTask(hWnd))
```

For the last two chapters, we have worked almost entirely with Windows files, using plain-vanilla DOS programs to examine them. For most of this investigation, Windows didn't even need to be running.

However, this technique has its limitations. Already, we needed to run Soft-ICE/Windows to help with our understanding of GetWindowTask(). Soft-ICE isn't a Windows application, but it reflects Windows as a dynamic environment, rather than as a static collection of files on disk. In the next chapter, we will stop looking at mere files and start examining Windows as it is when loaded into memory and running.

CHAPTER 4

Tools for Exploring Windows

Up until now, we've been exploring Windows by looking at its files. We've come a long way—finding undocumented functions, finding applications that call them, disassembling the functions, using the disassembly to piece together a picture of Windows' internal structures, and so on—but, as long as we look only at files, we have no way of *testing* whether our picture of undocumented Windows is an accurate one.

For example, we might disassemble KERNEL and examine the PostEvent() and WaitEvent() functions. Disassembly is just file manipulation, so Windows doesn't need to be running for us to disassemble one of its files, and the disassembler doesn't need to be a Windows application. By looking at the code for these functions, we could conclude that they work together to manipulate some sort of semaphore stored at offset 6 in a Windows task structure. But if we don't write a Windows program that actually tries to *use* these functions, it's all idle speculation.

In this chapter, we finally get around to *running Windows*. (What a concept!) We'll present a series of tools that let us try out undocumented Windows functions, browse its internal data structures, and trap interrupts and undocumented WM_ messages. These tools, and all the sample source code in this book, are written with the WINIO library, also presented in this chapter (and, along with the tools themselves, provided in library form on the accompanying disk). WINIO makes it easy to write Windows applications, with multiple windows, menus, clickable lines, and so on, but using main() rather than WinMain(), stdio functions such as printf(), and other conveniences.

Windows Spies, Walkers, and Debuggers

Before we start to develop our own home-brew utilities, though, let's take some time to survey the existing Windows snooping software.

Even though no longer essential to Windows software development, the Microsoft Windows Software Development Kit (SDK) comes with several programs that are useful for exploring Windows: HEAPWALK, SPY, CodeView for Windows, WDEB386, and the debug version of Windows.

HEAPWALK

HEAPWALK (Luke Heapwalker) displays a list of all items in the Windows global heap. For each item, HEAPWALK shows its handle, linear base address, size in bytes, allocation flags, the module name of its owner, and, in some cases, its type (such as "Module Database," "Task," "Code," "DGROUP," and so on). If a globally allocated item contains a local heap, you can do a LocalWalk on the item, bringing up a secondary window that displays the local heap.

In the global-walk window, you can doubleclick on any item to bring up a secondary window with a hex dump of the object (unfortunately, you can't seem to do this within a local-walk window). For example, double-clicking on any item labeled "Task" will display a hex dump of a Task Database structure. Without knowing anything more about this structure, you can inspect the hex dump and find that the Task Database includes a directory path, the module name of the task, a TD signature, and a PT signature.

HEAPWALK does an excellent job of labeling the objects it knows about (it will even pick up and display segment names from modules that include debug symbol tables, such as KERNEL, USER, and GDI in the debug version of Windows). However, it displays Task Queue structures merely as "USER Private," doesn't know about WND structures in the nondebug version of Windows, and, of course, doesn't know about any selectors that aren't on the Windows global heap (such as PSP selectors). HEAPWALK has "GDI LocalWalk" and "USER LocalWalk" options, but these work only on the USER and GDI *default* local heaps, not on the additional local heaps in 3.1 that help relieve the "free system resources" problem.

SPY

SPY displays information about windows: This part of SPY, as well as the program's name, is more or less a rip-off of Michael Geary's original SPY program, from the 1987 (yes, Windows has been around for a long time!) IBM special issue of *Byte*. When you click on a window in the SDK SPY, it displays the window's HWND handle, the module name of its owner, its parent, style, and class name.

For example, SPY will reveal that the main window in WinWord 1.x has the class name "OpusApp," that Visual Basic's class name is "ThunderForm," and that CorelDRAW's module name is "waldo." Such strings are important for Windows programs that communicate with other programs. (By the way, for a list of class names, module names, and DDE server names for key Windows applications, see the DDE chapter in Woody Leonhard's *Windows 3.1 Programming for Mere Mortals.*)

Besides displaying basic information about a window, SPY's main purpose is to trace WM_ messages, allowing you to see what messages are generated for various actions. However, the version of SPY that comes with the SDK doesn't show undocumented WM_ messages, such as WM_SYNCPAINT (0x0088), WM_ENTER-MENULOOP (0x0211), or WM_BEGINDRAG (0x022C).

Programmers sometimes use SPY or a similar program to determine the menu ID values used by an application such as Program Manager so that the application can be subclassed. By examining the wParam values for the WM_COMMAND messages triggered by selecting each menu item, you can produce a table of the application's menu values. However, message-watching utilities like SPY are usually overkill for this task. These values are almost always part of the program's menu resources, so it is much easier to get menu ID values by running the RESDUMP program from chapter 3. For example, the following shows that picking File New in Program Manager will generate a WM_COMMAND wParam=65h:

```
C:\BIN>resdump \win31\progman.exe
... some icons ...
MENU 5 (05h)
    POPUP "&File"
        101 (65h) "&New..."
        102 (66h) "&Open     Enter"
        103 (67h) "&Move... F7"
        104 (68h) "&Copy... F8"
        105 (69h) "&Delete  Del"
        106 (6Ah) "&Properties...    Alt+Enter"
        ... etc. ...
```

Thus, it is not necessary to run SPY, or even PROGMAN itself, to learn about an application's menu structure.

CodeView for Windows

CodeView for Windows (CVW) is a source-level debugger for Windows programs built with Microsoft C. It is not particularly convenient, but it can be used to do Windows snooping if nothing better is available. If your program calls an undocumented Windows function, you can trace into the function by pressing F8. The u command will unassemble any Windows API function, including an undocumented one, if you know the function's address. You can also set a breakpoint on an undocumented API function, again assuming you know its address. (To find an API function's address, you can write a simple Windows program that calls GetProcAddress() and prints out the segment:offset addresses of any API function you're interested in.)

WDEB386

For someone interested in the inner workings of Windows, particularly Enhanced mode Windows, Microsoft's WDEB386 is a far more interesting debugger than CVW. All the really good stuff is here! For example, these are some commands supported by WDEB386:

```
.dm     Display Module list
.dq     Display Task Queue list
dg      Display Global Descriptor Table (GDT)
di      Display Interrupt Descriptor Table (IDT)
dl      Display Local Descriptor Table (LDT)
```

```
dp          Display 386 page directory and page tables
dt          Display 386 Task State Segment (TSS)
dx          Display LOADALL buffer
.?          Display list of additional commands supported by the
            debug version of WIN386.EXE
```

Unfortunately, WDEB386 requires a second monitor and is awkward to use. Both problems, and more, are solved by NuMega's Soft-ICE/Windows debugger, described in detail later in this chapter.

Debug Version of Windows

The key ingredient in the Windows SDK, the one thing it includes that should make any Windows developer want to get the SDK even if he or she uses none of its other components, is the debug version of Windows. This consists of versions of KRNL286, KRNL386, USER, GDI, and MMSYSTEM that have been built with CodeView symbols. Unfortunately, the most interesting CodeView symbols, for undocumented and internal functions, have been deliberately mangled in the SDK (see the description of EXEDUMP -CVBLANKS in chapter 2).

In some cases, internal data structures are slightly larger in the debug than in the retail version of Windows. Such differences are indicated in this book's descriptions of these structures (for example, see the description of the DC structure in chapter 8). A program can test for the presence of debug Windows with GetSystemMetrics-(SM_DEBUG).

When running under the debug version of Windows, the ToolHelp library can provide tools with more information about USER objects such as windows, menus, and so on. The HEAPWALK utility is more informative when running under debug Windows, showing segment names for KERNEL, USER, and GDI, and showing object types for items in USER's local heap. There are also several API functions available in debug Windows that are not in the retail version.

Get the DDK!

As has been noted several times already in this book, the Microsoft Windows Device Driver Kit (DDK) is another key resource for anyone interested in undocumented Windows. To call this a "device driver" kit seriously underestimates its importance and limits its audience. The DDK actually has remarkably little to do with device-driver development as such; it's really a collection of additional Windows API functions that are lower-level and/or more powerful than the ones that come with the SDK.

For one thing, one of the key things you can do with the DDK is build Enhanced mode 32-bit virtual device drivers (VxDs). The .386 files that some applications install in your SYSTEM.INI file are VxDs; WIN386.EXE is a collection of VxDs. VxDs really aren't device drivers at all, but a different—and extremely powerful—

continued

continued

type of Windows program. Whenever something appears to be "impossible" in Windows, the solution often is to write a VxD. In particular, VxDs are essential for writing applications that tie together DOS and Windows. (If you want to learn a little bit about VxDs before buying the DDK, read Dan Norton's book, *Writing Windows Device Drivers*.)

Another reason to get the Windows 3.1 DDK is that it includes header files for many internal aspects of Windows, including:

- an "internal" version of WINDOWS.H, with about 300 items missing from the SDK version of WINDOWS.H. (This is somewhat like "WINDOWS.H: The Lost Recordings.")
- WINKERN.INC, with the global and local heap and arena structures
- TDB.INC, with the Task Database structure
- NEWEXE.INC, with the new-executable (NE) file format (sorry, EXE386.H, with the linear-executable (LE) format, is not included with the DDK; it certainly ought to be)
- WINNET.H, with the WNet (Windows/Network interface) and LFN (long filename) functions
- INT2FAPI.INC, with some of the INT 2Fh API for DOS programs running under Windows

In addition, the DDK includes disk upon disk of C and assembly-language *source code* for many (though by no means all) of the device drivers and VxDs that make up Windows, and includes a debug version of WIN386.EXE that provides many debugging commands that you can issue from either WDEB386 or Soft-ICE/Windows. ■

Other Snooping Utilities

If you have Borland C++, you don't need the SDK to produce and debug Windows applications. Everything you absolutely require for Windows software development comes with Borland C++. However, it does not come with the extensive documentation of the 3.1 SDK, and it is missing the extremely valuable debug version of Windows and some of the SDK tools such as HeapWalk. Probably the best way to do Windows development today is to use both Borland C++ and the SDK.

Instead of CVW, Borland C++ of course includes Turbo Debugger for Windows (TDW). As with CVW, you can unassemble, set breakpoints on, and trace into API functions, both documented and undocumented. However, as with CVW, you often have to know the function's segment:offset address beforehand.

Borland C++ comes with Resource Workshop, an excellent program for exploring, changing, and creating dialogs, menus, icons, cursors, bitmaps, fonts, and so on, somewhat similar to ResEdit on the Macintosh.

Borland C++ 3.1 comes with WinSpector, a post-mortem debugger similar, yet vastly superior, to Microsoft's Dr. Watson. (WinSpector was at one point known as Dr. Frank.) One of the parts of WinSpector is the BUILDSYM utility, which can create a debug .SYM file from an .EXE that has no debug information! BUILDSYM creates this debug information, seemingly "from nothing," using the symbolic information provided as part of the NE executable file format.

For watching WM_ messages, Borland C++ includes WinSight, which is vastly superior to Microsoft's SPY. WinSight knows about approximately 25 different undocumented WM_ messages and displays them differently from documented messages so that they stand out. WinSight will also pick up the names of messages that have been installed with RegisterWindowMessage(). WinSight uses indenting to show the nesting of messages, where one message will trigger others. For example, the following shows a WM_LBUTTONUP triggering a WM_SYSCOMMAND, which in turn triggers a WM_ENTERMENULOOP (shown in lowercase because this message is undocumented):

```
17C0 "File Manage" WM_LBUTTONUP Dispatched (22,18)
 17C0 "File Manage" WM_SYSCOMMAND Sent from self KeyMenu+0(Nowhere?) (32,0)
  17C0 "File Manage" wm_entermenuloop Sent from self 0000 0000:0000
  17C0 "File Manage" wm_entermenuloop  Returns 0
  ... etc.: WM_SETCURSOR, WM_INITMENU, WM_INITMENUPOPUP, WM_MENUSELECT...
```

Inside RegisterWindowMessage()

RegisterWindowMessage() is a documented function that, for once, behaves exactly as documented:

```
WORD FAR PASCAL RegisterWindowMessage(LPSTR lpszMsgName);
```

Nonetheless, there is something interesting about this function: If you run the EXEUTIL -DUPES utility from chapter 3 on the Windows 3.1 version of USER.EXE, you will find that RegisterWindowMessage() and RegisterClipboardFormat() are one and the same function, i.e., one piece of code has been given these two exported entry points.

If you then examine the code with Windows Source or another Windows disassembler, you will find that the function is nothing more than a wrapper around the KERNEL AddAtom() function. In other words, registered window messages and registered clipboard formats end up in USER's local atom table (which, incidentally, is not the same as the global atom table, even though that too is owned by USER).

continued

continued

A Windows message snooper such as WinSight can use this fact to locate strings for any messages in the range C000h through FFFFh. Given that RegisterWindowMessage() is simply a USER AddAtom(), the message number is no more and no less than a local atom, for which an associated string can be found with the GetAtomName() function.

But there's a catch: These registered messages are actually atoms in *USER's* atom table. GetAtomName() assumes that DS corresponds to the segment containing the atom table of interest, in the same way that LocalAlloc() assumes that DS corresponds to the segment containing your local heap. In your program, DS normally points to your own default data segment—not USER's. However, using a small wrapper of in-line assembler, you can write a segment-based version of GetAtomName() that works off any atom table:

```
WORD FAR PASCAL BasedGetAtomName(WORD wSeg,
    WORD wAtom, LPSTR lpszBuf, int cbBuf)
{
    WORD retval;
    _asm push ds
    _asm mov ds, wSeg
    retval = GetAtomName(wAtom, lpszBuf, cbBuf);
    _asm pop ds
    return retval;
}
```

(This code is almost identical to some commonly available functions for doing based memory allocation with LocalAlloc(); see "Porting DOS Programs to Protected-Mode Windows with the WINDOS Library," *Microsoft Systems Journal*, September-October 1991.)

To find names for messages in the range C000h through FFFFh, you would call BasedGetAtomName(), passing it USER's default data segment as the wSeg and the message number as wAtom. For example:

```
#define GET_USER_DS()\
  GetWindowWord(GetDesktopWindow(), GWW_HINSTANCE)

char buf[128];
BasedGetAtomName(GET_USER_DS(), message, buf, 128);
```

Naturally, a clipboard viewer could use the same piece of code to get the name for a registered clipboard format; after all, RegisterClipboardFormat() and Register-WindowMessage() are just two different names for the same thing.

GET_USER_DS() obviously only works with USER; to get the default data segment (DGROUP) for any module in the system, see the GetModuleDgroup() function shown in chapter 5.

To conclude, even a simple, properly documented function such as RegisterWindowMessage() turns out to have a lot of hidden, useful properties if you stare at it long enough. ■

A good way to watch undocumented message traffic with WinSight is to select the "Other" message category. In addition to the undocumented messages that WinSight knows about, others will be indicated, for example, WM_0x0032 (for WM_SET-HOTKEY). Interestingly, WM_OTHERWINDOWCREATED and WM_OTHER-WINDOWDESTROYED show up in WinSight in quotes, as "OTHER-WINDOWCREATED" and "OTHERWINDOWDESTROYED," indicating that these come from RegisterWindowMessage(). Another such message is "ACTIVATESHELLWINDOW". (See chapter 7 for further details.)

Another collection of Windows snooping utilities is MicroQuill's "Windows DeMystifiers," written by Jeff Richter, author of the excellent *Windows 3: A Developer's Guide* (chapter 1 of that book, "Anatomy of a Window," and chapter 6, "Tasks, Queues, and Hooks," are essential reading). The Windows DeMystifiers are excellent as enhanced versions of SPY, HEAPWALK, and so on: VOYEUR is a window-browsing and message-trapping utility, like SPY and WinSight; COLONEL (get it?) is an enhanced version of HEAPWALK; MECHANIC displays large amounts of information about device and driver capabilities, fonts, and objects for a given device or DC; and ECOLOGIST displays general information about the environment (such as memory availability, how many tasks are running, and the like).

VOYEUR at first seems to not "know" about undocumented messages. However, the program has a (undocumented!) feature to display these messages: If you hold down the Shift key while picking Message Selection... from its Messages menu, VOYEUR adds about 25 undocumented messages to its repertoire.

Soft-ICE/Windows

Soft-ICE/Windows (WINICE), from NuMega Technologies (Nashua, New Hampshire; 603-889-2386), pretty much replaces all of the above tools, and then some. It is the single, absolutely essential debugger and snooping utility for Windows developers. Here, we will be using WINICE's snooping capabilities rather than its debugging facilities, because snooping rather than debugging is the focus for this book. WINICE is a complete debugging environment; once you have it, you no longer need CVW, TDW, WDEB386, HEAPWALK, or SPY. You also no longer need a second debugging monitor, unless you want one: Unlike WDEB386, or older versions of CVW, WINICE is fully operational, and seems very stable, running on the same machine as Windows itself.

WINICE uses the built-in debug hardware of the 80386 and 80486 processors to provide debugging facilities that might otherwise require external hardware like an in-circuit emulator (ICE): hence the name Soft-ICE. For example, WINICE uses paging and the 386 debug registers to implement real-time memory-access breakpoints (several other debuggers do this too), uses 386 virtualization to implement breakpoints on I/O ports, and so on. WINICE isn't a Windows program; it runs before Windows. When you run WINICE from the DOS prompt, it loads Windows Enhanced mode (WINICE will not work with Windows Standard mode). You can go into WINICE any time by pressing its hot key (Ctrl-D by default). You don't need to be debugging a program to use WINICE.

Disassembly with WINICE

We already saw in chapter 3 that WINICE can be used to quickly unassemble undocumented API calls. We've mentioned that, in a pinch, you can do this with CVW or TDW, too. The difference in WINICE is that it "knows" a huge number of symbols for all the functions, both documented and undocumented, in KERNEL, USER, and GDI. For example

```
:u gettaskqueueds
KERNEL!GETTASKQUEUEDS
011F:00008775    MOV     DS,CS:[0030]
011F:0000877A    MOV     DS,[0248]
011F:0000877E    MOV     DS,[0020]
011F:00008782    RETF

:u getcurrenttask
KERNEL!GETCURRENTTASK
011F:0000842C    PUSH    ES
011F:0000842D    MOV     ES,CS:[0030]
011F:00008432    MOV     AX,ES:[0228]
011F:00008436    MOV     DX,ES:[0226]
011F:0000843B    POP     ES
011F:0000843C    RETF
```

Because Windows is running and we have a complete debugger at our disposal, we can, of course, inspect any variables that are used by the code we disassemble.

For example, above we see that GetCurrentTask() has an undocumented return value in DX. It's probably the beginning of the task list, but let's check. First, GetCurrentTask() loads ES from a value stored away in CS (yes, even protected-mode Windows stores data in its code segments), at offset 30h:

```
:dw 11f:30
011F:00000030 0137 ...
```

Now we can inspect the value at ES:[226h] and see if it looks as if it could be a task handle; assume we've already figured out that a valid task handle will have its module name at offset F2h, followed by the signature TD at offset FAh, followed by a PSP:

```
:dw 137:226
0137:00000226 0807 ...

:db 807:f2
0807:000000F2 57 49 4E 46 49 4C 45 00-54 44 00 00 00 00 CD 20  WINFILE.TD.....
```

Most excellent! It's definitely a task. Let's see if this is the beginning of a linked list of tasks, by looking at its first word and seeing if it corresponds to a valid task:

```
:dw 807:0
0807:00000000 14AF ...

:db 14af:f2
14AF:000000F2 57 49 4E 4F 4C 44 41 50-54 44 00 00 00 00 CD 20  WINOLDAPTD.....
```

It does. We can continue in this way until we reach the end of the list:

```
:dw 11bf:0
11BF:00000000 0000 ...
```

With WINICE 1.1, you can load the symbols for any other DLL or driver, such as SYSTEM, DISPLAY, KEYBOARD, MOUSE, and COMM. A debug version of these drivers is not required; the symbols come right out of the NE header. (See? The NE format really does give every single Windows executable the equivalent of a debug symbol table.) For example, the following shows that, at the base of Windows timers, there's just an INT 8 handler, installed with the good old DOS Set Interrupt Vector function (INT 21h AH=25h):

```
:u enablesystemtimers
SYSTEM!ENABLESYSTEMTIMERS
0157:000002E2    PUSH    DS
0157:000002E3    MOV     DS,CS:[0000]
0157:000002E8    CMP     BYTE PTR [005C],00
0157:000002ED    JNZ     030B
0157:000002EF    MOV     BYTE PTR [005C],01
0157:000002F4    MOV     AX,3508
0157:000002F7    INT     21
0157:000002F9    MOV     [005D],BX
0157:000002FD    MOV     [005F],ES
0157:00000301    MOV     AX,2508
0157:00000304    PUSH    CS
0157:00000305    POP     DS
0157:00000306    MOV     DX,0238
0157:00000309    INT     21
0157:0000030B    POP     DS
0157:0000030C    RETF
```

In the same way, we can look at the other Windows API: VxD calls, particularly those provided by the Windows Virtual Machine Manager (VMM). As far as WINICE is concerned, these are just more Windows API calls; WINICE doesn't make the common mistake of segregating these calls in some special DDK mode, where SDK programmers can't get at them:

```
:u get_cur_vm_handle
0028:800081AC    MOV     EBX,[80012944]
0028:800081B2    RET
```

```
:u get_sys_vm_handle
0028:800081BC    MOV     EBX,[80012948]
0028:800081C2    RET
```

Notice that WINICE handles 32-bit code. By the way, if you've been hearing a lot about the future of 32-bit Windows programming, you might note that you could be learning about 32-bit programming *today*, albeit at a somewhat low level, by taking a close look at VxDs.

Of course, if you are debugging a program, you get to use all of its symbols, too. WINICE understands both CodeView and Turbo Debugger symbol formats. The program you debug can be a Windows application, DLL, device driver, VxD, DOS program running in the Windows DOS box, or a 16-bit or 32-bit protected-mode DOS program (for example, a DOS-extended program or DPMI client).

WINICE Breakpoints

So far we've just examined WINICE's disassembly capabilities. Disassembling code isn't the best use of a debugger, though: Most of what's shown above (including dissessembly of VMM) can be done with a tool such as Windows Source (see chapter 3). Where WINICE really shines is in its extensive support for *breakpoints*:

```
BPX                     break point on execution
BMSG                    break point on Windows WM_ message
BPINT                   break point on interrupt
BPR                     break point on memory range read/write
BPRW                    range break point on Windows module or selector
BPMB,BPMW,BPMD          break point on memory byte, word, dword read/write
BPIO                    break point on I/O port access
CSIP                    instruction pointer (CS:IP) qualifier
```

For example, the following will trap all calls made by USER to the Get-TaskQueueES() function:

```
:csip user
:bpx gettaskqueuees
:x
```

Once a breakpoint has been triggered, you can see how it was called by using the STACK command (if you have a valid stack frame) or simply by browsing through the code. Many of the questions left unanswered in chapters 2 and 3, such as why USER shows so many references to MakeObjectPrivate(), or why GDI seems to unlock and relock objects so frequently, can be answered in this way, by watching the real, live system in action.

As an another example, in chapter 2 when EXEUTIL -UNDOC ran across calls to the GetProcAddress() function, it had to issue a warning because it had no way of knowing to *what* the program would want to dynamically link at run time (the function name could even be a string typed in by the user, as in our CALLFUNC program described later in this chapter). With WINICE, however, it's trivial to find out what GetProcAddress() is being used to link to:

```
:bpx getprocaddress
```

Even better, rather than set the breakpoint right on the first instruction in GetProc-Address(), it can be set a few instructions down, after the function has moved its function-name parameter into registers. Using the "display expression" (DEX) command, you can then instruct WINICE to display the passed-in function name every time the breakpoint is triggered. It turns out that, in 3.1 at any rate, programs mostly just use run-time dynamic linking to get at the Pen Windows RegisterPenApp( ) function. (This corresponds with what we saw when disassembling TASKMAN in chapter 3.)

WINICE is indispensable for investigating the behavior of undocumented functions. Although a disassembler such as Sourcer provides a detailed view of the code, that view is by its nature static. To understand how a function *behaves*, it is sometimes essential to trace it through at run time. WINICE can provide this dynamic and behavioral view of a function, particularly when used together with a function-call interpreter testbed such as CALLFUNC (described later in this chapter).

SysErrorBox( ) (see chapter 6) is a good example of a function that could have been difficult to crack. Since it is usually called only in response to a system error, you might use TDW or CVW to debug a program that deliberately crashed and then trace through the crash. However, these debuggers trap the crash and abort the program without allowing the debugging session to continue! And an error within Sys-ErrorBox, you would quickly discover, leaves little option of recovery short of a complete machine reset.

From a disassembly listing generated by Sourcer, we can see that the function returns with RETF 0Eh, removing seven words from the stack. These seven words represent the function's parameters (the Pascal calling convention, in which the called function pops its argument, makes disassembly a little easier). The disassembled listing for the function is long (some 13 pages), so rather than pore over it looking for clues, we might take an initial simplistic approach to the argument types and just try them. This first approach will probably be wrong, but it will help us get started toward understanding how the function *should* be called. Using CALLFUNC, which allows Windows API functions to be interactively typed in and called, we can formulate an experimental call, perhaps:

```
> user syserrorbox 0 0 0 0 0 0 0
```

Before pressing return, we need to set a breakpoint on the function itself so that we can trace through it. This as simple as pressing WINICE's hotkey and entering:

```
:bpx syserrorbox
:x
```

Now, back in CALLFUNC, we can press return, and we are immediately popped back into the debugger at the beginning of the SysErrorBox function. Pressing F10 (WINICE's default key assignments are similar to CodeView's), we arrive at the instructions:

```
MOV AX, [BP+10]
MOV DX, [BP+12]
```

These instructions indicate that the parameter at BP+10h, for a FAR PASCAL function expecting 14 bytes of parameters on the stack, is either a dword or a far pointer as the first parameter. Using the R (set register contents) command, we can reset IP to an address near the function's return and continue tracing, in order to return to CALLFUNC without blowing up. We might then try a string in the first position in another invocation of the function from the CALLFUNC prompt:

```
> user syserrorbox "Hello world!" 0 0 0 0 0
```

This time we may be able to trace through a bit further. After another few iterations, we will have arrived at a CALLFUNC command line of:

```
> user syserrorbox "Caption?" "Some text" 1 2 3
```

At this point the battle is nearly won. For the final results, see the description of SysErrorBox() in chapter 6.

This approach is a simplistic description of the process, but it serves to show how tools work together. It is possible to understand and document any undocumented function using other means, but the above approach, marrying a static listing with a flexible, stable debugger such as WINICE and a testbed program such as CALLFUNC, makes the task that much more enjoyable and significantly reduces the number of times a PC needs to be rebooted along the way!

As an example of a memory-access breakpoint, let's say you want to see whether any modules other than KERNEL grope Task Database structures. You could use the TASK command (see below) to get a listing of all running tasks and then set a memory range access breakpoint (BPR) on some TDB; a Task Database structure is 200h bytes (including the PSP stuck on the end), and in this example 807h is a valid HTASK:

```
:bpr 807:0 807:1ff rw
:csip not kernel
:x
```

The instant some piece of code other than KERNEL reads or writes anything in this 200-byte range, we trap to WINICE. Until then, our system is operating at full speed.

As a final example of WINICE breakpoints, BPINT lets you go exploring in the netherworld of Windows interrupts. For example, does the reserved DPMI function INT 31h AX=0701 (Discard Pages) ever get called?

```
:csip off
:bpint 31 ax=0701
:x
Break Due to BPINT 31 AX=0701 C=01
011F:00003BB6    INT     31
```

Yes, looks like as if does. But who calls it—that is, where's 011Fh?

```
:heap 11f
Han./Sel. Address     Length     Owner          Type       Seg/Rsrc
011F      00018440    0000CC80   KERNEL         Code       01
```

So, KERNEL calls this reserved DPMI function.

WINICE System-Information Commands

The HEAP command we just used is one of many commands that WINICE provides for displaying system information:

```
HWND        Display windows handles
CLASS       Display window class information
TASK        Display Windows task list
MOD         Display Windows module list
HEAP        Display Windows global heap
LHEAP       Display a Windows local heap
VM          Display information about DOS virtual machines
VXD         Display a map of virtual device drivers (VxDs)
GDT         Display Global Descriptor Table (GDT)
LDT         Display Local Descriptor Table (LDT)
IDT         Display Interrupt Descriptor Table (IDT)
TSS         Display Task State Segment (TSS), including the I/O permission
               bitmap, showing virtualized I/O ports
PAGE        Display page directory and page table information
MAP         Display memory map for this virtual machine
```

For example:

```
:task
TaskName    SS:SP       StackTop   StackBot   StackLow   TaskDB   hQueue   Events
WINOLDAP    146F:1D5A   1E82       0B18       16D4       14AF     1497     0000
WINFILE     17AF:3716   377C       1012       2546       0807     06BF     0000
DRWATSON    12CF:2A92   3B34       1BCA       25FA       12F7     12DF     0000
TASKMAN     1207:13A2   144E       00E4       0E48       1217     122F     0000
SH        * 1347:3BCC   3C54       28EA       378A       136F     1357     0000
```

Using the HEAP command shows that Task Databases are owned by themselves

```
:heap 14af
Han./Sel. Address     Length     Owner          Type       Seg/Rsrc
14AF      00025940    00000200   WINOLDAP       TaskDB
```

but, just as in HEAPWALK, Task Queue structures are shown as USER allocations, even though most of the code to manipulate them is in KERNEL. This reflects the lack of a clear division in Windows between KERNEL and USER:

```
:heap 1497
Han./Sel. Address     Length     Owner          Type       Seg/Rsrc
1497      00025B40    00000120   USER           Alloc
```

WINICE's GDT (Global Descriptor Table) command gives us a good idea of the Windows memory map:

```
:gdt
GDTbase=800715BC  Limit=010F
0008   Code16     Base=000157F0  Lim=0000FFFF  DPL=0   P    RE
0010   Data16     Base=000157F0  Lim=0000FFFF  DPL=0   P    RW
0018   TSS32      Base=8000DD74  Lim=00002069  DPL=0   P    B
0020   Data16     Base=800715BC  Lim=0000FFFF  DPL=0   P    RW
0028   Code32     Base=00000000  Lim=FFFFFFFF  DPL=0   P    RE
0030   Data32     Base=00000000  Lim=FFFFFFFF  DPL=0   P    RW
003B   Code16     Base=804A5B20  Lim=000004C7  DPL=3   P    RE
0043   Data16     Base=00000400  Lim=000002FF  DPL=3   P    RW
0048   Code16     Base=00013290  Lim=0000FFFF  DPL=0   P    RE
0053   Data16     Base=00000000  Lim=FFFFFFFF  DPL=3   P    RO
005B   Data32     Base=804A6000  Lim=00000FFF  DPL=3   P    RW
0060   Code32     Base=80059460  Lim=00001000  DPL=0   P    RE
0068   Code32     Base=80059451  Lim=00001000  DPL=0   P    RE
0073   Data16     Base=00000522  Lim=00000100  DPL=3   P    RW
0078   Code16     Base=0092C000  Lim=00033FFF  DPL=0   P    RE
0080   Data32     Base=0092C000  Lim=00033FFF  DPL=0   P    RW
0088   LDT        Base=80543000  Lim=00001FFF  DPL=0   P
0093   Data16     Base=00000000  Lim=FFFFFFFF  DPL=3   P    RW
009B   Data32     Base=805D0000  Lim=0000FFFF  DPL=3   P    RW
00A0   Reserved   Base=00000000  Lim=00000000  DPL=0   NP
... about a dozen more reserved descriptors ...
```

Here, we can see that selector 28h in Windows Enhanced mode is a code selector that maps the entire linear address space from 0 to 4 gigabytes. Selector 30h is an equivalent data selector. Selector 40h (shown here in DPL=3 form as 43h) maps 2FFh bytes at linear base address 400h; in other words, it's a bimodal selector to the BIOS data area (linear base address == selector << 4). Selector 20h maps the GDT itself. Selector 88h contains an LDT.

As noted earlier, WINICE can completely replace Microsoft's WDEB386. When used with the DDK debugging version of WIN386.EXE, WINICE provides instant access to WIN386 debug commands:

```
:.?
.VM [#] ------ Displays complete VM status
.VC [#] ------ Displays the current VMs control block
.VH ---------- Displays the current VM handle
.VR [#] ------ Displays the registers of the current VM (Prot mode only)
.VS [#] ------ Displays the current VM's virtual mode stack (Prot mode only)
.VL ---------- Displays a list of all valid VM handles
.T ---------- Toggles the trace switch
.S [#] ------ Displays short logged exceptions starting at #, if specified
.SL [#] ------ Displays long logged exceptions just #, if specified
.LQ ---------- Display queue outs from most recent
.DS ---------- Dumps the protected mode stack with labels
```

```
.MH [handle] - Displays Heap information
.MM [handle] - Displays Memory information
.MV ---------- Displays VM Memory information
.MS PFTaddr -- Display PFT info
.MF ---------- Display Free List
.MI ---------- Display Instance data info
.ML LinAddr -- Display Page table info for given linear address
.MP PhysAddr - Display ALL Linear addrs that map the given PhysAddr
.MD ---------- Change debug MONO paging display
.MO ---------- Set a page out of all present pages
.VMM --------- Menu VMM state information
.<dev_name> -- Display device specific info
:.vmm

        V M M   D E B U G   I N F O R M A T I O N A L   S E R V I C E S
[A]  System time
[B]  Time-slice information/profile
[C]  Dyna-link service profile information
[D]  Reset dyna-link profile counts
[E]  I/O port trap information
[F]  Reset I/O profile counts
[G]  Turn procedure call trace logging on
[H]  V86 interrupt hook information
[I]  PM interrupt hook information
[J]  Reset PM and V86 interrupt profile counts
[K]  Display event lists
[L]  Display device list
[M]  Display V86 break points
[N]  Display PM break points
[O]  Display interrupt profile
[P]  Reset interrupt profile counts
[Q]  Display GP fault profile
[R]  Reset GP fault profile counts
[S]  Toggle Adjust_Exec_Priority Log AND DISPLAY
[T]  Reset Adjust_Exec_Priority Log info
[U]  Toggle verbose device call trace
[V]  Fault Hook information


:.v86mmgr
Select desired V86MMGR component:
    [0]  - General info
    [1]  - Memory scan info
    [2]  - EMM driver info
    [3]  - XMS driver info
    [ESC] - Exit V86MMGR debug querry
:.dosmgr
Select desired DOSMGR function:
    [0]  Display DOS trace info
    [1]  Set DOSMGR queue_outs
    [ESC] - Exit DOSMGR debug querry
```

Some of the .vmm debug options let you profile the actual number of interrupts and exceptions generated inside Windows as part of its normal activity. The results are sometimes alarming and make you wonder how Windows could ever accomplish anything, with all the faults and exceptions that it intentionally generates internally. For example, Windows generates faults to make privilege-level transitions from Ring 3 (3.1) or Ring 1 (3.0), to Ring 0, and back again (the WINICE manual contains excellent discussions of these issues).

WINICE is able to completely take over for WDEB386 and CVW. In the debug version of Windows, for example, WINICE catches all RIP (rest in peace) codes, providing you with an opportunity to respond. WINICE does this by handling Windows INT 41h low-level debug calls. (The INT 41h low-level debug API is discussed briefly in chapter 5, in the entry for RegisterPtrace.)

Even though some of WINICE's capabilities may appear esoteric, this debugger gives you access to *all* of Windows. You can go exploring deep within VMM if you wish or just use it as a C source-level debugging replacement for CVW and TDW. Practically every Windows debugging tool, from the most common to the most esoteric, has been brought together into one program.

The WINIO Library

With the exception of the CORONER sample program in chapter 10, all the sample Windows programs in this book are written using a library called WINIO (sometimes also called WINDOS). The WINIO library functions are described in detail in Appendix A. As seen from a brief glance at the chapters on KERNEL, USER, and GDI, the source for these programs looks like old, pre-Windows C code: It uses main() and stdio functions such as printf(), getchar(), and the like. More than one reader has asked why we chose to code this entire book in "pseudocode," since obviously these *couldn't* be legitimate Windows programs.

They *are* legitimate Windows programs. WINIO provides a DOS-like procedural "cover" over the basic skeleton of an event-driven Windows application. You call printf() and, somewhere within the WINIO library, it turns into a TextOut(). What's more, anything you printf() to a window *stays there*; WINIO handles WM_PAINT messages automatically. At the same time, you get many of the benefits of Windows: backward scrolling, menus, and clickable lines (as in HEAPWALK) that can bring up additional windows. You can even handle WM_ messages without writing a switch/case statement. For example, the graphic at the top of page 152 shows part of what the WINWALK program from chapter 10 looks like to a user of the program.

This is a proper Windows application. If there is more data than can fit in a window (which is likely here, since it is a list of every item in the Windows global heap), the user can scroll through it. The user can resize the window. If part of the window is obscured by another window that subsequently stops obscuring it, the formerly obscured portion is properly repainted. In other words, messages such as WM_PAINT, WM_SIZE, and WM_VSCROLL are being handled properly.

Yet, here is how part of the same program looks to the programmer:

```
ge.dwSize = sizeof(ge);
ok = GlobalFirst(&ge, GLOBAL_ALL);
```

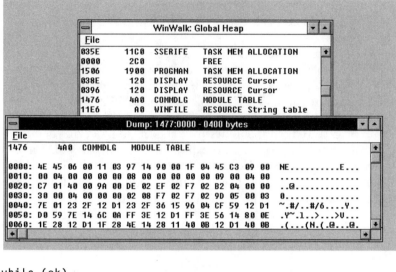

```
while (ok)
    {
    printf("%04X    %5lX  %-8s  %s\n",
        ge.hBlock, ge.dwBlockSize,
        GetModuleNameFromHandle(ge.hOwner),
        GetGlobalBlockType(ge.wType, ge.wData)
        );
    ok = GlobalNext(&ge, GLOBAL_ALL);
    }
```

Now imagine how this code would look if it directly called Windows API functions. The fact that we're walking the Windows global heap, using ToolHelp, printing out a description of each object, would be totally obscured by calls to BeginPaint(), EndPaint(), TextOut(), ScrollWindow(), SetScrollPos(), UpdateWindow(), and a host of other Windows API functions. WINIO will take care of all that.

All those Windows calls—the standard "boilerplate" needed in almost every Windows application—are part of a wonderful API that we can easily see ourselves using for the next five to ten years. Functions such as BeginPaint() and TextOut() are becoming part of an "industry standard architecture" much as the DOS INT 21h API has been. But they are best used as a *foundation* upon which to build higher level libraries; they are generally too low-level for direct use.

That a Windows application *does not have to* directly use the Windows API, that you can put a layer on top of this API, surprises so many Windows programmers that we could almost claim that this fact is "undocumented." Certainly Microsoft's SDK manuals never suggest that you could write a Windows application in any way other than peppering your code with direct calls to TextOut(), BeginPaint(), and so on.

The idea that a Windows program must contain direct, explicit Windows API calls—that it's not a "true" Windows application if it isn't descended from the original GENERIC.C—is part of the same *reverence* for the Windows API that we seek to undermine by disassembling this API and looking at the code. It may seem odd to introduce a way of *hiding* the Windows API, in a book otherwise devoted to *exposing* even lower level portions of it. However, revealing undocumented Windows API calls and then covering up the existing documented ones are really just two sides of the same coin: questioning the Windows API, instead of taking it on face value. The API is just code; we can do with it what we will.

In addition, there's no point in showing you example programs filled with calls to RegisterClass(), CreateWindow(), GetMessage(), and TextOut(): any Windows programmer has seen those a million times already. What you haven't seen probably are calls to SetInternalWindowPos() or GlobalMasterHandle(), or manipulation of the Task Database or WND structure, and we want these to stand out. WINIO gives us a way to write many Windows programs without each of them consuming several hundred lines of standard, boilerplate code. Although WINIO uses some neglected aspects of the Windows API, nothing in the implementation of WINIO itself has much to do with undocumented Windows. Therefore, we will not be discussing the *implementation* of WINIO here; its source code is not even included on the accompanying disk. Instead, .LIB files are included, for small-model and medium-model Microsoft C and Borland C++, and so are the necessary .H files.

Why didn't we just use the QuickWin library that comes with Microsoft C/C++ 7.0, or the EasyWin library that comes with Borland C++? Because neither library lets us do real Windows programming. In particular, Microsoft's documentation states that a QuickWin program cannot make any Windows API function calls! This immediately rules out QuickWin for anything other than porting DOS programs. EasyWin also was clearly designed only for porting simple DOS programs to Windows, not for writing Windows utilities.

If you are interested in how WINIO works, see our article, "Call Standard C I/O Functions from Your Windows Code Using the WINIO Library" (*Microsoft Systems Journal*, July 1991). WINIO has grown considerably since the MSJ article—it now includes multiple windows, clickable lines, menus, and many other features—but the basic architecture is the same. There is a further discussion in "Porting DOS Programs to Protected-Mode Windows with the WINDOS Library" (*Microsoft Systems Journal*, September-October 1991). We will discuss the implementation of WINIO in depth, and present its source code, in a forthcoming book, DOS *Programmer's Guide to Windows*.

An Interactive Command Shell

As our first example of a WINIO program, let's look at a stripped-down command shell for Windows. The shell supports the commands CD, DIR, and EXIT; you can change drives; most important, you can run any Windows program by typing its names, plus any arguments, on the command line. You will be able to see all this in the figure on top of page 154.

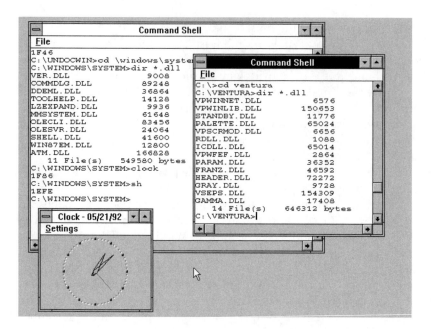

With WINIO, producing this useful program takes about 80 lines of code. Until the user exits, the program sits in a loop, each time printing a COMMAND.COM pg-style prompt, getting a line of input, and then performing some action based on the input. The action will usually be to pass the command line to WinExec():

```
/* SH.C -- Command Shell for Windows */

#include "windows.h"
#include <stdlib.h>
#include <string.h>
#ifdef __BORLANDC__
#define __MSC
#include <dir.h>
#else
#include <direct.h>
#define setdisk(x)          _chdrive((x)+1)
#endif
#include <dos.h>
#include "winio.h"

static HWND hwnd_sh;

int main()
{
    char buf[256] = {0};
    char orig[256] = {0};
    char *cmd, *args;

    hwnd_sh = winio_current();
```

```
    winio_settitle(hwnd_sh, "Command Shell");
    winio_setfont(hwnd_sh, ANSI_FIXED_FONT);

    for (;;)    // prompt-read-eval-exec loop
    {
        printf("%s>", getcwd(buf, 255));    // prompt
        gets(buf);                          // read
        if ((buf[0] == '\0') || (buf[0] == '\n'))
            continue;
        strcpy(orig, buf);  // unmodified buffer
        cmd = strupr(strtok(buf, " \t"));
        args = strtok(0, "\t");             // eval:
        if      (strcmp(cmd, "EXIT") == 0)  break;
        else if (strcmp(cmd, "CD") == 0)    chdir(args);
        else if (strcmp(cmd, "DIR") == 0)   do_dir(args);
        else if ((cmd[1] == ':') && (cmd[2] == 0))
            setdisk(toupper(s[0]) - 'A');
        else if (WinExec(orig, SW_SHOWNORMAL) <= 32) //exec
            puts("Bad command or file name");
        // SetActiveWindow(hwnd_sh);
    }

    winio_close(hwnd_sh);
    return 0;
}

int do_dir(char *s)
{
    struct find_t info;
    char wildcard[80];
    unsigned long bytes=0;
    unsigned attrib, files=0;
    strcpy(wildcard, s);
    if (! strchr(wildcard, '.'))
        strcat(wildcard, "*.*");
    attrib = _A_NORMAL | _A_SUBDIR | _A_RDONLY;
    if (_dos_findfirst(wildcard, attrib, &info) != 0)
        return 0;
    winio_setpaint(hwnd_sh, FALSE);
    do {
        if (info.attrib & _A_SUBDIR)
            printf("%-13s\t<DIR>\n", info.name);
        else
            printf("%-13s\t%9lu\n", info.name, info.size);
        files++;
        bytes += info.size;
    } while (_dos_findnext(&info) == 0);
    printf("%5u File(s)\t%lu bytes\n", files, bytes);
    winio_setpaint(hwnd_sh, TRUE);
    return 1;
}
```

The for (;;) makes it appear as if this program doesn't let other programs run. But other programs do run. Inside its versions of gets( ), printf( ), and other stdio functions,

WINIO calls the standard Windows message-retrieval functions. This is the key to writing procedural-looking code that still behaves correctly under Windows.

Note the calls to winio_setpaint() in the do_dir() function. Because WINIO supports backward scrolling, SH can speed up its output by turning off painting, blasting text to the WINIO buffer (simply by calling printf() with painting turned off), and then turning painting back on. Even if there are hundreds of file names displayed for a DIR command, the user can just scroll back to look at them. The result is Windows output that appears faster than DOS output.

SH.C #includes "winio.h" rather than <stdio.h>. In general, WINIO programs should use "winio.h" rather than <stdio.h>, not only so that they can access WINIO extensions such as winio_setpaint(), but also because most versions of <stdio.h> present getc() and putc() as macros rather than functions; these macros would not get routed to WINIO.

The SH program is interesting in its own right; Windows makes a fascinating environment for command shells. SH differs from COMMAND.COM running in a DOS box because it calls the Windows API function WinExec() and thereby performs actions that COMMAND.COM cannot, such as launching Windows applications. Also, because Windows maintains (in the Task Database) a separate current directory for each task, you can run multiple instances of SH, each with its own separate drive and directory. Finally, as a command processor for a multitasking environment, SH does not wait for the Windows programs it executes to complete; WinExec() executes Windows programs asynchronously. Thus, using SH is sort of like having a Unix shell with an & automatically tacked on the end of every line.

Incidentally, an early version of this program was called SHELL rather than SH. However, Windows 3.1 already has a module called SHELL, and you cannot load a module—even one that corresponds to a task rather than a DLL—if there's already a different one with the same module name. This behavior can drive you crazy if you've spent hours baffled by why your nice program called "SHELL" (or "SYSTEM" or "TIMER") simply will not run.

Going Resident

Our next program, even less ambitious than SH, helps make a key point about WINIO programs (and, in a way, about Windows programs in general). The program can be built, for example, with Borland C++:

```
// hello.c
// bcc -WS hello.c swindos.lib

#include "windows.h"
#include "winio.h"

main()
{
    printf("hello world!\n");
}
```

With WINIO, this really is a Windows program. You can resize the window, move it, iconize it, and close it. Most important, you can force it to repaint itself. But what happens when the program falls off the end of main()? Does it exit?

No, the program does *not* exit at this point. Instead, an atexit() handler installed by WINIO grabs control and, behind the scenes, puts the program into a conventional Windows Get/Translate/DispatchMessage loop. Whenever the window needs to be repainted, for example, a WM_PAINT handler in WINIO takes care of it. WINIO similarly handles many other WM_ messages automatically.

What happens, then, is that the WINIO program *goes resident*. Before main() is called, WINIO installs handlers for WM_ messages. Even after main() returns, these handlers are still in place, repainting the window, responding to WM_SIZE messages, and so on. Double clicking on the window's close box is what makes it exit.

In fact, this is no different from any other Windows program. In a way, all Windows programs are memory resident, and the Windows programming model represents the ultimate triumph of the TSR. You install some handlers and leave them to respond to different events. In a TSR, you wait for a hotkey press or a timer tick; in a Windows program you wait for a WM_KEYDOWN or a WM_TIMER; there's essentially no difference. *Only the size of the manuals has changed.* "Event-driven" programming sounds very new and different, but it's really just good old interrupt handling in yuppie attire.

Installing Event Handlers

Our next example makes this even clearer. NUMTASKS.C simply keeps track of how many tasks are running; the way it does this provides a good example of how to do event-driven programming with WINIO:

```
// NUMTASKS.C
#include "windows.h"
#include "winio.h"
#include "wmhandlr.h"

static WORD numtasks=0;

long on_time(HWND hwnd, unsigned message, WORD wParam, LONG lParam)
{
    WORD num;
    if ((num = GetNumTasks()) != numtasks)
    {
        numtasks = num;
        winio_clear();
        printf("%u tasks running\n", numtasks);
    }
    return 0;
}

main()
{
    HWND hwnd = winio_current();
    wmhandler_set(hwnd, WM_TIMER, on_time);
```

```
    if (! SetTimer(hwnd, 1, 1000, NULL)) // once a second
        fail("can't create timer");
    // go resident by falling off the end of main
}
```

In main(), NUMTASKS.C uses the documented Windows API function to create a timer that will go off once every 1000 milliseconds. In other words, once per second, NUMTASKS's window will receive a WM_TIMER message. NUMTASKS calls the winio_current() function to get its window handle; before main() is called, WINIO has already created a window for it in (you guessed it) WinMain(). NUMTASKS then calls the wmhandler_set() function to install a handler, named on_time(), for these WM_TIMER messages. The name "on_time" is meant to resemble the ON TIME GOSUB statement found in some versions of BASIC, because handling a WM_TIMER message in Windows is hardly different from writing an ON TIME GOSUB in BASIC.

NUMTASKS then returns from (actually, it just falls off the end of) main(). But the on_time() function is still resident. Every second, on_time() will be invoked. The on_time() function simply calls the Windows GetNumTasks() function to see if the number of tasks has changed. If it has, on_time() uses the winio_clear() and printf() functions to display the new number of tasks.

"On_time() will be invoked": the use of passive voice is a tip-off that we've left something out. There's a WndProc function inside WMHANDLR, which is the event-handling component of WINIO. This WndProc uses the WM_ message number (such as 0x113 in the case of WM_TIMER) as an index into a table of message-handling functions. Every time it receives a message, the WndProc calls the appropriate function out of the table.

When NUMTASKS called wmhandler_set(), it was simply changing the value of wmhandler_table[WM_TIMER]. To use wmhandler_set(), you need to #include "wmhandlr.h." Programs can change handlers on the fly. wmhandler_set() returns the value of the previously installed handler, which can be used to *chain* events. A lot nicer than a 14-page switch/case statement, no? And notice how we get to combine the best of both worlds here: linear, procedural programming (such as calling printf()), where it's convenient, and event-driven programming (installing on_time() to handle WM_TIMER messages), where that makes sense.

Naturally, a WINIO program can contain more than one message-handling function. Each WM_ message is handled in its own separate function; each one is installed with wmhandler_set(). For example:

```
static WMHANDLER prev_timer=0;
static WMHANDLER prev_size=0;
static WMHANDLER prev_cmd=0;

long on_time(HWND hwnd, unsigned message, WORD wParam, LONG lParam)
{
    // do something with WM_TIMER messages

    // chain to previous handler, if there is one
```

```
    return (prev_time) ? (*prev_time)(hwnd, message, wParam, lParam) : 0;
}
long on_size(HWND hwnd, unsigned message, WORD wParam, LONG lParam)
{
    // do something with WM_SIZE messages
    return (prev_size) ? (*prev_size)(hwnd, msg, wParam, lParam) : 0;
}
long on_cmd(HWND hwnd, unsigned message, WORD wParam, LONG lParam)
{
    switch (wParam)
    {
        // do something with WM_COMMAND messages
    }
    return (prev_cmd) ? (*prev_cmd)(hwnd, msg, wParam, lParam) : 0;
}
// ...
prev_time = wmhandler_set(hwnd, WM_TIMER, on_time);
prev_size = wmhandler_set(hwnd, WM_SIZE, on_size);
prev_cmd = wmhandler_set(hwnd, WM_COMMAND, on_cmd);
```

Putting together a Windows application as a collection of semi-independent, cooperating message handlers brings out its true nature far better than a massive, 14-page switch statement. It may well be more efficient, too, given how poorly most compilers do with switch statements.

This example also shows how a message handler can chain to the previous handler for the message. WINIO programs should always chain on any messages that WINIO itself handles (unless the program wishes to deliberately override WINIO's behavior). WINIO currently installs handlers for these messages:

WM_CHAR	WM_COMMAND	WM_DESTROY	WM_HSCROLL
WM_KEYDOWN	WM_KILLFOCUS	WM_LBUTTONDBLCLK	WM_PAINT
WM_SETFOCUS	WM_SIZE	WM_VSCROLL	

WINIO Menus

Because WINIO applications can handle WM_ messages, they can include many of the standard components of a Windows application. A program could call the Windows AppendMenu() function to add to WINIO's built-in menu (which includes a File... command for saving the contents of the window to a file) and use wmhandler_set() to install a WM_COMMAND handler for the user's menu selections.

Because this is such a common need, WINIO provides separate functions for menu handling: winio_hmenumain() retrieves a handle to the built-in WINIO menu, and winio_setmenufunc() installs a function to handle a menu selection. This approach also avoids the problem seen in the previous example, where we would have needed to use a switch statement to deal with the different wParam arguments to the WM_COMMAND handler. Switch statements are almost always a bad idea; we consider them harmful. Just as WMHANDLER keeps a table of message-handling functions, WINIO keeps a table of menu-handling functions.

The following, an altered version of the BASEMOVE.C example from chapter 5's entry on GetSelectorBase(), illustrates how the WINIO menu-handling functions are used together with the Windows API menu-handling functions. The BASEMOVE.C example needs to be run alongside some other program, such as HEAPWALK or SHAKER, that can shake up linear memory; in BASEMOV2.C, below, we give the program its own "GlobalCompact(-1)" menu selection:

```
/* basemov2.c -- use GetSelectorBase to show segment movement
   within the linear address space */

#include "windows.h"
#include "winio.h"
#include "wmhandlr.h"

/* in 3.0, undocumented function */
DWORD FAR PASCAL GetSelectorBase(WORD sel);

static WORD code, data;

void gc(HWND hwnd, int wID)
{
    printf("GC(-1) = %lu\n", GlobalCompact(-1L));
}

long on_time(HWND hwnd, unsigned message, WORD wParam, LONG lParam)
{
    static DWORD basecode, basedata;
    static DWORD prevcode = -1, prevdata = -1;

    if (((basecode = GetSelectorBase(code)) != prevcode) ||
        ((basedata = GetSelectorBase(data)) != prevdata))
    {
        printf("CS (%04x) = %08lx\tDS (%04x) = %08lx\n",
            code, basecode, data, basedata);
        prevcode = basecode;
        prevdata = basedata;
    }
    return 0;
}

#define MENUSTRING_GC    "&GlobalCompact(-1)"
#define IDM_GC           1

main()
{
    HWND hwnd = winio_current();
    HMENU hmenu = CreateMenu();
    HMENU hmenumain = winio_hmenumain(hwnd);
    AppendMenu(hmenumain, MF_STRING | MF_POPUP, hmenu, "&Test");
    AppendMenu(hmenu, MF_STRING | MF_ENABLED, IDM_GC, MENUSTRING_GC);
    winio_setmenufunc(hwnd, IDM_GC, gc);
    DrawMenuBar(hwnd);

    _asm mov code, cs
    _asm mov data, ds

    wmhandler_set(hwnd, WM_TIMER, on_time);
```

```
    if (! SetTimer(hwnd, 1, 1000, NULL)) // once a second
        fail("can't create timer");
}
```

The result, in 50 lines of code, is a menu-and timer-driven Windows application:

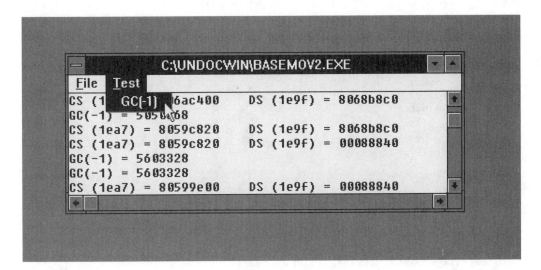

In the BASEMOVE.C example in the KERNEL chapter, we used a for (;;) loop to keep the example going; inside the loop, the program calls wmhandler_yield() to let other tasks run. This works, but it's better to make the program more *explicitly* event-driven, as we did above: The program installs its handlers and falls off the end of main().

WINIO Clickable Lines

Our final example shows how to build HEAPWALK-like WINIO programs. As noted earlier, in Microsoft's HEAPWALK (and in similar programs, such as Jeff Richter's COLONEL), you can click on a line to bring up a secondary window with more information about the chosen line. This is an excellent model for browsing/snooping utilities, and one we use in many of the larger examples in this book.

The winio_setlinefn() function lets you install a function that will get called whenever the user doubleclicks on a line in the WINIO window. WINIO calls your line-handling function with the line number and text of the clicked-on line, so you can use either one to figure out what the user is interested in. A line-handling function can pop up a new window, using the winio_window() function.

The following example, TASKWLK2, is an improved version of the TASKWALK program, used in chapter 5 to illustrate an undocumented return value from the GetCurrentTask() function. TASKWALK just walks the linked list of tasks once, printing out the handle and corresponding module name for each one. TASKWLK2 camps out on a timer, updating the list each time the number of tasks changes. (Rather than use a timer, TASKWLK2 could instead use the ToolHelp NotifyRegister() function and watch for NFY_STARTTASK and NFY_ENDTASK; see chapter 10.) The user can doubleclick on any task in the list to bring up a window with additional information, which in this case is just the task's present working directory (remember, Windows maintains multiple PWDs on a per-task basis; they're kept in each Task Database.) The task walk itself in this version is done using TOOLHELP:

```
/* TASKWLK2.C */

#include <string.h>
#include <dos.h>
#include "windows.h"
#include "toolhelp.h"
#include "winio.h"

/* 3.1 has doc function IsTask(), but it's not in
   3.0, so we use TOOLHELP (which works in 3.0) */
BOOL IsValidTask(WORD w)
{
    TASKENTRY te;
    te.dwSize = sizeof(TASKENTRY);
    return (TaskFindHandle(&te, w) != 0);
}

/* TOOLHELP doesn't provide this; good example of how
   UndocWin can be used in conjunction with TOOLHELP */
void GetTaskCurDir(HANDLE htask, char *buf)
{
    BYTE far *fp = MK_FP(htask, 0x66);  // offset of pwd in TDB
    buf[0] = *fp - 0x80 + 'A';          // drive letter
    buf[1] = ':';
    _fstrncpy(&buf[2], &fp[1], 0x44);
    buf[0x46] = '\0';
}

static HWND hwnd = 0;
static WORD volatile numtasks = 0;

/* Also printing linear base address for each TDB, to show that they
   are always allocated in conventional memory (first megabyte) */
extern DWORD FAR PASCAL GetSelectorBase(WORD wSel);

/* returns number of tasks found */
int taskwalk(void)
{
    WORD wNumTasks = 0;

    TASKENTRY te;
    te.dwSize = sizeof(TASKENTRY);
    if (TaskFirst(&te) == 0)
        return 0;

    winio_clear(hwnd);
    winio_setpaint(hwnd, FALSE); // no yield while walking task list
    for (;;)
    {
```

```
        printf("%04x\t%8s\t%08lx",
            te.hTask, te.szModule, GetSelectorBase(te.hTask));
        if (te.hTask == GetCurrentTask())
            printf(" <== current task");
        printf("\n");
        wNumTasks++;
        if (TaskNext(&te) == 0)
            break;
    }
    winio_setpaint(hwnd, TRUE);

    return wNumTasks;
}

long on_time(HWND hwnd, unsigned message, WORD wParam, LONG lParam)
{
    // sometimes task list is in unstable state (TOOLHELP
    // does nothing to compensate for this!)
    while (numtasks != GetNumTasks())
        numtasks = taskwalk();
    return 0;
}

void clickfunc(HWND hwnd, LPSTR line, int linenum)
{
    char buf[256];
    HANDLE htask;
    _fstrcpy(buf, line);
    sscanf(buf, "%04X", &htask);  // figure out which task was clicked on
    if (! IsValidTask(htask))
    {
        winio_warn(FALSE, buf, "Stale task list: no longer valid");
        numtasks = 0;             // force a new taskwalk
    }
    else
    {
        HWND prev = winio_setcurrent(winio_window(buf, 0, WW_HASMENU));
        GetTaskCurDir(htask, buf);
        printf("Current directory: %s\n", buf);
        winio_setcurrent(prev);
    }
}

main()
{
    hwnd = winio_current();
    winio_setlinefn(hwnd, clickfunc);
    numtasks = taskwalk();
    wmhandler_set(hwnd, WM_TIMER, on_time);
    if (! SetTimer(hwnd, 1, 1000, NULL)) // once a second
        fail("can't create timer");
    return 0;
}
```

One of the differences between TASWLK2 and TASKWALK is the call to winio_setlinefn(), passing in the address of the function clickfunc(). Whenever the user doubleclicks on a line in the displayed list of tasks, clickfunc() is called with the line number and the actual text of the line. clickfunc() uses the text, and the C sscanf() function, to figure out what task was clicked on. It then sees if this is still a valid task. (Yes, there's a stale data problem.) If it is, it calls winio_window() to create a new window, calls winio_setcurrent() so that stdout appears in that window, and prints out the specified task's current directory. The results look like this:

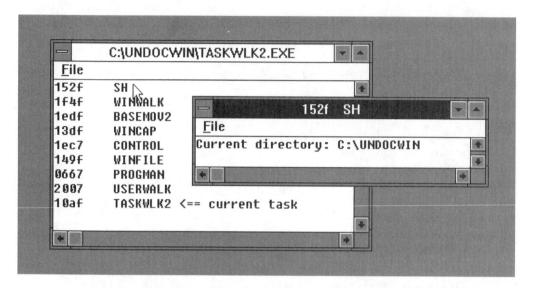

So what's this stale data problem? One of the problems with writing HEAP-WALK-like browsers, where the user is presented with a list of items that can be clicked on for information, is that the state of Windows could totally change from when the list was displayed to when the user decides he or she wants to know more. The item selected might no longer be valid.

HEAPWALK tries to avoid this situation by updating itself in an extremely annoying way. TASKWLK2 also tries to avoid this situation by updating itself, though we hope the effect is less annoying. TASKWLK2's on_time() function automatically generates a new display whenever the number of tasks changes.

However, KERNEL's task list itself can be in an unstable state when a task is in the middle of starting or exiting. This is why on_time() runs taskwalk() in a loop until the number of tasks it finds equals the number returned from the GetNumTasks() function. Note that this is necessary whether you're using ToolHelp, undocumented Windows, or (as here) a combination of the two.

The result is that the user should never be able to click on an invalid task. Still, it never hurts to be sure. In 3.1, we could use the documented IsTask() function to verify that we have a valid task handle, but because this isn't supported in 3.0, we've written our own. The functions IsValidTask(), GetTaskCurDir(), and GetTaskModule Name() have been given Windows-like names to suggest their general-purpose usefulness (or what would be their usefulness were they spruced up a bit and given some of what in 3.1 is called "parameter validation"—i.e., error checking of the sort that should have existed from the very beginning). General-purpose functions of this type are presented in HANDLES.C and HANDLES.H, in the introduction to chapter 5.

The point here was to illustrate WINIO. In less than 100 lines of C code, we've written a moderately useful program, which responds to user mouse input and which uses multiple windows. Think about what it would require to do this using only direct calls to the Windows API.

WINIO does have one annoying limitation in this area: The user has no visible clue that the lines are clickable. Unless you know this user-interface "idiom," or unless the program actually contains a direction such as "Click here to see more," the output looks just like a static list, not like something you can interact with.

Windows' built-in list boxes are an improvement here, but WINIO doesn't use list boxes because they're unsuitable for other things that WINIO does (such as providing a gets( ) function with which to produce programs such as SH and CALLFUNC). This reflects the generally frustrating nature of Windows' built-in controls: They are almost, but not quite, what one wants, and frequently it is more work to figure out how to change their behavior via subclassing than to come up with your own control. WINIO definitely needs more work in this area, but so does Windows itself; the built-in controls need to be more extensible, more customizable, and more "open."

See Appendix A for a user's guide to the WINIO library.

CALLFUNC: Dynamic Linking at Your Fingertips!

Having an "application framework" such as WINIO makes it much more likely that Windows programmers will experiment with the Windows API, trying things out for themselves, rather than just cuting and pasting blocks of code from the SDK samples.

However, even with WINIO, it seems like a hassle to have to write a five- or ten-line program, compile and link it, just to try out one or two Windows API calls. True, five or ten lines is an improvement over the non-WINIO 80 or 100, but it would be nice if, when you wanted to try out a Windows API call, perhaps even an undocumented one, you could just *type* the call in. Just as you do not have to write, compile, and link a program whenever you want to add some numbers, you should not have to write, compile, and link a program when you just want to call a Windows API function to see what it does.

In other words, it would be nice to have a Windows API interpreter: a calculator, if you will. Actually, there are many Windows programs today that can be used in this way. You might find this hard to believe, but Microsoft Word for Windows—a word processor, for heaven's sake—contains a complete programming language, Word Basic, that includes the ability to call Windows API functions "on the fly," without writing a program. You can even try out some undocumented Windows API functions with Word Basic. For example, if you have Word for Windows (or even the free WinWord "Working Model," which includes the complete Word Basic interpreter), you can just type the following few lines into a macro-editing window, press the Start button, and watch in amazement as the undocumented TileChildWindows() function gives Windows 3.1 the look and feel of Windows 1.0:

```
Declare Sub TileChildWindows Lib "user" (hwnd As Integer, action As Integer)
Declare Function GetDesktopWindow Lib "user" () As Integer
Sub MAIN
    TileChildWindows GetDesktopWindow, 1
End Sub
```

This is basically (sorry) the functionality that Windows programmers need in an API calculator: just a quick way to type in a few lines and see what they do.

Basic for Windows

Even if you're a C programmer and haven't touched Basic for years, it pays to become familiar with one or two of the many dialects of Basic for Windows. Basic has become the de facto Windows macro language. Learning about Basic for Windows is useful, not only because it's nice to know a noncompiled macro language when you just want to try out three lines of code, but also because the future of Windows programming may be dominated by the need to communicate with the "big" Windows applications, all of which have Basic or Basic-like macro languages.

The Microsoft Word for Windows 2.0 "working model," with the complete Word Basic interpreter, comes with Woody Leonhard's excellent (and extremely odd) book, *Windows 3.1 Programming for Mere Mortals* (Addison-Wesley, 1992).

Another Basic interpreter for Windows, Realizer, has a "limited" version that comes with Michael Hyman's book, *Windows 3.0 for BASIC Programmers* (Addison-Wesley, 1991). Like Word Basic, Realizer (even the limited version that comes with Hyman's book) allows full access to the Windows API, including undocumented calls. ∎

Even though Word Basic is in many ways a superb little language, it doesn't *quite* fit the bill as a Windows programmer's handy API calculator. Neither do the many other interpreted Windows languages currently available. While most provide a way to drop down to the Windows API, this is not their chief purpose. What we want is an interpreter whose *sole* purpose is to call Windows API functions on the fly.

CALLFUNC, a program provided on the accompanying disk, is just that: a small interpreter that lets the user type in Windows API calls. The following is a sample session using this API calculator:

```
> user getdesktopwindow
0x0e8c
> user tilechildwindows 0xe8c 0
0x0001
> kernel getcurrenttask %lx
14af1177
```

```
> user syserrorbox "System Error!" "Caption" 4 5 6
0x0001
> user iconsize %Fp
Couldn't find function
> user 86 %Fp
0020:0020
>
```

User input follows the > prompt, and the function return value or an error message follows on the next line. In these few lines, we first called the documented USER function GetDesktopWindow(), which expects no parameters, and which returned an HWND of 0x0E8C. We passed that HWND as an argument to the undocumented function TileChildWindows(). The log shows an apparent return of 0x0001, but actually the function returns nothing meaningful. However, we could observe the program's side effect which, as noted earlier, is to make Windows 3.1 look sort of like Windows 1.0.

On the following input line, we turn our attention to something entirely different and call the documented GetCurrentTask() function in KERNEL, using the %lx printf mask to print out its full DWORD return value. Next, we're distracted again and call the undocumented USER function SysErrorBox(). Note that we have passed several strings; CALLFUNC does some fairly primitive type assessment of parameters and passes far addresses to quoted strings if it encounters them.

Notice that the line "user iconsize %Fp" was unsuccessful because the above session was logged in version 3.1. As the entry for IconSize() in the USER chapter states, the entry point for the function still persists in 3.1, but it is named BEAR86. The next input line in the above log shows that calling the function through its ordinal number (86) was successful. At the end of the line, %Fp specifies the mask to be used to display the return value. In this case, we use %Fp, not because the function returns a far pointer, but because the mask provides a convenient way of showing a DWORD split into its low and high WORD components.

Because of its generality, CALLFUNC can also be used for tasks such as posting or sending messages to other windows: you just call PostMessage() or SendMessage() from the CALLFUNC command line. Used in this way, CALLFUNC is similar to the POSTMAN utility published in *Microsoft Systems Journal* (May 1991). You have to look up the WM_ message numbers yourself, though; in the following example, 0x102 is the "magic number" for WM_CHAR:

```
> ! notepad                              ;; launch notepad.exe
> user findwindow Notepad 0L             ;; FindWindow(class name)
0x1a3c                                   ;; notepad hwnd
> user getwindow 0x1a3c 5                ;; GetWindow(GW_CHILD)
0x1a90                                   ;; notepad edit control hwnd
> user postmessage 0x1a90 0x102 'h 0L    ;; PostMessage(WM_CHAR)
0x00c6
> user postmessage 0x1a90 0x102 'i 0L    ;; PostMessage(WM_CHAR)
0x0084
```

This launches Notepad, locates its main window by passing Notepad's class name to FindWindow(), calls GetWindow(GW_CHILD) to find HWND of its multiline edit control, and then sends the characters "h" and "i" which duly appear in Notepad.

This, of course, is exactly how the SendKeys() statement, found in every Windows macro language, is implemented.

In this example, we're sending WM_CHAR messages. Obviously we could send any other message we wanted, once we looked up its number in WINDOWS.H or some other handy source of Windows "magic numbers." We're calling PostMessage(), but we could as easily call SendMessage(). We're calling a function from USER, but we could as easily call a function from any other DLL. CALLFUNC really is general-purpose.

In essence, CALLFUNC is no different from the SH program whose source was shown earlier in this chapter, except that the CALLFUNC prompt is always an > and that, instead of interpreting its input as a command line to be passed to WinExec(), CALLFUNC treats each line of input as a function call of the following form, where <angle brackets> indicate required parameters, [square brackets] indicate optional parameters, and the | indicates a choice:

```
<modname> <funcname|ordinal> [args...] [%mask] [!]
```

The modname can be any valid Windows module name: KERNEL, USER, and GDI are the most common, but CALLFUNC can link to literally any module. If it's a DLL that's not already in memory, you need to provide its filename, such as "STRESS.DLL". CALLFUNC will pass this string off to GetModuleHandle() or LoadLibrary().

The funcname is any exported function name in the module. As an alternative, you can specify a *decimal* (not hexademical) ordinal number. CALLFUNC passes this string or ordinal off to the GetProcAddress() function.

All args to the function are typed in as strings, of course, but CALLFUNC uses some dumb rules to determine the actual type of each argument:

```
if first character of arg is a digit or '-'
    and if arg contains '.' then it's a floating-point number
    else if last character is an 'L' then it's a long
    else it's an unsigned word
else if first character is an apostrophe
    it's a single-byte character
else if it's the string @buf
    it's a far pointer to a 1k buffer built into CALLFUNC
otherwise
    it's a string (if within quotes, single arg)
```

For example, the following passes two four-byte parameters to the FindWindow() function in USER:

```
> user findwindow 0L "This is a test"
```

There are two exceptions to the args typing. First, if one of the arguments is the string @buf, then it turns into a far pointer to a 1K buffer within CALLFUNC. You can use this whenever you need some memory to be side-effected. For example

```
> user getwindowtext 0x1964 @buf 256
0x24
> dump @buf 0x24
1187:0056 | 43 61 6C 6C 66 75 6E 63 3A 20 64 6C 6C 20 66 75 | Callfunc: dll fu
1187:0066 | 6E 63 20 5B 61 72 67 73 2E 2E 2E 5D 20 5B 25 6D | nc [args...] [%m
1187:0076 | 61 73 6B 5D                                     | ask]
```

Second, if the first argument is the word "regs," then the next four arguments are assumed to be values for the AX, BX, CX, and DX registers. For example

```
> kernel dos3call regs 0x3000 0 0 0
0x0005
> kernel nohookdoscall regs 0x3000 0 0 0
0x0005
```

The optional %mask is any valid printf( ) mask. If no mask is specified, then the default "0x%04x" is used. For example

```
> kernel getversion
0x0a03
> kernel getversion %lx
5000a03
> kernel getversion 0x%lx
0x5000a03
> kernel getversion 0x%lXL
0x5000A03L
```

If the last argument is the character ! then CALLFUNC uses the cdecl calling convention rather than the default Pascal calling convention.

CALLFUNC relies on Windows run-time dynamic linking to turn the module name/function name pair into a callable far function pointer. Together, the three documented functions LoadLibrary( ), GetModuleHandle( ), and GetProcAddress( ) are sufficient to turn a pair of strings such as ("USER", "TILECHILDWINDOWS") into a function pointer that the program can call.

This same capability is found in OS/2 (where the functions are named DosGetModHandle( ), DosLoadModule( ), and DosGetProcAddr( )), and, in fact, CALLFUNC is the Windows adaptation of an OS/2 program that one of us did several years ago (see "Linking While the Program Is Running: Run-Time Dynamic Linking in OS/2," *Dr. Dobb's Journal*, November 1989).

Apart from providing dynamic linking at your fingertips, CALLFUNC has some other useful features. Before treating an input line as a function call, CALLFUNC checks to see if it is one of the built-in commands CLS, DUMP, EXIT, INFO, PRINTF, SEL, or !. CLS need not detain us for long; it does what its DOS namesake does; that is, it clears the display.

If the return value of a function is a global memory handle or a far pointer, DUMP is often useful for inspecting the contents of the corresponding memory. DUMP's syntax is

```
DUMP xxxx:xxxx [length]
```

where xxxx:xxxx is the starting address in hex seg:ofs to dump and the length is optional. If length is omitted, the DUMP command displays 64 bytes, corresponding to four lines of display output.

For example, we can use DUMP to follow the linked list of tasks:

```
> kernel getcurrenttask
0x1177
> kernel getcurrenttask %lx
14af1177
> dump 14af:00f2 16
14AF:00F2 | 57 49 4E 4F 4C 44 41 50 54 44 00 00 00 00 CD 20 | WINOLDAPTD.....
> dump 14af:0000 2
14AF:0000 | 07 08                                           | ..
> dump 0807:0000 2
0807:0000 | BF 11                                           | ..
> dump 11bf:0000 2
11BF:0000 | 77 11                                           | w.
> dump 1177:0000 2
1177:0000 | 00 00                                           | ..
```

DUMP uses the VERR and LSL instructions to check the validity of the specified pointer and length. Instead of xxxx:xxxx, you can specify @buf to view the side-effective buffer built into CALLFUNC.

EXIT terminates CALLFUNC's prompt-read-dynlink-printf loop. The CALL-FUNC window is kept open so you can save a log of your session. The window is closed by double clicking on its close box; this can also be used instead of EXIT.

INFO displays some Windows handles for this instance of CALLFUNC. Many functions, especially those in KERNEL, require valid task, instance, or other handles as parameters. INFO provides a ready source of such handles:

```
hwnd = 0x19ac
task = 0x11f7
module = 0x1207
instance (DS) = 0x11ce
PSP (PDB) = 0x11ef
task q = 0x11df
local heap = 0x2dd0
```

Here, "hwnd" refers to the window handle of the CALLFUNC main window; the handle is an offset into USER's default data segment. "Task," "module," "instance," "PSP," and "task q" are all global memory handles (see "Handle, handles, everywhere..." at the beginning of chapter 5). "Local heap" is the address within DS of the near heap information structure (see "Instance Data" in chapter 5). For example:

```
> kernel gettaskqueue 0x11f7    ;; get taskq from task
0x11df                          ;; ok
> kernel getexeptr 0x11ce       ;; get modhand from instance
0x1207                          ;; ok
> kernel getexeptr 0x11df       ;; get modhand from taskq
```

```
0x037f                             ;; hmm, what's that?
> kernel getmodulehandle user      ;; seem to remember taskq owned by USER?
0x037f                             ;; yes, taskq owned by USER!
```

PRINTF corresponds to the printf() function. It is useful when you want to see the decimal representation of a hex number or examine a far string. For example:

```
> printf %Fs @buf
This is a window title
```

Using the SEL command with a word value allows us to see if it corresponds to a valid selector. If it does, SEL also tells us a little more about it:

```
> sel 0x18d7
sel=0x18D7 size=512 data read/write
```

This tells us that 0x18d7 is indeed a valid selector, that the segment is 512 (decimal) bytes long, that it is a data rather than code segment, and that it is valid for reading and writing. Passing SEL a random value (almost always!) provokes the response "Invalid selector."

The ! is used as a convenient way to start other Windows programs from within CALLFUNC. Anything after the ! is treated as a command line to be passed to WinExec(). For example, the following commands both run CONTROL.EXE:

```
> ! control.exe
```

```
> kernel winexec control.exe 1
0x116e
```

CALLFUNC GP Fault Handling

CALLFUNC has one major limitation: It does not know anything about the functions you are calling. It just uses run-time dynamic linking to get a function pointer, pushes your arguments (converted to their appropriate types) on the stack, calls the function, and then uses the printf mask to display the return value in AX or DX:AX. By itself, this is not a limitation but a benefit: This ignorant pass-through design means that CALLFUNC will work with *any* API in a DLL, even one that may not have existed at the time CALLFUNC was compiled. This "late binding" is one of the great benefits of run-time dynamic linking.

However, precisely because CALLFUNC is just a pass-through mechanism, it can't help you with passing the correct number, or type, of arguments. Because almost all Windows API functions use the Pascal calling convention, in which the API function itself pops your arguments off the stack, passing in the wrong number of bytes will generally cause a (hopefully benign) general protection (GP) fault.

CALLFUNC uses the ToolHelp InterruptRegister() function to install a GP fault handler. If a GP fault occurs while CALLFUNC is in the middle of making your function call, it will attempt to recover by doing a Throw() to a Catch() that is

located just before the top of CALLFUNC's prompt-read-dynlink-printf loop. The
code looks like this:

```
CATCHBUF catchbuf = {0} ;
char *err_msg = 0;
BOOL in_dynlink = 0;
unsigned callfunc_ss = 0;

void _export far FaultHandler(void)
{
    static unsigned intnum, fault_ss;

    _asm mov ax, word ptr [bp+8]
    _asm mov intnum, ax
    _asm mov ax, word ptr [bp+14h]
    _asm mov fault_ss, ax

    if ((in_dynlink) && (intnum == 13) && (fault_ss == callfunc_ss))
    {
        err_msg = "GP fault!";
        Throw(catchbuf, 1); // longjmp off the interrupt callback
    }
    else
        return; // it's something other than a GP fault in CALLFUNC
}

main()
{
    char buf[256];
    FARPROC procinst_faulthandler;

    _asm mov callfunc_ss, ss
    procinst_faulthandler =
        MakeProcInstance((FARPROC) FaultHandler, __hInst);
    if (! InterruptRegister(0, procinst_faulthandler))
        puts("Can't register GP fault handler!");

    if (Catch(catchbuf) != 0)    //setjmp: come here with errors
        puts(err_msg);
    for (;;)
    {
        putchar('>'); putchar(' ');     // prompt
        gets(buf);                      // read
        // ... look for built-in commands, such as DUMP, SEL, etc.,
        // ... or for EXIT, which breaks out of loop
        in_dynlink++;
        do_dynlink(buf);                // dynlink, printf
        in_dynlink--;
    }

    FreeProcInstance(procinst_faulthandler);
}
```

If WINICE is also running, it will get the GP fault before CALLFUNC does. Just type "C" (continue) and CALLFUNC will then get to handle the fault; it will display a low-key "GP fault!" message and then await further input.

If Dr. Watson, WinSpector, or a similar interrupt-trapping program (such as our own CORONER) was running *before* you started CALLFUNC, once again it will get first crack at the fault before CALLFUNC (see the description of InterruptRegister() in chapter 10). Again, however, CALLFUNC will generally still be able to recover from the fault.

Giving programs the ability to handle their own GP faults is one of the great features of ToolHelp. Before ToolHelp, and in Microsoft's previous operating-system experiments (OS/2 1.x), trying to catch GP faults was a major chore (see, for example, "Stalking GP Faults," *Dr. Dobb's Journal*, January 1990 and February 1990). With ToolHelp, as the above code fragment shows, it is relatively simple and straightforward. Thanks, Microsoft!

Watching Undocumented WM_ Messages with SNOOP

Having taken a look at an API call interpreter, next up in our whirlwind tour of Windows diagnostic tools are the two event logging/tracing programs included with the book: SNOOP, which watches WM_ messages, including undocumented ones, and WISPY (I Spy for Windows), which watches interrupts and which is sort of a cheap Windows version of the popular INTRSPY program from *Undocumented DOS*.

In the world of networking, programs like SPY or SNOOP are called protocol analyzers or "sniffers." They report on various aspects of traffic on the net. Given that Windows is a message-based system, it is hardly surprising that it should require the same sort of traffic-reporting diagnostic tools as a network. Besides, there is a tremendous amount of "hook" functionality in the Windows API that practically begs to have this type of logging/tracing utility built on top of it. The existence of such API calls as SetWindowsHook() and SetWindowsHookEx(), or the ToolHelp function NotifyRegister(), sometimes seems like a solution in search of a problem. The problem then turns out to be how to write a Windows "sniffer."

Similar to the SDK Spy program, Borland's WinSight, and Richter's VOYEUR program, SNOOP reports on the WM_ messages received by one or more windows. Perhaps it should have been called YASP (Yet Another Spy Program). However, SNOOP differs from these other programs in a number of ways:

- Although able to report on any WM_ message, SNOOP is specially tailored for investigating undocumented messages. It works off two data files, WM_MSG.DAT and (by default) WM_UNDOC.DAT. When used with WM_UNDOC.DAT, SNOOP shows any messages, documented or undocumented, that are triggered during the processing of an undocumented message.

- The SNOOP data files can be customized, to tell SNOOP about WM_USER+ messages, about messages created with RegisterWindowMessage(), or about additional undocumented messages.

- SNOOP's "trace" option reports on which USER built-in WndProcs process a message. If a message arrives at DefWindowProc() or EditWindowProc(), for example, SNOOP can tell you.

- SNOOP uses an undocumented aspect of InSendMessage() (described in chapter 6) to locate the origin of sent messages.

- The effect and behavior of messages can be analyzed by filtering them out, i.e., not allowing them to reach either the target window or the default window procedures, and watching the resultant effect. In other words, SNOOP can be run in a massively intrusive "Heisenberg" mode.

- SNOOP devotes a separate tracing window to each window you are watching, making it useful as a tool for investigating undocumented inter-window protocols such as "drag and drop" in 3.0 and 3.1.

When SNOOP starts up, it shows an indented list of the window hierarchy. A menu item lets you "refresh" the list at any time (SNOOP does not automatically do this refresh, in the cool but slightly disconcerting way that WinSight does).

Double-clicking on any window in this display brings up another window in which messages will be logged. As noted above, you can watch message traffic for multiple windows at the same time; each one will get its own message-logging window. For example:

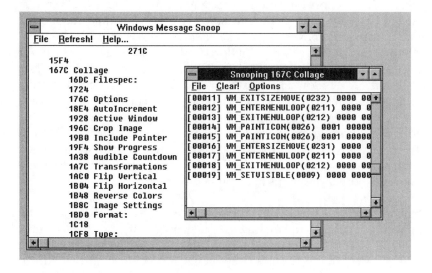

The messages that SNOOP logs to this window are determined by the contents of a data file. By default, SNOOP uses the file WM_UNDOC.DAT, to show all undocumented messages:

```
;; WM_UNDOC.DAT -- Undocumented Windows messages
WM_SIZEWAIT                     0004
WM_SETVISIBLE                   0009      ;; Documented in version 2.1 SDK
WM_SYSTEMERROR                  0017      ;; Documented in version 2.1 SDK
WM_PAINTICON                    0026      ;; 3.1 DDK WINDOWS.H -- doc in Win32  API
WM_ALTTABACTIVE                 0029      ;; ditto
WM_SETHOTKEY                    0032      ;; ditto -- doc in Win32 API
WM_GETHOTKEY                    0033      ;; ditto -- doc in Win32 API
WM_FILESYSCHANGE                0034      ;; cf. KERNEL FileCdr()
WM_ISACTIVEICON                 0035
WM_QUERYPARKICON                0036      ;; 3.1 DDK says WM_UNUSED0036
WM_QUERYSAVESTATE               0038
WM_???                          003A 003F
WM_TESTING                      0040
WM_OTHERWINDOWCREATED           0042      ;; Win32 WINUSER.H -- also RegisterWM
WM_OTHERWINDOWDESTROYED         0043      ;; Win32 WINUSER.H -- also RegisterWM
;; possibly WM_ACTIVATESHELLWINDOW  0044      ;; SetWindowsHook WH_SHELL
WM_HOTKEYEVENT                  0045      ;; Win32 WINUSER.H; not same as WM_HOTKEY
WM_???                          0049 0080
WM_SYNCPAINT                    0088      ;; cf. OS/2 PM CS_SYNCPAINT
WM_SYNCTASK                     0089      ;; WINUSER.H:  ST_BEGINSWP, ST_ENDSWP
WM_???                          008A 009F
WM_???                          00AA 00FF
WM_YOMICHAR                     0108      ;; Japan
WM_CONVERTREQUEST               010A      ;; Japan
WM_CONVERTRESULT                010B      ;; Japan
WM_INTERIM                      010C      ;; Korea
WM_???                          0109 010F
WM_SYSTIMER                     0118      ;; USER CreateSystemTimer()
WM_???                          0119 011E
WM_???                          0122 0130
WM_LBTRACKPOINT                 0131
WM_???                          0132 01FF
WM_???                          020A 020F
WM_ENTERMENULOOP                0211
WM_EXITMENULOOP                 0212
WM_NEXTMENU                     0213
WM_???                          0214 021F
WM_DROPOBJECT                   022A      ;; drag & drop
WM_QUERYDROPOBJECT              022B      ;; drag & drop
WM_BEGINDRAG                    022C      ;; drag & drop
WM_DRAGLOOP                     022D      ;; drag & drop
WM_DRAGSELECT                   022E      ;; drag & drop
WM_DRAGMOVE                     022F      ;; drag & drop
WM_ENTERSIZEMOVE                0231
WM_EXITSIZEMOVE                 0232
WM_???                          0234 027F
WM_KANJIFIRST                   0280
WM_KANJI???                     0281 029E
WM_KANJILAST                    029F
```

```
WM_???                          02A0 02FF
WM_INTERNAL_COALESCE_??         0390 039F
WM_INTERNAL_DDE_??              03E0 03EF

WM_CBT_RESERVED_??              03F0 03FF   ;; CBT = "computer-based training"
WM_USER                         0400 FFFF
```

Rather than watch undocumented messages, you can watch other message categories simply by specifying a different .DAT file on the SNOOP command line. For example, you might create a WM_KEY.DAT file, to watch all keyboard-related messages:

```
; WM_KEY.DAT
WM_KEYDOWN               0100
WM_KEYUP                 0101
WM_CHAR                  0102
WM_DEADCHAR              0103
WM_SYSKEYDOWN            0104
WM_SYSKEYUP             0105
WM_SYSCHAR              0106
WM_SYSDEADCHAR          0107
WM_YOMICHAR             0108        ;; Undocumented in 2.1, 3.x
```

This shows the syntax of each line in the file. Comments start with a semicolon in any position and are terminated by the end of the line, and blank lines are ignored. Each line describes a range of messages in the form "WM_name start-value [end-value]," where start-value and the optional end-value specify, in hex, the start and end of a range of values associated with WM_name. If an end-value is not specified, the entry describes a single value. WM_UNDOC.DAT has a number of lines designated WM_??? that use a range to describe values for which no messages names are currently known to exist. SNOOP uses the contents of this file as the list of messages to be displayed. If used to sniff out undocumented messages sent or posted to File Manager, for example, here is what SNOOP might find:

```
[00001] WM_GETHOTKEY(0033) 0000 00000000
        Sent by WINOA386
[00002] WM_SYNCPAINT(0088) 0017 00000000
        Sent by SNOOP
[00003] WM_SYNCPAINT(0088) 0017 00000000
        Sent by SNOOP
[00004] WM_ENTERMENULOOP(0211) 0000 00000000 Posted
[00005] WM_EXITMENULOOP(0212) 0000 00000000 Posted
[00006] WM_ENTERMENULOOP(0211) 0000 00000000 Posted
[00007] WM_EXITMENULOOP(0212) 0000 00000000 Posted
[00008] WM_SYNCPAINT(0088) 0017 00000000
        Sent by SNOOP
[00009] WM_FILESYSCHANGE(0034) 8056 00003D94 Posted
[00010] WM_FILESYSCHANGE(0034) 8043 00003DCC Posted
[00011] WM_FILESYSCHANGE(0034) 8056 00003D94 Posted
[00012] WM_FILESYSCHANGE(0034) 8043 00003DCC Posted
[00013] WM_GETHOTKEY(0033) 0000 00000000
        Sent by WINOA386
[00014] WM_GETHOTKEY(0033) 0000 00000000
        Sent by WINOA386
```

For further details on WM_GETHOTKEY, WM_SYNCPAINT, WM_ENTER/ EXITMENULOOP, and WM_FILESYSCHANGE, see chapter 7.

As the preceeding example shows, when a message has been issued with SendMessage() rather than with PostMessage(), SNOOP displays an additional line indicating where the message came from. The phase "Sent by" is somewhat misleading because, for example, SNOOP did not send File Manager a WM_SYNCPAINT message. However, SNOOP *was* the active task when some DLL (undoubtedly USER) sent File Manager a WM_SYNCPAINT; this message was generated when a SNOOP window was moved, revealing a previously obscured portion of File Manager.

How does SNOOP know what task was active at the time a message was sent? As is explained in chapter 6, the return value of the documented InSendMessage() function, if not zero, is actually the Task Queue handle of the task that sent the current message; this value comes straight out of a field in the Task Queue structure. This opens up the possibility of tracing back through the chain of SendMessage() calls. SNOOP uses essentially the following code:

```
#define TaskFromTaskQueue(tq)    *((WORD far *) MK_FP(tq, 2))

#define ModuleNameFromTask(t)    ((char far *) MK_FP(t, 0xF2))

#define TaskQueueOfSender(tq)    *((WORD far *) MK_FP(tq, 0x3A))

void PrintSenderChain(void)
{
    sender_taskq = InSendMessage();
    while ((sender_taskq != 0) && (sender_taskq != my_taskq))
    {
        sender_task = TaskFromTaskQueue(sender_taskq);
        printf("Sent by %.8Fs\n", ModuleNameFromTask(sender_task));
        sender_taskq = TaskQueueOfSender(sender_taskq); // follow chain
    }
}
```

Tracing Messages Through WndProc Calls
Selecting the Trace option from the SNOOP Options menu will produce a more detailed look at undocumented messages. Rather than just print the messages sent or posted to the window, SNOOP follows their progress through to Windows' built-in window procedures.

For example, here SNOOP is watching the same set of undocumented messages delivered to File Manager as before, but this time the Trace option is on:

```
[00018] WM_SYNCPAINT(0088) 0017 00000000
        Sent by SNOOP
   ->DefFrameProc h=1680 m=WM_SYNCPAINT(0088) w=0017 l=00000000
    ->MDIClientWndProc h=1680 m=WM_NCPAINT(0085) w=0001 l=00000000
    <-MDIClientWndProc ret 00000000 (h=1680 m=WM_NCPAINT)
    ->MDIClientWndProc h=1680 m=WM_ERASEBKGND(0014) w=0BB6 l=00000000
    <-MDIClientWndProc ret 00000001 (h=1680 m=WM_ERASEBKGND)
    ->DefMDIChildProc h=1774 m=WM_NCPAINT(0085) w=0001 l=00000000
```

```
   <-DefMDIChildProc ret 00000000 (h=1774 m=WM_NCPAINT)
   ->DefMDIChildProc h=1774 m=WM_ERASEBKGND(0014) w=0BAE l=00000000
   <-DefMDIChildProc ret 00000001 (h=1774 m=WM_ERASEBKGND)
 <-DefFrameProc ret 00000000 (h=1680 m=WM_SYNCPAINT)
[00019] WM_GETHOTKEY(0033) 0000 00000000
       Sent by WINOA386
   ->DefFrameProc h=1680 m=WM_GETHOTKEY(0033) w=0000 l=00000000
   <-DefFrameProc ret 00000000 (h=1680 m=WM_GETHOTKEY)
... etc ...
[00024] WM_ENTERSIZEMOVE(0231) 0000 00000000 Posted
   ->DefFrameProc h=1680 m=WM_ENTERSIZEMOVE(0231) w=0000 l=00000000
   <-DefFrameProc ret 00000000 (h=1680 m=WM_ENTERSIZEMOVE)
[00025] WM_EXITSIZEMOVE(0232) 0000 00000000 Posted
   ->DefFrameProc h=1680 m=WM_EXITSIZEMOVE(0232) w=0000 l=00000000
   <-DefFrameProc ret 00000000 (h=1680 m=WM_EXITSIZEMOVE)
[00026] WM_ENTERMENULOOP(0211) 0000 00000000 Posted
   ->DefFrameProc h=1680 m=WM_ENTERMENULOOP(0211) w=0000 l=00000000
   <-DefFrameProc ret 00000000 (h=1680 m=WM_ENTERMENULOOP)
[00027] WM_EXITMENULOOP(0212) 0000 00000000 Posted
   ->DefFrameProc h=1680 m=WM_EXITMENULOOP(0212) w=0000 l=00000000
   <-DefFrameProc ret 00000000 (h=1680 m=WM_EXITMENULOOP)
```

From this, we can see that the File Manager main window passes on WM_SYNC-PAINT, unchanged, to DefFrameProc(), which then turns it into WM_NCPAINT and WM_ERASEBKGRND messages for MDIClientWndProc() and DefMDI ChildProc(). The other undocumented messages—WM_GETHOTKEY, WM_ENT-ERSIZEMOVE, and so on—are all passed, unchanged, to DefFrameProc(), which appears to "eat" them.

SNOOP knows about the following window procedures:

```
DefWindowProc
DefDlgProc              (dialogs)
DefMDIChildProc         (MDI)
DefFrameProc            (MDI)
DesktopWndProc
EditWndProc             EDIT
ButtonWndProc           BUTTON
ComboBoxCtlWndProc      COMBOBOX
LBoxCtlWndProc          LISTBOX
MDIClientWndProc        MDICLIENT
MenuWndProc (3.1 BEAR306)
SBWndProc               SCROLLBAR
StaticWndProc           STATIC
```

To trace the course of a message through these WndProcs, SNOOP needs to have names, not only for the messages it is explicitly watching (generally the undocumented messages in WM_UNDOC.DAT), but for *all* messages. For example, SNOOP showed above that a WM_SYNCPAINT "becomes" a WM_NCPAINT and a WM_ERASEBKGRND. To show this, it has to know that message 85h is WM_NCPAINT and that 14h is WM_ERASEBKGND. SNOOP gets these "secondary" message numbers (i.e., messages it will display only during a trace) from the file WM_MSG.DAT. Like WM_UNDOC.DAT, this file can be changed by the user. Unlike

WM_UNDOC.DAT, though, you cannot specify a different file; you must have WM_MSG.DAT.

How does SNOOP intercept calls to functions like DefWindowProc() and EditWndProc()? Subclassing, using SetWindowsHookEx(WH_CALLWNDPROC) and/or SetWindowsHookEx(WH_GETMESSAGE), makes it relatively simple to intercept WM_ messages in Windows. (This is one reason why so many SPY programs have been written!)

Unfortunately, Windows hooks do not provide a way to see the return from a message. Without this, a message spy can't keep track of the nesting of messages. For this reason, message spies, including SNOOP, generally use window subclassing instead of, or in addition to, windows hooks. The term "subclass" isn't quite accurate here, because the window's messages are being passively intercepted, without changing the window's behavior (but, see the SNOOP Filter option below). Like subclassing, however, message spies use SetWindowLong(hwnd, GWL_WNDPROC).

To intercept calls to a built-in WndProc, SNOOP pretends to be a debugger: It puts INT 3 breakpoints (char 0CCh) on the first instruction of the WndProc. This same INT 3 technique is used by other programs that trap API calls, to do for function calls what programs like SPY and SNOOP do for WM_ messages. The BPX command in WINICE can also be used for the same purpose. For a slightly different approach, see the article "Intercepting DLL Function Calls" by Timothy Adams (*Windows/DOS Developer's Journal*, June 1992).

The ToolHelp InterruptRegister() function lets a Windows application handle INT 3; likewise, you can use DPMI to install a breakpoint handler. However, SNOOP has to get the opcode there in the first place. There are two issues here. First, because we are putting a breakpoint on a nonwritable code segment, we need a writable data alias for the segment. SNOOP uses the AllocCStoDSAlias() function (see chapter 5). Second, the code that we are attempting to modify may not even be in physical memory at the time! Happily, Windows provides a documented function that solves this problem—GetCodeHandle(), whose primary purpose is to provide information about the code segment in which a function resides, but which has the useful side effect of loading the code segment and marking it as recently used.

In order to better understand the nesting of events, SNOOP needs to record when one of these functions *returns*, as well as when it's called. When a SNOOP breakpoint is hit, at the same time that it gets ready to restart the call with the breakpoint temporarily removed, SNOOP fiddles with the return address on the stack so that the intercepted function will return to SNOOP rather than to the function's actual caller. In this way, SNOOP not only gets to reinsert its breakpoint, but, equally important, gets to track function exit as well as entry.

Deliberately-Intrusive Debugging

SNOOP's "Filter" option has no parallel in any other spy program that we know. If "Filter" is enabled from the SNOOP menu, the "primary" messages (that is, the ones specified in WM_UNDOC.DAT or in a different .DAT file you specify on the SNOOP command line) are filtered out, i.e., not allowed to reach the intended

WndProc! Such an option sounds ridiculous, but it is sometimes easy to deduce the behavior provoked by a particular message by seeing what happens if the message is no longer generated. SNOOP filtering certainly helped find the purpose of some of the undocumented messages described in chapter 7.

Watching Interrupts with WISPY

Our other traffic-reporting logging/tracing program is WISPY, the Interrupt Spy (or I Spy) for Windows. Although not script-driven like the popular INTRSPY program from *Undocumented DOS*, WISPY serves the same purpose: to report on software interrupts. Even though a list of software interrupts sounds as if it would contain nothing more than a lot of meaningless-looking hex dumps of the CPU registers, if formatted properly it can tell you what files have been opened, what programs have been executed, and so on.

Although the constraints of DOS TSR programming made INTRSPY a mostly noninteractive program that produces a log file, in Windows an interrupt spy can present its results in a window, in more-or-less real time, in much the same way that SNOOP shows WM_ messages.

On its command line, WISPY takes one or more numbers in decimal or C-style hex; these specify the interrupts to be watched. WISPY has built-in knowledge of specific functions, including some undocumented ones, that use INT 21h (DOS), INT 2Fh (multiplex), and INT 31h (DPMI). For other functions, WISPY will just show a register dump. For example:

```
                       WISPY 21h 2fh 31h
 File   Interrupts
<TASKMAN> Int 2Fh (4003) ENTER CRITICAL SECTION
<TASKMAN> Int 2Fh (4004) EXIT CRITICAL SECTION
<TASKMAN> Int 2Fh (4003) ENTER CRITICAL SECTION
<TASKMAN> Int 2Fh (4004) EXIT CRITICAL SECTION
<TASKMAN> Int 31h (0005) (RESERVED) UNLOCK SEL 118Fh
<TASKMAN> Int 31h (0202) GET EXCEPT VEC 06h
<TASKMAN> Int 31h (0203) SET EXCEPT VEC 06h 011F:196ch
<TASKMAN> Int 31h (0203) SET EXCEPT VEC 06h 011F:5fb1h
<TASKMAN> Int 21h (50) SET PSP 117f
<TASKMAN> Int 21h (00) AX=0001 BX=117f CX=119f DX=0000 DS=117f
<TASKMAN> Int 21h (3e) CLOSE 17
<TASKMAN> Int 31h (0703) DISCARD PAGES @806070e0 nbytes=06f20h
<TASKMAN> Int 31h (0703) DISCARD PAGES @806070e0 nbytes=06f20h
<TASKMAN> Int 21h (50) SET PSP 00af
<TASKMAN> Int 31h (0005) (RESERVED) UNLOCK SEL 119fh
<WINFILE> Int 2Fh (1689) W386_WIN_KERNEL_IDLE
<WINFILE> Int 2Fh (1689) W386_WIN_KERNEL_IDLE
<WINFILE> Int 2Fh (1689) W386_WIN_KERNEL_IDLE|
```

If you've used INTRSPY or any other DOS-based interrupt-watching utility (IBM once sold a nice one called PCWATCH), you may ask the obvious question, Why do we need WISPY at all? Why not just run INTRSPY before Windows and then inspect its log file after you leave Windows? After all, Windows is just another DOS program, right?

Aside from the obvious user-interface limitations of this approach, and the fact that some of us simply do not leave Windows (not without turning the machine off, anyhow), there's a more fundamental reason why a Windows-hosted interrupt spy is often useful for watching interrupts in Windows.

As an example, we can load INTRSPY before Windows and have it watch the DOS File Open (INT 21h AH=3Dh) and EXEC (INT 21h AH=4Bh) calls. We can then start Windows and run some program, such as Control Panel (CON-TROL.EXE). When we exit from Windows and look at the INTRSPY log, the portion relating to CONTROL looks something like this:

```
Open C:\WIN31\CONTROL.EXE
Open C:\WIN31\CONTROL.INI
Open C:\WIN31\SYSTEM\MAIN.CPL
Open C:\WIN31\SYSTEM\VER.DLL
Open C:\WIN31\SYSTEM\LZEXPAND.DLL
Open C:\WIN31\SYSTEM\COMMDLG.DLL
Open C:\WIN31\SYSTEM\SETUP.INF
Open C:\WIN31\SYSTEM\MOUSE.DRV
```

Actually, there's a lot more than this, since the Control Panel in Windows 3.1 is customizable with CPApplets; the INTRSPY log also shows CONTROL opening every. CPL file it can find: CPWIN386.CPL, DRIVERS.CPL, and so on. These .CPL files are actually DLLs, and it seems a little odd to see them being *opened* rather than . . . well, what is the DOS equivalent of a LoadLibrary()?

Seeing a LoadLibrary() at the Windows level turn into a File Open at the DOS level makes sense. But look at CONTROL.EXE in the INTRSPY log: It too appears, not as an EXEC, but as an OPEN. In fact, *any* Windows operation involving a file is, at the DOS level, going to look like a File Open. (If it gets to that level at all; in the future, we may see increased use of Microsoft's 32-bit FastDisk, which bypasses DOS altogether.)

But, if we run a Windows-hosted interrupt spy and then run CONTROL again, it shows up as an EXEC, just as one would have expected. Similarly, we could set an interrupt breakpoint in WINICE, using the expression BPINT 21 AH=4B, and it would catch the tail-end of every WinExec() call. In other words:

- WinExec() calls turn into INT 21h AH=4Bh (EXEC) calls, which can be caught by a Windows-hosted INT 21h spy.
- To a DOS-hosted INT 21h spy, these same WinExec() calls look like INT 21h AH=3Dh (OPEN) calls.

What's going on here? First, Windows is a protected-mode DOS extender. This means that it supports INT 21h services in protected mode. The DOS extender (WIN386 in Enhanced mode and DOSX in Standard mode) provides its own implementation for EXEC because MS-DOS unfortunately does not know how to EXEC protected-mode programs. The DOS extender's EXEC uses real-mode DOS's file services just to load (open, read, and close) the executable file into memory. DOS's EXEC services are unfortunately not useful for launching protected-mode applications. This is part of the reason why a Windows WinExec(), turned into a protected-mode INT 21h AH=4Bh, appears to DOS as a real-mode INT 21h AH=3Dh (OPEN). DOS also sees the WinExec() call's underlying file read and close calls, which the INTRSPY script happened not to be printing.

There's a second reason for the discrepancy between the Windows view and the DOS view. Even in the bad old days of real-mode Windows, we would have seen Windows EXECs turned into DOS OPENs. As we discussed in chapter 2, Windows uses the New Executable (NE) file format rather than the old DOS Mark Zbikowski (MZ) executable file format. DOS doesn't understand the NE format, so Windows has to take care of loading it (that's largely what Windows is for!). Windows relies on DOS for file services, so to implement its own NE-loading EXEC, it calls on DOS open, read, and close.

Because Windows and its underlying DOS substrate view the exact same operation in such different ways, we need a Windows-hosted, protected-mode interrupt spy. If we're watching interrupts from real mode, we're going to miss a lot of the action. Not only do we see DOS calls at too low a level, but some interrupts, such as DOS Protected-Mode Interface (DPMI) INT 31h calls, we're not going to see at all.

(On the other hand, while running INTRSPY before Windows isn't a good way to track Windows interrupts, it is an *excellent* way to find how Windows is booted on top of DOS in its various modes. It's also better than WISPY if you just want a log of all the files touched by Windows.)

WISPY helps provide an understanding of the software interrupts behind some familiar operations in Windows. We already saw that a WinExec() of CONTROL.EXE becomes a protected-mode INT 21h AH=4Bh call. But what else is going on? If we configure WISPY to watch not only INT 21h, but INT 2Fh (multiplex) and INT 31h (DPMI) as well, here's a small portion of what we see when CONTROL is being loaded from File Manager (WINFILE):

```
<WINFILE> Int 2Fh (1689) W386_WIN_KERNEL_IDLE
<WINFILE> Int 2Fh (1689) W386_WIN_KERNEL_IDLE
<WINFILE> Int 2Fh (1689) W386_WIN_KERNEL_IDLE
<WINFILE> Int 21h (4b) EXEC C:\WIN31\CONTROL.EXE
<WINFILE> Int 31h (0703) DISCARD PAGES @807c4b00 nbytes=055c0h
<WINFILE> Int 31h (0004) (RESERVED) LOCK SEL 11dfh
<WINFILE> Int 21h (55) (UNDOC) MK PSP 1effh size=0100h
<WINFILE> Int 21h (19) GET DISK
<WINFILE> Int 21h (47) GET CURR DIR
<WINFILE> Int 21h (19) GET DISK
<WINFILE> Int 21h (47) GET CURR DIR
<CONTROL> Int 31h (0004) (RESERVED) LOCK SEL 121fh
<CONTROL> Int 21h (25) SET VECT 00h 0377:1d17
<CONTROL> Int 21h (2f) GET DTA
<CONTROL> Int 21h (1a) SET DTA 11BF:2960
<CONTROL> Int 21h (4e) FIND FIRST C:\WIN31\CONTROL.INI
```

```
<CONTROL> Int 21h (1a) SET DTA 1EFF:0080
<CONTROL> Int 31h (0009) SET DESC ACCRGTS 00aeh 00f3h
... keep setting descriptor access rights ...
<CONTROL> Int 31h (0703) DISCARD PAGES @80685620 nbytes=0ac20h
<CONTROL> Int 31h (0004) (RESERVED) LOCK SEL 1f3fh
<CONTROL> Int 31h (0703) DISCARD PAGES @80685620 nbytes=0aa40h
<CONTROL> Int 31h (0005) (RESERVED) UNLOCK SEL 1f3fh
```

On the left, WISPY shows the module name of the current task at the time of the interrupt. It gets this using the expression MK_FP(GetCurrentTask(), 0xf2); see chapter 5 for details. This is not necessarily who issued the interrupt, since DLLs (which are not tasks) can issue interrupts. However, in this example it shows a clear transition from WINFILE (File Manager) to CONTROL, soon after the EXEC call.

Why do we see this sharp transition from WINFILE to CONTROL? Given Windows multitasking, shouldn't we see a *mix* of tasks running? The answer is that we should, and usually do, see such a mix in the WISPY trace. However, we're showing a very small block of time here: 30 interrupts out of about 300 that were logged while loading CONTROL. Furthermore, the experience of running Windows indicates that task-switching is effectively halted during task-loading, so the sharp transition here is (unfortunately) not at all surprising.

Wait a minute! Why doesn't WISPY itself always appear as the current task? After all, WISPY *has to be* the current task while it's displaying these lines on the screen. However, it is *not* necessarily the current task when its interrupt handler gets control. This interrupt handler (which is generic enough to handle any interrupt you mention on the WISPY command line) merely queues up information about the interrupt, including the name of the active task at the time, posts a message to WISPY's window, and then chains the interrupt. Sometime later, WISPY's GetMessage() call returns because of the posted message, and the information is pulled out of the queue and displayed. Any interrupts related to WISPY itself are discarded.

Let's examine the preceding WISPY log. Just before the EXEC call that launched CONTROL, KERNEL was twiddling its thumbs, issuing "KERNEL idle" calls (INT 2Fh AX=1689h). These are similar to the DOSINT 28h IDLE call. We will discuss IDLE calls in more detail below.

Shortly after the EXEC, someone, probably KERNEL (WINFILE was just the active task at the time), called the DPMI INT 31h AX=4 function. If you look in a copy of the DPMI specification, you will see this listed as "reserved and should not be called." Hmm, someone at Microsoft don't listen too good. There are actually four such reserved INT 31h functions, and Windows calls all of them:

```
RESERVED DPMI INT 31h FUNCTIONS
AX=0004h BX=selector to lock (won't be paged)
AX=0005h BX=selector to unlock
AX=0700h BX:CX=starting linear page number to mark as paging candidates
         SI:DI=number of pages to mark
AX=0701h BX:CX=starting linear page number to discard
         SI:DI=number of pages to discard
```

Actually, there are documented DPMI calls that do the same things as these functions. Windows probably just calls the reserved ones for what are usually called "historical reasons."

In any case, selector 11DFh is being locked. This selector, it turns out (we happened to see it in a WINICE display of tasks), is the Task Database for CONTROL. Thus, we found by accident what we probably could have guessed: A Task Database in Windows always uses locked memory. We can see this taking place in the trace produced by WISPY.

We can also see that someone, again probably KERNEL, is calling the undocumented DOS Create PSP function (INT 21h AH=55h). This is interesting because a Task Database (like the one that was just locked) already includes a PSP. Actually, using WINICE (again!) to display information about both this 1EFFh PSP selector and the 11DFh Task Database selector shows that, in fact, the PSP that's being created *is* the one that sits on the end of the Task Database: WINICE's LDT command shows the linear base address for any selector, and here it showed us that the PSP's base address is 100h bytes higher than the Task's. In other words, we're watching the Task Database, including its embedded PSP, being created!

We could keep going like this, looking at the WISPY trace and trying to make sense of it. But one thing already clear is that, with interrupts just as with API calls, there are plenty of obscure and undocumented functions to contend with. WISPY provides details on any that it knows.

What's most impressive about the WISPY log is the sheer *number* of interrupts that fly around in Windows. The 30 lines shown previously are a small fraction of what WISPY logs for the few seconds it takes to load CONTROL. Furthermore, for reasons that will be explained below, WISPY *misses* many, many interrupts. No wonder Windows has been called not just an event-driven operating system, but an interrupt-driven operating system.

In fact, Windows Enhanced mode deliberately generates many faults as part of its normal mode of operation, to move between privilege levels. When you add this steady three-degree-background-radiation of faults to the already enormous number of interrupts, the results are almost frightening. The debug version of WIN386 has a debug command (accessible via WINICE) to view interrupt and fault profiles; again, the results are not a pretty sight! It's a wonder that Windows gets anything done at all. The only possible explanation for the fact that Windows *does* manage to accomplish something is that it is run on very fast machines.

Starting a DOS Box

An interesting use for WISPY is to figure out what goes on when you start a DOS box in Enhanced-mode Windows. What pieces come together to produce a DOS box? Without going into the full details, here is WISPY 0x2F's part of the picture:

```
<WINFILE> Int 2Fh (1689) W386_WIN_KERNEL_IDLE
<WINFILE> Int 2Fh (1689) W386_WIN_KERNEL_IDLE
<WINOLDAP> Int 2Fh (1600) W386_GETVERSION
<WINOLDAP> Int 2Fh (1683) W386_GET_CUR_VMID
```

```
<WINOLDAP> Int 2Fh (1684) W386_GET_DEVICE_API dev=0x0017
<WINOLDAP> Int 2Fh (1684) W386_GET_DEVICE_API dev=0x000c
<WINOLDAP> Int 2Fh (1684) W386_GET_DEVICE_API dev=0x000d
<WINOLDAP> Int 2Fh (1684) W386_GET_DEVICE_API dev=0x000a
<WINOLDAP> Int 2Fh (1684) W386_GET_DEVICE_API dev=0x000a
<WINOLDAP> Int 2Fh (1684) W386_GET_DEVICE_API dev=0x000a
<WINOLDAP> Int 2Fh (4001) NOTIFY BACKGROUND SWITCH
<WINOLDAP> Int 2Fh (4002) NOTIFY FOREGROUND SWITCH
```

WINOLDAP (which is a task, not a DLL) makes a series of INT 2Fh calls. The interesting ones here are the 2F/1684 calls, which WINOLDAP uses to access the protected-mode APIs provided by four different Windows virtual device drivers. Which ones? We have to look up these device numbers in the VMM.INC file included with the DDK:

```
VDD_Device_ID        EQU 0000Ah    ; Virtual Display Device
VMD_Device_ID        EQU 0000Ch    ; Virtual Mouse Device
VKD_Device_ID        EQU 0000Dh    ; Virtual Keyboard Device
SHELL_Device_ID      EQU 00017h    ; SHELL Device
```

Add these to a grabber (such as V7VGA.3GR) and WINOLDAP (such as WIN-OA386.MOD), and starting a DOS box turns out to be a major piece of baroque orchestration.

Fixing WINIO

So far, we just wowed ourselves with the *level* of activity that WISPY reveals. But WISPY is genuinely useful on occasion. For example, the program helped us test a major change in the WINIO library, from which WISPY itself is built. The original version of the wmhandler_yield() function that we've used in this chapter once looked something like this:

```
void wmhandler_yield(void)
{
    MSG msg;
    while (PeekMessage(&msg, NULL, NULL, NULL, PM_REMOVE))
    {
        TranslateMessage(&msg);
        DispatchMessage(&msg);
    }
}
```

When a WINIO program returns from or falls off the end of main(), it goes into the following loop:

```
for (;;)
    wmhandler_yield();
```

This conforms to Windows programming conventional wisdom about using a PeekMessage() loop in programs that need to do "background processing." However, we then read four Microsoft KnowledgeBase articles that completely convinced us that using PeekMessage() in this way was an antisocial act:

- "DOS Idle Interrupts and Word for Windows" (Q69545)
- "Idle Interrupt (INT 28h) Under Windows 3.0" (Q75536)
- "Power-Friendly Applications"s (Q74528)
- "How to Use PeekMessage Correctly" (Q74042)

These Microsoft articles show that, during a PeekMessage() loop, the whole system is effectively parked inside your application. With GetMessage(), in contrast, when there are no messages for you, your application is parked inside the system. If there is nothing happening, the Reschedule() function in KERNEL can issue INT 28h (Idle) and INT 2Fh AH=1689 (Kernel Idle) calls, which can be used by TSRs or by power management on a notebook computer with a 386SL chip. We decided to rewrite wmhandler_yield() in this way:

```
void wmhandler_yield(void)
    {
    MSG msg;
    if (InSendMessage())     // yielding control during
        return;              // SendMessage can lead to deadlock
    for (;;)
    {
        if (! GetMessage(&msg, NULL, 0, 0))
            break;
        TranslateMessage(&msg);
        DispatchMessage(&msg);
        if (! PeekMessage(&msg, NULL, NULL, NULL, PM_NOREMOVE))
            break;
    }
}
```

Notice the change from while (PeekMessage()) to if (GetMessage()). (The addition of InSendMessage() was just another, unrelated addition that we realized was needed at the same time.)

WISPY provided the perfect vehicle for testing this change. Using a version compiled with the old WINIO, we ran WISPY 0x28, kept our hands off the keyboard, and waited to see if any INT 28h calls would be logged; none were. We then recompiled WISPY with the new, GetMessage-based WINIO, and again ran WISPY 0x28. The logged INT 28h calls poured forth in a torrent!

We then ran a similar test with WISPY 0x2F to see if the Kernel Idle call was getting through. Sure enough, with the new WINIO it was. In fact, since WISPY 0x2F will generally be used for purposes other than watching Kernel Idle calls, we had to introduce a -NOIDLE command-line option that suppresses these, so you can see the INT 2Fh calls you *are* interested in.

WISPY gives the Windows programmer a different perspective on what goes on in Windows. In some ways, WISPY's purpose is to make Windows a little *less* familiar-looking to the Windows programmer (though perhaps more familiar-looking to a DOS habitue). WinExecs show up as 21/4B calls; DPMI suddenly appears as a major player; all sorts of things you didn't want to even think about come into view. Who would have thought that the difference between GetMessage() and PeekMessage() was an intimate connection with the DOS INT 28h Idle interrupt? Actually, the Microsoft KnowledgeBase articles alerted us to this connection between message retrieval and INT 28h, but with WISPY we can *see* the difference between doing message retrieval the wrong way and doing it the right way.

All this serves to reinforce the fact that, for all its perceived differences, Windows is essentially a big DOS extender application, still dependent on DOS services to function.

Having sung the praises of WISPY, we have to note that the program as it stands now has a number of crushing limitations:

- It isn't script-driven like INTRSPY, so you cannot select what it displays at any granularity finer than the interrupt number. This is why the -NOIDLE hack was needed. Similarly, if you run WISPY 0x21 and the Windows Clock is running, all you ever see are DOS Get Date and Get Time calls. There's currently no way to write a script that filters these out, so watching INT 21h while Clock is running is a useless exercise.

- During the lag between when an interrupt occurs and when WISPY pulls it out of its queue for display, the contents of memory can change. Occasionally, WISPY displays stale data, or even garbage, in DS:DX.

- WISPY only traps interrupts on entry and then chains to the previous handler, using the _chain_intr() function provided with Microsoft C and Borland C++ 3.0. As a result, WISPY doesn't see interrupt returns and therefore can't present a *hierarchy* of interrupts, in the way that SNOOP does with WM_ messages.

- WISPY doesn't intercept the Windows Dos3Call() function. This function does *not* do an INT 21h; disassembly reveals that it directly *calls* KERNEL's INT 21h handler, using a PUSHF simulated interrupt. WISPY misses all Dos3Calls. In particular, every time a task terminates, it does so via the INT 21h AH=4Ch exit call; this call is made with Dos3Call() rather than with an actual INT 21h, so WISPY doesn't see it. You can, of course, watch Dos3Call() with WINICE:

```
:bpx Dos3Call
:dex 0 ds:dx
```

- Even more important, most of the code in KERNEL does not go through Dos3Call() or INT 21h at all. It just *calls* the INT 21h handler directly, with a simulated interrupt. Rather than pointing an interrupt at itself (WISPY uses the DOS Set Vector function), WISPY should just slap a breakpoint on the first instruction of the currently installed handlers for whatever interrupts it's supposed to be watching. That would get everything. You can do this today in WINICE:

```
:idt 21
0021  TrapG16  011F:00001B34  DPL=3  P
:bpx 11f:1b34
:dex 0 ds:dx
```

Stop the Presses!

Just as this book was going to press, we corrected this major limitation of WISPY. All it took was a call to the undocumented GetSetKernelDOSProc() function, which is described in chapter 5. Now WISPY hooks INT 21h differently from other interrupts: Instead of using the DOS Set Vector function (INT 21h AH=25h), it uses GetSetKernelDOSProc(). This one little undocumented call makes an enormous difference to WISPY's usability. For example, this version of WISPY helps investigate the Windows PSP problem, discussed in the chapter 5 entry on the PSP. ■

This completes our inspection tour of Windows logging/tracing programs. Basically, such a program sets up a series of semi-permanent breakpoints and prints something whenever the breakpoint is triggered. Other noninteractive debuggers like this are DDE watchers (these really seem like "protocol analyzers"), API call watchers, and programs that hang off the TOOLHELP NotifyRegister() function. Three such programs are the DBWIN application that comes (with source code) with the 3.1 SDK, the DRWATSON program, and our own CORONER, presented (with source code) in chapter 10. Like DRWATSON, CORONER uses NotifyRegister() to camp out on INT 0Dh, waiting for a GP fault to happen. Both programs log the "state of the world" at the time of the GP fault to a file. Clearly, there's room for additional utilities that do similar things with events other than UAEs.

Windows Browsers

Another type of tool for exploring Windows is the browser; HEAPWALK is the model for all such programs (HEAPWALK itself appears to be modeled on Macintosh programs such as "Uriah Heap"). Numerous programs of this kind appear, with source code, elsewhere in this book. In particular, check out the GDIWALK and USERWALK programs in chapters 6 and 8, the WINWALK program in chapter 10 and the MODWALK and TASKWALK programs in chapter 5.

CHAPTER ■ 5

KERNEL: Windows System Services

KERNEL is the Windows module responsible for the traditional operating-system services: memory management (which in Windows includes resource and atom-table management), loading of programs (which in Windows includes dynamic linking), scheduling of tasks, and so on. While Windows programs cooperate in Windows scheduling by calling USER functions such as GetMessage() and PeekMessage(), the scheduler itself lives in KERNEL.

One key component of any standalone operating system—file management—is *not* really performed by KERNEL, but instead is passed off to MS-DOS via INT 21h calls. The Windows DOS interface is located in KERNEL, and KERNEL performs a large amount of DOS Program Segment Prefix (PSP) manipulation so that multiple Windows tasks can safely do file I/O while running above a single copy of MS-DOS.

In other words, KERNEL provides the many operating-system services one would like to see in a protected-mode version of MS-DOS, but which DOS does not provide. KERNEL also provides the Windows interface to those few services (file I/O, PSP management) that DOS *does* provide.

Versions of KERNEL

Whereas the USER module is contained in the USER.EXE dynamic link library (DLL) USER.EXE and the GDI module is contained in GDI.EXE, the KERNEL module is not necessarily contained in KERNEL.EXE. A file name in Windows need not match the module name (see the explanation of the segmented-executable NE header in chapter 2). In fact, KERNEL.EXE is used only in the defunct Windows 3.0 real mode. Another version of the KERNEL module, the Windows 3.0 SDK file SKERNEL.EXE, operates only in 3.0 real mode and therefore can, like KERNEL.EXE, be safely ignored.

The two important versions of KERNEL are KRNL286.EXE and KRNL-386.EXE. KRNL286.EXE is used in Windows 3.0 and 3.1 Standard mode. The file

KRNL386.EXE is used in Windows 3.0 Enhanced mode and, in Windows 3.1, either in Enhanced mode or when running Standard mode on a 386 or higher processor. In other words, Windows 3.0 provides mode-specific versions of the KERNEL module; 3.1 provides processor-specific versions.

In addition to processor and Windows mode differences, it is important to note that there are both retail and debug versions of KRNL286.EXE and KRNL386.EXE. Thus, any use of undocumented features in KERNEL, particularly data structures, should keep track of the following differences:

- Windows 3.0 vs. 3.1
- Windows 3.0 Standard mode vs. Enhanced mode (real mode can be safely ignored)
- Windows 3.1 on an 80286 processor vs. an 80386+ processor
- Retail vs. debug

Spelling out the possibilities in gory detail, we get this list:

- Windows 3.0 Standard mode retail
- Windows 3.0 Standard mode debug
- Windows 3.0 Enhanced mode retail
- Windows 3.0 Enhanced mode debug
- Windows 3.1 286 retail
- Windows 3.1 286 debug
- Windows 3.1 386+ (Standard and Enhanced) retail
- Windows 3.1 386+ (Standard and Enhanced) debug

The combination of Windows 3.1 Standard mode on an 80386 or higher processor is particularly confusing. For example, the string displayed by the following code fragment contains "KRNL386.EXE," *not* "KRNL286.EXE":

```
char buf[128];
WORD wVersion = GetVersion();
LONG lFlags = GetWinFlags();
GetModuleFileName(GetModuleHandle("KERNEL"), buf, 128);
if (wVersion == 0x0a03)              // Windows 3.1
   if (lFlags & WF_STANDARD)         // Standard mode
      if (! (lFlags & WF_CPU286))    // must be on an 80386 or higher
         display(buf);               // "KRNL386.EXE"
```

This code implies that a feature of Windows 3.0 Enhanced mode may also be found in Windows 3.1 in Standard mode; for an example, see the entry on the Global Heap later in this chapter.

To check for a debug version of Windows, use the GetSystemMetrics() function:

```
if (GetSystemMetrics(SM_DEBUG) != 0)
    display("This is a Debug version of Windows");
```

KERNEL Data Structures

These differences affect undocumented data structures rather than undocumented functions. Using undocumented data structures is thus much more risky than using undocumented functions. Wherever possible, you should see if the documented ToolHelp interface (described in chapter 10) provides the information you need.

The key structures discussed in this chapter are these:

- Atom table
- Global heap and arena (also see GlobalMasterHandle)
- Instance data
- Local heap and arena
- Module table
- Task database
- Task queue structure (also see GetTaskQueue)

These structures are accessed by both documented and undocumented KERNEL functions. For instance, the undocumented GlobalMasterHandle() function returns a selector to the undocumented global heap structure; the documented Get-CurrentTask() function returns a selector to a task database whose structure is undocumented.

It is, of course, entirely appropriate that internal data structures such as these be undocumented; this is what the structured programming methodology of "information hiding" is all about. Programmers can call an interface function such as GlobalAlloc() or LocalAlloc() without having to know about the layout of the global and local heap and arena structures. You can use the atom-table functions without knowing, or caring, whether Windows resolves hash-table collisions using buckets or linear probing. Leaving these structures undocumented also allows Microsoft to change (and possibly even improve) the internals of future Windows versions.

Furthermore, a key programming principle is the ability to use a handle without knowing what the handle is. If one function returns a module handle and another function expects a module handle, your program should be able to act as a pipe, passing the handle (also known as a "magic cookie") from one function to the next, without knowing what this handle is.

In this chapter, though, we will tell you exactly what all these handles are, (that is, what data structures they point to). We think this is important for two main reasons:

1. The whole "you can use a handle without knowing what it points to" perspective (which we might call The Magic Cookie Philosophy) has to some extent backfired because programmers who don't know what these handles are inevitably get them confused. Even Microsoft has acknowledged that this is a problem in Windows programming, and it has issued an excellent technical note written by Bob Gunderson called "Modules, Instances, and Tasks" that tries to sort out what these handles are and how they relate.

2. The undocumented KERNEL data structures contain a wealth of information often unavailable elsewhere. A brief glance at this chapter's entries for the Task Database and Task Queue structures will probably convince you that, even though the principle of information hiding quite rightly holds that it is generally better *not* to know about something than it is to know about it, in the case of these Windows internal data structures, it is much better to know about these structures than to *not* know about them.

For example, let's say you are using the documented IsTask() function provided by Windows 3.1, and you would like to have equivalent functionality when running under Windows 3.0. You could play by the rules, see that there is no such function in Windows 3.0, and just give up. But once you know that the Task Database structure contains a 'TD' (4454h) signature at offset 0FAh, it is easy to write your own IsTask() that works under Windows 3.0.

```
#define TD_SIGN      0x4454   /* 'TD' = Task Database */
#define OFS_TD_SIGN 0xFA      /* location of 'TD' signature in Task DB */

extern DWORD FAR PASCAL GetSelectorLimit(WORD w);

BOOL IsValidTask(WORD w)
{
    WORD far *lpwMaybeTask;
    if (! w)
        return FALSE;
    if (GetSelectorLimit(w) < (OFS_TD_SIGN + 2))
        return FALSE;
    lpwMaybeTask = (WORD far *) MK_FP(w, OFS_TD_SIGN);
    return (*lpwMaybeTask == TD_SIGN);
}
```

This, in fact, is what KERNEL itself does in Windows 3.1, except that KERNEL uses the LSL instruction rather than the GetSelectorLimit function (note that there is still a danger of getting a segment not-present fault if a totally random bogus number is passed in).

```
ISTASK:
    mov ax, _w
```

```
    or ax, ax
    je fail            ; 0 is not a valid task handle
    lsl bx, ax         ; get the limit (size-1) of _w
    jne fail           ; fail if not even a valid selector
    cmp bx, OFCh
    jl fail            ; fail if less than OFCh bytes
    mov es, ax
    cmp word ptr es:[OFAh], 4454h
    jne fail           ; fail if no 'TD' signature at offset OFAh
    jmp short success
fail:
    xor ax, ax
success:
    retf 2
```

Thus, taking a two-byte number, seeing if it is a valid selector to a segment with at least 0FCh bytes, and seeing if it has the TD signature at offset 0FAh really is equivalent to calling IsTask() and can be extremely useful when IsTask() itself isn't available. So much for information hiding. Of course, if you don't care about 3.0 compatibility (you probably should, though), there is absolutely no reason to jump through these hoops.

Handles, Handles Everywhere

KERNEL functions return and expect several different types of handles, and as noted earlier it is easy to get them confused. Microsoft's documentation does not clearly spell out how they all interrelate. The major handles, with an example function that returns the handle, an example function that expects it as a parameter, and the data structure it corresponds to (explained in detail elsewhere in this chapter), are as follows:

	RETURNED FROM	EXPECTED BY	SELECTOR TO
hModule	GetModuleHandle	GetProcAddress	Module Table
hTask	GetCurrentTask	EnumTaskWindows	Task Database
hInstance	WinExec	MakeProcInstance	Instance Data (DGROUP)
hPDB	GetCurrentPDB		Program Segment Prefix (PSP)
hTaskQ	InsendMessage		Task Queue

Given one kind of handle, it is often important to know how to get a different kind. The following set of macros, functions, and comments attempts to present The Official Undocumented Windows Magic Handle Decoder Ring in handy two-dimensional form; in addition to showing the KERNEL handles, the USER hWnd handle is included, too. Note that some of these conversions are not true functions because, for example, a task can have more than one window or a module can have more than one task.

```
/*
HANDLES.H -- KERNEL-related handles

Macros and functions (see HANDLES.C) for:
    Task Database handles (HTASK)
    Task Queue handles
    Module Database handles (HMODULE)
    Instance (DGROUP) handles
    Window handles (HWND)
    PSP/PDB
    Selector validation

from "Undocumented Windows" by Schulman et al. (Addison-Wesley, 1992)
Chapter 5: KERNEL
Copyright (c) Andrew Schulman and Matt Pietrek 1992
*/

#ifdef __cplusplus
extern "C" {
#endif

#ifndef MK_FP
#define MK_FP(s,o) ((void far *) (((DWORD) (s) << 16) | (o)))
#endif
/* Convert a handle to a selector */
WORD HandleToSel(HANDLE h);

/* Turn hTask into hModule:  use WORD at offset 1Eh in the Task
Database (TDB) */
#define HMODULE_FROM_HTASK(hTask) \
    *((WORD far *) MK_FP(hTask, 0x1E))

/* Get module handle for current task */
#define GetCurrentModule() \
    HMODULE_FROM_HTASK(GetCurrentTask())

/* Turn hTask into hInstance:  use WORD at offset 1Ch in the TDB */
#define HINSTANCE_FROM_HTASK(hTask) \
    *((WORD far *) MK_FP(hTask, 0x1C))

/* Turn hTask into hWnd:  a task can have more than one window;
use the documented EnumTaskWindows() function */

/* Turn hTask into PSP:  use WORD at offset 60h in the TDB */
#define PSP_FROM_HTASK(hTask) \
    *((WORD far *) MK_FP(hTask, 0x60))

/* Turn hTask into hTaskQ:  use the undocumented GetTaskQueue()
function */

/* Turn hInstance into hModule:  use the GetInstanceModule()
```

macro provided with the Windows 3.1 SDK (WINDOWSX.H), or use the
undocumented GetExePtr() function. Remember that hInstance is
just a task's default data segment (DGROUP). */
#define HMODULE_FROM_HINSTANCE(hInstance) \
    GetModuleHandle(MK_FP(0, hInstance))

/* Turn hInstance into hTask */
WORD hTask_from_hInstance(WORD hInstance);

/* Turn hInstance into hWnd: use the "Turn hInstance into an
hTask" technique, then the "hTask into hWnd" technique */

/* Turn hInstance into PSP: get hTask from hInstance, then PSP
from hTask */
#define PSP_FROM_HINSTANCE(hInstance) \
    PSP_FROM_HTASK(hTask_from_hInstance(hInstance))

/* Turn hModule into hInstance: though note that this
is a true function only for DLLs (see IsModuleDLL()) */
WORD hInstance_from_hModule(WORD hModule);

/* a useful synonym */
#define GetModuleDgroup(hModule) \
    hInstance_from_hModule(hModule)

/* Turn hModule into hTask: not always possible, as multiple tasks
can share the same module table (see hModule into hInstance, above),
and because DLL modules do not have an hTask. If the load count at
offset 2 in the module table is 1, i.e., *((WORD far *)
MK_FP(hModule, 2)) == 1, the hTask can be obtained by first getting
the hInstance for the module (see "hModule into hInstance," above),
then getting the hTask from the hInstance (see "hInstance into
hTask," above) */

/* Turn hModule to hWnd: To obtain a list of windows associated with
an hModule, first use the "hModule into hTask" technique above, then
use the documented EnumTaskWindows() function to list the top-level
windows */

/* Turn hWnd into hTask: use the documented GetWindowTask() function */

/* Turn hWnd into hModule: get hTask from hWnd, then hModule
from hTask */
#define HMODULE_FROM_HWND(hWnd) \
    HMODULE_FROM_HTASK(GetWindowTask(hWnd))

/* Turn hWnd into hInstance: use the documented GetWindowWord(hwnd,
GWW_HINSTANCE) call */

/* Turn PDB (PSP) into hTask */
HANDLE hTask_from_PSP(WORD wPSP);

/* Turn PDB into hModule, hInstance, or hWnd: follow "PDB into hTask"
instructions above, then convert hTask */
#define HMODULE_FROM_PSP(wPSP) \

```
    HMODULE_FROM_HTASK(hTask_from_PSP(wPSP))

#define HINSTANCE_FROM_PSP(wPSP) \
    HINSTANCE_FROM_HTASK(hTask_from_PSP(wPSP))

/* Turn hTaskQ into hTask */
#define HTASK_FROM_HTASKQ(hTaskQ) \
    *((WORD far *) MK_FP(hTaskQ, 2))

/* Turn hTaskQ into hInstance, but don't use hInstance field in
Task Queue structure, which moves from 3.0 to 3.1 */
#define HINSTANCE_FROM_HTASKQ(hTaskQ) \
    HINSTANCE_FROM_HTASK(HTASK_FROM_HTASKQ(hTaskQ))

/* Turn hTaskQ into hModule: Useful for getting name of sender
from InSendMessage() */
#define HMODULE_FROM_HTASKQ(hTaskQ) \
    HMODULE_FROM_HINSTANCE(HINSTANCE_FROM_HTASKQ(hTaskQ))

/* Is handle for a DLL rather than a task? */
BOOL IsModuleDLL(HANDLE hModule);

/* C interface to protected-mode instructions; must compile
with 286 instructions (Borland -2, Microsoft -G2) */
BOOL verr(WORD wSel);    // verify for reading
BOOL verw(WORD wSel);    // verify for writing
WORD lsl(WORD wSel);     // load segment limit
WORD lar(WORD wSel);     // load access rights

/* for use with LAR */
#define CODEDATA_MASK   8
#define CODE            8
#define DATA            0

/* Are we using the 16-bit or 32-bit KERNEL?
Returns 16 for KRNL286, 32 for KRNL386, 0 for real mode */
int Kernel1632(void);

/* Does the far pointer point to a valid local heap info struct? */
BOOL IsValidLocalHeap(BYTE far *fp);

/* Is this handle for a Module Database? */
BOOL IsValidModuleHandle(HANDLE h);

/* Is this handle for a DOS Program Segment Prefix (PSP; alias PDB)? */
BOOL IsValidPSP(HANDLE h);

/* Is this handle for a Task Database?  3.1 has documented
IsTask(), but it's not in 3.0, so do our own */
BOOL IsValidTask(HANDLE h);

/* Not perfect, but a reasonable test:  a Task Queue
contains a valid task handle at offset 2 */
#define IsTaskQueue(h) \
    IsValidTask(HTASK_FROM_HTASKQ(h))
```

```c
#ifdef __cplusplus
}
#endif

/*
HANDLES.C -- KERNEL-related handles
from "Undocumented Windows" by Schulman et al. (Addison-Wesley, 1992)
Chapter 5: KERNEL
Copyright (c) Andrew Schulman and Matt Pietrek 1992
*/

#include <dos.h>
#include "windows.h"
#include "handles.h"

extern DWORD FAR PASCAL GetSelectorBase(WORD wSel);
extern DWORD FAR PASCAL GetSelectorLimit(WORD wSel);
extern WORD FAR PASCAL SetSelectorBase(WORD wSel, DWORD dwBase);
extern WORD FAR PASCAL SetSelectorLimit(WORD wSel, DWORD dwLimit);

/* Convert a handle to a selector, just the way ToolHelp
   does.  See WINMOD.C for explanation */
WORD HandleToSel(HANDLE h)
{
    static WORD wVers = 0;
    if (! wVers)     // one-time initialization
        wVers = (WORD) GetVersion();
    if (wVers == 3) // 3.0: handles = selectors+1
        return ((h & 2) == 2) ? h-1 : h;
    else            // 3.1++: handles = selectors-1
        return (h | 1);
}

/* Turn hInstance into hTask:  walk the task list (see sample
code in the entries for GetCurrentTask() and the Task Database),
searching for a TDB whose WORD at offset 1Ch matches the hInstance,
i.e., where HINSTANCE_FROM_HTASK(hTask) == hInstance */
WORD hTask_from_hInstance(WORD hInstance)
{
    DWORD (FAR PASCAL *GetCurrentTaskD)(void) = GetCurrentTask;
    DWORD dwTask = GetCurrentTaskD();
    HANDLE hTask = HIWORD(dwTask);        // get base of linked list
    for (;;)
    {
        if (HINSTANCE_FROM_HTASK(hTask) == hInstance)
            return hTask;

        /* Get handle of the next task from offset 0 in the Task DB */
        if ((hTask = *((WORD far *) MK_FP(hTask, 0))) == 0)
            break;
    }
    /* still here -- didn't find it */
    return 0;
}
```

```
/* Turn PDB (PSP) into hTask: this is for the truly masochistic. Use
GetSelectorBase() to obtain the linear address of the PSP. Subtract
100h, and create a new selector with the resulting base address. This
new selector points at the TDB, and the hTask can be found at offset
0Ch. It would be wise to "sanity check" by making sure that the WORD
at offset 0FAh is 'TD' */
HANDLE hTask_from_PSP(WORD wPSP)
{
    WORD hTask, hMyTask, wDS;
    _asm mov wDS, ds
    hMyTask = AllocSelector(wDS);    // use DS as model
    SetSelectorBase(hMyTask, GetSelectorBase(wPSP) - 0x100);
    SetSelectorLimit(hMyTask, 0x100);
    if (*((WORD far *) MK_FP(hMyTask, 0xFA)) != 0x4454) // 'TD'
    {
        FreeSelector(hMyTask);
        return 0;   // no 'TD' signature: something wrong
    }
    hTask = *((WORD far *) MK_FP(hMyTask, 0x0c)); // canonical hTask
    if (*((WORD far *) MK_FP(hTask, 0xFA)) != 0x4454)   // 'TD'
        hTask = 0;   // no 'TD' signature: something wrong
    FreeSelector(hMyTask);
    return hTask;
}


/* Turn hModule into hInstance: a module can have more than one
instance, unless if it's a DLL. Use offset 0Eh in the Module Table,
i.e., *((WORD far *) MK_FP(hModule, 0x0e)), to obtain the logical
segment number (1, 2, etc.) of the DGROUP for the module. Then, look
up the actual DGROUP selector in the segment portion of the module
table. Treat this DGROUP as the hInstance. If the module is for a
task rather than a DLL, the hInstance is for the most recent task
that's still using the module table, and is not correct for the
other invocations of the program.
    But a much simpler way is to get the hInstance returned from
LoadLibrary(). This is used in hInstance_from_hModule */
WORD hInstance_from_hModule(WORD hModule)
{
    char buf[128];
    WORD hInstance;
    GetModuleFileName(hModule, buf, 128);
    /* remember, module is already loaded */
    hInstance = LoadLibrary(buf);   // ref++
    FreeLibrary(hInstance);         // ref--
    return HIWORD((DWORD) GlobalLock(hInstance));
}


#define NEMAGIC       0x454E      /* new EXE magic id:  'NE'  */
#define NEFLAGS_OFS 0x0c          /* offset of flags in NE header */
#define DLL_FLAG      0x8000      /* is module a DLL? */

/* Is handle for a DLL rather than for a task? Use the flags at
    offset 0Ch in the Module Database */
```

```c
BOOL IsModuleDLL(HANDLE hModule)
{
    if (*((WORD far *) MK_FP(hModule, 0)) != NEMAGIC)
        return FALSE;    // it's not even a module, much less a DLL
    else
        return (*((WORD far *) MK_FP(hModule, NEFLAGS_OFS)) & DLL_FLAG);
}

/* C interface to protected-mode instructions; must compile
   with 286 instructions (Borland -2, Microsoft -G2) */

/* Verify for Reading (VERR) instruction */
BOOL verr(WORD wSel)
{
    if (! wSel) return 0;    /* workaround 386 bug: Hummel, p.584 */
    _asm verr word ptr wSel
    _asm je short ok
    return 0;    // not valid for reading
ok: return 1;    // is valid for reading
}

/* Verify for Writing (VERW) instruction */
BOOL verw(WORD wSel)
{
    if (! wSel) return 0;    /* workaround 386 bug: Hummel, p.585 */
    _asm verw word ptr wSel
    _asm je short ok
    return 0;    // not valid for writing
ok: return 1;    // is valid for writing
}

/* C interface to protected-mode Load Access Rights (LAR) instruction */
WORD lar(WORD wSel)
{
    if (! wSel) return 0;    /* workaround 386 bug: Hummel, p.448 */
    _asm lar ax, wSel
    _asm jne short error
    _asm shr ax, 8
    _asm jmp short no_error; /* value in AX */
error:
    return 0;
no_error:;
}

/* C interface to LSL (Load Segment Limit) instruction */
WORD lsl(WORD wSel)
{
    if (! wSel) return 0;    /* workaround 386 bug: Hummel, p.471 */
    _asm lsl ax, wSel
    _asm jne short error
    _asm jmp short no_error; /* value in AX */
error:
    return 0;
no_error:;
}
```

```
/* Are we using the 16-bit or 32-bit KERNEL?
   Returns 16 for KRNL286, 32 for KRNL386, 0 for real mode */
int Kernel1632(void)
{
    LONG lFlags = GetWinFlags();
    if (GetVersion() == 0x0003) // Windows 3.0: mode-dependent
    {
        if (lFlags & WF_STANDARD)        return 16;
        else if (lFlags & WF_ENHANCED)   return 32;
        else /* yuk! real mode! */       return 0;
    }
    else     // Windows 3.1+: processor-dependent
        return (lFlags & WF_CPU286) ? 16 : 32;
}
#define LHMAGIC      0x484C     /* 'LH' signature for Local Heap */
#define NEMAGIC      0x454E     /* new EXE magic id:  'NE'  */
#define PSPMAGIC     0x20CD     /* INT 20h instruction */
#define TDBMAGIC     0x4454     /* 'TD' signature for Task */

/* Does the far pointer point to a valid local heap info struct? */
BOOL IsValidLocalHeap(BYTE far *fp)
{
    WORD wMagicOffset = (Kernel1632() == 16) ? 0x22 : 0x28;
    return (*((WORD far *) &fp[wMagicOffset]) == LHMAGIC);
}

/* Is this handle for a Module Database? */
BOOL IsValidModuleHandle(HANDLE h)
{
    WORD far *fp;
    if (! verr(h))
        return 0;
    fp = MK_FP(h, 0);
    return (*fp == NEMAGIC);  // make sure starts with 'NE' signature
}

/* Is this handle for a DOS Program Segment Prefix (PSP; alias PDB)? */
BOOL IsValidPSP(HANDLE h)
{
    WORD far *fp;
    if (! verr(h))
        return 0;
    fp = MK_FP(h, 0);
    return (*fp == PSPMAGIC); // make sure starts with INT 20h
}

/* Is this handle for a Task Database?  3.1 has documented
   IsTask(), but it's not in 3.0, so do our own */
BOOL IsValidTask(HANDLE h)
{
    WORD far *fp;
    if (! verr(h))
        return FALSE;
    if (GetSelectorLimit(h) < 0xFC)
```

```
        return FALSE;
    fp = MK_FP(h, 0xFA);
    return (*fp == TDBMAGIC);
}
```

The following sample program exercises the handle-conversion macros and functions and can be used as the basis for an undocumented Windows "compatibility suite" to test out new or oddball versions of Windows. This program, like all the sample programs in this chapter, uses the WINIO library from chapter 4:

```
/*
TESTHAND.C -- test driver for HANDLES.H, HANDLES.C
from "Undocumented Windows" by Schulman et al. (Addison-Wesley 1992)
Chapter 5: KERNEL
*/

#include <stdlib.h>
#include <assert.h>
#include "windows.h"
#include "winio.h"
#include "handles.h"

main()
{
    extern HANDLE __hInst;  // in ARGCARGV.C
    HANDLE hTask, hModule, hModule2, hInstance, PSP;

    printf("Windows %d.%02d %s mode (%s)\n",
        LOBYTE(GetVersion()), HIBYTE(GetVersion()),
        (GetWinFlags() & WF_STANDARD) ? "Standard" : "Enhanced",
        (GetSystemMetrics(SM_DEBUG)) ? "DEBUG" : "RETAIL");

    hTask = GetCurrentTask();
    printf("hTask = %04x\n", hTask);

    hInstance = HINSTANCE_FROM_HTASK(hTask);
    printf("hInstance = %04x\n", hInstance);
    assert(hInstance == __hInst);

    hModule = HMODULE_FROM_HTASK(hTask);
    hModule2 = HMODULE_FROM_HINSTANCE(hInstance);
    printf("hModule = %04x\n", hModule);
    assert(hModule == hModule2);

    PSP = PSP_FROM_HTASK(hTask);
    printf("PSP = %04x\n", PSP);
    assert(PSP == GetCurrentPDB());

    assert(hTask_from_hInstance(hInstance) == hTask);
    assert(PSP_FROM_HINSTANCE(hInstance) == PSP);
    assert(hTask_from_PSP(PSP) == hTask);
    assert(HINSTANCE_FROM_PSP(PSP) == hInstance);
```

```
assert(IsValidModuleHandle(GetCurrentModule()));
assert(IsValidPSP(GetCurrentPDB()));
assert(IsValidTask(GetCurrentTask()));

return 0;
}
```

If all goes well, the program will do nothing more than display its own hTask, hInstance, hModule, and PSP. In the event of an error, an assert will be displayed.

KERNEL Exports and Imports

In Windows 3.0, KERNEL exports over 200 items; in 3.1, it exports over 400. Of these, about 100 are undocumented and are discussed at length in this chapter. Most of the exports from KERNEL are functions, but there are also several important constants (such as __AHINCR) and protected-mode selectors (such as __0000H).

As one would hope from a "kernel," KERNEL is considerably smaller than the other two key components of Windows. Whereas the retail (i.e., nondebug) USER.EXE is about 270K and GDI.EXE is about 160K, KRNL286.EXE is about 60K and KRNL386.EXE is about 90K. KERNEL is built from about sixty .OBJ modules.

In one sense, though, KERNEL is not a "kernel" at all. As noted in chapters 1 and 2, examination of the executable header for KERNEL makes it seem as if this module depends on no other modules. This is precisely what one expects from an operating-system kernel. However, in Windows there are documented functions, LoadLibrary() and GetProcAddress(), that allow a program or DLL to link to other modules it is running; these functions live in KERNEL and are used internally, by KERNEL itself, to tie into other parts of Windows, particularly USER. For example, the scheduler in KERNEL calls the IsUserIdle() function in USER; the undocumented DoSignal() function in KERNEL calls functions in USER, such as GetFocus(), IsWindow(), and GetWindowTask(); and the global-heap compacter in KERNEL calls the USER PostMessage() function to issue WM_COMPACTING messages.

In other words, KERNEL knows about WM_ messages and window handles! This is somewhat unavoidable, but the kernel's dependencies on other modules nonetheless makes Windows a lot less modular than one might like. It also shows that encapsulation is a lot harder to achieve in a large system, built over a long period of time (Windows has, after all, been under construction for at least seven years), than one might like.

KERNEL Initialization

Many of KERNEL's references to other modules are necessary to *bootstrap* Windows. Like all DLLs, KERNEL has a library-initialization entry point; when KERNEL is first loaded, this library-initialization routine runs. The entry point for KERNEL is in LDBOOT.OBJ and is called, not surprisingly, BOOTSTRAP. BOOTSTRAP and its helper routines load several Windows device drivers (the exact names for the drivers come from settings such as system.drv= and keyboard.drv= in the [boot] section of SYSTEM.INI). BOOTSTRAP also loads a "bootapp" whose default name is PROG-MAN.EXE; interestingly, the loading of "bootapp" is bypassed if the value of a variable "graphics" is zero (USER, KEYBOARD, GDI, and DISPLAY weren't loaded).

All of the modules loaded by the KERNEL BOOTSTRAP routine are, of course, segmented-executable NE files. Because KERNEL itself is also a segmented-executable NE and contains the dynamic-linking module loader that knows about the NE format, how is KERNEL itself loaded? After all, MS-DOS only knows how to load MZ executables and .COM files.

As explained in chapter 2, the NE format is a superset of the MZ format; every NE file also contains an MZ stub. When an NE file such as KRNL286.EXE or KRNL386.EXE is run under MS-DOS, it is the old-style MZ stub that runs. Normally, the old-style MZ stub prints out a message such as "This program requires Microsoft Windows."

In KRNL286.EXE and KRNL386.EXE, however, the stub (called KERNSTUB) opens the executable file (what would be argv[0] in a C program), reads in the MZ header, locates the NE header, and, within the NE header, locates the field that contains the library-initialization entry point CS:IP. It sets the AX register to the value 'OK' (4B4Fh), pushes the entry-point IP on the stack (the initial KERNEL segment is loaded into memory by the DOS loader, which has no idea that the segment is going to turn itself into a butterfly!), and RETFs to it; at this point, BOOTSTRAP starts running. In other words, the old-style MZ stub contains the absolute minimum necessary to start the segmented-executable loader process rolling.

Of course, there is a lot more to KERNEL initialization than the bootstrap loading of the dynamic-linking module loader. In particular, how does Windows get into protected mode? In Windows 3.0, this is taken care of by DOSX.EXE (Standard mode) or WIN386.EXE (Enhanced mode); when KRNL286.EXE or KRNL386.EXE starts running, the system is *already* in protected mode. DOSX.EXE and WIN386.EXE both contain DOS Protected-Mode Interface (DPMI) servers; one of the DPMI services is a function that switches the machine into protected mode, and the address of this function is retrieved by calling INT 2Fh AX=1687h. In Windows 3.0, not only is the DPMI server located in DOSX.EXE and WIN386.EXE, but so is the code that *calls* the DPMI mode-switch function. In Windows 3.1, on the other hand, KERNEL starts up in real (or virtual-8086) mode, and its BOOTSTRAP routine is responsible for calling the DPMI mode-switch function to put the system into protected mode. The mode-switching code itself, of course, continues to reside in DOSX.EXE and WIN386.EXE.

BOOTSTRAP also saves old interrupt vectors and DPMI exception vectors and installs new ones. The interrupts and exceptions handled by KERNEL include 0, 2, 4, 6, 7, 0Bh, 0Ch, 0Dh, 0Eh, 21h, 24h, 2Fh, 3Eh, 3Fh, and 75h.

Since the Windows DOS extender resides outside of KERNEL, in either DOSX.EXE (Standard mode) or WIN386.EXE (Enhanced mode), it may initially not be clear why KERNEL hooks INT 21h. After all, the DOS extenders in DOSX and WIN386 are responsible for catching protected-mode INT 21h calls generated by Windows programs and DLLs and translating them as appropriate into terms understandable by real-mode MS-DOS. But KERNEL needs an INT 21h handler to maintain PSPs for multiple Windows tasks and to track file-system changes (see the FileCdr( ) function).

Undocumented KERNEL Functions

As noted earlier, KERNEL exports about 100 undocumented functions and selectors; these can be divided into a number of rough categories.

SELECTOR MANAGEMENT

KERNEL.183	__0000H
KERNEL.193	__0040H
KERNEL.173	__ROMBIOS
KERNEL.172	AllocAlias
KERNEL.170	AllocCStoDSAlias
KERNEL.206	AllocSelectorArray
KERNEL.186	GetSelectorBase (documented in 3.1)
KERNEL.188	GetSelectorLimit (documented in 3.1)
KERNEL.345	IsSharedSelector
KERNEL.180	LongPtrAdd
KERNEL.321	PrestoChangoSelector (documented in 3.1)
KERNEL.196	SelectorAccessRights
KERNEL.187	SetSelectorBase (documented in 3.1)
KERNEL.189	SetSelectorLimit (documented in 3.1)

TASK AND TASK QUEUE MANAGEMENT

KERNEL.150	DirectedYield (documented in 3.1)
KERNEL.155	GetTaskDS
KERNEL.35	GetTaskQueue
KERNEL.118	GetTaskQueueDS
KERNEL.199	GetTaskQueueES
KERNEL.33	LockCurrentTask
KERNEL.122	IsTaskLocked
KERNEL.158	IsWinOldApTask
KERNEL.117	OldYield
KERNEL.31	PostEvent
KERNEL.32	SetPriority
KERNEL.34	SetTaskQueue
KERNEL.38	SetTaskSignalProc

| KERNEL.30 | WaitEvent (partially documented in 3.1) |

DEBUGGING, DIAGNOSTICS, TOOLHELP ASSIST

KERNEL.205	CVWBreak
KERNEL.314	DebugDefineSegment
KERNEL.329	DebugFillBuffer (K329)
KERNEL.328	_DebugOutput (K328)
KERNEL.340	DiagOutput
KERNEL.339	DiagQuery
KERNEL.327	HandleParamError (K327)
KERNEL.202	RegisterPtrace
KERNEL.332	THHook
KERNEL.341	ToolHelpHook

GP FAULT HANDLING

| KERNEL.342 | __GP |
| KERNEL.338 | HasGPHandler |

RESOURCE MANIPULATION

| KERNEL.168 | DirectResAlloc |

MODULE MANAGEMENT

KERNEL.354	GetAppCompatFlags
KERNEL.133	GetExePtr
KERNEL.105	GetExeVersion
KERNEL.167	GetExpWinVer

DOS INTERFACE AND WINOLDAP

KERNEL.76	DeletePathName
KERNEL.42	DisableDOS
KERNEL.41	EnableDOS
KERNEL.130	FileCdr
KERNEL.319	FlushCachedFileHandle
KERNEL.313	GetLastCriticalError
KERNEL.98	GetLastDiskChange
KERNEL.99	GetLPErrMode
KERNEL.311	GetSetKernelDOSProc
KERNEL.344	GetWinOldApHooks
KERNEL.101	NoHookDOSCall
KERNEL.75	OpenPathName
KERNEL.343	RegisterWinOldApHook
KERNEL.151	WinOldApCall
KERNEL.315	WriteOutProfiles

MEMORY MANAGEMENT

| KERNEL.403 | FarSetOwner (K403) |

KERNEL.404	FarGetOwner (K404)
KERNEL.316	GetFreeMemInfo
KERNEL.138	GetHeapSpaces
KERNEL.26	GlobalFreeAll
KERNEL.159	GlobalHandleNoRIP
KERNEL.28	GlobalMasterHandle
KERNEL.161	LocalCountFree
KERNEL.310	LocalHandleDelta
KERNEL.162	LocalHeapSize
KERNEL.14	LocalNotify
KERNEL.126	MemoryFreed

INITIALIZATION

KERNEL.116	InitLib
KERNEL.91	InitTask (partially documented in 3.1)
KERNEL.141	InitTask1

KERNEL MANIPULATION

KERNEL.125	DisableKernel
KERNEL.124	EnableKernel
KERNEL.2	ExitKernel

NOP

KERNEL.165	A20Proc
KERNEL.160	EMSCopy
KERNEL.157	GetCurPID
KERNEL.123	KbdRst

ROM WINDOWS

| KERNEL.326 | IsRomFile |
| KERNEL.323 | IsRomModule |

MISCELLANEOUS

KERNEL.351	Bunny_351
KERNEL.53	CallProcInstance
KERNEL.139	DoSignal
KERNEL.318	FatalExitHook
KERNEL.201	ReplaceInst
KERNEL.140	SetSigHandler
KERNEL.120	UndefDynlink

In addition to these undocumented functions, and the undocumented data structures discussed earlier, this chapter also covers documented functions whose true parameters and/or return value differ in some way from the documentation. For example, the GetCurrentTask() and GetModuleHandle() functions actually return two values packed into a DWORD, rather than a single WORD. Likewise, most functions that expect an hModule parameter can also be passed an hInstance, functions that expect an hTask parameter can instead be passed 0 to indicate the current task, and so on.

Using the Undocumented Functions

In addition to the general tips elsewhere in this book about using (and *not* using!) undocumented functions, a few points specifically about KERNEL are worth noting.

To use any of the selector-manipulation functions, you will need to remember that Windows is a protected-mode DOS extender and understand the connection between selectors and descriptors. For an introduction to this subject, we recommend the book *Extending DOS* (Second Edition), edited by Ray Duncan (see the bibliography).

In a number of cases undocumented KERNEL functions have the same functionality as DOS Protected-Mode Interface (DPMI) INT 31h calls. Microsoft documents only a handful of DPMI calls for use by Windows programs, but the DPMI INT 31h API, as documented in the 0.9 specification from Intel (again, see the bibliography) is available to the Windows programmer. You may want to consider using a documented DPMI 0.9 function rather than an equivalent undocumented Windows function.

The KERNEL itself uses DPMI and so, in several cases, an undocumented Windows function will be equivalent to a documented DPMI function. (On the other hand, there is plenty of code in both the 3.0 and 3.1 KERNEL that directly bangs on the Global Descriptor Table [GDT] and Local Descriptor Table [LDT], even where an equivalent DPMI function was available. These kids!)

As one example of the near-equivalence of DPMI and some undocumented KERNEL functions, the AllocSelectorArray() function described later works perfectly well in both Windows 3.0 and 3.1, but it *is* undocumented so you may want to consider using the documented DPMI INT 31h AX=0 (Alloc LDT Selectors) function instead. On the other hand, undocumented Windows functions are generally easier to use than DPMI functions, and many of the most useful DPMI calls don't appear in Microsoft's list of approved DPMI functions and/or may be unavailable in Standard mode.

In the following entries on undocumented KERNEL functions, you will sometimes note many different ways of performing the same operation. For example, there seem to be half a dozen different ways to create code/data aliases in Windows. You can call AllocCStoDSAlias(), for instance, or SelectorAccessRights(), or PrestoChangoSelector(), or ChangeSelector().

Finally, remember that the KERNEL sits on top of and relies on lower-level services from the Windows DOS extenders. In Enhanced mode, if something you need seems like a low-level system service that should be in KERNEL but isn't, remember to look at the virtual device driver (VxD) documentation, which comes with the Windows Device Driver Kit (DDK) and which is also described in Dan Norton's book,

Writing Windows Device Drivers. For example, *documented* memory management and scheduling services that are available at the VxD layer are not available even in the *undocumented* functions provided by KERNEL. Remember also to look at the DPMI 0.9 specification when hunting for kernel-like functions. Unlike the VxD API, these are also available in Windows Standard mode. Another place to look is the protected-mode 80x86 instruction set: in particular, look at LAR, LSL, SGDT, SIDT, SLDT, VERR, and VERW. Finally, and most important, check to see if the documented ToolHelp interface provides what you need; chapter 10 of this book provides an in-depth look at ToolHelp.

__0000H   KERNEL.183

```
EXTRN __0000H:ABS
```

0000H is not a function, but a two-byte selector exported by the Windows KERNEL. This protected-mode selector maps the 64K at absolute memory location zero. That is, you would use the value of __0000H, rather than 0, to create a far pointer to the first 64K of memory. A number of useful variables and data structures are kept by the ROM BIOS and MS-DOS in this area of memory, and these can be accessed from a protected-mode Windows program using __0000H. (For more information, see the "Absolute Memory Locations" section of the INTRLIST.EXE database on the disks accompanying *Undocumented DOS*.)

While most other KERNEL selectors (such as __B800H and __F000H) are documented by Microsoft, the extremely useful __0000H and __0040H are not.

The KERNEL selectors are necessary because Windows programs run in protected mode, where memory locations can't be addressed simply by creating a far pointer. To create a far pointer to real-mode address 0000:0522 (absolute memory location 522h), you cannot simply move zero into a segment register because this would cause a general-protection violation (UAE) in Windows Standard and Enhanced modes. Any pointer with a selector of zero is, by definition, a NULL pointer in protected mode. Instead, you can move the value of __0000H into a segment register, as shown in the next example.

According to the Microsoft Windows *Guide to Programming*, KERNEL selectors can be called only from an assembly-language module, where they must be declared with a statement such as EXTRN __0000H:ABS. As shown in the following example, however, a Windows program written in C or another high-level language can also access these selectors.

The value of __0000H will be some number such as 100Dh; this is a protected-mode selector whose corresponding descriptor has a linear base address of zero. Note that this is a *linear*, not a physical, address, but that these addresses are generally equivalent for at least the first 64K of memory. In 3.0, Enhanced mode memory below 64K is mapped 1:1 due to a 386 bug ("errata") that causes the paging hardware to fail in the first 64K. WINA20.386 checks for the presence of this errata, and in its absence hooks and replaces certain VMM services (such as MapIntoV86) so that mapping buffers for DPMI can be allocated below page 10h. Beyond the first 64K, virtual memory means that, in general, linear != physical addresses.

The size of the segment mapped by __0000H is 64K; this can be verified by using GetSelectorLimit(), which returns the maximum valid byte offset (size minus 1), as shown in the following conversation with the CALLFUNC program from chapter 4. This example also shows how to get the value of __0000H by discarding the HIWORD of the return value from GetProcAddress.

```
> kernel getmodulehandle KERNEL
0x00fd
> kernel getprocaddress 0xfd __0000H %Fp
FFFF:100D
> kernel getselectorbase 0x100d %lx
0
> kernel getselectorlimit 0x100d %lx
ffff
```

In other words, if you need to access data past the first 64K of the linear address space, you *cannot* use __0000H.

As an alternative to __0000H, you could allocate a selector and set its base address to zero, using either the undocumented SetSelectorBase() function or the DPMI Set Segment Base Address function (INT 31h AX=0007h).

Support: 3.0, 3.1
Used by: SIW (Norton System Information for Windows)
ASM example: Real-mode code such as the following, which intends to retrieve two bytes from the disk parameter table at real-mode address 0000:0522, would cause a general-protection fault (UAE) under Windows Standard or Enhanced mode:

```
xor ax, ax          ; ax = 0
mov es, ax
mov ax, es:[0522h]
```

Instead of moving zero into a segment register, move the value of __0000H; the actual value of __0000H need not concern the program.

```
extern __0000H:abs
; ...
mov es, __0000H
mov ax, es:[0522h]
```

C example: Real-mode code such as the following would cause a general-protection fault (UAE) under Windows Standard or Enhanced mode:

```
#define MK_FP(seg, ofs) \
    ((void far *) (((unsigned long) (seg) << 16) | (ofs)))
```

```
unsigned char far *fp = MK_FP(0, 0x522);
unsigned char foo = *fp;
```

Instead of using 0 as the segment, use the value of __0000H. One way to access __0000H is shown below, in a technique adapted from Dan Norton's *Writing Windows Device Drivers*. Note that the MK_FP() (make far pointer) macro remains valid in protected mode, so long as you pass in protected-mode selectors such as __0000H rather than real-mode paragraph addresses such as 0.

```
extern WORD _near _0000H;
WORD __0000H = (WORD) (&_0000H);
unsigned char far *fp = MK FP(__0000H, 0x522);
unsigned char foo = *fp;
```

Another way to access Windows variables such as __0000H from C is with GetProcAddress(). For example

```
#define GET_SEL(name) \
    ((WORD) (LOWORD(GetProcAddress(GetModuleHandle("KERNEL"), name))))

// ...
WORD __0000H = GET SEL("__0000H");
unsigned char far *fp = MK FP(__0000H, 0x522);
unsigned char foo = *fp;
```

Because the GET_SEL() macro discards the HIWORD of the four-byte return value from GetProcAddress(), the compiler may warn about "loss of segment." This is benign.

See also: SetSelectorBase, __0040H, __ROMBIOS

__0040H   KERNEL.193

```
EXTRN __0040H:ABS
```

__0040H is not a function but a two-byte selector exported by the Windows KERNEL. This protected-mode selector maps the BIOS data area in the 2FFh bytes at absolute memory location 400h, or real-mode addresses 0000:0400, 0040:0000, etc. You can use the value of __0040H, rather than paragraph 40h, to create a far pointer to the BIOS data area. A number of useful variables and data structures are kept in the BIOS data area, and these can be accessed from a protected-mode Windows program using either __0040H or __0000H.

Most of the remarks in the entry for __0000H also apply to __0040H. In particular, note that __0040H is superfluous because you can always use MK_FP(__0000H, 0x400). However, there are several important additional points about __0040H:

In Windows 3.0 and 3.1, accessing the BIOS data area with C code such as MK_FP(0x40, 0) does not cause a GP fault; neither does the following assembly-language fragment:

```
mov ax, 040h
mov es, ax
mov ax, es:[0C2h]
```

This code works in protected-mode Windows because selector 40h is transparent or bimodal. A bimodal selector is one in which the value of the selector is identical to its own base address, shifted right by 4:

```
sel == sel_base(sel) >> 4
```

Selector 40h is the *only* such bimodal selector in Windows. Because all bimodal selectors of interest would wind up in the GDT, bimodal selectors are almost always avoided in DPMI-compliant DOS extenders; the use of 40h in Windows is a very rare exception. Apparently, it persists because Rational Systems' DOS extender used in Lotus 1-2-3 Rel. 3.x relies on it.

It is a common mistake to think that because 0040:0000 correctly accesses the BIOS data area in protected-mode Windows, so must other segment:offset pairs that in real mode would be equivalent, such as 0000:0400. However, in protected mode 0040:0000 and 0000:0400 are *not* equivalent; although dereferencing the first does happen to work in Windows, dereferencing the second will cause a general-protection violation (UAE).

In Windows 3.0 *only*, the value of __0040H is itself 40h. In Windows 3.1, although selector 40h continues to be supported, the value of __0040H is *not* 40h, but merely some selector such as 101Fh whose value need not concern the application.

The size of the segment corresponding to __0040H is not 64K, as with the other KERNEL selectors; instead, it is 2FFh bytes, about the size of the BIOS data area itself. The Intel 80x86 LSL (load segment limit) instruction can be used to verify the size of the __0040H segment; the limit is the legal valid byte offset within the segment, or the size minus 1:

```
unsigned lsl(unsigned short sel)
{
    _asm xor ax, ax
    _asm lsl ax, word ptr sel
}

// ...
unsigned short __0040H = GET_SEL("__0040H");
unsigned size__0040H = lsl(__0040H) + 1;
```

The undocumented GetSelectorLimit() function can't be used to query the size of the __0040H selector because the bottom three bits of the number 40h are zero,

0040H

placing the corresponding descriptor in the Global Descriptor Table (GDT) rather than in the Local Descriptor Table (LDT). As described in the entry for this function, GetSelectorLimit() forces its parameter to be an LDT selector; using GetSelectorLimit(__0040H) will therefore produce incorrect results.

Support: 3.0, 3.1
Used by: NBWIN (Norton Backup for Windows), SIW (Norton System Information for Windows)
See also: __0000H, __ROMBIOS
Example: See the entry for __0000H

__AHINCR	**KERNEL.113**
__AHSHIFT	**KERNEL.114**

These constants exported from KERNEL are *not* undocumented, even though they are not listed in the Microsoft Windows *Programmer's Reference* or in WINDOWS.H. Instead, they are documented in the Windows *Guide to Programming*. These constants are used to move from one selector to the next in a "huge" (>64K) segment: __AHINCR is added to one selector to find the next selector; its value is simply 1 shifted left by __AHINCR (in C, __AHINCR == 1 << __AHSHIFT). In Windows 3.x, __AHSHIFT is always 3 and __AHINCR is thus always 8.

   For a sample use of __AHINCR, see the entry for AllocSelectorArray().

__GP	**KERNEL.342**

GP is not a function. Instead, it is a far pointer to a table of structures that appear in certain Windows 3.1 modules that perform parameter validation. The structures in the table are of this form:

WORD	segment selector
WORD	low offset
WORD	high offset
WORD	offset within segment of recovery function

   When a GP fault occurs in a module that has a __GP table (GDI, USER, KERNEL, PENWIN, DISPLAY, and MMSYSTEM are the only modules that are checked), the GP fault handler iterates through the table (the end of the table is marked with a 0 segment), checking to see if the faulting address is contained within the range specified by the segment and low/high offsets. If it is, then it assumed to be a recoverable parameter-validation fault, rather than an unrecoverable application error (UAE). The recovery address is where execution will resume after encountering a parameter validation fault. For example, the IsBadXXX() functions in the 3.1 KERNEL contain GP handlers.

Support: 3.1
See also: HasGPHandler, IsBadXXX
Example:

```
/* gp.c */

#include "windows.h"
#include "winio.h"

typedef struct {
    WORD seg, low, high, func;
    } GPTAB;

main(int argc, char *argv[])
{
    GPTAB far *__GP;
    GPTAB far *p;
    char *modname;

    modname = (argc < 2) ? "KERNEL" : argv[1];

    // MUST use GetProcAddress, because __GP in more than one module
    if (! (__GP = GetProcAddress(GetModuleHandle(modname), "__GP")))
        fail("Cannot locate __GP in module");

    printf("GP fault handling in %s\n", modname);
    for (p=__GP; p->seg; p++)
        printf("GP faults in %04x:%04x-%04x handled by %04x:%04x\n",
            p->seg, p->low, p->high, p->seg, p->func);
    return 0;
}
```

This example merely prints out the __GP table, by default in KERNEL (USER and GDI also have __GP tables). The output is quite boring and looks like this:

```
GP fault handling in KERNEL
GP faults in 0127:0137-0141 handled by 0127:0143
GP faults in 0117:0752-078d handled by 0117:0790
...
```

__ROMBIOS   KERNEL.173

```
EXTRN __ROMBIOS:ABS
```

This protected-mode selector maps 64K at absolute memory location 0F0000h (real-mode address F000:0000). It is identical to the selector __F000H, documented in the SDK *Guide to Programming*.

Support: 3.0, 3.1
See also: __0000H, __0040H

__WINFLAGS   KERNEL.178

```
EXTRN __WINFLAGS:ABS
```

This two-byte value exported from the Windows KERNEL is identical to the return value from the documented GetWinFlags() function.

In ROM (read-only memory) versions of Windows, however, __WINFLAGS might differ from GetWinFlags(): in ROM Windows, __WINFLAGS is statically fixed up in the ROM image, and bits other than WF_PMODE may be incorrect (see "Writing ROM Executables," Microsoft Windows Knowledge Base article Q75497).

Support: 3.0, 3.1
Example:

```
WF_PMODE EQU 1

EXTRN __WINFLAGS:ABS
; ...
mov ax, __WINFLAGS
test ax, WF_PMODE
jz short no_pmode  ;No pmode? I'm outta here!
```

A20Proc   KERNEL.165

In Windows 3.1 and 3.1, A20Proc performs no operation, but it expects one WORD argument (RETF 2). There is a similar NOP function, A20_Proc, in SYSTEM.DRV. The A20 line (which enables or disables access to memory above one megabyte, including the high memory area (HMA)) is handled elsewhere, for example, in HIMEM.SYS.

AllocAlias   KERNEL.172

```
WORD FAR PASCAL AllocAlias(sel);
WORD sel;       /* protected-mode selector */
```

This function is identical to the undocumented AllocCStoDSAlias() function; for more information, see the entry for AllocCStoDSAlias(). In Windows 3.0, the two functions even share a single entry point:

```
HANDLE kernel = GetModuleHandle("KERNEL");
if (GetProcAddress(kernel, "ALLOCALIAS") ==
    GetProcAddress(kernel, "ALLOCCSTODSALIAS"))
    msg("The functions are equivalent");
```

See also: AllocCStoDSAlias

AllocCStoDSAlias   KERNEL.170

```
WORD FAR PASCAL AllocCStoDSAlias(sel);
WORD sel;              /* protected-mode selector */
```

This function creates a "DS alias," a writeable data selector with the same base address and limit as a nonwriteable code selector. This provides a way to have self-modifying code in protected mode: the code can be modified using the allocated DS alias and executed using the original code selector.

The AllocDStoCSAlias() function, which creates an executable alias for a writeable data selector and which therefore can be used for executable data in protected mode, is documented by Microsoft. However, this seemingly quite similar Alloc-CStoDSAlias() function is not documented, and its use is discouraged in Microsoft KnowledgeBase article Q67165, "AllocCStoDSAlias() Not Documented and Not Supported":

"The AllocCStoDSAlias() function is used in the Windows version 3.00 COMM driver. This function is not documented and will not be supported in future versions of Windows.

The proper method for creating a code or data selector for a block of memory is to use the ChangeSelector() function. This function is documented in the *Windows Software Development Kit Reference Volume 1* version 3.0."

Unfortunately, while ChangeSelector() *is* documented in Windows 3.0, it is not actually available; you must instead use PrestoChangoSelector(), which was not documented until Windows 3.1.

Why is AllocCStoDSAlias() not documented, when the seemingly symmetrical function AllocDStoCSAlias() is? One possible reason is that these two functions *actually* aren't quite symmetrical. In Windows, code segments can be discarded and shared between multiple instances of an application; code is therefore supposed to be pure. The rules of protected mode forbid writing into a code segment *using a code selector*, but a DS alias obviously circumvents this protection. If an application uses a DS alias to *modify* a code segment, the Windows KERNEL has no way of knowing this has happened; modifications may be discarded, overwritten by another instance of the same program, or unintentionally shared with another instance. In contrast, creating CS aliases for data segments does not interfere with the sharing or discarding of code segments. (Note that OS/2 similarly has DosCreateCSAlias(), but no DosCreate-DSAlias() function.)

The DPMI Create Code Segment Alias Descriptor function (INT 31h AX=000Ah) also creates a data descriptor with the same base and limit as a specified code segment descriptor. The DPMI 0.9 specification notes that the alias "will *not* track changes to the code descriptor. In other words, if an alias descriptor is created, and then the base or limit of the code segment is changed, the alias descriptor's base or limit would not change." This presents the same problem as AllocCStoDSAlias, as indicated by the following session with the CALLFUNC interpreter from chapter 4:

```
> kernel getselectorbase 0x855 %lx      ;; 0x855 is program's code seg
7d0c0
> kernel alloccstodsalias 0x855         ;; get a DS alias
0x9d5
> kernel getselectorbase 0x9d5 %lx
7d0c0                                    ;; it has the same base address
> kernel globalcompact -1L
;; lots of hard disk activity here
> kernel getselectorbase 0x855 %lx
5e920                                    ;; it moved in linear addr space
> kernel getselectorbase 0x9d5 %lx
7d0c0                                    ;; oops:  the alias didn't move!!
> kernel freeselector 0x9d5
0x0000
```

Thus, to create reliable aliases under Windows, one *must* lock the original segment in the linear address space, using the documented GlobalPageLock() function. The Windows programmer's reference states that GlobalPageLock() is intended only for interrupt handlers, and for this reason, "must only be called from a DLL," but this isn't quite true (see the following example). GlobalPageLock() uses the undocumented DPMI Lock Selector Memory (INT 31h AX=0004h) function. The LockSegment() function sounds as if it would work, but it merely prevents the segment from being discarded and will not keep it from being moved about in the linear address space.

If locking the segment is unacceptable, your code will have to carefully manage the aliases itself. For example, a debugger might use AllocCStoDSAlias() to write breakpoints into a code segment. But the code segments may be discarded! WinDebug solves this problem with a cache that is used to rewrite breakpoints whenever a discarded segment comes back in. An interesting side effect is that this imposes an upper limit of 512 breakpoints when using a WinDebug-based debugger, such as CVW or TDW.

How about freeing the selector when done? According to a Microsoft Knowledge Base article (Q70810), "UAE Caused from Releasing Aliased Selector," you should *not* call FreeSelector() to release an aliased selector; Windows will supposedly free the selector automatically when the application terminates. This makes no sense at all and is not true. The confusion is further compounded in the Windows 3.1 SDK *Programmer's Reference*. The entry for FreeSelector() says that this function frees a selector originally allocated by AllocSelector() or AllocDStoCSAlias(). But, turning to the entry for AllocDStoCSAlias(), we find that "The application should not free the new selector by calling the FreeSelector function. Windows will free the selector when the application terminates." The two entries are in direct contradiction, and the one for AllocDStoCSAlias() is certainly wrong: Windows absolutely does *not* free selectors created with AllocDStoCSAlias() or AllocCStoDSAlias() when the application exits. You *must* call FreeSelector() before the application exits, or you will consume selectors. Heeding Microsoft's advice will merely turn your program into an unwitting clone of the STRESS program.

AllocCStoDSAlias

Support: 3.0, 3.1

Example: The following program, CODEDAT2.C, uses AllocCStoDSAlias() to demonstrate self-modifying code in protected-mode Windows (this is different from executable data, which is demonstrated in the CODEDATA.C example for the entry on PrestoChangoSelector()). Because Windows does not track changes to selector aliases, GlobalPageLock() *must* be used to lock the data segment down in the linear address space; in the sample program, GlobalCompact(-1) is used to try to shake it loose. All Windows-specific code is inside #ifdef WINDOWS; without this code, the program can also be run in real-mode DOS.

Note that the following code does *not* handle multiple instances properly; the code segment remains shareable, and subsequent instances of CODEDAT2.EXE will get incorrect values. This demonstrates that AllocCStoDSAlias(), or Presto-ChangoSelector(cs,ds) (as opposed to AllocDStoCSAlias() or PrestoChangoSelec-tor(ds,cs)) should really be used only in a DLL or device driver, where there is only one instance.

```c
/* CODEDAT2.C -- demonstration of self-modifying code */

#include <stdlib.h>
#ifdef WINDOWS
#include <dos.h>
#include windows.h"
#include "winio.h"

/* undocumented function */
WORD FAR PASCAL AllocCStoDSAlias(WORD code_sel);
#else
#include <stdio.h>
#endif

/* opcodes -- oper ax, addr */
#define ADD     0x03
#define OR      0x0b
#define AND     0x23
#define SUB     0x2b
#define XOR     0x33
#define CMP     0x3b

static unsigned char far *oper_byte = 0;

short math2(short oper, short op1, short op2)
{
    *oper_byte = oper;

    _asm jmp short go;      /* clear instruction prefetch! */
go:;

    _asm mov ax, op1        /* if need to set debug breakpoint, do here */
    _asm xor ax, op2        /* will be modified! */
    /* return result in AX */
}
```

AllocCStoDSAlias

```
main()
{
#ifdef WINDOWS
    WORD code_sel, data_sel;
    code_sel = FP_SEG((void far *) math2);
    GlobalPageLock(code_sel);   // still shareable!
    data_sel = AllocCStoDSAlias(code_sel);
    oper_byte = MK_FP(data_sel, FP_OFF((void far *) math2));

    /* now try to shake it loose */
    GlobalCompact(-1);
#else
    oper_byte = (unsigned char far *) math2;
#endif
    while (*oper_byte != XOR)
        oper_byte++;

#ifdef WINDOWS
    if (math2(AND, 1, 3) != 1)
    {
        extern HANDLE _hprevinst;   // ARGCARGV.C
        if (_hprevinst)
            return fail("Doesn't work with multiple instances!");
        else
            return fail("Inexplicable math failure!");
    }
#endif

    printf("1 && 3 ==> %d\n", math2(AND, 1, 3));
    printf("1 || 3 ==> %d\n", math2(OR, 1, 3));
    printf("1 ^ 3  ==> %d\n", math2(XOR, 1, 3));
    printf("1 + 3  ==> %d\n", math2(ADD, 1, 3));
    printf("1 - 3  ==> %d\n", math2(SUB, 1, 3));

#ifdef WINDOWS
    GlobalPageUnlock(code_sel);
    FreeSelector(data_sel);      // important to undo AllocCStoDSAlias()!
    // Win 3.1 QH says *NOT* to call FreeSelector. Huh?!
#endif

    return 0;
}
```

See also: AllocAlias, PrestoChangoSelector

AllocSelectorArray   KERNEL.206

```
WORD FAR PASCAL AllocSelectorArray(nSel);
WORD nSel;            /* number of selectors */
```

This function allocates a contiguous array of segment descriptors and returns a selector to the first descriptor in the array. It is equivalent to the DPMI Allocate LDT descriptors (INT 31h AX=0) function. The documented AllocSelector() function is simply the degenerate case of AllocSelectorArray(1).

The documented Windows constant __AHINCR (huge increment) can be used to move from one selector in the array to the next. The descriptors can be filled in with the SetSelectorBase() and SetSelectorLimit() functions, described later in this chapter.

There is no corresponding FreeSelectorArray() function. You must iterate over the individual selectors, as in the sample program below.

Support: 3.0, 3.1
Used by: WINMEM32.DLL
Example: The following program uses AllocSelectorArray() to create an array of far pointers, meg1, that maps the first megabyte of linear memory. Note that __AHINCR is used to move from one selector to the next, that SetSelectorBase/Limit are used to give each selector a linear base address and size, and that when finished the program deallocates the selector array by passing each element individually to the documented FreeSelector() function.

```
/* selarray.c */

#include <dos.h>
#include "windows.h"
#include "winio.h"

void fail(char *s) { puts(s); exit(1); }

#define NUM_SEL    (1024 / 64)

extern WORD FAR PASCAL AllocSelectorArray(WORD wSel);
extern DWORD FAR PASCAL GetSelectorBase(HANDLE h);
extern DWORD FAR PASCAL GetSelectorLimit(HANDLE h);
extern void FAR PASCAL SetSelectorBase(HANDLE h, DWORD dwBase);
extern void FAR PASCAL SetSelectorLimit(HANDLE h, DWORD dwLimit);

main()
{
    BYTE far *meg1[NUM_SEL];
    HANDLE first_sel, sel;
    WORD __AHINCR;
    int i;

    if ((first_sel = AllocSelectorArray(NUM_SEL)) == 0)
        fail("ran out of selectors");

    __AHINCR = LOWORD(GetProcAddress(GetModuleHandle("KERNEL"),
        "__AHINCR"));

    for (i=0; i<NUM_SEL; i++)
    {
```

```
        sel = first_sel + (i * __AHINCR);
        SetSelectorBase(sel, 64L * 1024L * i);
        SetSelectorLimit(sel, 0xFFFFL);
        meg1[i] = MK_FP(sel, 0);
    }

    for (i=0; i<NUM_SEL; i++)
        printf("%Fp\t%08lx\t%08lx\n",
            meg1[i],
            GetSelectorBase(FP_SEG(meg1[i])),
            GetSelectorLimit(FP_SEG(meg1[i])));

    /* here, could browse memory */

    for (i=0; i<NUM_SEL; i++)
        if (FreeSelector(FP_SEG(meg1[i])) != NULL)
            fail("FreeSelector failed");

    return 0;
}
```

This program does nothing with the allocated selector array besides displaying it:

```
081F:0000    00000000    0000ffff
0827:0000    00010000    0000ffff
082F:0000    00020000    0000ffff
   ....
088F:0000    000e0000    0000ffff
0897:0000    000f0000    0000ffff
```

See slso: SetSelectorBase/Limit

Atom Table

The Windows atom manager provides a mechanism for converting an ASCII string (atom name) into a 16-bit word (atom) that can be used as a more compact way to represent the string. Repeated calls to add the same string return the same ATOM handle. In addition to obvious functions such as AddAtom() and GlobalAddAtom(), the RegisterClass(), RegisterWindowMessage(), and RegisterClipboardFormat() functions also return ATOM handles. Both Dynamic Data Exchange (DDE) and Object Linking and Embedding (OLE) rely heavily on the atom-management API functions.

An ATOM is a representation of a near pointer to an ATOMENTRY structure (the C definition for which appears in the SDK include file WINEXP.H):

```
00   WORD        next -- pointer to next atom, or NULL
02   WORD        reference count
04   BYTE        length of string
05   BYTE[len]   ASCIIZ string
```

However, a string atom is always is the range C000h-FFFFh and isn't identical to its corresponding near pointer. The relationship between a string atom and its underlying near pointer is defined by the documented (but discouraged) GetAtomHandle() function. The existence of this function, a holdover from Windows 2.x, probably explains the presence of atom-manager structures in WINEXP.H; it's hard to use GetAtomHandle() without knowing the ATOMENTRY structure. Disassembly shows that GetAtomHandle() is an amazingly simple function:

```
GetAtomHandle proc far
    ; ...
    mov ax, _atom        ; [bp+6]
    cmp ax, 0C000h
    jb error
    shl ax, 1
    shl ax, 1
    jmp done
error:
    xor ax, ax
done:
    ; ...
GetAtomHandle endp
```

That's it! GetAtomHandle() takes any number greater than or equal to C000h, and shifts it left by two: the inevitable overflow results in a near pointer to the atom. Or, if an invalid parameter is passed in, it results in garbage that resembles a near pointer to an atom. No parameter validation is performed.

GetAtomHandle() checks for a value >= C000h because Windows, like OS/2 Presentation Manager, can have integer atoms which do *not* appear in an atom table. For example:

```
AddAtom("#12345") -> 0x3039
GetAtomName(0x3039, buf, 128) -> "#12345"
```

These integer atoms are used by built-in window classes that have names such as "#32769" (the desktop window class). For more information on integer atoms (which are not documented in the Windows SDK), see the chapter on atom tables in *Microsoft OS/2 Programmer's Reference*, Volume 1. Since integer atoms do not appear in the atom table, the remainder of this discussion assumes string atoms.

One can easily move between string atoms and near pointers:

```
/* similar to documented (but discouraged) GetAtomHandle(); assumes
    string atom; doesn't work with integer atoms */
#define AtomToHandle(atom)      ((WORD) (atom) << 2)    /* overflow */

#define HandleToAtom(handle)    (0xC000 | ((handle) >> 2))
```

Thus, we know that string atoms represent near pointers to ATOMENTRY structures. But, near pointers *into what*? Into a segment that contains an atom table. An

Atom Table

atom table in Windows is created with the InitAtomTable() function. If you call one of the atom-management functions and an atom table does not already exist in the DS segment, these functions will automatically call InitAtomTable() to create one.

An ATOMTABLE is nothing more than a hash table. Each entry in the hash table is a near pointer to an ATOM, or NULL. The ATOMs themselves are merely items in the local heap (any segment with an atom table must also contain a local heap, created with LocalInit()). The ATOMTABLE starts with a WORD containing the size of the hash table, which should be a prime number:

```
00  WORD       size; number (prime) of entries in hash table
02  (size * 2)  hash table; each entry an ATOMENTRY near*
```

Or, in pseudocode which is almost, but not quite, valid C:

```
typedef struct atomentry {
    struct atomentry near *next;
    WORD usage;
    BYTE len;
    BYTE name[len];
    } ATOMENTRY;

typedef struct {
    int numEntries;
    ATOMENTRY near *hashtab[numEntries];
    } ATOMTABLE;
```

In other words, ATOMTABLE is a prime number, numEntries, followed by the hash table itself, which has numEntries slots. Each slot holds zero or a near pointer to an ATOMENTRY. If more than one atom hashes to the same address, they are chained together to form a bucket, using ATOMENTRY's next field. For further details on hash tables, buckets, why the table size should be a prime number, and so on, see Donald Knuth, *Art of Computer Programming*, Volume 3 (Searching and Sorting), section 6.4 (Hashing). Windows uses a hash function based on the division method (hence the prime number) and does collision resolution by chaining (as opposed to linear probing or some other open-addressing scheme).

The default size of an atom table is 37 entries. Of course, the table can manage more than 37 strings. Let's say that a given table is currently managing about 100 atoms. On average, each entry in the hash table will contain a near pointer to an atom, which will be the first in a chain of about three atoms. The hash function used by Windows seems to do a good job of keeping each chain at about the average (number of strings / size of hash table) length. It also keeps similar items, such as "foobar" and "foboar", or "foobar" and "foobag", from hashing to the same address and thus winding up in the same bucket. FindAtom() searches should thus be relatively fast.

Unfortunately, as can be seen from the ATOMTABLE structure above, atom tables have no "signature." This probably explains, for example, why ToolHelp has no atom table-walking functions. However, there are a number of things about atom tables that make it possible to identify them in memory:

- Any segment containing an atom table will contain, at offset 8, a near pointer to the ATOMTABLE structure. (See Instance Data, later in this chapter.)
- Any segment containing an atom table must also contain a local heap (an individual ATOMENTRY is an item in the local heap; the ATOMTABLE just contains pointers to these items). Local heaps do have signatures (see Local Heap, later in this chapter).

In addition to local atom tables, Windows also has a global atom table, manipulated by documented functions such as GlobalAddAtom(). The global atom table, however, is really no different from a local atom table: USER's GlobalAddAtom() quickly turns into KERNEL's AddAtom(). The global atom table is located not in USER's default data segment (there's another, regular, non-global heap there), but in USER's global atom and text heap (see the discussion of USER heaps in the introduction to chapter 6).

Just like their related local-heap functions, all the atom-management functions in Windows work with near pointers; it is assumed that DS points to a segment containing an atom table. At first sight, this seems to indicate that you can only access one atom table, in your own default data segment. However, you can both create additional atom tables and access someone else's, merely by setting up DS around any calls to the atom-management functions; this is all that the global-atom functions in USER do. This is similar to the based-pointer scheme for suballocating out of multiple local heaps. For example, see the BasedGetAtomName() function in chapter 4's sidebar on RegisterWindowMessage(). Another example, BasedFindAtom(), appears in the ATOMWALK sample program below. Using these based atom functions merely requires that you know the segment for some existing atom table, or that you create a new one with a BasedInitAtomTable() function.

Support: 3.0, 3.1
See also: InitAtomTable, Instance Data, Local Heap
Example: The following program, ATOMWALK.C, enumerates the handle and string for each atom, in each atom table on the system. The global atom table is identified. A high-level view of the code looks like this:

```
For each global-heap entry reported by ToolHelp
    If it contains an atom table <--- this is the hard part!
        If it's the Global Atom Table, identify it
        For each entry in hash table
            If entry is in use
                Maybe show entry number
                For each atom in this bucket
                    Print atom handle, atom string
```

Atom Table

The output looks like this:

```
06a7 (C:\WIN31\SYSTEM\USER.EXE)
    c4ae    winio_wcmain
    c354    ComboLBox
    c43c    OTHERWINDOWCREATED
    c473    WOAFontPreview
    c58b    WFS_Search
    c455    tty
    c493    ACTIVATESHELLWINDOW
    ... etc. ...
37 hashtab entries, 40 atoms

050f (C:\WIN31\SYSTEM\GDI.EXE)
    c056    Small Fonts
    c127    MGXWMF.DRV
    c06b    Zapf Dingbats
    ... etc. ...
101 hashtab entries, 76 atoms

GLOBAL ==> 0287 (C:\WIN31\SYSTEM\USER.EXE) 37 entries
    c02a    SysCP
    c02e    SysBW
37 hashtab entries, 2 atoms
```

The program can be run with -BUCKET command-line switch to group together all atoms that hash to the same entry in the hash table. For example:

```
06a7 (C:\WIN31\SYSTEM\USER.EXE)
Bucket 1
    c4ae    winio_wcmain
Bucket 4
    c354    ComboLBox
Bucket 5
    c43c    OTHERWINDOWCREATED
    c473    WOAFontPreview
    c58b    WFS_Search
Bucket 6
    c455    tty
Bucket 8
    c493    ACTIVATESHELLWINDOW
    c57c    WFS_Dir
... etc. ...
37 hashtab entries, 40 atoms
```

The source code follows:

```
/* ATOMWALK.C -- show all atoms */

#include <stdlib.h>
#include <dos.h>
#include "windows.h"
#include "toolhelp.h"
```

Atom Table

```c
#include "winio.h"
#include "handles.h"

#pragma pack(1)

/* from WINEXP.H */
/* atom manager internals */
#define ATOMSTRUC struct atomstruct
typedef ATOMSTRUC *PATOM;
typedef ATOMSTRUC {
    PATOM chain;
    WORD  usage;              /* Atoms are usage counted. */
    BYTE  len;                /* length of ASCIZ name string */
    BYTE  name;               /* beginning of ASCIZ name string */
} ATOMENTRY;

typedef struct {
    int    numEntries;
    PATOM  pAtom[ 1 ];
} ATOMTABLE;

/* identical to documented (but discouraged) GetAtomHandle() */
#define AtomToHandle(atom)       ((WORD) (atom) << 2)    /* overflow */

#define HandleToAtom(handle)     (0xC000 | ((handle) >> 2))
/* NULL segment at offset 0 in a data segment with
   atom table or local heap */
typedef struct {
    WORD wMustBeZero;
    DWORD dwOldSSSP;
    WORD pLocalHeap;
    WORD pAtomTable;
    WORD pStackTop;
    WORD pStackMin;
    WORD pStackBottom;
    } INSTDATA;

/* There is no signature for atom tables, so seeing if you found one
   is tricky, and perhaps only probabilistically correct.  To be
   an atom table, there _must_ be a local heap (the atoms themselves
   are items in the local heap).  We can test for a correct local
   heap.  There must also be a valid NULL segment block at offset 0 */
ATOMTABLE far *GetAtomTable(GLOBALENTRY *pge)
{
    extern DWORD FAR PASCAL GetSelectorLimit(WORD sel);
    if ((pge->wType == GT_DGROUP) ||
        (pge->wType == GT_DATA) ||
        (pge->wType == GT_UNKNOWN)) // GlobalAllocs are GT_UNKNOWN
    {
        WORD sel = GlobalHandleToSel(pge->hBlock);
        INSTDATA far *lpInstData = MK_FP(sel, 0);
        DWORD limit = GetSelectorLimit(sel);
        if (verr(sel) &&
            (limit  > 16) &&
            (lpInstData->wMustBeZero == 0) &&
```

Atom Table

```
                    (lpInstData->pLocalHeap != 0) &&
                    (lpInstData->pLocalHeap < limit) &&
                    (lpInstData->pAtomTable != 0) &&
                    (lpInstData->pAtomTable < limit) &&
                     IsValidLocalHeap (MK_FP (sel, lpInstData->pLocalHeap)))
            {
                    return MK_FP(sel, lpInstData->pAtomTable);
            }
        }

    /* still here */
    return 0L;
}

ATOM BasedFindAtom(WORD wSeg, LPSTR lpsz)
{
    ATOM retval;
    _asm push ds
    _asm mov ds, wSeg
    retval = FindAtom(lpsz);
    _asm pop ds
    return retval;
}

static BOOL show_bucket = FALSE;

WORD print_bucket(WORD hash, ATOMENTRY far *pa)
{
    WORD num_atoms = 0;
    WORD seg = FP_SEG(pa);
    WORD ofs = FP_OFF(pa);
    if (show_bucket)
        printf("Bucket %u\n", hash);
    for (;;)    // print everything that hashes to this bucket
    {
        num_atoms++;
        printf("  %04x   %Fs\n", HandleToAtom(FP_OFF(pa)), &pa->name);
#ifdef PARANOID
        if (HandleToAtom(ofs) != BasedFindAtom(seg, &pa->name))
            fail("Something wrong!");
#endif
        if ((ofs = pa->chain) != 0)
            pa = MK_FP(seg, ofs);        // follow linked list
        else
            break;
    }
    return num_atoms;
}

main(int argc, char *argv[])
{
    ATOMTABLE far *lpAtomTable;
    GLOBALENTRY ge;
    HANDLE hUser;
    WORD num_atoms;
```

Atom Table

```c
    int ok;

    if (argc >= 2)
        if (strcmp(strupr(argv[1]), "-BUCKET") == 0)
            show_bucket = TRUE;

    hUser = GetModuleHandle("USER");
    ge.dwSize = sizeof(ge);
    winio_setbusy();
    winio_setpaint(__hMainWnd, FALSE);  // don't yield
    ok = GlobalFirst(&ge, GLOBAL_ALL);
    while (ok)
    {
        // for Atom Table structure, see WINEXP.H
        if (lpAtomTable = GetAtomTable(&ge))
        {
            char owner[128];
            int i;
            PATOM far *pa;
            WORD sel = FP_SEG(lpAtomTable);
            GetModuleFileName(ge.hOwner, owner, 128);
            if ((ge.hOwner == hUser) && (ge.wType != GT_DGROUP))
                printf("GLOBAL ==> ");  // identify Global Atom Table
            printf("%04x (%s)\n", sel, owner);
            num_atoms = 0;
            for (i=0, pa=&lpAtomTable->pAtom;
                 i<lpAtomTable->numEntries;
                 i++, pa++)
            {
                if (*pa != 0)
                    num_atoms += print_bucket(i, MK_FP(sel, *pa));
            }
            printf("%u hashtab entries, %u atoms\n\n",
                lpAtomTable->numEntries, num_atoms);
            printf("\n");
        }

        ok = GlobalNext(&ge, GLOBAL_ALL);
    }

    winio_setpaint(__hMainWnd, TRUE);
    winio_resetbusy();
    return 0;
}
```

Bunny_351   KERNEL.351

```c
void FAR Bunny_351(void);
```

Bunny_351() simply sets the KERNEL fault handler address to a different routine during the shutdown of Windows. The function is called when Windows shuts down and no more tasks are left. Apparently the function is a workaround for some bugs in applications that would otherwise cause the system to crash.

Perhaps of more interest than the details of the function itself are the origins of its name. Apparently a cast of stuffed animals lives among the Windows developers at Microsoft. Rumor has it that Bunny went to the "Land of Bug-Free Code" via a paper shredder. Besides Bunny, there's also Bear (see the USER BearNNN functions in chapter 6).

Support: 3.1

Burgermaster   206-827-9566

See: GlobalMasterHandle, Global Heap

CallProcInstance   KERNEL.53

```
LONG FAR PASCAL CallProcInstance(HWND hWnd, WORD wMessage,
    WORD wParam, LONG lParam);  /* ES:BX set to hInstance/lpfnWndProc */
```

This function is used internally by Windows 3.0 in the USER CallWindowProc(), DispatchMessage(), and SendMessage() functions; it thus is called constantly in the Windows 3.0 main loop. In Windows 3.1, CallProcInstance() still exists, but it appears to be unused (a function internal to USER, ValidateMessage(), is used instead). It's not clear why such a USER-dependent function resides in KERNEL in the first place.

CallProcInstance() expects to be called with ES:BX pointing to the hInstance/lpfnWndProc fields in a WND structure (at offset 38h in 3.0). The parameters on the stack are identical to the parameters expected by a WndProc. CallProcInstance sets DS to the hInstance and does a far jump to the lpfnWndProc.

Support: 3.0, 3.1 (not used in 3.1?)
See also: WND structure (USER)

CVWBreak   KERNEL.205

```
void FAR _interrupt CVWBreak(void);
```

CVWBreak() is used as part of the Windows debugging interface. The KEYBOARD function, EnableKBSysReq(), documented in the Windows Device Driver Kit (DDK), controls whether hitting Ctrl-Alt-SysReq will trigger a call to CVWBreak(). CVWBreak(), in turn, generates an INT 1, which can be caught by WINDEBUG.DLL (which in turn notifies Code View for Windows (CVW) or Turbo Debugger for Windows (TDW)), or by a debugger such as Soft-Ice for Windows (if the I1HERE ON option is specified). Alternatively, a Ctrl-Alt-SysReq can trigger an NMI (INT 2).

There should be no need to call CVWBreak() directly. Use the documented DebugBreak() function instead.

Support: 3.0, 3.1
Used by: KEYBOARD.DRV (see DDK source code \keyboard\enable.asm and \keyboard\trap.asm)

DebugDefineSegment   KERNEL.314

```
void FAR PASCAL DebugDefineSegment(lpName, wLogSeg, wSeg, wUnknown, wFlag)
LPSTR lpName;     /* module name of the segment owner, from task database */
WORD wLogSeg;     /* logical segment number from .EXE (0-based) */
WORD wSeg;        /* segment or selector value */
WORD wUnknown;
WORD wFlag;       /* data=1, code=0 */
```

This function is used by the memory management in KERNEL to provide segment information to an external debugger such as WDEB386 or Soft-Ice for Windows; it is little more than a C interface to one of the many INT 41h functions in the Windows low-level debug API (see RegisterPtrace); DebugDefineSegment() corresponds to the INT 41h Define Segment function:

```
AX = 50h
BX = wLogSeg
CX = wSeg
SI = wFlag
ES:(E)DI = lpName
INT 41h
```

Support: 3.1
See also: RegisterPtrace

DebugFillBuffer   KERNEL.329

```
void FAR PASCAL DebugFillBuffer(LPSTR lpBuffer, WORD wBytes);
```

The actual name of this export is K329. If the documented Windows 3.1 SetWinDebugInfo() DBO_BUFFERFILL option is set, this function is called to fill all of the buffer at lpBuffer with the byte 0F9h. The buffer is one that has been passed to a Windows API function such as GetWindowText(); DebugFillBuffer() helps ensure that all of the supplied buffer is writeable.

The 3.1 DDK version of WINDOWS.H contains the following definitions:

```
#define   DBGFILL_ALLOC   0xFD
```

```
#define    DBGFILL_FREE      0xFB
#define    DBGFILL_BUFFER    0xF9
#define    DBGFILL_STACK     0xF7
```

Support: 3.1

DeletePathName   KERNEL.76

```
WORD FAR PASCAL DeletePathname(lpPathName);
LPSTR lpPathName;    /* path name of file to delete */
```

This function appears in some versions of WINDOWS.H and WINEXP.H, but it is not documented—perhaps because it is so self-explanatory that it requires no documentation! The function sets AX=4100h and falls into the OpenPathname() function. The function deletes the named file; if it can't be deleted (file does not exist, or access denied), it returns -1.

Support: 3.0, 3.1

DiagOutput   KERNEL.340

```
void FAR PASCAL DiagOutput(char far *msg);
```

If Windows 3.1 has been started with the WIN /B boot-log option, this function writes a string to the BOOTLOG.TXT file; otherwise, it does nothing (thus, it is not necessary to call DiagQuery() before calling this function). Each time DiagOutput() is called, it opens BOOTLOG.TXT, writes out the string, and then closes BOOTLOG.TXT; thus, the log file may be useful for troubleshooting even if Windows has crashed.

Device drivers and DLLs that call DiagOutput() should generally output one "LoadStart = " message as soon as their initialization routine is called, and one "LoadSuccess = " or "LoadFailure = " message just before the initialization routine returns. Programs that intend to be run from the WIN.INI LOAD= or RUN= command line, or from the SYSTEM.INI SHELL= command line, should perhaps also call DiagOutput() in their initialization routine.

Support: 3.1
See also: DiagQuery
Example:

```
extern void FAR PASCAL DiagOutput(char far *msg);
char buf[128];
// ...
GetModuleFileName(hInstance, buf, 128); // can pass hInstance
DiagOutput("LoadStart = "); DiagOutput(buf); DiagOutput("\n");
```

```
// ... now do all the work of initializing ...
DiagOutput(success? "LoadSuccess = " : "LoadFailure = ");
DiagOutput(buf); DiagOutput("\n");
```

DiagQuery   KERNEL.339

```
BOOL FAR PASCAL DiagQuery(void);
```

This function returns TRUE if Windows 3.1 has been started with the WIN /B flag and FALSE otherwise. WIN /B enables boot log tracing, creating a file BOOTLOG.TXT with diagnostic boot-time messages such as "LoadStart = SYSTEM.DRV" and "LoadSuccess = SYSTEM.DRV." This file can be used to troubleshoot Windows boot problems.

DiagQuery() merely returns the value of an internal KERNEL variable, FDIAGMODE, which is set by an internal DiagInit() function.

Support: 3.1
See also: DiagOutput

DirectedYield   KERNEL.150

```
void FAR PASCAL DirectedYield(hTask);
HANDLE hTask;    /* Handle to a Task Database */
```

DirectedYield() is similar to the documented Yield() function, but it takes a parameter that specifies the handle of a task to which it yields. Thus, the calling application decides which Windows task gets to run next, rather than leaving this up to the Windows scheduler. The function could probably be used to implement coroutines in Windows, but it is generally used by Windows debuggers and development environments; it is called both by WINDEBUG.DLL and by Quick C for Windows (QC/W).

DirectedYield() is documented in Windows 3.1, but not in 3.0, where it also exists.

DirectedYield() is just a wrapper around the function OldYield(); the two functions communicate via a field at offset 0AAh in the Task Database.

To ensure that the task to which you are DirectedYielding runs make sure that it has a message in its queue. This, in turn, means ensuring that it has a queue in the first place (i.e., that it isn't still in the middle of executing its startup code). For example:

```
HANDLE hTask;
// ...
if (GetTaskQueue(hTask) != 0)
{
    PostAppMessage(hTask, WM_NULL, 0, 0L);
    DirectedYield(hTask);
}
```

In a debugger that uses WinDebug, you can use the Pid (process id) field in the WINDEBUG_BUF structure:

```
WINDEBUG_BUF wdbg;
// ...
PostAppMessage(wdbg.pid, WM_NULL, 0, 0L);
DirectedYield(wdbg.pid);
```

Support: 3.0, 3.1
See also: GetTaskQueue, OldYield, Task Database

DirectResAlloc   KERNEL.168

```
HANDLE FAR PASCAL DirectResAlloc(HANDLE hInstance, WORD wType,
    WORD wSize);
```

Whereas the documented AllocResource() function expects a resource identifier returned from FindResource(), which in turn expects to find resources in executable files, the undocumented DirectResAlloc() function is instead used when creating resources on the fly.

As part of this process, one obviously needs to allocate a block of global memory and copy the resource data into it; the documented GlobalAlloc() function is normally used to allocate global memory in Windows. However, when memory is allocated with GlobalAlloc(), it (with one important exception, noted below) becomes associated with the calling instance and is automatically freed when the instance terminates. Because resources are shareable among all instances of an application, they must be allocated differently: the memory must be associated, not with an instance, but with a module; it should only be freed when the very last instance of the module terminates, *not* when the instance that happened to allocate it terminates.

That in essence is what DirectResAlloc() does: provide a way to allocate global memory that is associated with a module rather than with an instance. Oddly enough, DirectResAlloc() nonetheless takes an hInstance as its first parameter; it automatically converts this to an hModule, using the undocumented GetExePtr() function (described later in this chapter).

It is not known what the second parameter is. The CreateCursorIconIndirect() function in USER passes in a wType of 0x10.

If successful, DirectResAlloc() returns a HANDLE, just like GlobalAlloc(). The calling function is expected to lock the handle with GlobalLock() and then copy the resource data into the resulting pointer. The handle can then be unlocked and subsequently treated like a normal resource that had been loaded out of an executable file.

Applications should generally not need to use DirectResAlloc() because GlobalAlloc() can also be made to do hModule- rather than hInstance-based allocation by using the (somewhat misnamed) GMEM_DDESHARE flag. A good discussion of this appears in Paul Yao's article, "Careful Windows Resource Allocation and Cleanup Improves Application Hygiene" (*Microsoft Systems Journal*, September 1991).

In addition, the owner of a memory block can be manipulated with the FarGetOwner() and FarSetOwner() functions, described later in this chapter. Interestingly, hInstance-based allocations seem to be stored with a PSP, rather than an actual hInstance, owner.

Support: 3.0, 3.1
Used By: USER, SHELL (3.1), PROGMAN (3.0 only), WINHELP
See also: FarSetOwner, CreateCursorIconIndirect (USER)

DisableDOS   KERNEL.42

```
void FAR PASCAL DisableDOS(void);
```

In Windows 3.0, after calling this function, any DOS INT 21h call, from any Windows application, will fail. Many existing applications will continue to work just fine, but you won't be able to start any new ones (the WinExec call requires DOS file I/O), and operations that require DOS, such as opening or saving files, will fail. DOS access can be turned back on with a call to EnableDOS().

DisableDOS() is used as part of normal Windows termination by the DisableKernel() function. DisableDOS() reinstalls the original interrupt handlers that KERNEL replaces as part of its startup: INT 0, 2, 4, 6, 7, 21h, 24h, 2Fh, 3Eh, and 75h.

There seems to be little reason to use this call, except perhaps to test the extent to which one's application is cut off, or dependent, on DOS.

In Windows 3.1, this function immediately returns. Much of its functionality appears to be present in DisableKernel(), however.

Support: 3.0
See also: DisableKernel, EnableDOS

DisableKernel   KERNEL.125

In Windows 3.0, this function calls DisableDOS(). In Windows 3.1, DisableKernel() executes the code described above for DisableDOS() in 3.0. However, EnableKernel() is a NOP in 3.1, so KERNEL can't be reenabled.

DoSignal   KERNEL.139

```
VOID FAR PASCAL DoSignal(void);
```

DoSignal() is used by KEYBOARD.DRV as a way of sending a Ctrl-Break to the task that has the focus window. Rather than generate an INT 1Bh, however, DoSignal() uses the signal handle stored at offset 26h in the Task Database (and settable via the SetSigHandler() function). Most Windows applications do not install signal handlers; the default signal handler points to an RETF instruction inside KERNEL.

Internally, DoSignal() uses the GetProcAddress() function to call several functions inside USER (KERNEL depends on non-KERNEL functionality). These functions are GetFocus() (to determine which window the Ctrl-Break belongs to), IsWindow() (to verify that this HWND is correct), and GetWindowTask() (to obtain the hTask corresponding to the focus HWND). With the hTask in hand, DoSignal() pushes 1 and 0 and calls through the function pointer stored in the task database. Most registers are saved around the call.

Support: 3.0, 3.1
Used by: KEYBOARD.DRV (see DDK source code \keyboard\trap.asm)
See also: SetSigHandler, Task Database
Example: If the following program is run without a command-line argument, it calls DoSignal(), and the signal is caught by a function installed with SetSigHandler(). If the program is run with a command-line argument (e.g., BREAK FOO), pressing Ctrl-Break terminates the program. The signal-handler function sets a global flag that is checked periodically within the program's main loop. Calling Windows API functions such as MessageBox() from within the signal handler will generally cause a protection violation if a genuine Ctrl-Break has been hit (as opposed to calling DoSignal), so the program calls MessageBox *outside* the signal-handling function.

```
/* break.c */

#include "windows.h"
#include "winio.h"

WORD (FAR PASCAL *SetSigHandler)(FARPROC newSignalHandler,
    DWORD FAR * lpOldSignalHandlerAddress,
    WORD FAR *lpOldSignalType, WORD signalType, WORD mustBeOne);

void (FAR PASCAL *DoSignal)(void);

int volatile do_abort = 0;

WORD FAR PASCAL _export ctrl_break_handler(WORD a, WORD b)
{
    MessageBeep(0); // seems ok to call, though most APIs aren't
    do_abort++;
}

main(int argc, char *argv[])
{
    FARPROC ctrl_break;
    DWORD dwOldProc;
    WORD wOldType;
```

```
    int do_dosignal = (argc < 2) ;
    HANDLE hKernel = GetModuleHandle("KERNEL");
    if (do_dosignal)
        if (! (DoSignal = GetProcAddress(hKernel, "DOSIGNAL")))
            fail("Can't find DoSignal");
    if (! (SetSigHandler = GetProcAddress(hKernel, "SETSIGHANDLER")))
        fail("Can't find SetSigHandler");
    ctrl_break = MakeProcInstance((FARPROC) ctrl_break_handler,
        __hInst);
    SetSigHandler((FARPROC) ctrl_break,
        &dwOldProc, &wOldType, 2, 1);    // install handler
    for (;;)
    {
        if (do_dosignal)
        {
            puts("This is a test of DoSignal!");
            DoSignal();
        }
        else
            puts("Hit Ctrl-Break!");

        if (do_abort)    // signal handler was called
        {
            if (MessageBox(NULL, "Ctrl-Break Pressed",
                "Test of SetSigHandler",
                MB_ABORTRETRYIGNORE) == IDABORT)
                break;           // abort
            else
                do_abort = 0;   // retry, ignore
        }
    }
    FreeProcInstance(ctrl_break);
    puts("Program aborted");
    return 0;
}
```

DOS3Call   KERNEL.102

```
void FAR Dos3Call(void);
```

Dos3Call() can be used as a direct replacement for INT 21h DOS calls; the function expects that all registers have been set up for an INT 21h. Dos3Call() is not undocumented, but the *Microsoft Windows Programmer's Reference* claims that "an application can call this function only from an assembly-language routine," which is certainly not true. For example:

```
WORD wDosVers;
void FAR Dos3Call(void) =
    GetProcAddress(GetModuleHandle("KERNEL"), "DOS3CALL");
// ...
_asm mov ax, 3000h
```

```
#ifdef OLDCODE
_asm mov int 21h
#else
Dos3Call();
#endif
_asm mov wDosVers, ax
```

While performing the same function as an INT 21h instruction, a call to Dos3Call() is considered more portable. On the other hand, DOS calls made with Dos3Call() will *not* be caught by an interrupt-snooping debugger such as this book's WISPY (I-Spy for Windows) or the BPINT (breakpoint on interrupt) command in Soft-ICE for Windows.

Support: 3.0, 3.1
See also: NoHookDosCall

EMSCopy   KERNEL.160

This function, a holdover from Windows 2.x expanded-memory support, does nothing in Windows 3.x. It expects to be called with 14 bytes worth of parameters.

EnableDOS   KERNEL.41

```
void FAR PASCAL EnableDOS(void);
```

In Windows 3.0, this function installs (or reinstalls) Windows interrupt handlers for INT 0, 2, 4, 6, 7, 21h, 24h, 2Fh, 3Eh, and 75h. After this function has been called, Windows applications can make DOS INT 21h calls; this undoes the effect of DisableDOS(), described earlier in this chapter. In Windows 3.1, the function immediately returns.

Support: 3.0
See also: DisableDOS, EnableKernel

EnableKernel   KERNEL.124

In Windows 3.0, this function undoes the work of DisableKernel(). In 3.1, it immediately returns.

ExitKernel   KERNEL.2

```
void FAR PASCAL ExitKernel(WORD wCode, WORD wReturnCode);
```

ExitKernel() is called by the documented ExitWindows() function and is used to shut down (and possibly restart) Windows. ExitKernel(), in turn, calls the KEYBOARD and

MOUSE Disable() functions and the SYSTEM DisableSystemTimers() function; it calls them through function pointers returned from GetProcAddress().

The second parameter to ExitKernel() is the same as the second parameter to ExitWindows(). The first parameter indicates whether Windows is supposed to exit and restart, or merely exit (in Windows 3.1, Microsoft documented that ExitWindows() can be passed the value EW_RESTARTWINDOWS (0x42) or EW_REBOOTSYSTEM (0x43)).

Support: 3.0, 3.1

FarGetOwner   KERNEL.404

```
WORD FAR PASCAL FarGetOwner(HANDLE h);
```

This function, available only in Windows 3.1, returns the owner of an item on the Windows global heap. The owner is sometimes a protected-mode PSP (PDB), and sometimes an hModule. In the case of blocks allocated with GlobalAlloc() (except when GMEM_DDESHARE is used), the owner is the protected-mode PSP. The return value of this function thus differs from that of GetExePtr(), which calls GetOwner() but which returns the corresponding hModule even where FarGetOwner() returns a PSP. The return value is 0 if the handle is invalid.

In Windows 3.0, the same functionality as FarGetOwner() is available by directly peeking at a Global Arena structure; this is all that FarGetOwner() does in Windows 3.1. In Standard mode, it returns the WORD at offset 1 in the Global Arena structure; in Enhanced mode, it returns the WORD at offset 12h. These same values can be used in Windows 3.0 (see the Global Arena entry).

Because this function is exported from KERNEL by ordinal only, it must also be imported by ordinal. For example:

```
WORD (FAR PASCAL *FarGetOwner)(HANDLE h);
// ...
FarGetOwner = GetProcAddress(hKernel, "#404");
printf("%04x owned by %04x\n", h, FarGetOwner(h));
```

Support: 3.1 only (unnamed export)
See also: FarSetOwner, GetExePtr, Global Arena

FarSetOwner   KERNEL.403

```
void FAR PASCAL FarSetOwner(HANDLE h, WORD wOwnerPSP);
```

Like FarGetOwner(), the FarSetOwner() function is available only as an unnamed export from Windows 3.1. It can be used to change the owner of a block on the

Windows global heap, for example, to pass ownership of a block from one task to another. The owner is specified using a protected-mode PSP, such as returned from the documented GetCurrentPDB() function, or as found at offset 60h in the Task Database.

When a task exits, Windows releases all the memory that the task allocated via GlobalAlloc(). However, if FarSetOwner() is used to pass ownership off to some other task, then the memory is *not* released until *that* task exits.

Support: 3.1 only (unnamed export)
See also: DirectResAlloc, FarGetOwner, GetExePtr, Global Arena

---

FatalExitHook   KERNEL.318

```
FARPROC FAR PASCAL FatalExitHook(FARPROC HookProc);
```

FatalExitHook() allows an application to install a system-wide hook that will be called whenever an application calls the documented FatalExit() function. If the address passed to FatalExitHook is 0L, it disables future callbacks. The return value is the address of the previous handler.

This function is new for Windows 3.1, and it appears to have been added to aid TOOLHELP.DLL in cleaning up programs that have called NotifyRegister() or InterruptRegister(). See chapter 10 on ToolHelp for further details.

The callback function is prototyped as follows:

```
BOOL FAR PASCAL FatalExitHookCallback(WORD exitCode);
```

Support: 3.1

FileCdr   KERNEL.130

```
DWORD FAR PASCAL FileCdr(FILECDRPROC lpfnNotifyProc);
```

FileCdr installs a callback function that will be called whenever there are changes to the file system, such as a file being created or deleted. The only known user of FileCdr is the Windows File Manager (WinFile). FileCdr will not install a new callback function if there is already a callback installed and the current hTask does not match the hTask of the program that called FileCdr originally. In other words, if WinFile is running, you can't use FileCdr—but there's more than one way to skin this cat, as we shall see.

Call FileCdr by passing in the far address of the callback function to be installed, or a NULL to deinstall the callback function that you have previously installed. The function returns a BOOL in the low-order WORD of the DWORD return indicating whether it performed the requested operation, i.e., there were no hTask clashes, and the high-order WORD is undefined. In version 3.1, if -1L is passed to the function, the address of the current callback function is returned. This provides an inquiry mode for the function, but note that this is not present in 3.0.

The callback function is prototyped as follows:

```
void FAR PASCAL FileCdrProc(WORD wActionCode, LPSTR lpszPath);
```

The wActionCode parameter identifies what has occurred, and lpszPath specifies the file or directory that it has occurred to. The action codes are AX values from the DOS INT21h functions that generated during file system operations; the following INT 21h functions are in the list of those that cause change, and therefore callbacks:

```
0x3C    Create file
0x39    Create directory
0x3A    Delete directory
0x41    Delete file
0x43    Get/set file attrs
0x56    Rename file/directory
0x57    Set file date/time
0x5A    Create unique file
0x5B    Create new file
0x6C    Extended open
```

Upon receiving one of these callbacks, WinFile allocates space to hold a copy of the passed string and copies the string into the local buffer. It then posts the undocumented WM_FILESYSCHANGE message (0x34, see chapter 7) to one of its windows. By using FileCdr, WinFile automatically tracks any file-system changes by Windows applications. In Standard Mode, WinFile has no way of tracking file system changes in the DOS box. To track changes by non-Windows applications running in Enhanced Mode DOS boxes, it must rely on the DOSMGR and DOSNET virtual device drivers in WIN386.EXE. This causes a sufficiently large performance hit that such tracking (enabled with the 'FileSysChange=ON' entry in the [Enhanced] section of SYSTEM.INI) is disabled by default, and the user must manually refresh the WinFile display by pressing F5 to pick up DOS-box changes.

FileCdr in both 3.0 and 3.1 is a very simple function in its implementation; this implementation provides all the information one needs to solve the problem mentioned at the end of the first paragraph. We present here a replacement for FileCdr() that can be used by one or more applications such that they can all receive notification of file system changes, even if WinFile is already running.

In essence, the pseudocode in KERNEL for FileCdr is:

```
static FARPROC lpfnFileCdrNotify = (FARPROC) 0;
static HANDLE hTaskFileCdr;

BOOL/FARPROC FileCdr(FARPROC lpfnNotifyNew)
{
```

FileCdr

```
#if (WINVER >= 0x0a03)
    if (lpfnNotifyNew == -1)
        return lpfnFileCdrNotify;
#endif

    if (lpfnFileCdrNotify && (hTaskFileCdr != GetCurrentTask()))
        return FALSE;

    lpfnFileCdrNotify = lpfnNotifyNew;
    hTaskFileCdr = GetCurrentTask();
    return TRUE;
}
```

where lpfnFileCdrNotify and hTaskFileCdr are static data items in KERNEL's DGROUP. These items may be accessed from the THHOOK_STRUCT described in the THHook entry later in this chapter. lpfnFileCdrNotify is at THHOOK_STRUCT offset 0x0185 in 3.0, and 0x00FE in 3.1; hTaskFileCdr is at THHOOK_STRUCT offset 0x0189 in 3.0, and 0x0102 in 3.1.

Armed with the known offsets relative to THHOOK_STRUCT in KERNEL's DGROUP of the callback function address and the handle of the task that owns the callback function, our implementation simply removes the task-matching performed by FileCdr, and uses side-effecting parameters, as in this pseudocode:

```
void GetSetFileCdr(bSet, *p_lpfnNotify, *p_hTask)
{
    FARPROC far *p_lpfnFileCdrNotify;
    HANDLE far *p_hTaskFileCdr;

    /* Get lpfnFileCdrNotify and hTaskFileCdr in KERNEL's
    /* DGROUP, into p_lpfnFileCdrNotify, p_hTaskFileCdr
        .
        .
        .
    if (bSet)
    {
        *p_lpfnFileCdrNotify = *p_lpfnNotify;
        *p_hTaskFileCdr = *p_hTask;
    }
    else
    {
        *p_lpfnNotify = *p_lpfnFileCdrNotify;
        *p_hTask = *p_hTaskFileCdr;
    }
}
```

The following program, STEALCDR, has a full implementation of the above. It saves away the current callback address and owning task handle, and plugs in its own. Whenever STEALCDR's callback function is called, it prints out the event that has taken place and chains to the previous, saved callback function. Other applications wishing to use GetSetFileCdr should also use this interrupt-chaining-like technique.

FileCdr

If WinFile was already loaded, it will continue to update its directory list boxes, because STEALCDR will "pass on" the notification. The only problem with this implementation is that, if WinFile is loaded *after* STEALCDR, WinFile will not receive file system change notifications. However, this would also have been the case had STEALCDR relied only on FileCdr.

STEALCDR's output simply logs file system changes as follows:

```
Module WINFILE, Delete file: C:\UNDOCWIN\TMP\AAA.AAA
Module WINFILE, Rename file: C:\UNDOCWIN\TMP\AAA.AAB
Module WINFILE, Get/set file attrs: C:\UNDOCWIN\TMP\AAA.AAA
Module WINFILE, Rename file/directory: C:\UNDOCWIN\TMP
Module NOTEPAD, Create file: C:\WIN31\TEMPRARY.TXT
Module NOTEPAD, Delete file: C:\WIN31\TEMPRARY.TXT
Module NOTEPAD, Create file: C:\WIN31\TEMPRARY.TXT
Module NOTEPAD, Create unique file: C:\UNDOCWIN\FOO\BDBKAACJ
Module NOTEPAD, Delete file: C:\UNDOCWIN\FOO\BDBKAACJ
Module WINFILE, Rename file/directory: C:\UNDOCWIN\FOO
Module STEALCDR, Create file: C:\UNDOCWIN\TMP\STEALCDR.LOG
```

STEALCDR operates identically in both 3.0 and 3.1. Note, too, that STEALCDR does not impact WinFile's Enhanced Mode ability to track file system changes in DOS boxes. Even if WinFile is loaded later, and therefore cannot track changes by Windows Apps, it will record DOS box file system changes.

Support: 3.0, 3.1
See also: THHook, WM_FILESYSCHANGE (chapter 7)
Example: STEALCDR takes over the file-system change notification hook, logs file-system change events, and chains on to the previous notification function:

```c
/* STEALCDR.C */

#include <windows.h>
#include <toolhelp.h>
#include <dos.h>
#include "winio.h"
#include "handles.h"

typedef void (FAR PASCAL *FILECDRPROC)(WORD wActionCode,
    LPSTR lpszPath);

void GetSetFileCdr(BOOL bSet, FILECDRPROC *lpfn, HANDLE *ph);
WORD far *GetTHH(void);

FILECDRPROC lpfnCallbackPrev = NULL;
FILECDRPROC lpfnCallbackOurs;
HANDLE hTaskPrev = NULL;
HANDLE hTaskOurs;
LPVOID lpTHH;

typedef struct { BYTE byAction; LPSTR szAction; } ACTION;
```

```
ACTION action[] = {
    { 0x3C, "Create file" },
    { 0x39, "Create directory" },
    { 0x3A, "Delete directory" },
    { 0x41, "Delete file" },
    { 0x43, "Get/set file attrs" },
    { 0x56, "Rename file/directory" },
    { 0x57, "Set file date/time" },
    { 0x5A, "Create unique file" },
    { 0x5B, "Create new file" },
    { 0x6C, "Extended open" },
    { 0, 0 } };

#define THH_OFS_FILECDR_30      0x0185
#define THH_OFS_FILECDR_31      0x00FE

void GetSetFileCdr(BOOL bSet, FILECDRPROC *lpfn, HANDLE *ph)
    {
    LPVOID lp = lpTHH;

    (DWORD) lp += (GetVersion() >= 0x0a03) ?
        THH_OFS_FILECDR_31 : THH_OFS_FILECDR_30;

    if (bSet)
        {
        *((FILECDRPROC FAR *) lp)++ = *lpfn;
        *((HANDLE FAR *) lp) = *ph;
        }
    else
        {
        *lpfn = *((FILECDRPROC FAR *) lp)++;
        *ph = *((HANDLE FAR *) lp);
        }
    }

void PutBackPrev(HWND hwnd)
    {
    // Deinstall our callback function and reinstall whoever was
    // there before if they are still there
    if (! IsValidTask(hTaskPrev))
        {
        lpfnCallbackPrev = NULL;
        hTaskPrev = NULL;
        }
    GetSetFileCdr(TRUE, &lpfnCallbackPrev, &hTaskPrev);

    FreeProcInstance(lpfnCallbackOurs);
    }

char *GetModuleNameFromTask(HANDLE handle)
    {
    TASKENTRY   te;
    static char name[40];

    te.dwSize = sizeof(te);
```

FileCdr

```
    if ( TaskFindHandle(&te, handle) )
        {
        lstrcpy(name, te.szModule);
        return name;
        }

    lstrcpy(name, "**UNKNOWN**");
    return name;
    }

void FAR PASCAL _export FileSysChange(WORD wActionCode, LPSTR lpszPath)
    {
    int i;
    static char buf[128];

    // Locate string representation of action code
    for (i = 0; action[i].byAction; i++)
        if (HIBYTE(wActionCode) == action[i].byAction) break;

    // We can't call anything that will use vsprintf, since it
    // relies on SS == DS which is not true in SMALL model
    wsprintf(buf,
        action[i].byAction ?
            "Module %s, %s: %s" :
            "Module %s, %04lX: %s",
        (LPSTR) GetModuleNameFromTask(GetCurrentTask()),
        action[i].byAction ?
            (DWORD) action[i].szAction :
            (DWORD) wActionCode,
        lpszPath);
    puts(buf);

    // Try to be generous by chaining to previous
    if (lpfnCallbackPrev)
        if (IsValidTask(hTaskPrev))
            (*lpfnCallbackPrev)(wActionCode, lpszPath);
        else
            {
            lpfnCallbackPrev = NULL;
            hTaskPrev = NULL;
            }
    }

int main()
    {
    lpfnCallbackOurs = (FILECDRPROC)
        MakeProcInstance((FARPROC) FileSysChange, __hInst);
    hTaskOurs = GetCurrentTask();

    if (! (lpTHH = GetTHH()))
        fail("Could not locate KERNEL's DGROUP.");

    GetSetFileCdr(FALSE, &lpfnCallbackPrev, &hTaskPrev);
    if (lpfnCallbackPrev != NULL)
        printf("Someone already had FileCdr; chaining\n");
```

FileCdr

```
    printf("Installing our callback function\n");
    GetSetFileCdr(TRUE, &lpfnCallbackOurs, &hTaskOurs);

    winio_onclose(__hMainWnd, (DESTROY_FUNC) PutBackPrev);
    return 0;
    }

#define THH_OFS_3_0                  0x10

WORD far *GetTHH(void)
    {
    HANDLE hMod = GetModuleHandle("KERNEL");

    return (GetVersion() >= 0x0a03) ?
        (WORD far *) GetProcAddress(hMod, "THHOOK") :
        MK_FP(GetModuleDgroup(hMod), THH_OFS_3_0);
    }
```

FlushCachedFileHandle   KERNEL.319

```
VOID FAR PASCAL FlushCachedFileHandle(HANDLE hModule);
```

To improve the response time of Windows, KERNEL maintains a cache of file handles to the most recently used executables (the cache size is controlled by the CachedFileHandles= setting in the [boot] section of SYSTEM.INI). This cache contains module handles with their associated DOS file handles. FlushCachedFileHandle() searches in this cache for the specified hModule and, if found, passes the associated file handle to the DOS Close File function (INT 21h AH=3Eh). This function is used by internal KERNEL routines such as LoadSegment(), SlowBoot(), and DelModule().

Support: 3.1

GetAppCompatFlags   KERNEL.354

```
DWORD FAR PASCAL GetAppCompatFlags(HANDLE hTask);
```

This function returns the Windows 3.1 "compatibility" flags for a given task (0 specifies the current task; GetAppCompatFlags(0) is equivalent to GetAppCompatFlags(GetCurrentTask()). If the task's module was built to target Windows 3.1, the compatibility flags will always be zero; only modules that target 3.0 can have nonzero compatibility flags. These are identical to the flags stored in the [Compatibility] section of WIN.INI:

```
[Compatibility]
TURBOTAX=0x00080000
```

```
W4GLR=0x4000
W4GL=0x4000
NETSET2=0x0100
GUIDE=0x1000
EXCEL=0x1000
. . . . .
```

Because this section is not documented in either the WININI.WRI file that comes with 3.1 or the (otherwise excellent) *Microsoft Windows Resource Kit* for 3.1, the meaning of these flags will be discussed below.

All GetAppCompatFlags() does is return the dwCompatFlags field from offset 4Eh in the Task Database for the specified task. That field is set by the function InitTask(), which calls GetProfileInt("compatibility", lpModuleName, 0); lpModule-Name comes from offset F2h in the Task Database; see the description of offsets 4Eh and F2h in the discussion of the Task Database later in this chapter. Thus, GetAppCompatFlags() simply retrieves exactly the same value as would the GetProfileInt() call, but it is much faster and works off the task handle rather than the module name. Note too that GetAppCompatFlags() returns a DWORD, whereas GetProfileInt() really returns only a WORD.

It needs to be fairly fast because GetAppCompatFlags() is used internally by Windows (though some functions inside Windows simply bypass the function, pulling the information directly out from offset 4Eh in the Task Database). For example, GlobalAlloc() in 3.1 calls the following code:

```
push 0                  ; hCurrentTask
nop
push cs                 ; far call translation
call GETAPPCOMPATFLAGS
test al, 1              ; GACF_IGNORENODISCARD (see below)
mov ax, [bp+0Ah]       ; alloc flags
jz skip
and al, 0DFh           ; GMEM_NODISCARD
skip:;
```

In other words, if the bottom bit of the compatibility flags is set for a given task's module, then GlobalAlloc() will mask off and ignore any GMEM_NODISCARD requests from that task.

While not documented in Windows or in the Windows Resource Kit, the [compatibility] flags appear in Microsoft KnowledgeBase article Q82860, from which the following is adapted:

The purpose of the compatibility flags is to work around problems that Windows applications built for 3.0 have under 3.1. Compatibility bits are predefined during Windows setup for the following applications: Publisher, MS Money, MS Works, WordPerfect, Freelance, CC Mail, Visual Basic, Ami Pro, Pixie, ObjectVision, Cricket Presents, Just Write, ExploreNet, Aporia, Packrat, Microcourier, Guide, Excel, Ascend, MGX Draw, AccPack, Charisma, Persuasion, Ingress, Lotus Notes, MS Draw, and Turbo Tax.

GetAppCompatFlags

Compatibility flags do not affect applications that target 3.1, only applications for 3.0 or earlier. As noted above, InitTask() in 3.1 checks the version and module name and, if the application targets 3.0, determines if any bits are defined for that name. If there are, these are stored in the Task Database, and then, at run time, each API function that has compatibility bits associated with it calls GetAppCompatFlags() or directly gropes the Task Database to see if these are in effect for the module of the calling task. Note that compatibility bits are only checked against application module names, not .DLL module names.

The following list of GACFs (GetAppCompatFlags) is revealing for several reasons. First, every application listed was in some sense doing something "wrong," or at least not following Microsoft recommendations to the letter (sometimes for good reason). In one sense, this list (like the [compatibility] section in WIN.INI itself) seems like a "hall of shame."

But in a complex environment such as Windows, such errors, assumptions, or workarounds are inevitable. In particular, some applications were working around bugs in 3.0, and now these applications would fall over in 3.1 because the bug has been fixed. Compatibility flags can be used to intentionally reinstate the 3.0 bug, as it were, on a per-module basis so that the application runs.

The entire [compatibility] scheme is also quite interesting because it shows the extent to which Microsoft is committed to running existing programs, even when their developers break rules, do things improperly, include workarounds, rely on undocumented behavior, and so on. The following point, from Gordon Letwin's *Inside OS/2*, seems appropriate here: "It may seem that if a popular application 'pokes' the operating system and otherwise engages in unsavory practice that the authors or users of the application will suffer because a future release . . . may not run the application correctly. To the contrary, the market dynamics state that the application has now set a standard, and it's the operating system developers who suffer because they must support that standard. Usually, that 'standard' operating system interface is not even known; a great deal of experimentation is necessary to discover exactly which undocumented side effects, system internals, and timing relationships the application is dependent on."

These flags appear, though without any explanation, in the 3.1 DDK version of WINDOWS.H.

Bit 0 (1)   **GACF_IGNORENODISCARD**

This bit ignores NODISCARD flag if passed to GlobalAlloc(). The Microsoft C 6.x runtime install library allocates global memory improperly by incorrectly specifying the GMEM_NODISCARD bit.

Bit 1 (2)   **GACF_FORCETEXTBAND**

This bit separates text band from graphics band. It forces a separate band for text, disallowing 3.1 optimization where text and graphics are printed in the same band. WordPerfect assumed text had to go in the second band; Freelance couldn't print presentation (.PRE) files.

GetAppCompatFlags

Bit 2 (4)   **GACF_ONELANDGRXBAND**

This bit allows one only graphics band and only one Landscape graphics band. Take as much memory as possible for this band; what doesn't fit in that band doesn't print. The compatibility switch doesn't completely fix the problem, only for certain memory configurations.

Bit 3 (8)   **GACF_IGNORETOPMOST**

This bit ignores topmost windows for GetWindow(HWND,GW_HWNDFIRST). CCMail would GP fault when running any Windows applet from CCMail because it assumed the applet it starts will be at the top of the window list when WinExec returns. Because of the addition of "topmost" windows in Windows 3.1, this isn't necessarily the case. The compatibility bit fixes this so GetWindow doesn't return a topmost window.

Bit 4 (10h)   **GACF_CALLTTDEVICE**

This bit sets the DEVICE_FONTTYPE bit in the FontType for TrueType fonts returned by EnumFonts(). AmiPro and WordPerfect assumed that TrueType fonts enumerated by the printer would have the device bit set, but TrueType fonts aren't device fonts. The compatibility bit fixes this by claiming that they are.

Bit 5 (20h)   **GACF_MULTIPLEBANDS**

This bit forces graphics output into more than one band when printing. Freelance wouldn't print graphics when there was enough memory, and UniDrv used only one band for printing. If the first band was the entire page, it didn't issue any graphics calls, thinking it was the text-only band. This bit forces UniDrv to use multiple bands.

Bit 6 (40h)   **GACF_ALWAYSSENDNCPAINT**

SetWindowPos() must send a WM_NCPAINT message to all children, disallowing the 3.1 optimization where this message is only sent to windows that must be redrawn. Some 3.0 applications used WM_NCPAINT to determine that they needed to reposition themselves at the top of the list. The bit is enabled for ObjectVision, Cricket Presents.

Bit 7 (80h)   **GACF_EDITSETTEXTMUNGE**

When this bit is set, strings that are passed to edit controls by WM_SETTEXT are forced to upper case. This would happen in 3.0 because of a bug; some applications worked around the bug and then broke in 3.1 when the bug was fixed. Essentially, this compatibility bit emulates the 3.0 bug so that the affected applications can work around it.

Bit 8 (100h   **GACF_MOREEXTRAWNDWORDS**

This bit adds four to the extra bytes (CBWNDEXTRA) in the window instance and class instance structures. In Windows 3.0, even if you didn't allocate extra window/class words, you could still access them and corrupt Windows internally. Windows 3.1 doesn't allow you to access extra words you didn't allocate. This switch forces extra words for all classes/windows created by the given application, because some applications relied on the ability to access the nonallocated bytes. For example, Aporia in RegisterClass() asks for

GetAppCompatFlags

one extra byte, then does a SetWindowWord() (two bytes), then a GetWindowLong (four bytes).

Bit 9 (200h)   GACF_TTIGNORERASTERDUPE

Don't enumerate duplicate bitmap fonts for TrueType fonts. Some applications (including WordPerfect and Visual Basic) get confused when fonts are enumerated for the same sizes as both bitmap and TrueType fonts.

Bit 10 (400h)   GACF_HACKWINFLAGS

Setting this compat flag causes GetWinFlags() to clear the WF_PAGING setting. However, no application seems to require this hack.

Bit 11 (800h)   GACF_DELAYHWHNDSHAKECHK

Don't check hardware handshaking (CTS and DSR) on SetCommState(); this reverts to (buggy) 3.0 behavior on which some applications (including Packrat) depended.

Bit 12 (1000h)   GACF_ENUMHELVNTMSRMN

This bit enumerates TmsRmn and Helv. Some applications break under 3.1 because they relied on the presence in 3.0 of the fonts "Helv" and "Tms Rmn" (such applications apparently include Spinnaker, Guide, Excel, and WordPerfect). Font substitution covers much of these problems, but Microsoft cannot legally enumerate the names "Helv" and "Tms Rmn" for future applications, so it was dropped. (Helvetica and Times Roman are registered trademarks of Linotype AG.) Windows 3.1 still has the exact same fonts, but under the names MS Sans Serif and MS Serif, and will enumerate them as Helv and Tms Rmn when this bit is set. Microsoft *is* allowed to do this, but solely for backward compatibility with existing 3.0 applications.

Bit 13 (2000h)   GACF_ENUMTTNOTDEVICE

This bit turns off DEVICE_FONTTYPE. Some applications (including PageMaker, Designer 3.1, MGXDraw, and Persuasion) fail to enumerate more than one size of True-Type fonts because they interpret the DEVICE_FONTTYPE flag incorrectly. They assume the font must be device resident and disregard the case where the font is downloaded (as TrueType can be). Therefore, when TrueType is correctly enumerated with the device bit set, the apps check the device capabilities to see if the printer can scale fonts. If the device cannot, the application assumes one size for the current font. This problem is not seen on PostScript printers, which can download and scale fonts, or on dot matrix printers, which cannot download fonts. This compatibility bit simply checks all the above conditions and selectively turns the DEVICE_FONTTYPE off.

Bit 14 (4000h)   GACF_SUBTRACTCLIPSIBS

This flag affects the way window invalidation works for non-WS_CLIPSIBLINGS parent windows and their children (e.g., dialog boxes and dialog controls). Normally, if two children of a non-WS_CLIPSIBLING parent overlap, and an area that contains both of those windows is invalidated (either by a call to InvalidateRect or through window rearrangement), both of the windows will get invalidated, even if one or both are WS_CLIP-SIBLINGS. With GACF_SUBTRACTCLIPSIBS, any sibling window underneath a

GetAppCompatFlags

WS_CLIPSIBLINGS window will *not* be invalidated in the part of the window that is beneath the WS_CLIPSIBLINGS window. This situation arises most commonly when windows that are supposed to appear overlapped don't seem to overlap properly. Applications that implement dropdown combo boxes as child windows of dialog boxes will exhibit this problem (e.g., Lotus Notes 2.1 drive dropdowns). It's often hard to tell whether a dropdown is implemented as a top-level window (e.g., the Windows system combo boxes) or as a child window—if there seem to be overlapping problems, then GACF_SUBTRACTCLIPSIBS could be the solution.

Bit 15 (8000h)   **GACF_FORCETTGRAPHICS**

Freelance wouldn't print TrueType unless "print TrueType as graphics" was selected.

Bit 16 (10000h)   **GACF_NOHRGN1**

This bit affects applications that depend on a bug in the 3.0 GetUpdateRect() function. Under 3.0, GetUpdateRect would not always return the rectangle in logical DC coordinates: if the entire window was invalid, the rectangle was instead sometimes returned in window coordinates. This bug was fixed for 3.0 and 3.1 apps in Windows 3.1: coordinates are *always* returned in logical coordinates. This bit intentionally reintroduces the bug in GetUpdateRect() for those applications such as Microsoft Draw that depend on this behavior.

Bit 17 (20000h)   **GACF_NCCALCSIZEONMOVE**

3.1 optimizes WM_NCCALCSIZE if a window was just moving, where 3.0 always sent it. This bit causes it to be sent always, as in 3.0, for applications such as Lotus Notes that depend on this behavior.

Bit 18 (40000h)   **GACF_SENDMENUDBLCLK**

This bit passes double-clicks on a menu bar to the app. With this bit set, if the user double clicks on the menu bar when a menu is visible, Windows ends processing of the menu and passes the double-click message on to the application. This allows JustWrite to detect double-click on the system menu of a maximized MDI child. The normal (and expected) behavior is for Windows to detect the double click on a sys menu of a maximized child and send the app a WM_SYSCOMMAND SC_CLOSE message, which is what happens with a nonmaximized MDI child window.

Bit 19 (80000h)   **GACF_30AVGWIDTH**

This bit changes the way Windows calculates average character width, so that 1040 forms from TurboTax will print correctly with a PostScript driver. When this bit is set, all fonts are scaled by 7/8. TurboTax has hardcoded the average widths it uses for selecting fonts; this broke when Windows changed the way it calculates average widths to match True-Type, resulting in an inability to print 1040 forms (when telling the IRS why your tax return is late, this one could possibly serve as the Windows equivalent of "the dog ate it").

GetAppCompatFlags

With all of these compatibility workarounds, if/when the application changes its behavior, it can mark itself as a 3.1-targeted application, so that the compatibility bits will no longer be used. If the application wants to continue to run in 3.0, WIN.INI can be edited or the application can change its module name (the compatibility settings work off the module name).

Support: 3.1 (for 3.0 apps only)
See also: InitTask, Task Database

GetCodeHandle   KERNEL.93

```
DWORD FAR PASCAL GetCodeHandle(lpProc);
FARPROC lpProc;      /* A procedure-instance address; but see below */
```

While documented, GetCodeHandle() has a variation that is undocumented: rather than pass it a far procedure-instance address, GetCodeHandle() can be called with a far pseudo-pointer containing a module handle and a logical segment number, for example, MK_FP(hModule, wSeg). Furthermore, while documented as returning only a WORD, GetCodeHandle() in fact returns a DWORD, with a segment handle in its LOWORD (AX) and a segment selector in its HIWORD (DX). This variation on GetCodeHandle() is used by WinDebug to convert logical segment numbers (1, 2, 3, etc.) into callable selectors.

One possible drawback is that, in a fine illustration of the so-called Heisenberg Principle (that is, merely looking at things changes them), after using GetCodeHandle() to convert a logical segment number into a selector, the segment will be loaded into memory if it wasn't there already.

Support: 3.0, 3.1
Example: The following program displays information about each segment (CODE or DATA) in a Windows module (the name of the module can be specified on the command line). GetCodeHandle() is passed the module handle and logical segment numbers, and it returns in its HIWORD a protected-mode selector to the segment. The number of segment numbers is established from offset 1Ch in the Module Table (see the description of the Module Table later in this chapter). The GetCodeInfo() function is used to get additional information about the segment; although documented, GetCodeInfo() is certainly *poorly* documented. (For more information, see the Microsoft Developer Knowledge Base article Q67650, "GetCodeInfo() Documented Incorrectly.")

```
/* walksegs.c */

#include <dos.h>
#include "windows.h"
#include "winio.h"
```

```
DWORD (FAR PASCAL *GetCodeHandleD)(WORD hMod, WORD wSeg);

/* GetCodeInfo is documented, but not very well */
typedef struct {
    WORD wOfs, wLen, wFlags, wAlloc, wHandle, wShift, wReserved[2];
    } CODEINFO;

main(int argc, char *argv[])
{
    char *modname;
    HANDLE hMod;
    WORD wSeg;
    WORD cSeg;
    DWORD dwCode;

    GetCodeHandleD = GetCodeHandle;

    modname = (argc < 2) ? "KERNEL" : argv[1];
    if (! (hMod = GetModuleHandle(modname)))
        fail("Cannot locate module");

    /* Get number of segments from offset 1Ch in Module Table */
    cSeg = *((WORD far *) MK_FP(hMod, 0x1c));

    printf("%s %04x\n", modname, hMod);
    for (wSeg=1; wSeg<=cSeg; wSeg++)
        if ((dwCode = GetCodeHandleD(hMod, wSeg)) < 32)
            printf("   Seg #%d\tError!!\n", wSeg);
        else
        {
            CODEINFO codeinfo;
            WORD wSel = HIWORD(dwCode); // code selector
            /* this alternate form of GetCodeInfo is documented */
            GetCodeInfo((FARPROC) MK_FP(hMod, wSeg), &codeinfo);
            printf("   Seg #%d\t%04x\tLen=%04xh\t%s\n",
                wSeg, wSel,
                codeinfo.wLen,
                (codeinfo.wFlags & 1) ? "DATA" : "CODE");
        }
    return 0;
}
```

The program displays a list of segments such as the following:

```
GDI 0367
    Seg #1    037f    Len=845eh    CODE
    Seg #2    0387    Len=10aeh    CODE
    Seg #3    038f    Len=2f9fh    CODE
    ....
    Seg #47   04ef    Len=04b0h    DATA
    Seg #48   04f7    Len=0b52h    DATA
```

GetCodeHandle

GetCurPID   KERNEL.157

```
DWORD FAR PASCAL GetCurPID(DWORD dw);
```

This function, a holdover from Windows 2.x, simply returns zero in Windows 3.x. It was designed for use with the (also defunct) EmsCopy() function. Windows applications needing a process ID should call GetCurrentTask() or GetCurrentPDB().

GetCurrentPDB   KERNEL.37

```
DWORD FAR PASCAL GetCurrentPDB(void);
```

Although the GetCurrentPDB() function is documented, its return value is specified as a WORD containing the current DOS Program Data Base (PDB), better known as the Program Segment Prefix (PSP). In fact, GetCurrentPDB() returns a DWORD, with the current PDB in the LOWORD (AX) and the value TOPPDB in the HIWORD (DX); TOPPDB (KERNEL's protected-mode PSP) is also contained in the THHOOK data structure, described later in this chapter. The current PDB is extracted from offset 60h of the current Task Database (CURTDB), also contained in the THHOOK structure.

Just as in plain-vanilla DOS, the PSP plays a crucial role in task management (such as it is) in Windows. For example, the file-handle table for each Windows task is kept in its PSP, just as in DOS. Similarly, memory allocations belong to a given PSP. Whenever a task is scheduled to run in Windows (i.e., becomes the current task), its PSP becomes the current PDB.

Because Windows is a protected-mode DOS extender, the PSP is, of course, a protected-mode data structure. The PSP handle itself is a protected-mode selector, and any addresses contained in the PSP are likewise protected-mode selectors or pointers. For example, the environment segment kept at offset 2Ch is actually a protected-mode selector, and the Job File Table (JFT) pointer at offset 34h is likewise a protected-mode selector:offset. Once you make these adjustments, the PSP structure given in *Undocumented DOS* (see the reference entry for INT 21h Function 26h (Create PSP) can be applied to Windows programs.

Windows uses some previously unused fields in the PSP. For example, offset 48h contains a flag whose bottom bit indicates whether the task is an old app (that is, a non-Windows DOS program; see the IsWinOldApTask() function described later in this chapter).

Support: 3.0, 3.1
See also: IsWinOldApTask, Task Database

GetCurrentTask   KERNEL.36

```
DWORD FAR PASCAL GetCurrentTask(void);
```

Although the GetCurrentTask() function is documented, its return value is specified as a WORD containing (as its name implies) a handle to the current task. In fact, GetCurrentTask() returns a DWORD, with the current task (CURTDB) in the LOWORD (AX) and the head of the task list (HEADTDB) in the HIWORD (DX). As shown in the following example, the value of HEADTDB is used to initiate a walk of the Windows task list. GetCurrentTask() does nothing more than retrieve the value of CURTDB and HEADTDB from the THHOOK data structure, described later in this chapter.

Furthermore, even though the GetCurrentTask() function is documented, its return value is described merely as "the handle of the currently executing task," without specifying exactly (or even vaguely) what it is a handle to. A task handle is, in fact, a selector to a Task Database structure, explained in detail later in this chapter. The Task Database also includes a protected-mode Program Segment Prefix (PSP) structure.

The handle of the current task is particularly useful to Windows DLLs (to find out who called it) and interrupt handlers (to find out who it interrupted). Calling this function from within a normal application will, of course, merely return the application's own task handle. This is generally useful only if the task handle is then used to access the Task Database or if the HIWORD of the GetCurrentTask() return value is used to access the entire task list.

There is no SetCurrentTask() function to match GetCurrentTask(). However, one could be created by setting (instead of just getting) the CURTDB field in the THHOOK structure. Even better, ToolHelp provides a documented function, TaskSwitch(), which does essentially the same thing as would SetCurrentTask(). As explained in chapter 10, TaskSwitch() enables an arbitrary section of code to be executed while running as an arbitrary task; code in one program can be executed while the current task belongs to some other program. Any DOS programmer who has used the Set PSP call (INT 21h AH=50h) will see why this could be useful.

Support: 3.0, 3.1
See also: Task Database, THHOOK
Example: This program walks the Windows task list, which is a linked list: as explained in the Task Database entry, the first WORD of each Task Database contains a selector to the next task in the list or 0 to indicate the end of the list. It is important not to change the state of the system while walking the list; the following program uses winio_setpaint(FALSE) to avoid any calls to PeekMessage() or Yield() that could alter the list. When done, the program verifies the number of tasks found against the documented GetNumTasks() function.

```
/* taskwalk.c */
```

```
#include <dos.h>
#include "windows.h"
#include "winio.h"

/* GetCurrentTask is documented, but only with WORD retval */
DWORD (FAR PASCAL *GetCurrentTaskD)(void);

main()
{
    DWORD dwTask;
    WORD wFirstTask, wNextTask;
    WORD wNumTasks;
    HWND hwnd;

    GetCurrentTaskD = GetCurrentTask;

    dwTask = GetCurrentTaskD();
    wFirstTask = HIWORD(dwTask);  // get base of linked list
    wNextTask = wFirstTask;
    wNumTasks = 0;
    hwnd = winio_current();
    winio_setpaint(hwnd, FALSE); // so we don't yield while walking task list!
    for (;;)
    {
        /*
            See the description of the Task Database data structure
            for an explanation of offsets 0 and 0F2h.
        */
        char far *fp;
        char modname[9], *p=modname;
        int i;
        /* Copy the modname name at offset 0F2h in the Task Database */
        for (i=0, fp=MK_FP(wNextTask,0xf2); i<8; i++, p++, fp++)
            *p = *fp;
        *p = '\0';
        printf("%04x %s", wNextTask, modname);
        if (wNextTask == GetCurrentTask())
            printf(" <== current task");
        printf("\n");
        wNumTasks++;
        /* Get the handle of the next task from offset 0 in the Task DB */
        wNextTask = *((WORD far *) MK_FP(wNextTask, 0));
        if (wNextTask == 0)
            break;
    }
    winio_setpaint(hwnd, TRUE);
    if (wNumTasks != GetNumTasks())
        fail("Wrong number of tasks!");
    return 0;
}
```

The program prints out a simple list of task handles and names; for example:

```
113F CLIPBRD
179F WINFILE
```

GetCurrentTask

```
141F WINOLDAP
11E7 CLOCK
108F TASKWALK <== current task
```

Many other programs that walk the Windows task list appear elsewhere in this book: the WINTASK program later in this chapter (see Task Database) provides far more information than TASKWALK. The WINWALK program in chapter 10 has a Task Walk that uses ToolHelp. The TASKWLK2 program in chapter 2 uses ToolHelp, and hangs off a timer, waiting for GetNumTasks() to change; at these times, the task list can be unstable (the number of tasks found by talking the task list is not the same as the number of tasks returned from GetNumTasks(), because the Windows scheduler is in the middle of rearranging the tasks in priority order; see Matt Pietrek's article "Inside the Windows Scheduler," *Dr. Dobb's Journal*, August 1992).

GetExePtr   KERNEL.133

```
WORD FAR PASCAL GetExePtr(HANDLE h);
```

GetExePtr() accepts handles of several different types and returns the corresponding module handle. Among the handles accepted by GetExePtr() are hModules (it simply returns the same hModule), hInstances, and global-heap handles returned from GlobalAlloc(). In other words, given an arbitrary handle to a global-heap item, GetExePtr() can return the module handle of the block's owner. Note that multiple instances of an application share a single module handle, so the value returned from GetExePtr() does not distinguish between multiple instances.

This is somewhat different from the value stored in the owner field of the Global Arena structure and returned from the undocumented FarGetOwner() function. GetExePtr() uses GetOwner() to get the owner PSP (PDB) for global heap items and then walks the task-database list, searching for the matching PSP.

GetExePtr() does *not* appear to accept either hTasks (which cause a debug break and return 0) or PSPs. Passing a Task Queue handle to GetExePtr() returns USER's module handle.

GetExePtr() is used extensively within KERNEL itself, for example, by the GetProcAddress(), DirectResAlloc(), and IsSharedSelector() functions. Functions that expect an hModule can generally also be passed an hInstance; the function will call GetExePtr() to convert the hInstance into an hModule.

Support: 3.0, 3.1
See also: FarGetOwner, Global Arena, Task Database
Example: The following rather feeble example uses WinExec() to launch two copies of the Windows Notepad. WinExec() returns an hInstance, which is then converted to an hModule, using GetExePtr(). Whereas multiple copies of an application obviously have different hInstances, they share the same hModule.

```
/* exeptr.c */

#include "windows.h"
#include "winio.h"

/* undocumented function */
WORD FAR PASCAL GetExePtr(HANDLE h);

main()
{
    char buf[128];
    HANDLE hInst1, hInst2, hMod1, hMod2;

    if ((hInst1 = WinExec("notepad.exe", SW_NORMAL)) < 32)
        fail("Can't exec");
    if ((hInst2 = WinExec("notepad.exe", SW_NORMAL)) < 32)
        fail("Can't exec");

    hMod1 = GetExePtr(hInst1);
    GetModuleFileName(hMod1, buf, 128);
    printf("hInst=%04x hMod=%04x %s\n", hInst1, hMod1, buf);

    hMod2 = GetExePtr(hInst2);
    GetModuleFileName(hMod2, buf, 128);
    printf("hInst=%04x hMod=%04x %s\n", hInst2, hMod2, buf);

    /* Multiple instances have same module handle */
    if ((hInst1 == hInst2) || (hMod1 != hMod2))
        fail("Something strange!");

    return 0;
}
```

The output from the program looks like this:

```
hInst=11fe hMod=11e7 C:\WINDOWS\NOTEPAD.EXE
hInst=110e hMod=11e7 C:\WINDOWS\NOTEPAD.EXE
```

GetExeVersion   KERNEL.105

```
WORD FAR PASCAL GetExeVersion(void);
```

This function returns the expected Windows version for the currently executing task; it merely returns the value from offset 1Ah in the Task Database of the current task: *((WORD far *) MK_FP(GetCurrentTask(), 0x1A)). The version number is returned in the same minor-major order as used by GetVersion() (for example, Windows 3.1 is 0x0A03h).

Support: 3.0, 3.1
See also: Task Database, GetExpWinVer

GetExpWinVer   KERNEL.167

```
WORD FAR PASCAL GetExpWinVer(HANDLE hModule);
```

This function returns the version number of Windows that the given module expects (requires as a minimum). This function can be used to distinguish among applications built for Windows 3.0, 3.1, or even 2.0. This value comes straight from offset 3Eh in the segmented-executable NE header (Module Table), so GetExpWinVer() strictly isn't necessary.

Unlike the documented GetVersion() function, which returns the Windows version number in minor/major order (for example, Windows 3.1 is 0A03h), GetExpWinVer() returns the expected Windows version in major/minor order (for example, 030Ah).

GetExpWinVer() and GetExeVersion() differ in that, while GetExpWinVer() gets the expected Windows version for an arbitrary module in the system, GetExeVersion() just gets it for the current task. Also, GetExpWinVer(GetCurrentModule()) (where GetCurrentModule() is a macro in HANDLES.H, in the introduction to this chapter) differs from GetExeVersion() in that one uses minor-major order and the other uses major-minor order. (Yawn!)

Support: 3.0, 3.1
See also: Module Table, GetExeVersion

GetFreeMemInfo   KERNEL.316

```
DWORD FAR PASCAL GetFreeMemInfo(void);
```

This function returns the number of unlocked and free pages; the information returned is a subset of that provided by the DPMI Get Free Memory Information (INT 31h AX=0500h) function. Unlike the underlying DPMI call, however, GetFreeMemInfo() is only available in Windows 3.1 on 80386 and higher processors (when using KRNL286.EXE, it simply returns 0FFFFFFFFh). It therefore makes more sense to use the DPMI call. Rather than directly call DPMI, you can also use the ToolHelp MemManInfo() function.

The DWORD returned from GetFreeMemInfo() contains the total number of unlocked pages in its LOWORD (AX) and the total number of free pages in its HIWORD (DX). Each page is 4K bytes.

Support: 3.1
See also: MemManInfo (ToolHelp)
Example: The following program uses both GetFreeMemInfo() and DPMI to report on available virtual memory:

```c
/* meminfo.c */

#include "windows.h"
#include "winio.h"

DWORD (FAR PASCAL *GetFreeMemInfo)(void);

typedef struct {
    DWORD dwLargestBlockBytes;
    DWORD dwMaxUnlockedPages;
    DWORD dwMaxLockedPages;
    DWORD dwLinAddrSpaceInPages;
    DWORD dwUnlockedPages;
    DWORD dwFreePages;
    DWORD dwPhysPages;
    DWORD dwFreeLinPages;
    DWORD dwPagingFilePages;
    BYTE reserved[0x0c];
    } DPMI_FREEMEM;

BOOL get_dpmi_freemem(DPMI_FREEMEM far *fpbuf)
{
    _asm push di
    _asm les di, fpbuf
    _asm mov ax, 0500h
    _asm int 31h
    _asm pop di
    _asm jc error
    return 1;
error:
    return 0;
}

#define SHOW(str, dw) \
    if (dw != -1L) \
        printf(str ## ": %lu bytes\n", dw)

main()
{
    DWORD dwInfo;
    WORD wTotalUnlocked;
    WORD wFreePages;

    DPMI_FREEMEM mem;
    if (get_dpmi_freemem(&mem))
    {
        // only first value is meaningful in Standard mode
        SHOW("Largest available free block", mem.dwLargestBlockBytes);
        SHOW("Linear address space", mem.dwLinAddrSpaceInPages * 4096);
        SHOW("Free address space", mem.dwFreeLinPages * 4096);
        SHOW("Size of paging file", mem.dwPagingFilePages * 4096);
        SHOW("Physical memory", mem.dwPhysPages * 4096);
    }

    GetFreeMemInfo = GetProcAddress(GetModuleHandle("KERNEL"),
```

GetFreeMemInfo

```
        "GETFREEMEMINFO");
    if (! GetFreeMemInfo)
        fail("This program requires Windows 3.1 or higher");
    dwInfo = GetFreeMemInfo();
    if (dwInfo == -1L)
        fail("GetFreeMemInfo doesn't apply in Standard mode");
    wTotalUnlocked = LOWORD(dwInfo);
    wFreePages = HIWORD(dwInfo);
    printf("Total Unlocked Pages = %04xh (%lu bytes)\n",
        wTotalUnlocked, (long) wTotalUnlocked * 4096L);
    printf("Total Free Pages = %04xh (%lu bytes)\n",
        wFreePages, (long) wFreePages * 4096L);
    return 0;
}
```

On a machine with 5 megabytes of physical memory and a permanent swap file of over 4 megabytes, sample output from the program looked like the following; note that Windows consistently reports the total linear address space as four times the available physical memory, regardless of the amount of disk space or the size of the permanent swap file:

```
Largest available free block: 14077952 bytes
Linear address space: 16105472 bytes
Free address space: 14221312 bytes
Size of paging file: 4993024 bytes
Physical memory: 4378624 bytes
Total Unlocked Pages: 0338h (3375104 bytes)
Total Free Pages: 01e1h (1970176 bytes)
```

GetHeapSpaces   KERNEL.138

```
DWORD FAR PASCAL GetHeapSpaces(hModOrInst)
HANDLE hModOrInst;        /* an hModule or an hInstance */
```

GetHeapSpaces() is the undocumented function that most applications use to compute free system resources, (i.e., the percentage of the USER and GDI heaps that remains unused). Chapter 1 of this book discusses the Saga of Free System Resources in detail.

Given a module handle or instance handle (the function figures out which is which by checking for an NE signature, in which case it knows it has a module handle), GetHeapSpaces() returns a DWORD whose HIWORD contains the total number of bytes in the module's local heap, and whose LOWORD contains the number of *free* bytes. This can be done for any module in the system that has a local heap (KERNEL doesn't). The free system resources percentage displayed by Program Manager and other Windows programs is the percentage free (free * 100 / total) for USER or GDI, whichever is smaller.

Windows 3.1 provides a documented GetFreeSystemResources() function. However, because this function is available only in 3.1, because it returns less information than GetHeapSpaces(), and because no one wants to change code that already works, most applications continue to use GetHeapSpaces(). Note, however, that GetHeapSpaces() produces a number that may be slightly off in 3.1 because, fortunately, some resources (menus in particular) have been moved out of USER's default local heap. Thus, GetHeapSpaces() in 3.1 may miscalculate the free percentage; on the other hand, the exact number generally isn't all that important, and the percentage of free resources may, in general, be a little less important in 3.1 anyway.

GetHeapSpaces() itself is implemented using an undocumented function: LocalCountFree(), described later in this chapter. GetHeapSpaces() gets the HIWORD of its return value from the documented GlobalSize() function and the LOWORD of its return value (the number of free bytes) from LocalCountFree().

```
push ds
mov ds, ax
call far ptr LocalCountFree
```

Example: The following program, SYSTRES, uses the GetHeapSpaces() function to compute Free System Resources. In 3.1, it also uses the documented GetFreeSystemResources() function. Interestingly, the results returned by the two different functions never seem to be off by more than 1%:

```
/* SYSTRES.C -- System Resources */

#include "windows.h"
#include "winio.h"

/* undocumented Windows call to use in 3.0 */
extern DWORD FAR PASCAL GetHeapSpaces(WORD hModule);

/* Windows 3.1 function may not be in WINDOWS.H */
WORD FAR PASCAL (*GetFreeSystemResources)(WORD wNum);

void heap_info(char *module, WORD *pfree, WORD *ptotal, WORD *ppercent)
{
    DWORD info = GetHeapSpaces(GetModuleHandle(module));
    *pfree = LOWORD(info);
    *ptotal = HIWORD(info);
    *ppercent = (WORD) ((((DWORD) *pfree) * 100L) / ((DWORD) *ptotal));
}

main()
{
    WORD user_free, user_total, user_percent;
    WORD gdi_free, gdi_total, gdi_percent;
    WORD min_percent, diff;
    WORD vers = (WORD) GetVersion();  // returns DWORD in 3.1

    heap_info("USER", &user_free, &user_total, &user_percent);
```

GetHeapSpaces

```
    heap_info("GDI", &gdi_free, &gdi_total, &gdi_percent);

    printf("Using GetHeapSpaces:\n");
    printf("USER heap: %u bytes free out of %u (%u%% free)\n",
        user_free, user_total, user_percent);
    printf("GDI heap: %u bytes free out of %u (%u%% free)\n",
        gdi_free, gdi_total, gdi_percent);
    min_percent = min(user_percent, gdi_percent);
    printf("Free system resources: %u%%\n", min_percent);

    if ((LOBYTE(vers) >= 3) && (HIBYTE(vers) >= 0x0a))  // 3.1+
    {   // What's this function doing in USER?!
        GetFreeSystemResources = GetProcAddress(GetModuleHandle("USER"),
            "GETFREESYSTEMRESOURCES");
        puts("\nUsing GetFreeSystemResources:");
        printf("USER heap: %u%% free\n", GetFreeSystemResources(2));
        printf("GDI heap: %u%% free\n", GetFreeSystemResources(1));
        printf("Free system resources: %u%%\n",
            GetFreeSystemResources(0));

        printf("\n");
        if (diff = GetFreeSystemResources(2) - user_percent)
            printf("USER off by %u%%\n", abs(diff));
        if (diff = GetFreeSystemResources(1) - gdi_percent)
            printf("GDI off by %u%%\n", abs(diff));
        if (diff = GetFreeSystemResources(0) - min_percent)
            printf("FSR off by %u%%\n", abs(diff));
        // no matter what, never find it off by more than 1%
    }

    return 0;
}
```

GetLastDiskChange   KERNEL.98

```
BYTE GetLastDiskChange(void);
```

This function, used by the defunct MSDOS.EXE shell, was apparently intended to report the current state of a removable drive. It returns the value of a KERNEL internal variable, but in Windows 3.0 and 3.1 this variable appears to never be set. If you need disk-change information, use the BIOS Get Disk Change Status function (INT 13h AH=16h).

GetLpErrMode   KERNEL.99

```
LPBYTE FAR PASCAL GetLpErrMode(void);
```

This function returns a long pointer to a byte inside of KERNEL's data segment; the byte indicates whether Windows is currently in error mode (that is, handling an INT

24h critical error). This is analogous to the critical-error flag that DOS TSRs often check (see *Undocumented DOS*, chapter 5). For example, the byte is 1 when a "System Error: cannot read from drive A:" message box is displayed. You can call the function once, and just dereference its returned pointer whenever you need the error mode:

```
BYTE far *lpErrMode = GetLpErrMode();
if (*lpErrMode == 1)
    // there's a critical error
```

Support: 3.0, 3.1
See also: SetErrorMode (documented)

GetModuleHandle   KERNEL.47

```
DWORD FAR PASCAL GetModuleHandle(lpModName);
LPSTR lpModName;     /* a module name such as "KERNEL," but see below */
```

Even though the GetModuleHandle() function is documented, it has several important aspects that are not documented. The return value is actually a DWORD, not a WORD. The HIWORD (DX) of the return value contains the handle of the first module in the system (usually KERNEL). This can be used to walk the Windows module-table list (see the following example); WinDebug uses GetModuleHandle() in this way. This undocumented DWORD return value from GetModuleHandle() is similar to GetCurrentTask(), described earlier in this chapter. The HIWORD of the return value from GetModuleHandle() is identical to the HEXEHEAD field in the THHOOK structure, described later in this chapter.

In addition to making a call such as GetModuleHandle("FOO"), where "FOO" is a far pointer to an ASCIIZ string, it can also be called with a DWORD whose LOWORD is 0 and whose HIWORD contains an hInstance (or, in fact, any handle decipherable by the undocumented GetExePtr() function, described elsewhere in this chapter, which GetModuleHandle() uses). For example, GetModuleHandle-(MK_FP(0, hInstance)) returns the same value as calling GetExePtr(hInstance) directly. In Windows 3.1 (WINDOWSX.H), the macro GetInstanceModule() is provided for turning an hInstance into an hModule:

```
#define GetInstanceModule(hInstance) \
    GetModuleHandle((LPCSTR) MAKELP(NULL, hInstance))
```

In fact, many KERNEL functions that expect an hModule can also be called with an hInstance. A Microsoft Technical Note by Bob Gunderson, "Modules, Instances, and Tasks," provides a good explanation of this:

> At this point you may be asking, "If an instance handle can be used in place of a module handle, why have module handles at all? Why not just

have instance handles and be done with it?" Good question. The answer is that it really doesn't matter. You can simply write applications using instance handles rather than module handles . . . This is good news because instance handles are much easier to obtain than module handles. For example, calling GetWindowWord with GWW_HINSTANCE obtains the instance handle of the application or the DLL that created a window. This instance handle can then be used to determine the module file name of the application that created the window. No equivalent way exists to do this using module handles.

Actually, module handles have a real use. Internally, Windows uses module handles to tag certain resources, such as window classes and hooks, that are associated with a module and not with a particular instance of a module. These resources are not freed until the last instance of the module is freed.

For a more complete explanation of the differences between modules, instances, and tasks, see the Task Database entry, which appears later in this chapter. For code that moves between these various handles, see HANDLES.H and HANDLES.C in the introduction to this chapter.

The Microsoft documentation describes the GetModuleHandle() return value merely as a module handle, without specifying really what this is a handle *to*. Of course, the whole point of handles is that they are "magic cookies," that one can use them without knowing what they point to. However, it is often useful to know that a module handle is a selector to a Module Table. See the entry on the Module Table data structure, later in this chapter.

The module-walking functions from ToolHelp provide equivalent, documented functionality; see chapter 10.

Support: 3.0, 3.1
See also: GetExePtr, Module Table
Example: This program walks the Windows module list, which is a linked list: as explained in the Module Table entry, offset 6 of each Module Table contains a selector to the next module in the list or 0 to indicate the end of the list. It is important not to change the state of Windows while walking the list, so the program below uses winio_setpaint(FALSE) to avoid any calls to PeekMessage() or Yield() until it has reached the end of the list. The program also checks for an NE signature at offset 0 in each supposed module table and uses the documented GetModuleFileName() function to retrieve its path name.

```
/* modwalk.c */

#include <dos.h>
#include "windows.h"
#include "winio.h"
```

```
/* GetModuleHandle is documented, but only with WORD retval */
DWORD (FAR PASCAL *GetModuleHandleD)(LPSTR lpModName);

main()
{
    extern WORD __hInst;
    DWORD dwMod;
    WORD wFirstMod, wNextMod;
    WORD wNumMods;
    WORD wThisMod;
    HWND hwnd;

    GetModuleHandleD = GetModuleHandle;

    dwMod = GetModuleHandleD("KERNEL");
    wFirstMod = HIWORD(dwMod);  // get base of module linked list
    wNextMod = wFirstMod;
    wNumMods = 0;
    wThisMod = GetModuleHandle(MK_FP(0, __hInst));  // same as GetExePtr
    hwnd = winio_current();
    winio_setpaint(hwnd, FALSE); // so we don't yield while walking mod list!
    for (;;)                     // walk linked list
    {
        /*
            For an explanation of offsets 0 and 6, see the description
            of the Module Table data structure
        */
        char filename[128];
        BYTE far *fpMod = MK_FP(wNextMod, 0);
        if (fpMod[0] != 'N' || fpMod[1] != 'E') // check 'NE' signature
            fail("Not a module!");
        GetModuleFileName(wNextMod, filename, 128);
        printf("%04x %s", wNextMod, filename);
        if (wNextMod == wThisMod)
            printf(" <== this module");
        printf("\n");
        wNumMods++;
        /* Get the handle of the next Mod from offset 6 in the ModTbl */
        wNextMod = *((WORD far *) MK_FP(wNextMod, 6));
        if (wNextMod == 0)
            break;
    }
    winio_setpaint(hwnd, TRUE);
    printf("%d modules\n", wNumMods);
    return 0;
}
```

The program prints out a simple list of module handles and names; for example:

```
010F C:\WINDOWS\SYSTEM\KRNL386.EXE
013F C:\WINDOWS\SYSTEM\SYSTEM.DRV
0147 C:\WINDOWS\SYSTEM\KEYBOARD.DRV
015F C:\WINDOWS\SYSTEM\MOUSE.DRV
01BF C:\WINDOWS\SYSTEM\VGAMONO.DRV
```

GetModuleHandle

```
....
1187 C:\WINDOWS\SYSTEM\MODWALK.EXE <== this module
49 modules
```

Also see the WINMOD example later in the chapter, and the WINWALK program in chapter 10.

GetProcAddress   KERNEL.50

```
FARPROC FAR PASCAL GetProcAddress(HANDLE hModule, LPSTR lpProcName);
```

This function is documented, but one way to call it is not: rather than pass in an lpProcName such as "FOO" or a decimal ordinal number such as MK_FP(0, 123), you can pass in a decimal ordinal number in string form such as "#123," as shown here:

```
void (FAR PASCAL *FooFunc)(WORD x);      // FOOBAR.123
HANDLE hFoobar = LoadLibrary("FOOBAR");
FooFunc = GetProcAddress(hFooBar, "#123");
```

This matches the behavior of the DosGetProcAddr() function in OS/2. This technique is used extensively within KERNEL itself to call functions in other Windows modules (KERNEL isn't a self-contained unit; it depends on other, supposedly higher level modules).

In addition, the hModule parameter, as with most Windows functions that expect an hModule, can instead be supplied with any handle, such as an hInstance, that KERNEL can resolve to an hModule via the undocumented GetExePtr() function. Like many other KERNEL functions, specifying 0 as the handle will cause the hModule of the current task to be used.

While GetProcAddress would appear to be an imposing piece of code, the divide-and-conquer approach makes its internal workings fairly simple. Since GetProcAddress can be passed either a function name, or an entry ordinal, the first order of business is to convert whatever the second parameter is, into a common form. Because every exported entry point in an EXE/DLL has an ordinal assigned to it, but not every entry point has a name, the common form is the ordinal value. The linker will assign ordinal values, even if you export by name.

If the entry-point parameter is either the function name, or a "#xxx" string, then a function that returns an ordinal value from either type of string is called. If the string is the "#xxx" integer-atom type, then the '#' is stripped off, and the string is converted to its binary value. Otherwise, the Resident names table in the module table is searched. If the name is not in the Resident names table, then the Non-Resident names table is loaded from disk (its file offset and size are stored in the ne_nrestab and ne_cbnrestab fields of the NE header/Module table) and is also searched. The passed-in function name string is uppercased during the search process.

GetProcAddress

After finding the ordinal value of the entry, it is necessary to find the corresponding address in memory. The function that performs this task searches through the entry table portion of the module table until the correct entry is found, or the end of the table is reached. (See the description of the Module table elsewhere in this chapter.) Upon finding the entry, the logical segment value is converted to an actual selector by looking it up in the segment table. If the segment is FIXED, but not yet loaded, it's brought in from the disk image.

Support: 3.0, 3.1

GetSelectorBase   KERNEL.186

```
DWORD FAR PASCAL GetSelectorBase(WORD wSel);
```

GetSelectorBase() returns the linear base address of a protected-mode selector. For example, a Windows program might access a data item through the pointer 11FF:0004; the value 11FFh is not a physical address, but essentially a table-lookup index. To get the underlying (though still not necessarily physical) address to which this pointer corresponds, you can use GetSelectorBase():

```
void far *fp;
// ...
dwBase = GetSelectorBase(FP_SEG(fp)) + FP_OFF(fp);
```

The selector you pass in *must* be located in the Local Descriptor Table (LDT). Selectors whose third bit is set (wSel & 4) are located in the LDT; if the third bit is clear (! (wSel & 4)), then the selector is in the Global Descriptor Table (GDT) and cannot be accessed via any function in the Get/SetSelectorBase/Limit family. For example, selectors 28h, 30h, and 40h cannot be accessed in this way. If you really need to access descriptors in the GDT, your best bet is probably to map the GDT into your address space and directly peek at the descriptors; a partial example is provided with the SetSelectorBase() function later in this chapter.

In Windows Standard mode, the base address will usually be within the range of physical memory installed. In Enhanced mode (or whenever paged virtual memory is supported), the base address returned from GetSelectorBase is *not* a physical address, but a "linear" address based on page tables. It is common to get addresses in the range of 2 gigabytes (e.g., 80673000h). Paging allows for a *sparse* address space, so this does not imply that you have 800 megabytes of virtual memory! (In fact, present versions of Windows don't support more than 64 megabytes of virtual memory: maximum Windows virtual memory is 4* physical memory; the maximum physical memory is 16 megabytes; however, the XMS 3.0 specification does provide for "super-extended memory" beyond 16 megabytes.)

While protected-mode programs can generally remain ignorant of the underlying addresses of their pointers, there are several important uses for linear-based addresses. For example, in Enhanced mode one interesting use that a Windows application might have for GetSelectorBase() is to share memory with a non-Windows application running in a DOS box. In Enhanced mode, each DOS box runs in its own virtual machine, with a separate address space from that used by the virtual machine in which Windows applications run. For example, 11FF:0004 in a Windows application has *no relation* to 11FF:0004 in a DOS box. But Windows applications and DOS boxes do, except for the first 64K, share a common *linear* address space. Thus, a Windows application might GlobalAlloc() a block of memory, GlobalPageLock() it, use GetSelectorBase() to find its linear address, and then pass the linear address (for example, on a WinExec() command line) to a DOS application. However, this application would need to be a protected-mode DOS application so that it could access linear addresses above 1 megabyte.

Even though documented in Windows 3.1, GetSelectorBase() was not documented in 3.0. Though it corresponds in functionality to DPMI function INT 31h AX=0600h, in Windows 3.0 GetSelectorBase() directly accesses the LDT:

```
GETSELECTORBASE proc far
    ENTER
    SAVE ds
    mov ds, cs:WIN_LDT
    mov bx, wSel      ; [bp+6]
    and bx, 0FFF8h    ; mask off bottom 3 bits, turning wSel into
                      ;    a byte offset into the LDT
    mov ax, [bx+2]
    mov dl, [bx+4]
    mov dh, [bx+7]
    RESTORE ds
    LEAVE 2
GETSELECTORBASE endp
```

Support: 3.0, 3.1
See also: GetSelectorLimit, SetSelectorBase
Example: The following program, BASEMOVE.C, uses GetSelectorBase to demonstrate that, even though the protected-mode selectors a program uses don't change, segments still move in the linear address space. GetSelectorBase() is called in a loop; whenever the base address for the program's CS or DS changes, the new value is displayed.

```
/* basemove.c -- use GetSelectorBase to show segment movement
   within the linear address space */

#include "windows.h"
#include "winio.h"
#include "wmhandlr.h"

/* undocumented function */
```

GetSelectorBase

```
DWORD FAR PASCAL GetSelectorBase(WORD sel);

main()
{
    DWORD basecode, basedata;
    DWORD prevcode = -1, prevdata = -1;
    WORD code, data;

    _asm mov code, cs
    _asm mov data, ds

    for (;;)
    {
        basecode = GetSelectorBase(code);
        basedata = GetSelectorBase(data);
        if (basecode != prevcode || basedata != prevdata)
            printf("CS (%04x) @ %08lx\tDS (%04x) @ %08lx\n",
                code, basecode, data, basedata);
        prevcode = basecode;
        prevdata = basedata;
        wmhandler_yield();
    }
}
```

BASEMOVE can be run with the Shaker program from the Windows SDK; if the Shaker "allocation granularity" is set to a high number such as 10K, BASEMOVE's CS and DS base addresses will change (of course, the values of CS and DS themselves never change in protected mode). Alternatively, BASEMOVE can be run while another program calls GlobalCompact(-1) in a loop or with the Windows 3.1 STRESS application. Output will look something like this:

```
CS (1207) @ 806907a0    DS (11ff) @ 80673000
CS (1207) @ 805b6e40    DS (11ff) @ 00078380
CS (1207) @ 805b3080    DS (11ff) @ 00078380
```

GetSelectorLimit   KERNEL.188

```
DWORD FAR PASCAL GetSelectorLimit(WORD wSel);
```

GetSelectorLimit() returns the limit of a protected-mode selector; this limit is the last legal offset within the corresponding segment. Except in the unlikely event that the segment has page (4K) granularity, this will be the last legal byte offset, so the limit is one byte less than the size of the segment.

While documented to some extent in Windows 3.1, this function was undocumented in 3.0. It corresponds in functionality to the Intel LSL (load selector limit) instruction, except that with GetSelectorLimit() 16-bit applications can still retrieve a limit greater than 64K, because in Enhanced mode GetSelectorLimit() itself uses 32-bit instructions.

```
GETSELECTORLIMIT proc far
    ; ...
    xor eax, eax
    lsl eax, wSel
    mov edx, eax
    shr edx, 10h
    ; ...
GETSELECTORLIMIT endp
```

The selector you pass in *must* be located in the Local Descriptor Table (LDT). Selectors whose third bit is set (wSel & 4) are located in the LDT; if the third bit is clear then the selector is in the Global Descriptor Table (GDT) and cannot be accessed via the Get/SetSelectorBase/Limit family. For example, selectors 28h, 30h, and 40h cannot be accessed in this way; use a check such as the following:

```
if ((sel & 4) != 0)
    it's an LDT selector: okay to use Get/SetSelectorBase/Limit
else
    it's a GDT selector
```

If you really need to access descriptors in the GDT, your best bet is probably to map the GDT into your address space and directly peek at the descriptors; a partial example is provided with the SetSelectorBase() function later in this chapter.

Dan Norton's book *Writing Windows Device Drivers* points out that USE32 segments might have page rather than byte granularity, and so the selector limit may indicate the size not in bytes but in 4K pages. It is thus safest to check the granularity bit, using a function such as SelectorAccessRights(); see the MyGetSelectorSize() function in the example below.

Support: 3.0, 3.1
See also: GetSelectorBase, SetSelectorLimit
Example: The following program uses GetSelectorLimit() to find the actual size in bytes of various KERNEL data structures:

```
/* sellimit.c */

#include <stdlib.h>
#include <dos.h>
#include "windows.h"
#include "winio.h"
#include "handles.h" //for lar()

extern DWORD FAR PASCAL GetSelectorLimit(WORD wSel);
extern DWORD FAR PASCAL GetSelectorBase(WORD wSel);
static WORD (FAR PASCAL *GetTaskQueue)(WORD hTask);
extern WORD FAR PASCAL SelectorAccessRights(WORD wSel,
    WORD wFlag, WORD wParam);
```

GetSelectorLimit

```
DWORD MyGetSelectorSize(WORD wSel)
{
    DWORD dwSize;
    WORD wRights;

    /* The Windows Get/SetSelectorBase/Limit functions can't
       handle selectors in the GDT */
    if ((wSel & 4) == 0)
        return 0L;                  // not an LDT selector

    /* Unfortunately, SelectorAccessRights() does not check the Zero
       flag after doing a LAR, so it can't be used to check if a
       selector is valid -- we'll use LAR ourselves to check */
    if ((wRights = lar(wSel)) == 0)
        return 0L;                  // invalid selector

    /* Add one to limit to get size */
    dwSize = GetSelectorLimit(wSel) + 1;

    /* Now we can use SelectorAccessRights to see if this (valid)
       selector has Page granularity */
    wRights = SelectorAccessRights(wSel, 0, 0);
    if (wRights & (1 << 15))        // page granularity bit set
        dwSize *= 4096;             // size was pages; turn into bytes

    return dwSize;
}

show_size(char *msg, HANDLE h)
{
    DWORD dwSize;
    if ((dwSize = MyGetSelectorSize(h)) == 0)
        printf("%s INVALID OR NOT IN LDT\n", msg);
    else
    {
        DWORD dwBase = GetSelectorBase(h);
        printf("%s size=%lu bytes @ %lxh\n", msg, dwSize, dwBase);
    }
}

main(int argc, char *argv[])
{
    extern WORD __hInst;

    HANDLE h = GlobalAlloc(GMEM_MOVEABLE, 1);
    char far *fp = GlobalLock(h);
    show_size("GlobalAlloc=1 byte; actually", FP_SEG(fp));
    GlobalUnlock(h);
    GlobalFree(h);

    show_size("Task Database", GetCurrentTask());

    show_size("PSP (PDB)", GetCurrentPDB());

    GetTaskQueue = GetProcAddress(GetModuleHandle("KERNEL"), "GETTASKQUEUE");
```

GetSelectorLimit

```
    show_size("Task Queue", GetTaskQueue(0));    // q for current tasknnnn

    show_size("Module Table",
        GetModuleHandle(MK_FP(0, __hInst)));    // hModule from hInstance

    return 0;
}
```

Under Windows 3.1 Enhanced mode, output from the program looked like this (note, by the way, that all these key data structures have been allocated in conventional memory, below 1 megabyte):

```
GlobalAlloc=1 byte; actually size=32 bytes @ 2bdc0h
Task Database size=512 bytes @ 2baa0h
PSP (PDB) size=512 bytes @ 2bba0h
Task Queue size=288 bytes @ 2bca0h
Module Table size=256 bytes @ 2bfe0h
```

Even though a single byte is allocated with GlobalAlloc(), GetSelectorLimit() shows that the resulting global-heap block is actually 32 bytes in size. A task handle corresponds to a 512-byte block of memory; this block overlaps the first 256 bytes of a PSP (PDB), which in Windows actually has 512 bytes allocated for it, though unfortunately only the first 256 are useful (thus, we're still stuck with command lines whose maximum length is 128 bytes).

GetSetKernelDosProc   KERNEL.311

```
FARPROC FAR PASCAL GetSetKernelDOSProc(FARPROC DosProc);
```

This function allows you to change the address of the INT 21h handler that Windows calls from such functions as Dos3Call() and NoHookDosCall(). The return value is the address of the previous handler. Both the function passed in, and the value returned, are protected-mode addresses.

Any Windows calls to Dos3Call() and NoHookDosCall() are *not* caught by an INT 21h handler (such as BPINT 21 in Soft-Ice for Windows). Therefore, GetSetKernelDosProc() is important for "spy" programs and other debuggers that want to catch *all* DOS calls made by Windows applications, even DOS calls made via Dos3Call() rather than via a direct INT 21h.

Support: 3.1
See also: Dos3Call, NoHookDosCall
Example: The following code fragment is excerpted from the source code for the WISPY (I Spy for Windows) sample program from chapter 4. If GetSet-KernelDosProc() is available, and the user asks to intercept INT 21h, then

GetSetKernelDOSProc() is used to hook the interrupt; otherwise the DOS Set Vector function (INT 21h AH=25h) is used:

```
/* excerpted from WISPY.C */

FARPROC (FAR PASCAL *GetSetKernelDosProc)(FARPROC DosProc) = 0;

typedef void (_interrupt _far *INTRFUNC)();
INTRFUNC get_vect(unsigned intno)
{
    if ((intno == 0x21) && GetSetKernelDosProc)
    {
        _asm cli
        FARPROC dos = GetSetKernelDosProc(0);
        GetSetKernelDosProc(dos);
        _asm sti
        return dos;
    }
    else
    {
        return _dos_getvect(intno);
    }
}

int set_vect(unsigned intno, INTRFUNC handler)
{
    if ((intno == 0x21) && GetSetKernelDosProc)
    {
        puts("Using GetSetKernelDosProc");
        GetSetKernelDosProc((FARPROC) handler);
        return TRUE;
    }
    else
    {
        _dos_setvect(intno, handler);
        return (get_vect(intno) == handler);
    }
}

typedef struct {
#ifdef __BORLANDC__
    unsigned bp,di,si,ds,es,dx,cx,bx,ax;
#else
    unsigned es,ds,di,si,bp,sp,bx,dx,cx,ax;  /* same as PUSHA */
#endif
    unsigned ip,cs,flags;
    } REG_PARAMS;

void _interrupt _far IntHandler(REG_PARAMS r)
{
    HANDLE task = GetCurrentTask();

    if (task != wispy_task)      /* don't show my own ints */
```

GetSetKernelDosProc

```
        // ...

    _chain_intr(old[intno]);
}

main(int argc, char *argv[])
{
    // ...
    GetSetKernelDosProc = GetProcAddress(GetModuleHandle("KERNEL"),
        "GETSETKERNELDOSPROC");

    for (i=1; i<argc; i++)
    {   // pseudocode: WISPY is actually a lot more complicated
        intno = atoi(argv[i]);
        old[intno] = get_vect(intno);
        set_vect(intno, IntHandler);
    }
```

GetTaskDS   KERNEL.155

```
WORD FAR PASCAL GetTaskDS(void);
```

This function returns the hInstance (default data segment, or DGROUP) of the currently executing task. It only makes sense to call this function from a DLL or an interrupt handler; otherwise, an application is merely inquiring after *its own* hInstance, which is already available as one of the parameters to WinMain( ).

Support: 3.0, 3.1
Example: The following macro passes the return value from GetTaskDS() to GetExePtr( ), turning the hInstance into an hModule:

```
#define GetCurrentModule()    (GetExePtr(GetTaskDS()))
```

GetTaskQueue   KERNEL.35

```
WORD FAR PASCAL GetTaskQueue(HANDLE hTask);
```

This function returns a handle to the Task Queue structure for the specified task (or, if hTask is 0, for the current task). Each task has a Task Queue containing pending messages; since each message contains an HWND, a WM_ message number, and so on, it is clear that KERNEL knows about such USER constructs.

For more information, see the entry on the Task Queue structure later in this chapter. In addition to getting the Task Queue belonging to a specified task, a task's Task Queue can be changed, using the SetTaskQueue function.

Support: 3.0, 3.1

See also: GetTaskQueueDS, GetTaskQueueES, SetTaskQueue, Task Queue
Example: The following short sample program will print the number of pending messages (usually zero!) for either the program itself, or for some other program whose window title you specify on the command line: FindWindow() returns an HWND, which GetWindowTask() turns into an HTASK, which GetTaskQueue() turns into a Task Queue handle:

```c
/* taskq.c */

#include <stdlib.h>
#include <dos.h>
#include "windows.h"
#include "winio.h"

typedef struct {
    WORD wNext;
    HANDLE hTask;
    WORD wSize;
    WORD wNumMsgs;
    // ... other fields:  see Task Queue ...
    } TASKQ;

WORD FAR PASCAL GetTaskQueue(HANDLE hTask);

main(int argc, char *argv[])
{
    HANDLE hTaskQ;
    TASKQ far *fpTaskQ;

    if (argc < 2)
        hTaskQ = GetTaskQueue(0);
    else
        hTaskQ = GetTaskQueue(GetWindowTask(FindWindow(0L, argv[1])));

    if (! hTaskQ)
        fail("Can't locate Task Queue");

    fpTaskQ = MK_FP(hTaskQ, 0);
    printf("Task: %04x\n", fpTaskQ->hTask);
    printf("Number of pending messages: %u\n", fpTaskQ->wNumMsgs);
    return 0;
}
```

A far more detailed example is provided in WINTASK.C, presented with the Task Database and Task Queue structures later in this chapter.

GetTaskQueueDS   KERNEL.118

```c
void FAR PASCAL GetTaskQueueDS(void);
```

GetTaskQueueDS() moves a selector to the Task Queue for the current task into the DS segment register. (The Task Queue structure is explained later in this chapter.)

This function is heavily used internally by KERNEL and by the message routines in USER. Because its purpose is to alter DS, DS must be saved and restored around calls to the function, as shown in the following example:

```
push ds
call far ptr GETTASKQUEUEDS
; ... access the task queue ...
pop ds
```

In general, it makes more sense to use the GetTaskQueue function.

Support: 3.0, 3.1
Used by: KERNEL, USER
See also: Task Queue, GetTaskQueue, GetTaskQueueES

GetTaskQueueES   KERNEL.119

```
void FAR PASCAL GetTaskQueueES(void);
```

GetTaskQueueES() moves a selector to the Task Queue for the current task into the ES segment register. (The Task Queue structure is explained later in this chapter.) The message routines in USER all call this function.

Support: 3.0, 3.1
Used by: USER
See also: Task Queue, GetTaskQueueDS

GetWinOldApHooks   KERNEL.344

```
FARPROC FAR *GetWinOldApHooks(void);
```

This function simply returns whatever value is set with RegisterWinOldApHook(). The only known code that calls this is WINOLDAP.MOD, which in 3.1 is the Standard mode program that runs DOS executables ("old apps"). WinOldApHook appears to be a mechanism for hooking the WinExec of "old" DOS applications.

Support: 3.1
See also: RegisterWinOldApHook

Global Arena Header

Each object allocated on the Windows global heap has a corresponding block of memory containing information about the block: its size, owner, GMEM_ flags, and so on. KERNEL uses this information to manage the global heap and to support API functions such as GlobalSize() and GlobalFlags(). This information structure is essentially a *header* for the actual data object and is called the Global Arena header.

You might think at first that such an arena header is unnecessary because in protected-mode Windows each global memory object has a corresponding descriptor in the Local Descriptor Table (LDT). However, the layout of protected-mode descriptors is fixed, is limited to 8 bytes, and does not include room for such Windows-specific information as the GMEM_ flags or the block's owner. Protected-mode descriptors include nothing more than a selector's base address, size, and access rights; Windows needs to keep around a lot more information about each block than that.

In a typical Windows session, there might be 400 to 600 of these Global Arena structures. They are chained together in a doubly linked list, with the first and last arena headers reachable from the Global Heap information structure (Burgermaster; see following description). The first and last arena headers are always "sentinels" used to make walking the linked list a little easier for the memory-management rover inside KERNEL. (For background reading in dynamic memory allocation, see Donald Knuth, *The Art of Computer Programming*, 2nd edition, Vol. I, section 2.5, "Dynamic Storage Allocation"; and Brian Kernighan and Dennis Ritchie, *The C Programming Language*, 2nd edition, section 8.7, "Example—A Storage Allocator.")

The structure of the Global Arena Header differs completely between the 16-bit KERNEL (KRNL286) and the 32-bit KERNEL (KRNL386).

In KRNL286, each Global Arena Header gets a separate selector. Thus, every time you do a GlobalAlloc() in Standard mode, *two* selectors must be allocated: one for your data and one for the arena header. As the following example shows, the arena header has a base address that is 16 bytes lower than that of the memory it controls; this example also illustrates the basics of accessing the Global Arena linked list off the Global Heap structure in the 16-bit KERNEL.

```
// KRNL286
WORD wGlobalHeap = HIWORD(GlobalMasterHandle()); // selector to Burgermaster
HEAPINFO far *lphi = MK_FP(wGlobalHeap, 0); // far ptr to Burgermaster
WORD wGlobalArena = lphi->first;    // sel to first Global Arena in list
GLOBAL_ARENA far *lpga = MK_FP(wGlobalArena, 0);  // far ptr to ditto
BYTE far *lpData;
HANDLE h;
// skip past first item in list, which is just a SENTINEL
// second item in list is sometimes Global Arena for BURGERMASTER itself
wGlobalArena = lpga->next;      // walk to next item in list
lpga = MK_FP(wGlobalArena, 0);  // far pointer to Global Arena
h = lpga->handle;               // extract handle from Global Arena
assert(GetSelectorBase(wGlobalArena) + 16 == GetSelectorBase(h));
lpData = GlobalLock(h);         // the data itself
```

In KRNL386, each Global Arena is just a block within the Global Heap information structure, so there is clearly no relationship between the location of a global memory object and the location of its corresponding arena header. (A separate data structure, the Selector Table, is used to get from an object to its arena header; see below.) The following example shows the basics of accessing the Global Arena linked list off the Global Heap structure in the 32-bit KERNEL.

Global Arena Header

```
// KRNL386
WORD wGlobalHeap = HIWORD(GlobalMasterHandle()); // selector to Burgermaster
HEAPINF032 far *lphi32 = MK_FP(wGlobalHeap, 0); // far ptr to Burgermaster
DWORD dwGlobalArena = lphi32->first;  // offset of first Global Arena
// fortunately, dwGlobalArena always seems < 0xFFFF
GLOBAL_ARENA_32 far *lpga32 = MK_FP(wGlobalHeap, dwGlobalArena);
BYTE far *lpData;
HANDLE h;
dwGlobalArena = lpga32->next;        // skip past first item (SENTINEL)
lpga32 = MK_FP(dwGlobalArena, 0);    // far pointer to a Global Arena
h = lpga32->handle;                  // extract handle from a Global Arena
lpData = GlobalLock(h);              // the data itself
```

Regardless of where it's located, the Global Arena plays a role somewhat similar to that of Memory Control Blocks (MCBs) in MS-DOS. In fact, MCBs in DOS are sometimes also called "Arena Headers"; the blocks of memory themselves are the arenas. This term doesn't quite work in Windows because, as noted previously, in the 32-bit Windows KERNEL the arena and its header are not contiguous.

The documented GLOBALENTRY structure in ToolHelp (see chapter 10) is an idealization of the Global Arena structure. ToolHelp is much easier and more reliable to work with than the actual Global Arena structures and should be used wherever possible.

KRNL286 Global Arena (size 10h bytes)

OFFSET	SIZE	DESCRIPTION
00	BYTE	Lock count for movable blocks
01	WORD	Owner of the block: a module handle, task handle, PSP, or special. Special blocks:
		0 free block
		-1 (FFFFh) sentinel block
		-3 (FFFDh) Burgermaster itself (KRNL286 only)
		-4 (FFFCh) "not there" (mapped to hardware)
		-5 (FFFBh) "phantom" (defunct EMS type?)
		-6 (FFFAh) "wraith" (?)
		-7 (FFF9h) "bogus" (temporarily allocated)
03	WORD	Size in 16-bit paragraphs (not bytes)
05	BYTE	Flags (note that the handle itself encodes whether the block is fixed or movable; see offset 0Ah below):
		04h DGROUP
		08h Discardable
06	WORD	Selector to previous Global Arena in doubly linked list; first (SENTINEL) points to self

Global Arena Header

08	WORD	Selector to next Global Arena in doubly linked list; last (SENTINEL) points to self
0A	WORD	Handle to this arena's memory object; the bottom two bits mark whether the block is fixed or movable:

	01	fixed (Windows 3.0: Ring 1)
	10	movable
	11	fixed (Windows 3.1: Ring 3)

0C	WORD	Selector to previous Global Arena in LRU (least recently used) chain
0E	WORD	Selector to next Global Arena in LRU chain

KRNL386 Global Arena (size 20h bytes)

OFFSET	SIZE	DESCRIPTION
00	DWORD	Offset of previous Global arena in doubly linked list; first (SENTINEL) points to self
04	DWORD	Offset of next Global area in doubly linked list; last (SENTINEL) points to self
08	DWORD	Linear base address of block (see GetSelectorBase())
0C	DWORD	Size of block in bytes (not paragraphs)
10	WORD	Handle to this arena's memory object; the bottom two bits mark whether the block is fixed or movable (see offset 0Ah for KRNL286 for bit patterns)
12	WORD	Owner of the block; a module handle, task handle, PSP, or special. See KRNL286 offset 01 for special block IDs.
14	BYTE	Lock count for movable blocks
15	BYTE	Number of times page locked (GlobalPageLock())
16	BYTE	Flags; see KRNL286 offset 05.
17	BYTE	Number of selectors required (used with huge blocks > 64K)
18	DWORD	Offset of previous Global Arena in LRU (least recently used) chain
1C	DWORD	Offset of next Global Arena in LRU (least recently used) chain

If the handle specified as the owner of a block is identical to the handle of the block itself, then the handle is an HTASK and the block is a Task Database:

```
if (arena->owner == arena->handle)
    assert(IsTask(arena->handle));
```

Global Arena Header

Blocks allocated with GlobalAlloc() are usually marked with an owner corresponding to the Program Segment Prefix (PSP) of the task that called GlobalAlloc().

The KRNL286 Global Arena does not include the base address of the block, similar to offset 08 in the KRNL386 Global Arena structure; use GetSelectorBase-(arena->handle) instead.

The flags field is not in the same form as the GMEM_ options passed to GlobalAlloc() or returned from GlobalFlags(). It is much easier to pass the handle to GlobalFlags() than to try to use the flags field.

The flags do not include a CODE vs. DATA indicator; use the LAR (Load Access Rights) instruction, or the undocumented SelectorAccessRights() function.

The Global Arena structure appears in the file WINKERN.INC, included with the Windows 3.1 DDK.

Support: 3.0, 3.1
See also: Global Heap, GlobalMasterHandle, Local Arena, Selector Table
Example: See COUNTMEM.C in description of Global Heap; the following structures are extracted from COUNTMEM.C.

```
#pragma pack(1)      /* align on BYTE boundaries, not WORD */

typedef struct {
    BYTE count;         // 0
    WORD owner;         // 1
    WORD paragraphs;    // 3
    BYTE flags;         // 5
    WORD prev;          // 6
    WORD next;          // 8
    WORD handle;        // 0A
    WORD lruprev;       // 0C
    WORD lrunext;       // 0E
    } GLOBAL_ARENA;

typedef struct {
    DWORD next;         // 0
    DWORD prev;         // 4
    DWORD base;         // 8
    DWORD bytes;        // 0C
    WORD handle;        // 10
    WORD owner;         // 12
    BYTE count;         // 14
    BYTE pglock;        // 15
    BYTE flags;         // 16
    BYTE selcount;      // 17
    DWORD lruprev;      // 18
    DWORD lrunext;      // 1C
    } GLOBAL_ARENA_32;
```

Global Arena Header

GlobalFreeAll   KERNEL.26

```
void FAR PASCAL GlobalFreeAll(WORD wPSP);
```

This function is used by KERNEL when a task terminates to free all global memory remaining owned by the task at the time it exited. The task is specified by its PSP (or 0, to indicate the PSP of the current task). Any global memory allocated by the task but owned by the module (e.g., memory allocated with DirectResAlloc() or with GlobalAlloc(GMEM_DDESHARE)) is, of course, not deallocated.

Support: 3.0, 3.1
See also: DirectResAlloc

GlobalHandleNoRIP   KERNEL.159

```
DWORD FAR PASCAL GlobalHandleNoRIP(WORD wMem);
```

GlobalHandleNoRIP() is a wrapper around the documented GlobalHandle() function. Like GlobalHandle(), it returns the handle of a global memory object whose selector is specified by the wMem parameter. However, it does this without running the risk of generating a Windows fatal exit or RIP ("rest in peace") code 0x280. GlobalHandleNoRIP() simply returns 0 if the parameter is invalid. The following shows the difference between the behavior of GlobalHandle() and GlobalHandle-NoRIP() when running under a debug version of Windows:

```
> kernel globalhandle 0x1234    ;; pass in a totally bogus selector
gdref: invalid handle 0000:1234 ;; internal gdref() function in KERNEL
FatalExit code = 0x0280         ;; GMEMHANDLE: Invalid global handle
Stack trace:
KERNEL:DEBUGBREAK+0184
KERNEL:ALLOCDSTOCSALIAS+0539    ;; (couldn't find any nearby symbols)
Abort, Break or Ignore?        ;; ignore
0x0000

> kernel globalhandlenorip 0x1234
0x0000
```

Thus, GlobalHandleNoRIP() can be used to test the validity of handles without causing a FatalExit for ones that prove to be invalid.

Support: 3.0, 3.1
Used by: WINDEBUG

Global Heap

Information about the Windows global memory heap is kept in a structure known as Burgermaster. (Burgermaster is also the name of a hamburger restaurant in Redmond.) The Global Heap information structure keeps a count of the number of items in the global heap (typically between 400 and 600), pointers to the first and last entries in the doubly-linked list of Global Arena structures, and so on. In the 32-bit KERNEL (KRNL386), the segment containing Burgermaster also contains the Global Arena headers themselves (see Global Arena).

A selector to the Global Heap information structure (this is getting long-winded, so let's just call it Burgermaster from here on) is returned from the undocumented GlobalMasterHandle() function; the undocumented THHOOK structure also includes a selector to Burgermaster.

It is sometimes claimed that, in protected mode, the Burgermaster goes away because its job is taken over by the protected-mode descriptor tables. This is not true; Burgermaster still exists in protected mode, and reports of its demise are very much exaggerated. Protected-mode descriptor tables do not include room for the sort of information that Windows needs. In addition to its protected-mode descriptor, each object on the Windows global heap has a lot of additional associated information, kept in its Global Area header; Global Arenas are reached via the fields named "first" and "last" in Burgermaster (or by using the Selector Table; see below).

The structure of Burgermaster is fundamentally the same in KRNL286 and KRNL386, except that the size of some fields, such as "first" and "last," changes from 16 bits in KRNL286 to 32 bits in KRNL386. As noted in the description of the Global Arena header earlier in this chapter, first and last are selectors in KRNL286, and 32-bit offsets in the Burgermaster segment in KRNL386.

The ToolHelp API (see chapter 10) provides a documented interface for walking the Global Heap; the idealized interface provided by ToolHelp should be used wherever possible rather than walking the actual Windows Global Heap structure described here.

In addition to objects in the global heap, Windows also maintains several selectors in the Global Descriptor Table (GDT). You can use a debugger with GDT-walking capabilities, such as Soft-ICE/Windows, to view the GDT. In addition to its GDT command, Soft-ICE also has an LDT command; this presents a different, worm's-eye, view of the Windows global heap from its HEAP command. For example:

```
:heap 00ae
Han./Sel. Address     Length      Owner             Type       Seg/Rsrc
00AE         0002A820    00000100    KERNEL            Alloc
:ldt 00ae
00AF   Data16     Base=0002A820  Lim=000000FF  DPL=3  P   RW
```

Each local heap has an associated information structure that closely resembles Burgermaster; see Local Heap.

The Global Heap structures are defined in the file WINKERN.INC, included with the Windows 3.1 DDK.

BURGERMASTER:

00	WORD	Non-zero enables heap checking (defunct?)
02	WORD	Freeze: non-zero prevents heap compaction
04	WORD	Number of entries in global heap (length of linked list)

-- KRNL286 --

06	WORD	Selector of first Global Arena in doubly-linked list (the first entry is always a SENTINEL)
08	WORD	Selector of last Global Arena in doubly-linked list (the last entry is always a SENTINEL)
0A	BYTE	Number of heap compactions; see MemoryFreed()
0B	BYTE	Current discard level
0C	WORD	Total bytes discarded so far; see MemoryFreed()
0E	WORD	Head of handle table list
10	WORD	Head of free handle table list
12	WORD	Delta: number of handles to allocate each time (MoreMasters)
14	WORD	Address of near procedures to expand handles
16	WORD	Address of statistics table (or zero)
18	WORD	Lock-out access to LRU chain from interrupt level (huh?)
1A	WORD	First handle in LRU chain (head of LRU chain is most recently used)
1C	WORD	Number of entries in LRU chain
1E	WORD	Number of paragraphs to reserve for discardable code
20	WORD	Fence for discardable code
22	WORD	Number of FREE blocks

-- KRNL386 --

06	DWORD	Offset within Burgermaster of first Global Arena in doubly-linked list
0A	DWORD	Offset within Burgermaster of last Global Arena in doubly-linked list
E	BYTE	Number of heap compactions; see MemoryFreed()
0F	BYTE	Current discard level
10	DWORD	Total bytes discarded so far; see MemoryFreed()
14	WORD	Always zero? (supposed to be handle table list head)
16	WORD	Always zero? (supposed to free handle table list head)
18	WORD	Always zero? (supposed to be handle delta)

Global Heap

1A	WORD	Always zero? (supposed to be near procedure to expand handles)
1C	WORD	Always zero? (supposed to be handle to statistics table)
1E	WORD	Lock-out access to LRU chain from interrupt level (huh?)
20	DWORD	Offset within Burgermaster of first handle in LRU chain (head of LRU chain is most recently used)
24	WORD	Number of entries in LRU chain
26	DWORD	Number of paragraphs to reserve for discardable code
2A	DWORD	Fence for discardable code
30	WORD	Number of FREE blocks

Support: 3.0, 3.1
See also: Global Arena, GlobalMasterHandle, Local Heap
Example: The following sample program, COUNTMEM.C, walks the Windows global heap, keeping a tally of the number of bytes and selectors allocated by each module. After walking the global heap, COUNTMEM displays the total allocation for each module, plus some grand totals. For example:

```
# Sel   Bytes (Discardable)
1      153920        0        BURGERMASTER
2          64        0        SENTINEL
8       83552    22976        C:\WIN31.B2\SYSTEM\KRNL386.EXE
52     175168    89920        C:\WIN31.B2\SYSTEM\GDI.EXE
6       21312    13568        C:\WIN31.B2\SYSTEM\MMSYSTEM.DLL
28      50944    38592        C:\WIN31.B2\SYSTEM\WINOA386.MOD
77     270304   178912        C:\WIN31.B2\SYSTEM\USER.EXE
128   1228128   280192        C:\WINWORD\WINWORD.EXE
59     120384    96800        C:\WIN31.B2\WINFILE.EXE
6       32960      352        C:\WIN31.B2\DRWATSON.EXE
10      86176    17632        C:\WINDOS\COUNTMEM.EXE
46     176768        0        FREE
27      27552    10976        C:\WIN31.B2\SYSTEM\VGAMONO.DRV
12      21024    18560        C:\WIN31.B2\SYSTEM\SHELL.DLL
3        1504        0        C:\WIN31.B2\SYSTEM\SYSTEM.DRV
8        5280     1344        C:\WIN31.B2\SYSTEM\KEYBOARD.DRV
3        9152     7712        C:\WIN31.B2\SYSTEM\MOUSE.DRV
..............
2        5760     5472        C:\WIN31.B2\SYSTEM\VGASYS.FON
2        4256     3968        C:\WIN31.B2\SYSTEM\COURE.FON
10      43296    36000        C:\WIN31.B2\SYSTEM\COMMDLG.DLL
2        4512     4224        C:\WIN31.B2\SYSTEM\VGAOEM.FON
3        9984     9600        C:\WIN31.B2\SYSTEM\SSERIFE.FON
3       12992        0        C:\WIN31.B2\SYSTEM\TOOLHELP.DLL
26        832        0        NOT_THERE

Total:        2497632 bytes (592 selectors)
Discardable:   893152 bytes
Free:          176768 bytes
Low memory:    703648 bytes
Code:         1011648 bytes
Data:         1643808 bytes
```

Global Heap

There are some interesting results here. For example, Microsoft Word for Windows (WINWORD) occupied over one megabyte of memory, less than one-quarter of it discardable. The core Windows DLLs—KERNEL, USER, and GDI—occupied a little over 500k, over half of it discardable. We also see that COUNTMEM.EXE itself is a pig, taking up more room (with less of it discardable!) than the KERNEL itself; this is largely because the default size of a WINIO buffer is 32k (oink! oink!).

The total "Free" memory displayed by COUNTMEM requires some explanation: this is merely the amount of free memory currently managed in the Global Heap; that is, memory that was at one point allocated and then freed. The Global Heap can grow; this is not reflected in the "Free" count. KERNEL grows the Global Heap by allocating memory via the DOS Protected-Mode Interface (DPMI) Allocate Memory call (INT 31h AX=0501). Watching DPMI calls with the WISPY utility from chapter 4, we can see that Windows grows the heap 128k (20000h) bytes at a time.

So much for what COUNTMEM does; how does it work? In main(), COUNTMEM uses HIWORD(GlobalMasterHandle()) to get a selector to Burgermaster. It also calls the function Kernel1632() to determine whether KRNL286 or KRNL386 is active; this will affect which structures the program uses later and how it walks the list of Global Arenas. Finally, main() calls walk_heap().

The walk_heap() function walks the linked list of Global Arenas, using a tight loop which does not yield control to other tasks. This is crucial, because if other tasks could run while COUNTMEM was walking the list, those other tasks could allocate memory and thereby change the list out from under us! Given that Windows has non-preemptive multitasking, all we need to do is simply *forget* to yield control; with preemptive multitasking, we would need to enter a critical section. By the way, this point about not yielding control while walking the heap is important even if you're using the ToolHelp GlobalFirst() and GlobalNext() functions. See the WINWALK program in chapter 10.

The code for walking the linked list of Global Arenas differs totally for the 16-bit and 32-bit versions of KERNEL. Not only do the Global Arena headers themselves differ, but, depending on the flavor of KERNEL, COUNTMEM must interpret the "first" field in Burgermaster and the "next" fields in the Global Arena headers differently.

For each Global Arena in the linked list, walk_heap() calls add(). The add() function uses the handle, owner, and size fields from the arena header to keep a running total. If the owner of a block is not a module handle, then the owner (either a task or PSP) is converted to a module handle, using hTask_from_PSP() and HMODULE_FROM_HTASK() from HANDLES.H in the introduction to this chapter.

The add() function passes the handles to GlobalFlags() and GetSelectorBase(), and uses the Intel LAR and VERR instructions on them as well. This shows that the arena->handles produced by walking the global heap can be used just like any other handles; you're not stuck getting all your information from the Global Arena headers themselves.

Global Heap

To try to produce an true picture of the memory consumption, COUNTMEM adds in the memory used by the Global Arena header itself. With KRNL286, it also remembers to add in the extra selector that's consumed by each Global Arena header:

```
/* COUNTMEM.C -- Totals memory consumption (bytes and selectors)
   of Windows modules, by walking Windows global heap

   The point of this code is to illustrate the arrangement of the
   Windows global heap info structure and arenas. If you actually
   want to walk the heap in commercial code, use ToolHelp, ok? Please?

   In ToolHelp, it's as simple as:
       GLOBALENTRY ge;
       BOOL ok;
       ge.dwSize = sizeof(ge);
       // don't yield until done
       ok = GlobalFirst(&ge, GLOBAL_ALL);
       while (ok)
       {
           add(ge.hBlock, ge.hOwner, ge.dwBlockSize);
           ok = GlobalNext(&ge, GLOBAL_ALL);
       }
       // okay to yield control again

   On the other hand, with ToolHelp it is too easy to forget to add
   in the size of the arenas themselves; in fact ToolHelp doesn't
   tell you the size of the arenas. For an example of where ToolHelp
   falls short, see the code in add() below with the comment "add
   this Global Arena to the totals for this owner." It would be nice
   if ToolHelp took this sort of thing into account.

   Andrew Schulman, March 1992; revised May 1992 */

#include <stdlib.h>
#include <string.h>
#include <assert.h>
#include <dos.h>
#include "windows.h"
#include "winio.h"
#include "handles.h"

static DWORD (FAR PASCAL *GlobalMasterHandle)(void);
static DWORD (FAR PASCAL *GetSelectorLimit)(WORD wSel);

#define GETPROC(modname, funcname) \
    GetProcAddress(GetModuleHandle(modname), (funcname))

#pragma pack(1)

/*  The only difference between HEAPINFO and HEAPINFO32
    is the size of fields such as "first" and "last". The
    following is borrowed from the Windows 3.1 DDK include
    file WINKERN.INC. However, not all of these fields
    appear to actually be used! */
```

Global Heap

```
#define DEFINE_HEAPINFO_STRUCT(STRUCTNAME, WORDDWORD) \
typedef struct { \
    WORD check; \
    WORD freeze; \
    WORD count; \
    WORDDWORD first; \
    WORDDWORD last; \
    BYTE ncompact; \
    BYTE dislevel; \
    WORDDWORD distotal; \
    WORD htable; \
    WORD hfree; \
    WORD hdelta; \
    WORD hexpand; \
    WORD pstats; \
    WORD lrulock; \
    WORDDWORD lruchain; \
    WORD lrucount; \
    WORDDWORD reserve; \
    WORDDWORD disfence; \
    WORD free_count;
    } STRUCTNAME;

DEFINE_HEAPINFO_STRUCT(GLOBAL_HEAP, WORD);
DEFINE_HEAPINFO_STRUCT(GLOBAL_HEAP_32, DWORD);

/*  The Global Arena structures are totally different
    for 16-bit and 32-bit KERNEL. */
typedef struct {
    BYTE count;
    WORD owner;
    WORD paragraphs;
    BYTE flags;
    WORD prev;
    WORD next;
    WORD handle;
    WORD lruprev;
    WORD lrunext;
    } GLOBAL_ARENA;

typedef struct {
    DWORD next;
    DWORD prev;
    DWORD base;
    DWORD bytes;
    WORD handle;
    WORD owner;
    BYTE count;
    BYTE pglock;
    BYTE flags;
    BYTE selcount;
    DWORD lruprev;
    DWORD lrunext;
    } GLOBAL_ARENA_32;
```

Global Heap

```c
/* special owner types; otherwise owner is module, task, or PSP */
#define SENTINEL          (-1)
#define BURGERMASTER      (-3)
#define NOT_THERE         (-4)
#define PHANTOM           (-5)
#define WRAITH            (-6)
#define BOGUS             (-7)
#define FREE              (0)

void walk_heap(WORD wGlobalHeap);
char *owner_name(WORD wOwner);
void add(HANDLE h, WORD wOwner, DWORD dwBytes);
void print_totals(void);

static HWND main_hwnd;
static WORD wGlobalHeap;        /* Burgermaster */
static int k1632;
static int arena_size;

main()
{
    main_hwnd = winio_current();

    k1632 = Kernel1632();
    if (k1632 == 16)
        arena_size = sizeof(GLOBAL_ARENA);
    else
        arena_size = sizeof(GLOBAL_ARENA_32);

    GlobalMasterHandle = GETPROC("KERNEL", "GLOBALMASTERHANDLE");
    GetSelectorLimit = GETPROC("KERNEL", "GETSELECTORLIMIT");

    // use HIWORD: take selector, not handle
    if (wGlobalHeap = HIWORD(GlobalMasterHandle()))
        walk_heap(wGlobalHeap);
    else
        fail("Cannot find Windows global heap");

    return 0;
}

void walk_heap(WORD wGlobalHeap)
{
    HWND hwnd;
    int i;

    winio_clear(main_hwnd);

    /* in 3.1+, BURGERMASTER itself is not in the linked list */
    if (GetVersion() >= 0x0a03)
        add(wGlobalHeap, BURGERMASTER,
            GetSelectorLimit(wGlobalHeap)+1);

    /* Turn off WINIO display while walking the global heap.
       WINIO yields when it displays, and we don't want to yield
```

Global Heap

```
                     here, because then other tasks might go and change the
                     state of the global heap while we're in the middle of
                     the walk. Actually, we're not doing output here, but it's
                     important to understand that YOU CANNOT YIELD IN THIS LOOP! */
                winio_setpaint(main_hwnd, FALSE);

            if (k1632 == 16)     // 16-bit KERNEL
            {
                GLOBAL_ARENA far *lpga;
                GLOBAL_HEAP far *lphi = MK_FP(wGlobalHeap, 0);
                WORD wSel = lphi->first;    // first entry
                WORD wCount = lphi->count;  // number of entries

                for (i=0; i<wCount; i++)
                {
                    /* In 16-bit KERNEL, lphi->first and lpga->next
                       are selectors to arenas. */
                    lpga = MK_FP(wSel, 0);
                    add(lpga->handle, lpga->owner,
                        (long) lpga->paragraphs << 4);
                    wSel = lpga->next;  // follow linked list
                }
            }
            else     // 32-bit KERNEL
            {
                GLOBAL_ARENA_32 far *lpga32;
                GLOBAL_HEAP_32 far *lphi32 = MK_FP(wGlobalHeap, 0);
                DWORD dwOffset = lphi32->first; // first entry
                WORD wCount = lphi32->count;     // number of entries

                for (i=0; i<wCount; i++)
                {
                    /* In 32-bit KERNEL, lphi32->first and lpga32->next
                       are not selectors, but offsets into the master table */
                    lpga32 = MK_FP(wGlobalHeap, dwOffset);
                    add(lpga32->handle, lpga32->owner, lpga32->bytes);
                    dwOffset = lpga32->next;    // follow linked list
                    if (dwOffset > 0xFFFFUL)
                        fail("Can't access all of heap from 16-bit code");
                }
            }
            winio_setpaint(main_hwnd, TRUE);

            print_totals();
}

typedef struct {
    WORD owner;
    WORD items;
    DWORD total;
    DWORD discard_total;
    DWORD code_total;
    } TOTAL;

#define MAX_TOTAL   1024
```

Global Heap

```
static TOTAL totals[MAX_TOTAL] = {0} ;
static int num_totals = 0;
static DWORD low_total = 0;        /* amount below 1 megabyte */
static DWORD code_total = 0;
static DWORD data_total = 0;

/* Add a Global Arena to the running total */
void add(HANDLE h, WORD wOwner, DWORD dwBytes)
{
    extern DWORD FAR PASCAL GetSelectorBase(WORD wSel);
    TOTAL *t;
    WORD wFlags;
    int i;
    /* If owner is a PSP or a task handle,
        find the corresponding module handle */
    if (IsValidPSP(wOwner))
    {
        HANDLE hTask;
        if (hTask = hTask_from_PSP(wOwner))
            wOwner = HMODULE_FROM_HTASK(hTask);
    }
    else if (IsValidTask(wOwner))
        wOwner = HMODULE_FROM_HTASK(wOwner);

    /* Find the owner in the table */
    for (i=0, t=totals; i<num_totals; i++, t++)
        if (t->owner == wOwner)
            break;
    if (i == num_totals)      // not in table yet
    {
        if (num_totals >= MAX_TOTAL)
            fail("totals overflow!");
        t = &totals[num_totals];
        t->owner = wOwner;
        num_totals++;
    }

    /* add this Global Arena to the totals for this owner */
    t->total += dwBytes;
    t->total += arena_size; // count the arena as part of total
    if (k1632 == 16)
        t->items += 2; // 16-bit KERNEL requires two selectors/block
    else
        t->items++;

    /* We could of course pull the flags right out of the Global
        Arena structure. But taking the handles produced by
        walking the Global Heap, and passing them to GlobalFlags(),
        shows that walking the heap could be used simply as a way to
        enumerate handles, leaving everything else to documented
        functions. */
    if (verr(wOwner)) // ensure has genuine owner before do GlobalFlags
        if (wFlags = GlobalFlags(h))
            if (wFlags & GMEM_DISCARDABLE)
```

Global Heap

```
                t->discard_total += dwBytes;

    /* To find out if it's CODE or DATA, we use the Intel LAR (Load
       Access Rights) instruction. We could also use the undocumented
       Windows SelectorAccessRights() function. */
    if ((lar(h) & CODEDATA_MASK) == CODE)
        code_total += dwBytes;
    else
        data_total += dwBytes;

    /* To find its linear base address, we use the undocumented
       Windows GetSelectorBase() function. If the base address is
       less than one megabyte, it's low memory (equivalent to a
       GlobalDosAlloc()) */
    if (GetSelectorBase(h) < 0x100000L)
        low_total += dwBytes;
}

void print_totals(void)
{
    TOTAL *t;
    DWORD total=0, discard=0, free_total=0;
    WORD items=0;
    int i;

    printf("# Sel\tBytes (Discardable)\n");

    for (i=0, t=totals; i<num_totals; i++, t++)
    {
        printf("%d\t%7lu    %7lu\t%s\n",
            t->items, t->total, t->discard_total,
            owner_name(t->owner));

        /* get the grand total */
        if (t->owner == FREE)
            free_total = t->total;
        else
        {
          total += t->total;
          discard += t->discard_total;
          items += t->items;
        }
    }

    /* display the grand total */
    printf("\n");
    printf("Total:       %8lu bytes (%d selectors)\n", total, items);
    printf("Discardable: %8lu bytes\n", discard);
    printf("Free:        %8lu bytes\n", free_total);
    printf("Low memory:  %8lu bytes\n", low_total);
    printf("Code:        %8lu bytes\n", code_total);
    printf("Data:        %8lu bytes\n", data_total);
}
```

Global Heap

```
char *owner_name(WORD wOwner)
{
    static char buf[128];

    switch (wOwner) // assumed to be module handle or special
    {
        case SENTINEL:      return "SENTINEL";
        case BURGERMASTER:  return "BURGERMASTER";
        case NOT_THERE:     return "NOT_THERE";
        case PHANTOM:       return "PHANTOM";
        case WRAITH:        return "WRAITH";
        case BOGUS:         return "BOGUS";
        case FREE:          return "FREE";
        default:
            if (IsValidModuleHandle(wOwner))
            {
                /* To get short name, could use
                    GetModuleNameFromHandle() in WINMOD.C */
                GetModuleFileName(wOwner, buf, 128);
                return buf;
            }
            else
                return "??";
    }
}
```

GlobalMasterHandle   KERNEL.28

```
DWORD FAR PASCAL GlobalMasterHandle(void);
```

GlobalMasterHandle() returns both a handle and a selector to the Global Heap information structure, also known as Burgermaster. The selector (pGlobalHeap) is returned in the HIWORD (DX) and is generally more useful than the handle (hGlobalHeap), returned in the LOWORD (AX); sometimes, though, the selector and the handle are identical. The values returned by GlobalMasterHandle() are identical to the fields pGlobalHeap and hGlobalHeap in the THHOOK structure (see below). In fact, all GlobalMasterHandle() does is return these values:

```
GlobalMasterHandle proc far
    mov ax, hGlobalHeap     ; THHOOK+0
    mov dx, pGlobalHeap     ; THHOOK+2
    retf
GlobalMasterHandle endp
```

The return value from this function is used for walking the Windows global heap. However, ToolHelp (see chapter 10) provides documented functions (Global Info(), GlobalFirst(), and GlobalNext()) that generally should be used in preference to walking the actual, live Windows global heap. On the other hand, different versions of the

Windows SDK HEAPWALK utility (Luke Heapwalker), the WINDEBUG library, and indeed, ToolHelp itself all rely on GlobalMasterHandle().

Walking the global heap is discussed at length in the descriptions earlier in this chapter for the Global Heap and Global Arena data structures. Briefly, GlobalMasterHandle() is used like this:

```
DWORD (FAR PASCAL *GlobalMasterHandle)(void);
WORD pGlobalHeap;
GlobalMasterHandle = GET_PROC("KERNEL", "GLOBALMASTERHANDLE");
if (pGlobalHeap = HIWORD(GlobalMasterHandle()))
    walk(MK_FP(pGlobalHeap, 0));
```

pGlobalHeap is a selector to a structure, the Global Heap information structure or Burgermaster, that changes from KRNL286 to KRNL386 (see Global Heap).

Support: 3.0, 3.1
Used by: HEAPWALK.EXE, WINDEBUG.DLL, \QCWIN\WINDBG.DLL, TOOLHELP.DLL
See also: Global Arena, Global Heap
Example: See COUNTMEM.C in description of Global Heap

HandleParamError   KERNEL.327

The function K327(), exported from KERNEL in Windows 3.1, has the internal, non-exported name HandleParamError(). Some __GP handlers jump to it.

Support: 3.1
See also: __GP

Handle Table

Handle Tables and the function DefineHandleTable() were present in Windows 2.x, but they were not documented by Microsoft until Windows 3.0, where they promptly became useless.

The definitive documentation on handle tables is the two-part article by Tim Paterson and Steve Flenniken, "Managing Multiple Data Segments Under Microsoft Windows," *Dr. Dobb's Journal*, February 1990 and March 1990. Microsoft's documentation for DefineHandleTable() is inadequate; to actually use the function, you would need the *Dr. Dobb's* articles. However, handle tables are relevant only in Windows real mode, which is not present in Windows 3.1 and not useful in Windows 3.0, where it is present. Those unfortunate souls needing to support Windows real mode should (a) really reconsider whether they need to support Windows real mode; (b) refer to the *Dr. Dobb's* article; and (c) really reconsider whether they need to support Windows real mode.

HasGPHandler   KERNEL.338

```
WORD FAR PASCAL HasGPHandler(DWORD gpAddress);
```

This function is called with the address of a faulting instruction. The function returns TRUE if the fault was caused by parameter validation; for example, the Windows 3.1 parameter-validation routines (the IsBadXXX() functions) signal error by causing a GP fault.

Using the CS component of the specified address, HasGPHandler() looks up the owning module of the code segment. It then compares the owner's module name to an internal table of names. The internal table contains the names of the Windows modules that have __GP tables defined (see __GP). If the owner of the faulting code segment is found in the table, then the address for __GP in that module is looked up.

Next, HasGPHandler() walks the __GP table, comparing the faulting CS:IP in gpAddress with each address range in the table. If the CS:IP is within one of the address ranges, then the address where execution should resume is returned; this WORD return value is an offset into the same segment as CS in the gpAddress parameter. If a handler cannot be found, the function returns 0.

In other words, HasGPHandler does roughly the following:

```
HasGPHandler(addr)
{
   hModule = owner(FP_SEG(addr));
   if (__GP = GetProcAddress(hModule, "__GP"))
      if (handler_ofs = in_gp(__GP, addr))
         return handler_ofs;
   /* still here */ return 0;
}
```

and would be used in roughly the following way:

```
if (handler_ofs = HasGPHandler(fault_addr))
{
   handler = MK_FP(FP_SEG(fault_addr), handler_ofs);
   (*handler)();
}
```

Support: 3.1
See also: __GP, IsBadXXX

InitAtomTable

```
WORD FAR PASCAL InitAtomTable(int size);
```

InitAtomTable() is documented as returning a BOOL; in fact, it returns a WORD that can be interpreted as a BOOL: a near pointer to the newly created atom table, or 0 if one couldn't be created. This return value is identical to the pAtomTable variable at offset 8 in the NULL segment (see Instance Data).

If pAtomTable is 0 when AddAtom() is called, then KERNEL automatically calls InitAtomTable().

Support: 3.0, 3.1
See also: Atom Table

InitLib   KERNEL.116

```
void FAR PASCAL InitLib(void);
```

InitLib() appears to be a relic from the Windows past. It was present in Windows 2.1, but it is not called in Borland's DLL startup code (C0D.ASM), nor in any known Windows 3.x DLL from Microsoft. For what it's worth, the function calls LocalInit(), passing 0 as the segment. This causes LocalInit() to assume that it should initialize whatever DS is currently pointing to. Windows 3.x DLLs typically call LocalInit() themselves, rather than relying on InitLib() to do this for them. InitLib() also sets ES to the KERNEL data segment.

InitTask   KERNEL.91

```
EXTRN INITTASK:FAR
```

InitTask() is the first function called in the startup code for a Windows application. For years undocumented, InitTask() and the other functions necessary for Windows startup code were finally documented by Microsoft as part of its "Open Tools" strategy; documentation for InitTask() now appears in the 3.1 SDK Overview article, "Windows Application Startup."

WinMain() is only the *perceived* entry point for a Windows program. The actual entry point for the program is specified in the ne_csip (initial CS:IP) field at offset 14h in the module's NE header (see Module Table). This initial CS:IP generally belongs to startup code supplied by the compiler. On entry to this code, the CPU registers contain the following information:

```
BX          Stack size
CX          Heap size
DI          hInstance
SI          hPrevInstance
ES          PSP
```

To turn itself into a legitimate Windows task, the first thing a Windows program's startup code must do is call InitTask(). For example, the following comes from the Borland C++ Windows startup code (which Borland provides in source code as C0W.ASM).

```
extrn INITTASK:far
; ...
call INITTASK
or ax, ax
jnz ok
```

InitTask() takes no explicit parameters, but the registers must be in the startup state shown above. On failure, InitTask() returns 0 in the AX register. On success, it sets up the registers with information to be passed on the stack to WinMain():

```
AX          1
CX          Stack limit in bytes
DX          nCmdShow parameter to WinExec() that started this task
ES:BX       lpCmdLine (ES = PSP, BX = 80h)
SI          hPrevInstance
DI          hInstance
```

InitTask() also initializes the pStackTop, pStackMin, and pStackBottom fields in the calling task's Instance Data area (NULL segment); see the description of Instance Data.

Dynamic link libraries (DLLs) are not tasks, so their startup code will not call InitTask().

In addition to calling InitTask(), a task's Windows startup code must also call the USER InitApp() function to create a message queue for itself. C startup code must initialize the C run-time library; C++ startup code must call any static constructors (it had better do this *after* calling InitTask() and InitApp(), by the way). Eventually, the startup code calls the application's WinMain() function, pushing the parameters expected by WinMain() on the stack.

Support: 3.0, 3.1
See also: InitApp (chapter 6), Instance Data, WaitEvent

InitTask1   KERNEL.141

```
void FAR PASCAL InitTask1(FARPROC fpDressedforSuccess);
```

InitTask1() sets the value of a function pointer, DressedForSuccess, which in turn would, if non-NULL, be called as part of task initialization. This function may be left over from experimentation involving the running of Windows applications under other operating environments.

Instance Data

An instance handle (hInstance) is actually a selector to a task's or DLL's default data segment (DGROUP). Although code and resources are shared between multiple instances of the same program, each instance gets its own DGROUP. It is therefore natural to use the DGROUP selector as a unique identifier for each instance. DLLs are not tasks and do not have multiple instances, but each DLL does have its own DGROUP, so here too the DGROUP selector can be used as a unique identifier for a module.

DGROUP is where the task's or DLL's near data (statics and consts), default local heap, and stack are kept. In addition, the first 16 (10h) bytes of DGROUP are reserved; they are generally formatted in the following way:

```
At offset 0 in default data segment:
00h      WORD          0000h
02h      DWORD         dwOldSSSP
06h      WORD          pLocalHeap
08h      WORD          pAtomTable
0Ah      WORD          pStackTop
0Ch      WORD          pStackMin
0Eh      WORD          pStackBottom
```

This structure is sometimes referred to as the NULL segment; the names of these fields often show up in CodeView debugging information in Windows executable files.

Not all default data segments in Windows have this structure. If the WORD at offset zero is not 0, then structure is not present. Similarly, if the WORD at offset 6 does not point to a valid Local Heap, then the structure is not present. Windows device drivers such as DISPLAY, KEYBOARD, and SYSTEM do not have NULL segments.

On the other hand, globally-allocated non-DGROUP blocks may also contain parts of the Instance Data structure, if the blocks have been treated with InitAtomTable() or LocalInit(); see offsets 6 and 8 below.

Bob Chiverton's article, "Shed Some Light on Your Windows Application's Default Data Segment with HeapPeep" (*Microsoft Systems Journal*, January/February 1992) contains an in-depth examination of the NULL segment.

00h   WORD   wMustBeZero

If the first WORD in the data segment is not zero, then the NULL segment structure is not present (however, pLocalHeap may still be present at offset 6; see below). See the function IsValidNULLSegment() in the following example.

02h   **DWORD**   **dwOldSSSP**

If the documented SwitchStackTo() function is called, the current SS:SP stack pointer is stored here, for later restoration by SwitchStackBack(). At other times, this field contains the number 5, left over from the C compiler's _rsrvptrs variable (the number of reserved pointers).

06h   **WORD**   **pLocalHeap**

This is a near pointer to a Local Heap information structure. Unfortunately, Windows modules that omit a local heap often fail to zero out this field. When using this field to locate a local heap, always look for the LH signature at offset 22h (Standard mode) or 28h (KRNL386) in the presumed local heap. See the IsValidLocalHeap() function in the following example, and the discussion of the Local Heap information structure later in this chapter.

 If LocalInit() is used to carve a local heap out of a globally allocated object (for example, as part of a suballocation scheme, then the WORD at offset 6 in the global object will contain a near pointer to the Local Heap information structure, even though other fields from the Instance Data (NULL segment) structure are not present. If *multiple* local heaps are created from a single globally allocated block, then offset 6 contains the address of the most recently created local heap's information structure.

08h   **WORD**   **pAtomTable**

This field will be zero until InitAtomTable() is called either directly by the task or indirectly by calling AddAtom() for the first time, at which point the field contains the same value as returned by InitAtomTable(): a near pointer to the task's atom table. See InitAtomTable() and Atom Table, elsewhere in this chapter.

 If InitAtomTable() is used to create an atom table in a globally-allocated, non-DGROUP block, then the WORD at offset 8 in the global object will contain a near pointer to the Atom Table, even though other fields from the NULL segment structure may not be present. Because atoms are items in the local heap, an atom-table pointer at offset 8 will always be accompanied by a local-heap pointer at offset 6.

0Ah   **WORD**   **pStackTop**

This is a near pointer to the end of the stack. The stack grows "down" (higher to lower address), so pStackTop is at a lower address than pStackBottom. This field will be zero in a DGROUP belonging to a DLL.

0Ch   **WORD**   **pStackMin**

This field is the "high-water mark" of actual stack use. Amount of stack used so far equals pStackBottom - pStackMin. This field will be zero in a DGROUP belonging to a DLL.

0Eh   **WORD**   **pStackBottom**

This field is a near pointer to the beginning of the stack. Maximum size of the stack equals pStackBottom - pStackTop. This field will be zero in a DGROUP belonging to a DLL.

Support: 3.0, 3.1

Instance Data

See also: InitTask, Local Heap

Example: The following program, NULLSEG, tries to examine the NULL segment corresponding to any module name specified on the command line. For example, NULLSEG USER displays the address of USER's default local heap and atom table (USER's local heap plays a major role in the notorious Windows "free system resources" problem; see GetHeapSpaces()).

If the specified module is not a DLL, then the program displays the NULL segment for only the first instance. This is just pure laziness: getting the DGROUP for a given task would involve nothing more than using the HINSTANCE_FROM_TASK() macro in HANDLES.H.

In any case, once the program has a DGROUP, it verifies that the DGROUP really contains a NULL segment. If it does, the fields in the structure are displayed. Note that DLLs do not have their own stacks, so the three stack-related fields in the NULL segment should be zero for DLLs.

```c
/* nullseg.c */

#include <stdlib.h>
#include <dos.h>
#include "windows.h"
#include "winio.h"
#include "handles.h"

typedef struct {
    WORD wMustBeZero;
    DWORD dwOldSSSP;
    WORD pLocalHeap;
    WORD pAtomTable;
    WORD pStackTop;
    WORD pStackMin;
    WORD pStackBottom;
    } INSTDATA;

extern DWORD FAR PASCAL GetSelectorLimit(WORD sel);

main(int argc, char *argv[])
{
    INSTDATA far *lpInstData;
    BYTE far *lpLocalHeap;
    HANDLE hModule, hDGroup;
    char *modname = (argc < 2) ? "NULLSEG" : argv[1] ;

    if (! (hModule = GetModuleHandle(modname)))
        fail("Can't locate %s", modname);
    if (! (hDGroup = GetModuleDGroup(hModule, TRUE)))
        fail("Can't locate %s's DGROUP", modname);
    if (! IsValidNULLSegment(hDGroup))
        fail("%s's DGROUP doesn't have a NULL segment", modname);

    lpInstData = MK_FP(hDGroup, 0);
    printf("dwOldSSSP = %Fp\n", lpInstData->dwOldSSSP);
```

Instance Data

```c
    if (lpInstData->pLocalHeap)
    {
        lpLocalHeap = MK_FP(hDGroup, lpInstData->pLocalHeap);
        printf("pLocalHeap = %Fp\n", lpLocalHeap);
        if (! IsValidLocalHeap(lpLocalHeap))
            printf("Not a valid local heap!\n");
    }
    else
        printf("No local heap\n");

    if (lpInstData->pAtomTable)
    {
        // for Atom Table structure, see WINEXP.H
        WORD far *lpAtomTable = MK_FP(hDGroup, lpInstData->pAtomTable);
        printf("pAtomTable = %Fp (%u atoms)\n", lpAtomTable,*lpAtomTable);
    }
    else
        printf("No atom table\n");

    printf("pStackTop    =   %04x\n", lpInstData->pStackTop);
    printf("pStackMin    =   %04x\n", lpInstData->pStackMin);
    printf("pStackBottom = %04x\n", lpInstData->pStackBottom);
    if (ModuleIsDLL(hModule))
    {
        if (lpInstData->pStackTop || lpInstData->pStackBottom ||
            lpInstData->pStackMin)
            printf("Error - DLLs don't have stacks!\n");
        else
            printf("DLL - no stack\n");
    }
    else
    {
        printf("Stack used =   %04x\n",
            lpInstData->pStackBottom - lpInstData->pStackMin);
        printf("Stack size =   %04x\n",
            lpInstData->pStackBottom - lpInstData->pStackTop);
    }

    return 0;
}

BOOL IsValidNULLSegment(HANDLE h)
{
    INSTDATA far *lpInstData;
    WORD pLocalHeap;
    if (! verr(h))
        return FALSE;
    if (GetSelectorLimit(h) < 16)
        return FALSE;
    lpInstData = MK_FP(h, 0);
    if (lpInstData->wMustBeZero != 0)
        return FALSE;
    if (lpInstData->pLocalHeap == 0)
```

Instance Data

```
        return TRUE;    // it's ok to not have a local heap!
    return IsValidLocalHeap(MK_FP(h, lpInstData->pLocalHeap));
}
```

NULLSEG reveals the following about several Windows modules:

- KERNEL—no local heap or atom table; stack fields are nonzero
- USER—has local heap and atom table; no stack; in 3.1, USER has *multiple* local heaps, only one of which resides in DGROUP
- GDI—no atom table in default data segment or stack; in 3.1, GDI can have *multiple* local heaps, only one of which resides in DGROUP
- KEYBOARD, DISPLAY, SYSTEM—no NULL segment
- WINFILE—stack about 10K bytes

IsBadReadPtr   KERNEL.334

```
BOOL FAR PASCAL IsBadReadPtr(BYTE far *fp, WORD wLen);
```

This function determines whether a block of memory is readable. The code for IsBadReadPtr() actually tries to read the byte at fp[wLen], and can generate a GP fault, which will be caught and handled by an __GP handler, without causing a UAE. For most purposes, the Intel VERR (verify for reading) and LSL (load selector limit) instructions are a better choice, particularly because IsBadReadPtr() is not supported in Windows 3.0; it can be defined using VERR and LSL:

```
BOOL MyIsBadReadPtr(BYTE far *fp, WORD wLen)
{
    WORD wSel = FP_SEG(fp);
    if (! (wSel && verr(wSel))) //verr() and lsl() in HANDLES.C
        return TRUE;
    else
        return (lsl(wSel)+1 < wLen);
}
```

Interestingly, the IsBadXXX() functions can still get an occasional UAE, due to segment-not-present (INT 11h) faults.

Support: 3.1
See also: __GP

IsBadStringPtr   KERNEL.337

```
BOOL FAR PASCAL IsBadStringPtr(BYTE far *fp);
```

IsBadStringPtr() determines whether a far pointer corresponds to a NULL-terminated (ASCIIZ) string. It scans up to 0FFFFh bytes for the 0 termination byte, using REPNE SCASB. This function can cause a GP fault, which will then be caught by an internal __GP handler without causing a UAE; the function will return TRUE if the passed-in parameter caused a GP fault.

Support: 3.1
See also: __GP

IsBadWritePtr   KERNEL.335

`BOOL FAR PASCAL IsBadWritePtr(BYTE far *fp, WORD len);`

This function determines whether a block of memory is writeable. To do this, it cleverly writes to the last byte of the supposed block, without actually changing anything: fp[len-1] |= 0. If the pointer is bad, this will generate a GP fault, which is caught by an internal __GP handler, without causing a UAE. For most purposes, the Intel VERW (verify for writing) and LSL (load selector limit) instructions are better suited for such tests, particularly because IsBadWritePtr() is not supported in Windows 3.0.

  IsBadWritePtr() is used within the 3.1 KERNEL by the lstrcpy() and lstrcat() functions.

Support: 3.1
See also: __GP

IsROMFile   KERNEL.326

`BOOL FAR PASCAL IsROMFile(HANDLE h);`

This function returns FALSE in non-ROM versions of Windows. In ROM versions of Windows, the return value determines whether the specified file is ROM- or disk-based.

  Code patching would, of course, be unavailable in a ROM-based file. For more information, see the Microsoft Developer Knowledge Base article Q75497, "Writing ROM Executables."

Support: 3.1
See also: IsROMModule

IsROMModule   KERNEL.323

`BOOL FAR PASCAL IsROMModule(HANDLE h);`

See the description of IsROMFile().

Support: 3.1
See also: IsROMFile

IsSharedSelector   KERNEL.345

```
BOOL FAR PASCAL IsSharedSelector(WORD wSel);
```

This function determines whether a selector is shared, that is, whether the selector belongs to a dynamic link library (DLL). It uses the undocumented GetExePtr() function (see above) to find the module handle to which the selector corresponds and then tests a flag word in the Module Table to see if it is a DLL rather than a task.

```
IsSharedSelector proc far
    push _wSel
    call GetExePtr
    or ax, ax
    je done
    mov es, ax
    xor ax, ax
    test word ptr es:[0Ch], 8000h
    je done
    inc ax
done:
    retf 2
IsSharedSelector endp
```

The function is provided only in Windows 3.1, but its functionality can be duplicated in Windows 3.0 using the above code, which, in turn, is simply ModuleIsDLL(GetExeptr(wSel)) (ModuleIsDLL() appears in HANDLES.H).

Support: 3.1
See also: GetExePtr, Module Table

IsTask

```
BOOL FAR PASCAL IsTask(HANDLE h);
```

This useful function, which determines whether the specified handle is actually a task handle (HTASK), that is, whether it is a selector to a valid Task Database, is documented in Windows 3.1, but it is not provided in Windows 3.0. However, it is easy to produce an implementation of this function that works under both Windows 3.0 and 3.1. The following is extracted from HANDLES.C:

```
#define TDBMAGIC_OFS    0xFA    // Offset of 'TD' signature
#define TDBMAGIC        0x4454  // 'TD' signature for Task Database

BOOL IsValidTask(HANDLE h)
{
    WORD far *fp;
    if (! verr(h))
```

```
        return FALSE;
    if (GetSelectorLimit(h) < 0xFC)
        return FALSE;
    fp = MK_FP(h, 0xFA);
    return (*fp == TDBMAGIC);
}
```

```
assert(IsValidTask(GetCurrentTask()));
```

See also: Task Database

IsTaskLocked   KERNEL.122

```
WORD FAR PASCAL IsTaskLocked(void);
```

IsTaskLocked() determines whether the *current* task is locked, that is, whether it is the only one in the system that will be scheduled. The function returns 0 if the current task is unlocked; otherwise it returns the task handle of the locked task. Tasks are locked with the undocumented LockCurrentTask() function (see below). IsTaskLocked() merely retrieves the value of a variable in KERNEL; this value is set by LockCurrentTask().

In Windows 3.1, the documented GetSystemDebugState() function can return SDS_TASKLOCKED; tasks can be locked in 3.1 with the documented LockInput() function.

Used by: WINDEBUG
Support: 3.0, 3.1
See also: LockCurrentTask

IsWinOldApTask   KERNEL.158

```
BOOL FAR PASCAL IsWinOldApTask(HANDLE hTask);
```

IsWinOldApTask() determines if a task belongs to the Windows WINOLDAP module, that is, if it is a DOS ("old") application. The task handle parameter can be created from a window handle, using the documented GetWindowTask() function. Thus, an IsDOSWindow() or IsDOSBox() function can easily be synthesized, as shown in the following example.

The value returned by IsWinOldApTask() is extracted from the PSP: WINOLDAP sets the bottom bit of the byte at offset 48h for "old apps."

Used by: TASKMAN
Support: 3.0, 3.1

Example:

```
#include "windows.h"

extern BOOL FAR PASCAL IsWinOldApTask(HANDLE hTask);

BOOL IsDOSBox(HWND hWnd)
{
    return IsWinOldApTask(GetWindowTask(hWnd));
}
```

K327—see HandleParamError
K328—see _DebugOutput
K329—see DebugFillBuffer
K403—see FarSetOwner
K404—see FarGetOwner

KbdRst   KERNEL.123

```
void FAR PASCAL KbdRst(void);
```

In Windows 3.x Standard and Enhanced modes, KbdRest() simply returns, without doing anything. The function is called from the INT 9 handler in KEYBOARD.DRV, and according to the source code for KEYBOARD provided with the Windows DDK (see \KEYBOARD\TRAP.ASM), the function has something to do with extended-memory reset.

KillTask

A function with the prototype BOOL FAR PASCAL KillTask(HANDLE) appears in the Windows 3.0 SDK file WINEXP.H under the heading "scheduler things that the world knows not." However, no such function is exported from KERNEL (the other two "scheduler things that the world knows not," WaitEvent() and PostEvent(), are genuine and are described later in this chapter).

To kill an application under Windows, you can PostMessage(hwnd, WM_QUIT) or PostAppMessage(hTask, WM_QUIT), depending on what kind of handle to the application you have. If a task does not respond, you can use the ToolHelp TerminateApp() function, which in effect does a SetCurrentTask followed by a FatalAppExit (see chapter 10).

LocalAlloc

```
HANDLE FAR PASCAL LocalAlloc(WORD wFlags, WORD wBytes);
```

Even though this function is documented, several aspects of LocalAlloc() are not documented:

LocalAlloc()'s return value appears not only in the AX register, but also in CX. We wouldn't think to mention this except that some Windows API functions (such as SetDCState() in GDI) *rely* on this behavior, so that LocalAlloc()'s return value can be tested with JCXZ. In fact, most LocalXXX() functions in Windows quite deliberately place their return value in CX as well as AX. Testing with JCXZ saves a few bytes, and a few nanoseconds, over the usual test with something like OR AX,AX/JNE.

More important, when (wFlags & LMEM_MOVEABLE), the HANDLE returned from LocalAlloc() takes on special meaning: instead of a "magic cookie" style HANDLE as used elsewhere in Windows, it is a HANDLE in the Macintosh sense: a doubly dereferenceable master pointer. In other words, LocalAlloc(LMEM_MOVE-ABLE, x) returns a pointer to a pointer to a block of memory:

```
HANDLE h = LocalAlloc(LMEM_MOVEABLE, wSomeSize);
// test return value (with JCXZ if you want to get cute)
// ...

#define PTR_FROM_LMEM_MOVEABLE(h) \
    *((BYTE **)(h)))

strcpy(PTR_FROM_LMEM_MOVEABLE(h), "This is a test");
```

Given the structure of movable handles (see Local Arena Header on the next page), it should be obvious how this works.

Code in USER, particularly for edit controls (and in Windows 3.0, for menu handles too), frequently uses this knowledge of how movable local handles are implemented. Instead of LocalLock/Unlock, one will instead see code like this:

```
mov bx, hMenu
mov bx, [bx]            ; local movable handle -> pointer
mov ax, [bx+SOME_OFFSET]
```

On the other hand, this particular block of code (lifted from the simple USER function GetMenuItemCount()) appears in 3.0 but not in 3.1. It's replaced in 3.1 by something quite a bit more complicated. Why? Due to the notorious free system resources problem, something needed to be moved out of USER's default data segment; menus were a perfect choice. In 3.1, therefore, the 64K barrier is less of a problem. However, note that something has been given up (as something always must be): keeping menus in USER's default data segment meant fast access, particularly with the PTR_FROM_LMEM_MOVEABLE() trick. Now system resources are less constrained, but access to things like menus is therefore necessarily less direct (see the discussion of USER heaps in the introduction to chapter 6).

Local Arena Header

Items in a Windows local heap are preceded by a four-byte arena header. For example, if LocalAlloc(LMEM_FIXED, x) returns the handle 3140h, you would find an arena header at 313Ch. The arena header simply contains pointers to the previous and next arena headers in the doubly linked list that makes up a local heap. The start and end of the linked list are pointed to by the fields "first" and "last" in the Local Heap information structure (see below).

Having said that a local arena header merely contains "previous" and "next" pointers, it's actually a little more complicated than that because the field holding the "previous" pointer does double duty, also encoding whether the arena is free or in use:

Local Arena Header

OFFSET	SIZE	DESCRIPTION
00	WORD	Near pointer to previous Local Arena in list; first arena in list points to self; EXCEPT, bottom bit of previous pointer encodes whether the current arena is free or in use. Thus, to get a pointer to the previous arena, you actually must mask off the bottom bit:

```
BOOL in_use = arena->prev & 1
WORD wPrev = arena->prev & ~1
```

OFFSET	SIZE	DESCRIPTION
02	WORD	Near pointer to next Local Arena in list; last arena in list points to self.

The *handle* corresponding to a given arena is simply the address of the arena, plus four (the size of a local arena header). For example, using an arena at 313Ch, LocalAlloc() would return 3140h.

The *size* of a block is the next pointer, minus the handle. In other words

```
typedef struct { WORD wPrev, wNext; } LOCAL_ARENA;

BOOL IN_USE(LOCAL_ARENA *la)      { return la->wPrev & 1; }
WORD PREV(LOCAL_ARENA *la)        { return la->wPrev & ~1; }
WORD NEXT(LOCAL_ARENA *la)        { return la->wNext; }
WORD LOC_HANDLE(LOCAL_ARENA *la) { return ((WORD) la) + sizeof(LOCAL_ARENA); }
WORD LOC_SIZE(LOCAL_ARENA *la)    { return NEXT(la) - LOC_HANDLE(la); }
```

Free arenas contain additional information in the data area immediately following the arena header; these free arenas are chained together in a free list:

Free Local Arena

OFFSET	SIZE	DESCRIPTION
00 (header+04)	WORD	Size of the free block, in bytes
02 (header+06)	WORD	Previous block in free list
04 (header+08)	WORD	Next block in free list

How do you get to the start of the free list? A look at the code for LocalCountFree() (see below) shows how: the root of the free list is contained in the data area for the very first local arena, which is always formatted in the following way:

First Local Arena

OFFSET	SIZE	DESCRIPTION
00 (header+04)	WORD	Number of items (repeat of field at offset 4 in Local Heap information structure?)
02 (header+06)	WORD	First item in list
04 (header+08)	WORD	First item in free list (see LocalCountFree())

The preceding all assume LMEM_FIXED allocations. LMEM_MOVABLE allocations have an additional level of indirection. If LocalAlloc(LMEM_MOVABLE, x) returns you the handle 3212h, then at offset 3212h in the data segment you will find the following four-byte structure:

Movable Handle

OFFSET	SIZE	DESCRIPTION
00	WORD	Near pointer to data area. See LocalAlloc() above for the implications of this.
02	BYTE	Flags
03	BYTE	Lock count (FFh = entry unused)

There is a table of these movable handles; the beginning of the table, and the next available slot, are pointed at from fields in the Local Heap information structure (see below). The first WORD in the table is the size of the table; LocalHandleDelta() determines the size of the table. The table resides in a normal LMEM_FIXED block; this block is not allocated until the first LMEM_MOVABLE request.

ToolHelp provides functions for walking idealized Local Heaps; these functions (LocalInfo(), LocalFirst(), and LocalNext(); see chapter 10) should be used in preference to walking real, live local heaps.

Local Arena Header

Support: 3.0, 3.1
See also: Global Arena, LocalAlloc, LocalCountFree, LocalHandleDelta, Local Heap
Example: The following program, LOCAL, displays either its own local heap or the local heap contained in a segment specified on the command line. For example:

```
Local Heap at 1097:2DD0
13 items in heap
2dc4 (2dc0)      0008 bytes      p=2dc0 n=2dcc    USE
2dd0 (2dcc)      004c bytes      p=2dc0 n=2e1c    USE
2e20 (2e1c)      0200 bytes      p=2dcc n=3020    USE
3024 (3020)      0080 bytes      p=2e1c n=30a4    USE
..........
39b0 (39ac)      0404 bytes      p=3942 n=3db4    USE
3db8 (3db4)      0000 bytes      p=39ac n=3db4    USE

Movable handle table: 3140, next=314e
32 movable handles
1097:3142 ==> 39b2 lock=2
1097:3146 ==> 3946 lock=1
1097:314A ==> 34e6 lock=0
```

LOCAL.C uses the pLocalHeap variable at offset 6 in the NULL segment to try to find the Local Heap information structure. In turn, it uses the Local Heap information structure (Burgerjunior?) to find the beginning and end of the linked list of Local Arenas. LOCAL.C detects whether it is running under KRNL286 or KRNL386 and uses the appropriate Local Heap information structure. LOCAL.C chases next pointers to walk the linked list of Local Arenas, unpacking each arena header's contents and passing them to show(). After walking the list of Local Arenas, LOCAL.C next works the movable handle table, printing each movable handle and its corresponding pointer:

```
/* local.c */

#include <stdlib.h>
#include <dos.h>
#include "windows.h"
#include "winio.h"
#include "handles.h"

#pragma pack(1)

/* Local Heap information structure -- similar to Global
   Heap information structure (Burgermaster). The KRNL286 and
   KRNL386 versions differ only in the size of the "first",
   "last", and "disctotal" fields */
#define DEFINE_LOCALHEAPINFO_STRUCT(STRUCTNAME, W_OR_DW) \
typedef struct { \
    WORD check; \
    WORD freeze; \
    WORD items; \
    W_OR_DW first; \
```

Local Arena Header

```
        W_OR_DW last; \
        BYTE numcompact; \
        BYTE disclevel; \
        W_OR_DW disctotal; \
        WORD movable_tbl; \
        WORD movable_next; \
        WORD delta; \
        WORD hexpand; \
        WORD pstats; \
        DWORD notifyfunc; \
        WORD sem; \
        WORD mingrow; \
        WORD minsize; \
        WORD signature; \
    } STRUCTNAME;

DEFINE_LOCALHEAPINFO_STRUCT(LOCAL_HEAP, WORD);
DEFINE_LOCALHEAPINFO_STRUCT(LOCAL_HEAP_32, DWORD);

/* Local Arena header is same for KRNL286 and KRNL386 */
typedef struct {
    WORD prev;        // includes USED/FREE in bottom bit
    WORD next;
    } LOCAL_ARENA;

typedef struct {
    WORD handle;
    BYTE flags;
    BYTE lock;
    } MOVABLE_HANDLE;

void show(WORD h, WORD size, WORD prev, WORD next, WORD in_use);
int axtoi(char *s);

main(int argc, char *argv[])
{
    extern WORD __hInst;
    LOCAL_ARENA far *lpla;
    WORD next, last, items, wMoveTab, wMoveNext, wMoveNum;
    WORD seg = HandleToSel((argc < 2) ? __hInst : axtoi(argv[1]));
    WORD heap = *((WORD far *) MK_FP(seg, 6));
    BYTE FAR *lpHeap = MK_FP(seg, heap);

    if (! IsValidLocalHeap(lpHeap))
        fail("Not a valid local heap!");
    printf("Local Heap at %Fp\n", lpHeap);

    if (Kernel1632() == 16)
    {
        LOCAL_HEAP far *lplh = lpHeap;
        next = lplh->first;
        last = lplh->last;
        items = lplh->items;
        wMoveTab = lplh->movable_tbl;
        wMoveNext = lplh->movable_next;
```

Local Arena Header

```
    }
    else
    {
        LOCAL_HEAP_32 far *lplh32 = lpHeap;
        next = lplh32->first;    // truncate to 16 bits
        last = lplh32->last;
        items = lplh32->items;
        wMoveTab = lplh32->movable_tbl;
        wMoveNext = lplh32->movable_next;
    }

    printf("%d items in heap\n", items);

    // show LMEM_FIXED allocations and FREE blocks
    while (last - next)
    {
        lpla = MK_FP(seg, next);        // far pointer to arena header
        show(next+4,                    // handle for this item (skip header)
            lpla->next - (next+4),     // size = next - this
            lpla->prev & ~1,           // prev (mask off USED/FREE bit)
            lpla->next,                // next
            lpla->prev & 1);           // IN USE or FREE (bottom bit of prev)
        next = lpla->next;
    }
    lpla = MK_FP(seg, last);
    show(last+4, 0, lpla->prev & ~1, lpla->next, lpla->prev & 1);

    // show LMEM_MOVABLE allocations
    printf("\nMovable handle table: %04x, next=%04x\n",
        wMoveTab, wMoveNext);
    wMoveNum = *((WORD far *) MK_FP(seg, wMoveTab));
    printf("%d movable handles\n", wMoveNum);
    if (wMoveNum)
    {
        MOVABLE_HANDLE far *tab = MK_FP(seg, wMoveTab+2);
        MOVABLE_HANDLE far *fp;
        int i;
        for (i=0, fp=tab; i<wMoveNum; i++, fp++)
            if (fp->lock != 0xFF)
                printf("%Fp ==> %04x lock=%d\n", fp, fp->handle,fp->lock);
    }
}

void show(WORD h, WORD size, WORD prev, WORD next, WORD in_use)
{
    printf("%04x (%04x)\t%04x bytes\tp=%04x n=%04x\t%s\n",
        h, h-4, size, prev, next, (in_use) ? "USE" : "FREE");
}

int axtoi(char *s)
{
    if (s[0]=='0' && s[1]=='x')
    {
        int ret;
```

Local Arena Header

```
        sscanf(s+2, "%x", &ret);
        return ret;
    }
    else
        return atoi(s);
}
```

LocalCountFree   KERNEL.161

```
void FAR PASCAL LocalCountFree(void);    /* DS = local heap */
```

LocalCountFree() returns the number of bytes free in the local heap specified in the DS register. This function is called by the (also undocumented) GetHeapSpaces() function (see above). Because the local heap is specified in DS, this function will normally return the number of bytes free in the *current* local heap. However, like other LocalXXX functions in Windows, LocalCountFree() can be forced to operate on other heaps (such as USER's, GDI's, and so on.) by setting and restoring DS around the function call. This is exactly what GetHeapSpaces() does:

```
push ds
mov ds, wSomeOtherLocalHeap
call far ptr LocalCountFree
pop ds
mov wFreeBytes, ax
```

To get the correct value of DS for other modules, see the GetModuleDgroup() function in HANDLES.C. Given DS, LocalCountFree() (like all LocalXXX functions) can find the Local Heap from offset 6 in Instance Data structure.

LocalCountFree() finds the number of free bytes by walking the given local heap's free list (see Local Arena Header, above):

```
LH_SIG      equ 484ch           ; 'LH'
P_FIRST     equ 6               ; offset of ptr to first item in heap
P_FREELIST  equ 8               ; offset of ptr in first Arena to free
list

IFDEF KRNL286
SIG_OFFSET  equ 22h             ; offset of 'LH' signature in Local Heap info
P_LAST      equ 8               ; offset of ptr to last item in heap
ELSE
SIG_OFFSET  equ 28h
P_LAST      equ 0Ah
ENDIF

LocalCountFree proc far
    mov di, [6]                 ; DS:[6] is pLocalHeap (see Instance Data)
                                ; DI now holds ptr to Local Info structure

    ; ...
```

```
        xor ax, ax                      ; set up return value of 0
        cmp word ptr [di+SIG_OFFSET], LH_SIG   ; check for 'LH' signature
        jne done                        ; not a local heap -- return 0
        mov si, [di+P_LAST]             ; SI = ptr to last item in heap
        mov di, [di+P_FIRST]            ; DI = ptr to first item in heap
                                        ; DI now hold ptr to first Local Arena
        ;;;; FIRST LOCAL ARENA IS SPECIAL; CONTAINS INFO IN DATA AREA
        mov di, [di+P_FREELIST]         ; DI = ptr to first item in free list
loop:
        ;;;; FREE BLOCKS HAVE ADDITIONAL INFO IN DATA AREA!
        cmp di, si                      ; at end of list?
        je done                         ; if so, return value in AX
        add ax, [di+4]                  ; SIZE
        sub ax, 0ah                     ; subtract size of header itself
        mov di, [di+8]                  ; DI = ptr to next item in free list
        jmp loop                        ; get next item
done:
        retf                            ; return value in AX
LocalCountFree endp
```

Support: 3.0, 3.1
See also: GetHeapSpaces, Instance Data, Local Arena, LocalHeapSize

---

LocalHandleDelta   KERNEL.310

```
short FAR PASCAL LocalHandleDelta(int nNewDelta);
```

This function was documented in Windows 2.x; it sets the number of movable handle-table entries to be allocated. (Each movable object in the local heap requires a four-byte handle-table entry; see Local Arena Header above.) Macintosh programmers will detect a similarity here to MoreMasters(). The function sets and returns the current handle delta from offset 12h or 18h in the Local Heap information structure; if nNewDelta is zero, the function returns the delta without setting a new one. The default handle delta is 20h.

Support: 3.1 (function was not exported from 3.0)
See also: Local Heap

Local Heap

Any task or DLL in Windows can have a local heap residing in its default data segment (DGROUP). In addition, any globally allocated block can be suballocated by turning it into a local heap, via a call to the documented LocalInit() function. In 16-bit Windows, the maximum size for a local heap is 64K bytes.

The location of a task or DLL's default local heap is specified by the variable pLocalHeap at offset 6 in the Instance Data area (see above). This variable points to a

Local Heap Information Structure, very similar to Burgermaster. The linked list of Local Arenas that makes up the local heap can be reached from "first" and "last" pointers located in this information structure.

Like Burgermaster, the Local Heap information structure (Burgerjunior?) shares roughly the same structure in KRNL286 and KRNL386, except that the "first," "last," and "disctotal" fields are WORDS in KRNL286 and DWORDs in KRNL386 (perhaps to allow the possibility of Local Heaps whose size is greater than 64K). One way that the Local Heap information structure differs from Burgermaster is that it contains an 'LH' signature at its end; this signature is used in the IsValidLocalHeap() function, used in the sample programs in other parts of this chapter.

The Local Heap structure appears in the file WINKERN.INC, included with the Windows 3.1 DDK.

ToolHelp (see chapter 10) provides documented functions for walking an idealization of the Local Heap; LocalInfo(), LocalFirst(), and LocalNext() should generally be used in preference to walking a real, live Local Heap.

Local Heap information structure

OFFSET	SIZE	DESCRIPTION
00	WORD	Non-zero enables heap checking (defunct?)
02	WORD	Freeze: non-zero prevents heap compaction (set and cleared by the extinct 2.x LocalFreeze() and LocalMelt() functions)
04	WORD	Number of items in heap: increases with every LocalAlloc() or AddAtom() (atoms are items in the local heap); LocalInit() initializes to four items

—KRNL286—

OFFSET	SIZE	DESCRIPTION
06	WORD	Near pointer to first Local Arena in list; format of data in first item is special
08	WORD	Near pointer to last Local Arena in list (heap size = last - first; see LocalHeapSize())
0A	BYTE	Number of heap compactions
0B	BYTE	Current discard level
0C	WORD	Total bytes discarded so far
0E	WORD	Near pointer to beginning of movable handle table, or zero if no movable handles allocated yet.

MOVABLE HANDLE TABLE

00	WORD	Number of entries in table

Followed immediately by entries:

EACH ENTRY

00	WORD	Handle (see LocalAlloc(), above)

02	BYTE	flags
03	BYTE	lock count (FFh if entry unused)
10	WORD	Next available movable handle table entry (see Local Arena); can be zero
12	WORD	Local handle delta; default 20h (see LocalHandleDelta())
14	WORD	Near pointer to expand function
16	WORD	Near pointer to statistics table, or zero
18	DWORD	Far pointer to LocalNotify function (see LocalNotify())
1C	WORD	Semaphore used internally by LENTER and LLEAVE
1E	WORD	Minimum amount to grow DS by; initialized by LocalInit() to 200h
20	WORD	Minimum size of heap
22	WORD	'LH' signature (484Ch)

—KRNL386—

06	DWORD	Near pointer to first Local Arena in list; format of data in first item is special
0A	DWORD	Near pointer to last Local Arena in list (local heap size = last - first; see LocalHeapSize())
0E	BYTE	Number of heap compactions
0F	BYTE	Current discard level
10	DWORD	Total bytes discarded so far
14	WORD	Near pointer to beginning of movable handle table; see KRNL286 offset 0E above; can be zero
16	WORD	Next available movable handle table entry (see Local Arena); can be zero
18	WORD	Local handle delta; default 20h (see LocalHandleDelta())
1A	WORD	Near pointer to expand function
1C	WORD	Near pointer to statistics table, or zero
1E	DWORD	Far pointer to LocalNotify function (see LocalNotify())
22	WORD	Semaphore used internally by LENTER and LLEAVE
24	WORD	Minimum amount to grow DS by; initialized by LocalInit() to 200h
26	WORD	Minimum size of heap
28	WORD	'LH' signature (484Ch)

Support: 3.0, 3.1
See also: Global Heap, Local Arena, LocalHandleDelta, LocalHeapSize, LocalNotify
Example: See the function IsValidLocalHeap() in HANDLES.C; see LOCAL.C in the entry for the Local Arena structure.

Local Heap

LocalHeapSize   KERNEL.162

```
WORD FAR PASCAL LocalHeapSize(void);    /* DS = local heap */
```

LocalHeapSize() returns the number of bytes (both allocated and free) in the local heap specified in the DS register. This function is called by the (also undocumented) GetHeapSpaces() function (see above). The function takes no parameters because it gets the caller's local heap from DS:[6]. Because the local heap is assumed to be specified in DS, this function will normally return the number of bytes free in the *current* local heap. However, like other LocalXXX functions in Windows, LocalHeapSize() can be forced to operate on other heaps (such as USER's, GDI's, etc.) by setting and restoring DS around the function call. This is exactly what GetHeapSpaces() does:

```
push ds
mov ax, some_local_heap
mov ds, ax
call far ptr LOCALHEAPSIZE
pop ds
mov heap_size, ax
```

LocalHeapSize() computes its return value by subtracting the value of the first entry in the local heap from the value of the last entry:

```
P_LOCALHEAP equ 6 ; offset in Instance Data (DS) of ptr to Local Heap info
P_FIRST equ 6     ; offset in Local Heap info struct of ptr to first
IFDEF KRNL286
P_LAST   equ 8    ; offset in Local Heap info struct of ptr to last
ELSE
P_LAST   equ 0Ah
ENDIF

LOCALHEAPSIZE    proc    far
    mov bx, ds:[P_LOCALHEAP]
    mov ax, [bx+P_LAST]
    sub ax, [bx+P_FIRST]
    retf
LOCALHEAPSIZE    endp
```

Support: 3.0, 3.1
See also: GetHeapSpaces, LocalCountFree, Local Heap

LocalNotify   KERNEL.14

```
FARPROC FAR PASCAL LocalNotify(FARPROC lpNotifyFunc);
```

This function was documented in Windows 2.x, but it is not documented in Windows 3.x, probably because the way that local heaps are generally used has changed, now that Windows (thanks to the incorporation of a DOS extender) usually has megabytes of memory available in the global heap.

LocalNotify() does nothing more than set the address of the local-heap notification handler in the Local Heap structure and (using XCHG) return the previous address:

```
; offset in Local Heap info struct of ptr to lpNotifyFunc
IFDEF KRNL286
P_NOTIFYFUNC      equ 18h
ELSE
P_NOTIFYFUNC      equ 1Eh
ENDIF

LOCALNOTIFY proc far
    mov bx, sp
    mov ax, ss:[bx+4]    ; lpNotifyFunc
    mov dx, ss:[bx+6]    ; lpNotifyFunc+2
    mov dx, ds:[6]       ; PLOCALHEAP
    xchg ax, [bx+P_NOTIFYFUNC]
    xchg dx, [bx+P_NOTIFYFUNC+2]
    retf 4
LOCALNOTIFY endp
```

The local-heap notification handler is called by KERNEL when certain actions occur, such as a request to increase the size of the local heap. According to the Windows 2.x documentation, this callback function must have the following form (before passing it to LocalNotify, the callback function must of course be "prepared" with MakeProcInstance() or you need to be using "smart callbacks"):

```
BOOL _export FAR PASCAL NotifyFunc(WORD wMsg, HANDLE hMem, WORD wArg);
```

The wMsg is a notification message (see below), hMem identifies the local memory object that generated the notification, and wArg supplies an argument to wMsg. According to some ancient "Microsoft University" course notes that one of the authors dug out from his basement, the wMsg notifications are as follows:

```
#define LN_OUTOFMEM    0    /* wArg = #bytes needed */
#define LN_MOVE        1    /* hMem = handle; wArg = old location */
#define LN_DISCARD     2    /* hMem = handle; wArg = discard flags */
```

Support: 3.0, 3.1
See also: Local Heap

LockCurrentTask   KERNEL.33

```
WORD FAR PASCAL LockCurrentTask(BOOL bLock);
```

This function either locks (block is nonzero) or unlocks (bLock is zero) the current task. "Locking" means that no other tasks can receive messages or get scheduled; the current application becomes "system modal." This behavior is clear in the following session with the CALLFUNC interpreter from chapter 4:

```
> kernel istasklocked
0x0000
> kernel getcurrenttask
0x84d
> kernel lockcurrenttask 1
0x84d
> kernel istasklocked
0x84d
;;; clock stops running; can't switch away to other apps; but
;;; CALLFUNC program is still fully operational
> kernel lockcurrenttask 0
0x0000
;;; clock jumps ahead to correct time; can switch away
> kernel istasklocked
0x0000
```

Note that it is not only user input to other tasks that is locked out, but *all* messages. This function is called by USER as part of system-modal MessageBox handling and by WINDEBUG (which in turn is used by Windows debuggers such as CVW and TDW).

Windows 3.1 has the documented LockInput() function; also documented in 3.1 is the GetSystemDebugState() function, one of whose return values is SDS_TASKLOCKED.

Support: 3.0, 3.1
Used by: USER, WINDEBUG
See also: IsTaskLocked

LongPtrAdd   KERNEL.180

```
void FAR PASCAL LongPtrAdd(DWORD dwLongPtr, DWORD dwAdd)
```

LongPtrAdd modifies the base address of a far pointer by adding its second parameter onto the current base address of the selector of the first parameter. The function is thus a base-relative variant of the SetSelectorBase() function (see discussion later in this chapter):

```
void MyLongPtrAdd(DWORD dwLongPtr, DWORD dwAdd)
{
    WORD wSel = FP_SEG(dwLongPtr);
    SetSelectorBase(wSel, GetSelectorBase(wSel) + dwAdd);
}
```

While similar functionality to LongPtrAdd is thus available elsewhere, setting a breakpoint on the function reveals that it is called frequently by the loader in KERNEL; it might be useful for segment arithmetic.

Support: 3.0/3.1
Example:

```
/* longptr.c */

#include <dos.h>
#include <assert.h>
#include <windows.h>
#include "winio.h"

extern void FAR PASCAL LongPtrAdd(DWORD fp, DWORD size);
extern DWORD FAR PASCAL GetSelectorBase(WORD sel);

#define ADD 0x30000L

main()
{
    WORD h = GlobalAlloc(GMEM_MOVEABLE, 0x1000L);
    void far *fp = GlobalLock(h);
    DWORD before, after;
    before = GetSelectorBase(FP_SEG(fp));
    LongPtrAdd(fp, ADD);
    after = GetSelectorBase(FP_SEG(fp));
    assert(after - before == ADD);
    GlobalUnlock(h);
    GlobalFree(h);
    return 0;
}
```

MemoryFreed   KERNEL.126

```
WORD FAR PASCAL MemoryFreed(WORD wAmount);
```

MemoryFreed() manipulates compaction/discarding fields in the Global Heap information structure (Burgermaster). If the 010th bit of [KERNEL_FLAGS+1] is turned off, the MemoryFreed() function returns 0. If the bit is turned on, the wAmount parameter comes into play. When wAmount is zero, the function simply returns the value in the low word of the discard_total field in Burgermaster (see Global Heap, above). If wAmount is nonzero, it is subtracted from the value in discard_total. Additionally, bit 0 of the ncompact field in Burgermaster is turned on. If the new discard_total falls below or equals zero, then the 010 bit is set. In other words:

```
MemoryFreed(wAmount)
{
```

MemoryFreed

```
    if (KERNEL_FLAGS+1 bit 010 is OFF)
        return 0;
    else if (wAmount == 0)
        return Burgermaster.distotal;
    else
    {
        if ((Burgermaster.distotal -= wAmount) <= 0)
            Burgermaster.ncompact |= 2;
        Burgermaster.ncompact |= 1;
    }
}
```

In other words, MemoryFreed( ) is related to global heap compaction.

Support: 3.0, 3.1
See also: Global Heap

Module Table

A module handle, returned from a KERNEL function such as GetModuleHandle( ), GetExePtr( ), or LoadModule( ), is actually a handle to a data structure called the Module Table. The Module Table is essentially an in-memory version of the "new" segmented-executable (NE) file header and contains the information necessary to do dynamic linking. The NE file header is documented in Ray Duncan's *Advanced OS/2 Programming* (it's essentially the same in Windows and OS/2 1.x), and in the Windows 3.1 SDK *Programmer's Reference, Volume 4: Resources*, chapters 6 and 7.

There are a number of key differences between the Module Table and the NE header, and the Module Table stands on its own as one of the key KERNEL internal data structures. In general, the organization of the Module Table is more straightforward than that of the NE header. Where the on-disk NE header appears to have been optimized (or is it pessimized?) to conserve disk space, the Module Table has been optimized for quick access.

With one exception in Windows 3.0 debug (see below), the structure of the Module Table has stayed unchanged from Windows 3.0 to Windows 3.1, making it relatively safe for programmers to use.

The Module Table is the central repository for anything related to an .EXE or .DLL that's currently in memory. Information about code and data segments, resources, the module filename, you name it, is in here. For application, the Module Table contains information that can be shared across multiple instances (though DLLs don't have multiple instances); per-instance information is kept in the Task Database.

For the purposes of this discussion, a module will refer to anything in the segmented-executable or new-executable format. When working with the Module Table, it is important to be familiar with the NE format. (See the discussion in chapter 2 and in the 3.1 SDK.)

Module Table

The most common modules you'll encounter are programs (.EXE), dynamic link libraries (.DLL), drivers (.DRV), and fonts (.FON). Other extensions, including .MOD, .CPL, and .IW, can also be used for modules. The important thing is that the file is in the NE format.

For programs and most DLLs, the Module Table is mainly used to keep track of the code and data segments and what selectors have been assigned to them. When KERNEL loads a program, and the program contains dynamic links to functions in a module that is already loaded (such as KERNEL itself), the information in the already-loaded module table is used to find the selector values assigned to the module's code segments. The KERNEL segment relocator patches these selector values into the newly loaded program's code, so that dynamic links become far calls that go directly to the module's code. This is a much cleaner interface than that of MS-DOS, which used interrupts and register values to connect the program to the operating system (of course, Windows *still* makes pretty heavy use of the interrupt calling convention too, for example, to call DOS and DPMI).

Other modules (.FON files in particular) exist purely to provide resources. The module table serves as an in-memory storage area for file offsets to resources, as well as to other tables in the NE file. If you're looking at a listing of all the modules in the system, don't be surprised to see some modules that have no code or data segments. On the other hand, there is the case of a well-known debugger that attempted to hide some critical code by placing it into a font file!

The Module Table is sometimes called a Module Database.

Module Table format

OFFSET	SIZE	DESCRIPTION
0	WORD	NE signature (454Eh)
2	WORD	load count of module
4	WORD	near * to entry table
		ENTRY TABLE
	WORD	First entry ordinal in bundle - 1
	WORD	Last entry ordinal in bundle (nEntries = last - first)
	WORD	near ptr to next bundle
		EACH ENTRY
	BYTE	type (actual number for fixed seg, or 0FFh for movable)
	BYTE	flags (1 = exported, 2 = shared data entry)
	BYTE	segNum (logical segment for entry)
	WORD	offset (offset of entry in segment)
6	WORD	selector of next module table. 0 indicates end of list

Module Table

8	WORD	near * to segment entry for DGROUP
0A	WORD	near * to load file information

LOAD FILE INFO

BYTE	length of load file info section, not counting itself
BYTE	flag: Bit 0 on in WIN 3.0 if loaded after ProgMan (inclusive)?
WORD	unknown
WORD	File date, in MS-DOS date format
WORD	File time, in MS-DOS time format
BYTE	file name in ASCIIZ format

0C	WORD	module flags (based on NE file flags)

FLAGS

8000h	Library module (0=task 1=DLL)
0800h	A self-loading application
0300h	Uses Windows display API services
0040h	Private allocation of memory
0010h	Will use LIM 3.2 EMS
0002h	Each instance of this module gets its own DGROUP (i.e., a task)
0001h	Each instance of this module shares the DGROUP (i.e., a DLL)

0E	WORD	logical segment number of DGROUP (1 based)
10	WORD	initial local heap size
12	WORD	initial stack size
14	DWORD	starting CS:IP (as a logical address)
18	DWORD	starting SS:SP (as a logical address)
1C	WORD	count of segments in the segment table
1E	WORD	count of entries in module reference table
20	WORD	size of nonresident names table on disk (see GetProcAddress)
22	WORD	near * to segment table

Segment table consists of a series of entries. The number is given by the WORD at offset 1Ch. Entries are sequentially numbered, starting at 1.

Format of a segment table entry is similar to the segment table entry in the NE file, but with the addition of a WORD at the end of each entry:

SEGMENT TABLE ENTRY

WORD	offset of segment within file on disk: shift left by align size at offset 32h
WORD	Size of segment on disk. 0 = 64K

Module Table

	WORD	flags: (bitfield)	
		0001h	DATA segment (0 indicates CODE)
		0008h	iterated segment
		0010h	movable
		0020h	shareable (should not be modified)
		0040h	preload
		0080h	read only
		0100h	has relocations
		1000h	discardable
	WORD	Initial size of segment when loaded (0 = 64K)	
	WORD	Handle or selector of segment in memory. (For fixed segments, a selector; else a handle. Zero indicates segment not loaded.)	
24	WORD	near * to resource table.	

RESOURCE TABLE FORMAT

WORD	alignment shift. (4 = 16 byte alignment, 9 = 512 byte alignment)

Immediately followed by:

FORMAT OF THE RESOURCE TYPE STRUCTURE

WORD	ID
WORD	number of info structs following this struct
WORD	far * to function containing resource handler

If the high bit of ID is set, this is an ordinal resource, and the bottom 8 bits indicate the type of the resource (an RT_ constant from WINDOWS.H):

Cursor	1
Bitmap	2
Icon	3
Menu	4
Dialog	5
String table	6
Font directory	7
Font	8
Accelerator	9
RC data	10 (user data)
Error table	11

Module Table

Group cursor   12
Unknown   13
Group icon   14
Name table   15 (eliminated in 3.1 NE files)
Version info   16 (3.1)
TrueType font   204 (CCh)

If the high bit is not set, a named resource; the value is an offset into the resource table.

FORMAT OF THE RESOURCE INFO STRUCT

WORD	offset in file, before alignment shift applied
WORD	length in file, before alignment shift applied
WORD	flags

1000h	Discardable
040h	preload
0020h	read only
0010h	movable
0004h	loaded in memory

WORD	resource number
WORD	handle to segment containing the resource in memory
WORD	usage count

26	WORD	near * to resident name table

A series of Pascal-style (counted) strings, one after the other. Get total length by subtracting the resident-names table offset from the module-reference table offset

28	WORD	near * to module reference table

Module reference table is an array of WORD's, each the module handle of the module to which it refers; access to the array is one-based

2A	WORD	near * to imported names table

This always points to a 0 byte, which should indicate the end of the table. However, for some unknown reason, the imported-name table always starts with a 0 byte, and then follows with Pascal-style (counted) strings

2C	DWORD	NE file offset of nonresident name table (see GetProcAddress)
30	WORD	count of movable entries
32	WORD	Sector alignment (i.e, 4 = segments in .EXE file aligned on 16-byte boundaries; 9 = aligned on 512-byte boundaries)
34	WORD	Always 0 in 3.0. In 3.1, set to 2 if a TrueType font. (In NE header, this field would be resource count.)
36	WORD	BYTE at offset 36h is operating-system flags (as in NE file)

Module Table

	0	unknown
	1	OS/2
	2	Windows
	3	European DOS 4
	4	WIN386

BYTE at offset 37h is "other flags" (as in NE file):

0001	long file names
0002	Win 2.x app o.k. for protected mode
0004	Win 2.x app o.k. for proportional font
0008	File has gangload area (i.e., area with all preload code segments ganged together, so they can be loaded in one shot)

EXCEPT in Win 3.0 Debug, WORD at offset 36h is same as WORD at offset 38h

38	WORD	Contains the same value as offset 2Ah (Imported Names Table)

EXCEPT in Win 3.0 Debug, contains near * to "other" segment table

"OTHER" SEGMENT TABLE FORMAT

WORD	unknown
	If CODE segment: 0 means not present, otherwise present
	if DATA segment: always 0
WORD	Always set to 0

3A	WORD	Always seems to hold the same value as offset 38h, except KERNEL
3C	WORD	Unknown; this field is the swap area size in NE header
3E	WORD	Expected windows version, as in NE file

Comments:

0   WORD

Like the module table in the NE file, the first two bytes contain the ASCII representation of NE; interpreted as a WORD, this is 454Eh. Internally, Windows uses these bytes as a signature to verify that it is looking at a valid module table.

2   WORD

The number of other modules that have references to this module. Usually KERNEL is the most popular module, with USER and GDI following close behind. When this value decrements to 0, Windows will remove the module from memory.

Module Table

4   **WORD**

This is a near pointer (relative to the module handle/selector) to the Entry Table for the module. The Entry Table in the module table bears little resemblance to the rather cryptic Entry Table found in the NE file. It appears that the in-memory Entry Table is optimized for quick lookup. All NULL bundle entries have been removed, and bundles with contiguous entry ordinals are combined. The bundles are organized as a null-terminated linked list. Each list node has a header that specifies the first and last entry ordinal in the node and a pointer to the next node. Once the appropriate node is found, the desired entry can quickly be found, as entries are contained in an array of fixed-sized structures that follows the node header. One frustrating note is that the segment portion of the entry point address is stored as a byte and is the *logical* segment number, rather then the actual selector in use. As a result, it is not possible to patch in another far address, from another module, for a given entry point. This makes it impossible to use the Entry Table to implement that badly-needed function in Windows, SetProcAddress().

6   **WORD**

This is the handle of the next module table. A value of 0 indicates that this is the last module in the list. ToolHelp uses this in its ModuleNext() function. The *start* of the Module Table linked list can be found by an undocumented use of GetModuleHandle() (see GetModuleHandle(), discussed previously).

8   **WORD**

For modules with a DGROUP, this contains a near pointer to the segment table entry for the DGROUP segment. The segment table is described in the discussion below of offset 22h.

0A   **WORD**

By passing GetModuleFilename() a module handle, you can get back the complete DOS file specification for the module's NE file. By using the information at this offset, you can get back a little more. Offset 0Ah is a near pointer to a block of memory that contains the file name, as well as its DOS date and time stamp. The first byte in the block contains the length of the remainder of the block, not counting itself. Offset 3 and 5 in the block contains the NE files date and time respectively, in the DOS bit encoded format. Presumably, this information is kept around so that Windows can verify that the NE file hasn't been changed since it was first loaded. Bringing up the rear is the fully qualified DOS file name. It appears that the data here is loosely modeled after the documented OFSTRUCT structure.

0C   **WORD**

Module flags: In general, these match the module flags that appear at the same offset in the NE file. It does appear that some bitfields are used for runtime flags that don't match up to anything in the on-disk NE header.

22   **WORD**

A near pointer to the segment table. The segment table contains not only attributes and file offsets for the code/data in the NE file, but also holds the handle that Windows has

Module Table

assigned to that segment. In short, this is where the correlation between a logical address and a selector is kept. If fact, Windows functions such as GetCodeHandle and GetCodeInfo use this table.

The CODE segments in a module are shared between all instances of the module. But what about non-shared segments, especially DGROUP? Each task (each instance of the module; for DLLs this is a non-issue) has its own DGROUP. The DGROUP's logical segment number if stored at offset 0Eh in the Module Table header, and this remains unchanged for each instance of the module. However, the actual selector value for DGROUP does change for each instance; this in fact is precisely what the hInstance is. Here, the segment table entry contains the value of the *last* (most recently loaded) DGROUP that was loaded for the module. If you close the second instance of an app, the DGROUP value is set back to its previous value (hPrevInstance). This implies that there is a DGROUP chain.

Segments are numbered starting at 1, so the logical segment 7 refers to the seventh entry in the segment table. Each segment table entry is 10 bytes in length. The first 8 bytes are identical to the segment table in the NE file. The remaining WORD is used for the global memory handle (or, for fixed segments, a selector) to the code/data. A value of 0 indicates that the segment has not been loaded yet; A nonzero value does not mean that the segment is present, though. To test for this, the LAR instruction should be used.

24   WORD

To quickly find resources, a condensed index of the resources in the NE file is kept in the Module Table. The WORD at this location is a near pointer to the resource table. Like the in-memory entry table, the resource table fortunately does not bear much resemblance to what's in the NE file. The first byte in the resource table is the alignment count. (See the NE file description for more information). The actual data for the resource index is then stored end to end, with no padding. For each collection of resource types (Icons, for instance), there is a fixed length header that identifies the resource type and tells how many individual resources are to follow. Immediately after the header is an array of fixed length structures, one per instance of the resource type. The end of the table is indicated by a zero value where the next resource type structure would otherwise be.

26   WORD

This is a near pointer to the resident names table; it is an exact duplicate of the table in the NE file.

28   WORD

Whereas the module reference table in the on-disk NE file contains offsets into the imported names table (to obtain the name of the fourth imported module, you'd look up the fourth word in the module reference table and add that to the base of the imported names table), in memory, the module reference table is much simpler. Instead of containing offsets, it contains the actual module handles of the imported modules.

Module Table

2A   **WORD**

This is a near pointer to the imported names table. For some reason (even in the NE file), the imported names table always starts with a 0 byte. According to the NE specification, this would indicate the end of the table. However, if you pretend that the next byte is the first byte, then everything appears as expected.

32   **WORD**

The align-shift value is used to compute offsets of the segments within the file. The segment table contains only a WORD to hold the file offset of a segment, yet the file, and the offset of the segment within the file, may be greater than 64k. The value at this field is used to shift-left segment file offsets; the shift is generally 4 or 9.

34   **WORD**

This WORD value is always set to 0 except when the module is a TrueType font under Windows 3.1. In this case, the value is 2.

36   **WORD or BYTE[2]**

In general, offsets 36h and 37h correlate to the "OS-type" and "other flags" fields of the NE file. However, under the debugging version of Windows 3.0, the two bytes are used as a near pointer to an undocumented table. This table parallels the segment table, but with the entries only two bytes in length. The low-order word is always 0, unless it is a code segment and the corresponding segment is present in memory. It is not known what the non-zero values are supposed to indicate. The high-order word is always 0.

38   **WORD**

If running under the Windows 3.0 debug version, this WORD points to the same table that the WORD at offset 36h points to. When running under the Window 3.0 retail version, or under 3.1, it contains the same value as offset 2Ah contains, namely the offset of the imported names table.

3C   **WORD**

This field always seems to contain a power of 2, and may actually be the maximum swap area size. This would correspond to the file-based NE image.

Support: 3.0, 3.1
See also: GetExePtr, GetModuleHandle
Example: The following sizable sample program, WINMOD, written using the WINIO library from chapter 4, demonstrates the use of the Module Table information presented above. First, WINMOD displays a list of all modules present in the system:

```
MODULE      HANDLE
KERNEL        00F7
SYSTEM        013F
KEYBOARD      0147
MOUSE         015F
DISPLAY       01BF
```

Module Table

```
....
CALLFUNC    11C7
WINMOD      119F
```

The user can click on any module name to bring up a window with additional information about the module. Note that this shows the module in memory, rather than the image on disk that an EXEDR-type program would show. For example, clicking on DISPLAY above creates a new window with the following information:

```
File                        C:\WIN31.B2\SYSTEM\VGAMONO.DRV  12-17-91   3:10
Usage count                 000D
DGROUP segment              0008
Initial heap size           0000
Initial stack size          0000
Starting CS:IP              0002:02C1
Starting SS:SP              0000:0000
Minimum Windows version     3.10
Flags                       LIBRARY USES_WINAPI SHARED_DATA
Non-res names offset        00584
Non-res names size          01B2

Segments:
  #  HNDL  FILE_SIZE  ALLOC_SIZE  TYPE
  01  01E7      333D       333D   CODE PRESENT
  02  01EE      02F5       02F5   CODE PRESENT
  ...............

Resources:
  ID: 800C Group Cursor         000B entries  fn(): 0117:7DF4
  ...............

  ID: 8002 Bitmap               001E entries  fn(): 0117:7DF4
  ...............

Referenced modules:
  HNDL   NAME
  0147   KEYBOARD
  00F7   KERNEL

Resident names:
  ORDN   NAME
  0000   DISPLAY
```

The program has one include file, MODTABLE.H:

```
// modtable.h
typedef struct {
    int    segment_type  : 1;   /* Segment type identification */
    int    unknown       : 2;   /* used by Windows for something*/
    int    iterated      : 1;   /* Segment is iterated         */
    int    movable       : 1;   /* Segment is movable          */
    int    pure          : 1;   /* Segment is shareable        */
    int    preload       : 1;   /* Segment is preload          */
    int    read_only     : 1;   /* Segment is read-only        */
```

Module Table

```
    int     reloc_info   : 1;   /* Segment has reloc info        */
    int     u1           : 3;
    int     discardable  : 1;   /* Discardable flag.             */
    int     u2           : 3;
} SEG_BITFIELD_FLAGS;

typedef struct {
    WORD    sector_offset;      /* Offset to logical sector      */
    WORD    segment_length;     /* Size in bytes of segment      */
    SEG_BITFIELD_FLAGS  flags;  /* flags for segment             */
    WORD    alloc_size;         /* Segment allocation size       */
    WORD    handle;
} MODULE_TABLE_SEGMENT_RECORD;

typedef enum {                  /* Segment type constants        */
  CODE      = 0x0000,           /* Code segment type             */
  DATA      = 0x0001,           /* Data segment type             */
} SEGMENT_TYPES;

typedef struct {
    WORD        ne_signature;
    WORD        ne_usage;
    WORD        ne_penttable;
    WORD        ne_pnextexe;
    WORD        ne_pautodata;
    WORD        ne_pfileinfo;
    WORD        ne_flags;
    WORD        ne_autodata;
    WORD        ne_heap;
    WORD        ne_stack;
    DWORD       ne_csip;
    DWORD       ne_sssp;
    WORD        ne_cseg;
    WORD        ne_cmod;
    WORD        ne_cbnrestab;
    WORD        ne_segtab;
    WORD        ne_rsrctab;
    WORD        ne_restab;
    WORD        ne_modtab;
    WORD        ne_imptab;
    DWORD       ne_nrestab;
    WORD        ne_cmovent;
    WORD        ne_align;
    WORD        ne_cres;
    unsigned char ne_exetyp;
    unsigned char ne_flagsother;
    union {
        WORD ne_pretthunks;    /* offset to return thunks       */
        WORD ne_gang_start;    /* start of gangload area        */
    } x;
    union {
        WORD ne_psegrefbytes; /* offset to segment ref. bytes */
        WORD ne_gang_length;  /* length of gangload area        */
    } y;
    WORD ne_swaparea;          /* minimum code swap area size   */
    WORD ne_expver;            /* expected windows version num */
```

Module Table

```
} MODULE_TABLE;

typedef struct _BUNDLE_HEADER {
    WORD      firstEntry;
    WORD      lastEntry;
    WORD      nextBundle;
} BUNDLE_HEADER;

typedef struct _ENTRY {
    BYTE      segType;
    BYTE      flags;
    BYTE      segNumber;
    WORD      offset;
} ENTRY;

typedef struct _RESOURCETYPE {
    WORD      ID;
    WORD      count;
    DWORD     function;
}RESOURCETYPE;

typedef struct _RESOURCEINFO {
    WORD      offset;
    WORD      length;
    WORD      flags;
    WORD      ID;
    WORD      handle;
    WORD      usage;
}RESOURCEINFO;

#define NENOTP            0x8000  /* Not a process (i.e. a library module)
*/
#define NESELFLOAD        0x0800  /* Self loading .EXE file */
#define NEAPPTYP          0x0700  /* Application type mask */
#define NEWINAPI          0x0300  /* Uses windowing API */
#define NEWINCOMPAT       0x0200  /* Compatible with windowing API */
#define NENOTWINCOMPAT    0x0100  /* Not compatible with windowing API */
#define NENONRES          0x0080  /* Contains nonresident code segments */
#define NELIM32           0x0010  /* Uses LIM 3.2 API */
#define NEPROT            0x0008  /* Runs in protected mode only */
#define NEPPLI            0x0004  /* Per-Process Library Initialization */
#define NEINST            0x0002  /* Instance data */
#define NESHARED          0x0001  /* Shared data */

// Target operating systems
#define NE_UNKNOWN        0
#define NE_OS2            1    /* Microsoft/IBM OS/2 / 
#define NE_WINDOWS        2    /* Microsoft Windows */
#define NE_DOS4           3    /* Microsoft European MS-DOS 4.x */
#define NE_DEV386         4    /* Microsoft Windows 386 */
```

WINMOD.C is presented below. The main() entry point (remember, WINIO applications use main(), not WinMain()) installs the function DumpModule() as a WINIO clickable-line handler; main() then calls the function ModuleWalk(). Module-

Module Table

Walk() uses an undocumented feature of GetModuleHandle() (see elsewhere in this chapter) to get a handle to the first module in the system. It then walks the linked list of Module Tables, printing the handle and name of each one, until it gets to the end of the list.

At this point, WINMOD returns from main(), where WINIO takes over, interacting with the user and calling the installed DumpModule() function whenever a module name is clicked. DumpModule() creates a new window and calls DisplayModule(), which in turn does most of the work of printing out the contents of the Module Table structure for the module that was clicked on. DisplayModule() calls DoSegment-Table(), DoResourceTable(), and DoResidentNamesTable() to each take care of their own part.

```c
//=================================
//  WinMod by Matt Pietrek, 1992
//  File: WINMOD.C
//=================================
#include <windows.h>
#include <stdio.h>
#include <string.h>
#include <dos.h>
#include "winio.h"
#include "modtable.h"

#define NE_SIGNATURE 0x454E

WORD WinVersion;

char *ResourceNames[] = {
    "Unknown",
    "Cursor",            // 1
    "Bitmap",            // 2
    "Icon",              // 3
    "Menu",              // 4
    "Dialog",            // 5
    "String Table",      // 6
    "Font Directory",    // 7
    "Font",              // 8
    "Accelerator",       // 9
    "RC Data",           //10
    "Error Table",       //11
    "Group Cursor",      //12
    "Unknown",           //13
    "Group Icon",        //14
    "Name Table",        //15
    "Version info"       //16
    };

//-----------------------------------------------
// Converts a global handle to a selector value.
// The proper way would be to use GlobalLock, but
// GlobalLock will RIP on certain selectors.
// ToolHelp does it like this, so...
```

Module Table

```
//-----------------------------------------------
WORD HandleToSel(HANDLE h)
{
    // In 3.1, handles = (selectors-1)
    // Valid selectors end in a 7 or a F
    // Thus, we can simply make sure the
    // lowest bit is turned on.
    //
    // In 3.0, handles = (selectors+1)
    // Valid selectors end in a 5 or a D
    // Decrement the handle if it's an
    // even value.

    if ( WinVersion == 0x030A )
        h |= 0x0001;
    else if ( WinVersion < 0x030A )
        if ( (h & 0x0002) == 0x0002 )
            h--;

    return h;
}


//-----------------------------------------------
// Given a module handle, return the
// name of the module.
//-----------------------------------------------
char *GetModuleNameFromHandle(HANDLE handle)
{
    static char name[129];
    char far *moduleTablePtr;
    WORD residentNamesOffset;
    BYTE cbModuleName;

    name[0] = 0;    // Null out the return string

    // create a pointer to the module table
    moduleTablePtr = GlobalLock(handle);
    GlobalUnlock(handle);
    if ( !moduleTablePtr )
        return name;

    // Verify that we're really looking at a module table, by
    // looking for the NE signature. If we are, get the
    // module name out of the resident names table.
    if ( *(WORD far *)moduleTablePtr == NE_SIGNATURE )
    {
        // Obtain the resident names table offset, and point to it
        residentNamesOffset = *(WORD far *)(moduleTablePtr + 0x26);
        moduleTablePtr += residentNamesOffset;

        // Get the length of the first entry, which is always
        // the module name.
        cbModuleName = *(BYTE far *)moduleTablePtr;
        moduleTablePtr++;
```

Module Table

```
            // Use the far string copy to move the name to our local
            // buffer. Then null terminate the local buffer copy.
            _fstrncpy(name, moduleTablePtr, cbModuleName);
            name[cbModuleName] = 0;
        }

        return name;
    }


    //----------------------------------------------
    // Display each entry in the resource table
    //----------------------------------------------
    void DoResourceTable(char far *ptr)
    {
        RESOURCETYPE far *type;
        RESOURCEINFO far *info;
        WORD align;
        char *resourceTypeName;
        WORD i;

        printf("Resources:\n");

        // Calculate the resource file alignment size
        align = 1 << (*(WORD far *)ptr);

        // Point past the alignment size field, to the first entry
        (char far *)type = ptr+2;

        // A resource type ID of 0 indicates the end of the list
        while ( type->ID != 0 )
        {
            // Determine what type this resource is
            if ( (type->ID & 0x7FFF ) <= 16 )
                resourceTypeName = ResourceNames[type->ID & 0x7FFF];
            else if ( type->ID == 0x80CC )
                resourceTypeName = "TrueType font";
            else
                resourceTypeName = "Unknown";

            // Display information common to all entry of this type
            printf("  ID: %04X %-20s %04X entries  fn(): %Fp\n",
                type->ID, resourceTypeName, type->count, type->function);

            // C pointer arithmatic at work here!!!
            (RESOURCETYPE far *)info = type+1;

            // Now iterate and display all the entries for this resource type.
            // The "info" pointer always points to the next resource instance
            // to be displayed and is updated with 'C' pointer arithmetic.
            for (i=0; i < type->count; i++)
            {
                printf("  Offs: %05lX  Len: %04lX  Flags: %04X"
                    "  Handle: %04X  Usage: %04X\n",
                    info->offset * (DWORD)align, info->length*(DWORD)align,
                    info->flags, info->handle, info->usage );
```

Module Table

```
            info++;
        }

        printf("\n");

        // The next resource type immediately follows the end
        // of the preceding resource. Use this info to point
        // to the next resource type section.
        type = (RESOURCETYPE far *)info;
    }

    printf("\n");
}

//-----------------------------------------------
// Display information about each segment in
// the modules segment table.
//-----------------------------------------------
void DoSegmentTable(void far *a, WORD count)
{
    MODULE_TABLE_SEGMENT_RECORD far *st = a;
    WORD segSel;
    WORD i;

    printf("Segments:\n");
    printf("  #  HNDL  FILE_SIZE  ALLOC_SIZE  TYPE\n");

    for ( i=1; i <= count; i++, st++)
    {
        printf
        (
            "  %02X  %04X       %04X        %04X  %s",
            i,
            st->handle, st->segment_length, st->alloc_size,
            st->flags.segment_type ? "DATA" : "CODE"
        );

        if ( st->handle == 0 )
            goto not_present;

        // Determine is the "present" bit is set in the
        // descriptor, and report accordingly
        segSel = HandleToSel(st->handle);
        asm     lar     ax, [segSel]
        asm     test    ax, 08000h
        asm     jz      not_present

        printf(" PRESENT");
        asm     jmp     done

        not_present:    printf(" NON-PRESENT");
        done:           printf("\n");
    }

    printf("\n");
```

Module Table

```
}

//------------------------------------------------
// Displays all the modules that are
// implicitly linked to.
//------------------------------------------------
void DoModuleTable(HANDLE far *modtab, WORD count)
{
    WORD i;

    printf("Referenced modules:\n");
    printf("  HNDL  NAME\n");

    for(i=0; i < count; i++)
        printf("  %04X  %s\n", modtab[i],
            GetModuleNameFromHandle(modtab[i]));

    printf("\n");
}


//------------------------------------------------
// Displays the resident names table. This
// table always contains the module name.
// DLLs should have WEPs in this table,
// and any function that is exported by name
// will appear in this table.
//------------------------------------------------
void DoResidentNamesTable(char far *t)
{
    char buffer[129];
    WORD ordinal;
    BYTE length;

    printf("Resident names:\n");
    printf("  ORDN  NAME\n");

    // A 0 byte indicates the end of the table.
    // Entries are a length byte, followed by
    // the string, followed by the entry ordinal
    while ( *t )
    {
        // Obtain the length of this name
        length = *(BYTE far *)t;

        // Copy the string to a local buffer,
        // and null terminate it.
        _fstrncpy(buffer, t+1, length);
        buffer[length] = 0;

        // The entry ordinal is a WORD immediately
        // following the name
        ordinal = *(WORD far *)(t + length + 1);
        printf("  %04X  %s\n", ordinal, buffer);

        // bump up the pointer to point to
```

Module Table

```
            // the next entry.
            t+= (length + 3);
    }

    printf("\n");
}

//---------------------------------------------
// High level function to display information
// about a module, based upon information in
// the module table
//---------------------------------------------
void DisplayModule(HANDLE hModule)
{
    int width = 25;
    MODULE_TABLE far *mt;
    WORD fileDate, fileTime;
    WORD sel = HandleToSel(hModule);
    unsigned char far *ptr = (unsigned char far *)mt = MK_FP(sel, 0);

    // Perform some weird contortions to extract the
    // filename and date/time. Date/Time fields
    // are in MS-DOS bit encoded format.
    printf("%-*s", width, "File");
    fileDate = *(WORD far *)(ptr+mt->ne_pfileinfo+4);
    fileTime = *(WORD far *)(ptr+mt->ne_pfileinfo+6);
    printf
    (
        "%Fs   %02u-%02u-%02u %2u:%02u\n",
        (ptr+mt->ne_pfileinfo+8),
        (fileDate >> 5) & 0xF, (fileDate & 0x1F), (fileDate >> 9) + 80,
        (fileTime >> 11), (fileTime >> 5) & 0x3F
    );

    printf("%-*s%04X\n", width, "Usage count", mt->ne_usage);
    printf("%-*s%04X\n", width, "DGROUP segment", mt->ne_autodata);
    printf("%-*s%04X\n", width, "Initial heap size", mt->ne_heap);
    printf("%-*s%04X\n", width, "Initial stack size", mt->ne_stack);
    printf("%-*s%Fp\n", width, "Starting CS:IP", mt->ne_csip);
    printf("%-*s%Fp\n", width, "Starting SS:SP", mt->ne_sssp);
    printf("%-*s%u.%02u\n", width, "Minimum Windows version",
        HIBYTE(mt->ne_expver), LOBYTE(mt->ne_expver));

    printf("%-*s", width, "Flags");
    if ( mt->ne_flags & NENOTP )              printf("LIBRARY ");
    if ( mt->ne_flags & NESELFLOAD )          printf("SELF_LOAD ");
    if ( (mt->ne_flags & NEAPPTYP) == 0x100 ) printf("NON_WIN_API ");
    if ( (mt->ne_flags & NEAPPTYP) == 0x200 ) printf("API_COMPAT ");
    if ( (mt->ne_flags & NEAPPTYP) == 0x300 ) printf("USES_WINAPI ");
    if ( mt->ne_flags & NENONRES )            printf("NON_RES_CODE ");
    if ( mt->ne_flags & NELIM32 )             printf("LIM32 ");
    if ( mt->ne_flags & NEPROT )              printf("PROT_MODE ");
    if ( mt->ne_flags & NEPPLI )              printf("PER_PROCESS_INIT
");
    if ( mt->ne_flags & NEINST )              printf("INSTANCE_DATA ");
```

Module Table

```c
    if ( mt->ne_flags & NESHARED )                        printf("SHARED_DATA ");
    printf("\n");

    printf("%-*s%05lX\n", width,"Non-res names offset", mt->ne_nrestab);
    printf("%-*s%04X\n", width, "Non-res names size", mt->ne_cbnrestab);

    printf("\n");

    // Only dump segment table if there are segments
    if ( mt->ne_cseg )
        DoSegmentTable(MK_FP(sel, mt->ne_segtab), mt->ne_cseg);

    // Calculate length of resource table. Only dump it if
    // it is a nonzero length
    if ( mt->ne_restab - mt->ne_rsrctab )
        DoResourceTable(MK_FP(sel,mt->ne_rsrctab));

    // Only dump module table if one or more entries
    if ( mt->ne_cmod )
        DoModuleTable( MK_FP(sel,mt->ne_modtab), mt->ne_cmod);

    DoResidentNamesTable( MK_FP(sel, mt->ne_restab) );
    printf("\n");
}

//----------------------------------------------
// Walks the list of modules in the system,
// calling DisplayModule to dump each one
// out in turn
//----------------------------------------------
void ModuleWalk(void)
{
    HANDLE   thisModule;
    WORD     hInstance;
    WORD     far *signature_word;

    // Get our instance handle, which is also our DS.
    // Hint: You can also obtain this value by using
    // the hInstance passed to WinMain. Also, some
    // compilers store the hInstance in a global
    // variable that is accessible to your code.
    asm      mov     [hInstance], DS

    // An undocumented use of GetModuleHandle. The
    // module handle associated with the passed-in
    // DS is returned in AX. The handle of the first
    // module in the system (KERNEL) is returned in DX
    GetModuleHandle( MK_FP(0, hInstance) );
    asm      mov     [thisModule], DX

    //  Turn off repainting while we blast out the info
    winio_setbusy();
    winio_setpaint(winio_current(), FALSE);

    printf("Double-Click on any line for detailed view\n\n");
```

Module Table

```
        printf("MODULE     HANDLE\n");

        // The list is terminated by a NULL next module handle
        while ( thisModule )
        {
            // Create a far pointer to the module table.
            // Verify that we have a valid table by
            // looking for the NE signature. Abort
            // if not found
            signature_word = MK_FP(thisModule, 0);
            if ( *signature_word != NE_SIGNATURE )
            {
                printf("Error in following module chain\n");
                break;
            }

            printf
            (
                "%-8s     %04X\n",
                GetModuleNameFromHandle(thisModule),
                thisModule
            );

            // The next module handle is at offset 6
            // in the module table
            thisModule = *(HANDLE far *)MK_FP(thisModule, 6);
        }

    // Turn the repainting back on, and position to the top of the list
    winio_setpaint(winio_current(), TRUE);
    winio_resetbusy();
    winio_home(winio_current());
}

#pragma argsused

void DumpModule(HWND hwnd, LPSTR line, int i)
{
    char moduleName[80];
    char buffer[80];
    HANDLE hModule;
    int returnCode;
    HWND newWindow;

    _fstrcpy(buffer, line);
    returnCode = sscanf(buffer, "%s %x", moduleName, &hModule);

    if ( returnCode != 2 )
    {
        MessageBox(NULL, "Not a valid line", "Error",
                    MB_OK | MB_ICONEXCLAMATION);
        return;
    }

    if ( GetModuleHandle(moduleName) != hModule )
```

Module Table

```
    {
        MessageBox(NULL, "Module no longer exists", "Error",
                    MB_OK | MB_ICONEXCLAMATION);
        return;
    }

    sprintf(buffer, "WinMod: %s", moduleName);

    newWindow = winio_window(buffer, 0x4000, WW_HASMENU);
    winio_setcurrent(newWindow);

    // Turn off repaints while blasting out the data
    winio_setbusy();
    winio_setpaint(winio_current(), FALSE);

    DisplayModule(hModule);

    // Turn repaints back on, and position to the top of the info
    winio_setpaint(winio_current(), TRUE);
    winio_resetbusy();
    winio_home(newWindow);
}

int main()
{
    // GetVersion returns in AX register. Flip the byte registers to
    // produce a sensible version, with the major revision in ah, and
    // the minor revision in AL. When done, store away in WinVersion.
    GetVersion();
    asm     xchg    ah, al
    asm     mov     [WinVersion], ax

    // Create the list of modules for the user to click on
    ModuleWalk();

    // Install a double click handler
    winio_setlinefn(winio_current(), DumpModule);

    return 0;
}
```

NoHookDOSCall   KERNEL.101

```
void FAR PASCAL NoHookDOSCall(void);
```

NoHookDOSCall() is almost identical to the documented function DOS3Call(): it is used to make DOS INT 21h calls, without putting an actual INT 21h instruction in your code. Both DOS3Call() and NoHookDOSCall() directly call the INT 21h handler inside KERNEL, without generating a software interrupt. Thus, these calls are slightly faster than a hard-wired INT 21h.

How is NoHookDOSCall( ) different from DOS3Call( )? Before calling the internal KERNEL function Real_DOS( ), DOS3Call( ) calls the WriteOutProfiles( ) function; NoHookDOSCall( ) does not. When the KERNEL DOS translation layer has been disabled via a call to DisableDOS( ), then NoHookDOSCall( ) and DOS3Call( ) behave essentially identically. The one remaining difference is that NoHookDOSCall( ) preserves the DS register across the DOS invocation.

Support: 3.0, 3.1
Used by: SYSTEM.DRV
See also: DisableDOS, DOS3Call, GetSetKernelDOSProc

NULL Segment—See Instance Data

OldYield   KERNEL.117

```
void FAR PASCAL OldYield(void);
```

OldYield( ) is the back end to the Yield( ) and DirectedYield( ) functions. DirectedYield(hTask), discussed earlier in this chapter, fudges with the stack, puts the passed hTask into the field at offset 0AAh in the Task Database (TDB), and JMPs to OldYield( ).

Yield( ) puts a zero in the same TDB field, checks to make sure there's a message queue for the task, and (if there is) JMPs to OldYield( ). (If there is no message queue, for example, if the task's startup code hasn't yet called InitApp( ), then Yield( ) calls through a function pointer to UserYield( ); see chapter 6.)

In most cases, you could get away with calling OldYield( ), instead of Yield( ), but there seems little reason to do so. On the other hand, many routines in USER appear to deliberately call OldYield( ) rather than Yield( ).

OldYield( ) checks to make sure that Windows is not already running the scheduler. It then increments the "waiting system event count" field at offset 6 in the TDB (this is the same field that PostEvent and WaitEvent use as a semaphore), calls the KERNEL scheduler, and then decrements the event count.

In other words, the code looks something like this:

```
DirectedYield proc far
    ; ...
    jmp OldYield
Yield:
    mov ds, ds:CURR_TASK
    cmp ds:TASK_QUEUE, 0
    jz OldYield
    jmp pYieldProc      ; UserYield(): only called if no task queue
OldYield:
    ; ...
    mov ds, ds:CURR_TASK
    inc ds:NEVENTS
```

```
    mov es, 0
    mov fs, 0
    mov gs, 0
    call Reschedule        ; the KERNEL scheduler
    dec ds:NEVENTS
    mov ax, FFFFh
DirectedYield endp
```

For more information on OldYield(), see Matt Pietrek's article "Inside the Windows Scheduler," *Dr. Dobb's Journal*, August 1992.

Support: 3.0, 3.1
See also: DirectedYield, PostEvent, Task Database, UserYield (USER), WaitEvent

---

OpenPathName   KERNEL.75

```
int FAR PASCAL OpenPathName(LPSTR lpPathName, int iAccessMode);
```

This uninteresting function has a function prototype in the Windows 3.0 SDK include file WINEXP.H, but it is otherwise undocumented—perhaps because its operation is so self-evident that no documentation is needed. Needless to say, OpenPathName() attempts to open the file lpPathName with the specified access mode. The function is essentially just a front-end to the DOS Open File function (INT 21h AH=3Dh); however, if the KERNEL internal variable fNovell is set, the function also calls INT 21h AX=4300 to get file attributes.

The proper way to open a file in Windows is with the OpenFile() function, or with your compiler's standard library functions such as open(), fopen(), or sopen(), or with DOS INT 21h AH=3Dh. There should be no reason to call OpenPathName(), which is included here only for completeness.

Support: 3.0, 3.1
See also: DeletePathName

PatchCodeHandle   KERNEL.110

```
void FAR PASCAL PatchCodeHandle(WORD hSeg);
```

PatchCodeHandle() was used in some versions of Microsoft Excel and Word for Windows as part of a mechanism to load themselves to run under Windows. Normally, KERNEL takes care of all the details of loading a Windows application or DLL once WinExec(), LoadLibrary(), or LoadModule() is called. However, some Windows applications bypass the KERNEL loader and take responsibility for loading themselves into memory.

Generally this is done to work around bugs in the KERNEL loader. Apparently, Excel contained a segment whose size was exactly right to trigger a boundary-condition bug in the Windows 3.0 loader. As another example, the Windows 3.0

loader does not properly load programs with huge (that is, greater than 64K) arrays. Huge arrays in 16-bit programs are composed of multiple 64K segments that must be loaded contiguously. Either Windows 3.0 does not do this contiguous loading or the Microsoft linker does not properly mark the segments as contiguous, or both, but in any case there's a problem. FORTRAN programs are highly likely to contain huge static arrays, and so the Microsoft FORTRAN QuickWin library is self-loading and includes calls to PatchCodeHandle().

In addition to working around bugs in the KERNEL loader, one might also have a self-loading Windows application to use a somewhat different (for example, compressed) executable file format from the segmented-executable (NE) one that Windows understands. Early versions of Word for Windows included "compressed relocation records." Just as compressed executables under MS-DOS (such as EXE files generated by PKLITE or by the shareware program LZEXE) must include their own loader that bypasses the DOS EXEC (INT 21h AH=4Bh) loader, compressed Windows executables would need to bypass the normal WinExec() loader.

The mechanism for producing self-loading Windows applications, including PatchCodeHandle(), was undocumented in Windows 3.0. However, it was part of Microsoft's "Open Tools" strategy and was documented in Windows 3.1 in an *Programmer's Reference* Overview article on "Self-Loading Windows Applications." Most of the self-loading Windows application mechanism involves functions that the application itself supplies; PatchCodeHandle() is supplied by KERNEL.

PatchCodeHandle(hSeg) walks the specified segment and patches function prologs. Any PUSH DS/POP AX/NOP sequence is patched to become either MOV AX, DGROUP or MOV AX, DS/NOP. This is the same function that the normal KERNEL segment loader uses. See the "Self-Loading Windows Applications" overview in the 3.1 SDK for more details.

PostEvent   KERNEL.30

```
BOOL FAR PASCAL PostEvent(HANDLE hTask);
```

This function, whose prototype appears in the SDK WINEXP.H as part of "scheduler things that the world knows not," wakes up the specified task (as with most functions that expect an hTask, zero can be used to indicate the current task). It does this simply by incrementing the event-count field at offset 6 in the Task Database:

```
POSTEVENT proc far
    call MOVE_HTASK_INTO_ES      ; ES = (hTask) ? hTask : GetCurrentTask()
    inc es:[6]                   ; incr event counter (ofs 6) in TASK_DB
    retf 2
POSTEVENT endp
```

A task blocks on an event by calling WaitEvent( ); the WORD at offset 6 in the Task Database thus acts as a semaphore. This mechanism is used during the startup of a Windows application; see the description of WaitEvent( ) for details.

Support: 3.0, 3.1
See also: Task Database, WaitEvent
Used by: PostMessage( ) and SendMessage( ) in USER
Example: See SEMTEST.C in the example for WaitEvent( )

PrestoChangoSelector   KERNEL.177

```
WORD FAR PASCAL PrestoChangoSelector(WORD wSelSource, wSelDest);
```

Like the documented ChangeSelector( ) function, PrestoChangoSelector( ) generates a code selector that corresponds to a given data selector, or a data selector that corresponds to a given code selector. For example:

```
WORD wData, wCode;
// ...
wCode = AllocSelector(wData);        // both are DATA right now
PrestoChangoSelector(wData, wCode); // now wCode is CODE
assert(verw(wData) && ! verw(wCode)); // wData writeable, wCode not
```

In Windows 3.0, Microsoft documented ChangeSelector( ), but the documentation mistakenly reversed the order of the wSelSource and wSelDest parameters, and, even worse, ChangeSelector( ) was mistakenly not exported from KERNEL. Thus, applications needing this functionality (or thinking they needed it, since AllocCStoDSAlias( ) and AllocDStoCSAlias( ) are almost always better choices) had to use the undocumented and curiously named PrestoChangoSelector( ).

In Windows 3.1, ChangeSelector( ) is documented correctly and is properly exported from KERNEL. PrestoChangoSelector( ) is identical to ChangeSelector( ), but without parameter validation. In fact, the ordinal number KERNEL.177 now belongs to ChangeSelector( ), so if your application calls PrestoChangoSelector( ) but is built with a 3.0 import library, you will end up getting the correct ChangeSelector( ) in 3.1. Explicitly calling ChangeSelector( ) will result in errors in Windows 3.0. Thus, if you want your application to run in both Windows 3.0 and 3.1, call Presto-ChangoSelector( ) rather than ChangeSelector( ). Better yet, use AllocDStoCSAlias( ) or AllocCStoDSAlias( ).

The seemingly silly name PrestoChangoSelector( ) actually makes complete sense once you see the function's implementation in Windows 3.0. The "presto chango" part is the use of XOR to flip a single bit in the access-rights field of the protected-mode descriptor:

```
PRESTOCHANGOSELECTOR proc far
```

```
        ENTER
        SAVE ds, si, di
        mov ds,cs:WIN_LDT
        mov es,cs:WIN_LDT
        mov si, wSourceSelector      ; [bp+8]
        mov di, wDestSelector        ; [bp+6]
        and si,0FFF8h                ; turn selector into LDT offset
        and di,0FFF8h                ; ditto
        mov ax,di
        mov cx,4
        cld
        rep movsw                    ; copy the 8-byte descriptor
        xor byte ptr [di-3],8        ; presto chango: flip the code/data bit
        MOV es, 0                    ; push 0 / pop es
        or  al,5
        RESTORE di, si, ds
        LEAVE 4
PRESTOCHANGOSELECTOR endp
```

Another trick employed in the above code is the transformation of a selector into a descriptor-table byte offset by ANDing the selector with 0FFF8h: descriptors are 8 bytes each, and the top 13 bits of a selector are an index into a descriptor table, so (wSel & ~8) does the trick. In Windows 3.1, KERNEL relies more (though by no means entirely) on DPMI calls, so PrestoChangoSelector() is more sedate:

```
PRESTOCHANGOSELECTOR proc far
    dpmicall GET_DESC, [bp+8]        ; 31/0B
    xor byte ptr [bp-3], 8           ; change the bit code<==>data
    dpmicall SET_DESC, [bp+6]        ; 31/0C
PRESTOCHANGOSELECTOR endp
```

Support: 3.0, 3.1
See also: AllocCStoDSAlias, SelectorAccessRights
Example: The following program, CODEDATA.C, uses PrestoChangoSelector() to demonstrate how data can be executed in protected-mode Windows (this is different from self-modifying code, which is demonstrated in the example for the entry on AllocCStoDSAlias()). Because Windows does not track changes to selector aliases, GlobalPageLock() *must* be used to lock the data segment down in the linear address space; in the sample program, GlobalCompact(-1) is used to try to shake it loose. All Windows-specific code is inside #ifdef WINDOWS; without this code, the program can also be run in real-mode DOS.

```
/* CODEDATA.C -- demonstration of executable data */

#include <stdlib.h>
#ifdef WINDOWS
#include <dos.h>
#include "windows.h"
#include "winio.h"
```

```
/* undocumented functions */
void FAR PASCAL PrestoChangoSelector(WORD sel1, WORD sel2);
DWORD FAR PASCAL GetSelectorBase(WORD sel);
#else
#include <stdio.h>
#endif

unsigned char data[] = {
    0xb8, 0x00, 0x00,   /* mov ax, 0000 */
    0x00, 0x00, 0x00,   /* oper ax, immed */
    0xcb,               /* retf */
    } ;

#define OPER        3       /* offset in data of operation byte */
#define AX_LO       1       /* ax operand lo byte */
#define IMMED_LO    4       /* immediate operand lo byte */

/* opcodes */
#define ADD     0x05
#define OR      0x0d
#define AND     0x25
#define SUB     0x2d
#define XOR     0x35
#define CMP     0x3d

void (far *code)(void);

short math(short oper, short op1, short op2)
{
    /*
        Compile code on the fly. For example, math(AND, 1, 3)
        becomes:

            B8 01 00        mov ax, 0001
            25 03 00        and ax, 0003
            CB              retf

        Code is compiled by putting values in data[] array; it is
        then immediately executed by calling (*code)() function ptr.
    */

    *((short *) &data[AX_LO]) = op1;
    *((short *) &data[IMMED_LO]) = op2;
    data[OPER] = oper;
    (*code)();
    /* return result in AX */
}

main()
{
#ifdef WINDOWS
    WORD data_sel, code_sel;

    data_sel = FP_SEG((void far *) data);
    GlobalPageLock(data_sel); // Windows will not track changes for aliases!!
```

PrestoChangoSelector

```
    code_sel = AllocSelector(data_sel);
    PrestoChangoSelector(data_sel, code_sel);
    code = MK_FP(code_sel, FP_OFF((void far *) data));  // Borland macros

    /* Now try to shake code & data loose by moving memory */
    GlobalCompact(-1L);

    if (GetSelectorBase(FP_SEG(code)) !=
        GetSelectorBase(FP_SEG(data)))
            return fail("Selectors out of sync!");
#else
    code = (void far *) data;
#endif

    printf("1 && 3 ==> %d\n", math(AND, 1, 3));
    printf("1 || 3 ==> %d\n", math(OR, 1, 3));
    printf("1 ^ 3  ==> %d\n", math(XOR, 1, 3));
    printf("1 + 3  ==> %d\n", math(ADD, 1, 3));
    printf("1 - 3  ==> %d\n", math(SUB, 1, 3));

#ifdef WINDOWS
    GlobalPageUnlock(data_sel);
    FreeSelector(code_sel);
#endif

    return 0;
}
```

Program Data Base (PDB)

The Windows PDB is really just a protected-mode DOS Program Segment Prefix (PSP). Each task's PDB is stored at offset 60h in its Task Database. See GetCurrentPDB(), discussed earlier in this chapter, and the description of the Task Database to follow.

The layout of the PSP (including undocumented fields) is given in *Undocumented DOS*, in the reference entry for INT 21h Function 26h (Create PSP).

There is one odd aspect of the behavior of the PSP under Windows: the scheduler in KERNEL doesn't switch PSPs when it switches tasks. According to a Microsoft KnowledgeBase article ("Passing File Handles from a TSR to a Windows Application," Q75257, 1 October 1991), the only time that a Windows application's PSP is selected as the current PSP is when the application actually makes a DOS call. Thus, a Windows program cannot assume that its PSP is the current PSP. If a program needs to *force* its current PSP to be the active PSP, it simply needs to make a DOS call, *any* DOS call (even Get Version or Get PSP will work; in other words, to do a Set PSP, you can do a Get PSP!).

It is difficult to demonstrate this behavior in a program. The Window GetCurrentPDB() function will always retrieve the current task's PDB, because it merely extracts the WORD from offset 60h in the current task, making it appear as if the current PSP is always correct. Similarly, calling the DOS Get PSP function (INT 21h AH=62h) involves a DOS call, and so switches to the correct PSP.

However, this behavior is confirmed by the WISPY program from chapter 4: you do not see the DOS Set PSP function (INT 21h AH=50h) called for a Windows program until the program makes some other DOS INT 21h call.

RegisterPtrace   KERNEL.202

```
void FAR PASCAL RegisterPtrace(FARPROC lpWinNotify);
```

This function installs a notification-handling function that will be called when interesting events occur. "Ptrace" means "process trace" and comes from the name of the key debugging interface in Unix. The Windows protected-mode debug interface, WinDebug(), is a hacked version of the DosPTrace() function from OS/2 1.x; WinDebug() uses RegisterPtrace(). The ToolHelpHook() function in Windows 3.1 is intended as a replacement for RegisterPtrace(). While RegisterPtrace() still persists in Windows 3.1, it is better to use ToolHelpHook() or, better yet, the documented notification functions provided in ToolHelp (see chapter 10).

Note that RegisterPtrace() does not return the address of the previously installed callback function. This makes it impossible to chain callbacks with RegisterPtrace(). Under Windows 3.0, this causes a problem between TOOLHELP and WINDEBUG: if WINDEBUG is already running (for example, you're using CVW or TDW), any calls to the ToolHelp RegisterNotify() function will fail.

Pass in 0L to remove the current handler.

The callback function receives notifications as follows, with all parameters passed in registers rather than on the stack:

```
void FAR Callback(void);
```

On entry:
AX = function number; these function numbers are the same as those used in the Windows INT 41h low-level debug interface. (For example, INT 41h AH=51h is the Move Segment notification function.)

00h   Output char (KERNEL wants you (the debugger) to output a char)
DS:DX =   char far *

01h   Input char (KERNEL wants you to get a character from the user)
On exit: return character is placed in AL

0Dh   Task going out
No args; call GetCurrentTask() to get its hTask

0Eh   Task coming in

No args; call GetCurrentTask() to get its hTask

12h   Output string (KERNEL wants you to output a string)

(3.0) DS:SI = far * to string
(3.1) ES:SI = far * to string

50h   Load segment (see DebugDefineSegment())

BX = segment number
CX = selector
DX = hInstance
SI = segment flags
ES:DI = module name

51h   Move segment

52h   Free segment

BX = freed selector

59h   Load task

CX:BX = CS:IP of start of new task

5Ch   Free segment

Same as 52h, except called only when KERNEL starts up. Called once for CS, and once for DS alias to CS.

60h   End of segment load

61h   End of segment discard

62h   App terminating

byte ptr [SP+06] = exit code

63h   Async stop (Ctrl-Alt-SysReg

64h   DLL loaded

CX:BX = CS:IP entry point
SI = Module Handle

65h   Module removed

ES = module handle

Support: 3.0, 3.1
See also: DebugDefineSegment, ToolHelpHook, ToolHelpNotifyRegister (chapter 10)

RegisterShield   KERNEL.210

```
void FAR PASCAL RegisterShield(FARPROC fpShield);
```

RegisterShield() is present only in the IBM OS/2 2.x version of Standard mode KER-
NEL (OS2K286.EXE). The function takes a far pointer to a callback "shield" function, which will be called whenever a task starts or stops. OS/2 uses this for
"autotermination" of virtual machines: rather than use a translation layer, OS/2 runs
Windows applications using an actual copy of Standard mode Windows (WIN-OS/2)
that runs in its own virtual machine (VM). This VM is automatically disappears when
the last Windows task exits. IBM uses the shield function to find when the last Windows task exited; basically, it is used for task counting.

   RegisterShield() can be called with a NULL pointer to reregister the shield callback function.

   Since it is built right into the OS/2 version of KERNEL, RegisterShield() can, in
addition to its intended use by IBM, be used as a WIN-OS/2 detection method (a
Windows application running on the OS/2 Presentation Manager desktop might do
DDE with PM applications, for example):

```
BOOL IsWinOS2(void)
{
    HANDLE hKernel = GetModuleHandle("KERNEL");
    return (GetProcAddress(hKernel, "REGISTERSHIELD") != 0);
}
```

   Normally, the DOS version number would be used for OS/2 detection (OS/2
2.0 presents itself as DOS version 20.0, so INT 21h AH=30h would return 14h (20)
in an OS/2 2.0 DOS box). However, the DOS version number can be changed on a
case-by-case basis, so the IsWinOS2() function above might be worthwhile as an alternate check.

Support: WIN-OS/2

RegisterWinOldApHook   KERNEL.343

```
BOOL FAR PASCAL RegisterWinOldApHook(FARPROC FAR * newHooks, WORD fPrevious);
```

This function is passed a pointer to an array of function pointers. If fPrevious is nonzero, then the pointer containing the array addresses is overwritten with the previous
value. If called in Standard mode, it always returns TRUE. If called in Enhanced
mode, it always returns FALSE.

   The passed-in function pointers are called by WINOA286.MOD in Windows 3.0,
and by WINOLDAP.MOD in Windows 3.1. These are the Standard mode managers
for DOS executables. But exactly what these functions are for is not known, as

RegisterWinOldApHook() itself doesn't appear to be called from anywhere. Since RegisterWinOldApHook() is in the WINEXEC module of KERNEL, perhaps it is used to hook the WinExec() of "old apps" in Standard mode.

Support: 3.1

ReplaceInst   KERNEL.201

In Windows 3.x Standard and Enhanced modes, this function performs no operation besides returning with a RETF 6.

Reserved1   KERNEL.77
Reserved2   KERNEL.78
Reserved3   KERNEL.79
Reserved4   KERNEL.80
Reserved5   KERNEL.87

In Windows 2.1, five ANSI-character handling functions were located in KERNEL: AnsiNext(), AnsiPrev(), AnsiUpper(), AnsiLower(), and lstrcmp(). In Windows 3.0, these documented functions were moved to the Windows USER module. To avoid breaking existing Windows 2.1 applications, however, these functions were left behind in KERNEL, though with their names changed to discourage any new use of the versions in KERNEL. The EXEUTIL -DIFFHDR program from chapter 2 reveals the following:

```
2.1 KERNEL.77 was AnsiNext;  3.0+ KERNEL.77 is Reserved1
                             3.0+ USER.472 is AnsiNext

2.1 KERNEL.78 was AnsiPrev;  3.0+ KERNEL.78 is Reserved2
                             3.0+ USER.473 is AnsiPrev

2.1 KERNEL.79 was AnsiUpper; 3.0+ KERNEL.79 is Reserved3
                             3.0+ USER.431 is AnsiUpper

2.1 KERNEL.80 was AnsiLower; 3.0+ KERNEL.80 is Reserved4
                             3.0+ USER.432 is AnsiLower

2.1 KERNEL.87 was lstrcmp;   3.0+ KERNEL.87 is Reserved5
                             3.0+ USER.430 is lstrcmp
```

SelectorAccessRights   KERNEL.196

```
WORD FAR PASCAL SelectorAccessRights(WORD wSel, WORD wOp, WORD wParam);
```

SelectorAccessRights() gets or sets access rights and related information for a given protected-mode selector. Access rights include the code/data and read/write permission bits.

```
#define AR_GET 0
#define AR_SET 1
```

If (wOp == AR_GET) then wParam is an ignored dummy value, and SelectorAccessRights() returns the current access rights. If (wOp == AR_SET) then wParam holds new access rights, and the function returns zero.

The access rights returned from this function are a slight variation on those found in a protected-mode descriptor and returned by the LAR (Load Access Rights) instruction (the following description comes from Dan Norton's book *Writing Windows Device Drivers*):

BIT	MASK	DESCRIPTION
0	1	(ignored) segment has been accessed
1	2	bit ON = if data, writeable; if code, readable
2	4	bit ON = if data, expand-down (stack); if code, conforming
3	8	bit ON = code; OFF = data
4	10h	bit ON = not a system descriptor (e.g., call gate)
5-11		(ignored)
12	1000h	(unused)
13	2000h	(ignored)
14	4000h	if expand-down, must match bit 15
15	8000h	bit ON = limit has page granularity; OFF = byte granularity

For example:

```
#define RIGHTS(wSel)        (SelectorAccessRights((wSel), 0, 0))
#define IS_CODE(wSel)       (RIGHTS(wSel) & 8)
#define IS_WRITEABLE(wSel)  ((! IS_CODE(wSel)) && (RIGHTS(wSel) & 2))
```

Unfortunately, SelectorAccessRights() only tells you something about a selector once you know that the selector itself is valid. SelectorAccessRights() is not useful for verifying if a specified selector is valid because the implementation in some versions of KERNEL uses the LAR instruction without checking the Zero flag afterward, thus causing completely bogus access rights to be returned. For example, SelectorAccessRights(1234, 0, 0) might return 4, whereas (assuming 1234 is an invalid selector) you would want it to return 0; 4 is returned because it happens to be sitting around in the AX register.

SelectorAccessRights

Validation of selectors should be done by directly using the LAR instruction and checking the Zero flag (see the lar( ) function in HANDLES.C), or by using the Windows 3.1 IsBadXXX functions.

Because other KERNEL functions (AllocCStoDSAlias, AllocDStoCSAlias, and PrestoChangoSelector) are dedicated to aliasing code segments into data and data segments into code, SelectorAccessRights() is probably best reserved for changing the read/write permission of segments: it can be used to make data segments read-only or code segments execute-only (no read). Also, the page/byte granularity bit may be of interest as 32-bit Windows programs become more prevalent.

Support: 3.0, 3.1
See also: AllocCStoDSAlias, AllocDStoCSAlias, GetSelectorLimit, IsBadXXX, PrestoChangoSelector
Example: See the example for GetSelectorLimit; the example uses Selector AccessRights( ) to get the byte/page granularity bit

Selector Table

Given a global memory handle, how do you find its corresponding Global Arena structure? You could, of course, walk the linked list of Global Arenas each time, looking for one whose handle field (that is, the value at offset 0Ah in KRNL286 and 10h in KRNL386) is identical to the handle you're holding. This would work, but it would be very slow, and it certainly *can't* be the method KERNEL itself uses; not even Windows is that . . . (okay, we won't say it).

With KRNL286, given a global memory handle, you can get to its Global Arena by taking the base address of the handle, subtracting 10h (the size of a Global Arena header in KRNL286) from it, and creating a new selector that would point to the Global Arena header. But this only works for the 16-bit KRNL286.

The 32-bit KRNL386 uses another data structure, called the Selector Table, to make it easy to find the Global Arena for a given selector; the Selector Table essentially contains a backlink from each selector to its Global Arena.

The Selector Table is located inside the Burgermaster segment; the KERNEL variable SelTableStart provides its address as a 32-bit offset into Burgermaster; this address will generally be greater than 64K. In Windows 3.1, SelTableStart and SelTableLen are available as fields in THHOOK (see later discussion); in Windows 3.0, SelTableStart is the DWORD located at offset 326h in KRNL386's default data segment, SelTableLen in the WORD at offset 324h. These values are hard-wired into TOOLHELP.DLL and are therefore reliable.

Most of the code below just sets up lpSelTab as a far pointer to the selector table; after that, the ARENA_FROM_SEL() macro takes a selector, masks the bottom three bits, divides by two, and uses the resulting value as an index into the Selector Table.

```
// KRNL386 only
BYTE far *lpSelTab;
WORD sel;
WORD SelTableLen;
DWORD SelTableStart;
WORD pGlobalHeap;

if (GetVersion() == 0x0003) // Windows 3.0
{
    extern DWORD FAR PASCAL GlobalMasterHandle(void);
    // GetModuleDGroup() -- see NULLSEG.C
    WORD wKernelDGroup = GetModuleDGroup(GetModuleHandle("KERNEL"), 0);
    SelTableLen = *((WORD far *) MK_FP(wKernelDGroup, 0x324));
    SelTableStart = *((DWORD far *) MK_FP(wKernelDGroup, 0x326));
    pGlobalHeap = HIWORD(GlobalMasterHandle());
}
else    // Windows 3.1+
{
    BYTE far *THHOOK = GetProcAddress(GetModuleHandle("KERNEL"),"THHOOK");
    SelTableLen = *((WORD far *) &THHOOK[0x16]);
    SelTableStart = *((DWORD far *) &THHOOK[0x18]); // 32-bit offset
    pGlobalHeap = *((WORD far *) &THHOOK[2]); // HIWORD(GlobalMasterHandle())
}

// SelTableStart is a 32-bit offset into Burgermaster (pGlobalHeap).
// It would be nice to say lpSelTab = MK_FP(pGlobalHeap, SelTableStart),
// but most Windows code is 16-bit. So we instead allocate a new
// selector with the same base and limit as the selector table
_asm mov sel, ds
sel = AllocSelector(sel);
SetSelectorBase(sel, GetSelectorBase(pGlobalHeap) + SelTableStart);
SetSelectorLimit(sel, SelTableLen);
lpSeltab = MK_FP(sel, 0);
// lpSeltab is now far* to selector table

// ...
#define ARENA_FROM_SEL(wSel) \
    *((DWORD far *) &lpSeltab[(wSel & 0xFFF8) >> 1])

// ...
DWORD dwArena = ARENA_FROM_SEL(wSel)
GLOBAL_ARENA_32 far *lpga32 = MK_FP(dwArena, 0);
assert(wSel == lpga32->handle);
```

Support: 3.0, 3.1
See also: Global Arena, Global Heap, THHOOK

SetPriority   KERNEL.32

```
int FAR PASCAL SetPriority(HANDLE hTask, WORD wPriority);
```

SetPriority() sets the "priority" field at offset 8 in the Task Database. Priority levels range from -32 to 15. The Task Database list is kept sorted in priority order.

In practice, it appears that SetPriority(hTask, 0) forces the task to run next. Low-priority is 1, and seems to mean that the task almost never gets scheduled. For example SetPriority(GetCurrentTask(), 1) (actually, we could just say SetPriority(0, 1) since 0 always works to specify the current task) will completely lock up the system until you either reboot, or pop into a debugger such as Soft-Ice for Windows and manually reset the word at offset 8 in the given Task Database back to zero.

Support: 3.0, 3.1
See also: Task Database

SetSelectorBase   KERNEL.187

```
WORD FAR PASCAL SetSelectorBase(WORD wSel, DWORD dwBase);
```

SetSelectorBase() is documented in Windows 3.1 but not in 3.0, where it also is provided; it sets the linear base address of a specified protected-mode selector. Even though the function has no useful return value, it is prototyped in the 3.1 WINDOWS.H as returning a WORD.

SetSelectorBase() is used, in conjunction with the SetSelectorLimit() and AllocSelector() functions, to "map" memory into the address space of a protected-mode Windows program. For example, where a real-mode program could access memory at location FFFF5h simply by forming the pointer FFFF:0005, a protected-mode Windows program must instead use a selector whose corresponding descriptor has a base address and limit that includes the desired address. SetSelectorBase() provides one very handy way to accomplish this. See the example that follows.

This function directly manipulates the Local Descriptor Table (LDT) and performs no error checking or validation of the selector you pass in; passing an invalid selector (or even a valid GDT selector) can crash the machine. To understand the implementation of SetSelectorBase(), it helps to know the layout of a protected-mode descriptor (the LDT and GDT are just arrays of these descriptors):

0	WORD	limit 0..15
2	WORD	base 0..15
4	BYTE	base 16..23
5	BYTE	access rights
6	BYTE	limit 16..19, rights (reserved 0 on 286)
7	BYTE	base 24..31 (reserved 0 on 286)

Because each descriptor is eight bytes, and because the bottom three bits of a selector are used to specify the privilege level (0-3) and the table (bit 2 ON means

LDT, OFF means GDT), these bottom three bits can be masked off to turn the selector into a descriptor-table offset:

```
SetSelectorBase proc far
    ; ...
    push DS
    mov ds, WIN_LDT             ; directly manipulate LDT
    mov bx, wSel                ; wSel assumed correct
    and bx, -8                  ; turn selector into offset
    mov ax, word ptr dwBase
    mov [bx+2], ax              ; base 0..15
    mov ax, word ptr dwBase+2
    mov [bx+4], al              ; base 16..23
    mov [bx+7], ah              ; base 24..31
    mov ax, wSel                ; returns passed-in selector (yawn)
    pop DS
    ; ...
SetSelectorBase endp
```

Thus, this function can only be used to set the base address for selectors belonging to the LDT; it does not work with GDT selectors. Again, bit 2 is OFF in GDT selectors and ON in LDT selectors; for example, 0040h is a GDT selector and 0044h is an LDT selector.

The specified base address is *linear*, not physical; if paging is on (either in Windows Enhanced mode or because a 386-based memory manager such as EMM386 is present), linear addresses will not be equivalent to physical addresses. Use the Virtual DMA Services (VDS; INT 4Bh) to access physical memory locations.

For most purposes, SetSelectorBase is functionally equivalent to the DPMI Set Segment Base Address function (INT 31h AX=0007h), but it is easier to use from a Windows program and possibly more portable (though it appears that all selector-manipulation functions, even documented ones, will be omitted from Win32).

Where possible, the Windows hard-wired selectors such as undocumented __0000H or documented __B800H should be used instead of allocating a new selector and setting its base with SetSelectorBase.

When finished with the selector, you should free it with the documented FreeSelector function.

Support: 3.0, 3.1
Used by: HEAPWALK.EXE, WINDEBUG.DLL, WINMEM32.DLL
See also: AllocSelector (documented), FreeSelector (documented), SetSelectorLimit, GetSelectorBase, __0000H
Example: The following program uses AllocSelector(), SetSelectorBase(), and SetSelectorLimit() to map the Global Descriptor Table (GDT) into the program's address space. Once mapped, the GDT can be mapped like any other block of data:

```
/* SETSBASE.C */

#include <windows.h>
```

```c
#include "winio.h"

#ifndef MK_FP
#define MK_FP(s,o) ((void far *) (((DWORD) (s) << 16) | (o)))
#endif

/* undocumented functions */
extern WORD FAR PASCAL SetSelectorBase(WORD sel, DWORD base);
extern WORD FAR PASCAL SetSelectorLimit(WORD sel, DWORD limit);

typedef unsigned char DESCRIPTOR[8];   /* just for purposes of this sample */

typedef struct { WORD limit; DWORD base; } GDTR;

/* C wrapper for the Intel SGDT instruction; must compile with
   286 instructions (-G2 in Microsoft C; -2 in Borland C++).
   Places the Global Descriptor Table (GDT) base and limit into
   the six-byte (FWORD PTR) structure pointed to by pgdtr */
void sgdt(GDTR far *pgdtr)
{
    _asm les bx, pgdtr
    _asm sgdt fword ptr es:[bx]
}

main()
{
    DESCRIPTOR far *gdt;
    GDTR gdtr;
    WORD sel;

    /* get the linear base address and size (limit) of the Global
       Descriptor Table (GDT), using the Intel SGDT instruction */
    sgdt(&gdtr);

    /* allocate a selector similar to our current DS
       (i.e., a data selector) */
    _asm mov sel, ds
    if ((sel = AllocSelector(sel)) == 0)
        fail("Cannot allocate a selector!");

    /* set the base and limit of the new selector */
    SetSelectorBase(sel, gdtr.base);
    SetSelectorLimit(sel, gdtr.limit);

    /* we now have a selector that maps the GDT into our address
       space; create a far pointer from this selector */
    gdt = MK_FP(sel, 0);

    /* the program now has a far pointer to the GDT and could
       manipulate it just like any other data. Here, we'll just
       print out some values */
    printf("GDT base=%08lx limit=%04x\n", gdtr.base, gdtr.limit);
    printf("GDT mapped as %Fp\n", gdt);
```

SetSelectorBase

```
    /* when done, free the selector! */
    FreeSelector(sel);
    return 0;
}
```

Running under Windows 3.0 Enhanced mode, the program produced the following output, indicating that the 0110h bytes (010Fh + 1) at linear address 8010011Ch were mapped in, and accessible to the program, with far pointer 14ED:0000:

```
GDT base=8010011c limit=010f
GDT mapped as 14ED:0000
```

SetSelectorLimit   KERNEL.189

```
WORD FAR PASCAL SetSelectorLimit(WORD wSel, DWORD dwLimit);
```

SetSelectorLimit() is somewhat documented in Windows 3.1, but not in 3.0; it sets the limit (last valid offset) for a specified protected-mode selector. Even though the function has no useful return value, it is prototyped in the 3.1 WINDOWS.H as returning a WORD. SetSelectorLimit() should be used in conjunction with SetSelectorBase() and AllocSelector(); the same limitations noted for SetSelectorBase() apply to SetSelectorLimit(), too.

This specified limit will almost always be a BYTE limit, that is, the offset of the last valid BYTE within the segment. For example, if for some reason you want to be able to *((WORD *) 0xFFFF) on a segment, then you will need to give it a limit of 10000h; *((DWORD *) 0xFFFF) would require a limit of 10002h. If somehow you have a segment with PAGE (4K) rather than BYTE granularity (see Get-SelectorLimit() and SelectorAccessRights()), then the limit specified is of course a PAGE limit.

The limit specified can be greater than 64K; however, there is an upper bound of one megabyte, which you can verify by doing a SetSelectorLimit(wSel, 0xFFFFFFFFL) and then doing a GetSelectorLimit(wSel); the returned limit will be 0xFFFF0L. This upper bound is imposed by the format of a protected-mode descriptor, which only contains 20 bits of addressing. Segments greater than one megabyte in size must have PAGE granularity. (See *Extending DOS*, chapter 1 for a more detailed explanation.)

Some implementations of SetSelectorLimit() look like this (see the descriptor of SetSelectorBase() for an explanation):

```
SetSelectorLimit proc far
    ; ...
    push ds
    mov ds, cs:WIN_LDT
    mov bx, wSel
    and bx, 0FFF8h              ; turn wSel into LDT offset
```

```
        mov ax, word ptr dwLimit
        mov [bx], ax                    ; limit 0..15
        mov ax, word ptr dwLimit+2
        and al, OFh                     ; truncate
        and byte ptr [bx+6], OFOh
        or [bx+6], al                   ; limit 16..19
        pop ds
        ; ...
SetSelectorLimit endp
```

In Windows 3.1, SetSelectorLimit() instead uses the DPMI Get Descriptor (INT 31h AX=0Bh) and Set Descriptor (INT 31h AX=0Ch) functions. SetSelectorLimit() should be equivalent in functionality to the DPMI Set Segment Limit (INT 31h AX=08h) function. However, KERNEL seems almost never to rely on one documented DPMI function, when multiple DPMI functions, or avoiding DPMI altogether, will do. Go figure.

Support: 3.0, 3.1
See also: GetSelectorLimit, SelectorAccessRights, SetSelectorBase
Example: See SETSBASE.C in the example for SetSelectorBase

SetSigHandler   KERNEL.140

```
WORD FAR PASCAL SetSigHandler(FARPROC newSignalHandler,
    DWORD FAR * lpOldSignalHandlerAddress, WORD FAR * lpOldSignalType,
    WORD signalType, WORD mustBeOne);
```

SetSigHandler() installs or removes a signal handler function for the currently running task. This signal handler is *not* the same as the "task signal handler" installed by SetTaskSignalProc. Instead, it is essentially a Ctrl-Break handler. See DoSignal() for a description of how the SetSigHandler() installed callback is invoked.

The fourth parameter to SegSigHandler (called signalType here), determines how the other parameters will be used. If signalType is 0, then the signal handler for the task will point to a default signal handler that simply RETFs. If signalType is 2, then a different handler is being installed.

Support: 3.0, 3.1
See also: DoSignal()
Example: See BREAK.C in the entry for DoSignal()

SetTaskQueue   KERNEL.34

```
HANDLE SetTaskQueue(HANDLE hTask, HANDLE hQueue);
```

SetTaskQueue() associates a specified Task Queue structure with a specified task; it does this simply by placing its hQueue parameter in the hQ field at offset 20h in the Task Database structure indicated by its hTask parameter. (If hTask is 0, SetTaskQueue() operates on the *current* task.) The function uses XCHG to return the previous value of the hQ field (or perhaps XCHG is just used to save a byte over MOV, and returning the previous value is a side effect).

This function is used indirectly by the documented SetMessageQueue() function in USER.

The calling function is responsible for preserving the linked list of Task Queues (see the wNext field at offset 0 in the Task Queue structure), and for setting the hTask field at offset 2 in the Task Queue. SetTaskQueue() does not take care of these for you.

Support: 3.0, 3.1
Used by: InitApp (USER)
See also: GetTaskQueue, Task Database, Task Queue

SetTaskSignalProc   KERNEL.38

```
FARPROC SetTaskSignalProc(HANDLE hTask, FARPROC lpSignalProc);
```

SetTaskSignalProc() allows an application to install a callback function for significant events in the life of a task. That is, the callback function is called when the task is about to be terminated (either willingly or unwillingly) and when a module is being loaded or unloaded.

The hTask parameter specifies the task the callback is installed for (as in all KERNEL functions that expect an hTask, zero can be used to specify the *current* task). The other parameter is the far address of the new callback function. SetTaskSignalProc() simply moves its lpSignalProc parameter into DX:AX and then does an XCHG with the DWORD at offset 2Ah in the Task Database. The return value, if nonzero, will thus be the address of the previous callback function; you can use this to "chain" from your handler to the previous one.

The callback function will be called with an event code in the BX register. The callback function is prototyped as:

```
void FAR PASCAL TaskSignalCallback(
    HANDLE   hTaskOrModule,
    WORD     wCode, // Same as BX; see below
    WORD     unknown,
    HANDLE   hInstance,
    HANDLE   hQueue
    );

Known values for BX and wCode:
0020h   task is being terminated
0040h   library is being loaded     (Call to USER SignalProc directly)
```

```
0080h    module is being unloaded    (Call to USER SignalProc directly)
0666h    task is terminating "violently" (i.e., a UAE)
```

For wCode 40h and 80h, only the hTaskOrModule parameter is significant; it holds a handle to the module being loaded. Also in these two cases, the signal handler installed by SetTaskSignalProc() is ignored, and the default signal procedure (SignalProc() in USER) is always called (KERNEL does a GetProcAddress() for SignalProc(), and then calls it directly!).

The fault handler in KERNEL contains the following code:

```
HANDLEFAULT:
    ; ...
    mov es, TASK_Q
    cmp word ptr es:[SIGNAL_PROC+2], 0
    je short no_sig_proc
    mov bx, 666h
    mov di, OFFFFh
    push es
    push bx
    push di
    push word ptr es:TASK_DS
    push word ptr es:TASK_QUEUE
    call word ptr es:SIGNAL_PROC
no_sig_proc:
    mov ax, 4CFFh        ; exit program
    int 21h
```

ToolHelp uses a signal proc to watch for the beastly wCode of 666h. When the signal proc is called, ToolHelp closes down any notify and interrupt handlers belonging to the faulting task.

Support: 3.0, 3.1
See also: SignalProc (USER), Task Database

Task Database (TDB)

A task handle, such as that returned from the GetCurrentTask() function, is a handle to a segment that contains information relevant to a particular instance of a program. This segment is the Task Database, or TDB for short. Among the vital information stored in a TDB is the current SS:SP of a nonactive task, the current state of the DOS file I/O structures, and a protected-mode DOS Program Segment Prefix (PSP; perversely called a Program Database or PDB in Windows). Because Windows is a multitasking system, each task must have its own "context." For example, it wouldn't do to have one application change the current directory behind another program's back, so KERNEL keeps *multiple* current directories, one per task. Where does it keep them? In the Task Database.

The structure of the Task Database has proved remarkably consistent between Windows 3.0 and 3.1, making it something that programmers can rely on relatively safely.

A constant source of confusion among Windows programmers is the distinction between a module handle, a task handle, and an instance handle. A module handle is a handle to a Module Table; the Module Table contains information that can be shared across multiple instances of an application. The Task Database, on the other hand, contains information specific to each instance of the application. If you run four copies of the Windows Notepad program, there will be one Module Table, but four different TDBs, each with its own current directory, open files, and more.

Not every module table has associated Task Databases. Windows DLLs, such as USER, KRNL386, GDI, and any other DLLs, have module tables, but they are not tasks. DLLs are simply application code that didn't get linked until run time. If you open a file while running in a DLL, the file is actually being opened by the task that called the DLL. Hence, the file handle is stored in the TDB for the calling task. If another task uses the same DLL, there will be a different TDB in use, so the file handles from the first TDB are not available. (Alert readers might now be saying, "But file handles are stored in the PSP!" Never fear. We'll come to that.)

An instance handle refers to a segment containing a DGROUP. In the case of a DLL, there is only one DGROUP, no matter how many tasks access the DLL. On the other hand, each running task has its own DGROUP (sometimes known as "instance data," hence the name). As a result, an hInstance is neither a task handle nor a module handle. For tasks, the hInstance is stored as part of the TDB. For DLLs, the hInstance is stored in the module table. In the previously mentioned Notepad example, there will be four hInstances, each stored in a separate TDB.

As a side note, resources are shared across multiple instances of a task (via the module table). Unfortunately, Microsoft chose to ask for an instance handle in its resource using functions [DialogBox(), etc.] rather than a module handle. No information about resources is stored in the DGROUP or the Task Database. The Windows internals have to take the passed-in hInstance and convert it to a module handle before it can access the resources.

The Task Database is always allocated in conventional (low) memory, using GlobalDosAlloc(), because each TDB contains a DOS Program Segment Prefix (PSP; called the PDB in Windows), which DOS can only access in the first megabyte of memory. The PSP is formatted with the undocumented DOS Create PSP function (INT 21h AH=55h). In Enhanced mode, the TDB is locked with the reserved DPMI function INT 31h AX=4, so that it won't be paged out of memory. (The WISPY program in chapter 4 was used to watch KERNEL as it creates a TDB.) Note that the TDB is created *before* a task starts running; the InitTask() function (discussed elsewhere in this chapter) does not create the TDB.

All Task Databases are kept in a singly-linked list, whose root is returned in the undocumented DX return value of the GetCurrentTask() function. The scheduler in KERNEL appears to maintain this task list sorted in priority order (see SetPriority()). When new tasks are being inserted into the list, there is a brief time during which it is

Task Database (TDB)

unstable: the number of tasks found by walking the list does not equal the value returned from the documented GetNumTasks() function (see the TASKWLK2 program in chapter 4).

The structure of the TDB appears in the header file TDB.INC, included with the Windows 3.1 DDK. The struct in TDB.INC contains some thread-related fields that we haven't seen referenced; these appear as "Unknown" in the structure below. That TDB.INC is included with the publicly-available DDK indicates that this structure is unlikely to change. This impression is also left by the remark in TDB.INC, "Don't you dare change anything in here or raor [Rao Remala?] will kill you; OLE depends on this." (In 3.0, OLE has to know if a task died; in 3.1, it uses the documented IsTask() function.)

It is often claimed that the TDB contains the CPU registers for a non-current task, but this is not true. The TDB does however contain (at offset 2) the SS:SP stack pointer from when the task was last switched away from, and the stack frame for a non-current task contains the switched-away CS:IP, used by the ToolHelpStack-TraceFirst/Next functions (see chapter 10). The TDB does also contain (at offset 14h) the 80x87 control word.

Task Database format (Windows 3.0 and 3.1)

OFFSET	SIZE	DESCRIPTION
0	WORD	Selector of next task. 0 = end of list
2	DWORD	SS:SP of the task when last switched away from
6	WORD	Semaphore (event count) used by PostEvent/WaitEvent
8	WORD	Priority
08	WORD	Priority
0A	WORD	Unknown; always 0; TDB.INC says "next thread"
0C	WORD	Selector for this TDB
0E	BYTE[6]	Unknown; always 0; TDB.INC says "thread_list," "thread_free," and "thread_count"
14	WORD	80x87 control word (FLDCW/FSTCW)
16	WORD	TDB.INC says "task flags", with WINOLDAP=1, OS2APP=8, and Win32s=10h (Win32s is Wind32 on top of 3.1)
18	WORD	Error mode; bit 1 (2h) indicates no "Display_Box_Of_Doom"
1A	WORD	Expected Windows version for task
1C	WORD	Instance handle for task
1E	WORD	Module handle for task
20	WORD	Selector of the task message queue
22	WORD	Selector of TDB of parent task
24	WORD	Some sort of flag relating to SetSigHandler
26	DWORD	SetSigHandler proc for task

Task Database (TDB)

2A	DWORD	Task signal proc
2E	DWORD	GlobalDiscard notification proc
32	DWORD	Interrupt 0 handler address
36	DWORD	Interrupt 2 handler address
3A	DWORD	Interrupt 4 handler address
3E	DWORD	Interrupt 6 handler address
42	DWORD	Interrupt 7 handler address
46	DWORD	Interrupt 3Eh handler address
4A	DWORD	Interrupt 75h handler address
4E	DWORD	Result of GetProfileInt(modName, "Compatibility", 0) (3.1)
52	BYTE[0Eh]	Unknown
60	WORD	Selector to PSP (PDB)
62	DWORD	Far ptr to Disk Transfer Area (DTA) or cmdline in PSP
66	BYTE	Current drive for task + 80h (80 = A:, 81 = B:, etc.)
67	BYTE[43h]	Current path for task (see previous field for drive letter)
AA	WORD	hTask of task that is being DirectedYield()'ed to
AC	WORD	Selector for segment containing referenced DLL list. Exists only before InitTask has been called.
AE	WORD	Offset of the DLL list in above segment.
B0	WORD	Code segment alias selector for this task database
B2	WORD	Selector to segment with additional MakeProcInstance() thunks; 0 if no segment necessary. Segment has the same basic format as offsets B2h - F1h.
B4	WORD	'PT' (5450h) signature for MakeProcInstance thunks
B6	WORD	Unknown; always 0
B8	WORD	Next available slot for MakeProcInstance() thunk. Subtract 6 from this value to get the actual offset where the next thunk will be stored.
BA	BYTE[38h]	Space for up to seven MakeProcInstance() thunks. Each thunk contains the original parameters to MakeProcInstance:

```
mov ax, hInstance
jmp far lpProc
```

F2	BYTE[08h]	Module name for task. No terminating 0 character if the module name is eight bytes in length
FA	WORD	'TD' (4454h) Task Database signature
100	BYTE[100h]	PSP for task. Word at offset 60h is a selector that points here.

Task Database (TDB)

Comments:

0   WORD

This is the selector of the next TDB in the system. Use the DWORD return value from GetCurrentTask() to get the first TDB, and then use this field to traverse the system walk list. A zero in this field marks the last task in the list. See GetCurrentTask(), discussed earlier in this chapter.

2   DWORD

Each task in the system has its own stack. Whenever Windows switches to a new task, the stack registers are loaded from this DWORD.

6   WORD

This field is the number of waiting events for this task in the system message queue. This field is *not* the same as offset 6 in the Task Queue. Instead, it can be thought of as a counting semaphore used between PostEvent() and WaitEvent(). See the entries in this chapter for PostEvent() and WaitEvent().

8   WORD

This field is the task priority, manipulated with the SetPriority() function. Priorities can range from -32 to 15, with lower numbers indicating higher priority. See the description of SetPriority(), discussed elsewhere in this chapter.

0C   WORD

This field is the selector value for this Task Database. Because you already know this value if you are reading this data, we presume it exists for sanity checks.

14   WORD

This contains the 80x87 control word (FLDCW) for the task. For a detailed discussion, see Paul Bonneau's "Q&A" on floating-point exceptions, in *Windows/DOS Developer's Journal*, May 1992, pp. 55–59.

1A   WORD

This field is the minimum Windows version under which a task expects to be running. This information can also be found in the module table with which the task is associated. It is in the same format as the return value from GetVersion().

1C   WORD

This field is the instance handle (also known as the hInstance, or DGROUP) for the task. The format of the DGROUP segment is covered earlier in this chapter, in the description of the Instance Data structure.

1E   WORD

The module handle (or hModule) for this hTask. As mentioned previously, it is possible for multiple TDBs to contain the same hModule in this field.

Task Database (TDB)

20   WORD

Very early in the creation of a task, a Task Queue is created for it by a call to InitApp().
The message queue exists in a segment set up just for that purpose. This WORD contains
the selector for this segment. The message queue, among other things, stores the messages that an application will be retrieving via GetMessage() or PeekMessage(). See the section on GetTaskQueue(), as well as the Task Queue description that follows.

22   WORD

The task handle for the "parent" of the task is stored here. Usually, the parent task is PRO-
GMAN.EXE or another Windows shell. However, if a program uses WinExec() or
LoadModule() to run another program, the program will be listed as the parent task.
(What if the parent of a program such as PROGMAN that has been loaded via the
SHELL= statement? This is a special case; the parent task is a selector to a segment that
was allocated by KERNEL at startup time.) See the description of WinExec() later in this
chapter for a sample use. Note that a parent task can terminate before its children; in this
case, the hParent field is no longer a valid task ID.

24   WORD

This field is some sort of "flag" value for the SetSigHandler() (whose address is stored at
offset 26h). If this value is not 2, the handler is not called.

26   DWORD

This field contains the address of a signal handler. This address can be changed via
SetSigHandler(), and the handler can be invoked via DoSignal(). The only known use of
this signal is by KEYBOARD.DRV, which uses it for sending a CTRL-BREAK to an application. The default handler is in KERNEL and simply RETFs. Ctrl-Break handling can be
installed by calling SetSignHandler(); see the descriptions of DoSignal() and
SetSigHandler() elsewhere in this chapter.

2A   DWORD

Contains the address of a signal handler that's called when an application is about to be
terminated and during library loads/unloads. The address can be set via
SetTaskSignalProc(). Windows 2.x also had undocumented SetTaskSwitchProc() and
SetTaskInterchange() functions.

32-4A   DWORD

Starting at offset 32h, there is a series of far function pointers that point to routines for
handling selected interrupts. The interrupts are:

0   (Divide by 0)
2   (NMI, or nonmaskable interrupt)
4   (INTO)
6   (Invalid opcode)
7   (Coprocessor not available)

Task Database (TDB)

3E   (Used by floating point emulators)

75   (Coprocessor error)

The INT 0 handler usually points to a routine in USER that displays a message box and then calls FatalAppExit. Programs that use WIN87EM will usually have the INT 3Eh handler pointing into one of their code segments. In the rest of the cases, the interrupt handlers point to a special segment belonging to KERNEL. This segment is a code segment, but it is just a table of identical instructions (such as HLT), one for each possible interrupt. The instruction is selected to force a transition to a handler in Windows.

4E   WORD

This field is only used in Windows 3.1. In the application's startup code, during the call to InitTask(), the field at offset 1Ah (the expected minimum Windows version) is examined. If the value is 0300h (meaning that the application targets Windows 3.0), then the following call is made:

```
GetProfileInt(moduleName, "Compatibility", 0)
```

The result of this call is stored in the field at offset 4Eh. The module name is extracted from the module name field at offset F2h. See GetAppCompatFlags(), above.

60   WORD

This field contains the selector for one of our favorite (and familiar) data structures. Microsoft calls it the Program Database, but it is more familiarly known as the PSP, or Program Segment Prefix. It is essentially the same PSP that you'll encounter with a DOS program, including the file handle tables. However, fields in the PSP that contain segment values under real-mode DOS contain protected-mode selector values here. As long as you don't play games with segment arithmetic, or try to use the selector values with real mode code, it's the same PSP you know and love (?!) from MS-DOS programming.

So where is the PDB itself stored in memory? It never shows up in HeapWalker, but if you look at TDBs, you'll notice that it's 200h bytes in size. The first 100h bytes are used by the data fields being discussed here. The second half of the TDB contains the PSP itself. The selector at offset 60h is just a selector with a base address 100h higher than the TDB's base address. Looking back, it seems like a pretty obvious place to put it.

62   DWORD

Contains a far pointer to the MS-DOS Disk Transfer Area (DTA). The default location for the DTA is at offset 80h in the PDB (see offset 60h). This is identical to the default location of the DTA in DOS.

66   BYTE[44h]

Starting at offset 66h is the current default drive/directory. The first BYTE contains the logical drive number, plus 80h. Thus, A: is 80h, B: is 81H, etc. The drive is immediately

Task Database (TDB)

followed by the current path and is NULL-terminated. This is one of two places where Windows maintains multiple current directories, on top of a single copy of MS-DOS. (The other place is in Enhanced mode, where each virtual machine has its own complete virtual DOS state.)

AA   WORD

If a task calls DirectedYield( ), the hTask to which it is yielding is stored in this WORD. If a task does a normal Yield( ), the value 0 is stored here. Don't look for this value to ever be nonzero unless you're debugging the KERNEL scheduler. It's always set back to 0 before the scheduler code exits.

AC   DWORD

This field is only valid when the task has just been created and is zeroed out by the call to InitTask( ). It contains a selector:offset to a NULL-terminated list of module handles. These module handles are for all the DLLs that this task is causing to be loaded. A helper function called by InitTask( ) iterates through each of the module handles, calls routines to find the entry point, and subsequently calls the DLL's initialization code. If any of the DLLs cannot load, the task is terminated by a call to DOS EXIT (INT 21h AH=4Ch), with a return code of F0h. After all the DLLs have been loaded, the segment containing the module handle list is GlobalUnlocked and GlobalFreed.

B0   WORD

This field is a code segment alias for the TDB. Why a code segment alias? A good question, with a good answer. When a program calls MakeProcInstance( ) to create an "instance thunk," the thunk is created in the TDB; to call the thunk, a code-segment alias is necessary (protected mode, remember?).

B2   WORD

This field is a selector for a segment with additional MakeProcInstance( ) thunks. There is a fixed amount of space for thunks in the TDB. If more thunks are requested than will fit in the TDB, an additional segment is allocated, and the thunks are continued in the new segment. The format of this segment is the same as the thunk section of the TDB (offsets B2h-F1h). This field is 0 if no segment has been allocated.

B4   WORD

As with many other Windows data structures, the MakeProcInstance( ) thunk portion of the TDB has a signature byte to allow for sanity checking. The WORD value at this address always contains 5450h, which appears as 'PT' when read as ASCII characters. Presumably, this stands for something like "Procedure Thunks" or "Process Thunks."

B8   WORD

If you subtract 6 from this WORD value, you'll have the offset where the next MakeProcInstance( ) thunk will be placed. If this location contains 0, than all available thunk spaces have been taken up. In this case, you must follow the linked list of MakeProcInstance( ) thunk segments, the head of which is given in offset B2h.

Task Database (TDB)

A BYTE[38h]

At this location we find room to store seven MakeProcInstance() thunks. The thunks have the following form:

```
MOV AX, hInstance_value          ; Second parameter to MakeProcInstance()
JMP FAR lpfnProgramProcedure     ; First parameter to MakeProcInstance()
```

F2 BYTE[8]

This field is the name of the module from which the task was loaded. If the module name is less than eight characters, the unused characters are NULL. Otherwise there is no NULL terminator. A DLL or interrupt handler that wants to know what program it was called from can call GetCurrentTask() and use this field to obtain the module name. If a module handle is desired, the WORD at offset 1Eh can be used.

FA WORD

Here we find the WORD signature for a TDB. The value is 4454h, which, if read as ASCII characters, displays as TD, for "Task Database" (or maybe someone at Microsoft is a secret admirer of "Turbo Debugger").

100 BYTE[100h]

Starting at offset 100h is the full and complete PSP (PDB) for the task. This region can also be accessed via the selector contained in the WORD at offset 60h. For the structure of the PSP itself, see *Undocumented DOS*, particularly the entry for INT 21h AH=26h (Create PSP). Just remember that in Windows, it's a protected-mode PSP. See also Program Database (PDB), in this chapter.

Example: The following program, WINTASK, illustrates both the Task Database and Task Queue structures. WINTASK starts by displaying the handle and name of each task running. More than one task can have the same name because each instance of a running application, such as NOTEPAD below, has its own separate Task Database:

```
TASK            HNDL
NOTEPAD         126F
WINFILE         179F
DRWATSON        1267
NOTEPAD         11AF
SH              12DF
WINOLDAP        141F
WINTASK         2007
```

If the user double clicks on any of these tasks, WINTASK brings up an additional window with more information on the task. For example, clicking on WINFILE above brings a window with additional information on the task running File Manager (because it was started from the SHELL= statement, its hParent field has no associated name and is not a valid task):

Task Database (TDB)

```
hTask                        179F
hInstance                    16EE
hModule                      053F (WINFILE)
PDB/PSP                      1797 <- Double-click here for PSP display
hParent                      0137 ()
Current directory            C:\WINDOS
SS:SP                        16EF:36EC
Waiting system events        0000
Priority                     0000
Expected Win version         3.10
SetSigHandler flag           0000
SetSigHandler Proc           0117:66A9
Signal Proc                  036F:09DE
Int 00 handler               036F:1E6F
Int 02 handler               003B:0004
Int 04 handler               003B:0008
Int 06 handler               003B:000C
Int 07 handler               003B:000E
Int 3E handler               003B:007C
Int 75 handler               003B:00EA

Message Queue:
hQueue                       06B7
Queue Size                   0008 messages
Message Size                 0016
Waiting messages             0000
Next Message offset          00F2
Next Free message offset     00F2

Messages:
OFFS  HWND  MSG   WPAR  LPARAM      TIME     POINT
006E  0FE4  0118  FFFD  036F36D8  0021F719   314.237
0084  0FE4  0118  FFFD  036F36D8  00221E5C   314.237
009A  0FE4  0118  FFFD  036F36D8  002245A0   314.237
00B0  17DC  0034  803C  00003B98  00224DC7   314.237
00C6  17DC  0113  0001  00000000  00225248   314.237
00DC  0FE4  0118  FFFD  036F36D8  00226CE3    92.218
00F2  0FE4  0118  FFFD  036F36D8  0021A892   314.237
0108  0FE4  0118  FFFD  036F36D8  0021CFD6   314.237
```

Finally, clicking on the PSP in this window brings up yet another window with some PSP information:

```
File handle count           001E
File handles:
 27 15 01 00 02 FF FF FF FF FF FF FF FF FF FF FF FF FF FF ...
Command line                ???
```

WINTASK.C uses three include files: TASKDB.H, TASKQ.H, and PSP.H. The file TASKQ.H is presented later in this chapter, with the description of the Task Queue structure.

Task Database (TDB)

```c
typedef struct
{
    WORD    next;                       // 0
    DWORD   sssp;                       // 2
    WORD    nevents;                    // 6
    WORD    priority;                   // 8
    WORD    unknown1;                   // A
    WORD    hTask;                      // C
    WORD    unknown2[3];                // E
    WORD    fpcw;                       // 14
    WORD    flags;                      // 16
    WORD    errmode;                    // 18
    WORD    expWinVer;                  // 1A
    WORD    hInstance;                  // 1C
    WORD    hModule;                    // 1E
    WORD    hQueue;                     // 20
    WORD    hParent;                    // 22
    WORD    SetSigHandlerFlag;          // 24
    DWORD   SetSigHandlerProc;          // 26
    DWORD   signalProc;                 // 2A
    DWORD   gdiscardProc;               // 2E
    DWORD   int0Proc;                   // 32
    DWORD   int2Proc;                   // 36
    DWORD   int4Proc;                   // 3A
    DWORD   int6Proc;                   // 3E
    DWORD   int7Proc;                   // 42
    DWORD   int3EProc;                  // 46
    DWORD   int75Proc;                  // 4A
    DWORD   Comptability;               // 4E
    char    unknown4[0x0E];             // 52
    WORD    pdb;                        // 60
    DWORD   dta;                        // 62
    BYTE    currDrive;                  // 66
    char    currDir[0x43];              // 67
    WORD    directedYieldHTask;         // AA
    WORD    libraryListSeg;             // AC
    WORD    libraryListOffset;          // AE
    WORD    codeAlias;                  // B0
    WORD    moreProcThunks;             // B2
    WORD    procThunksSig;              // B4
    WORD    unknown6;                   // B6
    WORD    nextAvailableThunk;         // B8
    char    procThunkData[0x38];        // BA
    char    moduleName[8];              // F2
    WORD    signature;                  // FA
} TASK_DB;

// psp.h
typedef struct _PSP
{
    WORD    signature;
    WORD    lastBlock;
    BYTE    r1;
    BYTE    dispatch[5];
    DWORD   int22;
```

Task Database (TDB)

```
        DWORD    int23;
        DWORD    int24;
        WORD     parent;
        BYTE     handles[20];
        WORD     environment;
        DWORD    saveStack;
        WORD     handleCount;
        DWORD    handleTablePtr;
        DWORD    sharePrevPSP;
        BYTE     r3[20];
        BYTE     int21Dispatch[3];
        BYTE     r4[9];
        BYTE     fcb1[16];
        BYTE     fcb2[16];
        DWORD    r5;
        BYTE     argLen;
        char     args[127];
}PSP;

// wintask.c
//=================================
//  WinTask, by Matt Pietrek, 1992
//  File: WINTASK.C
//=================================

#include <windows.h>
#include <stdio.h>
#include <string.h>
#include <ctype.h>
#include <dos.h>
#include "winio.h"

#include "taskdb.h"
#include "taskq.h"
#include "psp.h"

#define NE_SIGNATURE            0x454E
#define TDB_SIGNATURE           0x4454
#define TDB_SIGNATURE_OFFSET    0x00FA
#define TDB_MODULE_NAME_OFFSET  0x00F2
#define PSP_LENGTH              0x0100
#define PSP_SIGNATURE           0x20CD

WORD WinVersion;

//-------------------------------------------------
// Returns a BOOL indicating whether the passed
// in handle is an HTASK. In Windows 3.1, you
// could call IsTask()
//-------------------------------------------------
BOOL IsATask(HANDLE hTask)
{
    WORD segLen;
    BOOL segOK=FALSE;
    WORD far *signature;
```

Task Database (TDB)

```
    // Make sure that it's ok to read from the passed in handle/selector
    asm {
            mov     ax, [hTask]
            cmp     ax, 0
            je      mylabel
            lsl     bx, ax
            jnz     mylabel
            mov     [segLen], bx
            mov     [segOK], 1
    }

    mylabel:

    // Make sure that the segment is long enough, and then
    // look for the TD signature
    if ( !segOK || (segLen < TDB_SIGNATURE_OFFSET+2) )
        return FALSE;

    signature = MK_FP(hTask, TDB_SIGNATURE_OFFSET);
    return (*signature == TDB_SIGNATURE) ? TRUE : 0;
}

BOOL IsAPSP(HANDLE hPSP)
{
    WORD segLen;
    BOOL segOK=FALSE;
    WORD far *signature;

    // Make sure that it's ok to read from the passed in handle/selector
    asm {
            mov     ax, [hPSP]
            cmp     ax, 0
            je      mylabel
            lsl     bx, ax
            jnz     mylabel
            mov     [segLen], bx
            mov     [segOK], 1
    }

    mylabel:
    // Make sure that the segment is long enough, and then
    // look for the TD signature
    if ( !segOK || (segLen < PSP_LENGTH) )
        return FALSE;

    signature = MK_FP(hPSP, 0);
    return (*signature == PSP_SIGNATURE) ? TRUE : 0;
}

//----------------------------------------------
// Given a module handle, return the name
// of the module.
//----------------------------------------------
char *GetModuleNameFromHandle(HANDLE handle)
{
```

Task Database (TDB)

```
    static char name[129];
    char far *moduleTablePtr;
    WORD residentNamesOffset;
    BYTE cbModuleName;

    name[0] = 0;     // Null out the return string

    // create a pointer to the module table
    moduleTablePtr = GlobalLock(handle);
    GlobalUnlock(handle);
    if ( !moduleTablePtr )
        return name;

    // Verify that we're really looking at a module table, by
    // looking for the NE signature. If we are, get the
    // module name out of the resident names table.
    if ( *(WORD far *)moduleTablePtr == NE_SIGNATURE )
    {
        // Obtain the resident names table offset, and point to it
        residentNamesOffset = *(WORD far *)(moduleTablePtr + 0x26);
        moduleTablePtr += residentNamesOffset;

        // Get the length of the first entry, which is always
        // the module name.
        cbModuleName = *(BYTE far *)moduleTablePtr;
        moduleTablePtr++;

        // Use the far string copy to move the name to our local
        // buffer. Then null terminate the local buffer copy.
        _fstrncpy(name, moduleTablePtr, cbModuleName);
        name[cbModuleName] = 0;
    }

    return name;
}

//---------------------------------------------
// Given a task handle, return back the name
// of the module that it's an instance of
//---------------------------------------------
char *GetModuleNameFromTaskHandle(HANDLE hTask)
{
    static char buffer[10];
    buffer[0] = 0;
    if ( IsATask(hTask) )
    {
        _fstrncpy(buffer, MK_FP(hTask, TDB_MODULE_NAME_OFFSET), 8);
        buffer[8] = 0;
    }
    return buffer;
}

void DisplayMessage(MSG far *msg)
{
    WORD offset = FP_OFF(msg);
```

Task Database (TDB)

```
    // If Win 3.1, adjust the offset to display the true
    // start of the message
    if (WinVersion == 0x030A)
        offset -= 4;

    printf("%04X  %04X  %04X  %04X  %08lX  %08lX  %4d.%d\n",
            offset,
            msg->hwnd, msg->message,
            msg->wParam, msg->lParam,
            msg->time, msg->pt.x, msg->pt.y);
}

#define WIDTH 25

void DoTaskQueue(HANDLE hQueue)
{
    MESSAGEQUEUE far *mq;
    WORD    sel;
    WORD    msgCount;
    MSG     far *firstMsg;
    char    far *currMsgOffset;
    BOOL    win31=FALSE;
    WORD    i;

    if ( WinVersion > 0x030A )
    {
        printf("Cannot dump task queue. Windows version is too new\n");
        return;
    }

    win31 = ( WinVersion == 0x030A) ? TRUE : FALSE;
    sel = hQueue;
    mq = MK_FP(sel, 0);
    firstMsg = MK_FP(sel, (win31) ? 0x6E : 0x5A);
    msgCount = (mq->endOfQueue - FP_OFF(firstMsg)) / mq->msgSize;

    printf("%-*s%04X messages\n", WIDTH, "Queue Size", msgCount);
    printf("%-*s%04X\n", WIDTH, "Message Size", mq->msgSize);
    printf("%-*s%04X\n", WIDTH, "Waiting messages", mq->msgCount);
    printf("%-*s%04X\n", WIDTH, "Next Message offset", mq->nextMessageOffset);
    printf("%-*s%04X\n", WIDTH,
        "Next Free message offset", mq->nextFreeMessageOffset);
    printf("\n");
    printf("Messages:\n");
    printf("OFFS  HWND   MSG  WPAR    LPARAM       TIME  POINT\n");

    currMsgOffset = (char far *)firstMsg;
    if ( win31 )
        currMsgOffset += 4;

    for ( i=0; i < msgCount; i++ )
    {
        DisplayMessage( (MSG far *)currMsgOffset );
        currMsgOffset += mq->msgSize;
    }
}
```

Task Database (TDB)

```
        printf("\n");
}

void DisplayTask(HANDLE hTask)
{
    WORD sel = hTask;
    TASK_DB far *tdb = MK_FP(sel, 0);

    printf("%-*s%04X\n", WIDTH, "hTask", tdb->hTask);
    printf("%-*s%04X\n", WIDTH, "hInstance", tdb->hInstance);
    printf("%-*s%04X (%s)\n", WIDTH, "hModule",
        tdb->hModule, GetModuleNameFromHandle(tdb->hModule));

    printf("%-*s%04X <- Double-click here for PSP display\n",
        WIDTH, "PDB/PSP", tdb->pdb);

    printf("%-*s%04X (%s)\n", WIDTH, "hParent",
        tdb->hParent,  GetModuleNameFromTaskHandle(tdb->hParent));

    printf("%-*s%c:%Fs\n", WIDTH, "Current directory",
            (tdb->currDrive-0x80) + 'A', tdb->currDir );
    printf("%-*s%Fp\n",  WIDTH, "SS:SP", tdb->sssp);
    printf("%-*s%04X\n", WIDTH, "Waiting system events", tdb->nevents);
    printf("%-*s%04X\n", WIDTH, "Priority", tdb->nevents);

    printf("%-*s%u.%02u\n", WIDTH, "Expected Win version",
        HIBYTE(tdb->expWinVer), LOBYTE(tdb->expWinVer) );

    printf("%-*s%04X\n", WIDTH, "SetSigHandler flag", tdb->SetSigHandlerFlag);
    printf("%-*s%Fp\n", WIDTH, "SetSigHandler Proc", tdb->SetSigHandlerProc);
    printf("%-*s%Fp\n",  WIDTH, "Signal Proc", tdb->signalProc);

    printf("%-*s%Fp\n",  WIDTH, "Int 00 handler", tdb->int0Proc);
    printf("%-*s%Fp\n",  WIDTH, "Int 02 handler", tdb->int2Proc);
    printf("%-*s%Fp\n",  WIDTH, "Int 04 handler", tdb->int4Proc);
    printf("%-*s%Fp\n",  WIDTH, "Int 06 handler", tdb->int6Proc);
    printf("%-*s%Fp\n",  WIDTH, "Int 07 handler", tdb->int7Proc);
    printf("%-*s%Fp\n",  WIDTH, "Int 3E handler", tdb->int3EProc);
    printf("%-*s%Fp\n",  WIDTH, "Int 75 handler", tdb->int75Proc);

    printf("\nMessage Queue:\n");
    if ( tdb->hQueue )
    {
        printf("%-*s%04X\n", WIDTH, "hQueue", tdb->hQueue);
        DoTaskQueue(tdb->hQueue);
    }
    else
        printf("No message queue for task\n");
}

void DisplayPSP(HANDLE hPSP)
{
    WORD i;
    char c;
    WORD sel = hPSP;
```

Task Database (TDB)

```
    PSP far *psp = MK_FP(sel, 0);

    printf("%-*s%04X\n", WIDTH, "File handle count", psp->handleCount);

    printf("File handles:\n");
    for ( i = 0; (i < psp->handleCount) && (i < 20 ); i++)
        printf(" %02X", psp->handles[i]);
    printf("\n");

    printf("%-*s", WIDTH, "Command line", psp->handleCount);
    if ( psp->argLen == 0 )
        printf("<none>");
    else
        for ( i = 0; i < psp->argLen; i++)
        {
            c = psp->args[i];
            c = isascii(c) ? (isprint(c) ? c : '.') : '.';
            printf("%c", c);
        }
    printf("\n");
}

void TaskWalk(void)
{
    HANDLE thisTask;
    WORD far *signature;

    // Undocumented way to get the first task in the system
    GetCurrentTask();
    asm     mov     [thisTask], DX
    if ( !thisTask )
        return;

    // Turn off repaints while we output the info
    winio_setbusy();
    winio_setpaint(winio_current(), FALSE);

    printf("Double-Click on any line for detailed view\n\n");
    printf("TASK     HNDL\n");

    while ( thisTask )
    {
        // Verify that we're looking at a valid TDB
        signature = MK_FP(thisTask, 0xFA);
        if ( *signature != TDB_SIGNATURE )
        {
            printf("Error in following task chain\n");
            break;
        }

        printf("%-8s  %04X\n",
            GetModuleNameFromTaskHandle(thisTask), thisTask);

        // Extract the next task in the linked list
        thisTask = *(HANDLE far *)MK_FP(thisTask, 0);
```

Task Database (TDB)

```
    }

    // Turn the repaints back on
    winio_resetbusy();
    winio_home(winio_current());
}

void DumpPSP(HWND hwnd, LPSTR line, int i)
{
    char moduleName[80];
    char buffer[80];
    HANDLE hPSP;
    int returnCode;
    HWND newWindow;

    // Make a local copy of the line, and then extract the
    // relevant info from the line.
    _fstrcpy(buffer, line);
    returnCode = sscanf(buffer, "PDB/PSP %x", &hPSP);

    // Make sure that a valid line was pressed, and that the
    // task still exists. Get out if either is not true
    if ( returnCode != 1 )
    {
        MessageBox(NULL, "Not a valid line", "Error",
                    MB_OK | MB_ICONEXCLAMATION);
        return;
    }

    if ( !IsAPSP(hPSP) )
    {
        MessageBox(NULL, "Task/PSP no longer exists", "Error",
                    MB_OK | MB_ICONEXCLAMATION);
        return;
    }

    // Create the window for the PSP display. Give it
    // an appropriate title.
    GetWindowText(hwnd, buffer, sizeof(buffer));
    sscanf(buffer, "WinTask: %s", moduleName);
    sprintf(buffer, "WinTask PSP: %s", moduleName);
    newWindow = winio_window(buffer, 0x0400, WW_HASMENU);
    winio_setcurrent(newWindow);

    // Turn off repaints
    winio_setbusy();
    winio_setpaint(winio_current(), FALSE);

    DisplayPSP(hPSP);

    // Turn repaints back on, and position at the top of the info
    winio_setpaint(winio_current(), TRUE);
    winio_resetbusy();
    winio_home(newWindow);
}
```

Task Database (TDB)

```
void DumpTask(HWND hwnd, LPSTR line, int i)
{
    char moduleName[80];
    char buffer[80];
    HANDLE hTask;
    int returnCode;
    HWND newWindow;

    // Make a local copy of the line, and then extract the
    // relevant info from the line.
    _fstrcpy(buffer, line);
    returnCode = sscanf(buffer, "%s %x", moduleName, &hTask);

    // Make sure that a valid line was pressed, and that the
    // task still exists. Get out if either is not true
    if ( returnCode != 2 )
    {
        MessageBox(NULL, "Not a valid line", "Error",
                   MB_OK | MB_ICONEXCLAMATION);
        return;
    }

    if ( !IsATask(hTask) )
    {
        MessageBox(NULL, "Task no longer exists", "Error",
                   MB_OK | MB_ICONEXCLAMATION);nnnn
        return;
    }

    // Create the window for the new task display. Give it
    // an appropriate title.
    sprintf(buffer, "WinTask: %s", moduleName);
    newWindow = winio_window(buffer, 0x1000, WW_HASMENU);
    winio_setcurrent(newWindow);

    // Turn off repaints
    winio_setbusy();
    winio_setpaint(winio_current(), FALSE);

    DisplayTask(hTask);

    // Turn repaints back on, and position at the top of the info
    winio_setpaint(winio_current(), TRUE);
    winio_resetbusy();
    winio_home(newWindow);

    winio_setlinefn(winio_current(), DumpPSP);
}

int main(int argc, char *argv[])
{
    // GetVersion returns in AX register. Flip the byte registers to
    // produce a sensible version, with the major revision in ah, and
    // the minor revision in AL. When done, store away in WinVersion.
    GetVersion();
```

Task Database (TDB)

```
asm     xchg    ah, al
asm     mov     [WinVersion], ax

// Create the list of tasks for the user
// to double click on.
TaskWalk();

// Install a double click handler
winio_setlinefn(winio_current(), DumpTask);

return 0;
}
```

WINTASK is structured much like the WINMOD program shown earlier in this chapter in the Module Table example; WINTASK too is a WINIO program with clickable-line handlers. The program's main() entry point installs DumpTask() as a clickable-line handler, and calls TaskWalk() to print out a list of task names and handles. When main() returns, WINIO takes over. Any time the user clicks on a task, the function DumpTask() is called.

DumpTask() verifies that the task still exists, creates a new window, calls DisplayTask(), and installs DumpPSP() as a handler for a clicked-on PSP field. DisplayTask() displays information on the selected Task Database. It calls DoTask Queue() to display information on the associated Task Queue; for each message in the queue, DoTaskQueue() calls DisplayMessage(). If the user clicks on a PSP, DumpPSP() calls DisplayPSP() to show the PSP's file handles and command line.

Task Queue

Windows is often referred to as an "event driven" operating system (it's also referred to as a lot of other things, but they're not printable). The events are in the form of messages that are dispatched to window procedures. Messages can be delivered with SendMessage(), which directly calls the appropriate window procedure (switching tasks if needed), or with PostMessage(), which puts the message in a task's message queue. Actually, SendMessage() can be a lot more complicated than a simple call, and also uses the task queue; see below. This message queue resides in the Task Queue structure, maintained by KERNEL.

Very early in the life of each task, a Task Queue is created when its startup code calls the USER function InitApp(). The Task Queue resides in its own segment; the WORD at offset 20h in the Task Database contains a selector to the Task Queue segment. Functions such as GetTaskQueue() in KERNEL and InSendMessage() in USER return a handle to a Task Queue.

A task dispatches messages to its various window procedures by calling the documented USER function DispatchMessage(). The messages themselves thus originally go to the task, not to the windows. In fact, you can get messages without even having a window: the documented PostAppMessage() function posts messages by specifying an hTask rather than an hWnd. (While you can post messages to a task, though, you can't *send* messages; that requires an hWnd on the receiving end.)

Because messages are really posted to a task, not a window, it makes sense that the Task Queue itself is a KERNEL rather than a USER data structure. On the other hand, many routines inside USER have intimate knowledge of the Task Queue structure; these include ReplyMessage(), InSendMessage(), GetMessageTime(), GetMessagePos(), and PostQuitMessage(). In fact, some of the Task Queue fields seem to belong exclusively to these USER functions. For example, one field (offset 28h in Windows 3.0, and 2Ch in 3.1) belongs to the PostQuitMessage() message function.

Actually, it is difficult to decide whether the Task Queue is a KERNEL or a USER data structure. Really, it's shared between the two modules, and in fact provides most of the glue between KERNEL and USER. The GetTaskQueue() and SetTaskQueue() functions are in KERNEL, but the Task Queue itself is created by the InitApp() function in USER (see chapter 6), so that GetExePtr(hTaskQ) == GetModuleHandle("USER").

Unlike the Task Database and other structures in Windows, the Task Queue does not contain a "signature." This makes it difficult to write a fully-reliable IsTaskQueue() function. However, every Task Queue contains (at offset 2) a back pointer to its Task Database, so this, along with the fact that Task Queues are owned by USER, can be used to write a function that works well in practice:

```
BOOL IsTaskQueue(HANDLE h)
{
    if (h == 0)
        return FALSE;
    if (GetExePtr(h) != GetModuleHandle("USER"))
        return FALSE;
    return (IsTask(*((WORD far *) MK_FP(h, 2))));
}
```

Messages cannot be posted to a task which does not yet have a Task Queue, that is, whose startup code has not yet reached the call to InitApp(). The GetTaskQueue() function can be used to determine if a task's queue exists yet. In Windows 3.1, the documented function GetSystemDebugState() can return the value SDS_NOTASKQUEUE if the current task's queue does not yet exist.

All Task Queue segments are linked together in a list (see offset 0 in the structure), and the root of the list is stored in USER's fixed (not DGROUP) data segment (at offset E6h in 3.1). Task Queues are always allocated in low memory.

By default, the Task Queue can hold eight messages. However, this can be changed with an undocumented (and not very useful) DefaultQueueSize= setting in WIN.INI.

The Task Queue segment contains not only the space for messages themselves to be stored, but also other message-related information. For example, the documented GetMessageTime() and GetMessagePos() functions produce their return values by simply retrieving them from fields in the Task Queue. Windows API functions dealing

Task Queue

with messages can get most of what they need right from this structure; they don't need much "outside" information. Any C++ programmer would instantly recognize the Task Queue structure and code as an object just waiting to happen.

Each Task Queue includes near pointers that point into the actual message storage area of the queue segment. The message storage area is very similar in concept to the circular keyboard buffer maintained by the ROM BIOS. The near pointers in the message queue are vital to maintaining the correct message order and ensuring that the buffer does not overflow.

If SendMessage() is called for a window that's in the same task, the message does not go into the message queue; instead, Windows directly calls the appropriate Window procedure. However, when a SendMessage call needs to switch between two tasks, the message parameters are stored in the message queue, though in an area separate from the queue of posted messages.

Certain messages (such as mouse movement messages) are not stored in the task's message queue. Instead, they are stored in a system-wide hardware-event queue managed by USER and are retrieved by the message functions when there are no events left in the task's message queue. The system queue is set up and maintained by the same code that handles the task queues, but the format of messages in the system queue is different. (See System Message Queue in chapter 6.)

In the following list of the Task Queue fields, note that the structure splits at offset 1Ah between Windows 3.0 and 3.1; also, fields whose use is unknown are not listed.

Task Queue format

OFFSET	SIZE	DESCRIPTION
00	WORD	Selector of next message queue
02	WORD	hTask of task that owns this queue
04	WORD	Size of a message in this queue
06	WORD	Number of messages waiting to be retrieved
08	WORD	Offset of next message to be retrieved
0A	WORD	Offset of next available message slot
0C	WORD	Offset of the end of the queue
0E	DWORD	Value returned by GetMessageTime()
12	DWORD	Value returned by GetMessagePos()
16	WORD	Reserved? Sometimes the offset of the last message retrieved
18	DWORD	Information returned by GetMessageExtraInfo() in 3.1

—Win 3.0—

1A	DWORD	SendMessage() lParam
1E	WORD	SendMessage() wParam
20	WORD	SendMessage() msg

Task Queue

22	WORD	SendMessage( ) hWnd
28	WORD	PostQuitMessage has been sent flag—wPostQMsg
2A	WORD	PostQuitMessage exit code—wExitCode
36	WORD	hInstance of task
38	WORD	Expected Windows version from NE file
3A	WORD	InSendMessage return value (Task Queue of sender, not BOOL)
3C	WORD	Task Queue handle of next sender to reply to
3E	WORD	Task Queue handle of next sender to be serviced
42	WORD	Queue status (see GetQueueStatus( ), chapter 6)
44	WORD	Queue state flags
5A	WORD	Start of message area in Windows 3.0

—Win 3.1—

1E	DWORD	SendMessage( ) lParam
22	WORD	SendMessage( ) wParam
24	WORD	SendMessage( ) msg
26	WORD	SendMessage( ) hWnd
2C	WORD	PostQuitMessage has been sent flag—wPostQMsg
2E	WORD	PostQuitMessage exit code—wExitCode
36	WORD	Expected Windows version from NE file in Windows 3.1
38	WORD	InSendMessage return value (Task Queue of sender, not BOOL)
3A	WORD	Task Queue handle of next sender to reply to
3C	WORD	Task Queue handle of next sender to be serviced
44	WORD	Queue status (see GetQueueStatus( ), chapter 6)
42	WORD	Queue state flags
6E	WORD	Start of message area in Windows 3.1

Comments:

00   WORD

This is the selector value for the next message queue. New entries are added to the list by adding the queue to the front of the list.

02   WORD

Contains the TDB selector of the task that owns this queue. From KERNEL's perspective, this seems silly because, to get a task queue, you need to have a TDB in the first place. However, for USER this field plays a crucial role: the WND structure (chapter 6) contains an hTaskQ, but not an hTask. Thus, to get the TDB corresponding to a WND (i.e., the operation of the documented GetWindowTask( ) and undocumented GetTaskFromHwnd( ) functions), the Task Queue itself must contain a backlink to its TDB. Furthermore, InSendMessage( ) returns an hTaskQ, so *((WORD far *)

Task Queue

InSendMessage(), 2) gets the hTask of the sender. The SendMessage2() and ReplyMessage() functions in USER use offset 2 in an hWnd's hTaskQ to get a TDB to pass to the SetPriority() function. In other words, this field represents one of the crucial links in Windows.

04   WORD

This is the size of a message in this queue, in bytes. In windows 3.0, this size is 12h bytes, which is exactly enough to contain a MSG structure (defined in WINDOWS.H). Under Windows 3.1, this field contains 16h, with four unknown bytes, perhaps for GetMessageExtraInfo(). In the System Message Queue (see chapter 6), this holds the size of an EVENTMSG structure (plus, in 3.1, the same four additional bytes).

06   WORD

This field contains the number of messages in the queue that have not been retrieved yet. Note that this is completely different from the field at offset 6 in the Task Database structure.

08   WORD

This field is the offset of the next message that will be retrieved by a GetMessage or PostMessage. Every time a message is retrieved, this value is incremented by the WORD value at offset 4. When this value reaches the end of the queue (see offset 0Ch), then it is "wrapped" around to the lowest message slot offset.

0A   WORD

This WORD contains the offset of the next available message slot in the queue. The message code inside of KERNEL will fail a call to PostMessage if putting a message in the queue would overwrite an earlier message that hasn't been retrieved yet.

0C   WORD

This WORD points to the address immediately after the message storage area. By using this value, along with the offset of the first message slot and the message size, it is possible to figure out how many messages this queue can hold. The default is eight messages, but it can be altered with SetMessageQueue() (which, in turn, calls SetTaskQueue() to create a new Task Queue structure).

16h   WORD

This meaning of this value is currently unknown, but in some queues it contains the offset of the last message that was retrieved. At other times, it contains 0 or 1.

1Ah(3.0), 1Eh(3.1)   WORD

At this address, you'll find the parameters of the last SendMessage() to this task. The twist is that the parameters appear in reversed order: lParam, wParam, msg, hWnd. When using these values, bear in mind that SPY-like programs have a tendency to execute SendMessages in a DLL hook procedure. In this case, the SendMessage() would be coming from the hooked windows task, rather then from the SPY task. Thus, it is possible to

Task Queue

see values in this field that you wouldn't ordinarily expect to see coming from the application.

3Ah (3.0), 38h (3.1)   WORD

The InSendMessage() function is documented as returning a BOOL, but in fact it returns a HANDLE: the Task Queue of the sender (see chapter 6). That is, the message recipient's Task Queue contains the Task Queue of the message's sender. This can be used to chase down the ultimate origin of sent messages. (See SNOOP in chapter 4.)

3Ch (3.0), 3Ah (3.1)   WORD

3Eh (3.0), 3Ch (3.1)   WORD

These fields also relate to SendMessage(). SendMessage() is often described as involving just a simple far call to a WndProc, in contrast to the queueing mechanism used by PostMessage(). But this simplicity is only present when a task calls SendMessage() to send a message to a window in the same task. If sending messages to another task's window, SendMessage() will involve a task switch, and will make heavy use of the Task Queue.

SendMessage() saves the task queue handle in the field at 3C/3A (task queue handle of next sender to reply to) in the receiver's (send-to) task queue, then sets that field to the current task queue handle; then it sets the field at offset 3E/3C (task queue handle of next sender to be serviced) in the current (sent-from) task queue structure to the saved task queue handle. This constitutes a LIFO queue for SendMessage calls. SendMessage() also sets the field at offset 38/3A (task queue handle of sender) in the receiver's structure.

42h (3.0), 44h (3.1)   WORD

This field appears to contain a copy of many of the flags below (at offset 44h in 3.0 and 42h in 3.1), but it is reset to zero (using XCHG) when either GetInputState() or GetQueueStatus() is called (GetInputState == GetQueueStatus & 5). The field would therefore appear to signify what has changed since either of the last of these was called. See GetQueueStatus() in chapter 6.

44h (3.0), 42h (3.1)   WORD

Queue state flags, indicating in shorthand, the types of messages in the queue, and other information about the state of the task queue structure. The following bits are known:

QS_MSEWAITING (0x0001).   A Mouse message is present in the queue.

QS_KBDWAITING (0x0002).   A Keyboard message is present in the queue.

QS_MSGPOSTED (0x0004).   A Posted message is present in the queue.

QS_TMRWAITING (0x0008).   A WM_TIMER or WM_SYSTIMER (see the entry in chapter 7, and SetSystemTimer in chapter 6) message is present in the queue.

QS_PNTWAITING (0x0010).   A WM_PAINT message is present in the queue.

QS_NULWAITING (0x0020).   A WM_NULL message is present in the queue. See DirectedYield() for an example of why this message may be present.

Task Queue

QS_SNDWAITING (0x0040).

The field at offset 3Ch is non-NULL, i.e., a SendMessage is pending.

QS_SNDCOMPLETE (0x0080).

SendMessage appears to wait until this flag is set before returning.

QS_PARAMAREAFREE (0x0100).

SendMessage appears to wait until this flag is set before placing the message and parameters in the receiver's task queue structure message area.

Support: 3.0, 3.1
See also: GetTaskQueue, SetTaskQueue, Task Database, GetQueueStatus (chapter 6), GetTaskFromHwnd (chapter 6), InSendMessage (chapter 6)

Example: See WINTASK.C in entry for Task Database. That program relies on the following include file, TASKQ.H. Note that this structure only includes the fields unchanged between Windows 3.0 and 3.1:

```
// taskq.h -- common fields for Windows 3.0, 3.1
typedef struct
{
    WORD    Next;                       // 0
    WORD    hTask;                      // 2
    WORD    msgSize;                    // 4
    WORD    msgCount;                   // 68
    WORD    nextMessageOffset;          // 8
    WORD    nextFreeMessageOffset;      // 0A
    WORD    endOfQueue;                 // 0C
    DWORD   GetMessageTimeRetval;       // 0E
    DWORD   GetMessagePosRetval;        // 12
    WORD    messageQueueStart;          // 16
}   MESSAGEQUEUE;
```

THHook   **KERNEL.332**

```
THHOOK_STRUCT far *THHOOK;
```

THHOOK is not a callable function, but a far pointer to a structure in KERNEL's data segment. In a way, THHOOK is analogous to the MS-DOS List of Lists (INT 21h AH=52h, described in *Undocumented DOS*). Like the List of Lists, THHOOK provides direct access to the system's internal variables.

"TH" stands for ToolHelp, which uses this entry point to access several key KERNEL variables; this is the only thing it has in common with ToolHelpHook().

A program wishing to use THHOOK can use GetProcAddress to obtain the base address of the structure:

```
THHOOK = GetProcAddress(GetModuleHandle("KERNEL"), "THHOOK");
```

THHook

This function was not available in Windows 3.0, but don't despair just yet: in Windows 3.0, this same structure exists at offset 10h in the KERNEL data segment. As shown in the example that follows, in Windows 3.0, you can thus use GetModuleHandle() and the hInstance field in the module table to obtain the corresponding address in Windows 3.0.

Once your program has the THHOOK pointer, it can use the following offsets to obtain the desired information. Most of the values in the THHOOK structure either are available elsewhere or have a purpose that is unknown (the names comes from CodeView symbols in a debug version of KERNEL from the Windows SDK):

00h   hGlobalHeap

This is the handle to the Global Heap information structure (BURGERMASTER). It is identical to the LOWORD of the return value from GlobalMasterHandle().

02h   pGlobalHeap

This is the selector of the Global Heap information structure (BURGERMASTER). It is identical to the HIWORD of the return value from GlobalMasterHandle().

04h   hExeHead

This is the handle to first Module Table in linked list of modules. It is identical to the HIWORD of the return value from GetModuleHandle().

06h   hExeSweep

This offset is unknown and doesn't appear to be used.

08h   TopPDB

KERNEL's protected-mode PDB (PSP). It is identical to the HIWORD of the return value from GetCurrentPDB().

0Ah   HeadPDB

This is a handle to the first PDB (PSP) in the list.

0Ch   TopSizePDB

This offset is unknown and does not appear to be used; value 0.

0Eh   HeadTDB

This is a handle (hTask) to first Task Database (TDB) in linked list of tasks. It is identical to the HIWORD of the return value from GetCurrentTask().

10h   CurTDB

This is a handle (hTask) to current Task Database (TDB). It is identical to the LOWORD of the return value from GetCurrentTask().

12h   LoadTDB

This offset is unknown and does not appear to be used, but it value is usually 0.

THHook

14h   LockTDB

This is a handle to locked task, or zero. It is identical to return value from IsTaskLocked().

16h   SelTableLen (3.1)

This is the length of the selector lookup table (see Selector Table). In 3.0, this variable is not located in THHOOK: instead, it is at KERNEL_DGROUP+324.

18h   SelTableStart (3.1)

This DWORD is the address of the selector lookup table (see Selector Table), as a 32-bit offset within the Burgermaster segment. In 3.0, this variable is not located in THHOOK: instead, it is at KERNEL_DGROUP+326.

There are many other variables located further on in the table, but only the above have been verified for both Windows 3.0 and 3.1. Other interesting variables in 3.1 include these:

20h	WORD	wWinVer	useful for sanity checking
28h	WORD	hGDI	
2Ah	WORD	hUSER	
2Ch	WORD	hShell	definitely 3.1 specific!
34h	BYTE	Graphics	USER, KEYBOARD, GDI, DISPLAY loaded?
44h	DWORD	Dressed_for_Success	see InitTask1
48h	WORD	InDOS	
5Ah	WORD	CurDTA	Disk Transfer Area
5Eh	WORD	Cur_DOS_PDB	
60h	WORD	Win_PDB	for PSP switching
66h	BYTE	DOS_Version	useful for sanity checking
67h	BYTE	DOS_Revision	useful for sanity checking
69h	BYTE	fNovell	Running under Novell
73h		DebVar	debug variables?
9Bh	BYTE	fFarEast	Asian version of Windows?

The above variables can change at any moment, perhaps even with minor slip-stream releases of Windows, and are probably highly unreliable. Some of the known values (such as wWinVer, hGDI and hUSER, DOS_Version and DOS_Revision) could perhaps be used to check if the offsets are moderately reliable. For example, if pulling wWinVer out of the table produces different results from calling GetVersion(), then everything in the table is clearly unreliable.

The FileCdr() function uses two variables which can be expressed as offsets from THHOOK: see the description of FileCdr() earlier in this chapter.

THHook

Support: 3.1 (but see note and example for 3.0)
See also: GetCurrentTask, GetCurrentPDB, GetModuleHandle, GlobalMasterHandle, IsTaskLocked, Selector Table
Example:

```c
/* THHOOK.C */

#include <stdlib.h>
#include <dos.h>
#include "windows.h"
#include "winio.h"
#include "handles.h"

typedef struct {
    WORD hGlobalHeap;       // 0
    WORD pGlobalHeap;       // 2
    WORD hExeHead;          // 4
    WORD hExeSweep;         // 6
    WORD TopPDB;            // 8
    WORD HeadPDB;           // 0a
    WORD TopSizePDB;        // 0c
    WORD HeadTDB;           // 0e
    WORD CurTDB;            // 10
    WORD LoadTDB;           // 12
    WORD LockTDB;           // 14
    WORD SelTableLen;       // 16
    DWORD SelTableStart;    // 18
    } THHOOK_STRUCT;


main()
{
    THHOOK_STRUCT far *THHOOK;
    WORD wVers;

    wVers = GetVersion();
    if (wVers == 0x0003)    // 3.0
    {
        WORD wKernel, wKernelDgroup;
        wKernel = GetModuleHandle("KERNEL");
        printf("KERNEL = %04x\n", wKernel);
        if (! (wKernelDgroup = GetModuleDGroup(wKernel)))
            fail("Can't get KERNEL DGROUP");
        THHOOK = MK_FP(wKernelDgroup, 0x10);
    }
    else    // 3.1+
    {
        THHOOK = GetProcAddress(GetModuleHandle("KERNEL"), "THHOOK");
        if (! THHOOK)
            fail("Can't locate THHOOK");
    }
```

THHook

```
    printf("hGlobalHeap = %04xh\n", THHOOK->hGlobalHeap);
    printf("pGlobalHeap = %04xh\n", THHOOK->pGlobalHeap);
    printf("hExeHead = %04xh\n", THHOOK->hExeHead);
    printf("hExeSweep = %04xh\n", THHOOK->hExeSweep);
    printf("TopPDB = %04xh\n", THHOOK->TopPDB);
    printf("HeadPDB = %04xh\n", THHOOK->HeadPDB);
    printf("TopSizePDB = %04xh\n", THHOOK->TopSizePDB);
    printf("HeadTDB = %04xh\n", THHOOK->HeadTDB);
    printf("CurTDB = %04xh\n", THHOOK->CurTDB);
    printf("LoadTDB = %04xh\n", THHOOK->LoadTDB);
    printf("LockTDB = %04xh\n", THHOOK->LockTDB);
    printf("SelTableLen = %04xh\n", THHOOK->SelTableLen);
    printf("SelTableStart = %08lxh\n", THHOOK->SelTableStart);

    return 0;
}
```

Thunk

Windows programming books generally devote several pages to the subject of "thunks." Unfortunately, these discussions were originally written for Windows real mode and have not, in general, been adequately updated for protected mode. Fortunately, all that's required to bring these discussions up to date is to remove a lot of material (protected mode has really simplified Windows programming by vastly reducing the amount you need to understand about its internals).

There are three kinds of thunks; only one kind matters anymore. "Call thunks" and "return thunks" are gone in protected mode; good riddance. Call thunks were really just overlays with a fancy name and, in fact, used the exact same INT 3Fh mechanism as the Microsoft linker's overlay manager. This is not necessary in protected mode because the processor provides a Segment Not Present fault (INT 0Bh).

All that's left in protected-mode Windows are "instance thunks," created with a call to MakeProcInstance(). Even these are less important now, as compilers such as Borland C++ have "smart callbacks" that make it unnecessary to call MakeProcInstance(). In fact, as we'll see on the following page, instance thunks were *never* necessary.

Multiple instances of a Windows program can be running at the same time. Each has its own default data segment (DGROUP); the hInstance identifier is, in fact, nothing more than the value of DGROUP for a given instance. Some mechanism is needed so that, when Windows invokes a callback function (that is, uses your application as if it were a subroutine library), the function can access the default data segment. But we've just said that this data segment will differ for each instance of the program!

Compilers such as Microsoft C have a keyword _loadds that sounds as if it would work in this situation: the DS register is automatically loaded with the value of DGROUP on entry to the function; the value of DGROUP is stored right in the code as part of a MOV DS, SOME_CONSTANT instruction. But code in Windows is shared between multiple instances, so having the value of DGROUP embedded right in the code segment obviously won't work; being in protected mode doesn't solve the problem.

This is the problem that MakeProcInstance() is designed to solve. MakeProcInstance() has the following function prototype:

```
FARPROC MakeProcInstance(FARPROC lpProc, HANDLE hInstance);
```

The function takes a function pointer and an hInstance (the value of DGROUP for a particular instance of a program) and returns an "instance thunk," which is another function pointer, but one that somehow ties the passed-in procedure, lpProc, to a particular instance of the calling program. How it does this is quite simple: an "instance thunk" is eight bytes of code that contain the original parameters to MakeProcInstance():

```
MOV AX, hInstance
JMP FAR lpProc
```

The original function pointed to by lpProc must help too, by doing a PUSH DS/MOV DS, AX in its prolog. (See the Microsoft SDK overview article, "Windows Prologs and Epilogs.")

As noted earlier in this chapter, instance thunks are stored in the Task Database. See the discussion of the Task Database, particularly offsets B2h, B4h, B8h, and BAh.

All the above sounds quite necessary: MakeProcInstance() is needed so that each instance gets its own unique little header that Windows can patch. But as Michael Geary explained in his documentation for FIXDS 2.0 (April 1989), these instance thunks were *never* necessary!

So, all that work is necessary, right? Wrong. Despite all the work that MakeProcInstance() and EXPORTS go through to put the correct value into the DS register, THAT VALUE WAS JUST SITTING IN ANOTHER REGISTER WAITING TO BE USED. Which register? SS.

Remember that in a Windows application, SS == DS. Let me repeat that, SS == DS. Now, does any of the function prolog code or the instance thunk code do anything to SS? Nope. Whenever any of your application code is running, and whenever Windows calls one of your window functions or callback functions, SS contains your data segment address. The prolog code and instance thunks don't have anything to do with this; Windows' task manager puts the right value into SS before it lets your task run. If it didn't, the SS == DS assumption would be violated.

You can probably guess by now what FIXDS does. It patches all FAR function prologs to look like this:

```
mov     ax, ss
nop
inc     bp
```

Thunk

```
push    bp
mov     bp, sp
push    ds
mov     ds, ax
```

Now this prolog works for *all* FAR functions. Since SS, by definition, always has the correct data segment value, this prolog will put the correct value into DS. It doesn't matter whether it's a function you call directly or whether it is called back from Windows. . . .

The folks at Microsoft didn't believe me when I told them about the technique that FIXDS uses. After studying it a bit, they realized that of course it works. If it didn't, every application that's been compiled with the SS == DS assumption would have failed. Perhaps there's hope that a future version of Windows or the C compiler will have something like this built in.

FIXDS is what you get when you use Borland C++ "smart callbacks." Essentially, the value of SS is copied into DS. Wouldn't it be nice if Windows just did this to begin with? MakeProcInstance() could just become an undocumented function, and new Windows programmers wouldn't have to initiated into its mysteries.

All that's left is to explain the term "thunk" itself. While discussions of thunks can be found in most books on programming-language theory and in books on Lisp (such as the superb *Structure and Interpretation of Computer Programs* by Abelson and Sussman), the best definition of the term appears in Eric Raymond's *New Hacker's Dictionary* (MIT Press, 1991).

ToolHelpHook   KERNEL.341

```
FARPROC FAR PASCAL ToolHelpHook(FARPROC lpfnNotifyHandler);
```

This function is essentially a 3.1 replacement for RegisterPtrace(). Like RegisterPtrace(), this function installs a notification-handling function that will be called when interesting events occur. ToolHelp, which provides *documented* notification services, attempts to use ToolHelpHook(); only if it can't (3.0), does it call RegisterPtrace().

RegisterPtrace() continues to exist alongside ToolHelpHook() in Windows 3.1, but there are a few differences between the two worth noting. ToolHelpHook() returns the address of the previously installed handler; RegisterPtrace() does not. This allows a program to tap into the "notification stream," and, when it's done, restore the previous notification handler.

Second, there are two new notifications specific to Windows 3.1 that can be received:

```
66h - Log error
    CX = Error code
    DX:BX = pointer to error code dependent info

67h - Log param error
    ES:BX = pointer to error structure
    Error Structure :
        WORD      ErrorCode
        DWORD     lpfnErrorAddress
        DWORD     lpBadParameter
    ; NOTE: This is the NFYLOGPARAMERROR struct without size DWORD
```

For other notifications, see the description of RegisterPtrace() earlier in this chapter.

Internally, KERNEL maintains two function pointers, one set via RegisterPtrace(), the other set via ToolHelpHook(). Additionally, two flags are used to tell whether RegisterPtrace() and ToolHelpHook have been called with nonzero parameters; calling RegisterPtrace() and ToolHelpHook() with a 0L disables further notifications.

If both NotifyRegister() and ToolhelpHook() have been called, the order of calling the notification callback function varies. In most cases, the ToolHelpHook() callback function is called, and the RegisterPtrace() function is not. However, for a task-load notification (59h), both callbacks are called, and for an Asynch Stop notification (63h), the RegisterPtrace() callback is called instead of the ToolHelpHook() callback.

Support: 3.1
See also: RegisterPtrace, ToolHelp (chapter 10)

UndefDynlink   KERNEL.120

If a Windows executable (application or DLL) contains a module.ordinal dynlink link that can't be resolved, the KERNEL segment relocator calls UndefDynlink(). UndefDynlink(), in turn, calls FatalExit(), generating RIP ("rest in peace") code 404h.

For example, if your application contains a hard-wired (load-time) dynamic link to a Windows 3.1 function but is run under Windows 3.0, UndefDynlink() will be called, and your application will be terminated. This is a hazard of load-time dynamic linking. Note that calling GetVersion(), and only calling the function if the appropriate version of Windows is present, won't help: the problem isn't the actual call to the function, but the dynamic link to it that's embedded inside the executable file.

To avoid calling functions that aren't present, and thereby avoid a possible UndefDylink FatalExit, the solution is to use run-time dynamic linking:

```
#ifdef NOT_VERY_DYNAMIC
// use load-time dynamic linking; risk UndefDynlink FatalExit
extern WORD FAR PASCAL SomeWindowsAPIFunction(WORD wParam);
#else
```

```
// use run-time dynamic linking; if functions return 0, handle
// the problem myself, or ask user what to do, etc.
static WORD (FAR PASCAL *SomeWindowsAPIFunction)(WORD wParam) = 0;
// ...
if (SomeWindowsAPIFunction == 0)     // one-time initialization
{
    HANDLE hModule = GetModuleHandle(lpSomeModuleName);
    if (hModule == 0)   // not already loaded; try to load
        hModule = LoadLibrary(lpSomeModuleName);
    if (hModule == 0)   // really can't find it
        // can't find module -- do something intelligent
    SomeWindowsAPIFunction = GetProcAddress(hModule, lpSomeFunctionName);
    if (SomeWindowsAPIFunction == 0)
        // can't find function -- do something intelligent
}
#endif
// ...
WORD wRet = SomeWindowsAPIFunction(wArg);  // f() equiv to (*f)()
```

Support: 3.0, 3.1

WaitEvent   KERNEL.30

```
BOOL FAR PASCAL WaitEvent(HANDLE hTask);
```

WaitEvent() is one of three functions that Windows application startup code must call; the other two are InitApp() in USER and InitTask() in KERNEL. This startup code is supplied by compilers for Windows, and is responsible for calling an application's WinMain() function.

Though crucial to running applications under Windows, all three startup functions (including WaitEvent()) were undocumented through Windows 3.0; they are now documented in a 3.1 SDK *Programmer's Reference* overviews article titled "Windows Application Startup." A function prototype for WaitEvent() however, did, appear (along with PostEvent() and the non-existent KillTask()) in the Windows 3.0 SDK header file WINEXP.H, under the heading "scheduler things that the world knows not." In addition, Borland C++ includes commented Windows startup code in the file \BORLANDC\LIB\STARTUP\C0W.ASM.

WaitEvent() checks if an event has been posted to the specified task (0 is used to indicate the current task). If an event has been posted (see PostEvent(), described earlier in this chapter), WaitEvent() clears the event and returns control to the application. If no event has been posted (i.e., the event counter at offset 6 in the Task Database is zero), the function suspends execution of the application by calling the internal KERNEL function Reschedule(), which is the Windows task scheduler. WaitEvent() returns nonzero if Reschedule() scheduled another application; otherwise, it returns zero:

```
extrn WAITEVENT:far
; ...
push 0
call WAITEVENT
or ax, ax
jnz resched        ; nonzero if rescheduled (Open Tools)
```

WaitEvent() is used in startup code to clear the initial event that started the task. It can also be used in conjunction with PostEvent(), as shown in the example below. Note, however, that if you call WaitEvent() from an application that has the input focus, do not expect to be able to manually switch away to another application so it can call PostEvent(). Once an application is waiting, it really waits. The code that calls PostEvent() must already be running in the background.

The "event" referred to here is really just the signaling of a semaphore, and it has no relation to Windows messages; the semaphore is the WORD at offset 6 in the Task Database. WaitEvent(), together with a timer, could be used as the basis for a Windows implementation of the OS/2 DosSemWait() function; PostEvent() could be used to build something like DosSemWake().

For more information on WaitEvent() and PostEvent(), see Matt Pietrek's article "Inside the Windows Scheduler," *Dr. Dobb's Journal*, August 1992.

Support: 3.0, 3.1
See also: PostEvent, Task Database
Example: The first instance of the following program, SEMTEST, starts up a second instance using WinExec(argv[0]). The second instance blocks at random times by calling WaitEvent(); the first instance at random wakes the second instance at random times by calling PostEvent().

```
/* semtest.c */

#include <stdlib.h>
#include <time.h>
#include "windows.h"
#include "winio.h"
#include "handles.h"

/* from WINEXP.H -- "scheduler things that the world knows not" */
BOOL far PASCAL WaitEvent(HANDLE);
BOOL far PASCAL PostEvent(HANDLE);

void waste_time()    // waste a random amount of time
{
    static time_t t = 0;
    int i;

    if (t == 0)      // one-time initialization
        srand(time(&t));

    for (i=rand(); i--; )
```

```
        GetVersion();
}

main(int argc, char *argv[])
{
    extern HANDLE __hPrevInst;  // in ARGCARGV.C
    HANDLE hSecondInst, hSecondTask;
    int i;

    if (! __hPrevInst)
    {
        winio_settitle(winio_current(), "SEMTEST - First Task");
        if ((hSecondInst = WinExec(argv[0], SW_NORMAL)) < 32)    // fork
            fail("Could not EXEC second task");
        hSecondTask = hTask_from_hInstance(hSecondInst);
        for (i=10; i--; )
        {
            waste_time();
            puts("I'm about to wake second task");
            PostEvent(hSecondTask);
            puts("I woke second task");
        }
    }
    else    // I must be the second task
    {
        winio_settitle(winio_current(), "SEMTEST - Second Task");
        for (i=10; i--; )
        {
            waste_time();
            puts("I'm about to wait");
            WaitEvent(0);
            puts("Thanks, I needed that");
        }
    }
    puts("done");
    return 0;
}
```

WinExec

```
WORD FAR PASCAL WinExec(LPSTR lpCmdLine, int nCmdShow);
```

Although WinExec() is, of course, documented (it would be difficult to get much done in Windows if it wasn't), its return value is documented merely as a success/failure indicator. In fact, if WinExec() returns a number greater than 32, the number is the DGROUP (hInstance) of the EXECed program. If WinExec() is used to start a DOS program, the return value is an hInstance for WinOldAp. (For this reason, WinExec() can return a value greater than 32 even if the DOS program did not successfully start: it still probably succeeded in starting the WINOLDAP program, and this is what the WinExec() return value reflects.)

WinExec

For example, Windows programs that EXEC other programs could possibly use this return value to periodically check (once a second on a WM_TIMER, for example) to see if the EXECed program has terminated; use the WinExec() return value along with GetNumTasks(). Note, however, that hInstances *can* get reused in Windows. Microsoft has a technical note ("How to Determine When Another Application Has Finished," Q67673) that proposes several other, equally dubious techniques. A better approach is provided by Walt Oney's ExecWait() function, which uses the ToolHelp NotifyRegister() function to wait for NFY_EXITTASK (see "Parlez-vous Windows?," *Windows Tech Journal*, April 1992).

In any case, there are other uses for the WinExec() return value. Windows programs that trap interrupts can call GetCurrentTask() at the time the interrupt occurs (given the utter simplicity of GetCurrentTask(), it can safely be called at interrupt time), and then use the HINSTANCE_FROM_HTASK() macro in the introduction to this chapter to compare against the WinExec() return value. For example:

```
HANDLE hInstanceOfSomeApp = WinExec("SomeApp", SW_NORMAL);
// ...
void interrupt far some_interrupt_handler(REGS r)
{
    if (HINSTANCE_FROM_HTASK(GetCurrentTask()) == hInstanceOfSomeApp)
        // we are interested in handling this interrupt
        do_something(&r);
    else
        // this is from some other app we don't care about
        _chain_intr(previous_handler);
}
```

In summary, the WinExec() return value provides a handle to whom you EXECed. If you need a handle of who EXECed *you*, check out the hParent field at off-set 22h in the Task Database, described earlier in this chapter. For example:

```
/* error checking omitted for brevity */
#define GetParentTask(hTask) \
    (*((WORD far *) MK_FP(hTask, 0x22)))

GetTaskName(HANDLE hTask, char *buf)
{
    _fstrncpy(buf, MK_FP(hTask, 0xF2), 8);
    buf[8] = '\0';
}

// who EXECed me?
char buf[9];
GetTaskName(GetParentTask(GetCurrentTask()), name);
printf("My parent is %s\n", buf);
```

Note, however, that a parent task can exit before its children, making the hParent field invalid. You really do need to check for this to make any of the above meaningful: see the IsValidTask() function in HANDLES.C.

WinExec

WinOldApCall   KERNEL.151

```
void FAR PASCAL WinOldApCall(WORD wMode);
```

"Old apps" is what Microsoft has called DOS applications since the mid-1980s (funny, DOS still hasn't disappeared!). WinOldApCall() is called by the Windows WINOLDAP module; it is *not* a routine to call WINOLDAP. WinOldApCall() is called by the Standard mode version of WINOLDAP, WINOA286.MOD (3.0) or WINOLDAP.MOD (3.1), but not by the Enhanced mode version, WINO-A386.MOD.

If wMode is nonzero, all cached files currently open are closed. If wMode is zero, then several KERNEL internal variables are loaded into registers before returning. Aside from WinOldApCall() itself, the names in the following pseudo-disassembly are not exported from KERNEL; they are available only in debug versions of KERNEL with CodeView symbols:

```
WINOLDAPCALL proc far
    ; ...
    cmp word ptr wMode, 0
    je short load_regs
    push WIN_PDB
    push TOPPDB
    call far ptr CLOSECACHEDFILES
    pop WIN_PDB
    jmp short done
load_regs:
    mov ax, SELLOWHEAP              ; selector to lower-640k heap?
    mov bx, CPLOWHEAP
    mov cx, SELHIGHHEAP
    mov dx, SELWOAPDB              ; PSP for use by WINOLDAP?
    mov di, FILEENTRYSIZE
done:
    ; ...
loc_2747:
    pop ds
    retf    2
WINOLDAPCALL endp
```

The values of the returned variables are meaningful only in Standard mode.

Support: 3.0, 3.1

WriteOutProfiles   KERNEL.315

```
void FAR PASCAL WriteOutProfiles(void);
```

WriteOutProfiles() flushes .INI (profile file) changes out to disk. This function is called in the KERNEL INT 21h handler, during a task switch and inside the

ExitKernel() function. Note that it is *not* called from WriteProfileString(); thus, .INI file changes are momentarily cached. Note also that WriteOutProfiles() is called by DOS3Call(), but not by NoHookDOSCall().

Support: 3.1
See also: NoHookDOSCall

CHAPTER ■ 6

USER: Microsoft Windows User Interface

USER is the largest of the core modules of Windows. Probably close to two-thirds of the functions called from a typical application are exported from USER. It contains the window manager and the messaging subsystem, on which applications that run in the Windows environment are founded. It also manages menus, controls, dialog boxes, timers, and many other general services of mundane but central interest to all application programs.

The USER.EXE module is shipped in a debug version with the Microsoft SDK. This is considerably larger and slower than the retail module, as are the debug versions of KERNEL and GDI, but unlike those modules, USER data structures do not change in the debug version. Nor do any of the undocumented features of USER need any direct awareness of either processor or mode, a logical development for a module that presents an interface at this level. However, some structures *have* been altered between versions 3.0 and 3.1; therefore, the same general caveats concerning direct manipulation of undocumented structures apply here, as in the introduction to the previous chapter, though to a lesser extent. And again, you will see in some of these structures a gold mine of information unavailable from any other source that may make it worthwhile or essential that you use them.

USER Data Structures

Behind each of the many types of documented and undocumented handles that USER recognizes is an internal, undocumented structure. As in the other modules, the handles are returned by documented functions and are the means by which structures are hidden. The classic example in USER is the CreateWindow function that returns an HWND, perhaps the most universal of Windows currencies. The structure for which the HWND is a handle (which we have dubbed, perhaps unsurprisingly, the WND) is not documented, and it is the only USER structure that has changed extensively between versions 3.0 and 3.1. Microsoft could not have changed a documented structure in that way for version 3.1 and still allowed 3.0 applications to run.

As an example of the norm, however, the undocumented DragObject function sends messages to accepting windows with a handle to an undocumented structure (DRAGINFO) as its wParam. Even though the drag-and-drop protocol is superseded in version 3.1 by one that uses a documented function and handle interface, the 3.0 protocol, and its undocumented structure, continue to be supported, virtually unchanged, in version 3.1.

These are some of the most important structures covered in this chapter:

- Window information and state structure (WND)
- Class information for a window instance (CLASS)
- Menu and item structures (MENU)
- Drag-and-drop information in 3.0 (DRAGINFO)
- Drop data used in documented 3.1 drag-and-drop (DROPINFO)
- Cursor and icon in-memory resource information (CURSORICONINFO)

USER Heaps

As will be described in greater depth in the USER Objects entry, USER handles fall into two groups: those that are essentially global memory handles, such as HICON and HCURSOR, which are allocated using GlobalAlloc or DirectResAlloc; and those, such as HWND and HMENU and the undocumented HCLASS (see the WND entry later in the chapter) that are near pointers to blocks of memory in USER's local heap containing the associated object structures, allocated using LocalAlloc. By default, a Windows executable has a single default heap segment. It is a 16-bit segment, so it can be a maximum of 64K in size. Since Window and Menu structures, as we will see, are the most frequently needed USER objects, and since their handle types are pointers into this one 64K segment, it is not difficult to imagine how a few resource-intensive applications could quickly consume USER's heap.

In version 3.0, as can be verified by using the USERWALK program described later, USER actually has two heap segments. The default heap is used for storage of USER objects, as described above, and the second is used for the Global Atom table and USER string storage. The documented GlobalAddAtom, GlobalDeleteAtom, and GlobalFindAtom functions operate on this alternate heap segment. Within USER, however, there is also a set of unexported Textxxx functions that operate on this secondary heap. TextAlloc and TextFree (these names are presumed, not known) switch DS to this alternate heap segment before calling the KERNEL LocalAlloc and LocalFree functions, respectively.

It is obvious that this shared use of the Global Atom segment was intended to remove the possibility of a system resource crunch. It is also apparent from the addition of two more heap segments in version 3.1 that it did not remove the problem but simply eased or delayed it a little.

The USERWALK program's Analyze Heap option, when run in version 3.0, shows why at least one object type has been broken out into its own heap in version 3.1:

```
User Heap Analysis
Heap at 06F5 is 31526 bytes:
        NORMAL              Total: 3658 bytes (11%)
        Class               Total: 1852 bytes (5%)
        Window              Total: 8116 bytes (25%)
        Menu                Total: 10292 bytes (32%)
        FREE                     : 7608 bytes (25%)

Heap at 07E5 is 4208 bytes:
        NORMAL              Total: 4184 bytes (99%)
        FREE                     : 24 bytes (1%)
Total USER memory in heaps is 35734 bytes
```

In the above display, the first heap is the default heap, and the second is the Global Atom/Text heap. Microsoft Word for Windows, File Manager, Program Manager, and the SDK Dialog Editor were all loaded. Menus account for more of the USER heap than Window and Class structures combined. This is especially astonishing in that the Program Manager configuration that was running contained several program group windows, each of which had more than 20 applications in it. In version 3.0, Program Manager allocates a window for every program icon in every active (not minimized) program group.

As a result, in version 3.1 menu structures are stored in a separate heap, greatly improving system resource availability. Note that the corresponding USERWALK Heap Analysis display for version 3.1, with the same applications running as above, appears to show a small part of the menu heap being used by menus:

```
User Heap Analysis
Heap at 079D is 8588 bytes:
        NORMAL              Total: 1716 bytes (19%)
        Class               Total: 1416 bytes (16%)
        Window              Total: 2628 bytes (30%)
        FREE                     : 2828 bytes (33%)

Heap at 02DD is 3476 bytes:
        NORMAL              Total: 3412 bytes (98%)
        FREE                     : 64 bytes (2%)

Heap at 031D is 1296 bytes:
        NORMAL              Total: 376 bytes (29%)
        FREE                     : 920 bytes (71%)

Heap at 0325 is 9536 bytes:
        NORMAL              Total: 7440 bytes (78%)
        Menu                Total: 908 bytes (9%)
        FREE                     : 1188 bytes (13%)
Total USER memory in heaps is 22896 bytes
```

This is due to the fact that, in version 3.1, the menu item structure array has been broken out into a separate allocation (see the Menu object entry later in this chapter), and only the menu header structure is identifiable. In fact, the whole of that heap is used for menu structures.

Another indication of the resource appetite of menus is the separating out of menu item strings into their own heap in version 3.1, bringing the heap total to four. This menu strings heap, at 2DDh in the previoua display, contains only menu item strings and is responsible for 3.4k of the total 18k allocated heap space.

It should be noted that a fifth USER heap segment has also been seen while running USERWALK. Although it is not known what it is used for, it never contains any of the currently recognized USER object types and is transient in nature; it is often not present but may be allocated, used, and then freed.

USER Objects

USER has a number of important structures that are undocumented but accessible. These include the window class, window instance, property, menu, menu item, cursor, icon, drag-and-drop, and the system message queue. There are certainly others, but they are less important and less accessible.

The structures listed above fall into two categories: those that reside in the global heap and those that reside in a USER local heap segment.

Global Heap Objects

What characterizes these structures is that they are relatively stable; they are not frequently allocated and freed. Their location on the Global Heap avoids any problems associated with local-heap overload.

Cursors, Icons	Described in the CURSORICONINFO structure entry (CURSICON.H). Examples of its use are given in the CreateCursor, IconIndirect, and DumpIcon entries.
Drag and Drop	Described in the DRAGINFO and DROPINFO structure entries (DRAGDROP.H). Examples of their use are given in the DragObject entry.
Message Queue	Described in the Task Queue structure entry in the KERNEL chapter (TASKQ.H).
System Message Queue	Described in the System Message Queue entry.

User Local Heap Objects

Structures stored in USER's local heap space are an essential element in what are termed System Resources, which were discussed at some length in chapter 1. Free System Resource availability has been perceived by Microsoft as being a problem that lies mainly in USER; between versions 3.0 and 3.1, USER grew at least two extra heap segments. Many of the structures stored in USER's local heaps, though by no means all, are frequently created and destroyed, and are required to be always quickly accessible in order for Windows performance to remain acceptable.

Class   described in the CLASS structure entry
Windows and Properties described in the WND structure entry
Menus and Items   described in the MENU structure entry

All the above structures and associated constants and flags are available in USER-OBJ.H:

```
/* WND.H */

#define    CLASS_MAGIC      0x4B4E     // NK
#define    MENU_MAGIC       0x554D     // MU

/* === UNDOCUMENTED STRUCTURES === */

// Window class structure held in USER's near heap

typedef struct {
    HANDLE   hcNext;              // 00h Next entry in the class linked list
    WORD     wSig;                // 02h Should contain 0x4b4e ("NK")
    ATOM     atomCls;            // 04h Atom for class name string (USER heap)
    HANDLE   hDCE;               // 06h Handle to DCE when CS_CLASSDC, or NULL
    WORD     cClsWnds;           // 08h Count of windows with this class
    WNDCLASS wc;                 // 0Ah Incomplete copy from RegisterClass
    WORD     eExtra[1];          // 24h Class extra user data from here
    } CLASS, NEAR * HCLASS;

// Window structure for 3.0 held in USER's local heap

typedef struct {
    HWND     hwndNext;           // 00h Next in top level window linked list
    HWND     hwndChild;          // 02h first child window
    HCLASS   hClass;             // 04h Class info for this window
    HANDLE   hProp;              // 06h Handle of property list
    HWND     hwndLastActive;     // 08h hwnd of last active popup
    HANDLE   hScroll;            // 0Ah USER local handle used for scrolling?
    HANDLE   hmemTaskQ;          // 0Ch Window task/application message queue
    HRGN     hrgnUpdate;         // 0Eh Current invalid region for window
    HANDLE   hDCE;               // 10h handle to DCE when CS_OWNDC, or NULL
    HMENU    hmenuSystem;        // 12h System menu handle
    HWND     hwndOwner;          // 14h Owning application window
    RECT     rectWindow;         // 16h Non-client window coordinates
    RECT     rectClient;         // 1Eh Client window coordinates
    HPALETTE hPalette;           // 26h Logical palette used during paint
    WORD     wFlags;             // 28h bits 9/10 used in WM_USER+260 drag/drop
    DWORD    rgfExStyle;         // 2Ah
    DWORD    rgfStyle;           // 2Eh
    WORD     wID_Menu;           // 32h ID if control otherwise menu handle
    HANDLE   hText;              // 34h handle of window text in text heap
```

```
        HWND    hwndParent;      // 36h for child windows
        HANDLE  hInstance;       // 38h application instance handle
        FARPROC lpfnWndProc;     // 3Ah ProcInstance of WndProc for window
                                 // 3Eh user data area (array size >= 0 )
    } WND_3_0 /* , NEAR * HWND */ ;


// Window structure for 3.1 held in USER's local heap
// Note that, for no apparent reason, all fields in the structure
// apart from the first two, which provide navigation through the
// window hierarchy, have changed position, including those accessible
// by GetWindowWord/GetWindowLong.

typedef struct {
    HWND    hwndNext;        // 00h Next in top level window linked list
    HWND    hwndChild;       // 02h first child window
    HWND    hwndParent;      // 04h
    HWND    hwndOwner;       // 06h for child windows
    RECT    rectWindow;      // 08h Non-client window coordinates
    RECT    rectClient;      // 10h Client window coordinates
    HANDLE  hmemTaskQ;       // 18h Window task/application message queue
    HRGN    hrgnUpdate;      // 1Ah
    HCLASS  hClass;          // 1Ch Class info for this window
    HANDLE  hInstance;       // 1Eh application instance handle
    FARPROC lpfnWndProc;     // 20h ProcInstance of WndProc for window
    DWORD   dwFlags;         // 24h
    DWORD   rgfStyle;        // 28h
    DWORD   rgfExStyle;      // 2Ch
    WORD    wID_Menu;        // 30h ID if control otherwise menu handle
    HWND    hText;           // 32h handle of window text in text heap
    HANDLE  hScroll;         // 34h USER local handle used for scrolling
    HANDLE  hProp;           // 36h handle of property list
    HWND    hwndLastActive;  // 38h hwnd of last active popup
    HMENU   hmenuSystem;     // 3Ah System menu handle
                             // 3Ch user data area
        } WND_3_1 /* , NEAR * HWND */ ;

// Menu item substructure valid for 3.0 and 3.1
typedef struct {
    WORD    wFlags;          // 00h Flags
    WORD    hIDorPopup;      // 02h Item ID or popup menu handle
    RECT    rectCapture;     // 04h Item area in screen coords.
    WORD    xTab;            // 0Ch tab position in string
    HANDLE  hCheckedBmp;     // 0Eh Bitmap to use for checked
    HANDLE  hUncheckedBmp;   // 10h Bitmap to use for unchecked
    HANDLE  hStrOrBmp;       // 12h Handle to string or bitmap
    WORD    xULStart;        // 14h Start of underline
    WORD    cxULLen;         // 16h Length of underline (width of char)
    WORD    cbItemLen;       // 18h Length of item if string or NULL
    } ITEM, FAR *LPITEM;     // 1Ah Total

// Menu structure
typedef struct {
    WORD    wFlags;          // 00h flags
    WORD    iCurrSel;        // 02h Currently selected item or -1
```

```
        WORD     iCurrPopup;       // 04h Current popup or -1 if curr not popup
        WORD     cbMenu;           // 06h Size of this structure + items
        WORD     cxWidth;          // 08h Menu width in pixels
        WORD     cyHeight;         // 0Ah Menu height in pixels
        WORD     cItems;           // 0Ch Count of items following
        HWND     hwndOwner;        // 0Eh Owning window
                                   // 10h start of array of ITEMs
            } MENU_3_0 /* , *HMENU */ ;
typedef struct {
    HMENU   hmenuNext; // 00h Next in linked list of menus
    WORD    wFlags;           // 02h flags
    WORD    wMagic;           // 04h Signature/magic (0x554D == 'MU')
    HANDLE  hTaskQ;           // 06h Owning task queue handle ???
    WORD    cxWidth;          // 08h Width (0 if Sys Menu box)
    WORD    cyHeight;         // 0Ah Height (0 if Sys Menu box)
    WORD    cItems;           // 0Ch Count of items
    HWND    hwndOwner;        // 0Eh Owning window
    HANDLE  hItems;           // 10h hItems
    WORD    w12;              // 12h ??? (Usually 0)
                              // 14h Total
            } MENU_3_1 /* , *HMENU */ ;

typedef void FAR *LPMENU;

// Window Properties structures
typedef struct {
    ATOM    atomID;           // 00h Atom containing property identifier
    HANDLE  hData;            // 02h User supplied data handle
    WORD    wFlags;           // 04h Flags:
    } PROPERTY;               //      0x000B = Always set...
                              //      0x0010 = Internal property
                              //      0x0100 = Identifier was string
                              //               not atom


typedef struct {
    WORD    cProps;           // 00h Count of properties in array at 02h
                              // 02h Start of array of PROPERTY structures

        } PROPLIST;

// USER DC Entry structure
typedef struct {
    HANDLE  hdceNext;         // 00h Next in linked list of DCEs
    HWND    hwnd;             // 02h Currently owning window
    HDC     hDC;              // 04h HDC that this entry refers to
    BYTE    byFlags;          // 06h Flags:
                              //      0x01 - For client area use
                              //      0x02 - For window area use
                              //      Others ???
    BYTE    byInUse;          // 07h 0 = free, 1 = in use
    BYTE    byDirty;          // 08h 1 = window needs update, 0 = does not
    BYTE    by0A;             // 09h ???
    WORD    xOrigin;          // 0Ah DC Origin X
    WORD    yOrigin;          // 0Ch DC Origin Y
    HWND    hwndTop;          // 0Eh Parent window (also using this entry?)
    HRGN    hVisRgn;          // 10h Visible region
        } DCE, *HDCE;         // 12h TOTAL
```

USERWALK

USERWALK is a program that walks the USER heap segments and lists all the entries in each. Using the technique already seen in many of the utilities and example programs that accompany this book, double-clickable lines allow navigation through the structures in the heap.

The source code for USERWALK is too large to be included here, although it is available on the accompanying disk. It is worth discussing one or two points that arose during its development and that are brought out by its use.

USERWALK starts with a display listing local memory handles within the default USER local heap and then lists the handles in any other USER heaps. The following is an excerpt (unabridged, it would run to five pages) from the display generated using the retail version of Windows 3.1 in 386 Enhanced mode with one DOS box, Program Manager and Word for Windows loaded:

```
USER heap in segment 079dh:
(Double-click to view a block)
HANDLE   ADDR   SIZE   TYPE
0AC8     0AC8   0008   NORMAL
0AD4     0AD4   002C   NORMAL
0B04     0B04   0010   NORMAL
0B18     0B18   0010   NORMAL
0B2C     0B2C   0010   NORMAL
0B40     0B40   0010   NORMAL
0B54     0B54   0010   NORMAL
0B68     0B68   0024   Class
0B90     0B90   004C   NORMAL
         . . .
2694     2694   003C   Window
26D4     26D4   0044   NORMAL
0000     271C   0504   FREE
2C24     2C24   0048   Window
2C70     2C70   0048   Window
2CBC     2CBC   0048   Window
2D08     2D08   0048   Window
0000     2D54   0960   FREE

USER heap in segment 02ddh:
(Double-click to view a block)

HANDLE   ADDR   SIZE   TYPE
0018     0018   0008   NORMAL
0024     0024   002C   NORMAL
0054     0054   000C   NORMAL
0064     0064   0008   NORMAL
         . . .
110C     110C   000C   NORMAL
111C     111C   000C   NORMAL
112C     112C   000C   NORMAL
```

```
113C    113C    0014    NORMAL
1154    1154    0010    NORMAL
1168    1168    0010    NORMAL
117C    117C    0018    NORMAL
1198    1198    0014    NORMAL
11B0    11B0    0018    NORMAL
11CC    11CC    0014    NORMAL
11E4    11E4    0010    NORMAL
11F8    11F8    0014    NORMAL
1210    1210    0010    NORMAL
1224    1224    000C    NORMAL
0000    1234    0320    FREE
```

USER heap in segment 031dh:
(Double-click to view a block)

HANDLE	ADDR	SIZE	TYPE
001C	001C	0008	NORMAL
0028	0028	002C	NORMAL
0058	0058	004C	NORMAL
00A8	00A8	000C	NORMAL
00B8	00B8	000C	NORMAL
00C8	00C8	0010	NORMAL
. . .			
01CC	01CC	001C	NORMAL
01EC	01EC	0020	NORMAL
0000	0210	0624	FREE

USER heap in segment 0325h:
(Double-click to view a block)

HANDLE	ADDR	SIZE	TYPE
0018	0018	0008	NORMAL
0024	0024	002C	NORMAL
0054	0054	0014	Menu
006C	006C	0014	Menu
0084	0084	00EC	NORMAL
. . .			
0000	1A8C	0034	FREE
1AC4	1AC4	0014	Menu
0000	1ADC	0018	FREE
1AF8	1AF8	0104	NORMAL
1C00	1C00	0188	NORMAL
1D8C	1D8C	0154	NORMAL
1EE4	1EE4	0154	NORMAL
203C	203C	0138	NORMAL
2178	2178	0120	NORMAL
229C	229C	00EC	NORMAL
238C	238C	0034	NORMAL
23C4	23C4	0084	NORMAL
0000	244C	0044	FREE
2494	2494	0068	NORMAL
0000	2500	0394	FREE

This is the bleak view of the heap. Hundreds upon hundreds of entries, with the only break in the NORMALs being the occasional Class, Window, or Menu entry. Indeed, in the unabridged list, 90% of the lines listed are type NORMAL. The reason for this is that USER in the retail version of 3.0 only gives a signature to the CLASS structure. In the retail 3.1 version, two structures, CLASS and MENU, have signatures. No other object types, including WND structures, have any intrinsic form of identification.

Since a window is always an instance of a window class, however, every WND structure must contain a valid hClass field. By testing whether a block of memory contains a handle to a valid CLASS structure, which can at least be identified, at the appropriate offset (i.e., the offset of the WND structure hClass field) we can validate, indirectly, whether it is a window structure, even though it has no signature.

By contrast, in both 3.0 and 3.1 debug versions, blocks of memory in the default USER heap are allocated not by LocalAlloc but by UserLocalAlloc, which is an undocumented, unexported cover function over LocalAlloc. In addition to the wFlags and wSize parameters passed to LocalAlloc, UserLocalAlloc takes a byBlockType parameter that contains one of the ToolHelp documented User object type constants. UserLocalAlloc adds 4 to the size of the allocation before passing the call through to LocalAlloc and, upon return, uses the first of these extra four bytes as storage for the byBlockType. (As a side note, it does not appear to use any of the other three bytes.) In the debug version, then, the object type *is* stored with the object in a way that ToolHelp can use it. For this reason, the display under the debug version of 3.0 or 3.1 shows a much richer variety of block types in the heaps.

Back with USERWALK, double clicking on any of the lines in the above list will generate a window containing a formatted display of the local block that the line describes. For example, double clicking on one of the Window entries in the default heap would generate a window that might look like this:

```
Window handle 261C @ 079D:261C for 68 bytes

Lines marked '->' may be double clicked
for expansion

Window Title: USER Heap Walker: Heap Segments
Window Class: winio_wcmain

WND:


->          hwndNext        : 22D8
->          hwndChild       : 0000
->          hwndParent      : 0E8C
->          hwndOwner       : 0000
            rectWindow      : (100, 75, 700, 525)
            rectClient      : (106, 119, 678, 503)
            hTaskQ          : 2557
            hrgnUpdate      : 0000
->          hClass          : 2290
            hInstance       : 2546
```

```
       lpfnWndProc    : 2487:34BB
       dwFlags        : 0000000F
       rgfStyle       : 14FF0000
       rgfExStyle     : 00000000
->     wID_Menu       : 1150
       hText          : 01EC
       hScroll        : 2330
->     hProp          : 0000
->     hwndLastActive : 261C
->     hmenuSystem    : 0000
```

As you can see, the display is an exact dump of the structure as defined in the WND entry in this chapter. Further, the lines in the display that start with '->' may again be, you guessed it, double-clicked. This will produce a formatted display of the object in the line that has been selected. In the new display there may be more double-clickable lines. This makes it very easy to follow the relationship between structures. The only limit to this journey is the availability of Free System Resources required for each window.

In the main heap display, double clicking on a NORMAL block generates a raw hex-dump window. NORMAL indicates that we don't really know what the block is.

From the main menu bar, the View menu allows the selection of an alternative route into USER's heaps. Selecting Window Hierarchy from the View menu brings up a display similar to that used by the SNOOP program discussed in chapter 4. It is a hierarchy of all the windows in the system:

```
0E8C  [#32769]
   0F0C  [#32768]
   0ECC  [#32771]
   271C  [#32772]
   261C USER Heap Walker: Window Hierarchy [winio_wcmain]
   22D8  [#32772]
   1C84 Microsoft Word - CHAP6.DOC [OpusApp]
      1D30  [OpusPmt]
      1F34  [a_sdm_Microsoft Wor]
         2CBC  [savebits_lbox_Micro]
            2D08  [ScrollBar]
         1F78  [OpusFedt]
         1FBC  [OpusFedt]
         2C24  [savebits_lbox_Micro]
            2C70  [ScrollBar]
      1CE8  [OpusIcnBar]
      2000  [OpusStat]
      2040  [OpusDesk]
         18E8 CHAP6.DOC [OpusMwd]
            2398  [a_sdm_Microsoft Wor]
               2108  [savebits_lbox_Micro]
                  2154  [ScrollBar]
               23DC  [OpusFedt]
            24AC  [OpusRSB]
            2460  [OpusRSB]
            2080  [OpusWwd]
```

```
                2354  [OpusIcnBar]
                    2420  [OpusRul]
      2694  [#32772]
      1168 Program Manager [Progman]
          11DC  [MDIClient]
              0F78 UndocWin tools [PMGroup]
              12D0  [#32772]
              16A8  [#32772]
              1640 Games [PMGroup]
              1600  [#32772]
              1598 StartUp [PMGroup]
              1558  [#32772]
              14F0 Other Development [PMGroup]
              1360  [#32772]
              1310 Undocwin Examples [PMGroup]
              14B0  [#32772]
              1448 Accessories [PMGroup]
              1408  [#32772]
              13A0 SDK Tools [PMGroup]
              24F8  [#32772]
              16E8 Main [PMGroup]
      20C8  [#32772]
      1818 DOS Prompt [tty]
      0FF8 [#42]
```

In the Window Hierarchy display, which progressively increases the level of indentation for each level of child window that USERWALK encounters, each window handle is displayed along with its window caption, if it has one, and its window class next to it within square brackets. From any window entry in the display, the trusty double-click mechanism launches us into the same heap navigation capabilities that we had from the Heap Segments display.

The Refresh main menu selection regenerates the current view. If you double click on an item and a message box pops up to tell you that the handle you have just selected is no longer valid, it is time to use the Refresh option. Many of the object types in USER's heaps are allocated with the LMEM_MOVEABLE flag, and periodically the heap will be compacted as blocks are freed and allocated, changing the location of other blocks and possibly invalidating information currently held inside USERWALK.

The other important option from the main menu bar is Analyze Heaps. Earlier, we used the Analyze Heaps window to understand how USER heap usage contributed to the Windows Free System Resources problem. Choosing Analyze Heaps causes a window to be created that contains a breakdown of heap usage by heap segment (so there will be two subheads in the display in version 3.0, and four or more subheads in version 3.1). This report aggregates memory block sizes by object type within heap segment, and displays the heap consumption for each object type represented in terms of bytes and as a percentage of the heap segment size.

The report is intended to give a feel for what proportion of which heaps are taken by what sorts of system resource.

USER Exports and Imports

USER is made of approximately 150 object modules containing a total of more than 3,000 exported and internal (nonexported) functions. These fall into the following rough groups, in no particular order:

- Window and desktop management
- Dialog and control management
- Resource management
- Menu and accelerator management
- Task management and messages
- Window class maintenance
- Clipboard management
- Device drivers and timer management
- Network API
- Comms API
- Language and ANSI support
- USER initialization and exit routines
- String and other miscellaneous functions

As with KERNEL, most of the object modules that compose USER are hidden. In fact, in version 3.1 almost all of the documented exports are exported from a single object module, LAYER.OBJ. This presents an apparently neat and tightly controlled exported function interface.

USER Undocumented Functions

USER's undocumented functions in 3.0 and 3.1 can be roughly categorized as follows:

WINDOW AND DESKTOP MANAGEMENT

CalcChildScroll	PaintRect
CascadeChildWidows	RepaintScreen
CompUpdateRect	ScrollChildren
CompUpdateRgn	SetDesktopPattern
ControlPanelInfo	SetDeskWallpaper
DragDetect	SetGridGranularity
DragObject	SetInternalWindowPos
FillWindow	SetWC2
GetDesktopHwnd	SnapWindow
GetInternalWindowPos	SwitchToThisWindow
GetNextQueueWindow	TileChildWindows
GetWC2	

DIALOG AND CONTROL MANAGEMENT

ContScroll   GetFilePortName
GetControlBrush   SysErrorBox

RESOURCE MANAGEMENT

CreateCursorIconIndirect   LoadCursorIconHandler
DumpIcon   LoadDIBCursorHandler
GetIconID   LoadDIBIconHandler
IconSize   LoadIconHandler

MENU AND ACCELERATOR MANAGEMENT

EndMenu   MenuItemState
LookupMenuHandle   SetSystemMenu

TASK MANAGEMENT AND MESSAGES

BroadcastMessage   PostMessage2
GetMessage2   SendMessage2
GetQueueStatus   SignalProc
GetTaskFromHwnd   UserYield
IsUserIdle   WinOldAppHackOMatic
LockMyTask

DEVICE DRIVERS AND TIMER MANAGEMENT

DisableOEMLayer   KillTimer2
EnableOEMLayer   SetEventHook
GetMouseEventProc   SetGetKbdState
GetTimerResolution   SetSystemTimer
KillSystemTimer   SetTimer2

USER AND APPLICATION INITIALIZATION AND EXIT ROUTINES

FinalUserInit   OldExitWindows
InitApp

STRING AND OTHER MISCELLANEOUS FUNCTIONS

IsTwoByteCharPrefix   _wsprintf
StringFunc   XCStoDS
TabTheTextOutForWimps

USER Composition

In version 3.0, USER exports are fairly evenly distributed among its object files. In 3.1 however, most of the API exports of USER are now in a single LAYER.OBJ. Using the same model as KERNEL, parameter validation is performed in LAYER, and then code in the appropriate object file is called. Not all of the exports have been moved into LAYER—it is as if the exercise of moving the entry points could not be finished in time.

Using Undocumented USER Functions

Most undocumented USER functions appear to be no more and no less resilient to parameter abuse than their legitimate siblings and, with the exception of CascadeChildWindows and TileChildWindows, have not changed in either parameter usage or function between versions 3.0 and 3.1.

Many of the examples in this chapter use the function CheckOrdName() to verify that the named function exists in the expected module at the expected ordinal number:

```
/* CHECKORD.C */

BOOL CheckOrdName(char *szFunction, char *szModule, int nOrdinal)
    {
    HANDLE hModule;
    FARPROC lpfnByName;
    FARPROC lpfnByOrd;
    char achTitle[80];

    sprintf(achTitle, "%s() [%s.%d]", szFunction, szModule, nOrdinal);
    winio_settitle(__hMainWnd, achTitle);
    hModule = GetModuleHandle((LPSTR) szModule);
    lpfnByName = GetProcAddress(hModule, (LPSTR) szFunction);
    lpfnByOrd = GetProcAddress(hModule, (LPSTR) ((DWORD) nOrdinal));
    printf("hModule = %04X, by name = %Fp, by ord = %Fp\n\n",
            hModule, lpfnByName, lpfnByOrd);
    if (hModule == NULL)
        printf("Module %s not loaded!\nAborting\n", szModule);
    else if (lpfnByName == NULL)
        printf("Function %s not found in module %s!\n"
            "Aborting\n", szFunction, szModule);
    else if (lpfnByOrd == NULL)
        printf("Ordinal %d not found in module %s!\n"
            "Aborting\n", nOrdinal, szModule);
    else if (lpfnByName != lpfnByOrd)
        printf("Function %s not found at ordinal %d!\n"
            "Aborting\n", szFunction, nOrdinal);
    else
        return TRUE;

    return FALSE;
    }
```

BearNNN   Lore

In some cases, indicated in the individual entries, a function that had a sensible name in version 3.0 has been renamed in version 3.1 to BearNNN where NNN is the ordinal number of the entrypoint. The underlying function, however, has usually not changed and, when referenced using the ordinal value, works as in version 3.0. Other functions have never had any other name than Bear-something. But where does the prefix 'Bear' come from?

Bear (and Bunny in KERNEL) immortalize a couple of stuffed productivity enhancements in one developer's office, which apparently acted as problem-solving aids by providing punchbag-style psychological relief at times of stress.

See also: SetSystemTimer, GetSystemTimer, IconSize, IsTwoCharPrefix, SetDeskWallPaper

---

BozosLiveHere   USER.301

```
long FAR PASCAL BozosLiveHere(HWND, WORD, WORD, DWORD)
HWND hwnd;
WORD wMsg;
WORD wParam;
DWORD wParam;
```

This function in version 3.1 has the same ordinal entry point as the function EditWndProc in 3.0. It is apparently never intended to be called, since it outputs the string "USER: Invalid function called. System state potentially trashed," but then passes control to an internal edit class window procedure function. Since none of the other built-in class window procedure functions is exported in 3.1, it is unclear why this one alone received the special treatment (and name).

BroadcastMessage   USER.355

```
void FAR PASCAL BroadcastMessage(HWND, WORD, WORD, DWORD)
HWND hwnd;          /* hwnd of window sending message */
WORD wMessage;      /* Message */
WORD wParam;      /* additional message info */
DWORD lParam;      /* additional message info */
```

This function allows an application to post a message to all current top-level windows. It provides no more and no less functionality than PostMessage with the hwnd parameter set to 0xFFFF; PostMessage tests for this condition and branches to Broadcast-Message.

BroadcastMessage special cases two messages, WM_WININICHANGE and WM_DEVMODECHANGE. For these two, it replaces the lParam parameter, which it expects to receive containing an LPSTR pointing at a WIN.INI string, with a HANDLE to a block of global memory containing a copy of the string. (It is interesting, incidentally, that the documentation for these two messages does not mention that this is a possibility.)

After the special casing, BroadcastMessage does a PostMessage from a callback function passed to EnumWindows.

Support: 3.0, 3.1
Example: The following would minimize all windows on the desktop:

```
BroadcastMessage(my_hwnd, WM_SYSCOMMAND, SC_ICON, 0);
```

CalcChildScroll   USER.462

```
void FAR PASCAL CalcChildScroll(HWND, WORD)
HWND hwnd;                    /* Window to calculate for */
WORD wScroll;                 /* Combination of SB_HORZ and SB_VERT */
```

This function sets scroll bars in an MDI application parent window as a result of the movement of child windows or the resizing of the parent. It will remove the scroll bars if all the children fit within the parent client area or add scrollbars if a child is moving horizontally or vertically out of the parent client area.

The wScroll parameter must contain one or both of the documented constants SB_HORZ and SB__VERT, and determines which direction scrolling is to be calculated. It is called by the undocumented function ScrollChildren, and directly from within the MDIClientWndProc function.

Support: 3.0, 3.1

CascadeChildWindows   USER.198

```
void FAR PASCAL CascadeChildWindows(HWND [, WORD])
HWND hParent;     /* Window whose children are to be cascaded */
WORD wAction;     /* How to cascade [3.1 only] */
```

This function arranges the positions of child windows of the specified parent into a cascaded formation. CascadeChildWindows() was apparently written for MDI and is called by PROGMAN.EXE and FILEMAN.EXE. It takes the window handle of the owning, or parent, target window as its first, and in 3.0 only, parameter.

Note that an attempt, under version 3.0, to

```
CascadeChildWindows(FindWindow(NULL, "Program Manager"));
```

will not achieve the expected result, as the Program Group windows are not actually direct child windows of the Program Manager main window but rather MDI client windows. The above statement with Microsoft Word for Windows as the target application, however, leads to interesting results! Many of the characteristic pieces of the

Word main document window are forced into positions and shapes that they were obviously never intended to assume.

The second parameter is only present in 3.1 and affects whether disabled windows are cascaded. If the wAction parameter is set to MDITILE_SKIPDISABLED (0x0002), defined in the 3.1 WINDOWS.H, only child windows of the currently active child window of the specified hParent are cascaded. Note that although the wAction field may contain either MDITILE_HORIZONTAL or MDITILE_VERTICAL, these have no effect with CascadeChildWindows.

CascadeChildWindows, like all window-positioning functions, is implemented using the BeginDeferWindowPos, DeferWindowPos, and EndDeferWindowPos functions.

Support: 3.0, 3.1 (see notes)
Note: The second parameter is not present in 3.0.
Used by: PROGMAN.EXE, FILEMAN.EXE
See also: TileChildWindows
Example: Cascades the windows on the desktop. When run in 3.1, alternately cascades horizontally and vertically:

```
CASCCHLD.C */

#include <windows.h>
#include "winio.h"

/* undocumented function -- no function prototype
   because it differs between 3.0 and 3.1 */
extern void FAR PASCAL CascadeChildWindows();

#include "checkord.c"

int main()
    {
    WORD wVer = (WORD) GetVersion();

    if (! CheckOrdName("CascadeChildWindows", "USER", 198))
        return 0;

    winio_setecho(winio_current(), FALSE);

    for (;;)
    {
        puts("Press a key to cascade the desktop");
        getchar();

        if (wVer == 0x0003)
            CascadeChildWindows(GetDesktopWindow());
        else
            CascadeChildWindows(GetDesktopWindow(), 0);
    }

    }
```

CascadeChildWindows

CLASS   Structure

The Class Instance structure is referenced by the hClass field of the WND structure. Unlike the WND structure, the CLASS structure did not change between versions 3.0 and 3.1.

```
typedef struct tagCLASS {
    HANDLE      hcNext;
    WORD        wSig;
    ATOM        atomCls;
    HANDLE      hDCE;
    WORD        cClsWnds;
    WNDCLASS    wc;
    WORD        wExtra[1];
    } CLASS, NEAR * HCLASS;
```

The above structure contains the following known fields. Fields not described here are not yet understood.

FIELD	DESCRIPTION
hcNext	A list of CLASS structures is maintained in USER's default heap segment. This field provides linkage to the next entry in the list, which is terminated by a value of NULL.
wSig	A signature identifying the structure type. Sometimes known as "magic," this field is used for validation and should always contain 0x4b4e ("NK"), presumably the initials of the developer (Neil Konzen?).
atomCls	A local USER atom containing the window class name.
hDCE	Handle of the DCE structure used by the class if CS_CLASSDC is specified, NULL otherwise. See the DCE structure entry later in this chapter.
cClsWnds	The number of windows of this class in existence.
wc	An incomplete copy of the WNDCLASS structure passed to the RegisterClass function when the class was registered; the lpszMenuName and lpszClassName fields are both always NULL.
wExtra	Start of the instance data for the class instance, as specified in the documented WNDCLASS structure passed to the RegisterClass call.

Selecting the "Class Walk" option from the WINWALK program in chapter 10 (or doing an equivalent ToolHelp class walk with the ClassFirst() and ClassNext() functions) shows that USER has the following built-in window classes:

Button
ComboBox
ComboLBox
Edit
ListBox
MDIClient
ScrollBar
Static
#32768 (PopupMenu)
#32769 (Desktop)
#32770 (Dialog)
#32771 (WinSwitch)
#32772 (IconTitle)

When a class has a name such as #32XXX, the name is an integer atom (see the Atom Table entry in chapter 5). The string names provided for these in the list above come from the excellent WinSight program that comes with Borland C++ 3.0.

Note: Along with many other USER structures, the USERWALK program may be used to show the contents of CLASS structures. The WINWALK program in chapter 10 uses ToolHelp to walk the linked list of classes.
See also: DCE, WND

CompUpdateRect   USER.316

```
void FAR PASCAL CompUpdateRect(HWND, LPRECT, BOOL, WORD)
HWND hwnd;         /* window handle */
LPRECT lpRect;     /* pointer to RECT to adjust update region with */
BOOL bErase;       /* erase the background upon repaint */
WORD wType;        /* type of operation to perform */
```

This function adds or subtracts the specified rectangular region to or from the window's update region. It is the engine behind the documented InvalidateRect/-ValidateRect functions. The wType field accepts a number of bit flags:

```
    CUR_VALIDATE            (0x8000)
```

The specified rectangle is to be *subtracted* from the update region (i.e., validated, as by ValidateRect). If this flag is zero, the rectangle is *added* to the update region (i.e., invalidated, as by InvalidateRect).

```
    CUR_???                 (0x4000)
    CUR_CHILDREN            (0x0004)
```

Add/subtract the specified rectangle to child window update regions, except as defined by CUR_NOTCLIPCHILDREN.

```
CUR_NOTCLIPCHILDREN      (0x0001)
```

If the window style includes WS_CLIPCHILDREN, do not change their update region.

Because CompUpdateRect performs the functionality of ValidateRect/Invalidate-Rect, and because it is not exported in 3.1, there does not appear to be any good reason to call this function directly.

Support: 3.0
See also: CompUpdateRgn

CompUpdateRgn   USER.317

```
void FAR PASCAL CompUpdateRgn(HWND, HRGN, BOOL, WORD)
HWND hwnd;       /* window handle */
HRGN hRgn;       /* handle of region to adjust update region with */
BOOL bErase;     /* erase the background upon repaint */
WORD wType;      /* type of operation to perform */
```

This function adds or subtracts the specified region to or from the window's update region; it is the engine behind the documented InvalidateRgn/ValidateRgn functions. The wType field accepts a number of bit flags, only one of which is currently understood:

```
CUR_VALIDATE            (0x8000)
```

The specified region is to be *subtracted* from the update region (i.e., validated, as by ValidateRgn). If this flag is zero, the region is *added* to the update region (invalidated, as by InvalidateRgn).

```
CUR_???                 (0x4000)
CUR_CHILDREN            (0x0004)
```

Add/subtract the specified region to child window update regions, except as defined by CUR_NOTCLIPCHILDREN.

```
CUR_NOTCLIPCHILDREN     (0x0001)
```

If the window style includes WS_CLIPCHILDREN, do not change their update region.

Because it performs the functionality of ValidateRgn/InvalidateRgn, and because it is not exported in 3.1, there does not appear to be any good reason to call this function directly.

Support: 3.0
See also: CompUpdateRect

ControlPanelInfo   **USER.273**

```
void FAR PASCAL ControlPanelInfo(int, WORD, LPSTR)
int nInfoType;          /* Control panel setting number */
WORD wData;             /* Update data for some settings */
LPSTR lpBuffer;         /* Buffer for control panel setting data */
```

This function, called by CONTROL.EXE in Windows 3.0 to get/set six settings, allows certain desktop Control Panel settings to be queried and updated. The settings that can be modified by this function are not closely related. They are (with the names of the corresponding icons in Control Panel) as follows:

- Warning beep ON/OFF (Sound)
- Mouse tracking speed (Mouse)
- Window border width (Desktop)
- Key repeat rate (Keyboard)
- Language driver (International)
- Icon spacing (Desktop)

The setting and the action (set/get) is defined by the nInfoType parameter. The value of this parameter takes one of the following values, and behaves as described:

`CPI_GETBEEP (1)`

treats the two bytes pointed to by lpBuffer as a BOOL and sets its value to TRUE or FALSE depending on whether warning beeps are enabled or not. wData is ignored.

`CPI_SETBEEP (2)`

uses the value of wData (which should be TRUE or FALSE) to enable or disable warning beeps. lpBuffer is ignored.

`CPI_GETMOUSE (3)`

treats the six bytes pointed to by lpBuffer as an array of three WORDs which represent the mouse tracking speed. The Control Panel dialog controlling this setting uses a horizontal scrollbar with seven possible positions. The algorithm linking the Control Panel's seven speeds and the values of the three words works as follows. At the lowest speed, all three words are set to 0. For the next three 'notches' (n=1, 2, and 3), the third word is set to a 1, the second to a 0, and the first is set to the value of 13 - (3 * n). For the last, fastest notches (n=4, 5, and 6), the third word is set to 2, the first to 4, and the second to 24 - (3 * n)..! wData is ignored.

CPI_SETMOUSE (4)

treats the six bytes pointed to by lpBuffer as an array of three WORDs, as above, which should contain values as described in the above formula. wData is ignored. The update takes immediate effect.

CPI_GETBORDER (5)

treats the two bytes pointed to by lpBuffer as a WORD and sets its value to the currently established window border width in pixels. wData is ignored.

CPI_SETBORDER (6)

updates (all windows are updated immediately) the window border width from wData. The value is coerced into the range 1 - 50 before being used. lpBuffer is ignored.

CPI_GETKEYBOARDSPEED (10)

treats the two bytes pointed to by lpBuffer as a WORD and sets its value to the current keyboard typematic repeat rate. wData is ignored.

CPI_SETKEYBOARDSPEED (11)

updates keyboard typematic repeat rate from wData. The value is coerced into the range 1 - 32 before being used. lpBuffer is ignored.

CPI_LANGDRIVER (12)

loads the language driver DLL whose name is specified in lpBuffer. wData is ignored.

CPI_ICONSPACING (13)

either gets or sets the desktop icon spacing used for arranging the desktop and Program Manager group windows. If the lpBuffer parameter is *not* NULL, the call is assumed to be a 'get,' and the two bytes pointed to by lpBuffer are treated as a WORD whose value is set to the current icon spacing in pixels. For a 'get,' wData is ignored. If the lpBuffer parameter *is* NULL, the call is assumed to be a 'set,' and the value of wData is used to set the new icon spacing. Note, however, that a NULL value of wData is ignored.

ControlPanelInfo

Support: 3.0, 3.1

Note: Although this function is exported in versions 3.0 and 3.1, it has been superseded in 3.1 by the much more comprehensive, and documented, SystemParametersInfo function.

Example: The following example shows the use of some of the function's options.

```c
/* CPNLINFO.C */

#include <windows.h>
#include <ctype.h>
#include <stdlib.h>
#include "winio.h"

/* undocumented function */
extern WORD FAR PASCAL ControlPanelInfo(int nInfoType,
    WORD wData, LPSTR lpBuf);

#define CPI_GETBEEP             1
#define CPI_SETBEEP             2
#define CPI_GETMOUSE            3
#define CPI_SETMOUSE            4
#define CPI_GETBORDER           5
#define CPI_SETBORDER           6
#define CPI_GETKEYBOARDSPEED    10
#define CPI_SETKEYBOARDSPEED    11
#define CPI_LANGDRIVER          12
#define CPI_ICONSPACING         13


#include "checkord.c"

int main()
    {
    WORD wBuf[3];
    char bBuf[80];
    int n;

    // Ord/name check
    if (! CheckOrdName("ControlPanelInfo", "USER", 273))
        return 0;

for(;;){
    ControlPanelInfo(CPI_GETBEEP, 0, (LPSTR) &wBuf);
    printf("\nWarning beeps    : %s\n",
                    wBuf[0] ? "Enabled" : "Disabled");

    ControlPanelInfo(CPI_GETMOUSE, 0, (LPSTR) &wBuf);
    printf("Mouse speed      : %d (%d %d %d)\n",
            wBuf[2] == 0 ? 1 :
            wBuf[2] == 1 ? (16 - wBuf[0]) / 3 :
            wBuf[2] == 2 ? (27 - wBuf[1]) / 3 : -1,
            wBuf[0], wBuf[1], wBuf[2]);

    ControlPanelInfo(CPI_GETBORDER, 0, (LPSTR) &wBuf);
    printf("Border Width     : %d pixels\n", wBuf[0]);
```

ControlPanelInfo

```
ControlPanelInfo(CPI_GETKEYBOARDSPEED, 0, (LPSTR) &wBuf);
printf("Key repeat rate   : %d\n", wBuf[0]);

ControlPanelInfo(CPI_ICONSPACING, 0, (LPSTR) &wBuf);
printf("Icon spacing      : %d\n", wBuf[0]);

printf("enter type to set (w, m, b, k, i): ");

switch (toupper(getchar()))
    {
    case 'W' :
        printf("\nToggling Warning Beep switch.\n");
        ControlPanelInfo(CPI_GETBEEP, 0, (LPSTR) &wBuf);
        wBuf[0] ^= 1;
        ControlPanelInfo(CPI_SETBEEP, wBuf[0], NULL);
        break;
    case 'B' :
        printf("\nEnter border width in pixels (1-50) : ");
        gets(bBuf);
        ControlPanelInfo(CPI_SETBORDER, atoi(bBuf), NULL);
        break;
    case 'M' :
        printf("\nEnter speed (1-7) : ");
        gets(bBuf);
        if ((n = atoi(bBuf)) == 0) n = 1;
        else
        if (n > 7) n = 7;
        if (n == 1)
            { wBuf[2] = 0; wBuf[1] = 0; wBuf[0] = 0; }
        else
        if (n < 5)
            { wBuf[2] = 1; wBuf[1] = 0; wBuf[0] = 16 - (3 * n); }
        else
            { wBuf[2] = 2; wBuf[1] = 27 - (3 * n); wBuf[0] = 4; }
        ControlPanelInfo(CPI_SETMOUSE, 0, (LPSTR) &wBuf);
        break;
    case 'K' :
        printf("\nEnter keyboard typematic repeat rate (1-31) : ");
        gets(bBuf);
        ControlPanelInfo(CPI_SETKEYBOARDSPEED, atoi(bBuf), NULL);
        break;
    case 'I' :
        printf("\nEnter desktop icon spacing in pixels : ");
        gets(bBuf);
        ControlPanelInfo(CPI_ICONSPACING, atoi(bBuf), NULL);
        break;
    default :
        printf("\n");
    }
}

return 0;
}
```

ControlPanelInfo

ContScroll   USER.310

```
void FAR PASCAL ContScroll(HWND, WORD, WORD, DWORD)
HWND hwnd;        /* window owning scrollbars */
WORD wMsg;        /* unreferenced */
WORD wParam;      /* unreferenced */
DWORD lParam;     /* unreferenced */
```

This is the function which implements continuous scrolling when the user presses the left mouse button over the arrow button at either end of a scrollbar and holds it down.

This function is called from within the default scrollbar WndProc. When the left mouse button is initially pressed, a WM_VSCROLL or WM_HSCROLL message (as appropriate) is sent, and a timer is set up with a period of 200 milliseconds using the undocumented function SetSystemTimer. The callback function installed for the timer is ContScroll. Unless the user releases the left mouse button, in which case the timer is cancelled, ContScroll receives control.

It then resends the WM_xSCROLL message, and resets the timer frequency to 50 ms. The initial delay before repeat of 200 ms, and the repeat rate of 50 ms are hard-coded constants. Releasing the left mouse button discontinues the repeating action.

Support: 3.0

CreateCursorIconIndirect   USER.408

```
HANDLE FAR PASCAL CreateCursorIconIndirect(HANDLE, LPCURSORICONINFO,
    LPSTR, LPSTR)
HANDLE hInstance;
LPCURSORICONINFO lpInfo;     /* pointer to bitmap info */
LPSTR lpANDBits;             /* pointer to bitmap data */
LPSTR lpXORBits;             /* pointer to masking bits */
```

This function creates a bitmap resource to be associated with the specified instance.

This function is called by the documented CreateCursor and CreateIcon functions, and it can be used to create both cursors and icons on the fly. It returns a HANDLE that can be used as an HICON or an HCURSOR as appropriate.

Rather than use GlobalAlloc to allocate the memory for storage of the bitmap, the function uses the undocumented KERNEL function DirectResAlloc (see chapter 5). This allows the icon or cursor to be shared by multiple instances of a task. This is necessary for class icons and cursors and ensures that the memory is not freed on termination of hInstance as would happen if GlobalAlloc were used.

Use of this function is not recommended, because it affords no more capability than the CreateCursor and CreateIcon functions, and it requires the use of the undocumented CURSORICONINFO structure. This structure is the header for both Cursor

and Icon resources in memory, and is described in more detail in the
CURSORICONINFO entry in this chapter:

```
/* CURSICON.H */

typedef struct {
    POINT    pntHotSpot;      /* Cursor hot spot (ignored for icon) */
    WORD     nWidth;          /* Width of bitmap in pixels */
    WORD     nHeight;         /* Height of bitmap in pixels */
    WORD     nWidthBytes;     /* width of bitmap in bytes */
    BYTE     byPlanes;        /* number of bit planes */
    BYTE     byBitsPix;       /* number of bits per pixel */
    } CURSORICONINFO, FAR *LPCURSORICONINFO;
```

Return: If successful, returns a non-NULL HANDLE that may be cast to an HICON
or an HCURSOR; if unsuccessful, returns NULL.

See also: CURSORICONINFO, DumpIcon

Example: Creates a gunsight cursor on the fly from a monochrome bitmap using
CreateCursorIconIndirect:

```
/* CICONIND.C */

#include <windows.h>
#include "wmhandlr.h"
#include "winio.h"

/* undocumented CURSORICONINFO structure */
#include "cursicon.h"

WORD awANDBits[64] = /* AND bit mask for gunsight cursor */
       {    0x0100, 0xffff, 0xfd7e, 0xffff,
            0xfd7e, 0xffff, 0x0d60, 0xffff,
            0xed6e, 0xffff, 0xed6e, 0xffff,
            0x6d6c, 0xffff, 0x0101, 0xffff,
            0x6d6c, 0xffff, 0xed6e, 0xffff,
            0xed6e, 0xffff, 0x0d60, 0xffff,
            0xfd7e, 0xffff, 0xfd7e, 0xffff,
            0x0100, 0xffff, 0xffff, 0xffff,
            0xffff, 0xffff, 0xffff, 0xffff,
            0xffff, 0xffff, 0xffff, 0xffff,
            0xffff, 0xffff, 0xffff, 0xffff,
            0xffff, 0xffff, 0xffff, 0xffff,
            0xffff, 0xffff, 0xffff, 0xffff,
            0xffff, 0xffff, 0xffff, 0xffff,
            0xffff, 0xffff, 0xffff, 0xffff,
            0xffff, 0xffff, 0xffff, 0xffff};

WORD awXORBits[64] = {0}; /* no XOR bits needed for gunsight cursor */

/* undocumented function */
extern HANDLE FAR PASCAL CreateCursorIconIndirect(HANDLE hInstance,
```

CreateCursorIconIndirect

```
        LPCURSORICONINFO lpInfo, LPSTR lpANDbits, LPSTR lpXORbits);

#include "checkord.c"

HANDLE hNewCursor, hOldCursor;
WMHANDLER prev_lbuttondown, prev_lbuttonup;
CURSORICONINFO iconinfo;

long my_lbuttondown(HWND hwnd, WORD wMsg, WORD wParam,
    DWORD lParam)
    {
    printf("Changing the cursor to a 'rifle sight'.\n");
    hOldCursor = SetClassWord(winio_current(), GCW_HCURSOR, hNewCursor);
    SetCapture(hwnd);
    SetCursor(hNewCursor);
    return (*prev_lbuttondown)(hwnd, wMsg, wParam, lParam);
    }

long my_lbuttonup(HWND hwnd, WORD wMsg, WORD wParam,
    DWORD lParam)
    {
    printf("Changing back to the regular cursor.\n");
    SetClassWord(hwnd, GCW_HCURSOR, hOldCursor);
    ReleaseCapture();
    SetCursor(hOldCursor);
    return (*prev_lbuttonup)(hwnd, wMsg, wParam, lParam);
    }

int main()
    {
    // Ord/name check
    if (! CheckOrdName("CreateCursorIconIndirect", "USER", 408))
        return 0;

    iconinfo.pntHotSpot.x = 7;
    iconinfo.pntHotSpot.y = 7;
    iconinfo.nWidth = 32;
    iconinfo.nHeight = 32;
    iconinfo.nWidthBytes = 4;
    iconinfo.byPlanes = 1;
    iconinfo.byBitsPix = 1;

    // Create a cursor
    if ((hNewCursor = CreateCursorIconIndirect(__hInst, &iconinfo,
        (LPSTR) &awANDBits, (LPSTR) &awXORBits)) == NULL)
        {
        printf("Could not create a cursor.\n");
        return 0;
        }

    prev_lbuttondown = wmhandler_set(winio_current(),
        WM_LBUTTONDOWN, (WMHANDLER) my_lbuttondown);
    prev_lbuttonup = wmhandler_set(winio_current(),
        WM_LBUTTONUP, (WMHANDLER) my_lbuttonup);
```

CreateCursorIconIndirect

```
printf("Press the left mouse button to use a\n"
    "cursor created by CreateCursorIconIndirect().\n"
    "Release the button to restore the regular cursor\n\n"
    "Close the window to exit\n\n");

return 0;
}
```

CURSOR   **Structure**

A cursor is a global memory resource, and the HCURSOR associated with it is a global memory handle. The global memory block it refers to contains a monochrome bitmap with an undocumented CURSORICONINFO header structure. See the CURSORICONINFO and DumpIcon entries in this chapter.

CURSORICONINFO   **Structure**

This structure (included in CURSICON.H, used in the CreateCursorIconIndirect and DumpIcon example programs in this chapter) is the header of the resource format used to store both cursors and icons in memory. It is different from the file-based resource header structures principally because, once loaded, the bitmap has been processed from a possibly Device Independent Bitmap (DIB) format into a device dependent format.

It is located at offset 0 of a global memory block and is immediately followed by the bits of the device dependent bitmap as documented in the BITMAP structure entry in the SDK Reference Vol. 2.

The handle to the block is an HICON or an HCURSOR.

```
typedef struct {
    POINT   pntHotSpot;
    WORD    nWidth;
    WORD    nHeight;
    WORD    nWidthBytes;
    BYTE    byPlanes;
    BYTE    byBitsPix;
    } CURSORICONINFO, FAR *LPCURSORICONINFO;
```

The structure contains the following fields:

FIELD	DESCRIPTION
pntHotSpot	If the bitmap is to be used as a cursor, this field contains the pixel coordinates within the bitmap of the "hotspot," or the focal point of the cursor. If the structure refers to an icon this field is ignored.
nWidth	Width of the bitmap in pixels

nHeight	Height of the bitmap in pixels
nWidthBytes	Width of the bitmap in bytes
byPlanes	Number of bit planes in the bitmap. For a cursor, which must be monochrome, this will always be 1.
byBitsPix	Number of consecutive bits representing one pixel. For a cursor, this will always be 1.

Support: 3.0, 3.1
See also: CreateCursorIconIndirect, DumpIcon, LoadCursorIconHandler

---

DCE   Structure

The DCE (DC Entry) is used by USER to track one of a number of DCs that USER shares among applications. At startup, USER calls the GDI function CreateDC() five times, to obtain five DCs, and initializes a DCE for each. The key GetDC(), GetWindowDC(), and BeginPaint() functions (which are in USER, not GDI) all return a DC recorded in one of the DCEs.

For windows created with the CS_OWNDC or CS_CLASSDC class styles, additional DCs are obtained and corresponding DCEs created as needed.

That the structure has the name DCE is confirmed by the documentation for the TOOLHELP LOCALENTRY structure, which recognizes it as LT_USER_DCE of the USER local heap object types. The assumption that the E in DCE stands for Entry, however, may well be erroneous since the five DCEs are maintained (in both 3.0 and 3.1) as a singly linked list in USER's default local heap, rather than, as the word "entry" might suggest, in a static array.

```
typedef struct {
    HANDLE  hdceNext;   // 00h Next in linked list of DCEs
    HWND    hwndCurr;   // 02h Currently owning window
    HDC     hDC;        // 04h HDC that this entry refers to
    BYTE    byFlags;    // 06h Flags:
                        //        0x01 - For client area use
                        //        0x02 - For window area use
                        //        Others ???
    BYTE    byInUse;    // 07h 0 = free, 1 = in use
    BYTE    byDirty;    // 08h 1 = window needs update, 0 = does not
    BYTE    byOA;       // 09h ???
    WORD    xOrigin;    // 0Ah DC Origin X
    WORD    yOrigin;    // 0Ch DC Origin Y
    HWND    hwndTop;    // 0Eh Parent window (also using this entry?)
    HRGN    hVisRgn;    // 10h Visible region
} DCE, *HDCE;          // 12h TOTAL
```

The structure contains the following known fields:

FIELD	DESCRIPTION
hdceNext	Pointer to the next DCE in the linked list. The list is terminated by a NULL in this field.

hwndCurr	Window that is using the DC, or NULL
hDC	DC for the entry (see chapter 8)
byFlags	These bit flags appear to describe the use to which the DC is being put. Only two bits are known:
0x01	DC used for Client area
0x02	DC used for Window area
	Others are known to be used but are not currently understood.
byInUse	This flag indicates whether this DCE is in use (1) or free (0)
byDirty	If this field contains 1, the associated region needs updating, i.e., is invalid
xOrigin	Appears to be the x-coordinate of the top left of the window/client area.
yOrigin	Appears to be the y-coordinate of the top left of the window/client area.
hwndTop	Top level window of hwndCurr
hVisRgn	Visible region of window

Support: 3.0, 3.1
See also: WND and CLASS structures in this chapter, DC in chapter 8

DCHook   USER.362

```
BOOL FAR PASCAL DCHook(HDC, WORD, DWORD, DWORD)
HDC hDC;            /* display context */
WORD code;         /* DC hook callback code */
DWORD data;        /* DC hook data */
DWORD lParam;      /* DC hook lParam */
```

This is a hook function that USER installs with the GDI SetDCHook() function.

Support: 3.1
See also: SetDCHook (chapter 8)

DisableOEMLayer   USER.4

```
void FAR PASCAL DisableOEMLayer(void);
```

This function disables the Windows OEM device interface. It disables the keyboard, mouse and display drivers, and the system timer and restores the prior (probably non-graphics) video mode with a screen clear. In addition, it uses an internal call, InternalBroadcastDriverMessage, to signal to all system drivers that the

OEM layer is going down. If there is a network driver present, it too is notified. This effectively leaves the machine in "raw" DOS but still in protected mode.

See the discussion in EnableOEMLayer for more information.

Used by: WINOLDAP.MOD, WINOA286.MOD but **not** WINOA386.MOD
Support: 3.0, 3.1
See also: EnableOEMLayer, and Death, Resurrection (chapter 8)
Example: See EnableOEMLayer

DragDetect   USER.465

```
BOOL FAR PASCAL DragDetect(HWND, LPRECT)
HWND hwnd;              /* window handle */
LPPOINT lpPoint;       /* POINT from which to test drag */
```

This function can be used in a window function to determine whether a "drag" has taken place.

It should be called from within the handling of a WM_LBUTTONDOWN message. The function creates a small rectangular area surrounding the coordinates pointed at by lpPoint and then captures the cursor using SetCapture. Using a PeekMessage (WM_MOUSEXXX) loop, it then waits for one of two conditions to be met: if the user moves the mouse out of the small rectangle without releasing the left button, the function releases the capture and returns TRUE (drag in progress); if, however, the left mouse button is released while the mouse is still within the rectangle, the function returns FALSE (no drag).

The rectangular area is created by creating a rectangle of zero size at the coordinates of lpPoint and then calling InflateRect to inflate it to twice the width of a window border in both dimensions.

Within USER, DragDetect is called from one place: if a listbox control is created with an extended style of WES_NOTIFYDRAG (see the rgfExStyle field of the WND structure in this chapter), the listbox class window procedure calls DragDetect from within its WM_LBUTTONDOWN handling as part of a decision as to whether to send a WM_BEGINDRAG message (see chapter 7) to its parent widow.

Interestingly enough, it is not called by either Program Manager or File Manager. One might have expected them to call this function in preparation for a drag-and-drop session (see DragObject in this chapter).

Return: TRUE if the mouse is being dragged, otherwise FALSE
Support: 3.0, 3.1
See also: DragObject, WM_BEGINDRAG (chapter 7)

DRAGINFO   Structure

The DRAGINFO structure (included in DRAGDROP.H, which is used in the DragObject example programs in this chapter) is a major component of the 3.0 drag-and-drop protocol. It contains information about the dragged "object," and a far pointer to it is passed to a receiving application window in the lParam parameter of the undocumented WM_DRAGQUERYACCEPT and the WM_DRAGDROP messages (see chapter 7).

```
typedef struct {
    HWND hwndSource;
    HANDLE h1;
    WORD wFlags;
    HANDLE hList;
    HANDLE hOfstruct;
    int    x, y;
    long lUnknown;
    } DRAGINFO, FAR * LPDRAGINFO;
```

The structure contains the following fields:

FIELD	DESCRIPTION
hwndSource	The window from which the object is being dragged
wFlags	One of the following undocumented constants (defined in DRAGDROP.H) indicating the type of object being dragged: DRAGOBJ_PROGRAM (0x0001) single file name whose extension is among those listed in the 'Programs=' entry in the [Windows] section in WIN.INI DRAGOBJ_DATA (0x0002) single file name that is not a program DRAGOBJ_DIRECTORY (0x0003) a single subdirectory name DRAGOBJ_MULTIPLE (0x0004) two or more of any combination of the above three types As well as one of the above values, the wFlags field will contain the DRAGOBJ_EXTERNAL (0x8000) flag, if the window that receives one of the above messages is not owned by the same application instance as the sending application.
hList	A fixed local memory handle (near pointer) in the source window application data segment to a string containing the list of objects being dragged

hOfstruct   A global memory handle to a documented OFSTRUCT structure if
                            a single file is being dragged and if the filename extension has an
                            association. Otherwise, this field contains NULL

Support: 3.0, 3.1
See also: DragObject

DragObject   USER.464

```
DWORD FAR PASCAL DragObject(HWND, HWND, WORD, WORD, NPSTR, HCURSOR)
HWND hwndScope;         /* Scope in which dragging can occur */
HWND hwndObj;           /* Window initiating the DragObj call */
WORD wObjType;          /* One of the DRAGOBJ_ constants (see below) */
WORD hOfstruct;         /* handle to global OFSTRUCT or NULL */
NPSTR szList;           /* list of file/dir objects */
HCURSOR hDragCursor;    /* cursor or icon to be used during drag */
```

This function implements the server component of drag-and-drop in 3.0. It is called
by both Program Manager and File Manager. An object is an executable file, a non-
executable (data) file, a directory name, or a list of any combination of these.

Drag-and-drop is a documented feature for 3.1 applications wishing to be "clients"
(that is, to receive dragged objects) and is implemented cleanly in its approved guise.
However, the requirements of an application wishing to be a server (that is, provide
the user objects to drag) still are not documented. This function provides the means
by which both the documented protocol in 3.1, and the undocumented protocol in
both 3.0 and 3.1 described below, are implemented.

A drag-and-drop server application calls this function in response to a user initiated drag operation, usually from within the window procedure's WM_LBUTTON-
DOWN handling. That a drag is in progress can be determined using the
undocumented DragDetect function (see the DragDetect entry in this chapter).

The hwndScope parameter appears to limit which windows in the window hierarchy will be notified that there is a drag in progress and asked whether they want to
accept a drop. Passing the return from the documented GetDesktopWindow() function will ensure that all windows have the opportunity to become a client for the drop.
The hwndObj parameter is the handle of the window initiating the drag and from
which the object is being dragged.

If the object being dragged is a single file, as defined in the following paragraph,
the caller may provide an hOfstruct parameter containing a global memory handle to a
block of memory containing a documented OFSTRUCT structure describing the file.
Otherwise this parameter should be NULL.

The wFlags parameter is used to specify the type of object that is being dragged
and whether the messages should be sent to external applications. Only if the high bit
of this parameter is set can another application be notified of the drag and accept the
drop. If the high bit is not set, the drag is for internal consumption only; Program

DragObject

Manager always issues the call with the high bit set off, so drags from it are never notified to other applications. wFlags should contain *one* of the following constants ORed with DRAGOBJ_EXTERNAL (0x8000) to allow dragging outside the source application.

DRAGOBJ_PROGRAM (0x0001)	The object is a single executable file (.EXE, .COM, .DLL or .BAT).
DRAGOBJ_DATA (0x0002)	The object is a single file other than an executable.
DRAGOBJ_DIRECTORY (0x0003)	The object is a fully qualified directory name.
DRAGOBJ_MULTIPLE (0x0004)	The object is a list of files and directories.

As the user drags the "object," the function sends an undocumented message, WM_QUERYDROPOBJECT (see chapter 7), to the window under the current cursor position, i.e., the potential client. DefWindowProc, which normally handles this message, returns 0. As long as the underlying window returns 0 to this message, the cursor remains the "no-entry" type. The client window function may return 1 to the message, however, signaling acceptance of the dragged object. The message provides information to assist in deciding whether to accept. First, the wParam parameter contains a 1 if the current dragged position is over a nonclient area and a 0 if it is over the client area. Second, the lParam parameter contains a pointer to an undocumented DRAGINFO structure, described earlier. From this structure, the window can determine

- what type of object is being offered (program or data file, directory, or multiple file selection, as defined in the wFlags parameter to the DragObject call),
- the list of file/directory names,
- if a file, whether an association exists for it
- if a file, the full qualified file name.

In addition, in 3.0, another undocumented message, WM_USER+260, is repeatedly sent to the window under the cursor. The purpose of the message is unclear (wParam and lParam are always both 0). Because this message is not used in 3.1, and because not accepting it in 3.0 does not affect the operation of the protocol, it appears safe to ignore.

Upon receipt of the acceptance, DragObject now sends the undocumented WM_DRAGSELECT message to the client, signaling that conditions are go for a drop. This message acts as a flip-flop if the user drags the object out of the window; the window will receive another WM_DRAGSELECT, this time signaling that the drag-drop is off. If the user brings the object back into the window, yet another WM_DRAGSELECT is sent to it, signaling that the drag-drop is on again.

DragObject

After acceptance, and as the object is dragged, the function continues to send the WM_QUERYDROPOBJECT messages, but now it also sends undocumented WM_DRAGMOVE messages. (See chapter 7.)

Finally, when the user releases the left mouse button, "dropping" the file(s), the undocumented WM_DRAGDROP message is sent to the window. The wParam indicates the window that issued the DragObject() call, and the lParam parameter again holds the DRAGINFOPTR pointer.

The DRAGINFO structure, described in the DRAGINFO entry, contains a handle at offset 2 that should be a near pointer into the server application's near heap. This points at a null terminated string containing a list of one or more files and directories, each with a trailing space, composing the list of objects being dragged. Note that when File Manager is the server, directories in the list are fully qualified, but that files are simple file names without paths. The files and directories can be extracted from the list by simple parsing, using the separating space characters as delimiters.

The only way for a client to derive the path to the files in a list from File Manager appears to rely on knowledge that the window from which the user has dragged the objects has the directory and file spec in the caption bar; thus, we can get hold of it by calling GetWindowText on the hwndSource field of the DRAGINFO structure and parsing the directory from the returned string. In order to remain compatible with File Manager, other server applications appear to have to emulate this characteristic. This is illustrated in the example programs that follows. It is likely that there is a more practical and elegant solution to the problem, but it is not currently known.

In version 3.1, DragObject also sends a documented message, WM_DROPFILES, to the client window when the left mouse button is released. The wParam to the message is described in the version 3.1 SDK as a handle to a reserved structure. That structure is documented in the DROPINFO entry in this chapter.

An interesting feature that DragObject displays is hidden in the last parameter it is called with and that was not described above. The hDragCursor parameter accepts a handle to a cursor *or an icon!* If an icon, an internal routine, sadly not exported even by ordinal (it shows up in some CodeView symbol tables for debug versions of USER), called ColorToMonoIcon, generates a cursor-compatible monochrome bitmap from the supplied, color, icon. The DRAGOBJ example program uses the class icon for WINIO applications as the drag "cursor."

Note that the cursor that is used within the function to signify that a drag has not been accepted, the 'No Entry' universal-no sign, is a resource that can be accessed from within applications. It is, in versions 3.0 and 3.1, a USER.EXE resource with ID 100. Thus, a handle to it can be obtained by code similar to

```
hcrsNoEntry = LoadCursor(GetModuleHandle("USER.EXE"), MAKEINTRESOURCE(100));
```

The two example programs in this entry both make extensive use of the DRAGDROP.H file, which follows. The structures defined are described in the DRAGINFO and DROPINFO entries in this chapter; the messages are described in chapter 7.

```
/* DRAGDROP.H */


/* === UNDOCUMENTED MESSAGES === */

#define WM_DROPOBJECT        0x022A
#define WM_QUERYDROPOBJECT   0x022B


#define WM_BEGINDRAG         0x022C
#define WM_DRAGLOOP          0x022D


#define WM_DRAGSELECT        0x022E
#define WM_DRAGMOVE          0x022F


#ifndef WM_DROPFILES
#define WM_DROPFILES         0x0233
#endif


/* === UNDOCUMENTED CONSTANTS === */

// Used in the wFlags field of the DRAGINFO sructure
#define DRAGOBJ_PROGRAM     0x0001     // A single executable
#define DRAGOBJ_DATA        0x0002     // A single 'other' file
#define DRAGOBJ_DIRECTORY   0x0003     // A single pathed directory
#define DRAGOBJ_MULTIPLE    0x0004     // Any combination 2 or more
#define DRAGOBJ_EXTERNAL    0x8000     // ORed with one of the above

// Used as the return to the source (caller of DragObject)
#define DRAG_PRNT 0x544e5250          //'PRNT'
#define DRAG_FILE 0x454c4946          //'FILE'

/* === UNDOCUMENTED STRUCTURE === */

// Structure pointed at by lParam of WM_DRAGDROP
typedef struct {
    HWND hwndSource;   // File Manager window that owns source listbox
    HANDLE h1;         // Handle of drag icon ???
    WORD wFlags;       // One of the DRAGOBJ_ constants below. They
                       // include a top bit set, indicating drag
                       // is allowed outside source app (FileMan).
    char *szList;      // near pointer to list of files.
    HANDLE hOfstruct;  // handle to a global OFSTRUCT. If a list, or
                       // file has no association, FileMan sets
                       // this to NULL.
    int    x, y;       // Position of cursor in client coords at drop
    long lUnknown;     // ????
    } DRAGINFO, FAR * LPDRAGINFO;

// Structure in global memory - handle in wParam of WM_DROPFILES in 3.1
typedef struct {
    WORD wOfsFirst;    // Offset of the first filename in the block
    WORD xDrop;        // X coordinate of the drop point
    WORD yDrop;        // Y coordinate of the drop point
    BOOL bClient;      // 1 if Dropped on client area, 0 if NonClient
```

DragObject

```
    char chBuffer[1]; // Buffer with null-terminated list
                      //   of null-terminated strings
    } DROPINFO, FAR * LPDROPINFO;
```

Return: In 3.0, the return is either 1, indicating that the drop was successful, i.e., a client application accepted the dragged objects, or 0, indicating that the objects were not accepted by a client. In 3.1, the return is either one of the DRAG_PRNT or DRAG_FILE constants defined in the preceeding file, or 1 if the drop was not accepted by a client.

Support: 3.0, 3.1

See also: DRAGINFO, DROPINFO, and chapter 7

Note: For additional information on undocumented aspects of both client and server ends of the 3.1 drag-and-drop protocol, see Jeff Richter, "Drop Everything: How to Make Your Application Accept and Source Drag-and-Drop Files," *Microsoft Systems Journal* (May-June, 1992).

Example A: The following drag-and-drop "client" program accepts all object types and lists the names of those dropped on it. It responds to both 3.0 and 3.1 drag-and-drop protocols:

```
/* DDCLIENT.C */

#include <windows.h>
#include <string.h>
#include "wmhandlr.h"
#include "winio.h"
#include "dragdrop.h"
#ifndef __BORLANDC__
#define MK_FP(a,b)  ((void far *)(((unsigned long)(a) << 16) | (b)))
#endif

#define AboutBoxString    \
    "DDClient\n\nDragObject client example program"

BOOL tInClientArea = FALSE;

// We also get documented drag-and-drop in 3.1
// Here we don't use the documented API, but rather manipulate the
// undocumented DROPINFO structure directly.
long my_dropfiles(HWND hwnd, WORD wMsg, WORD wParam, DWORD lParam)
    {
    LPDROPINFO lpDropInfo;
    int i = 0;
    LPSTR lpszFile;

    printf("WM_DROPFILES received\n");

    lpDropInfo = (LPDROPINFO) GlobalLock(wParam);
    lpszFile = (LPSTR) &lpDropInfo->chBuffer;

    while (*lpszFile)
        {
```

```
        i++;
        printf("%02d File name : %Fs\n", i, lpszFile);
        lpszFile = (LPSTR) ((DWORD) lpszFile + lstrlen(lpszFile) + 1);
        }

    GlobalUnlock(wParam);

    // Replicates the functionality of DragFinish!
    GlobalFree(wParam);

    return 1;
    }

// Handles WM_DROPOBJECT - Sent when user releases left button
// inside our client area.
long drop_handler(HWND h, WORD wMsg, WORD wParam, DWORD lParam)
    {
    LPOFSTRUCT lpofstruct;
    LPDRAGINFO lpDragInfo;
    LPSTR lpTail, lpHead, lpFileName;
    WORD wSourceDS;
    int i = 0;
    char szPath[120];
    char *szFile;
    BOOL bPath;
    static const char *szObjType[] = {"executable", "data/text file",
        "directory", "multiple files/dirs"};

    // Reset ready for next drag/drop
    tInClientArea = FALSE;

    lpDragInfo = (LPDRAGINFO) lParam;

    // Get source app (File Manager, presumably) DS
    wSourceDS = (GetWindowWord(lpDragInfo->hwndSource, GWW_HINSTANCE)
        & 0xfffc) | 1;

    // Use wFlags field (without top bit, and decremented to
    // zero-base) as index to get object type string.
    printf("Drop in progress...\n"
        "----------------------------\n"
        "Object type  : %s\n",
        szObjType[(lpDragInfo->wFlags - 1) & 3]);

    // hOfstruct only non-NULL when a single file, and
    // extension has association
    if (lpDragInfo->hOfstruct)
        {
        lpofstruct = (LPOFSTRUCT) MK_FP(lpDragInfo->hOfstruct, 0);
        printf("01 File name : %Fs\n\t(Extension has association)\n"
            "----------------------------\n"
            "Drop completed successfully\n\n",
            lpofstruct->szPathName);

        return DRAG_FILE;
```

DragObject

```
        }

    // This returns a list of files and complete directory paths
    // by forming a far pointer into the source application's near
    // heap and parsing to space characters. If a list item has no
    // path, we assume that the source app is or emulates FileMan,
    // and use the source window title to obtain the directory.
    // This technique is not only a hack, but it only works in v3.0!
    // In 3.1 we can use the documented API.

    if ((GetWindowText(lpDragInfo->hwndSource,
            (LPSTR) szPath, sizeof(szPath))) ||
        (GetWindowText(GetParent(lpDragInfo->hwndSource),
            (LPSTR) szPath, sizeof(szPath))))
        {
        szFile = szPath + strlen(szPath);
        while (szFile && (*szFile != '\\')) szFile--;
        ++szFile;
        }
    else
        szFile = szPath;

    lpTail = (LPSTR) MK_FP(wSourceDS, (WORD) (lpDragInfo->szList));

    do {
        // Separate out next 'token', record whether it contains a path
        lpHead = lpTail;
        bPath = FALSE;
        while (*lpTail != ' ')
            if (*lpTail++ == '\\')
                bPath = TRUE;

        *lpTail = 0;

        // if list item has no path, use szPath.
        if (! bPath)
            {
            lstrcpy((LPSTR) szFile, lpHead);
            lpFileName = (LPSTR) &szPath;
            }
        else
            lpFileName = lpHead;

        printf("%02d %s : %Fs\n",
            ++i,
            bPath ? "Directory" : "File name",
            lpFileName);

        *lpTail++ = ' ';

        } while (*lpTail);

printf("----------------------------\n"
        "Drop completed successfully\n\n");
```

DragObject

```
    return DRAG_FILE;
    }


// Handles WM_QUERYDROPOBJECT - Sent whenever the object being
// dragged moves over our window.
long query_handler(HWND h, WORD w, WORD wParam, DWORD lParam)
    {
    LPDRAGINFO lpDragInfo;

    lpDragInfo = (LPDRAGINFO) lParam;

    // Dragged icon has reached client area (wParam == 0).
    // Since lParam is a DRAGINFOPTR, we can decide whether we
    // want to accept on the basis of file-type, and whether or
    // not 'associated'. This code is only here to illustrate
    // the point, and is a pointless and redundant test,
    // and accepts all object types.
    if ((wParam == 0) &&
        (lpDragInfo->wFlags == DRAGOBJ_PROGRAM) ||
        (lpDragInfo->wFlags == DRAGOBJ_DATA) ||
        (lpDragInfo->wFlags == DRAGOBJ_DIRECTORY) ||
        (lpDragInfo->wFlags == DRAGOBJ_MULTIPLE) ||
        (lpDragInfo->hOfstruct != NULL))
        return 1;
    else
        return 0;
    }

// Handles WM_DRAGSELECT - Sent whenever the object being
// dragged moves into or out of our client area. We don't actually
// need to handle this one.
long select_handler(HWND h, WORD w1, WORD w2, DWORD l)
    {
    printf("Drag %s\n",
        (tInClientArea ^= 1) ? "in progress" : "suspended");

    return 1;
    }

// Handles WM_DRAGMOVE - Sent whenever the object being
// dragged is dragged after we have signaled acceptance of it.
// We don't actually need to handle this one, either.
long move_handler(HWND h, WORD w1, WORD w2, DWORD l)
    {
    return 1;
    }

int main()
    {
    winio_settitle(__hMainWnd, "Drag'n'Drop Client");
    winio_about(AboutBoxString);

    wmhandler_set(__hMainWnd, WM_DROPOBJECT,
        (WMHANDLER) drop_handler);
```

DragObject

```
wmhandler_set(__hMainWnd, WM_QUERYDROPOBJECT,
    (WMHANDLER) query_handler);
wmhandler_set(__hMainWnd, WM_DRAGSELECT,
    (WMHANDLER) select_handler);
wmhandler_set(__hMainWnd, WM_DRAGMOVE,
    (WMHANDLER) move_handler);
wmhandler_set(__hMainWnd, WM_DROPFILES,
    (WMHANDLER) my_dropfiles);

printf("Waiting for drag'n'drop messages...\n\n");

return 0;
}
```

Example B: The following drag-and-drop "server" program allows input of one or more file names as a list of objects. Dragging from any position in the window allows the currently defined set of objects to be dragged over, and dropped on, a drag-and-drop client.

```
/* DDSERVER.C */

#include <windows.h>
#include <string.h>
#include "wmhandlr.h"
#include "winio.h"
#include "dragdrop.h"
#ifndef __BORLANDC__
#define MK_FP(a,b)  ((void far *)(((unsigned long)(a) << 16) | (b)))
#endif

/* Compile with 3.0 SDK, run with 3.0/3.1 */
extern DWORD FAR PASCAL DragObject(HWND hwndScope, HWND hwndOwner,
    WORD wFlags, WORD hOfstruct, char *szList, HCURSOR hDragCursor);

char filelist[128];
char szSaveTitle[128];
WMHANDLER prev_lbuttondown, prev_lbuttonup, prev_mousemove;
HCURSOR hDragCursor;
BOOL bDrag = FALSE;
WORD wDragType;
HANDLE hOfstruct = 0;
LPOFSTRUCT lpof;
int cObjs;
char *szArgv0;

#include "checkord.c"

BOOL do_DragObject(void)
    {
    DWORD lRet;

    puts("Dragging...");
    GetWindowText(__hMainWnd, szSaveTitle, sizeof(szSaveTitle));
```

DragObject

```
    lRet = DragObject(GetDesktopWindow(), __hMainWnd, wDragType,
        hOfstruct, (char *) &filelist, hDragCursor);
    SetWindowText(__hMainWnd, szSaveTitle);
    printf("Returned %08lX\n", lRet);

    switch (lRet)
        {
        case DRAG_PRNT :
            printf("Dropped onto a print oriented app.\n");    break;
        case DRAG_FILE :
            printf("Dropped onto a file oriented app.\n");    break;
        case 1 :
            printf("Drop accepted (rejected if v3.1).\n");    break;
        default :
            printf("Drop not completed.\n");        return FALSE;
        }
    return TRUE;
    }

void do_31Protocol(void)
    {
    DWORD pntDrop;
    HANDLE hDropInfo;
    DWORD dwSizeBlk;
    LPDROPINFO lpDropInfo;
    int i;
    LPSTR lpsz;
    char *sz;
    char szBuf[80];
    HWND hwndDrop;

    pntDrop = GetMessagePos();

    // Estimate size of allocation needed. This should be plenty.
    dwSizeBlk = (DWORD) cObjs * 128;

    hDropInfo =
        GlobalAlloc(GMEM_DDESHARE | GMEM_ZEROINIT, dwSizeBlk);

    lpDropInfo = (LPDROPINFO) GlobalLock(hDropInfo);

    lpDropInfo->wOfsFirst = 8;
    lpDropInfo->xDrop = LOWORD(pntDrop);
    lpDropInfo->yDrop = HIWORD(pntDrop);
    lpsz = (LPSTR) &lpDropInfo->chBuffer;

    // WinFile emulation!
    lstrcpy((LPSTR) &szBuf, szArgv0);

    // remove filename to leave \ terminated path
    *(strrchr(szBuf, '\\') + 1) = 0;
    sz = filelist;

    // copy in complete pathed filenames
    for (i = 0; i < cObjs; i++)
```

DragObject

```
        {
        lstrcpy(lpsz, (LPSTR) &szBuf);
        lstrcat(lpsz, (LPSTR) strtok(sz, " "));
        lpsz = (LPSTR) ((DWORD) lpsz + lstrlen(lpsz) + 1);
        sz = NULL;
        }
    for (; i > 0; i--)
        filelist[strlen(filelist)] = ' ';

    GlobalUnlock(hDropInfo);

    // Find out who to send WM_DROPFILES to
    hwndDrop = WindowFromPoint(MAKEPOINT(pntDrop));

    SendMessage(hwndDrop, WM_DROPFILES, hDropInfo, 0L);

    // In case the client app doesn't follow the rules
    GlobalFree(hDropInfo);
    }

BOOL free_sel(HWND hwnd)
    {
    GlobalFree(hOfstruct);
    return TRUE;
    }

long my_lbuttondown(HWND hwnd, WORD wMsg, WORD wParam,
    DWORD lParam)
    {
    // Only allow dragging if there is something to drag
    if (filelist[0])
        bDrag = TRUE;
    return (*prev_lbuttondown)(hwnd, wMsg, wParam, lParam);
    }

long my_lbuttonup(HWND hwnd, WORD wMsg, WORD wParam,
    DWORD lParam)
    {
    bDrag = FALSE;
    return (*prev_lbuttonup)(hwnd, wMsg, wParam, lParam);
    }

long my_mousemove(HWND hwnd, WORD wMsg, WORD wParam,
    DWORD lParam)
    {
    if (bDrag)
        {
        // Avoid 'reentrancy'
        bDrag = FALSE;
        if (do_DragObject())
            do_31Protocol();
        }
    return (*prev_mousemove)(hwnd, wMsg, wParam, lParam);
    }
```

DragObject

```
int main(int argc, char *argv[])
    {
    int i;
    char *sz;

    if (! CheckOrdName("DragObject", "USER", 464))
        return 0;

    // for later WinFile emulation (!)
    szArgv0 = argv[0];

    prev_lbuttondown = wmhandler_set(__hMainWnd, WM_LBUTTONDOWN,
        (WMHANDLER) my_lbuttondown);
    prev_lbuttonup = wmhandler_set(__hMainWnd, WM_LBUTTONUP,
        (WMHANDLER) my_lbuttonup);
    prev_mousemove = wmhandler_set(__hMainWnd, WM_MOUSEMOVE,
        (WMHANDLER) my_mousemove);
    winio_onclose(__hMainWnd, (DESTROY_FUNC) free_sel);

    // Use the class icon for the drag cursor
    hDragCursor = GetClassWord(__hMainWnd, GCW_HICON);

    // Allocate ourselves a global block for a single file
    hOfstruct = GlobalAlloc(GMEM_DDESHARE, sizeof(OFSTRUCT));

    while (TRUE)
        {
        printf("Enter file(s) and/or dir(s)\n"
            "separated by a single space:\n");
        gets(filelist);
        strupr(filelist);

        // Ensure it is space char terminated
        if (filelist[strlen(filelist) - 1] != ' ')
            strcat(filelist, " ");
        printf("List is <%s>\n", filelist);
        for (i = 0, cObjs = 0; filelist[i]; i++)
            if (filelist[i] == ' ') cObjs++;

        // Detect the 'object' type
        if (cObjs > 1)
            wDragType = DRAGOBJ_MULTIPLE;
        else
        if (filelist[strlen(filelist) - 2] == '\\')
            wDragType = DRAGOBJ_DIRECTORY;
        else
            {
            lpof = (LPOFSTRUCT) GlobalLock(hOfstruct);
            OpenFile((LPSTR) &filelist, lpof, OF_PARSE);
            printf("Filename parsed to: %Fs\n",
                (LPSTR) &lpof->szPathName);
            if ((sz = strchr(filelist, '.')) &&
                ((strncmp((char *) (sz+1), "EXE", 3) == 0) ||
                (strncmp((char *) (sz+1), "BAT", 3) == 0) ||
                (strncmp((char *) (sz+1), "COM", 3) == 0)))
                wDragType = DRAGOBJ_PROGRAM;
```

DragObject

```
        else
            wDragType = DRAGOBJ_DATA;
        wDragType |= DRAGOBJ_EXTERNAL;
        GlobalUnlock(hOfstruct);
        }
    }
    return 0;
    }
```

DROPINFO   Structure

A drag-and-drop client protocol is documented in version 3.1 for those applications that want to accept files dragged by the user from File Manager. The documented WM_DROPFILES message passes to the receiving application a handle to an undocumented, "internal" structure in the global heap. This DROPINFO structure contains information about the file/directories that are being dropped, together with the coordinates in the window at which the object(s) were dropped, and is acted upon by the documented DragFinish and DragQueryFiles functions. It is created by the DragObject function in version 3.1.

The DROPINFO structure, described below, is created by the undocumented DragObject function in version 3.1 at the same time as it creates the undocumented DRAGINFO structure described elsewhere in the chapter. In the same way as the DRAGINFO structure is referenced via the lParam of the undocumented WM_QUERYDROPOBJECT and WM_DROPOBJECT messages (see chapter 7), a handle to the DROPINFO structure is passed via the wParam of the documented WM_DROPFILES message.

```
typedef struct {
    WORD wOfsFirst;
    WORD xDrop;
    WORD yDrop;
    BOOL bClient;
    char chBuffer[1];
    } DROPINFO, FAR * LPDROPINFO;
```

The structure contains the following fields:

FIELD	DESCRIPTION
wOfsFirst	The offset in the structure of the first file name string. Viewed alternatively, it is the length of the header.
xDrop	Client window X coordinate of the drop point
yDrop	Client window Y coordinate of the drop point
bClient	TRUE (1) if drop was in client area of window, FALSE (0) if not.
chBuffer	Variable length buffer containing a list of null terminated strings. The list is terminated by a final, NULL string.

Support: 3.1
See also: DRAGINFO, DragObject

DumpIcon   USER.459

```
DWORD FAR PASCAL DumpIcon(LPCURSORICONINFO, WORD FAR *,
        LPSTR FAR *, LPSTR FAR *)
LPCURSORICONINFO lpInfo;      /* Pointer to Cursor/Icon info */
WORD FAR *lpLen;              /* Pointer to header length word */
LPSTR FAR *lpXORBits;        /* Receives pointer to buffer */
LPSTR FAR *lpANDMask;        /* Receives pointer to buffer */
```

DumpIcon dissects the structure pointed to by lpInfo and returns ("dumps") information about it.

This function works with both cursor and icon resources. The word pointed to by
the lpLen parameter is filled with the length of the CURSORICONINFO structure;
the pointer pointed to by the lpXORBits parameter is set to the address of the XOR
bitmap; and the pointer pointed to by the lpANDBits parameter is set to the address
of the AND bitmap.

Return: On failure, the function returns 0. Otherwise, the low word of the return
specifies the size in bytes of a single plane of the bitmap. The high word specifies the
size in bytes of the entire bitmap. In the case of a cursor, which can currently be only
black and white, these will always be the same. In the case of an icon, the high word
will be bPlanes * lowWord.
Support: 3.0, 3.1
Used by: Program Manager
Note: Uses the undocumented CURSORICONINFO structure.
See also: CreateCursorIconIndirect, CURSORICONINFO
Example: Uses DumpIcon to display information about the WINIO class icon and
cursor.

```
/* DUMPICON.C */

#include <windows.h>
#include "winio.h"

/* undocumented structure--see CURSORICONINFO */
#include "cursicon.h"

/* undocumented function */
extern DWORD FAR PASCAL DumpIcon(LPCURSORICONINFO lpInfo,
    WORD FAR *lpLen,          // Length of header
```

```
    LPSTR FAR *lpXORBits,     // Pointer to XOR bits
    LPSTR FAR *lpANDMask      // Pointer to AND bits
    );

#include "checkord.c"

int main()
    {
    DWORD dwSize;
    WORD wHdrLen;
    LPSTR lpXOR;
    LPSTR lpAND;

    // Ord/name check
    if (! CheckOrdName("DumpIcon", "USER", 459))
        return 0;

    if ((dwSize = DumpIcon(
            (LPCURSORICONINFO) LockResource(
                (HANDLE) GetClassWord(winio_current(), GCW_HCURSOR)),
            (WORD FAR *) &wHdrLen,
            (LPSTR FAR *) &lpXOR,
            (LPSTR FAR *) &lpAND)) == 0)
        {
        printf("Could not DumpIcon the class cursor.\n");
        return 0;
        }

    FreeResource((HANDLE) GetClassWord(winio_current(), GCW_HCURSOR));

    printf("Dump of the winio_app class CURSOR\n"
           "----------------------------------\n"
           "Header length       : %d bytes\n"
           "Single plane size   : %d\n"
           "Full bitmap size    : %d\n"
           "XOR bitmap address  : %Fp\n"
           "AND bitmap address  : %Fp\n\n",
               wHdrLen, (WORD) dwSize,
               (WORD) (dwSize >> 16), lpXOR, lpAND);

    if ((dwSize = DumpIcon(
            (LPCURSORICONINFO) LockResource(
                (HANDLE) GetClassWord(winio_current(), GCW_HICON)),
            (WORD FAR *) &wHdrLen,
            (LPSTR FAR *) &lpXOR,
            (LPSTR FAR *) &lpAND)) == 0)
        {
        printf("Could not DumpIcon the class icon.\n");
        return 0;
        }

    FreeResource((HANDLE) GetClassWord(winio_current(), GCW_HICON));

    printf("Dump of the winio_app class ICON\n"
           "--------------------------------\n"
```

```
"Header length        : %d bytes\n"
"Single plane size     : %d\n"
"Full bitmap size      : %d\n"
"XOR bitmap address    : %Fp\n"
"AND bitmap address    : %Fp\n\n",
     wHdrLen, (WORD) dwSize,
     (WORD) (dwSize >> 16), lpXOR, lpAND);

    printf("Program terminated");
    return 0;
}
```

EnableOEMLayer   USER.3

```
void FAR PASCAL EnableOEMLayer(void);
```

This function enables the Windows OEM device interface, i.e., the interface between the Windows device independent API and BIOS and DOS device drivers. While the OEM layer is disabled, access to devices is not available from the messaging interface; any application that disables the OEM layer must use traditional interrupts for console communication, for example.

When the OEM layer is reenabled, the screen is restored to graphics mode and the OEM layer takes over control of device management. Specifically, the GDI layer is resurrected with a call to the undocumented Resurrection function, and then input from the mouse, keyboard, and system timer is reenabled. System device drivers are notified that the OEM layer is coming up using a call to InternalBroadcastDriverMessage, (which is not exported). If there is a network device driver, it too is notified. Finally, the desktop is repainted; the message interface again becomes the means by which applications communicate with devices.

In real mode (Windows 3.0 only) and Windows standard mode, which runs in the 286 protected mode of the 80286/80386 processors, this is the means by which the Windows "Old App" (DOS) control application (WINOLDAP/WINOA286) disables/enables the Windows device layer to allow traditional DOS applications to run.

In 386 Enhanced mode, where Windows runs in the V86 mode of the 80386 processor, DOS applications run in separate virtual machines (VM) and can be "windowed" and preemptively multitasked. In this mode, the control program (WINOA386) does *not* use Enable/DisableOEMLayer(), which do, however, still work.

Used by: WINOLDAP.MOD, WINOA286.MOD, but **not** WINOA386.MOD
Support: 3.0, 3.1.
See also: DisableOEMLayer, and Death, Resurrection (chapter 8)
Example: Uses DisableOEMLayer and EnableOEMLayer to switch into full screen text mode from within a Windows application.

```c
/* OEMLAYER.C */

#include <windows.h>
#include <dos.h>
#include "winio.h"

/* undocumented functions */
extern void FAR PASCAL EnableOEMLayer(void);
extern void FAR PASCAL DisableOEMLayer(void);

#include "checkord.c"

void b800display(char *szDisplay)
    {
    unsigned lineofs = 0, charofs = 0, scrsel;

    printf("Screen Selector is %04x\n",
    scrsel = (WORD)
            GetProcAddress(GetModuleHandle("KERNEL"), "__B800h"));

    for (; *szDisplay; szDisplay++)
        switch (*szDisplay) {
            case '\r' : charofs = 0; break;
            case '\n' : lineofs += 160; break;
            default :
                *(WORD FAR *) MK_FP(scrsel, lineofs+charofs) =
                            0xe00 | *szDisplay;
                charofs += 2;
            }
    }

int main()
    {
    // Ord/name check
    if (! (CheckOrdName("EnableOEMLayer", "USER", 3)) &&
            (CheckOrdName("DisableOEMLayer", "USER", 4)))
        return 0;

    DisableOEMLayer();
    b800display("\n"
        "The OEM layer has been disabled, and normal Windows\r\n"
        "keyboard and display handling have been suspended.\r\n"
        "Direct writes to b800:0 are being used to display this,\r\n"
        "and a call to Int 16h will be used to get your keystroke.\r\n"
        "\r\n"
        "Press a key to return.");

    _asm {
        mov ah, 0
        int 16h
        }

    EnableOEMLayer();

    printf("\n\nProgram terminated");
```

EnableOEMLayer

```
return 0;
}
```

EndMenu   USER.187

```
void FAR PASCAL EndMenu(void);
```

EndMenu allows an application to take down the current user menu or ensure that there is no currently active menu. It can be used by applications to take down a menu when an event occurs that requires attention. The function releases captives, inverts bits, kills timers, and does whatever else is needed to get Windows out of menu "mode."

The following example uses a timer event to cancel the current menu. Note that EndMenu does not take any HWND or HMENU parameters. It ends the current menu active in the system, independent of application, as shown by running the example program and minimizing it. Any subsequent application or system menu activated in any application on the desktop will be taken down from the timed calls to EndMenu.

This function is called extensively by Microsoft's own Windows applications, although it is not known why. It is also called by DefWindowProc().

Used by: Excel, VisualBasic, WinWord
Support: 3.0, 3.1
Example:

```
/* ENDMENU.C */

#include <windows.h>
#include "winio.h"

/* undocumented function */
extern void FAR PASCAL EndMenu(void);

#include "checkord.c"

HANDLE hTimer;
FARPROC lpfnTimerFunc;

WORD FAR PASCAL TimerFunc(HWND hwnd, WORD wMsg,
    int nIDEvent, DWORD dwTime)
    {
    EndMenu();
    return 1;
    }

BOOL CleanUp(HWND hwnd)
    {
    FreeProcInstance(lpfnTimerFunc);
```

```
    KillTimer(winio_current(), hTimer);
    return TRUE;
    }

int main()
    {
    HMENU hMenu, hPopup;

    // Ord/name check
    if (! CheckOrdName("EndMenu", "USER", 187))
        return 0;

    lpfnTimerFunc = MakeProcInstance((FARPROC) TimerFunc, __hInst);

    hPopup = CreateMenu();
    AppendMenu(hPopup, MF_GRAYED | MF_STRING,
        1, "Watch me disappear...");
    AppendMenu(hPopup, MF_GRAYED | MF_STRING,
        2, ".. within 3 seconds.");

    hMenu = winio_hmenumain(winio_current());
    AppendMenu(hMenu, MF_ENABLED | MF_STRING | MF_POPUP,
        hPopup, "Click Me");

    hTimer = SetTimer(winio_current(), 10, 3000, lpfnTimerFunc);

    winio_onclose(winio_current(), (DESTROY_FUNC) CleanUp);

    printf("\nClick once on the menu selection \"Click Me\" above,\n"
        "leaving the popup visible. Within a couple of seconds\n"
        "the popup will disappear by itself. This is caused by\n"
        "a call to EndMenu() within a timer event handler.\n\n"
        "Close the window to exit.");

    return 0;
    }
```

FarCallNetDriver   USER.500

```
void FAR FarCallNetDriver(void);
// takes function pointer offset in BX
// all parameters to WNet* function are already on stack
```

Most of the WNet* functions in USER, which are documented in the Windows
Device Driver Kit (DDK) *Device Driver Adaptation Guide*, use the FarCallNetDriver()
function to call through to the actual WNet* functions in a network device driver
(such as NETWARE.DRV, MSNET.DRV, or LANMAN.DRV). This function is used
in both 3.0 and 3.1, but is only exported in 3.0.

   USER links to the network driver at run-time, using GetProfileString() to get the
driver name from the network.drv= setting in the [boot] section of SYSTEM.INI,

LoadLibrary() to turn the driver name into a module handle, and GetProcAddress() to get a far function pointer for each WNet* function supported by the driver. The functions supported by the driver are returned from its WNetGetCaps() function, which USER calls. The function pointers are placed in a table which FarCallNetDriver() uses to JMPF to the appropriate function in the driver:

```
00h    IWNETOPENJOB
04h    IWNETCLOSEJOB
08h    IWNETABORTJOB
0Ch    IWNETHOLDJOB
10h    IWNETRELEASEJOB
14h    IWNETCANCELJOB
18h    IWNETSETJOBCOPIES
1Ch    IWNETWATCHQUEUE
20h    IWNETUNWATCHQUEUE
24h    IWNETLOCKQUEUEDATA
28h    IWNETUNLOCKQUEUEDATA
2Ch    IWNETGETCONNECTION
30h    WNETGETCAPS2
34h    IWNETDEVICEMODE
38h    IWNETBROWSEDIALOG
3Ch    IWNETGETUSER
40h    IWNETADDCONNECTION
44h    IWNETCANCELCONNECTION
48h    IWNETGETERROR
4Ch    IWNETGETERRORTEXT
50h    WNETENABLE
54h    WNETDISABLE
5Ch    WNETWRITEJOB
60h    WNETCONNECTDIALOG
64h    WNETDISCONNECTDIALOG
68h    WNETCONNECTIONDIALOG
6Ch    WNETVIEWQUEUEDIALOG
70h    WNETPROPERTYDIALOG
74h    WNETGETDIRECTORYTYPE
78h    WNETDIRECTORYNOTIFY
7Ch    WNETGETPROPERTYTEXT
```

Functions prefaced IWNET* rather than WNET* are "internal" versions of the exported functions. In 3.1, the exported function (in LAYER) does parameter validation, and then (assuming all parameters are kosher) jumps to the internal version. Thus, those functions marked WNET* rather than IWNET* above do not have the parameter-validation layer.

WNet* functions not appearing at all in this table are implemented by USER itself. These include the undocumented WNetErrorText() function and the documented WNetRestoreConnection() function. If WNetRestoreConnection() is called in a funny way (described in the DDK) by the 3.1 File Manager, WNet-RestoreConnection() performs initialization.

Support: 3.0 (also present in 3.1, but not exported)
See also: WNetErrorText

FarCallNetDriver

FFFE_FarFrame   USER.341

```
FFFE_FarFrame proc far
;; cs:ip on the stack points to two bytes:
;; first is count of words of local stack space needed by function
;; second is count of words of function parameters expected on the stack
```

FFFE_FarFrame appears to be a special case of the WinFarFrame function (see the WinFarFrame entry) for a special _FFFE code segment in USER.EXE. As with WinFarFrame there is a corresponding set of three routines, which are not exported but which might be named FFFE_NearFrame, FFFE_FarFrameUndo, and FFFE_NearFrameUndo.

_FFFE appears to be a segment that is relocated to high memory in real mode.

Support: 3.0
See also: WinFarFrame

FillWindow   USER.324

```
void FAR PASCAL FillWindow(HWND, HWND, HDC, HANDLE)
HWND hwndParent;        /* handle of parent or NULL */
HWND hwnd;              /* handle of target window */
HDC hDC;                /* window display context */
HANDLE hBrush;          /* handle of brush to fill with */
                        /* OR CTLCOLOR_ constant */
```

FillWindow paints the window specified by hwnd using hBrush. If hwndParent is not NULL, the hBrush parameter may specify one of the documented CTLCOLOR_ control type constants for the child window, in which case a WM_CTLCOLOR is sent to the parent window to allow it to set the brush type that is to be used.

This function is used extensively within USER itself. Calls to FillWindow can be seen in the sources for DefWindowProc (DEFWND.C) and DefDlgProc (DEFDLG.C), supplied with the SDK, in the handling of WM_ERASEBKGND and WM_ICON-ERASEBKGND messages, and appears to be used for a similar purpose, namely to paint backgrounds, in other built-in window class WndProcs. FillWindow() calls the undocumented PaintRect() function, which in turn calls the documented FillRect() function.

Support: 3.0, 3.1
Note: If the hBrush parameter specifies a CTLCOLOR_ constant and the hwndParent parameter is NULL, the function fails benignly, but with *no indication*.

Example:

```
/* FILLWIND.C */

#include <windows.h>
#include "wmhandlr.h"
#include "winio.h"

/* undocumented function */
extern void FAR PASCAL FillWindow(HWND hwndParent, HWND hwnd,
    HDC hDC, HANDLE hBrush);

#include "checkord.c"

long dblclk(HWND hwnd, WORD wMsg, WORD wParam, DWORD lParam)
    {
    HDC hDC = GetDC(hwnd);
    FillWindow(NULL, hwnd, hDC, GetStockObject(DKGRAY_BRUSH));
    ReleaseDC(hwnd, hDC);
    puts("The rest of the window should now be dark gray");
    puts("Double click on a text line to do it again");
    return 1;
    }

int main()
    {
    // Ord/name check
    if (! CheckOrdName("FillWindow", "USER", 324))
        return 1;

    wmhandler_set(winio_current(),
        WM_LBUTTONDBLCLK, (WMHANDLER) dblclk);

    puts("Double click on a text line to turn the window dark gray");
    puts("Close the window to exit");

    return 0;
    }
```

FinalUserInit   USER.400

```
void FAR PASCAL FinalUserInit(void);
```

Called by KERNEL, this function allows USER to create the desktop background at the end of the Windows initialization process and before the shell, such as Program Manager, is loaded. FinalUserInit calls various GDI functions to create the desktop bitmap and paint the initial background, and then calls the apparent GDI parallel of this function, FinalGdiInit, as the last step.

Support: 3.0, 3.1
Called by: KERNEL

GetControlBrush   USER.326

```
HANDLE FAR PASCAL GetControlBrush(HWND, HDC, WORD)
HWND hwnd;              /* Window owning the control */
HDC hDC;               /* Device context to use */
WORD wControlType;     /* Control type (static, button, edit, etc) */
```

This function retrieves the handle of the brush in use for the given control type within the specified device context of the specified window. The function is implemented using SendMessage (WM_CTLCOLOR).

The wControlType parameter expects values from the CTLCOLOR_ series of documented constants.

Return: A HANDLE to the brush, or NULL if any of the parameters is invalid or not found
Support: 3.0, 3.1
Used by: Excel

GetDesktopHwnd   USER.278

```
HWND FAR PASCAL GetDesktopHwnd(void);
```

GetDesktopHwnd is an undocumented alias for the documented GetDesktopWindow function.

Return: the HWND of the desktop window.
Support: 3.0, 3.1

GetFilePortName   USER.343

```
WORD FAR PASCAL GetFilePortName(LPOFSTRUCT)
LPOFSTRUCT lpofstruct;         /* OFSTRUCT buffer for user specified file */
```

This function displays a "Print to File" dialog box and returns the user-specified file information into the OFSTRUCT pointed at by the lpofstruct parameter.

In the Connect dialog box in the Printers section of the Control Panel, a list of Ports is available to which a printer driver can be connected. After others, recognizable as actual PC hardware ports, such as LPT:, LPT2:, COM1: etc., is listed the FILE: port. The printer driver itself does not need to know about the port through which its output is to be sent, and the FILE: port is treated no differently at this stage than the others, even though the destination of output is a file, not a device. Instead, the port to be used for output is passed by the driver in its call to the GDI OpenJob function when an application initiates a print job. OpenJob calls GetFilePortName through a far pointer initialized presumably at GDI startup time. (So, GDI *does* call into USER, at least for this one case.)

The function creates the user-specified file if it does not already exist; if it does exist, the user is presented with an "Overwrite File" dialog box soliciting permission for the file to be truncated. If the user cancels the operation, the function returns the documented constant SP_USERABORT; otherwise it returns TRUE.

Return: TRUE (1) if the user completes the operation, SP_USERABORT(-3) if the Cancel button is pressed or the user presses Escape
Support: 3.1
Example: The following program uses GetFilePortName to obtain a print file name:

```
/* FPRTNAME.C */

#include <windows.h>
#include <string.h>
#include "winio.h"

/* undocumented function */
extern WORD FAR PASCAL GetFilePortName(LPOFSTRUCT lpofstruct);

#include "checkord.c"

int main()
    {
    WORD wRet;
    OFSTRUCT ofstruct;

    if (! CheckOrdName("GetFilePortName", "USER", 343))
        return 0;

    printf("This program demonstrates the\n"
        "GetFilePortName function which\n"
        "puts up a \"Print to File\" dialog box.\n\n");
    winio_setecho(winio_current(), FALSE);

    for (;;)
        {
        wRet = GetFilePortName((LPOFSTRUCT) &ofstruct);

        printf("GetFilePortName returned %d\n", wRet);
        if (wRet == 1)
            printf(
                "In the OFSTRUCT:\n"
                "structure length: %d\n"
                "fixed disk file : %s\n"
                "dos error code  : %d\n"
                "full file name  : %s\n",
                ofstruct.cBytes,
                ofstruct.fFixedDisk ? "Yes" : "No",
                ofstruct.nErrCode,
```

GetFilePortName

```
            ofstruct.szPathName);

    printf("\nPress a key to do it again\n"
        "or close the window to exit\n\n");
    getchar();
    }

    return 0;
    }
```

GetIconID

```
WORD FAR PASCAL GetIconID(HANDLE, DWORD)
HANDLE hResource;       /* Resource handle of cursor/icon */
DWORD dwResType;        /* 1 (cursor) or 3 (icon) */
```

This function returns the ID number of the selected icon *or cursor* resource in the resource directory of the associated program file. It is called from within the documented LoadIcon function and by the Windows 3.1 Object Packager.

This function was present in 3.0 but not exported. It appears that it has been exported specifically for Object Packager as a means for it to relate an HICON back to the **id** that the icon has in the owning application's resource table.

Return: ID number of the specified resource in the program file resource directory
Used by: PACKAGER.EXE
Support: 3.1

GetInternalWindowPos

```
WORD FAR PASCAL GetInternalWindowPos(HWND, LPRECT, LPPOINT)
HWND hwnd;              /* window to get info on */
LPRECT lprectWnd;       /* RECT to receive window coords */
LPPOINT lppointIcon;    /* POINT to receive icon position */
```

This function returns information about the specified window's active coordinates, its icon position when iconized, and its current state. Specifically, the lprectWnd parameter points to an application-supplied RECT buffer that the function fills with the current screen coordinates that the window occupies when it is not iconized or maximized. The lppointIcon points to an application-supplied POINT buffer that the function fills with the top left screen coordinates of the icon position that the window occupies when minimized. The function return indicates the window's current state (hidden, normal, minimized, or maximized).

Note that in Windows 3.1 the documented GetWindowPlacement function, together with the WINDOWPLACEMENT structure, provides the same capability through a slightly different interface. However, since most Program Manager replacements written for Windows 3.0 rely on GetInternalWindowPos, it continues to exist, still undocumented, in version 3.1 and even, it appears, in the Win32 NT version of USER.

Return: One of the ShowWindow constants, reflecting the current state of the window (SW_HIDE, SW_SHOWNORMAL, SW_SHOWMINIMIZED, or SW_SHOWMAXIMIZED)

Support: 3.0, 3.1

Notes:

1. Until a window has been iconized, its icon position will be reported as (-1, -1). Similarly, until a window has been activated, its window coordinates will be reported as (-1, -1, -1, -1).

2. The function has no way of reporting an invalid hwnd parameter other than to return 0, or SW_HIDE.

Used by: PROGMAN.EXE, Norton Desktop

See also: SetInternalWindowPos

Example: See SetInternalWindowPos later in this chapter for an example illustrating both GetInternalWindowPos and SetInternalWindowPos.

GetMessage2   USER.323

```
BOOL FAR PASCAL GetMessage2(LPMSG, HWND, WORD, WORD, WORD, BOOL)
LPMSG lpMsg;       /* message structure to receive available message */
HWND hwnd;         /* window for which message is being retrieved */
WORD wFilterMin;   /* lowest message to be retrieved */
WORD wFilterMax;   /* highest message to be retrieved */
WORD wRemove;      /* Remove and/or yield, or neither (PM_ constants) */
BOOL bWait;        /* wait if no messages or return immediately */
```

This function is the back end to the documented PeekMessage and GetMessage functions. The PeekMessage function pushes an extra FALSE (do not wait) bWait parameter onto the stack and then jumps to this function; GetMessage pushes a PM_REMOVE wRemove parameter and a TRUE (wait for a message) bWait parameter and falls through to this function.

It is neither recommended nor necessary to use this function; it is included here only for completeness.

Return: If bWait was FALSE, returns TRUE if a message was waiting in the task message queue in the specified range, for the specified window. If bWait was TRUE, returns FALSE unless the message retrieved was WM_QUIT, in which case it returns TRUE! Alternatively, and more legibly, in pseudocode:

```
if (bWait)
    return bMessageWaiting;
else
    return (msg == WM_QUIT);
```

Support: 3.0

GetMouseEventProc   USER.337

```
FARPROC FAR PASCAL GetMouseEventProc(void);
```

This function returns the address of the mouse interrupt handler, Mouse_Event (described later in this chapter). The mouse interrupt handler is called asynchronously, directly in response to mouse moves and mouse button presses.

To be strictly accurate, Mouse_Event is not an interrupt handler but is called from the interrupt handler in MOUSE.DRV. It is possible, as shown in the example below, to feed or simulate mouse events by calling the function directly. (The 3.1 SDK says that you can't use the documented hardware_event() function to do this.) An assembler procedure header for the MouseEventProc is shown below. It takes parameters passed in registers:

```
MouseEventProc       proc far
;; AX:        Event type - may contain one or other or both (ORed) of ME_MOVE
;; and one of the ME_ button constants
;; BX:        relative horizontal mouse movement if (AX & ME_MOVE), signed.
;; CX:        relative vertical mouse movement if (AX & ME_MOVE), signed.
;; DX:        unknown. always contains 2.
```

If synchronous event generation into a specific window is sufficient, using SendMessage to generate mouse movements is the recommended course. This function, however, enables the asynchronous generation of mouse events, without regard to the window that will receive them. The events go into the System Message Queue.

It is interesting that there is no parallel function for obtaining the USER keyboard event handler, Keybd_Event, described later in this chapter. However,

```
lpKbdEventProc =
  GetProcAddress(GetModuleHandle("USER"), "Keybd_Event");
```

appears to work, and

```
lpMseEventProc =
  GetProcAddress(GetModuleHandle("USER"), "Mouse_Event"));
```

appears to be functionally equivalent to GetMouseEventProc.

Return: A FARPROC address of the USER mouse event handler
Support: 3.0, 3.1
See also: SetEventHook, Keybd_Event, Mouse_Event, System Message Queue
Example: Moves the mouse in a rectangular path using GetMouseEventProc.

```
/* GTMSEVNT.C */

#include <windows.h>
#include "winio.h"

#ifdef __BORLANC__
#define _asm asm
#endif

#define ME_MOVE      0x01
#define ME_LDOWN     0x02
#define ME_LUP       0x04
#define ME_RDOWN     0x08
#define ME_RUP       0x10

FARPROC lpfnMouseEventProc;
FARPROC lpfnTimerFunc;
int i;
int xInc;
int yInc;
HANDLE hTimer;


/* undocumented function */
extern FARPROC FAR PASCAL GetMouseEventProc(void);

#include "checkord.c"

BOOL StopMoving(HWND hwnd)
    {
    KillTimer(winio_current(), hTimer);
    FreeProcInstance(lpfnTimerFunc);
    return TRUE;
    }

WORD FAR PASCAL TimerFunc(HWND hwnd, WORD wMsg, int id, DWORD dwTime)
    {
    if (++i & 7)
        {
        // This trickery simply moves the mouse in a rectangular path
        if ((xInc = 32 - (((i >> 3) & 3) * 16)) == 32)
            xInc = 0;
        if ((yInc = 32 - ((((i + 24) >> 3) & 3) * 16)) == 32)
            yInc = 0;
        }
```

GetMouseEventProc

```
    _asm {
        mov     ax, ME_MOVE;
        mov bx, xInc;
        mov     cx, yInc;
        mov dx, 2;
        call    dword ptr [lpfnMouseEventProc];
        }

    return 1;
    }

int main()
    {
    // Ord/name check
    if (! CheckOrdName("GetMouseEventProc", "USER", 337))
        return 0;

    lpfnTimerFunc = MakeProcInstance((FARPROC) TimerFunc, __hInst);

    printf("Mouse event proc is at %Fp\n",
        lpfnMouseEventProc = GetMouseEventProc());

    printf("The mouse will now move as if by magic!\n\n");

    hTimer = SetTimer(winio_current(), 1, 30, lpfnTimerFunc);

    winio_onclose(winio_current(), (DESTROY_FUNC) StopMoving);

    printf("\nClose window to exit! (Use F4)");

    return 0;
    }
```

GetNextQueueWindow   USER.274

```
HANDLE FAR PASCAL GetNextQueueWindow(HWND hwnd, int nWhichWay);
HWND hwnd;                       /* relative to this window */
int nWhichWay;                   /* Next(0)/Prev(> 0) queued window */
```

The USER window manager maintains all application and unowned windows in the system in what is known as Z order. This list reflects a window's position 'down' from the top of the desktop. The z order is primarily controlled by the documented SetWindowPos function, which appears to be called in response to any window rearrangement operation, including calls of documented functions such as Bring-WindowToTop and ShowWindow, and user operations such as the use of the Alt-Tab keystroke.

GetNextQueueWindow returns the last active window in the hierarchy of windows from the next (lower, or further from the desktop) or previous (higher, or closer to the desktop) top-level application window in the z order, using the hwndLastActive

field of the WND structure, described elsewhere in this chapter, and a GetWindow
(GW_HWNDPREV/NEXT) loop.

The example program below uses another undocumented function, Switch-
ToThisWindow, to activate the next or previously queued window.

Return: HWND of the next/previous active window
Support: 3.0
Used by: WINOA386.MOD
Example: Uses SwitchToThisWindow to activate the window returned by GetNext-
QueueWindow.

```c
/* GETNEXTQ.C */

#include <windows.h>
#include <ctype.h>
#include "winio.h"

/* undocumented functions */
extern HANDLE FAR PASCAL GetNextQueueWindow(HWND hwnd, int nWhichWay);
extern void FAR PASCAL SwitchToThisWindow(HWND hwnd, BOOL tRestore);

#define GNQW_PREVIOUS    1
#define GNQW_NEXT        0

#include "checkord.c"

int main()
    {
    // Ord/name check
    if (! CheckOrdName("GetNextQueueWindow", "USER", 274))
        return 0;

    printf("About to use SwitchToThisWindow() to\n"
        "switch to the next/previous queued window\n");

    printf("Press N or P for Next or Previous window : ");

    SwitchToThisWindow(
        GetNextQueueWindow(winio_current(),
            toupper(getchar()) == 'N' ? GNQW_NEXT : GNQW_PREVIOUS,
            TRUE);

    printf("\n\nProgram terminated");
    return 0;
    }
```

GetQueueStatus   **USER.334**

```c
WORD FAR PASCAL GetQueueStatus(void);
```

This function returns the queue status flags at offset 42h (3.0) or 44h (3.1) in the calling task's Task Queue structure (see the Task Queue entry in chapter 5).

GetQueueStatus is almost identical to the documented GetInputState function; GetQueueStatus returns the entire QueueStatus word, where GetInputState masks off all but the QS_MSEKBDWAITING and QS_TIMERWAITING bits. GetInputState is implemented as GetQueueStatus( ) & 5.

The documented GetInputState has been touted as a way to significantly improve system performance (see Microsoft's Knowledge Base article, "Use of GetInputState() Is Faster Than Using PeekMessage"). Normally, an application that needs to perform some processing while waiting for a message will use the PeekMessage function. GetInputState, which is a very small and efficient function, provides a very cheap way to determine if there are any user input or timer messages waiting, instead of using the more processor-intensive PeekMessage function.

GetQueueStatus appears to offer the same advantages as GetInputState, and more. Instead of the subset of messages notified by GetInputState, GetQueueStatus reports on all waiting messages.

Return: The application task's QueueStatus word
Support: 3.0, 3.1
See also: Task Queue structure in chapter 5

GetTaskFromHwnd   USER.117

```
HANDLE FAR PASCAL GetTaskFromHwnd(HWND)
HWND hwnd;          /* window */
```

GetTaskFromHwnd is functionally identical to the documented GetWindowTask(); it returns the task handle of the task owning the specified window. Because GetWindowTask is documented, is supported in Windows 3.1, and appears internally to be a simpler implementation, there is little point in using GetTaskFromHwnd.

Both functions work by following a chain of handles back from the WND structure of the supplied window handle. The hmemTaskQ field of the WND structure is used to locate the task queue structure for the task. At offset 2 in that structure (see the Task Queue structure in chapter 5) is the Task Database handle, otherwise known as the task handle.

Return: The HANDLE of the task owning the specified window
Support: 3.0

GetTimerResolution   USER.14

```
DWORD FAR PASCAL GetTimerResolution(void);
```

The return value indicates the number of microseconds per timer tick. The number returned in versions 3.0 and 3.1 is 1000, suggesting that events may be timed to 1 millisecond. In practice, of course, timer ticks occur no more frequently than 18.2 times per second, as dictated by the PC clock, unless the timer chip has been reprogrammed.

For more information on the clock in Windows, see chapter 9.

Return: The number of wishful-thinking microseconds per timer tick
Support: 3.0, and documented in 3.1
Used by: Excel

GetUserLocalObjType   USER.480

```
WORD FAR PASCAL GetUserLocalObjType(HANDLE)
HANDLE hObj;           /* handle to object */
```

In the debug version of USER.EXE, this function returns the type of the object whose handle is specified. The object types appear to be those that are defined in TOOLHELP.H, i.e.:

```
#define LT_USER_CLASS              1
#define LT_USER_WND                2
#define LT_USER_STRING             3
#define LT_USER_MENU               4
#define LT_USER_CLIP               5
#define LT_USER_CBOX               6
#define LT_USER_PALETTE            7
#define LT_USER_ED                 8
#define LT_USER_BWL                9
#define LT_USER_OWNERDRAW          10
#define LT_USER_SPB                11
#define LT_USER_CHECKPOINT         12
#define LT_USER_DCE                13
#define LT_USER_MWP                14
#define LT_USER_PROP               15
#define LT_USER_LBIV               16
#define LT_USER_MISC               17
#define LT_USER_ATOMS              18
#define LT_USER_LOCKINPUTSTATE     19
#define LT_USER_HOOKLIST           20
#define LT_USER_USERSEEUSERDOALLOC 21
#define LT_USER_HOTKEYLIST         22
#define LT_USER_POPUPMENU          23
#define LT_USER_HANDLETABLE        32
```

The streamlined code for the retail version, however, as follows, suggests a uniform type for all USER objects:

```
XOR AX, AX
RETF 2;
```

Although it would seem logical that it would, this function does not get called during an iteration over the USER heap (see chapter 10), indicating perhaps that ToolHelp performs its own detective work on USER heap block types.

In fact, ToolHelp's detective powers are only marginally better than GetUserLocalObjType in the retail version. This is borne out in the examples of display logs from the USERWALK program presented in the USER Objects entry in this chapter.

The reason for ToolHelp's object-type blindness, the unresponsiveness of the GetUserObjType function in the retail version, and the richness of their output in the debug version lies in the way that memory for objects is allocated in USER. In the 3.1 debug version of USER, memory allocations are made using UserLocalAlloc, a function that is not exported and not present in the retail version. UserLocalAlloc is a cover over LocalAlloc but with an additional parameter, which is the object type to be allocated. UserLocalAlloc allocates four bytes more than it is asked to and stores the object type as the first of these. (The other three do not appear to be used currently.)

In the retail version, by way of contrast, the objects themselves (except in the cases of the CLASS and MENU structures) contain no signature or magic by which an application might validate them or tell them apart. Compare this with the broad support for object types provided for GDI in both the retail and debug versions (see chapter 8).

Return: Always 0 in the retail version, or an object type as defined in TOOLHELP.H in the debug version
Support: 3.1
See also: USERWALK, GDIWALK

GetWC2   USER.318

```
DWORD FAR PASCAL GetWC2(HWND, int)
HWND hwnd;         /* window handle */
int nOffset;       /* offset from end of WND or WNDCLASS structure */
// CL contains bits indicating Class or Window, WORD or DWORD
```

This function is the engine behind GetWindowLong, GetWindowWord, GetClassWord, and GetClassLong. Those functions present two entry points that set bits in CL (0x80 indicates get from class structure, not window structure; 0x01 indicates DWORD required, not WORD, although this bit is ignored) before falling through to GetWC2. They present only two entry points because GetWindowWord and GetWindowLong are aliases for the same entry point, as are GetClassWord and GetClassLong; the WINDOWS.H prototypes for the four functions define the respective return types, although there is always a full DWORD returned in DX:AX.

Return: DWORD from the offset within either the window or class structure for the window
Support: 3.0

ICON   Structure

An icon is a global memory resource, and the HICON associated with it is a global memory handle. The global memory block that it refers to contains a device-dependent color bitmap with an undocumented CURSORICONINFO header structure. See the CURSORICONINFO and DumpIcon entries in this chapter, and the USERWALK program.

IconSize   USER.86

```
DWORD FAR PASCAL IconSize(void);
```

This function returns the width and height of an icon in pixels as defined by the display resolution and driver. These values are identical to GetSystemMetrics (SM_CXICON) and GetSystemMetrics (SM_CYICON). They come from the display driver's OEMBIN structure.

Return: Double word containing, in the high and low words, the width and height respectively of an icon in pixels
Note: In 3.1, the entry point still exists, but it is named BEAR86.
Support: 3.0, 3.1 (see Note)
See also: BearNNN

InitApp   USER.5

```
BOOL FAR PASCAL InitApp(HANDLE)
HANDLE hInstance;          /* Instance handle of uninitialized module */
```

Called from within the compiler's startup code, InitApp performs the Windows task manager checks and initializations for the new application instance, including loading resource handlers (such as LoadCursorIconHandler, described later in this chapter), setting the SignalProcs for the task, creating the task queue, and inserting the task into the task manager's list.

Note: This function is covered in the Open Tools documentation for 3.1 and is the subject of a Microsoft overview article on Windows Startup.

Return: TRUE (1) if successful or FALSE (0) if not, in which case the application instance fails to load. If successful, the application start time is returned in the DX:CX register pair.
Support: 3.0, 3.1
See also: InitTask, Task Queue structure (both in chapter 5), LoadCursorIcon-Handler

---

InsendMessage   USER.192

```
HANDLE FAR PASCAL InSendMessage(void);
```

This function is documented in both versions 3.0 and 3.1 of the SDK as returning a BOOL indicating whether the current processing is within a SendMessage call, rather than, for example, a PostMessage call.

The documentation is not complete, however. The documented return value actually holds the Task Queue handle of the application that issued the SendMessage. The function calls the undocumented GetTaskQueueES function (see chapter 5) to obtain the task queue handle of the currently executing task and returns the value at offset 3Ah (version 3.0) or 38h (version 3.1) within that Task Queue structure.

Return: Task Queue handle of task that sent message, or NULL if not in SendMessage.
See also: Task Queue (chapter 5)

IsTwoByteCharPrefix   USER.51

```
BOOL FAR PASCAL IsTwoByteCharPrefix(char)
char cChar;          /* character to test */
```

This function returns TRUE if the specified character is a two-byte (e.g., Unicode) character prefix code. This function will only return TRUE when a language driver that supports Unicode or some other two-byte character set is installed.

IsTwoByteCharPrefix() tests the passed-in character against the Begin/End_First /Second_range fields in the keyboard driver's KBINFO structure (which is documented in the DDK).

Note: In 3.1, the entry point still exists, but it is named BEAR51. The function entry point should therefore be obtained by ordinal rather than by name in applications intended to work in Windows 3.0 and 3.1. The following code fragment will achieve this:

```
       .
       .
       .
   {
   BOOL (FAR PASCAL *lpfnIsTwoByteCharPrefix)(char);
```

```
    char cTest;
    BOOL bIsTwoByteCharPrefix;
        .
    lpfnIsTwoByteCharPrefix =
        GetProcAddr(GetModuleHandle("USER"), (LPSTR) (DWORD) 51);
        .
    bIsTwoByteCharPrefix = (*lpfnIsTwoByteCharPrefix)(cTest);
        .
    }
```

Support: 3.0, 3.1 (see Note)
See also: IsDBCSLeadByte (documented), BearNNN

IsUserIdle   USER.59

```
BOOL FAR PASCAL IsUserIdle(void);
```

This function, which indicates the level of end-user keyboard and mouse activity, is called (via a function pointer returned from GetProcAddress) from the KERNEL scheduler. It allows Windows to perform housekeeping while the user is not typing or using the mouse. The KERNEL scheduler uses the return value from IsUserIdle() to determine whether to set the Win_Idle_Mouse_Busy_Bit when calling the Win_Kernel_Idle (INT 2Fh AX=1689h) function (see INT2FAPI.INC in the DDK).

IsUserIdle() can be called asynchronously, for example, from within a CreateSystemTimer callback function (see chapter 9).

In 3.1, this function is responsible for triggering screen-saver applications. When no activity is detected (IsUserIdle() returns TRUE), and the duration since the time of last activity exceeds that specified in the ScreenSaveTimeOut= entry in WIN.INI, a WM_SYSCOMMAND with wParam=SC_SCREENSAVE is sent to the screen-saver application window. If, on the other hand, activity is detected, the time of last activity is reset to the current time. (For more on screen savers, see chapter 14 of the 3.1 SDK Overviews manual.)

Return: FALSE if input is pending; TRUE if no input
Support: 3.0, 3.1

Keybd_Event   USER.289

```
Keybd_Event    proc  far
;; AX = Virtual Key code
;; BL = OEM Scan code
;; BH = 1 if Enhanced key
```

This function is the handler for keyboard events, invoked by the keyboard driver's INT 9 hardware interrupt handler. It generates a System Message Queue entry for key press/release events.

While there does not appear to be a comparable function to GetMouseEventProc for the keyboard, this function can be called in 3.1 to generate system-level keystroke events. If there is a direct equivalent in version 3.0, it is not exported.

This function is described, though without a name, in the Keyboard Drivers chapter of the DDK. The address of Keybd_Event is passed to a keyboard driver when its Enable() function is called.

Support: 3.1
See also: Mouse_Event, GetMouseEventProc, System Message Queue
Example: Uses Keybd_Event to generate Alt-Tab keystrokes, causing a cycling through the active windows.

```c
/* KBDEVENT.C */

#include <windows.h>
#include "winio.h"
#ifdef __BORLANDC__
#define _asm asm
#endif

HANDLE hTimer;

#define KE_RELEASE 0x8000

/* undocumented function */
extern void FAR PASCAL Keybd_Event(void);

FARPROC lpfnTimerFunc;

#include "checkord.c"

BOOL StopCycling(HWND hwnd)
    {
    FreeProcInstance(lpfnTimerFunc);
    KillTimer(winio_current(), hTimer);
    return TRUE;
    }

WORD FAR PASCAL TimerFunc(HWND hwnd, WORD wMsg, int id, DWORD dwTime)
    {
    _asm mov ax, VK_MENU;
    _asm xor bx, bx;
    Keybd_Event();
    _asm mov ax, VK_TAB;
    _asm xor bx, bx;
    Keybd_Event();
    _asm mov ax, VK_TAB + KE_RELEASE;
    _asm xor bx, bx;
```

```
    Keybd_Event();
    _asm mov ax, VK_TAB;
    _asm xor bx, bx;
    Keybd_Event();
    _asm mov ax, VK_TAB + KE_RELEASE;
    _asm xor bx, bx;
    Keybd_Event();
    _asm mov ax, VK_MENU + KE_RELEASE;
    _asm xor bx, bx;
    Keybd_Event();

    return 1;
    }

int main()
    {
    // Ord/name check
    if (! CheckOrdName("Keybd_Event", "USER", 289))
        return 0;

    lpfnTimerFunc = MakeProcInstance((FARPROC) TimerFunc, __hInst);
    printf("We will now cycle through the Windows tasks...\n\n");
    hTimer = SetTimer(winio_current(), 1, 2000, lpfnTimerFunc);
    winio_onclose(winio_current(), (DESTROY_FUNC) StopCycling);
    printf("\nClose window to exit.");
    return 0;
    }
```

KillSystemTimer   USER.182

```
BOOL FAR PASCAL KillSystemTimer(HWND, WORD)
HWND hwnd;                    /* Window owning timer */
WORD wTimer;                  /* timer returned by SetSystemTimer */
```

This function kills a system timer created using SetSystemTimer(). It operates in exactly the same way as the documented function KillTimer(), except that it only kills system (reserved) timers. See the discussion of SetSystemTimer().

Return: TRUE (1) if the timer was successfully killed, otherwise FALSE (0).
Note: In 3.1, the entry point still exists, but it is named BEAR182. The function entry point should therefore be obtained by ordinal rather than by name in applications intended to work in Windows 3.0 and 3.1. The example program for SetSystemTimer illustrates this.
Support: 3.0, 3.1 (see Note)
See also: SetSystemTimer, BearNNN
Example: See the example for SetSystemTimer.

KillTimer2   USER.327

```
BOOL FAR PASCAL KillTimer2(HWND, WORD)
HWND hwnd;        /* window owning timer */
WORD wIDEvent;    /* timer event id */
// CX contains BOOL bSystem
```

This function is the back end to the documented KillTimer and undocumented KillSystemTimer functions.

KillTimer sets CX to 0 and jumps to this function; KillSystemTimer sets CX to 1 and falls through to this function. The bSystem parameter in CX specifies whether the timer was created using CreateTimer (bSystem == FALSE) or SetSystemTimer (bSystem == TRUE).

It is neither necessary nor recommended to call this function; it is included here only for completeness.

Return: TRUE (1) if the timer event was killed or FALSE (0) if not
Support: 3.0
See also: SetTimer2, KillSystemTimer

LoadCursorIconHandler   USER.336

```
HANDLE FAR PASCAL LoadCursorIconHandler(HANDLE, HANDLE, HANDLE)
HANDLE hGlobMem;      /* global memory to use or NULL */
HANDLE hInstance;     /* instance whose file contains resource */
WORD wResIndex;       /* index of resource in the file */
```

Loads an old-style 16-color bitmap from the resource file associated with the specified application instance and returns an HICON or HCURSOR depending on resource type. If a cursor, the bitmap is converted to monochrome. If hGlobMem is NULL, the function allocates memory for the resource. If the memory allocated to hGlobMem is not sufficient for the bitmap, the function reallocates the block.

This function is installed by InitApp at application startup using the documented SetResourceHandler function in KERNEL as the resource load handler for cursor and icon resources for instances of applications built for Windows versions earlier than 3.0. When the application makes a call to LoadCursor or LoadIcon to load a cursor or icon, the handler is invoked. (See the documentation for SetResourceHandler.)

Return: An HICON or HCURSOR, depending on the type of resource loaded, if successful; NULL if not
Support: 3.0, 3.1
See also: InitApp, LoadDIBIconHandler, LoadDIBCursorHandler

LoadDIBCursorHandler   USER.356

```
HANDLE FAR PASCAL LoadDIBCursorHandler(HANDLE, HANDLE, HANDLE)
HANDLE hGlobMem;        /* global memory to use or NULL */
HANDLE hInstance;       /* instance whose file contains resource */
WORD wResIndex;         /* index of resource in the file */
```

Loads a new-style device independent bitmap (DIB) cursor from the resource file associated with the specified application instance and returns an HCURSOR. If hGlobMem is NULL, the function allocates memory for the resource. If the memory allocated to hGlobMem is not sufficient for the bitmap, the function reallocates the block.

This function is installed by InitApp at application startup using the documented SetResourceHandler function in KERNEL as the resource load handler for cursor resources for instances of applications built for Windows versions 3.0 and later. When the application makes a call to LoadCursor, the handler is invoked.

Return: An HCURSOR if successful; NULL if not
Support: 3.0, 3.1
See also: InitApp, LoadCursorIconHandler, LoadDIBIconHandler

LoadDIBIconHandler   USER.357

```
HANDLE FAR PASCAL LoadDIBIconHandler(HANDLE, HANDLE, HANDLE)
HANDLE hGlobMem;        /* global memory to use or NULL */
HANDLE hInstance;       /* instance whose file contains resource */
WORD wResIndex;         /* index of resource in the file */
```

Loads a new-style device independent bitmap (DIB) icon from the resource file associated with the specified application instance and returns an HICON. If hGlobMem is NULL, the function allocates memory for the resource. If the memory allocated to hGlobMem is not sufficient for the bitmap, the function reallocates the block.

This function is installed by InitApp at application startup using the documented SetResourceHandler function in KERNEL as the resource load handler for cursor resources for instances of applications built for Windows versions 3.0 and later. When the application makes a call to LoadCursor, the handler is invoked.

Return: An HICON if successful or NULL if not
Support: 3.0, 3.1
See also: InitApp, LoadCursorIconHandler, LoadDIBIconHandler

LoadIconHandler   USER.456

```
HICON FAR PASCAL LoadIconHandler(HANDLE, BOOL)
HANDLE hResource;       /* resource containing icon bitmap */
BOOL bNew;              /* device independent icon bitmap */
```

This function appears to turn an old- or new-style (device dependent or independent) bitmap into a 16-color bitmap suitable for use as an icon; note that it converts the bitmap in place, reallocating global memory for the bitmap if appropriate.

Program Manager, for example, uses this function to obtain icons from executable files without regard to the icon type.

LoadIconHandler is a very small function. It simply passes control to one of two local, unexported functions depending on the value of bNew. If bNew is FALSE, the function called is the back end of the processing of the undocumented LoadCursorIconHandler function; otherwise, it calls a function that is shared by the undocumented LoadDIBIconHandler and LoadDIBCursorHandler functions. Either way, these back-end functions convert a loaded resource into the appropriate format for the display device, looking after such things as converting a 32 x 32 icon into a 32 x 16 icon on low-resolution systems, and converting a color bitmap into monochrome cursor.

Return: HICON of a device-dependent icon if successful or NULL if not
Used by: PROGMAN.EXE, SHELL.DLL, WINHELP.EXE
Support: 3.0, 3.1

LockMyTask   USER.276

```
void FAR PASCAL LockMyTask(BOOL)
BOOL bLock;          /* TRUE = Lock, FALSE = Unlock */
```

This function locks the specified task. LockMyTask is essentially a cover on the undocumented Kernel function LockCurrentTask, which it calls as its first action. Having called the Kernel routine to unlock the task, the function unlocks the System Messsage queue (see the System Message Queue entry in this chapter).

Support: 3.0, 3.1
See also: LockCurrentTask (chapter 5), SystemMessageQueue

LookupMenuHandle   USER.217

```
HMENU FAR PASCAL LookupMenuHandle(HMENU, int)
HMENU hMenu;    /* Root level menu handle */
int nID;        /* Menu item id */
```

This function returns the handle of the menu in which the specified item can be found. It searches down a tree of popup menus from the supplied menu handle, looking for specified menu item id.

Return: HMENU of the owning menu or NULL if the id cannot be found
Note: Under 3.0, no checking is done on the supplied menu handle other than for NULL. Specifying a nonzero invalid menu handle will cause a UAE.
Support: 3.0, 3.1
See also: MENU structure

MENU   Structures

The MENU structure is where USER keeps information about a top-level or popup menu. In version 3.0, the structure stores information about the menu and its associated component items (with one important exception, which will be clarified in a moment) as a single contiguous block in the default USER local heap segment. The documented HMENU handle is in that version, therefore, a near pointer to a single block of memory in the default USER heap segment. This is the handle returned by the documented CreateMenu function and acted upon by the AppendMenu, InsertMenu, DeleteMenu, DestroyMenu, etc., functions.

The exception mentioned above relates to the storage of the menu item strings. These are stored in a separate heap reserved for the Global Atom table and USER strings. In version 3.0, this heap is used almost exclusively for menu item strings, and in version 3.1 the menu strings are in a separate heap segment.

In version 3.1 there are three main differences in the way that menus and their associated structures are treated by USER. First, menu structures are now in their own local heap segment (see the discussion of USER local heaps in the introduction to this chapter).

Secondly, the array of ITEM structures associated with a MENU structure (both structures are shown below) are now stored separately, although within the same heap segment.

Finally, the MENU structure in version 3.1 contains a signature 'MU'; there is no signature or magic in the 3.0 structure and therefore no easy way of validating an HMENU. The lack of a signature was presumably an oversight in 3.0; the addition of this field and the appearance in version 3.1 of the documented IsMenu function is obviously no coincidence. However, it is possible to use the properties of the 3.0 menu structure to validate HMENUs, and this is how the USERWALK program recognizes menus in version 3.0.

```
// Menu item substructure valid for 3.0 and 3.1
typedef struct {
    WORD    wFlags;
    WORD    wIDorPopup;
    RECT    rectItem;
    WORD    xTab;
    HANDLE  hCheckedBmp;
    HANDLE  hUncheckedBmp;
    HANDLE  hAtomOrBmp;
    WORD    xULStart;
    WORD    cxULLen;
    WORD    cbItemLen;
    } ITEM, NEAR * HITEM;
```

LookupMenuHandle

The structure contains the following fields:

FIELD	DESCRIPTION
wFlags	Flags describing the item. These are MF_ constants present in WINDOWS.H, some of which are not documented:

       MF_SEPARATOR
       MF_ENABLED
       MF_GRAYED
       MF_DISABLED
       MF_UNCHECKED
       MF_CHECKED
       MF_USECHECKBITM
       MF_STRING
       MF_BITMAP
       MF_OWNERDRAW
       MF_POPUP
       MF_MENUBARBREAK
       MF_MENUBREAK
       MF_UNHILITE
       MF_HILITE

FIELD	DESCRIPTION
wIDorPopup	The menu item ID as specified in the wIDNewItem parameter to the InsertMenu function, or, if for a popup menu, the popup's menu handle
rectItem	The position and size of the items rectangle in the menu in screen coordinates
xTab	The tab position in effect for the item
hCheckedBmp	Handle of the 'checkmark' bitmap
hUncheckedBmp	Handle of the bitmap to be used when the item is not checked. This is normally NULL.
hAtomOrBmp	Normally an atom handle for the menu item string, but may be the handle of a bitmap for owner-draw
xULStart	If a string item, and an Alt key accelerator is in effect for the item, the x coordinate relative to the left of the item of the beginning of the underline
xULLen	The length of the underline. This will be the width of the underlined character.
cbItemLen	Length of the item string

LookupMenuHandle

```
// Menu structure for 3.0
typedef struct {
    WORD    wFlags;
    WORD    iCurrSel;
    WORD    iCurrPopup;
    WORD    cbMenu;
    WORD    cxWidth;
    WORD    cyHeight;
    WORD    iMaxItems;
    HWND    hwndOwner;
    ITEM    item[1];
    } MENU_3_0, NEAR * HMENU;

//Menu structure for 3.1
typedef struct {
    HMENU   hmenuNext;
    WORD    wFlags;
    WORD    wSig;
    HANDLE  hTaskQ;
    WORD    cxWidth;
    WORD    cyHeight;
    WORD    cItems;
    HWND    hwndOwner;
    HANDLE  hItems;
    WORD    w12h;
    } MENU_3_1, NEAR * HMENU;
```

The above structures contain the following fields. Any field that does not appear below is not currently understood:

FIELD	DESCRIPTION
hmenuNext	This field only appears in the 3.1 MENU structure. A list of MENU structures is held in the version 3.1 USER menu heap (see the introduction to this chapter) and the hmenuNext field points to the next menu in the list. The list is terminated by a value of NULL in this field.

wFlags	Contains one or more of the following MF_ flags. These are present in WINDOWS.H, but not documented:
	    MF_SYSMENU
	    MF_HELP
	    MF_MOUSESELECT

wSig	Only present in version 3.1, this field contains 0x554D ("NK"), presumably the initials of Neil Konzen, as the signature, or magic, for the structure.
iCurrSel	Only present in version 3.0, this field contains the index of the last ITEM structure selected from the menu, or -1 if no selection has yet been made.

LookupMenuHandle

iCurrPopup	Only present in version 3.0, this field contains the index of the ITEM structure for the last active popup submenu, or -1 if none has yet been active.
hTaskQ	Only present in version 3.1, this field contains the Task Queue handle of the task that owns the menu.
cbMenu	Only present in version 3.0, this field contains the combined size of the MENU structure and all the ITEM structures that follow it.
cxWidth	The width of the bounding rectangle that surrounds the menu, in pixels.
cyHeight	The height of the bounding rectangle that surrounds the menu, in pixels.
iMaxItem	Only present in version 3.0, but in the same location as the similar cItems field present in the version 3.1 structure, this field contains one less than the number of elements in the array of ITEM structures associated with the menu, i.e., the maximum index into the array. This property together with the contents of the cbMenu field is relied upon by the validation used by the USERWALK program to identify a MENU in version 3.0. The program assumes that if (cbMenu == ((iMaxItem + 1) * sizeof(ITEM))) the structure is a MENU. This appears to be a reliable identification test.
cItems	Only present in version 3.1, this field contains the number of elements in the array of ITEM structures associated with the menu.
hwndOwne	The window that owns this menu
hItems	Only present in version 3.1, this field contains the menu heap handle of the block of memory containing the array of ITEM structures associated with the menu.

See also: USER Objects

MenuItemState   USER.329

```
WORD FAR PASCAL MenuItemState(HMENU, WORD, WORD)
HMENU hmenu;          /* menu handle */
WORD wIDItem;         /* menu item/position */
WORD wFlags;          /* combination of MF_ flags */
// CL contains mask to filter MF_ flags
```

This function changes the state of the specified menu item as specified by the wFlags parameter and filtered by the mask in CL, and it returns the previous state of the masked bits.

This function is called by the documented functions EnableMenuItem and CheckMenuItem. They effectively act as different prologs to MenuItemState, simply setting different masks into CL on the way in to that function.

EnableMenuItem sets CL = 3, masking the MF_ENABLED and MF_GRAYED bits. CheckMenuItem sets CL = 8, masking the MF_CHECKED bit. Note that both mask out the MF_BYPOSITION bit, which cannot be set but controls interpretation of the wIDItem parameter.

The function operates on the wFlags field of the ITEM structure indexed (if MF_BYPOSITION), or identified (if not), by the wIDItem parameter in the array associated with the MENU structure pointed to by the hmenu parameter.

Return: The previous state of the flags masked by CL
Support: 3.0
See also: MENU and ITEM structures

Mouse_Event   USER.299

```
Mouse_Eventproc far
;; AX = mouse event
;; BX = horizontal displacement if (AX & ME_MOVE)
;; CX = vertical displacement if (AX & ME_MOVE)
;; DX = button state
;; SI = mouse event flags
```

This function is the handler for mouse events. It is invoked (usually) by the mouse driver MOUSE.DRV within its IRQ 2 hardware interrupt handler. It generates a System Message Queue entry for button press/release events and generates a new, or updates the existing, mouse movement queue entry. Note that this function ensures that there is only one mouse movement message in the queue at one time.

This is the function whose address is returned by the undocumented GetMouseEventProc function. See the description of that function for an example of how this function might be called by an application to generate system-level mouse events.

This function is described, though without a name, in the Mouse Drivers chapter of the DDK manual. The address of Mouse_Event is passed to a mouse driver when its Enable() function is called.

Support: Code present in 3.0, 3.1, but only visible as a USER.EXE export in 3.1
See also: Keybd_Event, GetMouseEventProc, System Message Queue
Example: See example code for GetMouseEventProc.

OldExitWindows   USER.2

```
void FAR PASCAL OldExitWindows(void);
```

This function terminates the calling Windows application by invoking Int 21h/Function 4Ch. This function is a hangover from version 2.1 and persists all the way into 3.1, presumably to provide compatibility for 2.1 applications that call it.

New applications should use the documented ExitWindows function.

Support: 3.0, 3.1

PaintRect   USER.325

```
void FAR PASCAL PaintRect(HWND, HWND, HDC, HANDLE, LPRECT)
HWND hwndParent;        /* handle of parent or NULL */
HWND hwnd;              /* handle of target window */
HDC hDC;                /* window display context */
HANDLE hBrush;          /* handle of brush to fill with */
                        /* OR CTLCOLOR_ constant */
LPRECT lpRect;          /* Rectangle to paint */
```

PaintRect fills a rectangular area defined by the RECT pointed at by lpRect on the window specified by hwnd using hBrush. If hwndParent is not NULL, the hBrush parameter may specify one of the documented CTLCOLOR_ control type constants for the child window, in which case a WM_CTLCOLOR is sent to the parent window to allow it to set the brush type to be used. PaintRect() calls the documented FillREct() function.

Support: 3.0, 3.1
Used by: FillWindow()
Notes: If the hBrush parameter specifies a CTLCOLOR_ constant and the hwndParent parameter is NULL, the function fails benignly, but with *no indication*.
Example:

```
/* PAINTRCT.C */

#include <windows.h>
#include "wmhandlr.h"
#include "winio.h"

/* undocumented function */
extern void FAR PASCAL PaintRect(HWND hwndParent, HWND hwnd,
    HDC hDC, HANDLE hBrush, LPRECT lpRect);
#include "checkord.c"

long dblclk(HWND hwnd, WORD wMsg, WORD wParam, DWORD lParam)
    {
    RECT rect;
    HDC hDC = GetDC(hwnd);

    GetClientRect(hwnd, (LPRECT) &rect);
    rect.left += 20;
    rect.right -= 20;
```

```
    rect.top += 10;
    rect.bottom -= 10;
    PaintRect(NULL, hwnd, hDC,
        GetStockObject(DKGRAY_BRUSH), (LPRECT) &rect);
    ReleaseDC(hwnd, hDC);
    puts("A rectangular area in the window is now dark gray");
    puts("Double click on a text line to do it again");
    return 1;
    }

int main()
    {
    // Ord/name check
    if (! CheckOrdName("PaintRect", "USER", 325))
        return 0;

    wmhandler_set(winio_current(),
        WM_LBUTTONDBLCLK, (WMHANDLER) dblclk);

    puts("Double click on a text line to fill a dark gray rectangle");
    puts("Close the window to exit");

    return 0;
    }
```

PostMessage2   USER.313

```
DWORD FAR PASCAL PostMessage2(HANDLE, WORD, WORD, DWORD)
HANDLE hWndTask;     /* target task/window */
WORD wMsg          /* message */
WORD wParam;       /* additional message info */
DWORD lParam;       /* additional message info */
// CL contains BOOL bTaskMessage
```

This function is the back end to documented PostAppMessage and PostMessage functions.

PostAppMessage sets CL to 1 before jumping through to this function; PostMessage sets CL to 0 and then, if the hwnd parameter is not 0xFFFF (in which case it jumps to BroadcastMessage), it falls through to this function. The value of CL is used to determine whether the HANDLE parameter is a task handle or a window handle, in which case the extra step of extracting the task handle from the window structure (see the WND structure) needs to be performed.

PostMessage2 is included here only for completeness.

Return: The return value reflects the outcome of the target window's processing of the message and depends on the message being sent.
Support: 3.0
See also: BroadcastMessage

ScrollChildren   USER.463

```
void FAR PASCAL ScrollChildren(HWND, WORD, WORD, DWORD)
HWND hwnd;          /* parent window */
WORD wMsg;          /* WM_HSCROLL or WM_VSCROLL */
WORD wParam;        /* SB_ value from WM_?SCROLL message */
DWORD lParam;       /* unreferenced */
```

This function scrolls MDI client windows within a parent window that is being scrolled. ScrollChildren is designed to be called from within a WndProc scrollbar event handler and is used by MDIClientWndProc. It is also called directly from Program Manager, for example, to realign the iconic application windows within a parent application group window in response to a user scroll operation. The function is implemented using the documented ScrollWindow() function.

Support: 3.0, 3.1
Used by: USER.EXE, PROGMAN.EXE
See also: CalcChildScroll

SendMessage2   USER.312

```
DWORD FAR PASCAL SendMessage2(HWND, WORD, WORD, DWORD,
                    LPVOID, WORD)
HWND hwnd;          /* target window */
WORD wMsg;          /* message */
WORD wParam;        /* additional message info */
DWORD lParam;       /* additional message info */
LPVOID lp1;         /* unknown - always NULL */
WORD w1;            /* unknown - unreferenced - always 0 */
```

This function is the back end to the documented SendMessage function. It is called only by SendMessage and takes two additional, vestigial parameters, which SendMessage always sets to 0. It is included here only for completeness.

Return: The return value reflects the outcome of the target window's processing of the message and depends on the message being sent.
Support: 3.0

SetDeskPattern   USER.279

```
BOOL FAR PASCAL SetDeskPattern(void);
```

This function activates the desktop background pattern specified in the WIN.INI file. SetDeskPattern() is called by the Control Panel (CONTROL.EXE) in version 3.0. It takes no parameters and obtains the pattern that is to be used as desktop background from the Pattern entry of the [Desktop] section in WIN.INI. The Control Panel program therefore performs a WriteProfileString(), to record a new user pattern selection, before issuing the SetDeskPattern() call.

The WIN.INI entry contains a sequence of eight decimal numbers representing the eight bytes that make up the pattern (which is used to create a bit blt source within the SetDeskPattern() call). The Control Panel program selection "50% Gray," for example, leads to the WIN.INI entry "Pattern=170 85 170 85 170 85 170 85" where 170 represents 128+32+8+2 (a byte code with bits 7, 5, 3, and 1 on) and 85 represents 64+16+4+1 (a byte code with bits 6, 4, 2, and 0 on). The alternating bit patterns result in a close crosshatch.

Return: If a pattern was specified in WIN.INI, returns 1; otherwise returns 0
Support: 3.0, 3.1 (see Note)
Notes:
  1. The call will not fail no matter what the line contains: a nonnumeric token in the line results in a default 0 for the byte code; missing tokens are also assumed to be zeroes.
  2. The functionality provided by SetDeskPattern has been subsumed into the documented SystemParametersInfo function in Windows 3.1. In 3.1, the entry point still exists, but it is named OldSetDeskPattern. The function entry point should therefore be obtained by ordinal rather than by name in applications intended to work in both Windows 3.0 and 3.1. The example below illustrates this technique.

Used by: CONTROL.EXE (3.0 only)
See also: SetDeskWallPaper, SetGridGranularity, ControlPanelInfo
Example:

```
/* DTPATTRN.C */

#include <windows.h>
#include "winio.h"

/* undocumented function */
BOOL (FAR PASCAL *lpfnSetDeskPattern)(void);

int main()
    {
    char buf[128];

    // Get function address
    lpfnSetDeskPattern =
        GetProcAddress(GetModuleHandle("USER"), (LPSTR) (DWORD) 279);

    for (;;)
        {
        /* prompt for the pattern */
        puts("Enter 8 bytes of (decimal) pattern data:");
        gets(buf);
```

SetDeskPattern

```
    /* record the pattern in the win.ini file ....*/
    WriteProfileString("Desktop", "Pattern", buf);

    /* ... and call the SetDeskPattern function */
    if ((*lpfnSetDeskPattern)())
        {
        InvalidateRect(GetDesktopWindow(), NULL, TRUE);
        printf("Desktop pattern successfully changed\n");
        }
    else
        printf("Could not change desktop pattern.\n");
    }

printf("Program terminated");
return 0;
}
```

SetDeskWallPaper   USER.285

```
BOOL FAR PASCAL SetDeskWallPaper(LPSTR)
LPSTR lpszBmpFileName;    /* name of the wallpaper bitmap file */
```

This function loads the named file as the desktop background wallpaper.

SetDeskWallPaper is called by Control Panel (CONTROL.EXE) in version 3.0 to set the .BMP bitmap file to be used as the desktop background wallpaper. The call will fail if the named file is not found or does not contain a valid bitmap. Note that the call only *loads* the file but does not refresh the visible desktop. Neither does it record the new choice in the WIN.INI file.

If the lpszBmpFileName is parameter is -1, the function retrieves the name of the current bitmap file specified in the 'Wallpaper' entry in the [Desktop] section of WIN.INI. The example below calls InvalidateRect() on the desktop window to cause the new wallpaper to take immediate effect.

According to Neil Rubenking's book on TPW, SetDeskWallpaper() doesn't always load the palette of 256-color bitmaps properly, and can fail when loading RLE files. Always use SystemParametersInfo() when possible.

Return: If the wallpaper was successfully changed, returns 1; otherwise, if the file name or content was invalid or the file could not be located, returns 0.
Support: 3.0, 3.1 (see Note)
Note: The functionality provided by SetDeskWallpaper has been subsumed into the documented SystemParametersInfo function in Windows 3.1. In 3.1, the entry point still exists, but it is named BEAR285. The function entry point should therefore be obtained by ordinal rather than by name in applications intended to work in both Windows 3.0 and 3.1. The following example illustrates this technique.
Used by: CONTROL.EXE (3.0 only)
See also: SetDeskPattern, SetGridGranularity, ControlPanelInfo, BearNNN
Example:

```
#include <windows.h>
```

SetDeskWallPaper

```
#include "winio.h"

/* undocumented function */
BOOL (FAR PASCAL *lpfnSetDeskWallPaper)(LPSTR lpszBmpFileName);

int main()
    {
    char bmpfilename[64];

    // Get function address
    lpfnSetDeskWallPaper =
        GetProcAddress(GetModuleHandle("USER"), (LPSTR) (DWORD) 285);

    for (;;)
        {
        /* prompt for the filename */
        puts("Enter name of .BMP file to use:");
        gets(bmpfilename);

        /* break on empty filename */
        if (bmpfilename[0] == 0)
            break;

        /* otherwise call the SetDeskWallPaper function */
        if ((*lpfnSetDeskWallPaper)(bmpfilename))
            {
            /* Save name of bitmap in WIN.INI */
            WriteProfileString("Desktop", "Wallpaper", bmpfilename);
            InvalidateRect(GetDesktopWindow(), NULL, TRUE);
            puts("Desktop wallpaper successfully changed.\n");
            }
        else
            puts("Could not change desktop wallpaper.\n");
        }

    puts("Program terminated");
    return 0;
    }
```

SetEventHook   USER.321

```
void FAR PASCAL SetEventHook(FARPROC)
FARPROC lpfnEventHook; /* Pointer to the event hook function */
```

This function allows mouse and keyboard events to be intercepted asynchronously and filtered. SetEventHook is used by Windows debuggers to intercept mouse and keyboard events. Even though it is now documented (see the following), it is included here because it was undocumented for 3.0 and because the existing documentation gives no sample source code.

Note that the lpfnEventProc passed to the function in the following example below is not created using MakeProcInstance. This occurs because our event hook function is written in assembler and already includes appropriate prolog code to establish DS upon entry.

Support: 3.0, *documented* in 3.1.

Note:

1. This function was undocumented in 3.0 but is included in the Open Tools documentation.

2. In 3.0, the interface to the event hook function contained two bugs.

   a. Bit 0 of BH is supposed to contain the enhanced key flag, but BX is destroyed before it reaches the hook function.

   b. The Carry flag is set by the event hook function to indicate that the Mouse event is to be discarded instead of being passed on to the application. However, mouse events are *always* ignored on return from the hook function; leaving the Carry flag clear upon exit from the hook function therefore has no effect.

3. Behavior between 3.0 and 3.1 changed. In 3.0, mouse and keyboard events pass through the event hook procedure first and, if not ignored, are passed into the System Message Queue. In 3.1, they pass through the System Message Queue first and, if used, do not get passed to the hook function. This is noticeable in the example program in that under 3.0 it is impossible to pull down the system menu by pressing Alt + Space.

Used by: CVW.EXE, TDW.EXE

See also: System Message Queue

Example:

```
/* SETEHOOK.C */

/* MUST be compiled SMALL model because of */
/* model dependency in EVNTHOOK.ASM */

#include <windows.h>
#include "winio.h"

/* undocumented function */
extern void FAR PASCAL SetEventHook(FARPROC lpfnEventHook);

/* the Assembler routine from EVNTHOOK.ASM */
extern void far EventHook(void);

char * szEvent[] = { "WM_KEYUP", "WM_KEYDOWN", "WM_MOUSEMOVE",
    "WM_LBUTTONDOWN", "WM_LBUTTONUP", "WM_RBUTTONDOWN",
    "WM_RBUTTONUP", "WM_MBUTTONDOWN", "WM_MBUTTONUP", "WM_???" };

int wEvent = -1;
int wKeyInfo = -1;
```

SetEventHook

```c
int     iEvent;

#include "checkord.c"

BOOL DeinstHook(HWND hwnd)
    {
    puts("Deinstalling event hook function...");
    SetEventHook(NULL);
    puts("...successfully deinstalled.");
    return TRUE;
    }

int main()
    {
    // Ord/name check
    if (! CheckOrdName("SetEventHook", "USER", 321))
        return 0;

    printf("");
    puts("Installing an event hook function...");
    SetEventHook((FARPROC) EventHook);
    puts("...successfully installed.");

    // Make sure that we always unhook...
    winio_onclose(winio_current(), (DESTROY_FUNC) DeinstHook);

    for (;;)
        {
        if ((wEvent == -1) && (wKeyInfo == -1))
            continue;

        switch (wEvent) {
            case WM_KEYUP:        iEvent = 0;        break;
            case WM_KEYDOWN:      iEvent = 1;        break;
            case WM_MOUSEMOVE:    iEvent = 2;        break;
            case WM_LBUTTONDOWN:  iEvent = 3;        break;
            case WM_LBUTTONUP:    iEvent = 4;        break;
            case WM_RBUTTONDOWN:  iEvent = 5;        break;
            case WM_RBUTTONUP:    iEvent = 6;        break;
            case WM_MBUTTONDOWN:  iEvent = 7;        break;
            case WM_MBUTTONUP:    iEvent = 8;        break;
            default:              iEvent = 9;
            }

        if (iEvent < 2)
            printf("%s - Scan=0x%02X, VK code=0x%02X\n",
                    szEvent[iEvent],
                    HIBYTE(wKeyInfo), LOBYTE(wKeyInfo));
        else
            puts(szEvent[iEvent]);

        if ((wEvent == WM_KEYDOWN) &&
            (LOBYTE(wKeyInfo) == VK_ESCAPE))
            {
            puts("** ESC pressed");
```

SetEventHook

```
            DeinstHook(NULL);
            winio_onclose(winio_current(), (DESTROY_FUNC) NULL);
            break;
            }
        wEvent = -1;
        wKeyInfo = -1;
        }

    puts("\nProgram terminated");
    return 0;
    }

;; EVNTHOOK.ASM ;;
;; Event hook function - subroutine of SETEHOOK.C ;;
    .286P

        PUBLIC      _EventHook
        EXTRN       _wEvent : word
        EXTRN       _wKeyInfo : word

DGROUP      GROUP       _DATA
_DATA       segment         WORD PUBLIC 'DATA'
_DATA       ends

_TEXT       segment         BYTE PUBLIC 'CODE'

_EventHook      proc far
        assume  cs:_TEXT, ds:_DATA
        push    ds
        pusha
        mov     si, _DATA
        mov     ds, si
        mov     word ptr [_wEvent], ax
        mov     word ptr [_wKeyInfo], cx
        popa
        pop     ds
        ret
_EventHook      endp
_TEXT   ends
        end
```

SetGetKbdState   USER.330

```
void FAR PASCAL SetGetKbdState(LPSTR)
LPSTR lpKeyState;          /* buffer to set/get state from/into */
// CL holds BOOL bSet
```

This function is the back end to documented GetKeyboardState and SetKeyboardState functions. GetKeyboardState sets CL to 0 and falls through to this function; SetKeyboardState sets CL to 1 and falls through to this function. The bSet parameter

SetGetKbdState

in CL is used to determine whether to copy from the system keyboard state buffer or into it.

It is neither recommended nor necessary to call this function; it is included here only for completeness.

Support: 3.0
Note: In version 3.1, this same entry point corresponds to the documented GetFreeSystemResources function.

SetGridGranularity   USER.284

```
void FAR PASCAL SetGridGranularity(int)
int nGranularity;          /* level of granularity (see text) */
```

This function sets the desktop window grid granularity. It is called by the Windows 3.0 Control Panel program CONTROL.EXE and allows the desktop grid granularity to be set in whole screen byte increments or to be disabled (for the grid to be 1 pixel). For values of nGranularity > 0, the grid is set to nGranularity * 8 pixels horizontally and vertically. If nGranularity is 0, the grid is set to 1 pixel. The function works by setting a global variable that is used by many other routines in USER.

When the grid is enabled, windows are aligned on byte boundaries. This improves Windows repainting performance because no shifting of bitmap bits needs to be performed.

Used by: CONTROL.EXE
Support: 3.0
Note: The functionality provided by SetGridGranularity has been subsumed into the documented SystemParametersInfo function in Windows 3.1.
Example:

```
/* GRIDGRAN.C */

#include <windows.h>
#include <stdlib.h>
#include "winio.h"

/* undocumented function */
extern void FAR PASCAL SetGridGranularity(int nGran);

#include "checkord.c"

int main()
    {
    char buf[128];

    // Ord/name check
```

```
        if (! CheckOrdName("SetGridGranularity", "USER", 284))
            return 0;

        /* prompt for the pattern */
        printf("Enter granularity: ");
        gets(buf);

        /* ... and call the SetDeskPattern function */
        SetGridGranularity(atoi(buf));
        printf("Grid granularity changed\n");

        printf("\nResize or move the window; if you entered\n"
            "a value > 0, the window should 'snap' to grid\n"
            "positions, and window repainting should be faster\n"
            "If you entered 0, the window should move smoothly\n"
            "again but performance will be (unnoticeably?) degraded.\n\n"
            "Program terminated");

        return 0;
        }
```

SetInternalWindowPos   USER.461

```
void FAR PASCAL SetInternalWindowPos(HWND, WORD, LPRECT, LPPOINT)
HWND hwnd;
WORD wStatus;          /* new status for window */
LPRECT lprectWnd;      /* RECT with new window coords or NULL */
LPPOINT lppointIcon;   /* POINT with new icon position or NULL */
```

This function allows modification of a window's screen positions and status.

SetInternalWindowPos is significantly more powerful than the similar sounding and documented SetWindowPos. SetInternalWindowPos allows a window's desktop icon position, its active position and size, and its current status (active/inactive, maximized/minimized/normal, etc.) to be set from a single call. In contrast, SetWindowPos, which SetInternalWindowPos calls as one of its last actions, allows a window's normal position and size, and its z-order position to be modified (see GetNextQueueWindow for more discussion of z ordering).

The wStatus parameter takes the SW_ constants as used by the documented ShowWindow() function. The lprectWnd parameter may be NULL, in which case the current window coordinates remain unchanged; otherwise, it points at an application-supplied RECT structure containing the new coordinates that the window is to occupy when neither iconized nor maximized.

The lppointIcon parameter may be NULL, in which case the current Icon position is unchanged; otherwise, it points at an application-supplied POINT structure containing the new x and y coordinates of the top left of the window's icon when minimized. If the lppointIcon parameter is not NULL, but the supplied x coordinate is -1, the window's icon position will again remain unchanged.

Note that in Windows 3.1 the documented SetWindowPlacement function, together with the WINDOWPLACEMENT structure, provides the same capability through a slightly different interface. However, since most Program Manager replacements originally written for Windows 3.0 rely on SetInternalWindowPos, it has been allowed to continue to exist, still undocumented, in version 3.1.

Return: Void
Support: 3.0, 3.1
Used by: PROGMAN.EXE, Norton Desktop
See also: GetInternalWindowPos
Example: Uses GetInternalWindowPos and SetInternalWindowPos to arrange window positions.

```c
/* GETIWPOS.C */

#include <windows.h>
#include <stdlib.h>
#include <string.h>
#include "winio.h"

/* undocumented functions */
extern WORD FAR PASCAL GetInternalWindowPos(HWND hwnd,
    LPRECT lprectWnd, LPPOINT lppointIcon);
extern BOOL FAR PASCAL SetInternalWindowPos(HWND hwnd,
    WORD wStatus, LPRECT lprectWnd, LPPOINT lppointIcon);

char *szWndStatus[] =
    {   "0 - hidden", "1 - normal/restored", "2 - minimized",
        "3 - maximized", "4 - restore inactive", "5 - show",
        "6 - minimize", "7 - minimize inactive",
        "8 - show inactive", "9 - restore"};

#include "checkord.c"

int main()
    {
    char achInput[80];
    WORD wStatus;
    HWND hwnd;
    RECT rectWindow;
    POINT pointIcon;
    char *szStr;
    char *szTok;
    int iWrk[4];
    int i;

    // Name/ordinal checks
    if (! (CheckOrdName("GetInternalWindowPos", "USER", 460) &&
            CheckOrdName("SetInternalWindowPos", "USER", 461)))
        return 0;

    for (;;)
```

SetInternalWindowPos

```
    {
    // Prompt for window to look at
    puts("Enter the window title of a window");
    gets(achInput);

    if (achInput[0] == 0)
        break;

    // Get its handle
    if ((hwnd = FindWindow(NULL, achInput)) == 0)
        {
        printf("Couldn't locate <%s>....\n", achInput);
        continue;
        }

    // Get current minimized, maximized, and normal
    // position data, and current status
    wStatus = GetInternalWindowPos(hwnd,
        (LPRECT) &rectWindow, (LPPOINT) &pointIcon);
    printf("Window is currently %s.\n", szWndStatus[wStatus]);
    printf("Window coordinates are %d, %d, %d, %d,\n",
        rectWindow.left, rectWindow.top,
        rectWindow.right, rectWindow.bottom);
    printf("Icon position is %d, %d.\n\n",
        pointIcon.x, pointIcon.y);

    // Prompt for new normal window coordinates
    puts("Enter new window coordinates");
    puts("or <CR> to leave unchanged:");
    szStr = gets(achInput);
    if (! *szStr)
        goto lIconPos;
    i = 0;
    while ((i < 4) && (szTok = strtok(szStr, ", \t")))
        {
        iWrk[i++] = atoi(szTok);
        szStr = NULL;
        }
    while (i < 4) iWrk[i++] = 0;
    memcpy(&rectWindow, &iWrk, sizeof(RECT));

lIconPos:
    // Prompt for top left coordinates of minimized icon position
    puts("Enter new icon coordinates");
    puts("or <CR> to leave unchanged:");
    szStr = gets(achInput);
    if (! *szStr)
        goto lWinStatus;
    i = 0;
    while ((i < 2) && (szTok = strtok(szStr, " ")))
        {
        iWrk[i++] = atoi(szTok);
        szStr = NULL;
        }
    while (i < 2) iWrk[i++] = 0;
```

SetInternalWindowPos

```
        pointIcon.x = iWrk[0];
        pointIcon.y = iWrk[1];

    lWinStatus:
        // Prompt for new window status
        puts("Enter new window status");
        printf("%s\t%s\t%s\n%s\t%s\t%s\n%s\t%s\n"
                "or <CR> to leave unchanged:\n", szWndStatus[0],
                szWndStatus[1], szWndStatus[2], szWndStatus[3],
                szWndStatus[4], szWndStatus[5], szWndStatus[6],
                szWndStatus[7], szWndStatus[8], szWndStatus[9]);
        szStr = gets(achInput);
        if (! *szStr)
            goto lSetIWPos;
        wStatus = atoi(szStr);

    lSetIWPos:
        // and update window position and status data
        SetInternalWindowPos(hwnd, wStatus,
                (LPRECT) &rectWindow, (LPPOINT) &pointIcon);
        puts("SetInternalWindowPos executed.\n");
        }

    printf("Program terminated");
    return 0;
    }
```

SetSystemMenu   USER.280

```
BOOL FAR PASCAL SetSystemMenu(HWND, HMENU)
HWND hwnd;          /* window to receive a new system menu */
HMENU hMenu;        /* handle of new menu */
```

This function sets the system menu of the specified MDI client window to the supplied menu and destroys any previous system menu handle.

This function is called by MDIClientWndProc and does not work for anything other than MDI client windows; the documented GetSystemMenu, Append/Insert/DeleteMenu, and ShowMenu combination is adequate for all non-MDI purposes.

Return: TRUE (1) if the function was successful, FALSE (0) if not
Support: 3.0, 3.1

SetSystemTimer   USER.11

```
BOOL FAR PASCAL SetSystemTimer(HWND, int, WORD, FARPROC)
HWND hwnd;                  /* Window to own timer */
int nIDEvent;               /* timer identifier */
WORD wElapse;               /* milliseconds between events */
FARPROC lpTimerProc;        /* function to receive timer events */
```

This function allows an application to create a timer even when regular application timers are not available.

USER provides 16 application timers in version 3.0, and 32 in version 3.1. Timers are entries in an array of structures within USER's default DS. However, the array is not 16 entries in size in version 3.0, it is 18. In version 3.1 it is 34. the extra two entries in both versions are only available to this function, not to the documented SetTimer function.

This mechanism allows SetSystemTimer to draw from the same pool as SetTimer but allows for a timer to always be available for internal uses, such as the caret or scroll message auto repeats.

This function should not be confused with the undocumented CreateSystemTimer function in SYSTEM. The terminology is inconsistent between the two modules; a SYSTEM system timer is an asynchronous timer, but a USER system timer is a synchronous timer available to the system (as opposed to applications).

The lpTimerProc callback function is called with the same parameters as SetTimer. Note that if timer events are to be received from the message loop, the message sent by the timer is the undocumented WM_SYSTIMER (0x0118) (see chapter 7).

A timer created using SetSystemTimer is subsequently destroyed using its complementary function, KillSystemTimer.

Return: A timer identifier if successful, or NULL if unsuccessful
Note: In 3.1, the entry point still exists, but it is named BEAR11. The function entry point should therefore be obtained by ordinal rather than by name in applications intended to work in Windows 3.0 and 3.1. The example below illustrates this.
Support: 3.0, 3.1 (see Note)
Used by: Excel
See also: CreateSystemTimer, KillSystemTimer, WM_xxxx
Example: Allocates all available application timers, then allocates another timer using SetSystemTimer:

```
/* STSYSTMR.C */

#include <windows.h>
#include "wmhandlr.h"
#include "winio.h"

/* undocumented functions */
WORD (FAR PASCAL *lpfnSetSystemTimer)(HWND hwnd, int nIDEvent,
                        WORD wElapse, FARPROC lpTimerFunction);
BOOL (FAR PASCAL *lpfnKillSystemTimer)(HWND hwnd, WORD wTimer);

#define WM_SYSTIMER        0x0118

#define MAXTABLE 64        // Overgenerous!

WORD hSysTimer;
WORD hRegTimer[MAXTABLE] = {0};
```

SetSystemTimer

```
long do_systimer(HWND hWnd, WORD wMsg, WORD nIDEvent, DWORD lParam)
    {
    printf("hWnd=0x%04X, wMsg=0x%04X, nIDEvent=0x%04X, lParam=0x%08lX\n",
              hWnd, wMsg, nIDEvent, lParam);
    return 0;
    }

BOOL ResetTimer(HWND hwnd)
    {
    if (hSysTimer)
        (*lpfnKillSystemTimer)(hwnd, hSysTimer);
    return TRUE;
    }

int main()
    {
    int i;

    (FARPROC) lpfnSetSystemTimer =
        GetProcAddress(GetModuleHandle("USER"), (LPSTR) 11L);
    (FARPROC) lpfnKillSystemTimer =
        GetProcAddress(GetModuleHandle("USER"), (LPSTR) 182L);

    if ((! lpfnSetSystemTimer) || (! lpfnKillSystemTimer))
        fail("Could not locate Set/KillSystemTimer functions!\n");

    puts("Allocating timers...");

    for (i = 0; i < MAXTABLE; i++)
        {
        if (! (hRegTimer[i] = SetTimer(__hMainWnd, i+1, 10000,
                (FARPROC) 0L)))
            break;
        }
    printf("\nUsed SetTimer() to allocate all timers\n"
        "(there were %d available).\n\n", i);
    printf("We can still allocate a timer, however, using\n"
        "SetSystemTimer(). An event will be generated\n"
        "every second.\n"
        "Close the window to terminate.\n\n");

    wmhandler_set(__hMainWnd, WM_SYSTIMER, (WMHANDLER) do_systimer);

    hSysTimer = (*lpfnSetSystemTimer)(__hMainWnd, 0xDADA, 1000, NULL);
    if (hSysTimer == NULL)
        printf("Could not create system timer!\n");
    else
        printf("Timer handle is %04X\n\n", hSysTimer);

    printf("Freeing up %d regular timers.\n", i);
    for (i = 0; i < MAXTABLE; i++)
        if (hRegTimer[i])
            KillTimer(__hMainWnd, hRegTimer[i]);
        else
            break;
```

SetSystemTimer

```
winio_onclose(__hMainWnd, (DESTROY_FUNC) ResetTimer);

return 0;
}
```

SetTimer2   USER.328

```
HANDLE FAR PASCAL SetTimer2(HWND, WORD, WORD, FARPROC)
HWND hwnd;               /* window owning timer */
WORD wIDEvent;          /* timer event id */
WORD wElapse;           /* milliseconds between events */
FARPROC lpTimerFunc;    /* timer event handler or NULL */
// CX contains BOOL bSystem
```

This function is the back end to documented SetTimer and undocumented Set-SystemTimer functions.

CreateTimer sets CX to 0 and jumps to this function; SetSystemTimer sets CX to 1 and falls through to this function. The bSystem parameter in CX specifies whether the timer is to be drawn from the application subset of the timer array (see the discussion of SetSystemTimer), in which case bSystem is FALSE, or from the entire array, in which case bSystem is TRUE.

The bSystem parameter in CX also determines whether the message that is posted to the calling applications message queue is to be the undocumented WM_SYSTIMER (0x0118) message (see chapter 7) or the documented WM_TIMER message.

It is neither necessary nor recommended to call this function, and it is included here only for completeness.

Return: A HANDLE to a timer, or NULL if the function was unsuccessful
Support: 3.0
See also: KillTimer2, SetSystemTimer, WM_SYSTIMER

SetWC2   USER.319

```
DWORD FAR PASCAL SetWC2(HWND, int, DWORD)
HWND hwnd;          /* window handle */
int nOffset;        /* offset from end of WND or WNDCLASS structure */
DWORD dwData;       /* new data to update structure at offset */
// CL contains bits indicating Class or Window, WORD or DWORD
```

This function is the engine behind SetWindowLong, SetWindowWord, SetClassWord, and SetClassLong. Those functions present four entry points that set bits in CL (0x80 indicates get from class structure, not window structure; 0x01 indicates DWORD required, not WORD) before falling through to SetWC2.

Return: Previous DWORD from the offset within either the window or class structure for the window
Support: 3.0
Note: In version 3.1, this same ordinal entry point corresponds to the documented function ScrollWindowEx.

SignalProc   USER.314

```
void FAR PASCAL SignalProc(HANDLE, WORD, WORD, HANDLE HANDLE)
HANDLE hTaskQueue;      /* task queue of task */
WORD wSigType;         /* 0x20, 0x40, 0x80 or 0x666 */
WORD wExitFn;          /* 0, 0x4c00 or 0xffff */
HANDLE h1;             /* unknown */
HANDLE hCurrent;       /* task queue of currently executing task */
```

This function is USER's standard handler for KERNEL-generated task initiation/switch/termination signals.

This function is installed using the undocumented KERNEL function SetTaskSignalProc. It receives control at task initiation (wSigType == 0x0040), Task Manager task switch (wSigType == 0x0020), abnormal task event (wSigType == 0x0666—the satanic flavor of which is unlikely to be coincidental!), and task termination (wSigType == 0x0080).

Support: 3.0, 3.1
See also: SetTaskSignalProc (chapter 5)

SnapWindow   USER.281

```
BOOL FAR PASCAL SnapWindow(HWND)
HWND hwnd;             /* Window to be snapped */
```

This function takes a snapshot of the specified window and records it as a bitmap in the clipboard. It uses the window coordinates to determine what proportion of the screen to clip. Any of the window that is hidden on the desktop will remain hidden in the clipboard rendition.

This function allows, for example, a screen capture facility to be built into an application. SnapWindow(GetActiveWindow()) will capture the current window, and SnapWindow(GetDesktopWindow()) will capture the entire screen to the clipboard. In Windows 3.0 these are the calls that are triggered by the PrtScr and Shift-PrtScr keystrokes, respectively.

The function continues to exist in version 3.1 but is not exported, even by ordinal.

Return: TRUE (1) if the Window was snapped, FALSE (0) if unsuccessful
Support: 3.0

Example:

```
/* SNAPWIND.C */

#include <windows.h>
#include "winio.h"

/* undocumented functions */
extern BOOL FAR PASCAL SnapWindow(HWND hwnd);

#include "checkord.c"

int main()
    {
    HWND hwnd;
    char achWindowTitle[128];

    // Ord/name check
    if (! CheckOrdName("SnapWindow", "USER", 281))
        return 0;

    for (;;)
        {
        puts("Enter the window title of the application window");
        gets(achWindowTitle);

        if ((hwnd = FindWindow(NULL, achWindowTitle)) == 0)
            printf("Couldn't locate <%s>.\n", achWindowTitle);
        else
        if (SnapWindow(hwnd))
            printf("Window has been snapped into the clipboard.\n");
        else
            printf("Could not SnapWindow().\n");
        }

    printf("Program terminated");
    return 0;
    }
```

StringFunc   **USER.470**

```
LPSTR|int FAR PASCAL StringFunc(LPSTR[, LPSTR])
LPSTR strInput;    /* source string (Reserved5) or char pointer */
LPSTR strComp;     /* comparison string (Reserved5 only) */
// CX contains function type (1-5 corresponding to KERNEL
// functions Reserved1 thru Reserved5)
```

This function is called from the Kernel functions Reserved1 thru Reserved5. These calls are obsolete and date from 2.1 when the functionality of the functions AnsiNext, AnsiPrev, AnsiUpper, AnsiLower, and lstrcmp resided in KERNEL. This function now provides a gateway by which KERNEL can provide backward compatibility for those applications that still use the ReservedN functions. The ReservedN functions place a function code in CX and call StringFunc, which uses the value in CX to perform an indexed jump to the appropriate routine.

The strComp parameter is only present from the Reserved5 call (lstrcmp), in which case the return value is of type int, as documented for the lstrcmp function. Otherwise, for Reserved1 thru Reserved4 (the Ansi- functions), the strComp parameter is not present. For these calls, the strInput parameter and return value are as specified in the documentation of the AnsiPrev, AnsiNext, AnsiUpper, and AnsiLower functions.

It will never be necessary to call this function directly.

Return: As specified in the SDK for the documented functions AnsiPrev, AnsiNext, AnsiUpper, AnsiLower, and lstrcmp
Support: 3.0, 3.1
See also: Reserved1 thru Reserved5

SwitchToThisWindow   USER.172

```
void FAR PASCAL SwitchToThisWindow(HWND, BOOL)
HWND hwnd;              /* Window to switch to */
BOOL bRestore;         /* Restore it? */
```

SwitchToThisWindow() is nothing if not self-documenting. It switches focus to the task owning the specified window, activates it and restores it. The Task Manager "Switch To" button calls this function directly.

If the window is iconized,and the bRestore parameter is TRUE (1), the function restores the Window to normal size. If the bRestore parameter is FALSE (0), the window is activated, but it is left at its current size and state.

Support: 3.0, 3.1
Notes: For an additional example, see GetNextQueueWindow().
Example: Installs a timer which constantly switches focus to the program.

```
/* SWTOTHIS.C */

#include <windows.h>
#include "winio.h"

/* undocumented function */
extern void FAR PASCAL SwitchToThisWindow(HWND hwnd, BOOL tRestore);

#include "checkord.c"

WORD hTimer;
FARPROC lpfnTimerFunc;

WORD FAR PASCAL TimerFunc(HWND hWnd, WORD wMsg,
```

```
    int nIDEvent, DWORD dwTime)
    {
    SwitchToThisWindow(winio_current(), TRUE);
    return 1;
    }

BOOL ResetTimer(HWND hwnd)
    {
    FreeProcInstance(lpfnTimerFunc);
    KillTimer(winio_current(), 0xDADA);
    return TRUE;
    }

int main()
    {
    // Ord/name check
    if (! CheckOrdName("SwitchToThisWindow", "USER", 172))
        return 0;

    lpfnTimerFunc = MakeProcInstance((FARPROC) TimerFunc, __hInst);

    if ((hTimer = SetTimer(winio_current(), 0xDADA,
        3000, lpfnTimerFunc)) == NULL)
        {
        printf("Could not SetTimer()!\nProgram terminating.");
        return 0;
        }

    winio_onclose(winio_current(), (DESTROY_FUNC) ResetTimer);

    printf("Minimize this window, and within 5 seconds,\n"
            "it will restore itself using a call to\n"
            "SwitchToThisWindow() within a timer event.\n\n"
            "Close the window to terminate");

    return 0;
    }
```

SysErrorBox   USER.320

```
int FAR PASCAL SysErrorBox(LPSTR, LPSTR, WORD, WORD, WORD)
LPSTR lpMessage;        /* Error message text */
LPSTR lpTitle;          /* Error box title */
WORD wLButton;          /* Left button type */
WORD wMButton;          /* Middle button type */
WORD wRButton;          /* Right button type */
```

This function puts up an asynchronous message box with up to three buttons and returns the user response.

This function allows a low-level error to be reported immediately. It allows one, two, or three buttons to appear on the message box, with one of them optionally the default selection. If a button is wanted in one of the three positions, its associated parameter should be *one* of the SEB_ constants defined in the example below, optionally ORed with the SEB_DEFAULT to make it the default selection (giving it initial keyboard focus). If a button is not wanted in a particular position, its associated position parameter should be set to 0.

The function returns 1, 2, or 3 depending on which button was actually selected by the user.

This function can be used whatever state Windows is in because it does not rely on being able to send or receive messages but rather implements its own event handling within the function.

Return: 1, 2, or 3 depending on user button selection

Support: 3.0, 3.1

Note: This function is not reentrant and is used in the case of application fatal errors by Windows itself. If any of the parameters is invalid, the system will be unstable and will in all certainty crash either immediately or very soon after.

Example:

```
/* SYSERRBX.C */
#include <dos.h>
#include <windows.h>
#include "winio.h"

/* undocumented function */
extern int FAR PASCAL SysErrorBox(LPSTR msg, LPSTR title,
    WORD lButton, WORD mButton, WORD rButton);

#define SEB_OK        1
#define SEB_CANCEL    2
#define SEB_YES       3
#define SEB_NO        4
#define SEB_RETRY     5
#define SEB_ABORT     6
#define SEB_IGNORE    7

#define SEB_DEFAULT    0x8000

#include "checkord.c"

int main()
    {
    int nResult;

    // Ord/name check
    if (! CheckOrdName("SysErrorBox", "USER", 320))
        return 0;

    nResult = SysErrorBox("Press one of these buttons.",
                "SysErrorBox() Test",
                SEB_ABORT, SEB_RETRY, SEB_IGNORE | SEB_DEFAULT);
```

SysErrorBox

```
printf("You pressed the %s button\n",
        nResult == 1 ? "left" :
        nResult == 2 ? "middle" :
                "right");

printf("\nProgram terminated");
return 0;
}
```

System Message Queue   Structure

Windows contains two different kinds of message queues: the Task Queue and the System Message Queue. As is discussed in chapter 5 (KERNEL), each task has its own private Task Queue. There is one system-wide message queue, used essentially as a buffer for hardware events. The hardware_event() function, documented in the 3.1 SDK, places messages in the System Message Queue. So do the Keybd_Event() and Mouse_Event() functions, discussed elsewhere in this chapter. The System Message Queue is sometimes also referred to as the hardware event queue.

The System Message Queue has the same basic structure as the Task Queue (see chapter 5), but with a few differences:

- The System Message Queue can generally hold more messages than a Task Queue. By default, the System Message Queue can hold 120 messages. However, this can be changed with the undocumented TypeAhead= setting in the [windows] section of WIN.INI. In contrast, a Task Queue by default holds only eight messages, though this too can be changed with an undocumented DefaultQueueSize= setting in WIN.INI. Thus, a perverse WIN.INI might create huge Task Queues and a smaller System Message Queue:

```
[windows]
;;; don't do this!
TypeAhead=60
DefaultQueueSize=80
```

- Whereas the Task Queue holds an array of 12h-byte MSG structs (plus, in 3.1, room for GetMessageExtraInfo, for a total of 16h bytes per Task Queue message), the System Message Queue holds an array of 0Ah-byte EVENTMSG structs (plus, in 3.1, room for GetMessageExtraInfo, for a total of 0Eh bytes per system message).
- Because it does not correspond to the Task Database, the System Message Queue's hTask field (offset 2) does not contain a task handle.
- The System Message Queue is not on the linked list of Task Queues. Thus, its Next field (offset 0) is NULL.

But Task Queues and the System Message Queue at least share the following generic Queue structure:

```
00h      WORD      Next            Always NULL in System Message Queue
02h      WORD      hTask           System Message Queue has no hTask
04h      WORD      msgSize         3.0 SysMsgQ=0Ah, 3.1=0Eh; TaskQ=12h
06h      WORD      msgCount        Number of unretrieved messages
08h      WORD      msgOffset       start + (msgSize * msgCount)
0Ah      WORD      freeOffset      Offset of next free slot
0Ch      WORD      endQueue        ????
... etc. ...
???      ????      msgArray        size = msgSize * ??
```

USER keeps a selector to the System Message Queue in its non-default fixed DATA segment, at offset 2 in 3.0 and offset 0 in 3.1.

Support: 3.0, 3.1
See also: Keybd_Event, Mouse_Event, SetEventHook in this chapter; Task Queue structure in chapter 5
Example: The following program, SYSMSG, hangs off the timer, printing out any pending messages in the System Message Queue as raw bytes.

```c
/* SYSMSG.C -- inspect System Message Queue */

#include <stdlib.h>
#include <dos.h>
#include "windows.h"
#include "toolhelp.h"
#include "winio.h"
#include "wmhandlr.h"

#define DEFAULT_NUMMSG          120

typedef struct {
    WORD     Next;                   // 0
    WORD     hTask;                  // 2
    WORD     msgSize;                // 4
    WORD     msgCount;               // 6
    WORD     nextMessageOffset;      // 8
    WORD     nextFreeMessageOffset;  // 0A
    WORD     endOfQueue;             // 0C
    DWORD    GetMessageTimeRetval;   // 0E
    DWORD    GetMessagePosRetval;    // 12
    WORD     messageQueueStart;      // 16
    } QUEUE;

long on_time(HWND hwnd, unsigned message, WORD wParam, LONG lParam);

static BYTE far *fpMsgs;
static QUEUE far *SysMsgQ;
static WORD hSysMsgQ;

WORD GetSystemMessageQueue(void)
{
    GLOBALENTRY ge;
```

System Message Queue

```
        WORD SysMsgQOfs;
        WORD wVers;
        BOOL ok;
        WORD hUser = GetModuleHandle("USER");
        WORD UserOtherDS = 0;
        // use ToolHelp to find USER's non-default data segment
        ge.dwSize = sizeof(ge);
        ok = GlobalFirst(&ge, GLOBAL_ALL);
        while (ok)
        {
            if (ge.hOwner == hUser)
                if (ge.wType == GT_DATA)     // not GT_DGROUP!
                {
                    UserOtherDS = ge.hBlock;
                    break;
                }
            ok = GlobalNext(&ge, GLOBAL_ALL);
        }
        if (UserOtherDS == 0)
            return 0;   // couldn't locate USER's non-DGROUP DS

        /* printf("USER's other DS: %04x\n", UserOtherDS); */

        // get selector to System Message Queue from ofs 2 (3.0) or 0 (3.1)
        wVers = (WORD) GetVersion();
        SysMsgQOfs = -1;
        if (LOBYTE(wVers) == 3)
        {
            if (HIBYTE(wVers) == 0)        // 3.0
                SysMsgQOfs = 2;
            else if (HIBYTE(wVers) == 10)   // 3.10
                SysMsgQOfs = 0;
        }
        if (SysMsgQOfs == -1)
            return 0;   // unknown Windows version
        return *((WORD far *) MK_FP(UserOtherDS, SysMsgQOfs));
    }

main()
{
    char buf[128];
    WORD cMsg, QOfs;

    if ((hSysMsgQ = GetSystemMessageQueue()) == 0)
        fail("Can't find System Message Queue");
    SysMsgQ = MK_FP(hSysMsgQ, 0);

    // figure out number of messages
    cMsg = GetProfileInt("windows", "TypeAhead", DEFAULT_NUMMSG);

    // figure out offset of actual queue within System Msg Queue struct
    QOfs = SysMsgQ->endOfQueue - (cMsg * SysMsgQ->msgSize);
    fpMsgs = MK_FP(hSysMsgQ, QOfs);

    // show where SysMsgQ is, and how big it is
```

System Message Queue

```
        sprintf(buf, "SysMsgQ: %u %u-byte messages @ %Fp",
            cMsg,               // number of messages can hold (default 120)
            SysMsgQ->msgSize, // size of each message (3.0: 0Ah, 3.1: 0Eh)
            fpMsgs);          // far ptr to actual message within struct
    winio_settitle(__hMainWnd, buf);
    wmhandler_set(__hMainWnd, WM_TIMER, on_time);
    if (! SetTimer(__hMainWnd, 1, 250, NULL))
        fail("can't create timer");
    return 0;
}

long on_time(HWND hwnd, unsigned message, WORD wParam, LONG lParam)
{
    BYTE far *fp;
    WORD numpending, nextmsg;
    int i, j;

    nextmsg = SysMsgQ->nextMessageOffset;

    // how many unretrieved messages are in the queue?
    numpending =
        (SysMsgQ->nextFreeMessageOffset - nextmsg) /
        SysMsgQ->msgSize;

    // if any pending messages, show them
    if (! numpending)
        return 0;

    winio_setpaint(__hMainWnd, FALSE);
    printf("%u messages pending: %04X-%04X\n",
        numpending, nextmsg, SysMsgQ->nextFreeMessageOffset);

    for (i=0, fp=MK_FP(hSysMsgQ, nextmsg); i<numpending; i++)
    {
        for (j=0; j<SysMsgQ->msgSize; j++, fp++)
            printf("%02X ", *fp);
        printf("\n");
    }
    winio_setpaint(__hMainWnd, TRUE);

    return 0;
}
```

TabTheTextOutForWimps   USER.354

```
DWORD FAR PASCAL TabTheTextOutForWimps(HDC, int, int, LPSTR, int,
                              int, LPINT, int, BOOL)
HDC hDC;              /* device context */
int X;               /* start X coordinate */
int Y;               /* start Y coordinate */
LPSTR lpString;      /* string to draw */
int nCount;          /* string length */
int nTabPositions    /* number of tab stop positions in array */
LPINT lpnTabStops;   /* array of tab stop positions */
```

TabTheTextOutForWimps

```
int nTabOrigin;          /* where to start expanding tabs from */
BOOL bDraw;              /* actually draw the string ? */
```

This function writes a string on the specified display, expanding tabs to positions specified in the supplied array of tab stops. This function is the engine called by the documented USER functions TabbedTextOut and GetTabbedTextExtent. The final parameter specifies whether it should actually draw the string or not, allowing it to do double duty for the above two functions.

The function is included solely for interest, since no more can be achieved with it than can be achieved with the two documented functions; it does not appear in 3.1 (presumably 3.1 programmers are no longer wimps...).

Return: The dimensions of the string as it would appear on the display, with the height and width in the high and low words, respectively, of the DWORD
Support: 3.0

TileChildWindows   USER.199

```
void FAR PASCAL TileChildWindows(HWND [, WORD])
HWND hParent;      /* Window whose children are to be tiled */
WORD wAction;      /* How to tile [3.1 only] */
```

This function arranges the positions of child windows of the specified parent into a tiled formation.

TileChildWindows() was apparently written for the MDI function group and is called by PROGMAN.EXE and FILEMAN.EXE, both of which are MDI applications. It takes the window handle of the owning, or parent, window as its first—and in version 3.0, only—parameter.

Note that an attempt, in version 3.0, to

```
TileChildWindows(FindWindow(NULL, "Program Manager"));
```

will not achieve the expected result, as the Program Group windows are not actually direct child windows of the Program Manager main window, but rather are MDI client windows.

The second parameter is present only in version 3.1 and affects whether disabled windows are tiled. If the wAction parameter is set to MDITILE_SKIPDISABLED (0x0002), defined in the version 3.1 WINDOWS.H, only child windows of the currently active child window of the specified hParent are tiled. The wAction field may also contain one of either MDITILE_HORIZONTAL or MDITILE_VERTICAL. These, as their names imply, control the direction in which the tiling operation proceeds.

Return: Void
Support: 3.0, 3.1 (see Notes)
Note: The second parameter is not present in 3.0.
Used by: PROGMAN.EXE, FILEMAN.EXE
See also: CascadeChildWindows
Example:

```
/* TILECHLD.C */

#include <windows.h>
#include "winio.h"

/* undocumented function */

/* Declaring a void parameter list allows us to call the function */
/* with the appropriate number of arguments for either 3.0 or 3.1 */
extern void FAR PASCAL TileChildWindows();

#include "checkord.c"

int main()
    {
    WORD wVer = (WORD) GetVersion();

    // Ord/name check
    if (! CheckOrdName("TileChildWindows", "USER", 199))
        return 0;

    winio_setecho(winio_current(), FALSE);

    for (;;)
        if (wVer == 0x0003)
            {
            puts("Press a key to tile the desktop.");
            getchar();

            TileChildWindows(GetDesktopWindow());
            }
        else
            {
            puts("Press a key to tile the desktop horizontally.");
            getchar();

            TileChildWindows(GetDesktopWindow(), MDITILE_HORIZONTAL);

            puts("Press a key to tile the desktop vertically.");
            getchar();

            TileChildWindows(GetDesktopWindow(), MDITILE_VERTICAL);
            }

    printf("Program terminated");
    return 0;
    }
```

TileChildWindows

UserSeeUserDo

USER.216

```
DWORD FAR PASCAL UserSeeUserDo(WORD, WORD, WORD, WORD)
WORD wReqType;          /* request type */
WORD wParam1;           /* depends on wReqType */
WORD wParam2;           /* unused - reserved for future expansion? */
WORD wParam3;           /* depends on wReqType */
```

This function provides access to the USER default local heap. (In version 3.1 USER has multiple heaps—see the discussion in the USER Heaps section of the introduction to this chapter.) It is used by TOOLHELP.DLL in version 3.1 (see chapter 10). UserSeeUserDo recognizes five request types in the wReqType. Use of the other parameters depends on the request type (except for the wParam2 argument, which is not used by any of the currently defined request types).

USUD_LOCALALLOC (0x0001)

allocates some memory from the USER module default local heap. The wParam1 argument contains the flags to be passed to the documented LocalAlloc function for the allocation, and wParam3 specifies the size of the block to allocate.

It returns the allocated handle in the low word if the LocalAlloc was successful, NULL if it failed.

USUD_LOCALFREE (0x0002)

frees a block of memory in the USER module default local heap. The wParam1 argument contains the USER local memory handle to be freed.

It returns NULL in the low WORD if the LocalFree was successful, or the specified handle if it failed.

USUD_LOCALCOMPACT (0x0003)

generates a free block of the specified size in the USER module default local heap. The wParam3 argument specifies the size of the required free block, to be passed to LocalCompact, then returns the size of the largest free block in the USER module default local heap in the low word.

USUD_LOCALHEAP (0x0004)

returns the selector for the USER module default local heap in the low word. This can be combined with a local memory handle such as an HWND, or a handle returned from the USUD_LOCALALLOC request described above, to form a far pointer into the USER heap.

```
USUD_FIRSTCLASS (0x0005)
```

returns the HCLASS for the first class entry in the linked list of class structures. See the CLASS entry in this chapter.

If the request type does not correspond to one of the above values, the call signifies an invalid request type by returning -1.

In the debug version of USER, allocations made by UserSeeUserDo are identified by an allocation type of LT_USER_USERSEEUSERDOALLOC (see chapter 10).

Return: Depends on the request type, as specified above
Support: 3.1
See also: GdiSeeGdiDo (chapter 8), CLASS structure, GetUserLocalObjType

---

UserYield   USER.332

```
void FAR PASCAL UserYield(void);
```

This function is called from the documented KERNEL function Yield(). UserYield almost immediately calls the undocumented KERNEL function OldYield(). UserYield() checks the queue status fields in the current task's Task Queue.

Support: 3.0, 3.1
See also: OldYield (chapter 5)

WinFarFrame   USER.340

```
WinFarFrame proc far
;; cs:ip on the stack points to two bytes:
;; first is count of words of local stack space needed by function
;; second is count of words of function parameters expected on the stack
```

WinFarFrame is an assembler routine that prepares a stack frame for a near function that is called using a far call. In WINSTACK.ASM, from which WinFarFrame is exported, there is a companion routine, which is not exported but which is presumably called WinNearFrame, which performs the same functionality for near functions that are called using a near call. WinNearFrame is not exported because it does not need DS to be set up by the loader.

It is not known why they exist, but a clue must lie in the fact that in version 3.0, which supports real mode, almost every function in USER is a near function and calls one or the other of the WinXXXFrame routines; in version 3.1, however, all traces of the routines themselves, and the mechanism that they implement, have disappeared, as has support for real mode.

At offset 0 at the beginning of every code segment in 3.0 USER, the following code appears:

```
NearFuncEntry:
    push cs
    jmp far WinNearFrame
NearFuncExit:
    push cs
    jmp far WinNearUndoFrame

FarFuncEntry:
    push cs
    jmp far WinFarFrame
FarFuncExit:
    push cs
    jmp far WinFarUndoFrame
```

At the beginning of every far function, the following code appears:

```
call FarFuncEntry        ;; or NearFuncEntry for a near function
db     nLocalWords
db     nParamWords
```

When WinXXXFrame is called, it establishes BP; subtracts the appropriate number of bytes from SP to allow for local variables as defined by the nLocalWords byte; stores on the stack the number of words by which the stack must be adjusted to account for parameters, as defined by the nParamWords byte; puts the address of the appropriate XXXFuncExit label on the stack; and, in the case of WinFarFrame, establishes DS and saves SI and DI.

When the function returns via a RETN instruction, the WinXXXFrameUndo function is called. It restores BP, removes the parameters from the stack, and in the case of WinFarFrameUndo, restores SI, DI, and DS.

Support: 3.0
See also: FFFE_FarFrame

WinOldAppHackOMatic   USER.322

```
DWORD FAR PASCAL WinOldAppHackOMatic(DWORD)
DWORD dwFlags;          /* flags to be set - must be 1 */
```

This function is only called by WINOA386.MOD, i.e., only in 386 Enhanced mode. It sets a global flag in USER's DS which tells USER to check the Alt key state to allow for DOS box system menu options (such as Alt-Tab to switch task focus and Alt-Enter to switch between full screen and windowed modes) to be processed.

Return: Always returns 0
Support: 3.0, 3.1
Used by: WINOA386.MOD

WND   Structure

This is the structure that contains information and state about a window. It is maintained in USER's default near heap segment, and is certainly one of the most important undocumented Windows structures. The ubiquitous HWND is a handle to this structure. The structure changed significantly between versions 3.0 and 3.1.

Window structure in version 3.0:

```
typedef struct tagWND {
    HWND          hwndNext;
    HWND          hwndChild;
    HCLASS        hClass;
    HANDLE        h1stProp;
    HWND          hwndLastActive;
    HANDLE        hmemScroll;
    HANDLE        hmemTaskQ;
    HRGN          hrgnPaint;
    HANDLE        hDCE;
    HMENU         hmenuSystem;
    HWND          hwndOwner;
    RECT          rectWindow;
    RECT          rectClient;
    HPALETTE      hPalette;
    WORD          wFlags;
    DWORD         rgfExStyle;
    DWORD         rgfStyle;
    WORD          wID_Menu;
    HANDLE        hBuffer;
    HWND          hwndParent;
    HANDLE        hInstance;
    FARPROC       lpfnWndProc;
    // User data starts here
    } WND_3_0;
```

Window structure in version 3.1:

```
typedef struct tagWND {
    HWND          hwndNext;
    HWND          hwndChild;
    HWND          hwndParent;
    HWND          hwndOwner;
    RECT          rectWindow;
    RECT          rectClient;
    HANDLE        hmemTaskQ;
    HRGN          hrgnUpdate;
    HCLASS        hClass;
    HANDLE        hInstance;
    FARPROC       lpfnWndProc;
    DWORD         dwFlags;
    DWORD         rgfStyle;
    DWORD         rgfExStyle;
    WORD          wID_Menu;
    HANDLE        hBuffer;
```

```
HANDLE        hmemScroll;
HANDLE        h1stProp;
HWND          hwndLastActive;
HMENU         hmenuSystem;
// User data starts here
} WND_3_1;
```

The preceeding versions of the structure contain the following fields:

FIELD	DESCRIPTION
hwndNext	Next sibling window at the same hierarchical level
hwndChild	First child window belonging to this window. Other children of this window will appear in the hierarchy as siblings to this window.
hClass	Handle to an undocumented CLASS structure in the internal stored list of window classes
h1stProp	Local handle within USER's heap to the head of a chain of property entries associated with the window, added through calls to SetProp; NULL if no properties are associated with the window
hwndLastActive	Window handle of the last popup window owned by this window that was active, as returned by the GetLastActivePopup function
hmemScroll	It is not fully understood what the memory (always 16 bytes) that this handle references is for, but it appears to have something to do with window scrolling. It is known to be at the root of an infamous bug in USER in version 3.0 involving multiline edit controls (see Paul Borneau's "Windows Q&A" columns in the December 1991, April 1992, and June 1992 issues of *Windows/DOS Developer's Journal.*) The field was used to store a handle allocated during an initialization that was erroneously performed twice. The second handle overwrote the first, which was orphaned, leading eventually to a Windows out of memory lock-up
hmemTask	A global memory handle for the application's Task Queue data structure
hrgnUpdate	Accumulated window update region, built up through calls to InvalidateRgn and InvalidateRect, and cleared by EndPaint
hDCE	Handle of the DCE structure used by the window, if the window class included the CS_OWNDC style, otherwise NULL. See the DCE structure entry earlier in this chapter (3.0 only).
hmenuSystem	The handle of the system menu for a MDI client window, or the copy of the default system menu current for the window, as returned by GetSystemMenu with a bRevert parameter of FALSE (see SDK documentation for GetSystemMenu)
hwndOwner	Window handle of the owning window
rectClient	RECT containing screen coordinates of client area

WND

rectWindow	RECT containing screen coordinates of nonclient area
hPalette	Handle to the logical palette to be used during window, or NULL
wFlags	Unknown—bits 9/10 set/reset in response to return from WM_USER+260 (see DragObject)
rgfExStyle	Undocumented Extra Style bits. These include, among other unknown flags

> WES_NOTIFYDRAG (0x00000002) — This must be set in order for LBWndProc to send a WM_BEGINDRAG message if a drag operation is started within a listbox control (see WM_BEGINDRAG in chapter 7)
>
> WES_ALWAYSONTOP—This style is documented in 3.1 and keeps a window at the top of the z order, i.e., always on top of the desktop

rgfStyle	See SDK documentation for CreateWindow window styles
wID_Menu	See SDK documentation for CreateWindow child control window IDs. In the case of child control windows, this field is a control ID. Otherwise, if the window has a menu, it will contain an HMENU; otherwise NULL.
hBuffer	Appears to be an alternative global handle for the window text (for edit controls?)
hwndParent	See SDK documentation for the CreateWindow function hwndParent parameter
hInstance	See SDK documentation for the CreateWindow hInstance parameter. This field contains the hInstance with which the window is associated.
lpfnWndProc	See SDK documentation for the WNDCLASS structure lpfnWndProc field. This field contains the procedure instance of the window's WndProc
wExtra	See SDK documentation for the WNDCLASS structure cbWndExtra field. This field marks the start of the window instance data area, if extra bytes were defined for the window.

Note: The structure changed completely between versions 3.0 and 3.1. It appears that the number, type, and usage of the fields in the structure have remained constant, but that the field order has been extensively changed. In fact, the only fields that have remained in the same position in the structure are the first two, hwndNext and hwndChild. These are the fields used to navigate the hierarchy of windows in the system and which relate child windows to parents. Frequently, code within USER needs to trace windows up to the top level window for a particular application instance. This is frequently done in-line, rather than through a call to a single function, perhaps to avoid too much 3.0 code modification, which these two fields were spared in 3.1.

WND

The reordering is puzzling for another reason: in version 3.0, the functions GetWindowWord and GetWindowLong took Windows SDK defined constants such as GWL_WNDPROC or application-supplied positive offsets. The positive offsets allowed access to instance data that an application can attach to a window. The pre-defined constants, on the other hand, are negative offsets defined in WINDOWS.H. The code in 3.0 for the two functions, which shared the same entry point, needed only to apply the given offset from the end of the window structure directly and retrieve a double word (the prototype for GetWindowWord makes it return only a word, although a full double word is available in DX:AX).

The code for these functions in 3.1 has become more complex. Instead of the direct application of the supplied offset (after simple range validation) to the structure as in 3.0, it is now checked for being positive or negative. If positive, the function acts as in 3.0. However, if negative, it is scanned for in a lookup table in CS. When located, the resultant new offset is extracted and is then used against the structure.

Note: See also Paul Bonneau's "3.1's Internal Window Structure," *Windows/DOS Developer's Journal*, June 1992. Bonneau mentions the possibility of a four-byte block *before* the WND in 3.1 debug.

See also: CLASS structure, MENU structure
Example: See the USERWALK program

WNetErrorText   USER.499

```
WORD FAR PASCAL WNetErrorText(WORD nError, LPSTR lpBuffer, WORD
nBufferSize);
```

This is the only undocumented WNet* function. All others are documented in chapter 5 of the Windows DDK *Device Driver Adapation Guide,* and in the DDK header file WINNET.H. (A few are also documented in the 3.1 SDK.) WNetErrorText() appears in WINNET.H as "internal." A comment in WINNET.H simply says "stuff in user, not driver, for shell apps." Indeed, the function is called by File Manager.

Also unlike most other WNet* functions in USER, which simply use FarCallNetDriver() to pass through to their respective functions in a network driver such as LANMAN.DRV, MSNET.DRV, or (most likely!) NETWARE.DRV, the code for WNetErrorText() actually resides in USER.

WNetErrorText() differs from the documented WNetGetErrorText() function only in that the textual description of the error may be loaded from a stringtable resource in USER, rather than from the driver itself. USER's stringtable in 3.1 includes relating to errors while restoring network connections. An improvement in 3.1 was support for network connections in File Manager and Print Manager.)

For descriptions of other WNet* functions, see the *DDK Device Driver Adaptation Guide* and Ralph Davis's book *The Windows Programmer's Guide to Networking* (Addison-Wesley, forthcoming 1993).

Support: 3.1
Used by: WINFILE (File Manager)
See also: FarCallNetDriver

XCStoDS USER.315

```
WORD FAR PASCAL XCStoDS(void);
```

This function returns the value of USER's default DS selector.

It can be used in conjunction with the HANDLE of any USER object that is stored in the USER default heap (see the introduction to this chapter for a discussion of USER heaps and object types), such as a documented HWND or an undocumented HCLASS, to generate a far pointer. This can in turn be used to inspect the contents of USER data structures. The function depends on the function prolog to set up DS on entry, after which it simply pushes DS and pops AX.

It should be pointed out that USER's default DS selector can instead be obtained by calling GetWindowWord(GetDesktopWindow(), GWW_HINSTANCE), all the pieces of which are documented. Since this works not only in 3.0, but also in 3.1 (where XCStoDS() is not available), this is the recommended method for obtaining USER's DS.

ToolHelp (see chapter 10) provides a way of locating all USER global heap blocks. Those that are local heaps can then be determined using techniques described in the entry for Local Heaps in chapter 5, or simply by testing if the ToolHelp LocalFirst() function succeeds when passed a given global-heap handle. For example:

```
GLOBALENTRY ge;
BOOL ok;
HANDLE hUser = GetModuleHandle("USER");
ge.dwSize = sizeof(ge);
ok = GlobalFirst(&ge, GLOBAL_ALL);
while (ok)
{
    if (ge.hOwner == hUser) // locate all blocks belonging to USER
    {
        LOCALENTRY le;
        le.dwSize = sizeof(le);
        if (LocalEntry(&le, ge.hBlock))
        {
            // it's a USER local heap
        }
    }
    ok = GlobalNext(&ge, GLOBAL_ALL);
}
```

The following example masquerades under the name XCSTODS.C but does not call XCStoDS at all; instead, it illustrates the alternate, GetWindowWord, approach.

Using the undocumented WND structure, it lists a hierarchical tree of parent and child window handles with their titles without using GetWindow, EnumWindows, or EnumChildWindows.

Return: The USER default DS selector.
See also: Chapter 10, Local Heaps (chapter 5), and the introduction to this chapter
Example: The following is an example of how to avoid having to use XCStoDS!

```c
/* XCSTODS.C */

#include <windows.h>
#include <dos.h>
#include <string.h>
#include "winio.h"

#define MK_FP(a,b)  ((void far *)(((unsigned long)(a) << 16) | (b)))

/* Undocumented WND structure */
#include "wnd.h"

/* undocumented function that could be used in 3.0 */
// extern WORD FAR PASCAL XCStoDS(void);

WORD selUserDS;
char strIndent[30] = {0};
char strText[128];

void printtree(WORD wndofs)
    {
    // We only need WND fields which coincide in 3.0 and 3.1
    WND_3_0 far *hwnd;

    for (;;)
        {
        hwnd = MK_FP(selUserDS, wndofs);
        GetWindowText((HWND) wndofs, (LPSTR) &strText, 128);
        printf("%sWindow %04X is %s\n", strIndent, wndofs, strText);
        if (hwnd->hwndChild != NULL)
            {
            int i = strlen(strIndent);
            strcat(strIndent, "  ");
            printtree(hwnd->hwndChild);
            strIndent[i] = 0;
            }
        if ((wndofs = hwnd->hwndNext) == NULL)
            break;
        }
    }
int main()
    {
    // The following line will only work in 3.0
    //     selUserDS = XCStoDS();
    // whereas the following line will work in 3.0 and 3.1
```

XCStoDS

```
// ( and in 3.1 only because WND structures are store in USER's
// default local heap; other structures reside in other heaps)
selUserDS = GetWindowWord(GetDesktopWindow(), GWW_HINSTANCE);

// Now we need to adjust the selector privilege level for 3.0
selUserDS &= 0xfffc;
selUserDS |= 1;

// Build the list, then paint it
winio_setpaint(winio_current(), FALSE);
printtree(GetDesktopWindow());
puts("\n\nEnd *********");
winio_setpaint(winio_current(), TRUE);
winio_home(winio_current());
return 0;
}
```

CHAPTER 7

Undocumented Windows Messages

The header files included with the SDK contain about 130 window message (WM_) constants. The file WM_UNDOC.H, which can be found on the disk that accompanies this book, defines another 25 or so undocumented messages. Some of these undocumented messages implement an interface that is directly related to an undocumented function. An example of this would be the WM_SYSTIMER message (0x0118) which is sent to a window in response to system timer events from a timer created in a call to the undocumented SetSystemTimer function. Since Microsoft did not want to document the SetSystemTimer function, it would make even less sense for them to document the WM_SYSTIMER message, which is only defined to implement that function's message-based callback.

Others are generated in response to system events such as the user clicking on a window's system menu bar. In this case, for example, USER generates an undocumented WM_ENTERMENULOOP message. Since it is 100% reliable, and always accompanied by a subsequent WM_EXITMENULOOP, it is less clear why it was this message would not be documented.

Still others remain a mystery, although proof that they exist is provided by the fact that there are #defines for them commented with the legend "Internal" in the WINDOWS.H file that is shipped with the 3.1 DDK. A few, such as the WM_PAINTICON message, which is present but undocumented in version 3.0, have been included in the preliminary Win32 API documentation, and in the Win32 include file WINUSER.H.

For further discussion of Windows messages, see the SNOOP utility and its WM_UNDOC.DAT file, discussed in chapter 4.

WM_ACTIVATESHELLWINDOW?   (0x0044?)

Windows message 44h is possibly WM_ACTIVATESHELLWINDOW. See WM_OTHERWINDOWCREATED for further details.

WM_ALTTABACTIVE   (0x0029)

This message is believed to be sent to certain types of dialog windows when the user is using Alt-Tab to switch focus away from the dialog window.

Support: 3.0, 3.1

WM_BEGINDRAG   (0x022C)

This message appears on first sight to be part of the drag-and-drop protocol since it its name and number fit neatly into the range of messages associated with the undocumented DragObject function (see chapter 6). However, while it is related to dragging, it is not used by that function, nor is it a part of the protocol. It is instead sent by a child listbox class control window to its parent window if the user starts to drag the listbox selection bar. The message is rarely seen, however, since the other criterion for its generation is that the child window must have the undocumented extended window style WES_DRAGDETECT (0x00000002) set. This style cannot be set simply by using code such as:

```
SetWindowLong (hwndLBox, GWL_EXSTYLE, GetWindowLong() | WES_DRAGDETECT);
```

since calls to modify the dwExStyle appear to be filtered (see the WND structure in chapter 6). Instead, the rgfExStyle field of the WND structure must be modified directly.

Support: 3.0, 3.1

WM_CBT_RESERVED_FIRST   (0x03F0)
WM_CBT_RESERVED_LAST   (0x03FF)

These are placeholders, not messages, to mark the range of message numbers reserved by Windows for use in Computer Based Training (CBT) applications such as WinTutor.

CBT is documented in the Windows 3.1 SDK, in the discussion of SetWindows Hook(WH_CBT). It is possible that the WM_CBT messages correspond to the WH_CBT codes in WINDOWS.H; for example, Windows message 03F0h might be WM_CBT_MOVESIZE:

```
HCBT_MOVESIZE        0
HCBT_MINMAX          1
HCBT_QS              2
```

```
HCBT_CREATEWND       3
HCBT_DESTROYWND      4
HCBT_ACTIVATE        5
HCBT_CLICKSKIPPED    6
HCBT_KEYSKIPPED      7
HCBT_SYSCOMMAND      8
HCBT_SETFOCUS        9
```

Support: 3.0, 3.1

WM_CONVERTREQUEST (0x010A)

This message is documented in Kanji Windows and sent during the processing of the Kanji Windows function ConvertRequest( ). For more information, see "Bringing Windows to the Expanding Japanese Market," *Microsoft Systems Journal,* March 1988.

Support: Kanji Windows
See also: WM_CONVERTRESULT, WM_KANJIFIRST,

WM_CONVERTRESULT (0x010B)

This message is documented in Kanji Windows and sent during the processing of the Kanji Windows function ConvertRequest( ).

Support: Kanji Windows
See also: WM_CONVERTREQUEST, WM_KANJIFIRST,

WM_DRAGLOOP (0x022D)

This message is sent by the undocumented DragObject function to the window associated with the current drag-and-drop "session" whenever the cursor moves. It provides the source window with an indication of whether the object is currently accepted by the window under the cursor.

Parameter	Description
wParam	TRUE (1) if the object has been accepted by the window under the cursor, or FALSE (0) if notlParam
	The high word contains the global memory handle to the DRAGINFO structure originally supplied to the DragObject function. The low word is always 0. In standard or enhanced mode, therefore, lParam can be used directly as a far pointer to the DRAGINFO structure.

Support: 3.0, 3.1
See also: DRAGINFO (chapter 6), DragObject (chapter 6), WM_DROPOBJECT, WM_QUERYDROPOBJECT, WM_DRAGSELECT, WM_BEGINDRAG, WM_DRAGMOVE

WM_DRAGMOVE   (0x022F)

This message is sent by the undocumented DragObject function to the window under the cursor when the user drags the object, once the window has signaled acceptance of the drop by responding to the WM_QUERYDROPOBJECT message.

Parameter	Description
wParam	Always 0
lParam	The high word contains the global memory handle to the DRAGINFO structure originally supplied to the DragObject function. The low word always 0. In standard or enhanced mode, therefore, lParam can be used directly as a far pointer to the DRAGINFO structure.

Support: 3.0, 3.1
See also: DRAGINFO (chapter 6), DragObject (chapter 6), WM_DROPOBJECT, WM_QUERYDROPOBJECT, WM_DRAGSELECT, WM_BEGINDRAG, WM_DRAGLOOP

WM_DRAGSELECT   (0x022E)

While an object is being dragged, and once a window has signaled acceptance of the drop in the 3.0-type drag-and-drop protocol (which continues to work in 3.1),by responding to the WM_QUERYDROPOBJECT message, it will receive this message when the cursor is dragged out of, or into, the window area. It can be used by the "client" window to keep track of whether the object is over the window.

Parameter	Description
wParam	0 if the cursor is leaving the window, or 1 if it is entering the window
lParam	The high word contains the global memory handle of the DRAGINFO structure describing the object(s) being dragged. The contents of the low word are not understood. Since it is not always 0, lParam cannot be used directly as a far pointer to the DRAGINFO structure.

Support: 3.0, 3.1

See also: DRAGINFO (chapter 6), DragObject (chapter 6), WM_DROPOBJECT, WM_QUERYDROPOBJECT, WM_DRAGLOOP, WM_BEGINDRAG, WM_DRAGMOVE

WM_DROPOBJECT   (0x022A)

This message is sent by the undocumented DragObject function to the window under the cursor when the user releases the left mouse button, signifying that the object has been dropped. It will only be sent to a 3.0-type drag-and-drop protocol client window that has previously signaled acceptance of the drop by responding to a WM_QUERYDROPOBJECT message. The lParam parameter will point to the same DRAGINFO structure as that of the WM_QUERYDROPOBJECT message.

Parameter	Description
wParam	HWND of source window
lParam	The high word contains a global memory handle to a DRAGINFO structure describing the object(s) being dropped. The low word is always 0. In standard or enhanced mode, therefore, lParam can be used directly as a far pointer to the DRAGINFO structure.

Return: In version 3.0, the return is either TRUE (1) signifying that the object has been dropped, or FALSE (0) signifying that the drop was unsuccessful. In version 3.1, the DWORD returned contains a four-character identifier of either 'FILE' (0x454c4946) or 'PRNT' (0x544e5250) if successful; any other value signifies an unsuccessful drop.
Support: 3.0, 3.1
See also: DRAGINFO (chapter 6), DragObject (chapter 6), WM_QUERYDROP-OBJECT, WM_DRAGLOOP, WM_DRAGSELECT, WM_BEGINDRAG, WM_DRAGMOVE

WM_ENTERMENULOOP   (0x0211)

When the user clicks on the system menu bar of a window, this message is placed in the window's message queue. When the system menu is taken down, a WM_EXITMENULOOP message is posted to the Window. The two messages are always paired; a window will never receive two WM_ENTERMENULOOP messages without an intervening WM_EXITMENULOOP message, for example.

Parameter	Description
wParam	Always NULL
lParam	Always NULL

Support: 3.0, 3.1
See also: WM_EXITMENULOOP

WM_ENTERSIZEMOVE (0x0231)

This message is generated when the user initiates a move or size operation. This includes a click or drag of the caption bar, the window border, either of the Move or Size system options, or the window icon when the window is minimized. The corresponding message for signaling termination of the operation, WM_EXITSIZEMOVE, will only be generated if the operation was initiated by a direct click on the caption bar or the window border, or if the operation results in a change in window position or size. This means that the two messages can not reliably be used as a start/stop indication of window size or move operations.

The documented WM_WINDOWPOSCHANGING and WM_WINDOWPOS-CHANGED messages in version 3.1 provide slightly different functionality. There is no documented equivalent in 3.0.

Parameter	Description
wParam	Always NULL
lParam	Always NULL

Support: 3.0, 3.1
See also: WM_EXITSIZEMOVE

WM_EXITMENULOOP (0x0212)

When the user clicks on the system menu bar, a WM_ENTERMENULOOP message is placed in the window's message queue. When the user has selected an option from the option menu, or has cancelled the menu, this message, WM_EXITMENULOOP, is posted. The two messages are always paired; a window will never receive two WM_ENTERMENULOOP messages without an intervening WM_EXITMENULOOP message, for example.

Parameter	Description
wParam	Always NULL
lParam	Always NULL

Support: 3.0, 3.1
See also: WM_ENTERMENULOOP

WM_EXITSIZEMOVE (0x0232)

This message is generated when the user completes a move or size operation. This includes a click or drag of the caption bar, the window border, or after selection of the Move or Size system options actually leads to a change in window position or size. It will always have been preceded by a WM_ENTERSIZEMOVE message. Note that the reverse is *not* true; in other words a WM_ENTERSIZEMOVE message will not always be followed by a WM_EXITSIZEMOVE message. This message is still supported in version 3.1, although the documented WM_WINDOWPOSCHANGED provides better and more consistent functionality in that version, as described in the entry for WM_ENTERSIZEMOVE.

Parameter	Description
wParam	Always NULL
lParam	Always NULL

Support: 3.0, 3.1
See also: WM_ENTERSIZEMOVE

WM_FILESYSCHANGE   (0x0034)

This message is used internally by WinFile and, if "FileSysChange=ON" is specified in the [Enhanced] section of SYSTEM.INI, broadcast by WINOA386. WinFile sends itself WM_FILESYSCHANGE messages from within a callback function installed using the undocumented FileCdr function. The callback is notified of file system changes by Windows apps. WinFile also intercepts WM_FILESYSCHANGE messages generated by WINOA386 in response to file system changes by DOS applications. It uses the message, from either source, to update its directory listboxes. See the FileCdr entry in chapter 5 for more information.

Parameter	Description
wParam	A numeric code identifying the action that caused the file system change. Only the following are known:

0	Create file
1	Delete file
2	Rename file/directory
3	Create unique file
7	Create directory
8	Delete directory

lParam	Not known, except that the high word in version 3.0 always contains 0, and in 3.1 always contains a valid selector.

Support: 3.0, 3.1
See also: FileCdr chapter 5)

WM_GETHOTKEY (0x0033)

This message is documented in Win32 but is also available, undocumented, in versions 3.0 and 3.1. An application sends WM_GETHOTKEY to find out its currently-assigned hot key. Hot keys are known as application "shortcut" keys in the user's documentation for Program Manager; shortcut keys can be set in the Program Item Properties dialog box. The hot key is a Ctrl-, Alt-, and/or Shift-key combination that, when pressed, activates the application and restores its top-level window. The message returns the VK_ and shift key values of the currently assigned hot key, or NULL if one is not currently assigned:

```
wVK_Curr = SendMessage(hwnd, WM_GETHOTKEY, 0, 0L);
```

The low byte contains the VK_ code for the key, and the high byte contains the shift state, as described in the SDK documentation for the VkKeyScan function. An application might send this message to obtain and display the current hot key assignment before allowing a user to change it.

The returned shift state flags will always contain the Alt-key bit flag set (0x0400), since hot keys are a type of system key not accessible directly to applications.

A new hot key can be assigned using the WM_SETHOTKEY message.

Support: 3.0, 3.1
See also: WM_SETHOTKEY

WM_INTERIM (0x010C)

This message appears in the Korean language (Hangeul) version of Windows only.

Support: Hangeul Windows

WM_INTERNAL_COALESCE_FIRST (0x0390)
WM_INTERNAL_COALESCE_LAST (0x039F)

These are placeholders, not messages, to mark the range of message numbers 0390h through 039Fh reserved by Windows. Their purpose is not currently understood by us. This range appears, marked "internal," in the version of WINDOWS.H included with the 3.1 DDK.

Support: 3.0, 3.1

WM_INTERNAL_DDE_FIRST   (0x03E0)
WM_INTERNAL_DDE_LAST   (0x03EF)

These are placeholders, not messages, to mark the range of message numbers 03E0h through 03EFh, reserved by Windows. Their purpose is not currently understood by us, aside from the obvious relation to Dynamic Data Exchange (DDE). This range appears, marked "internal," in the version of WINDOWS.H included with the 3.1 DDK.

Support: 3.0, 3.1

WM_ISACTIVEICON   (0x0035)

This message is placed in the message queue of an iconic MDI client window whenever there is a change in its status. In version 3.0, the message is sometimes sent to the window, and sometimes posted. It appears to be similar in purpose to the WM_SETFOCUS and WM_KILLFOCUS messages but operates within an MDI application only, allowing the application main window to hold system focus but still provide a separate document focus within the application when it is active.

Return: The return is only meaningful when the message has been sent to a window rather than posted and is therefore not used in version 3.1, even though DefMDIChildProc continues to return a valid value. If FALSE (0), the target window is not the active, i.e., currently selected, icon. If TRUE (1), the target window is the active icon.

Parameter	Description
wParam	Always NULL
lParam	Always NULL

Support: 3.0, 3.1

WM_KANJIFIRST   (0x0280)
WM_KANJILAST   (0x029F)

These are placeholders, not messages, to mark the range of message numbers 0280h through 029Fh, used in Kanji Windows (Japan).

In the Korean-language version of Windows, this same range is identified with WM_HANGEULFIRST and WM_HANGEULLAST.

Support: Kanji Windows, Hangeul Windows
See also: WM_CONVERTRESULT, WM_CONVERTREQUEST

WM_LBTRACKPOINT   (0x0131)

This message is placed in the message queue of the window that owns a listbox control whenever the user selects an entry in the list. It appears to provide supplementary functionality to the LBN_SELCHANGE notification messages sent to parents of list box controls when the LBS_NOTIFY style is specified.

As can be seen from the parameters below, this message provides information about the position of the mouse and the entry in the listbox being selected. However, there is no indication, if the listbox is one of many in a dialog window, which control is providing the notification. For this, the documented LBS_NOTIFY message should be used.

Parameter	Description
wParam	Item number in the list that has been selected
lParam	Contains the coordinates of the position of the cursor at selection relative to the top left of the listbox, with the x-coordinate in the low word and the y-coordinate in the high word.

Support: 3.0, 3.1

WM_MM_RESERVED_FIRST   (0x03A0)
WM_MM_RESERVED_LAST   (0x03DF)

These are placeholders, not messages, that mark the range of message numbers, 03A0h through 03DFh, reserved for the Multimedia extensions to Windows. The actual message numbers appear in MMSYSTEM.H:

Joystick messages: 0x03A0 through 0x03B8
MCI message: 0x03B9
Waveform output: 0x03BB through 0x03BD
Waveform input: 0x03BE through 0x03C0
MIDI input: 0x03C1 through 0x03C6
MIDI output: 0x03C7 through 0x03C9

Support: Multimedia Windows

WM_NCPAINT (0x0085)

Although this message is documented in the SDK, the documentation is incomplete. In both 3.0 and 3.1, the documentation states that neither wParam nor lParam are used. While lParam is always zero and is indeed not used, in 3.0, wParam is used internally to hold a rectangular clipping region to be applied to the paint operation. In 3.1, wParam sometimes contains a 1. The code in USER that handles this message appears to recognize 1 as signifying that the window frame is to be painted but that there is no clipping region. Although it is never seen, a NULL clipping region handle would appear to cause no frame update. This logic appears to be present in the 3.0 code as well. A clue to the fact that there is a relationship between clipping regions and WM_NCPAINT lies in the Comments section of the documentation, where, after no mention of clipping or clipping regions, it offers the following, seemingly irrelevant, advice: "Remember that the clipping region for a window is always rectangular, even if the shape of the frame is altered."

Parameter	Description
wParam	HRGN for clipping region or 1.
lParam	Always NULL.

The return from the message is ignored.

Support: 3.0, 3.1

WM_NEXTMENU (0x0213)

This message was undocumented in version 2.1and does not appear in versions 3.0 or 3.1.

WM_OTHERWINDOWCREATED (0x0042)

Under certain circumstances, this message is posted to top-level windows and to windows without owners, whenever a new window is created. However, while the message number quoted above appears to be the intrinsic message number, Windows also registers "OTHERWINDOWCREATED", "OTHERWINDOWDESTROYED," and "ACTIVESHELLWINDOW" messages using the RegisterWindowMessage() function (and therefore having message numbers >= 0xC000 produced "on the fly").

These three messages appear to be related to SetWindowsHook(WH_SHELL), which is documented in the 3.1 SDK's entry for ShellProc(). WINDOWS.H defines the following WH_SHELL codes:

```
HSHELL_WINDOWCREATED          1
HSHELL_WINDOWDESTROYED        2
HSHELL_ACTIVATESHELLWINDOW    3
```

The WM_OTHERWINDOWxxx messages are documented in the Win32 API, and appear in the Win32 include file WINUSER.H.

Parameter	Description
wParam	HWND of newly created window
lParam	Always NULL

Support: 3.1
See also: WM_OTHERWINDOWDESTROYED

WM_OTHERWINDOWDESTROYED   (0x0043)

Under certain circumstances, this message is sent to top-level windows and windows without owners whenever a window in the system is destroyed.

However, while the message number quoted above appears to be the intrinsic message number, Windows also registers an "OTHERWINDOWDESTROYED" message using the RegisterWindowMessage function, and may be used instead.

See the WM_OTHERWINDOWCREATED entry, and the 3.1 SDK entry for SetWindowsHook(SH_SHELL) and ShellProc( ).

This message is documented in the Win32 API and appears in WINUSER.H.

Parameter	Description
wParam	HWND of window being destroyed
lParam	Always NULL

Support: 3.1
See also: WM_OTHERWINDOWCREATED

WM_PAINTICON   (0x0026)

This message is posted to a window's message queue whenever its icon needs to be painted. This occurs whenever a window is minimized; when its icon is moved; and when its icon is revealed after having been partially or completely hidden. It is only sent to iconic windows with class icons. All other iconic windows receive WM_PAINT messages instead.

The wParam and lParam parameters are always NULL, except in version 3.0, where wParam is sometimes 1.

This message is documented in the Win32 API, and appears in WINUSER.H.

Support: 3.0, 3.1

WM_QUERYDROPOBJECT (0x022B)

This message is sent by the undocumented DragObject function to the window under the cursor when an object is being dragged. A window responding to the 3.0-type drag-and-drop protocol that wishes to accept the dragged object will return TRUE on receipt of this message, otherwise it returns FALSE. The DRAGINFO pointed at by the lParam parameter may be used to decide whether to accept the object.

Parameter	Description
wParam	0 if cursor is over client area, 1 if over non-client area.
lParam	The high word contains a global memory handle to a DRAGINFO structure describing the object(s) being dragged. The low word is always 0. In standard or enhanced mode, therefore, lParam can be used directly as a far pointer to the DRAGINFO structure.

Return: TRUE (1) if the receiver wishes to accept the dragged objects, FALSE (0) if not
Support: 3.0, 3.1
See also: DragObject (in chapter 6), WM_DROPOBJECT, WM_DRAGLOOP, WM_DRAGSELECT, WM_BEGINDRAG, WM_DRAGMOVE

WM_QUERYPARKICON (0x0036)

This message is placed in the message queue of a top-level window that is about to be minimized. It is unclear what its purpose is, but one could speculate that it may originally have been intended as a means of allowing an application to specify whether/where it should be minimized.

An entry for this message number appears in the version of WINDOWS.H that ships with the version 3.1 SDK as WM_UNUSED0036.

Parameter	Description
wParam	Always NULL
lParam	Always NULL

Support: 3.0

WM_QUERYSAVESTATE   (0x0038)

This message was undocumented in version 2.1. It is not known what the purpose of it was, but it is not seen in versions 3.0 or 3.1.

WM_SETHOTKEY   (0x0032)

This message is documented in the Win32 API but is also available, undocumented, in versions 3.0 and 3.1. An application sends WM_SETHOTKEY to define the hot key to be assigned to the application. The hot key is an Alt-, Ctrl-, and/or Shift-key combination that, when pressed at the keyboard, activates the application and restores its top-level window; in the user's documentation for Program Manager, hotkeys are referred to as application "shortcut" keys.

The message expects the new hotkey VK_ and shift key values in wParam, and returns one of four return codes, as illustrated in this code fragment:

```
ret = SendMessage(hwnd, WM_SETHOTKEY, VkKeyScan(chHotKey) | 0x400, 0L);
switch (ret)
{
    case 2 :  printf("OK (another app owned the hot key)\n"); break;
    case 1 :  printf("OK\n"); break;
    case 0 :  printf("Invalid hwnd\n"); break;
    case -1 : printf("Invalid hot key value\n"); break;
}
```

The low byte of wParam contains the VK_ code for the key, and the high byte contains the shift state, as described in the SDK documentation for the VkKeyScan function.

The shift state flags should always contain the Alt- key bit flag set (0x0400), since hot keys are a type of system key, much like menu accelerator keys, not accessible directly to applications.

Support: 3.0, 3.1
See also: WM_GETHOTKEY

WM_SETVISIBLE   (0x0009)

This message was documented in version 2.1 and is sent to a window just before it is made visible or invisible by a call to ShowWindow, or by the user iconizing or restoring the window.

Parameter	Description
wParam	Nonzero if the window is being made visible, zero if the window is being made invisible
lParam	Not used

Support: 3.0 (not in 3.1)

WM_SIZEWAIT   (0x0004)

This message was undocumented in version 2.1. It is not known what its purpose was, but it is not seen in versions 3.0 or 3.1.

WM_SYNCPAINT   (0x0088)

This message is sent or posted to a window when part of its window area is overlayed by another window that is about to be updated. It is not known what determines whether the message is sent or posted.

This appears to be similar to the window style CS_SYNCPAINT in OS/2 Presentation Manager. According to Charles Petzold's *Programming the OS/2 Presentation Manager*, "When CS_SYNCPAINT is set, WM_PAINT messages are sent directly to a window procedure when part of the window becomes invalid. When this bit is *not* set, WM_PAINT messages are posted to the message queue and retrieved later. The CS_SYNCPAINT bit is used mostly with small control windows that must be repainted immediately."

Parameter	Description
wParam	Unknown
lParam	The high word is always 0. The low word appears to be 1 when the window is minimized, otherwise it appears to be an HDC.

Support: 3.0, 3.1

WM_SYNCTASK   (0x0089)

This message was undocumented in version 2.1. It is not known what the purpose of it was, but it is not seen in versions 3.0 or 3.1. The Win32 include file WINUSER.H, while not containing an identifier for WM_SYNCTASK itself, does contain the following; "SWP" presumably stands for SetWindowPos:

```
/* WM_SYNCTASK Commands */
#define ST_BEGINSWP      0
#define ST_ENDSWP        1
```

WM_SYSTEMERROR   (0x0017)

This message was documented in version 2.1 and was sent to all top-level windows when Windows ran out of memory in response to a request to GlobalAlloc, or GlobalReAlloc upwards, a block of memory.

Parameter	Description
wParam	Always 8 (DOS 'Out of memory' error code)
lParam	Not used

WM_SYSTIMER   (0x0118)

This message is to SetSystemTimer (see chapter 6) when the documented WM_TIMER message is to SetTimer, i.e., it is the message that is placed in a window's message queue in response to system timer events. Like WM_TIMER messages, WM_SYSTIMER messages are only generated if no callback function was specified in the call to SetSystemTimer, i.e., the last parameter to the call was NULL.

   If generated, they are posted to the application message queue.

Parameter	Description
wParam	Event ID as specified in the call to SetSystemTimer
lParam	Always NULL

Support: 3.0, 3.1

WM_TESTING   (0x0040)

This message is not seen in either the retail or debug versions of 3.0 or 3.1. It is not known what its purpose is.

WM_YOMICHAR   (0x0108)

The purpose of this message is not currently understood, although it is known to be seen only in Kanji Windows and is perhaps associated with WIFEMAN (Windows Intelligent Font Environment).

Support: 3.0, 3.1

Built-in WndProcs

The Windows SDK provides the source for two of the documented functions that handle messages that an application does not wish to intercept. They are the DefWindowProc and DefDlgProc functions which process messages for application windows and dialogs respectively. It is interesting that neither of what are the two most fundamental WndProcs handle any undocumented messages.

Two other functions, DefFrameProc and DefMDIChildProc, for which source code was not provided with the SDK, handle MDI messages not processed by the MDI application window procedure. USER.EXE also contains WndProcs for each of the built-in control classes and some other special 'window' types including the MDI client window type. These functions include EditWndProc, StaticWndProc, LBoxCtlWndProc, ComboBoxWndProc, ButtonWndProc and SBWndProc, MDIClientWndProc, MenuWndProc, MB_DlgProc (for MessageBox dialogs), and DesktopWndProc, all of which are undocumented.

Some of these are exported in 3.0; all are present, but none are exported in 3.1, except for EditWndProc(), which is exported under the name BozosLiveHere(). In any case, far pointers to all these functions can be acquired using GetWindowLong-(GWL_WNDPROC) or GetClassInfo().

The SNOOP utility, presented in chapter 4, can be used to trace and filter messages through all the built-in WndProcs.

Undocumented Control Messages

The following identifiers appear, marked "internal," in the version of WINDOWS.H shipped with the 3.1 DDK. Unfortunately, no more is known about them at this time, except for EM_SCROLL, which may be the same as the EM_SCROLL documented in the Win32 API:

Edit control messages
EM_SCROLL	WM_USER+5
EM_GETTHUMB	WM_USER+14

Listbox messages
LB_ADDFILE	WM_USER+23
LB_SETANCHORINDEX	WM_USER+29
LB_GETANCHORINDEX	WM_USER+30

Listbox/Combobox messages
LBCB_CARETON	WM_USER+36
LBCB_CARETOFF	WM_USER+37

CHAPTER ■ 8

GDI

GDI provides the visual link between Windows and the outside world. It manages the display and other output devices by communicating with device drivers. These device drivers are DLLs that control specific types of devices which fall into two categories: display drivers, which always have the generic module name "DISPLAY" (and a file name such as VGA.DRV, V7VGA.DRV, or 8514.DRV); and printer drivers, such as HPPCL.DRV, PSCRIPT.DRV, or TTY.DRV.

Keeping the device specific component of device management in a device driver layer allows GDI to present a device-independent interface both to USER and to applications. GDI deals with objects like pens, brushes, bitmaps, colors, fonts, regions, and the device context. These objects are at a lower level than those presented by USER. Thus GDI does not know about "windows," that is, those things referred to by HWNDs, or icons, cursors, menus, and so on, whereas USER and applications need to know about GDI objects. In principle, an entirely different GUI standard could have been, and could be, implemented on top of GDI.

The GDI interface to USER and applications consists of function calls and object handles. The handles are near pointers to objects in GDI's default heap segment. The GDI functions provide the means by which USER and applications create, manipulate, and destroy these objects. CreatePen, for example, creates a pen object, and returns a handle to it (HPEN); CreateBrush creates a brush object and returns a handle to it (HBRUSH), and so on. HDCs, however, are not treated in quite the same way. As will be discussed in more length in the DC entry in this chapter, applications normally obtain the handle to a display device context from USER functions such as BeginPaint and GetDC, *not* from the GDI function CreateDC.

The list of exported GDI functions, aggregated over versions 3.0 and 3.1, contains about 380 entry points, of which some 80 are undocumented. These numbers show a better documented-to-undocumented ratio than either the USER or KERNEL modules.

GDI Data Structures

GDI maintains a number of different data structures in its default near heap. These structures, which represent the objects that GDI makes available to USER and applications, are consistent in their use of a standard header structure, and in the use of "magic," or signature words, to identify them. This makes it possible to determine, given a handle to any object in the default heap, what the object is.

Many of the undocumented structures are simply internal copies of documented structures passed to API functions such as CreatePenIndirect or CreateBrushIndirect. So, for example, an undocumented FONTOBJ structure, referenced by a documented HFONT handle, is made up of a GDIOBJHDR structure (described below), followed by the LOGFONT structure passed to CreateFont.

The object header structure is the same size but has different fields in versions 3.0 and 3.1. In version 3.0, objects are identified by a type number, as follows:

Pen	1
Brush	2
Font	3
Palette	4
Bitmap	5
Region	6
DC	7
Disabled DC	8
MetaDC	9
Metafile	10
Metafile DC	11

These object types, as found in the GDI object header in version 3.0, are identical to those in the TOOLHELP.H GDI heap object type defines (with one exception—ToolHelp makes no mention of the Metafile DC, type 11).

In version 3.1, objects have signatures that are effectively type numbers made to look like 2-character strings:

Pen	0x4F47 ('GO')
Brush	0x4F48 ('HO')
Font	0x4F49 ('IO')
Palette	0x4F4A ('JO')
Bitmap	0x4F4B ('KO')
Region	0x4F4C ('LO')
DC	0x4F4D ('MO')
Disabled DC	0x4F4E ('NO')

MetaDC	0x4F4F ('OO')
Metafile	0x4F50 ('PO')
Metafile DC	0x4F51 ('QO')

These signatures are also overloaded with flags, of which only one is really understood. Version 3.1's undocumented MakeObjectPrivate function, described later in the chapter, ORs in 0x2000 to indicate that an object is private. This has the effect of turning the 'O' into an 'o' in each of the above strings. In addition, another flag (0x8000) is known to exist in both 3.0 and 3.1, although its purpose is less obvious. It appears to signify that the object is currently selected into a DC. The permutations of these two flags, with the base signature of a Pen, for example, lead to the possible signature field values of 'GO,' 'Go,' 'GÏ,' and 'Gï'.

In the list of object signatures above, there is a profusion of Metas: MetaDC, Metafile, and Metafile DC. In addition, as we will see below, there is a wMetaList field in the object header structure. The MetaDC is very rarely seen, and remains a mystery. The Metafile DC is a DC created using CreateMetaFile, and which will provide the device context for the Metafile operations. In the hMetaFile field of the DC is a handle to a Metafile object. The Metafile object is the in-memory representation of a Metafile, documented in the SDK. Interestingly, the Metafile is stored in the global heap, and does not contain the object header. It is not clear, therefore, why ToolHelp has a local-heap entry entry constant LT_GDI_METAFILE.

The header structure is described in more detail in the GDI Object Header entry later in the chapter.

GDIWALK

The GDIWALK program, similar to the USERWALK program described in chapter 6, provides visual clarification of how GDI object structures are constructed and how they fit together. The primary undocumented data structure that GDI has to offer is the DC—the device context. The HDC is, of course, documented, but what it points to, the DC, isn't. The DC holds device-specific and GDI state information required for an output operation. In the same way as the WND structure provides the focal point for many of the USER object types, the DC contains references to almost all of the GDI object types. Say that the DC, found some 12 lines from the end, with the handle 0BC6, is selected from the following excerpt of a GDIWALK main display run in version 3.1:

```
GDI heap in segment 4bach:
(Double-click to view a block)

HANDLE  ADDR  SIZE  TYPE
GDI heap in segment 05eeh:
(Double-click to view a block)
HANDLE  ADDR  SIZE  TYPE
. . . just an example. . .
```

```
0BF6    1D26    001A    Brush
0BF2    1D46    001A    Brush
0BEE    1D66    001A    Brush
0C4A    1D86    001A    NORMAL
0BDA    1DA6    0026    Region
0BD6    1DD2    00CE    DC
0BD2    1EA6    0012    NORMAL
0BCE    1EBE    0046    NORMAL
0BCA    1F0A    0026    Region
0BC6    1F36    00CE    DC
0000    2008    0010    FREE
0C8A    201E    0046    NORMAL
0000    2068    0048    FREE
0C7E    20B6    002A    Bitmap
0BB2    20E6    00CE    DC
0C6E    21BA    0026    Bitmap
0BAA    21E6    00CE    DC
0000    22B8    0028    FREE
0BA2    22E6    00CE    DC
0C62    23BA    0026    Bitmap
0B9A    23E6    00CE    DC
        .    .    .
```

The following window might then appear:

```
DC handle 0BC6 @ 05ED:1F36 for 206 bytes

Lines marked '->' may be double clicked for expansion


GDIOBJHDR:
        hNext           : 0000
        wMagic          : 6F4D ("Mo")
        dwCount         : 42
        wMetaList       : 0000
        DC:
        byFlags         : 01
        byFlags2        : 00
->      hMetaFile       : 0000
->      hrgnClip        : 0000
        hPDevice        : 07A7
->      hLPen           : 0AE2
->      hLBrush         : 0AC6
->      hLFont          : 0AFA
->      hBitmap         : 0C6E
->      dchPal          : 0B06
        hLDevice        : 0B7A
        hRaoClip        : 0BCA
        hPDeviceBlock   : 0B7E
        hPPen           : 0BD2
        hPBrush         : 0BCE
        hPFontTrans     : 0B8E
        hPFont          : 17E6
        lpPDevice       : 02E7:0000
        pLDevice        : 26EA
        pRaoClip        : 0000
```

```
            pPDeviceBlock    : 2666
            pPPen            : 1EB0
            pPBrush          : 1ECE
            pPFontTrans      : 25BA
            lpPFont          : 17E7:0042
            nPFTIndex        : 0000
            fnTransform      : 0000:0000
            wROP2            : 000D
            wBkMode          : 0001
            dwBkColor        : 3FFFFFFF
            dwTextColor      : 20000000
. . . about 50 fields omitted...
            lpfnNotify       : 0000:0000
            dwHookData       : 0000:0000
            wDCGlobFlags     : 0003
```

The DC is a large structure which changes from one Windows version to the next. It not only changed between versions 3.0 and 3.1, but also differs between retail and debug versions of 3.1. Direct use of the information in the DC can not be done without much coding effort. The situation in 3.1 is further complicated, not only for the DC, but for all GDI object structures, by the fact that the GDIOBJHDR structure is equally unstable; in the debug version, the structure grows by 4 bytes, as described in the GDI Object Header entry in this chapter. For a description of each of the fields in the DC, refer to the DC entry.

Selecting one of the clickable fields (whose lines are indicated with a '->') in the GDIWALK display will bring up another window with the underlying structure. The hLPen field shown in the last window, for example, might lead to:

```
Pen handle 0AE2 @ 05ED:37DE for 22 bytes

GDIOBJHDR:
        hNext            : 0BD2
        wMagic           : CF47 ("Gï")
        dwCount          : 8
        wMetaList        : 0000 LOGPEN:
        lopnStyle        : 0000
        lopnWidth        : (0, 0)
        lopnColor        : 00000000
```

The header file that contains the undocumented GDI structure definitions used by GDIWALK is reproduced here:

```
/*  GDIOBJ.H - GDI object structures */


typedef struct tagGDIOBJHDR {
    HANDLE      hNext;       // 00h Handle to next (sometimes flags in 3.0)
    WORD        wMagic;      // 02h Obj type in 3.0, Magic in 3.1
    DWORD       dwCount;     // 04h Sequence number
    WORD        wMetaList;   // 08h
    } GDIOBJHDR, FAR *LPGDIOBJHDR;   // 0Ah total
```

```
typedef struct tagGDIOBJ31DBG {
    HANDLE      hNext;          // 00h Handle to next (sometimes flags in 3.0)
    WORD        wMagic;         // 02h Obj type in 3.0, Magic in 3.1
    DWORD       dwCount;        // 04h Sequence number
    WORD        wMetaList;      // 08h
    WORD        wSelCount;      // 0Ah Count of times selected???
    HANDLE      hOwner;         // 0Ch Owning task
    } GDIOBJ31DBG, FAR *LPGDIOBJ31DBG;  // 0Eh total

// NOTE all offsets after 'header' from here on in this file will be
// 4 bytes more when 3.1 DEBUG version is running

typedef struct tagBRUSHOBJ {
    GDIOBJHDR   header;         // 00h
    LOGBRUSH    logbrush;       // 0Ah
    COLORREF    crHatchBk;      // 12h extra DWord for hatched brush color
    } BRUSHOBJ, FAR *LPBRUSHOBJ; // 1Ah total

typedef struct tagPENOBJ {
    GDIOBJHDR   header;         // 00h
    LOGPEN      logpen;         // 0Ah
    } PENOBJ, FAR *LPPENOBJ;    // 16h total

typedef struct tagPALETTEOBJ {
    GDIOBJHDR   header;         // 00h
    LOGPALETTE  logpalette;     // 0Ah
    } PALETTEOBJ, FAR *LPPALETTEOBJ;// size depends on size of logpalette

typedef struct tagFONTOBJ {
    GDIOBJHDR   header;         // 00h
    LOGFONT     logfont;        // 0Ah
    } FONTOBJ, FAR *LPFONTOBJ;  // size depends on strlen(typeface name)

typedef struct tagBITMAPOBJ {
    GDIOBJHDR   header;         // 00h
    HANDLE      hmemBitmap;     // 0Ah
    BOOL        bSelected;      // 0Ch Currently selected into a DC ???
    HDC         hdc;            // 0Eh DC last selected into ???)
    } BITMAPOBJ, FAR *LPBITMAPOBJ;

typedef struct tagDC {
    GDIOBJHDR   header;         // 00h
    BYTE    byFlags;            // 0Ah
    BYTE    byFlags2;           // 0Bh
    HANDLE  hMetaFile;          // 0Ch
    HRGN    hrgnClip;           // 0Eh handle to (reclangular) clip region
    HANDLE  hPDevice;           // 10h Phys device handle
    HANDLE  hLPen;              // 12h Log. pen
    HANDLE  hLBrush;            // 14h Log. brush
    HANDLE  hLFont;             // 16h Log. Font
    HANDLE  hBitmap;            // 18h Selected bitmap
    HANDLE  dchPal;             // 1Ah Selected palette
    HANDLE  hLDevice;           // 1Ch Log. device
    HRGN    hRaoClip;           // 1Eh clip region
    HANDLE  hPDeviceBlock;      // 20h
```

```
    HANDLE    hPPen;                // 22h Phys. pen
    HANDLE    hPBrush;              // 24h Phys. brush
    HANDLE    hPFontTrans;          // 26h
    HANDLE    hPFont;               // 28h Phys. font
    LPVOID    lpPDevice;            // 2Ah
    WORD      pLDevice;             // 2Eh near pointer to log. device info
    WORD      pRaoClip;             // 30h near pointer to clip region
    WORD      pPDeviceBlock;        // 32h near pointer to GDIINFO
    WORD      pPPen;                // 34h
    WORD      pPBrush;              // 36h
    WORD      pPFontTrans;          // 38h near pointer to hPFontTrans
    LPVOID    lpPFont;              // 3Ah Font engine entrypoint
    int       nPFTIndex;            // 3Eh
    LPVOID    Transform;            // 40h

/* Begin DRAWMODE structure — see DDK doc */
    WORD      wROP2;                // 44h Raster Op drawing mode
    WORD      wBkMode;              // 46h Background mode (opaque/transparent)
    DWORD     dwBkColor;            // 48h Phys. Background color
    DWORD     dwTextColor;          // 4Ch Phys. text color
    int       nTBreakExtra;         // 50h Text padding: ExtTextOut justification
    int       nBreakExtra;          // 52h pad per break = nTBreakExtra/BreakCount
    WORD      wBreakErr;            // 54h SetTextJustify called with nBreakExtra=0?
    int       nBreakRem;            // 56h remainder of TBreakExtra/nBreakCount
    int       nBreakCount;          // 58h Count of break characters in string
    int       nCharExtra;           // 5Ah Per char additional padding
    DWORD     crLbkColor;           // 5Ch Logical background color
    DWORD     crLTextColor;         // 60h Logical text color
/* End DRAWMODE structure */
    int       LCursPosX;            // 64h Log curs pos X
    int       LCursPosY;            // 66h Log curs pos Y
    int       WndOrgX;              // 68h window origin X
    int       WndOrgY;              // 6Ah window origin Y
    int       WndExtX;              // 6Ch window width
    int       WndExtY;              // 6Eh window height
    int       VportOrgX;            // 70h viewport origin X
    int       VportOrgY;            // 72h viewport origin Y
    int       VportExtX;            // 74h viewport width
    int       VportExtY;            // 76h viewport height
    int       UserVptOrgX;          // 78h (USER/user ??) viewport origin X
    int       UserVptOrgY;          // 7Ah (USER/user ??) viewport origin Y
    WORD      wMapMode;             // 7Ch mapping mode
    WORD      wXFormFlags;          // 7Eh
    WORD      wRelAbs;              // 80h Relative/absolute mode
    WORD      wPolyFillMode;        // 82h Polygon fill mode
    WORD      wStretchBltMode;      // 84h Bitblt stretch mode
    BYTE      byPlanes;             // 86h for DC
    BYTE      byBitsPix;            // 87h for DC
    WORD      wPenWidth;            // 88h pen width in pix
    WORD      wPenHeight;           // 8Ah pen width in pix
    WORD      wTextAlign;           // 8Ch Text alignment flags
    DWORD     dwMapperFlags;        // 8Eh
    WORD      wBrushOrgX;           // 92h brush origin X
    WORD      wBrushOrgY;           // 94h brush origin Y
    WORD      wFontAspectX;         // 96h one half of font aspect ratio
```

```
        WORD      wFontAspectY;     // 98h other half of font aspect ratio
        HANDLE    hFontWeights;     // 9Ah handle to font weights
        WORD      wDCSaveLevel;     // 9Ch depth of stack of saved DCs
        WORD      wcDCLocks;        // 9Eh count of locks on DC
        HRGN      hVisRgn;          // A0h Handle to visible region
        WORD      wDCOrgX;          // A2h DC origin X
        WORD      wDCOrgY;          // A4h DC origin Y
        FARPROC   lpfnPrint;        // A6h print driver entrypoint
        WORD      wDCLogAtom;       // AAh Logical device driver name atom
        WORD      wDCPhysAtom;      // ACh Physical device name atom
        WORD      wDCFileAtom;      // AEh FILE: port file name atom
        WORD      wPostScaleX;      // B0h
        WORD      wPostScaleY;      // B2h
        union DC_TAIL {
            struct {                    // 3.0 fields from here
                WORD      wB4;          // B4h
                RECT      rectB6;       // B6h rect
                WORD      wDCGlobFlags; // BEh Bit 0 indicates DC dirty
                WORD      wC0;          // C0h
            } tail_3_0;                 // 3.0 size: C2h total
            struct {                    // 3.1 fields from here
                RECT      rectBounds;   // B4h Bounds rect
                RECT      rectLVB;      // BCh
                FARPROC   lpfnNotify;   // C4h Hook func
                LPSTR     lpHookData;   // C8h hook data
                WORD      wDCGlobFlags; // CCh Bit 0 indicates DC dirty
                HDC       hDCNext;      // CEh Next DC in linked list - Debug only
            } tail_3_1;                 // 3.1 size: CEh total nondebug, D6h debug
        };
    } DC, FAR *LPDC;

typedef struct tagRGNOBJ {
    GDIOBJHDR    header;            // 00h
//  RGN          rgn;              // 0Ah
    } RGNOBJ, FAR *LPRGNOBJ;
```

There is no specific provision for the 3.1 debug version of the object header structure within the object structures; they all assume the retail version of the header structure, GDIOBJHDR. Since the 3.1 debug version of the structure is 4 bytes larger, code such as the following should be used to adjust the alignment of pointers to address fields in the object structures following the header:

```
LPGDIOBJ31DBG lphdr;
LPDC lpdc;

lphdr = (LPGDIOBJ31DBG) MK_FP(default_gdi_heap_seg, address_of_dc);

if ((GetVersion == 0x0a03) && GetSystemMetrics(SM_DEBUG))
    lpdc = (LPDC) lphdr;
else
    (BYTE FAR *) lpdc = (BYTE FAR *) lphdr +
        sizeof(GDIOBJ31DBG) - sizeof(GDIOBJHDR);
```

```
/* Use lphdr for access to object header structure fields, and
   lpdc for access to DC fields */
   .
   .
   .
```

Why didn't we use #ifdef DEBUG for the extra fields in the 3.1 debug version of this structure? The developers of GDI itself could, and presumably do, use #ifdef DEBUG to *build* the two versions of GDI with different structures. But if you think about it, this isn't going to help when we want to write one program that *uses* GDI, and that needs to work with either the debug or retail version.

GDI Heaps

In version 3.0, GDI uses a single heap segment for all local allocations and object storage, as well as for the GDI module atom table.

In version 3.1, GDI has two heap segments. The default heap segment still contains all local allocations and object storage, but the GDI module atom table has been moved into its own, secondary heap segment. Comparing this growth with that of USER's heap segments indicates that the resource problem was not as severe in GDI as in USER. It was/is, in fact, really a problem in USER. See the introduction to Chapter 6 for a corresponding disussion of USER heap spaces.

GDI Exports and Imports

In version 3.0, the retail GDI.EXE is 129K in size and made of just over 100 object files; in version 3.1, it is up to a whopping 219K and now comprises just under 150 object files. Apart from its overall growth, the GDI module has followed the same pattern as USER. In other words, most of the exported entry points have been gathered into a single LAYER.OBJ in version 3.1, whereas they were spread over all of the object files in version 3.0.

It is also interesting to note that the number of exports increased from 235 in version 3.0 to 284 in version 3.1. Of the 49 new functions, most are undocumented— not an encouraging trend.

On the bright side, however, this latest batch of functions includes one with the name "FixUpBogusPublisherMetaFile," which, at 27 characters, noses ahead of a crowded field by one character and takes the prize for Longest Windows API Function Name.

The following is a list of the main GDI function groupings, in no particular order:

- device context and device management
- Palette management
- Visible region (VisRgn) manipulation

- Font management
- Bitmap manipulation
- Viewport, region, and rectangle manipulation
- Metafile manipulation
- Vector drawing operations
- Printing
- Miscellaneous

GDI Undocumented Functions

GDI is unlike USER, for example, in that some of its exports that are not documented in the SDK *are* documented in the DDK. These include the DMxxx functions, such as DMBitBlt and DMColorInfo, and most of the spooler interface functions, such as OpenJob and CloseJob. To avoid redundancy, we have not documented them here. Refer to the DDK documentation to obtain more information on any of these functions. As we did in the introduction to chapter 7, let's categorize the remaining undocumented GDI functions under general headings:

DEVICE CONTEXT AND DEVICE MANAGEMENT

SetRelAbs	SetDCState
GetRelAbs	IsDCCurrentPalette
SetDCOrg	GetDCHook
InternalCreateDC	SetDCHook
GSV	SetHookFlags
WordSet	Death
IsDCDirty	Resurrection
SetDCStatus	Brute
GetDCState	

PALETTE MANAGEMENT

GdiSelectPalette	DeviceColorMatch
GdiRealizePalette	

VISIBLE REGION (VISRGN) MANIPULATION

ExcludeVisRect	SaveVisRgn
IntersectVisRect	RestoreVisRgn
OffSetVisRgn	InquireVisRgn
SelectVisRgn	StuffVisible

FONT MANAGEMENT

DeleteAboveLineFonts	GetCurLogFont
ConvertOutlineFontFile	MFDrawText
GetPhysicalFontHandle	UnicodeToAnsi

BITMAP MANIPULATION

SelectBitmap
BitmapBits
CompatibleBitmap
CreateRealBitmapIndirect

CreateUserBitmap
CreateRealBitmap
CreateUserDiscardableBitmap
GdiMoveBitmap

VIEWPORT, REGION, AND RECTANGLE MANIPULATION

DPXlate
SetWinViewExt
ScaleExt
LVBUnion

RectStuff
OffSetOrg
GetClipRgn
StuffInRegion

METAFILE MANIPULATION

IsValidMetafile
FixUpBogusPublisherMetaFile
Vector drawing operations
RealizeDefaultPalette

PixToLine
RCos
RSin
FastWindowFrame

PRINTING

AbortDoc
QueryAbort

GetSpoolJob
QueryJob

MISCELLANEOUS

EnumCallBack
Copy
GdiInit2
FinalGdiInit
FTrapping0
MakeObjectPrivate

GdiTaskTermination
SetObjectOwner
GdiSeeGdiDo
IsGdiObject
ShrinkGdiHeap

Using Undocumented GDI functions

The undocumented functions described in this section can be used in the same way as any documented function unless otherwise noted. Parameter validation may sometimes be less stringent (hard to imagine in version 3.0, where parameter validation is already notoriously skimpy) than for documented functions, but this should not deter careful programmers. In GDI, where even most 3.0 structures referred to by handles contain an embedded signature, more type validation is possible than in USER, where structures are difficult to identify intrinsically.

BitmapBits   GDI.46

```
LONG FAR PASCAL BitmapBits(HBITMAP, DWORD, LPSTR)
HBITMAP hBitmap;      /* Identifies the bitmap */
DWORD dwCount;        /* size of lpBits buffer */
LPSTR lpBits;         /* Points to a bitmap bits buffer */
// CX contains a switch value specifying Get/Set functionality
```

This function is the back end to the documented GetBitmapBits and SetBitmapBits functions. Those functions are just entry points that set CX and jump to this function.

The value set into CX is the address of one of two tiny functions that establish DS:SI and ES:DI appropriately for either Get or Set operation. It appears that originally, the code for BitmapBits called the value in CX directly. Although the two functions are still present, they are no longer called. Instead, a separate piece of code now compares the value in CX and sets up DS:SI and ES:DI in-line.

It should never be necessary to call this function directly, and it is included here for completeness only.

Return: Number of bytes of dwCount used if successful, 0 if not.
Support: 3.0

BITMAPOBJ   structure

This is the structure behind the documented HBITMAP handle. Like other GDI object types, it is stored in GDI's default heap segment:

```
typedef struct tagBITMAPOBJ {
    GDIOBJHDR    header;
    HANDLE       hmemBitmap;
    BOOL         bSelected;
    HDC          hdc;
    } BITMAPOBJ, FAR *LPBITMAPOBJ;
```

where:

- hmemBitmap is a handle to bitmap resource
- bSelected is TRUE if the bitmap is currently selected, FALSE if not
- hdc is the handle of the DC into which the bitmap is selected if the bSelected field is TRUE.

The structure is identified by a wMagic field in the GDIOBJHDR structure of 5 in version 3.0, and "KO" (0x4F4B) in 3.1.

See also: GDI object header structure

BRUSHOBJ ⠀⠀⠀⠀⠀⠀⠀⠀⠀⠀⠀⠀⠀⠀⠀⠀⠀⠀⠀⠀ structure

This is the structure behind the documented HBRUSH handle. It is stored in GDI's default heap segment, and is made up of three parts: the undocumented GDIOBJHDR structure described in the GDI object header entry later in this chapter; the LOGBRUSH structure; and an extra COLORREF containing the hatch color for a hatched brush:

```
typedef struct tagBRUSHOBJ {
    GDIOBJHDR    header;
    LOGBRUSH     logbrush;
    COLORREF     crHatchBk;
    }  BRUSHOBJ, FAR *LPBRUSHOBJ;
```

The structure is identified by a wMagic field in the GDIOBJHDR structure of 2 in version 3.0, and "HO" (0x4F48) in 3.1.

See also: GDI object header structure

Brute ⠀⠀⠀⠀⠀⠀⠀⠀⠀⠀⠀⠀⠀⠀⠀⠀⠀⠀⠀⠀⠀⠀⠀⠀ GDI.213

This function is behind the so called "dot matrix" DMxxxx printer driver entry points (DMExtTextOut, DMGetCharWidth, DMStretchBlt, and DMColorInfo), described in the DDK. We have shown no prototype for it because it takes no parameters of its own, nor does it return anything. The entry points that lead into it have different numbers and types of parameters and return different types. Each entrypoint sets a value into CX and jumps to this function. The value in CL determines the number of bytes on the stack that this entrypoint requires for arguments. CH determines the function ID and is actually an offset within a call table. The call table provides entry points to a printer driver DLL. Thus, Brute is the interface function to printer drivers.

Support: 3.0, 3.1

CompatibleBitmap ⠀⠀⠀⠀⠀⠀⠀⠀⠀⠀⠀⠀⠀⠀⠀ GDI.157

```
HBITMAP FAR PASCAL CompatibleBitmap(HDC, int, int)
HDC hDC;                /* target device context */
int nWidth;             /* width of the bitmap in bits */
int nHeight;            /* height of the bitmap in bits */
/* CX contains additional parameter information */
```

CompatibleBitmap provides the setup code behind the documented Create-CompatibleBitmap and CreateDiscardableBitmap functions and the undocumented

CreateUserDiscardableBitmap function. These entry points set additional information into CX and then jump to CompatibleBitmap, which establishes DS, performs some other initializations, and then calls CreateRealBitmap.

This function is included for completeness only; it should never be necessary to call it directly. Note that internal code is unchanged in version 3.1, but that this entrypoint is no longer exported.

Return: A handle to the created bitmap or NULL if an error is encountered
Support: 3.0
See also: CreateUserDiscardableBitmap, CreateRealBitmap

ConvertOutlineFontFile   GDI.312

```
DWORD FAR PASCAL ConvertOutlineFontFile(LPSTR, LPSTR, LPSTR);
```

It is unclear what this function was ever intended to achieve. It first appears in 3.1, but there is no functional code associated with it, only normal compiler prolog and epilog. The function prototype appears in the 3.1 DDK version of WINDOWS.H.

Copy   GDI.250

```
void FAR PASCAL Copy(LPVOID, LPVOID, int)
LPVOID lpDest;          /* Copy to here */
LPVOID lpSrce;          /* Copy from here */
int nBytes;             /* Number of bytes to copy */
```

This little piece of rocket science is an inefficient challenger to the C library function _fmemcpy. It is unclear why this function, which persists into 3.1, lives in GDI and not KERNEL, if it is needed at all. It does not ever appear to be called by any of the system executables, and it is not referenced from within GDI itself.

Its inefficiency is due to the byte size string move instruction used in this function, rather than the word size used in most C library memory-to-memory copies. The code for Copy is essentially:

```
        mov     cx, word ptr nBytes
        les     di, dword ptr lpDest
        lds     si, dword ptr lpSrce
        rep     movsb
```

By its simplicity and lack of optimization, this code suggests that it originally served a noncritical, utilitarian purpose.

Consequently, there appears to be no reason to use this function in preference to _fmemcpy.

Support: 3.0, 3.1

CreateRealBitmapIndirect   GDI.406

```
HBITMAP FAR PASCAL CreateRealBitmapIndirect(LPBITMAP, HANDLE)
LPBITMAP lpBitmap;      /* Bitmap structure */
HDC hDC;                /* hDC for compatibility - may be NULL */
/* CX contains additional parametric information */
```

This function creates a bitmap and returns a handle to it. It is the engine behind the documented CreateBitmap, CreateBitmapIndirect, CreateCompatibleBitmap, and CreateDiscardableBitmap functions, as well as the undocumented CreateRealBitmap, CreateUserBitmap, CompatibleBitmap, and CreateUserDiscardableBitmap functions.

All these functions, except for CreateBitmapIndirect, allocate an internal BITMAP structure on the stack before passing control to CreateRealBitmapIndirect.

This function is included for completeness only; there should never be any need to call it directly.

Return: A handle to the created bitmap
Support: 3.0
See also: CreateRealBitmap

CreateRealBitmap   GDI.408

```
HBITMAP FAR PASCAL CreateRealBitmap(WORD, WORD, WORD, WORD,
        DWORD, HDC)
WORD xWidth;            /* width of bitmap */
WORD yWidth;            /* height of bitmap */
WORD nPlanes;           /* number of bit planes */
WORD nBitsPix;          /* bits per pixel */
LPSTR lpBits;           /* pointer to bitmap bits */
HDC hDC;                /* hDC for compatibility - may be NULL */
/* CX contains additional parametric information */
```

This function creates a bitmap and returns a handle to it. It is the engine behind the documented CreateBitmap, CreateCompatibleBitmap, and CreateDiscardableBitmap functions, as well as the undocumented CreateUserBitmap, CompatibleBitmap, and CreateUserDiscardable Bitmap functions.

This function is included for completeness only; there should never be any need to call it directly.

Return: A handle to the created bitmap
Support: 3.0
See also: CreateRealBitmapIndirect

CreateUserBitmap   GDI.407

```
HBITMAP FAR PASCAL CreateUserBitmap(WORD, WORD, WORD, WORD,
    DWORD)
WORD xWidth;          /* width of bitmap */
WORD yWidth;          /* height of bitmap */
WORD nPlanes;         /* number of bit planes */
WORD nBitsPix;        /* bits per pixel */
LPSTR lpBits;         /* pointer to bitmap bits */
```

This function is a special version of CreateBitmap used by USER. It appears to operate in almost exactly the same way as CreateBitmap. Both functions place a value in CX and call CreateRealBitmap.

It is only called from one place in USER, and appears to be used to prepare a bitmap for use in the creation of grayed menu entries. It is unclear why USER required a separate entrypoint.

This function is included for completeness only; there should never be any need to call it directly.

Return: A handle to the created bitmap
Support: 3.0, 3.1
See also: CreateUserDiscardableBitmap

CreateUserDiscardableBitmap   GDI.409

```
HBITMAP FAR PASCAL CreateUserDiscardableBitmap(HDC, WORD, WORD)
HDC hDC;              /* device context */
WORD yWidth;          /* width of bitmap */
WORD yHeight;         /* height of bitmap */
```

This function is a USER.EXE-specific version of the CreateDiscardableBitmap function, and appears to operate in almost exactly the same way as CreateDiscardable-Bitmap.

It is called from one place: a non-exported function that appears to save the underlying screen of a new window before it is painted for the first time (CS_SAVEBITS?). As with CreateUserBitmap, it is unclear why there is a special version for USER.

This function is included for completeness only; there should never be any need to call it directly.

Return: A handle to the created bitmap or NULL if an error is encountered
Support: 3.0, 3.1
See also: CreateUserBitmap

DC   Structure

The documented GetDC, BeginPaint, GetWindowDC and CreateMetaFile functions return a handle to a device context (HDC). Although those functions are fully documented in the Windows SDK documentation, the structure to which the returned handle refers is undocumented and is kept in GDI's local heap. That structure is defined in the GDIOBJ.H file and is described below.

This use of a handle is nothing new to Windows; the HWND is used principally outside of USER, by an application, and the WND structure is kept in USER's default local heap. The application need never direct access to the structure, but holds onto the handle, and passes it back to USER when some operation needs to be performed on a window. The analogy with GDI is that the HDC is used principally outside GDI, but the DC structure is kept and manipulated in GDI's default heap segment.

However, the situation with DC's is not quite as simple as that. If you were to use the tools described in chapter 2 to generate a complete list of all GDI.EXE module exports, documented and undocumented, you would find no reference to the above documented functions. You will instead find them among the exports from the USER module. CreateDC, which is called less frequently than the above functions, *is* a GDI export. CreateDC is functionally similar, in very general terms, to the documented USER CreateWindow function. In essence, both functions allocate a structure in their respective module's default heap, initialize it from the parameters passed to the function, and return a handle to it.

In fact, during USER startup, and after GDI has been loaded, USER (*not* GDI) calls CreateDC five times to allocate five DC's as an initial pool of HDC's for screen update. It stores these for shared use by all applications. GetDC, BeginPaint, and GetWindowDC simply return an unused entry from the list of stored DC handles (see the DCE structure entry in chapter 6). This reason for this approach is no doubt the size of the DC. At close to 210 bytes, the DC is a large structure. Allowing one dedicated DC structure per window would consume a lot of GDI resources (heap space) in a moderately loaded system, and would be wasteful. Given that relatively few applications are updating the screen at a given moment, the 'pool' approach appears to be efficient in terms of GDI resource usage. It incurs a performance penalty, however, in that the DC must be re-initialized before every painting operation. The CS_OWNDC and CS_CLASSDC class styles (see SDK for the WNDCLASS structure) provide for a specific window or class of windows to have its own dedicated DC.

The DC changed between versions 3.0 and 3.1, mainly through the addition of fields at the end of the structure, for the implementation of DC hooks (discussed in the SetDCHook entry in this chapter). However, in the debug version of the 3.1 GDI.EXE, the OBJECTHDR structure is four bytes longer, pushing all offsets in the rest of the DC out 4 bytes. Structure sizes are:

3.0 Retail	0xC2 (194) bytes
3.0 Debug	0xC2 (194) bytes

3.1 Retail	0xCE (206) bytes
3.1 Debug	0xD6 (214) bytes

The wMagic field in the GDIOBJHDR structure in version 3.0 contains the type number 7, 8, 9 or 11 (for a regular DC, a disabled DC, a MetaDC or a Metafile DC respectively). In 3.1 it contains the equivalent signature: 'MO,' 'NO,' 'OO,' or 'QO'. (Disabled and Meta DCs are currently not understood.)

Most of the names below are derived from symbols extracted from a debug version of 3.1 GDI.EXE. The offsets are for retail Windows; add 4 for debug Windows in 3.1.

```
typedef struct tagDC {
    GDIOBJHDR  header;           // 00h
    BYTE    byFlags;             // 0Ah
    BYTE    byFlags2;            // 0Bh
    HANDLE  hMetaFile;           // 0Ch
    HRGN    hrgnClip;            // 0Eh handle to (reclangular) clip region
    HANDLE  hPDevice;            // 10h Phys device handle
    HANDLE  hLPen;               // 12h Log. pen
    HANDLE  hLBrush;             // 14h Log. brush
    HANDLE  hLFont;              // 16h Log. Font
    HANDLE  hBitmap;             // 18h Selected bitmap
    HANDLE  dchPal;              // 1Ah Selected palette
    HANDLE  hLDevice;            // 1Ch Log. device
    HRGN    hRaoClip;            // 1Eh clip region
    HANDLE  hPDeviceBlock;       // 20h
    HANDLE  hPPen;               // 22h Phys. pen
    HANDLE  hPBrush;             // 24h Phys. brush
    HANDLE  hPFontTrans;         // 26h
    HANDLE  hPFont;              // 28h Phys. font
    LPVOID  lpPDevice;           // 2Ah
    WORD    pLDevice;            // 2Eh near pointer to log. device info
    WORD    pRaoClip;            // 30h near pointer to clip region
    WORD    pPDeviceBlock;       // 32h near pointer to GDIINFO
    WORD    pPPen;               // 34h
    WORD    pPBrush;             // 36h
    WORD    pPFontTrans;         // 38h near pointer to hPFontTrans
    LPVOID  lpPFont;             // 3Ah Font engine entrypoint
    int     nPFTIndex;           // 3Eh
    LPVOID  Transform;           // 40h
    /* Begin DRAWMODE structure - see DDK doc */
    WORD    wROP2;               // 44h Raster Op drawing mode
    WORD    wBkMode;             // 46h Background mode (opaque/transparent)
    DWORD   dwBkColor;           // 48h Phys. Background color
    DWORD   dwTextColor;         // 4Ch Phys. text color
    int     nTBreakExtra;        // 50h Text padding: ExtTextOut justification
    int     nBreakExtra;         // 52h pad per break = nTBreakExtra/BreakCount
    WORD    wBreakErr;           // 54h SetTextJustify called with nBreakExtra=0?
    int     nBreakRem;           // 56h remainder of TBreakExtra/nBreakCount
    int     nBreakCount;         // 58h Count of break characters in string
    int     nCharExtra;          // 5Ah Per char additional padding
    DWORD   crLbkColor;          // 5Ch Logical background color
```

```
DWORD    crLTextColor;      // 60h Logical text color
/* End DRAWMODE structure */
int      LCursPosX;         // 64h Log curs pos X
int      LCursPosY;         // 66h Log curs pos Y
int      WndOrgX;           // 68h window origin X
int      WndOrgY;           // 6Ah window origin Y
int      WndExtX;           // 6Ch window width
int      WndExtY;           // 6Eh window height
int      VportOrgX;         // 70h viewport origin X
int      VportOrgY;         // 72h viewport origin Y
int      VportExtX;         // 74h viewport width
int      VportExtY;         // 76h viewport height
int      UserVptOrgX;       // 78h (USER/user ??) viewport origin X
int      UserVptOrgY;       // 7Ah (USER/user ??) viewport origin Y
WORD     wMapMode;          // 7Ch mapping mode
WORD     wXFormFlags;       // 7Eh
WORD     wRelAbs;           // 80h Relative/absolute mode
WORD     wPolyFillMode;     // 82h Polygon fill mode
WORD     wStretchBltMode;   // 84h Bitblt stretch mode
BYTE     byPlanes;          // 86h for DC
BYTE     byBitsPix;         // 87h for DC
WORD     wPenWidth;         // 88h pen width in pix
WORD     wPenHeight;        // 8Ah pen width in pix
WORD     wTextAlign;        // 8Ch Text alignment flags
DWORD    dwMapperFlags;     // 8Eh
WORD     wBrushOrgX;        // 92h brush origin X
WORD     wBrushOrgY;        // 94h brush origin Y
WORD     wFontAspectX;      // 96h one half of font aspect ratio
WORD     wFontAspectY;      // 98h other half of font aspect ratio
HANDLE   hFontWeights;      // 9Ah handle to font weights
WORD     wDCSaveLevel;      // 9Ch depth of stack of saved DCs
WORD     wcDCLocks;         // 9Eh count of locks on DC
HRGN     hVisRgn;           // A0h Handle to visible region
WORD     wDCOrgX;           // A2h DC origin X
WORD     wDCOrgY;           // A4h DC origin Y
FARPROC  lpfnPrint;         // A6h print driver entrypoint
WORD     wDCLogAtom;        // AAh Logical device driver name atom
WORD     wDCPhysAtom;       // ACh Physical device name atom
WORD     wDCFileAtom;       // AEh FILE: port file name atom
WORD     wPostScaleX;       // B0h
WORD     wPostScaleY;       // B2h
union DC_TAIL {
    struct {                      // 3.0 fields from here
        WORD     wB4;             // B4h
        RECT     rectB6;          // B6h rect
        WORD     wDCGlobFlags;    // BEh Bit 0 indicates DC dirty
        WORD     wC0;             // C0h
        } tail_3_0;               // 3.0 size: C2h total

    struct {                      // 3.1 fields from here
        RECT     rectBounds;      // B4h Bounds rect
        RECT     rectLVB;         // BCh
        FARPROC  lpfnNotify;      // C4h Hook func
        LPSTR    lpHookData;      // C8h hook data
        WORD     wDCGlobFlags;    // CCh Bit 0 indicates DC dirty
```

DC

```
            HDC       hDCNext;        // CEh Next DC in linked list - Debug only
         } tail_3_1;                  // 3.1 size: CEh total nondebug, D6h debug
      };
   } DC, FAR *LPDC;

typedef struct tagRGNOBJ {
   GDIOBJHDR    header;               // 00h
// RGN          rgn;                  // 0Ah
   } RGNOBJ, FAR *LPRGNOBJ;
```

The structure contains the following fields. Fields not described here are not understood:

header
: All GDI object types contain a header structure that, among other things, contains a signature indicating the object's type. See the OBJECTHDR structure later in this chapter.

byFlags
: Flags, only one of which is currently understood: Bit 2 (0x04) signifies that the VisRgn for DC has changed, and that the DC is, as a result, dirty. This causes the RaoRgn (see the hRaoClip field below) to be recomputed, and the DC to be updated. This flag is modified, among other places, by the undocumented USER function DCHook through a call to the undocumented SetHookFlags function.

byFlags2
: Flags, which are not currently understood.

hMetaFile
: If this is a metafile playback (as in PlayMetaFile), this field contains the metafile handle.

hrgnClip
: This field contains the handle to the currently selected clip region for the DC.

hPDevice
: This contains the handle of the driver-specific PDEVICE info (see DDK documentation) stored in the GDI default heap.

hLPen
: Logical pen currently selected. See the PEN structure in this chapter.

hLBrush
: Logical brush currently selected. See the BRUSH structure in this chapter.

hLFont
: Logical font currently selected. See the FONT structure in this chapter.

hBitmap
: Handle to the currently selected bitmap, or NULL.

dchPal
: Logical palette currently selected or NULL. See the PALETTE structure in this chapter.

hLDevice
: Logical device. This is a handle to a block of memory in the default GDI heap segment, whose structure is currently not understood, except that it appears to be an array of driver entry points.

hRaoClip	This is the handle to a region that describes the intersection of the clip region and the visible region of the DC. This region used to be calculated on the fly, but is now precomputed to improve performance at a slight cost in heap space. The name apparently honors the Microsoft developer who originated the field (Rao Remala). See the SelectVisRgn entry in this chapter.
hPDeviceBlock	This field appears to be a handle to the GDIINFO structure for the device driver for the DC. See DDK documentation for more information on the GDIINFO structure.
hPPen	Handle to a driver-specific physical structure, stored in the GDI default heap, representing the logical pen stored in the hLPen field (see the DDK documentation for more information).
hPBrush	Handle to a driver-specific physical structure, stored in the GDI default heap, representing the logical brush stored in the hLBrush field (see the DDK documentation for more information).
hPFontTrans	Handle to a structure in the GDI default heap segment. It is not known what the structure is for, except that it is obviously related to Font transformations.
hPFont	Module handle of selected font; this value is returned by GetPhysicalFontHandle( ).
lpPDevice	Physical address of the device-specific PDEVICE info structure. This appears to be a far pointer to the PDEVICE structure whose handle is stored in the hPDevice field.
pLDevice	Near pointer to a logical device structure. This contains the return from a call to LocalLock the handle in the hLDevice field.
pRaoClip	This field contains the return from a call to LocalLock the handle in the pRaoClip field, or NULL.
pPDeviceBlock	This field contains the return from a call to LocalLock the handle in the hPDeviceBlock field.
pPPen	This field contains the return from a call to LocalLock the handle in the hPPen field.
pPBrush	This field contains the return from a call to LocalLock the handle in the hPBrush field.
pPFontTrans	This field contains the return from a call to LocalLock the handle in the hPFontTrans field.
lpPFont	This field contains a pointer into the block of memory to which the hPFont field contains a handle. The offset part of the pointer always appears to be 42h.

DC

The next 12 fields correspond to the DRAWMODE structure documented in the DDK. The fields are broken out here for clarity.

wROP2	This field stores the drawing mode selected using the documented SetROP2 function.
wBkMode	This field stores the background mode selected using the documented SetBkMode function.
dwBkColor	This field stores the device driver-specific, 32-bit representation of the crBkColor field below.
dwTextColor	This field stores the device driver-specific, 32-bit representation of the crLTextColor field below.
nTBreakExtra	This field stores the nBreakExtra parameter set using the documented SetTextJustification function (see the SDK documentation's description of SetTextJustification for more information).
nBreakExtra	This field stores the number of fill pixels per character to be used by TextOut. It is the quotient of the nTBreakExtra and nBreakCount fields rounded down.
wBreakErr	Contains an error code if SetTextJustification is called with nBreakExtra set to zero.
nBreakRem	This field stores the remainder of the division performed to calculate the nBreakExtra field above.
nBreakCount	This field stores the nBreakCount parameter set using the documented SetTextJustification function.
nCharExtra	This field stores the nCharExtra parameter passed to (see the SDK documentation's description of SetTextCharacterExtra for more information).
crLBkColor	This field stores the background color selected using the documented SetBkColor function.
crLTextColor	This field stores the background color selected using the documented SetTextColor function.
LCursPosX	The current logical cursor X coordinate position. This field is affected by the documented LineTo function, and by the TextOut function, if the TA_UPDATECP flag has been set using the documented SetTextAlign function.
LCursPosY	The current logical cursor Y position (see LCursPosX above).
WndOrgX	The X coordinate of the window origin, as set using the documented SetWindowOrg function.
WndOrgY	The Y coordinate of the window origin, as set using the documented SetWindowOrg function.
WndExtX	The width of the window, as set using the documented SetWindowExt function.

DC

WndExtY	The height of the window, as set using the documented SetWindowExt function.
VportOrgX	The X coordinate of the origin of viewport origin, as set using the documented SetViewportOrg function.
VportOrgY	The Y coordinate of the origin of viewport origin, as set using the documented SetViewportOrg function.
VportExtX	The width of the viewport, as set using the documented SetViewportExt function.
VportExtY	The height of the viewport, as set using the documented SetViewportExt function.
UserVptOrgX	It is not known what this field is used for.
UserVptOrgY	It is not known what this field is used for.
wMapMode	This field stores the mapping mode as set using the documented SetMapMode function.
wXFormFlags	It is not known what this field is used for.
wRelAbs	This field stores the coordinate mode set by the undocumented SetRelAbs function (see the SetRelAbs entry in this chapter).
wPolyFillMode	This field stores the polygon-filling mode set by the documented SetPolyFillMode function.
wStretchBltMode	This field stores the coordinate mode set by the undocumented SetRelAbs function (see the SetRelAbs entry in this chapter).
byPlanes	This appears to hold information related to the last bitmap selected into the DC, in this case the number of bit planes.
byBitsPix	This appears to hold information related to the last bitmap selected into the DC, in this case the number of bit planes.
wPenWidth	This field is derived from the x component of the lopnWidth field of the documented LOGPEN structure component, of the undocumented PEN structure, referred to by the hLPen parameter in this structure.
wPenHeight	This field is derived from the y component of the lopnWidth field of the documented LOGPEN structure component, of the undocumented PEN structure, referred to by the hLPen parameter in this structure.
wTextAlign	This field stores the text alignment flags set by the documented SetTextAlign function.
dwMapperFlags	This field stores the font mapper flags set by the documented SetMapperFlags function.
wBrushOrgX	This field stores x coordinate of the origin of the currently selected brush for the DC (see the hLBrush field above), set by the documented SetBrushOrg function.

DC

wBrushOrgY	This field stores y coordinate of the origin of the currently selected brush for the DC (see the hLBrush field above), set by the documented SetBrushOrg function.
wFontAspectX	This field contains the x dimension of the font aspect ratio of the currently selected font. It is zero for bitmap fonts.
wFontAspectY	This field contains the x dimension of the font aspect ratio of the currently selected font. It is zero for bitmap fonts.
wFontWeights	This field appears to contain the font weight for the currently selected font, but is often zero, even for stroked or TrueType fonts.
wDCSaveLeve	This field is incremented and decremented by the documented SaveDC and RestoreDC functions respectively. It indicates the 'stack depth' of saved DCs for this DC.
wcDCLocks	It is not known what this field is used for.
hVisRgn	This field contains the handle for the visible region (VisRgn) of the DC. See the undocumented SelectVisRgn function in this chapter for information about visible regions.
wDCOrgX	This field stores the x coordinate of the origin of the DC in pixels.
wDCOrgY	This field stores the x coordinate of the origin of the DC in pixels.
lpfnPrint	This field appears to contain the address of the printer driver entrypoint.
wDCLogAtom	This field contains a GDI local atom handle containing the name of the device driver module. In the case of a display DC, the atom will contain "DISPLAY".
wDCPhysAtom	This field contains a GDI local atom handle (presumably containing the name of the physical device) or NULL.
wDCFileAtom	This field contains a GDI local atom handle (presumably containing the name of the File port filename when printing to a file) or NULL.
wPostScaleX	It is not known what this field is used for.
wPostScaleY	It is not known what this field is used for.
rectBounds	It is not known what this field is used for.
rectLVB	This field contains the rectangle that bounds the update region of the DC. It is updated by the undocumented SetDCStatus function described later in this chapter.
lpfnNotify	This field stores the address of a DC hook, or callback function, installed using the undocumented SetDCHook function (see SetDCHook later in this chapter). Those DCs created at USER startup contain the address of the undocumented USER function DCHook in this field.

DC

dwHookData | This field stores the hook data parameter passed to the SetDCHook function.

wDCGlobFlags | Mostly unknown flags. The flag at bit 0, however, is known to indicate whether the DC is "dirty," that is, whether it needs updating. This bit is tested and reset by the undocumented IsDCDirty function described later in this chapter.

See also: DCSAVE structure

DCSAVE   Structure

The DCSAVE structure is a subset of a DC structure used to store state saved using the documented SaveDC or undocumented GetDCState functions, and subsequently restored using the documented RestoreDC or undocumented SetDCState functions. GetDCState and SetDCState are described later in this chapter.

The DCSAVE structure, like the DC structure, is affected by the change in GDI object header structure size between retail and debug versions in 3.1. Apart from that change, the structure is stable:

3.0 Retail   0xAA (170) bytes
3.0 Debug   0xAA (170) bytes
3.1 Retail   0xAA (170) bytes
3.1 Debug   0xAE (174) bytes

A DCSAVE structure is allocated in the default GDI heap using the documented SaveDC and undocumented GetDCState functions. These call an internal function, SaveDCState, that allocates space for the DCSAVE structure; copies the first 160 bytes (162 in 3.1 debug) of the DC into the DCSAVE; copies the wDCOrgX and wDCOrgY fields; makes a copy of the clip region, and saves its handle in the hrgnClip field of the DCSAVE.

The structure is comprised of the first 70 fields of a DC, from "header" up to "wDCLocks," followed by the wDCOrgX and wDCOrgY fields of a DC. See the DC structure entry above for information on the individual fields.

See also: DC structure, GetDCState, SetDCState

Death   GDI.121

```
void FAR PASCAL Death(HDC)
HDC hDC;           /* handle of desktop device context */
```

This function, called from the undocumented DisableOEMLayer function, disables the GDI display driver. This returns the display to the default text mode defined for the device, normally 80x25 in 16 colors.

Used by: USER.EXE
Support: 3.0, 3.1
See also: Resurrection, DisableOEMLayer, EnableOEMLayer

DeleteAboveLineFonts   GDI.186

```
void FAR PASCAL DeleteAboveLineFonts(void);
```

This function is called as part of the USER task termination procedure in versions 2.1 and 3.0, although its purpose is not understood.

Support: 3.0

DeviceColorMatch   GDI.449

```
DWORD FAR PASCAL DeviceColorMatch(COLORREF, LP???)
COLORREF crSource;      /* color to be matched */
LP??? lp;
```

This function is not currently understood, although it appears to validate whether a device is capable of rendering the specified color.

Support: 3.0, 3.1

DPXlate   GDI.138

```
BOOL FAR PASCAL DPXlate(HDC, LPPOINT, int)
HDC hDC;                /* device context */
LPPOINT lpPoints;       /* Array of points to be translated */
int nPoints;            /* number of points in array */
// DX contains the address of the internal function
// to perform the translation
```

This function is the back end to the documented LPtoDP and DPtoLP functions. Those functions set into DX the address of a near function to perform the appropriate translation (that is, from logical to device points or from device to logical points) and then jump to this function.

This function performs a check on the hDC parameter, loads the address of the array of points into ES:DI and the number of points into CX, and then calls the routine specified in DX. Upon return, it sets the return value to TRUE. This suggests that the LPtoDP and DPtoLP functions will only fail if the hDC is invalid, contrary to the documentation, which suggests that they can fail if not all the points are converted.

Just as an aside, the DPXlate function contains an interesting piece of code that does not have any immediately obvious value (symbol names are our own):

```
        .
        .
        ;; DX contains function to call
        call near DontKnowWhy       ;; pushes ret addr then continues
DontKnowWhy:
        pop bx                      ;; pops ret addr from call (DontKnowWhy)
        sub bx, offset DontKnowWhy;; must result in bx = 0
        add dx, bx                  ;; dx never modified by the above
        call dx
        .
```

Return: FALSE (0) if the hDC parameter is not valid, otherwise returns TRUE (1)
Support: 3.0

EngineXXX   GDI.300-314

The 3.1 version of GDI contains exports for the following functions:

EngineDeleteFont	GDI.301
EngineEnumerateFont	GDI.300
EngineExtTextOut	GDI.314
EngineGetCharWidth	GDI.303
EngineGetGlyphBMP	GDI.305
EngineMakeFontDir	GDI.306
EngineRealizeFont	GDI.302
EngineSetFontContext	GDI.304

These are TrueType service functions that GDI provides for use by non-raster printer drivers. For example, to print TrueType fonts on a PostScript printer, the PostScript driver must convert TrueType into a downloadable font format that the printer accepts; the EngineXXX functions simplify this task by providing the driver with information about the TrueType font, bitmaps for an individual glyph (character or symbol), and so on.

These functions are mentioned briefly in the 3.1 DDK (*Device Driver Adaptation Guide*, chapter 4), but no function prototypes are given. The true documentation for these functions appears to be the source code for the PostScript driver, which comes with the 3.1 DDK. (Use the Source, Luke!) \PRINTERS\PS35\TRUETYPE.H contains function prototypes, and \PRINTERS\PS35\TTFONT.C contains code that uses these functions. The prototypes are:

```
WORD FAR PASCAL EngineDeleteFont(LPFONTINFO);
WORD FAR PASCAL EngineEnumerateFont(LPSTR, FARPROC, DWORD);
WORD FAR PASCAL EngineGetCharWidth(LPFONTINFO, BYTE, BYTE, LPINT);
int  FAR PASCAL EngineGetGlyphBmp(WORD, LPFONTINFO, WORD, WORD, LPSTR,
     DWORD, LPBITMAPMETRICS);
WORD FAR PASCAL EngineRealizeFont(LPLOGFONT, LPTEXTXFORM, LPFONTINFO);
WORD FAR PASCAL EngineSetFontContext(LPFONTINFO, WORD);
```

The prototype for another appears in the 3.1 DDK version of WINDOWS.H:

```
typedef UINT FAR* LPFONTDIR;
DWORD FAR PASCAL EngineMakeFontDir(HDC, LPFONTDIR, LPCSTR);
```

In general, application programs should not need to use these functions. Windows 3.1 has documented functions for querying TrueType information, such as GetRasterizerCaps(), GetGlyphOutline(), and GetOutlineTextMetrics().

Interestingly, GDI.EXE in Windows 3.0 had an embedded FONTENG.DLL. Running a strings utility on 3.0 GDI.EXE turns up the following:

```
InquireFontEngine
fontdir
FONTENG.DLL
StartFontEngine
EnumerateEFontsHeaders
RealizeThatFont
GetEFontStructSize
DeleteEFont
MicroSoft (c) 1989 - This is an awesome engine font!!
```

These do not show up in the normal NE header for GDI.EXE. Perhaps they are functions that realize GDI's bitmap fonts from .FON files.

This all also relates to a component of Kanji Windows: WIFEMAN, "Font Driver Mgr for Windows Intelligent Font Environment." This DLL contains functions for manipulating font contexts, getting widths, and so on.

EnumCallback   GDI.158

```
int FAR PASCAL EnumCallback(LPLOGFONT, LPTEXTMETRICS, WORD, LPSTR)
LPLOGFONT lpLogFont;
LPTEXTMETRICS lpTextMetrics;
WORD wFontType;
LPSTR lpData;
```

The purpose of this function is not clear. It appears to be a vestigial internal callback function intended for invocation by EnumFonts. However, it is not referenced internally within the primary Windows modules, and it disappears in version 3.1. It is included here only for completeness; there should be no reason to call it directly.

Return: Unknown
Support: 3.0

ExcludeVisRect   GDI.73

```
int FAR PASCAL ExcludeVisRect(HDC, LPRECT)
HDC hDC;            /* device context */
LPRECT lprect;      /* rectangle to exclude */
```

This function removes the rectangular area from the visible region of the DC. It operates in exactly the same way as the documented ExcludeClipRect function, except that instead of operating on the current clipping region for the device context, it operates on the visible region, contained in the hVisRgn field of the DC structure.

See SelectVisRgn for a discussion of visible regions.

Return: One of the documented constants COMPLEXREGION, NULLREGION, SIMPLEREGION, or ERROR
Support: 3.0, 3.1
See also: SelectVisRgn, OffsetVisRgn, SaveVisRgn, RestoreVisRgn, IntersectVisRect, DC structure

FastWindowFrame   GDI.400

```
BOOL FAR PASCAL FastWindowFrame(HDC, LPRECT,  int, int, DWORD)
HDC hDC;            /* device context */
LPRECT lprect;      /* coordinates of frame */
int xWidth;         /* pixel width of frame uprights */
int yWidth;         /* pixel width of frame horizontals */
DWORD dwROP3;       /* ternary raster operation */
```

This function allows fast rectangular frames to be bitblt'ed onto a device context. The USER window manager code uses this function for the frame that appears when a window is dragged across the desktop, for example.

The dwROP3 parameter is one of the ternary raster operation constants defined in WINDOWS.H.

This function corresponds to one of the required GDI display driver entry points, FastBorder (ordinal 17), and is passed on by GDI to the driver. See the DDK documentation for more information.

ExcludeVisRect

Return: Nonzero if the frame could be painted, zero if not

Support: 3.0, 3.1

Example: Uses FastWindowFrame to implement a crude exploding window

```c
/* FASTWFRM.C */

#include <windows.h>
#include <wmhandlr.h>
#include <winio.h>

/* Undocumented function */
extern BOOL FAR PASCAL FastWindowFrame(HDC hDC, LPRECT lpRect,
    int xWidth, int yWidth, DWORD dwROP3);

WMHANDLER wmsize_old;

#include "checkord.c"

long my_wmsize(HWND hwnd, WORD wMsg, WORD wParam, DWORD lParam)
    {
    HDC hDC;
    RECT rect;
    int nFrames, i, xWidth = 2, yWidth = 2;

    GetClientRect(hwnd, &rect);

    yWidth = (rect.bottom - rect.top);
    xWidth = (rect.right - rect.left);

    rect.left = (xWidth / 2) - 1;
    rect.right = (xWidth / 2) + 1;
    rect.top = (yWidth / 2) - 1;
    rect.bottom = (yWidth / 2) + 1;

    if (yWidth > xWidth)
        {
        nFrames = (xWidth / 2) - 1;
        yWidth /= xWidth;
        xWidth = 1;
        }
    else
        {
        nFrames = (yWidth / 2) - 1;
        xWidth /= yWidth;
        yWidth = 1;
        }

    hDC = GetDC(hwnd);

    for (i = 0; i < nFrames; i++)
        {
        FastWindowFrame(hDC, &rect, 2, 2, DSTINVERT);
        FastWindowFrame(hDC, &rect, 2, 2, DSTINVERT);
        rect.left -= xWidth;
```

FastWindowFrame

```
            rect.right += xWidth;
            rect.top -= yWidth;
            rect.bottom += yWidth;
            }

     ReleaseDC(hwnd, hDC);

     return (*wmsize_old)(hwnd, wMsg, wParam, lParam);
     }

int main()
     {
     if (! CheckOrdName("FastWindowFrame", "GDI", 400))
         return 1;

     wmsize_old = wmhandler_set(__hMainWnd, WM_SIZE,
                                (WMHANDLER) my_wmsize);
     printf("Resize this window, and\n"
            "an exloding frame will fill it out!\n\n"
            "Close the window to exit\n");

     return 0;
     }
```

FinalGdiInit   GDI.405

```
void FAR PASCAL FinalGdiInit(HBRUSH)
HBRUSH hPattern;              /* default desktop background */
```

This function is called by USER as the last call of its initialization. It appears to set the default brush to be used to paint the desktop background.

   Subsequent invocations of the function have no effect.

Used by: USER.EXE
Support: 3.0, 3.1

FixUpBogusPublisherMetaFile   GDI.464

```
int FAR PASCAL FixUpBogusPublisherMetaFile(LPMETAFILE)
LPMETAFILE lpMetaFile;   /* contents of the Metafile */
```

The purpose of this function is not known; its name gives a general idea of its raison d'etre, of course, but is not quite long enough to indicate the exact nature of the problem in the metafile from the offending publisher. Ventura?

   It is called from the documented GetClipboardData function in the USER module. It is very unlikely that there will ever be a need to call this function directly.

Return: 1, 0, -1, -2, or -3.
Used by: USER.EXE
Support: 3.1

FONTOBJ   structure

This is the structure behind the documented HFONT handle. It is stored in GDI's
default heap segment, and is made up of two parts: the undocumented GDIOBJHDR
structure described in the GDI object header entry later in this chapter; and the
LOGFONT structure:

```
typedef struct tagFONTOBJ {
    GDIOBJHDR    header;
    LOGFONT      logfont;
    }   FONTOBJ, FAR *LPFONTOBJ;
```

The structure is identified by a wMagic field in the GDIOBJHDR structure of 3 in
version 3.0, and "JO" (0x4F49) in 3.1.

See also: Introduction to the chapter, GDI object header structure

fTrapping0   GDI.355

fTrapping0 is a WORD variable in the GDI data segment. When GDI initializes, it
uses DPMI to hook processor exception 0 (divide by zero). During certain GDI operations, the value of fTrapping0 is set to 1. If an exception 0 occurs while flag is set to
1, then GDI attempts to clean up the exception, and continue. If the value is 0, it
chains it on to whatever handler was previously installed. fTrapping0 is inspected by
both TOOLHELP and CVWIN.DLL. If fTrapping0 is set, they both chain on the
exception.
    The value of this variable can be retrieved using GetProcAddress:

```
#define GET_VAL(modname, varname) \
  ((WORD) (LOWORD(GetProcAddress(GetModuleHandle(modname), name))))

WORD fTrapping0 = GET_VAL("GDI", "FTRAPPING0");
```

GDI Object header   structure

GDI objects are structures stored, with the exception of BITMAPs (which are stored
in the global heap), in GDI's default local heap segment. They consist of a header followed by either a documented or undocumented structure specific to the object being

represented. For example, an HPEN is a handle to an undocumented PEN structure that is made up of the GDIOBJHDR structure followed by a documented LOGPEN structure; the GDIOBJHDR structure contains a signature word at offset 2 that identifies the structure as a pen. This pattern is completely consistent among all GDI object types, and makes it very easy to identify and validate object handles programmatically from within applications.

This property is used by ToolHelp to fill the wType field of the LOCALENTRY structure provided by the LocalFirst/LocalNext heap walking functions (see chapter 10). So that ToolHelp continues to function, it is likely that the GDIOBJHDR structure will remain fairly stable. It should also be said, however, that if all that you need from the header structure is the object type field, it is advisable to use ToolHelp. There is one caveat, however: ToolHelp does not recognize the handle to Metafile DC (type 11 in 3.0, 'QO', 0x4F51 in 3.1).

The structure is 10 bytes long (14 in 3.1 debug version):

```
typedef struct tagGDIOBJHDR {
    HANDLE        hNext;
    WORD          wMagic;
    DWORD         dwCount;
    WORD          wMetaList;
/* additional 3.1 debug fields from here */
    WORD          wSelCount;
    HANDLE        hOwner;
    } GDIOBJHDR, FAR *LPGDIOBJHDR;
```

Note the presence of the extra fields at the end of the 3.1 debug version of the structure. In the file GDIOBJ.H presented in the introduction to this chapter, the 3.1 debug version of the structure is separately defined as GDIOBJ31DBG.

The structure contains the following fields. Fields not described here are not currently understood:

FIELD	DESCRIPTION
hNext	This field is used to provide linked lists of objects. For example, the documented SaveDC function stores a stack of saved DCSAVE structures linked through this field. Lists are terminated by a NULL in this field. In version 3.0, this field appears occasionally to be used to store transient flags.
wMagic	The "magic," or type identifier, changed between versions 3.0 and 3.1. In 3.0, the type was a simple numeric value in the range 1-11 as follows:

Pen	1
Brush	2
Font	3
Palette	4

GDI Object header

Bitmap	5
Region	6
DC	7
Disabled DC	8
MetaDC	9
Metafile	10
Metafile DC	11

In 3.1, the numeric is expanded into a word length string identifier, presumably to make it easier to spot during debugging, as follows:

Pen	0x4F47 ('GO')
Brush	0x4F48 ('HO')
Font	0x4F49 ('IO')
Palette	0x4F4A ('JO')
Bitmap	0x4F4B ('KO')
Region	0x4F4C ('LO')
DC	0x4F4D ('MO')
Disabled DC	0x4F4E ('NO')
MetaDC	0x4F4F ('OO')
Metafile	0x4F50 ('PO')
Metafile DC	0x4F51 ('QO')

In addition, the wMagic field is used to store at least two bit flags. These occupy positions that allow the signature to be masked and validated independently of the flags' value. Specifically, in both 3.0 and 3.1, bit 15 of this field is set while an object is selected into a DC. In version 3.1 only, bit 13 is set if the object is private (see the MakeObjectPrivate function later in this chapter). The IsGdiObject function uses this field to test the validity of a GDI object handle (see IsGdiObject later in this chapter).

dwCount	This field contains a sequence number reflecting the count of objects created before this one.
wSelCount	This field only exists in the 3.1 debug version, and tracks the number of times that an object has been selected into a DC.
hOwner	This field only exists in the 3.1 debug version, and contains the handle of the task that was current when the object was created. It can be modified using the SetObjectOwner function, described later in the chapter.

GDI Object header

GdiInit2

```
HANDLE FAR PASCAL GdiInit2(HANDLE, HANDLE)
HANDLE h1;          /* GDI object */
HANDLE h2;          /* Global data */
```

It is not known exactly what this function is for. It is invoked by the USER clipboard manager when a GDI object, such as a bitmap, is copied from the clipboard. The h1 parameter refers to the GDI object handle. The h2 parameter may be 0, -1, or a global memory handle. If 0, the function returns the global memory handle of the data associated with the object. If h2 is -1, the global memory handle associated with the object is set to NULL and the return is undefined. Otherwise, the global memory handle associated with the object is set to h2, and h2 is returned.

Return: The global memory handle associated with h1, unless h2 is -1, in which case it is undefined (see text)
Used by: USER.EXE
Support: 3.0, 3.1

GdiMoveBitmap

```
void FAR PASCAL GdiMoveBitmap(HBITMAP)
HBITMAP hBitmap;      /* handle of bitmap to be moved */
```

This function causes the global memory associated with the bitmap to be moved into lower memory using the documented GlobalWire and GlobalUnWire functions.

It is called during USER's startup processing, and from FinalUserInit, to ensure that USER bitmaps, such as the gray bitmap used for disabled menu item text, are kept low in memory.

Used by: USER.EXE
Support: 3.0, 3.1

GdiRealizePalette

```
DWORD FAR PASCAL GdiRealizePalette(HDC)
HDC hDC;                /* Device context to own palette */
```

This function realizes the logical palette in effect for the specified device context. It is the GDI module entrypoint behind the documented USER function RealizePalette.

There is no reason to call this function directly; it is included here for completeness only.

Return: The low word of the return contains the number of entries mapped to different entries in the system palette; it is not known what the high word contains.
Support: 3.0, 3.1
See also: The DC structure

GdiSeeGdiDo   GDI.452

```
DWORD FAR PASCAL GdiSeeGdiDo(WORD, WORD, WORD, WORD)
WORD wReqType;          /* request type */
WORD wParam1;           /* depends on wReqType */
WORD wParam2;           /* unused - reserved for future expansion? */
WORD wParam3;           /* depends on wReqType */
```

This function provides access to the GDI local heap. Like UserSeeUserDo (chapter 6) it is used by TOOLHELP in version 3.1. GdiSeeGdiDo recognizes four request types in the wReqType. The use of other parameters depends on the request type (except for the wParam2 argument, which is not used by any of the currently defined request types; it is perhaps being reserved for future use).

GSGD_LOCALALLOC   (0x0001)
This parameter allocates some memory from the GDI module local heap. The wParam1 argument contains the flags to be passed to the documented LocalAlloc function for the allocation, and wParam3 specifies the size of the block to allocate.

It also returns the allocated handle in the low word if the LocalAlloc was successful, NULL if it failed. The high word will always be zero.

GSGD_LOCALFREE   (0x0002)
This parameter frees a block of memory in the GDI module local heap. The wParam1 argument contains the GDI local memory handle to be freed.

It also returns NULL in the low word if the LocalFree was successful, or the specified handle if it failed. The high word will always be zero.

GSGD_LOCALCOMPACT   (0x0003)
This parameter generates a free block of the specified size in the GDI module local heap. The wParam3 argument specifies the size of the required free block, to be passed to LocalCompact.

It also returns the size of the largest free block in the GDI module local heap in the low word. The high word will always be zero.

GSGD_LOCALHEAP   (0x0103)
This parameter returns the selector for the GDI module local heap in the low word. This can be combined with a local memory handle, such as an HDC, or a handle returned from the GSGD_LOCALALLOC request described above, to form a far pointer into the GDI heap.

The high word will always be zero.

If the request type does not correspond to one of the above values, the call signifies an invalid request type by returning -1.

Return: Depends on the request type, as specified above
Support: 3.1
See also: UserSeeUserDo (chapter 6), ToolHelp (chapter 10)

GdiSelectPalette   GDI.361

```
HPALETTE FAR PASCAL GdiSelectPalette(HDC, HPALETTE)
HDC hDC;                /* Device context to own palette */
HPALETTE hPalette;      /* Handle of palette to be selected */
```

This function selects a logical palette to be in effect for the specified device context. It is the GDI module entrypoint behind the documented USER function SelectPalette. The bForceBackground parameter of that call is processed within the USER code before control is passed to the GDI routine to actually select the palette.

There is no reason to call this function directly; it is included here for completeness only.

Return: The HPALETTE previously in effect for the device context
Support: 3.0, 3.1
See also: The DC structure

GdiTaskTermination   GDI.460

```
void FAR PASCAL GdiTaskTermination(HANDLE)
HANDLE hTask;           /* terminating task */
```

USER calls this function in GDI upon task termination. In the retail version, the function does nothing. The debug GDI.EXE, however, contains calls to KERNEL.328 (see K328, chapter 5) to output a debug string if any GDI objects owned by the specified task remain. The GDI object header structure in the debug executable contains two extra fields, one of which (hOwner) is the task handle of the task that created the object. It is this additional field that allows this test to be performed in the debug version.

Used by: USER.EXE
Support: 3.1
See also: GDI Object Header

GetClipRgn   GDI.173

```
HRGN FAR PASCAL GetClipRgn(HDC)
HDC hDC;          /* Get clipping region for this DC */
```

This function returns a handle to the clipping region in effect for the specified DC. This corresponds to the clipping region handle previously defined for the DC through a call to the documented SelectClipRgn function.

   This function, like most of the GetXXX functions in GDI, is a very simple implementation. It sets the offset of the hrgnClip field in the DC into CX and falls through to the undocumented GSV function (which is present in both 3.0 and 3.1, but only exported in 3.0) described later in this chapter.

   A slight variation on this function appears in the Win32 API.

Return: HRGN for the clipping region in effect for the device context, NULL if none
Used by: USER.EXE
Support: 3.0, 3.1
See also: GSV, DC structure

GetCurLogFont   GDI.411

```
HFONT FAR PASCAL GetCurLogFont(HDC)
HDC hDC;          /* device context */
```

This function returns the current logical font selected for the specified device context. This will previously have been created by one of the documented CreateFont or CreateFontIndirect functions, or it will be one of the stock fonts.

   This function, like most of the GetXXX functions in GDI, is a very simple implementation. It sets the offset of the hLFont field in the DC into CX and falls through to the undocumented GSV function (which is present in both 3.0 and 3.1, but only exported in 3.0) described later in this chapter.

   It is, as with GetClipRgn above, unclear why this function is not documented in the SDK.

Return: a handle to the logical font in effect for the device context or NULL if the device context is invalid
Used by: USER.EXE
Support: 3.0, 3.1
See also: DC structure, GSV

GetDCHook   GDI.191

```
DWORD FAR PASCAL GetDCHook(HDC, FARPROC FAR *)
HDC hDC;                  /* device context */
FARPROC FAR *lpfnHook;   /* ptr to buffer to receive address */
```

This function returns the address of the currently installed hook function for the specified HDC and the value of the dwHookData associated with it. For more information on the DC hook, see SetDCHook later in this chapter.

GetDCHook( ) places the contents of the lpfnNotify field of the DC structure in the buffer pointed to by the lpfnHook parameter, and returns the contents of the dwHookData field. If the specified HDC is invalid, the return is undefined.

Return: The value of the dwHookData field from the DC structure.
Used by: USER.EXE
Support: 3.1
See also: SetDCHook, SetHookFlags

GetDCState   GDI.179

```
HDCS FAR PASCAL GetDCState(HDC)
HDC hDC;                  /* device context */
```

This function saves some of the specified device context into a DCSAVE structure in the local GDI heap and returns a handle to it to allow for a subsequent restore using SetDCState.

The DCSAVE structure is a subset of the DC structure, and has the same signature as a full DC.

This function is very similar to the documented SaveDCe function; both GetDC-State and SaveDC call an unexported internal function, SaveDCState, to make the selective copy of the DC. There are differences is the behaviors of there two functions. GetDCState is simply an exported far cover over SaveDCState, whereas SaveDC inserts the handle returned be SaveDCState into a linked list 'stack' based on the hNext field of the specified DC's GDI Object header and increments the wDCSaveLevel field of the DC.

USER calls this function once when creating an initial pool of five DCs to obtain an initial DCSAVE containing the default DC state. It then uses SetDCState to re-initialize a DC when it is released, for example by ReleaseDC, using the saved DCSAVE. See the SetDCState entry for more information.

Return: handle to a DCSAVE structure if the DC is valid, otherwise NULL.
Used by: USER.EXE
Support: 3.0, 3.1
See also: SetDCState, DC and DCSAVE structures

GetKerningPairs   GDI.332

```
int FAR PASCAL GetKerningPairs(HFONT, int, LPSTR)
HFONT hFont;          /* physical font handle */
int nEntries;         /* number of pairs to retrieve */
LPSTR lpBuffer;       /* buffer to hold retrieved pairs */
```

Kerning pairs are adjustments to interletter spacing in a font. For example, the word LAYAWAY requires kerning between almost every pair of letters. This function appears to be a variation on the Control(GETPAIRKERNTABLE) subfunction, documented in the DDK. Whereas GETPAIRKERNTABLE returns a four-byte KERNPAIR struct for each kerning pair on a device, this function returns nEntries * a six-byte struct for a given font. The Win32 API specification indicates that GetKerningPairs() will be part of the API.

GetPhysicalFontHandle   GDI.352

```
HANDLE FAR PASCAL GetPhysicalFontHandle(HDC)
HDC hDc;              /* device context */
```

This function returns the module handle of the font selected into the specified DC. The function merely returns the value of the hPFont field at offset 28h (2Ch in 3.1 debug) in the DC. It does not check if the passed-in DC is valid.

Return: Font module handle or NULL if the logical font handle is invalid
Support: 3.0, 3.1

GetRelAbs   GDI.86

```
int FAR PASCAL GetRelAbs(HDC)
HDC hDC;              /* Get the coordinate mode for this DC  */
```

This function returns ABSOLUTE or RELATIVE, corresponding to the coordinate mode for the specified DC. The coordinate mode determines whether coordinates are relative to the origin of the Device Context or the current position. This affects the behavior of the LineTo and PolyLine functions.

The function operates in the same way as other GDI GetXXX functions; it places the offset of the wRelAbs field in the DC into CX and drops through to the undocumented GSV function, described later in this chapter.

Return: ABSOLUTE (1) or RELATIVE (2) (defined in WINDOWS.H) unless the DC is NULL, in which case returns NULL
Support: 3.0, 3.1

Note: This function was documented in 2.1. The documentation of the return value states that it is NULL if *the DC is invalid*. The code (in 3.0 at least) actually checks only for a zero hDC parameter.
See also: DC structure, SetRelAbs, GSV

GetSpoolJob GDI.245

```
DWORD FAR PASCAL GetSpoolJob(int, LONG)
int nOption;      /* spool-job request option */
LONG p;           /* parameter */
```

Most Print Manager spooling functions, such as OpenJob(), CloseJob(), and DeleteJob(), are documented in the DDK (*Device Driver Adaptation Guide*, chapter 4). However, some of these functions, including GetSpoolJob(), seem only to appear in the 3.1 DDK include file SPOOL.H.

GetSpoolJob() takes one of the following SP_ or CP_ constants as its first parameter. The other parameter, and the function return value, depend on the individual request. The CP_ constants are used by Control Panel for modifying the printer setup:

```
#define SP_PRINTERNAME       20
#define SP_REGISTER          21
#define SP_CONNECTEDPORTCNT  25
#define SP_QUERYDISKUSAGE    26
#define SP_DISKFREED         27
#define SP_INIT              28
#define SP_LISTEDPORTCNT     29
#define CP_ISPORTFREE        30
#define CP_REINIT            31
#define SP_TXTIMEOUT         32
#define SP_DNSTIMEOUT        33
#define CP_CHECKSPOOLER      34
#define CP_SET_TT_ONLY       35
#define CP_SETSPOOLER        36
#define CP_SETDOSPRINT       37
```

For SP_PRINTERNAME (20), the second parameter is an LPSTR that points to a buffer to receive a NULL-terminated list of NULL-terminated strings. Upon return, the buffer will be filled with the names of the supported printers. The first two bytes of the buffer should be initialized as a WORD value specifying the size in bytes of the buffer.

Used by: Print Manager, Control Panel
Support: 3.0, 3.1
See also: QueryJob

GSV   GDI.137

```
DWORD FAR PASCAL GSV(HDC)
HDC hDC;              /* device context */
// CL contains the offset into the DC structure
```

This function is the engine behind the undocumented and documented GetXXX functions that operate on a device context (for example, GetTextColor, GetBkMode, GetViewPortOrg, and GetRelAbs). Those functions are entrypoint labels that set an offset into CL and fall through to this function.

The phrase "fall through" should be explained; it is more accurate than you might think. The code for the various functions that use GSV reveal an unusual technique which is worth a brief diversion. The code for the entrypoints which use GSV is arranged as follows:

```
GetClipRgn proc far
    mov cl, OEh
    db   3Dh          ;; 3D is OpCode for cmp ax, immediate-word-value
GetROP2 proc far
    mov cl, 44h
    db   3Dh
GetTextAlign proc far
    mov cl, 8Ch
    db   3Dh
    .
    .
GetTextColor proc far
    mov cl, 60h
GSV proc far
    mov ax, hInstance
    push bp
    mov bp, sp
    push ds
    mov bx, [bp+6]
    .
    .
```

One might think upon first inspection that the above code would always, no matter which function was called, lead to CL being finally loaded with 60h, and that therefore all of the functions would return the contents of the crLTextColor field of the DC (crLTextColor is the WORD at offset 60h in the DC). The intervening 3Dh byte between each of the entrypoints, however, is the opcode for CMP AX, imm-word-value. Thus, for example, the processor interprets the opcodes from the GetClipRgn entrypoint, as:

```
GetClipRgn proc far
    mov cl, OEh
    cmp ax, 44B1h
    cmp ax, 8CB1h
```

```
    .
    .
    .     cmp ax, 60B1h
GSV proc far
    mov ax, hInstance
    push bp
    mov bp, sp
    push ds
    mov bx, [bp+6]
    ...
```

where the CMP AX, 44B1h and so on has no effect apart from setting flags over and over. Note that the 44B1h word corresponds to the instruction MOV CL, 44h that aligns with the entrypoint for GetROP2. In the same way, the entrypoint for GetTextAlign (which was buried in the CMP AX, 8CB1h instruction above) will appear to the processor as:

```
GetTextAlign proc far
    mov cl, 8Ch
    cmp ax, 82B1h
    cmp ax, 84B1h
    .
    .
```

In this way, only the function being called sets CL. This mechanism requires no JMP instructions. It is an interesting optimization, although it is not clear that it yields great savings in machine cycles. In fact, generating all those CMP instructions would seem worse than taking the JMP. This technique is used in other places throughout Windows, not just in GDI.

The code is almost unchanged in 3.1, but the function is not exported. The function is included here for completeness and should not be called directly.

Return: DWORD in DX:AX. Even if the API function returns a WORD, there is always a full DWORD available in DX:AX when GSV returns.
Support: 3.0
See also: DC structure, GetRelAbs, GetClipRgn

InquireVisRgn   GDI.131

```
HRGN FAR PASCAL InquireVisRgn(HDC)
HDC hDC;              /* Get handle to visible region for this DC */
```

This function returns a handle to the region describing the visible region of the specified DC. The visible region describes that part of a window that is not overlayed by other windows or the bounds of the screen.

This function operates in the same way as many of the documented and undocumented GetXXX functions; it sets the offset of the hVisRgn field of the DC structure into CX and falls through to the undocumented GSV function.

See SelectVisRgn for a discussion of visible regions.

Return: HRGN for visible region of display
Used by: USER.EXE
Support: 3.0, 3.1
See also: SelectVisRgn, OffsetVisRgn, SaveVisRgn, RestoreVisRgn, IntersectVisRect, DC Structure

---

InternalCreateDC   GDI.118

```
HDC DAR PASCAL InternalCreateDC(LPSTR, LPSTR, LPSTR, LPDEVMODE)
LPSTR lpDriverName;     /* filename of device driver */
LPSTR lpDeviceName;     /* device name */
LPSTR lpOutputl;        /* file or device name for output */
LPDEVMODE lpInitData;   /* pointer to DEVMODE containing initial data */
```

This function is an internal entrypoint to the documented CreateDC function.

InternalCreateDC implements and stores the driver and device names in local GDI atoms, then branches into the code for CreateDC.

This function is not exported, but it continues to exist in version 3.1. In version 3.1 another function, ATMInternalCreateDC (although not exported), also branches into the CreateDC code, apparently to support the rasterization of Adobe Type Manager (ATM) fonts.

There is no need to call this function directly, and it is included here only for completeness.

Return: HDC for created device context if successful, NULL if not
Support: 3.0

IntersectVisRect   GDI.98

```
int FAR PASCAL IntersectVisRect(HDC, int, int, int, int)
int x1;           /* left of rectangle */
int y1;           /* top of rectangle */
int x2;           /* right of rectangle */
int y2;           /* bottom of rectangle */
```

This function forms the intersection of the current visible region and the rectangle (x1, y1, x2, y2) to create a new visible region. All subsequent output is clipped to this new visible region.

This function operates in much the same way as the documented IntersectClipRect. Where IntersectClipRect operates on the current clipping region for the device context, IntersectVisRect operates on the current visible region. Both functions are simply entry points into the same code, using a technique described in this section in which a control parameter is set into CX. In this case, that parameter is the offset of the appropriate region handle (hrgnClip or hVisRgn respectively) in the DC structure.

Note that as a result of either function being called, the RaoRgn is recomputed. This region defines the intersection of the clipping and visible regions. See the discussion of the hRaoClip field of the DC in the DC structure entry earlier in this chapter.

For a description of visible regions, see SelectVisRgn.

Return: One of the documented constants ERROR, NULLREGION, SIMPLEREGION, COMPLEXREGION
Used by: USER.EXE
Support: 3.0, 3.1
See also: DC Structure, SDK documentation for IntersectClipRect function

IsDCCurrentPalette   GDI.412

```
BOOL FAR PASCAL IsDCCurrentPalette(HDC)
HDC hDC;       /* device context */
```

This function returns TRUE if the palette currently selected for the DC (using the documented SelectPalette function) is the same as the current foreground palette. It allows the window manager to avoid the inefficiency of realizing the same palette that is currently in effect at paint time.

Because many Windows applications do not use anything other than the default palette, this function allows the window manager to optimize screen updating performance.

Return: TRUE (1) if the logical palette for the device context is the same as the currently active palette, FALSE (0) if not
Used by: USER.EXE
Support: 3.0, 3.1

IsDCDirty   GDI.169

```
int FAR PASCAL IsDCDirty(HDC, LPRECT)
HDC hDC;               /* Is this DC dirty */
LPRECT lpRectDirty;    /* Buffer to receive RECT that needs updating */
```

This function returns TRUE if the DC is dirty (that is, if any part of the specified device context has been updated) and returns, in lpRect, the bounding rectangle of the area that needs to be repainted. Otherwise, if the DC has been repainted, the function returns FALSE, and resets the RECT structure to 0.

The DC is dirty if bit 0 of the wDCGlobFlags field of the DC structure is set.

This function is *not*, whatever its name might imply, without impact. It always calls SetDCStatus(hDC, 0, NULL), which resets the DC to a clean state.

Return: TRUE (1) if the specified DC needed to be updated, FALSE (0) if not, or -1 if the HDC is NULL. If TRUE, the RECT buffer addressed by lpRectDirty on return contains the coordinates of the part of the DC that needed painting.
Used by: USER.EXE
Support: 3.0, 3.1
See also: DC structure, SetDCStatus

IsGdiObject   GDI.462

```
BOOL FAR PASCAL IsGdiObject(HANDLE)
HANDLE hObject;           /* object */
```

This function checks the supplied handle to see if it is a valid GDI object handle. It decides this by looking at the signature word at offset 2 in the GDI object header and applying a set of validity tests to it.

This function only works with GDI objects stored in the GDI default near heap. The METAFILE object structure is stored in the global heap, and a separate function, IsValidMetafile, is used to validate metafile handles. See the IsValidMetafile entry below for more information.

An object that has previously been marked as private will nevertheless be visible to any task that passes the private object handle to this function.

Essentially, the function checks that

```
((pobj->wMagic & 0x5fff)-0x4F47 /* 'GO' */)
```

is in the range 0 to 9.

Return: TRUE if the supplied handle refers to a valid GDI object, FALSE if not.
Support: 3.1
See also: DC structure, MakeObjectPrivate, SetObjectOwner, IsValidMetafile

IsValidMetafile   GDI.410

```
BOOL FAR PASCAL IsValidMetafile(HANDLE)
HANDLE hMetaFile;           /* metafile */
```

This function checks the validity of the specified metafile. The first three fields of the METAFILE structure associated with the hMetaFile parameter are checked. If they are in range, the function returns TRUE; otherwise, it returns FALSE.

The METAFILE structure is stored in the global heap, unlike other GDI objects. For this reason, the IsGdiObject function does not work with Metafile handles.

Return: TRUE (1) if the metafile is valid, FALSE (0) if not.
Used by: USER.EXE
Support: 3.0, 3.1

LvbUnion   GDI.171

```
BOOL FAR PASCAL LvbUnion(HDC, int, int, int, int)
HDC hDC;                    /* device context */
int xLeft;                  /* left x coord of rectangle */
int yTop;                   /* top y coord of rectangle */
int xRight;                 /* right x coord of rectangle */
int yBottom;                /* bottom y coord of rectangle */
```

This function is called from several places within GDI, and although it is exported in 3.0, it is not called by any other Windows modules. The function is not exported in version 3.1.

It is used to update the rectLVB field of the DC. This field contains the bounding rectangle of the region of the DC that requires update. The function takes the union of the existing rectLVB and the rectangle formed by the xLeft, yTop, xRight, and yBottom parameters, and updates the rectLVB with the result.

Return: Always appears to return TRUE (1).
Support: 3.0

MakeObjectPrivate   GDI.463

```
BOOL FAR PASCAL MakeObjectPrivate(HANDLE, BOOL)
HANDLE hObject;             /* GDI object */
BOOL bPrivate;              /* TRUE if make private, FALSE if make public */
```

This function marks a GDI object as private or public in version 3.1.

At offset 2 in the GDI object header is the wMagic field, which contains the object signature and a set of flags. This function sets or resets the 0x2000 bit flag depending on the value of the bPrivate parameter. This marks the object as private or public, and also has the side-effect of making the second character of the signature lower case. It then returns the previous state of that flag. See the GDI Data structures section of this chapter's introduction for a discussion of GDI object signature types.

It is not clear how the object can be associated with a particular owning task since this function does nothing more than the procedure described above. It does not, for example, attempt to obtain the current task and store it with the object.

Note that, presumably because there is no owner stored with the object, it will still be validated by the undocumented IsGdiObject function, discussed earlier in this chapter.

Return: TRUE if the object was previously private, FALSE if not
Support: 3.1
See also: IsGdiObject, SetObjectOwner, GDI Object Header, GDI Data Structures (Introduction to this chapter)

METAFILEDC   structure

This structure is created by the documented CreateMetaFile function if its lpFilename parameter is NULL. The structure is a DC with a different signature.

```
typedef struct tagMETAFILEDC {
    GDIOBJHDR    header;
//  MFDC         mfdc;    // This structure is not currently understood
    }   METAFILEDC, FAR *LPMETAFILEDC;
```

The structure is identified by a wMagic field in the GDIOBJHDR structure of 11 in version 3.0, and "QO" (0x4F51) in 3.1.

See also: GDI object header structure

MFDrawText   GDI.347

```
BOOL FAR PASCAL MFDrawText(HDC, LPSTR, int, LPRECT, WORD)
HDC hDC;            /* device context */
LPSTR lpString;     /* string to be printed */
int nLength;        /* number of chars to draw, or -1 for all */
LPRECT lpClip;      /* clipping rectangle */
WORD wFlags;        /* DT_ flags */
```

This function appears to be identical to the documented DrawText function in all but name. It is not referenced internally within any of the primary Windows modules.

Return: The height of the text
Support: 3.0

OffsetOrg GDI.143

```
DWORD FAR PASCAL OffsetOrg(HDC, int, int)
HDC hDC;                  /* device context */
int xOffset;             /* x offset */
int yOffset;             /* y offset */
/* CX contains additional parametric information */
```

OffsetOrg provides the functionality behind the documented OffsetWindowOrg and OffsetViewportOrg functions. These two functions set the offset of the WndOrgX and VportOrgX fields, respectively, in the DC into CX and then jump to this entrypoint. It is not clear why it is exported in version 3.0.

    This function is included for completeness only and should never need to be called directly.

Return: A DWORD containing, in the low order word, the x-coordinate, and in the high word, the y-coordinate of the previous origin
Support: 3.0

OffsetVisRgn GDI.102

```
int FAR PASCAL OffsetVisRgn(HDC, int, int)
HDC hDC;                  /* device context */
int xOffset;             /* X direction offset */
int yOffset;             /* Y direction offset */
```

This function displaces the visible region of the specified device context xOffset pixels along the x-axis and yOffset units along the y-axis.

    It is called by an unknown internal function in version 3.0 of USER, and does not appear to be called by any of the primary Windows modules in version 3.1.

Return: One of the documented constants COMPLEXREGION, NULLREGION, SIMPLEREGION, or ERROR
Used by: USER.EXE (3.0 only)
Support: 3.0, 3.1
See also: InquireVisRgn, SelectVisRgn, SaveVisRgn, RestoreVisRgn, IntersectVisRect

QueryAbort GDI.155

```
BOOL FAR PASCAL QueryAbort(HDC, HANDLE);
HDC hDC;          /* print device context */
*/ HANDLE hJCB;     /* job control block handle */
```

Most Print Manager spooling functions, such as OpenJob(), CloseJob(), and DeleteJob(), are documented in the DDK (*Device Driver Adaptation Guide*, chapter 4). However, some of these functions, including QueryAbort(), seem only to appear in the 3.1 DDK include file SPOOL.H. QueryAbort() appears to return TRUE if an abort has been issued for the specified print job control block. The JCB structure is declared in SPOOL.H.

Support: 3.0, 3.1
See also: GetSpoolJob, QueryJob

QueryJob GDI.248

```
BOOL FAR PASCAL QueryJob(int, HANDLE)
int nOption;          /* query type */
HANDLE hJCB;          /* handle to JCB */
```

This function provides two inquiries, depending on the value of the nOption parameter, as follows:

QJ_GETJOBACTIVE (0x001E)

This option uses the size of the global memory allocation associated with the specified JCB (Job Control Block) to determine whether it is active. The JCB itself is actually a global memory handle shifted right by 1 bit! If the size of the block is greater than 327 bytes, the function returns TRUE (1); otherwise, it returns FALSE (0).

QJ_GET??? (0x1002)

This option returns TRUE if at least one of two unknown GDI global data items is non-zero. If both are zero, it returns FALSE. For this option, the hJCB parameter is not used.

Support: 3.0, 3.1
See also: GetSpoolJob

PALETTEOBJ structure

This is the structure behind the documented HPALETTE handle. It is stored in GDI's default heap segment, and is made up of two parts: the undocumented GDIOBJHDR structure described in the GDI object header entry later in this chapter, and the documented LOGPALETTE structure:

```
typedef struct tagPALETTEOBJ {
    GDIOBJHDR    header;
    LOGPALETTE   logpalette;
    }  PALETTEOBJ, FAR *LPPALETTEOBJ;
```

The structure is identified by a wMagic field in the GDIOBJHDR structure of 4 in version 3.0, and "JO" (0x4F4A) in 3.1.

See also: GDI object header structure

PENOBJ   structure

This is the structure behind the documented HPEN handle. It is stored in GDI's default heap segment, and is made up of two parts: the undocumented GDIOBJHDR structure described in the GDI object header entry later in this chapter; and the documented LOGPEN structure:

```
typedef struct tagPENOBJ {
    GDIOBJHDR    header;
    LOGPEN       logpen;
    }   PENOBJ, FAR *LPPENOBJ;
```

The structure is identified by a wMagic field in the GDIOBJHDR structure of 1 in version 3.0, and "GO" (0x4F47) in 3.1.
For additional information, see the GDI object header entry later in this chapter.

See also: GDI object header structure

PixToLine   GDI.164

```
void FAR PASCAL PixToLine(??? FAR *, int, int, int, int, ??? FAR *)
```

This function is not currently understood. It is not called by any of the primary Windows modules, and the code does not appear to exist in version 3.1.

Support: 3.0

RestoreVisRgn   GDI.130

```
WORD FAR PASCAL RestoreVisRgn(HDC)
HDC hDC;              /* Restore the visible region for this DC */
```

This function restores the visible region saved by a prior call to SaveVisRgn(). The call frees the memory associated with the saved visible region, and returns the type of the restored region, or ERROR if there is either no saved VisRgn, or the HDC is invalid.
There is no hVisRgnSave field in the DC, nor is there a separate stack of saved VisRgns. It appears that the save and restore mechanism is implemented using a linked

list stack of HRGN handles in the first field of the header of the region structure of the original VisRgn. RestoreVisRgn "pops" the previous HRGN from the head of the linked list into the hVisRgn field of the DC, and frees the memory allocated for the previous hVisRgn.

See SelectVisRgn for a discussion of visible regions.

Return: Region type of the restored region, or ERROR if either the DC is invalid, or there is no saved VisRgn associated with it.

Used by: USER.EXE

Support: 3.0, 3.1

See also: SaveVisRgn, InquireVisRgn, OffsetVisRgn, SelectVisRgn, IntersectVisRect, DC Structure

---

RCos   GDI.177

```
int FAR PASCAL RCos(int, int)
int nRadius;           /* hypotenuse */
int n10thDegrees;      /* angle in 10th degrees */
```

This is an integral cosine function with scaling. This function uses a lookup table and integer-only math to provide a very useful, very fast trigonometric drawing aid [$r * cos(a)$].

The function is not exported in 3.1, and the code appears to no longer exist.

Support: 3.0

Return: The integer result of nRadius * cos(n10thDegrees/10)

See also: RSin

Example: Uses RSin and RCos to draw fast stars on a window

```
/* RSIN.C */

#include <windows.h>
#include <wmhandlr.h>
#include <winio.h>

/* Undocumented functions */
extern int FAR PASCAL RSin(int nRadius, n10thDegrees);
extern int FAR PASCAL RCos(int nRadius, n10thDegrees);

WMHANDLER prev_paint;

#include "checkord.c"

long DrawStar(HWND hwnd, WORD wMsg, WORD wParam, DWORD lParam)
    {
    RECT rectClient;
    long ret;
```

```
        HDC hDC;
        POINT middle;
        int nRadius;
        int d;
        TEXTMETRIC tm;

        ret = (*prev_paint)(hwnd, wMsg, wParam, lParam);

        GetClientRect(hwnd, (LPRECT) &rectClient);

        hDC = GetDC(hwnd);

        SelectObject(hDC, GetStockObject(BLACK_PEN));

        GetTextMetrics(hDC, &tm);

        middle.x = (rectClient.right - rectClient.left) / 2;
        middle.y = (rectClient.bottom - (rectClient.top
                        + tm.tmHeight + tm.tmExternalLeading)) / 2;
        nRadius = min(middle.x, middle.y) - 2;
        middle.y += tm.tmHeight + tm.tmExternalLeading;

        for (d = 0; d < 90; d++)
            {
            MoveTo(hDC, middle.x, middle.y);
            LineTo(hDC, middle.x + RSin(nRadius, d * 40),
                        middle.y + RCos(nRadius, d * 40));
            }

        ReleaseDC(hwnd, hDC);

        return ret;
        }

int main()
    {

    if (! CheckOrd("RSin", "GDI", 178))
        return 1;

    if (! CheckOrd("RSin", "GDI", 178))
        return 1;

    prev_paint = wmhandler_set(winio_current(),
                        WM_PAINT, (WMHANDLER) DrawStar);

    printf("The star is drawn using RSin and RCos.");

    return 0;
    }
```

RCos

RealizeDefaultPalette

GDI.365

```
int FAR PASCAL RealizeDefaultPalette(HDC)
HDC hDC;          /* device context */
```

This function restores the system default logical palette into the specified device context and realizes it. This function combines the functionality of the following three lines of code:

```
hPal =  GetStockObject(DEFAULT_PALETTE);
SelectPalette(hDC, hPal, FALSE);
RealizePalette(hDC);
```

Return: The number of entries in the default palette that were mapped to different entries in the system palette
Used by: USER.EXE
Support: 3.0, 3.1

RectStuff

GDI.142

```
int FAR PASCAL RectStuff(HDC, int, int, int, int)
HDC hDC;          /* device context */
int x1;           /* left of rectangle */
int y1;           /* top of rectangle */
int x2;           /* right of rectangle */
int y2;           /* bottom of rectangle */
/* CX and DX contain additional parametric information */
```

RectStuff provides the functionality behind the documented IntersectClipRect and ExcludeClipRect functions and the undocumented IntersectVisRect function. These establish values in CX and DX, and fall through to RectStuff. There is also prolog code for what would be an ExcludeVisRect function, although the code is unused, and there is no documented or undocumented or internal function by that name.

RectStuff takes a function code in CL (1 = Intersect, 2 = Exclude), and the offset of the appropriate field in CH (hrgnClip or hVisRgn). The parameter in DX is not understood. It is only used when CL is 1 (Include/ExcludeClipRect) and is passed to an internal CheckMetaFile function.

It is unclear why it was exported in versions 2.1 and 3.0. The code remains in version 3.1, but the label is no longer exported.

The only reason to call this function directly would be to implement a version of the "missing" function ExcludeVisRect alluded to above (for version 3.0 only). The following code could be used as a basis for such a function:

```
ExcludeVisRect proc far
        mov cl, 4
```

```
        mov ch, offset hVisRgn ;; This will vary between retail and debug
        jmp far RectStuff
ExcludeVisRect endp
```

Return: One of the documented constants COMPLEXREGION, ERROR, NULLREGION, or SIMPLEREGION
Support: 3.0
See also: IntersectVisRect, DC Structure

RGNOBJ   structure

This is the structure behind the documented HRGN handle. It is stored in GDI's default heap segment, and is made up of two parts. The first is the undocumented GDIOBJHDR structure described in the GDI object header entry later in this chapter, and the second, which contains the actual region data, is not currently understood:

```
typedef struct tagRGNOBJ {
    GDIOBJHDR   header;
//  REGION      region;    // This structure is not currently understood
    }   RGNOBJ, FAR *LPRGNOBJ;
```

The structure is identified by a wMagic field in the GDIOBJHDR structure of 6 in version 3.0, and "LO" (0x4F4C) in 3.1.

See also: GDI object header structure

Resurrection   GDI.122

```
void FAR PASCAL Resurrection(HDC, WORD, WORD, WORD, WORD, WORD, WORD)
HDC hDC;            /* Handle of desktop device context */
WORD w1;            /* unknown - set to 0 */
WORD w2;            /* unknown - set to 0 */
WORD w3;            /* unknown - set to 0 */
WORD w4;            /* unknown - set to 0 */
WORD w5;            /* unknown - set to 0 */
WORD w6;            /* unknown - set to 0 */
```

This function, called from the undocumented EnableOEMLayer function, enables the GDI graphics driver. The driver in turn sets the display adapter to the active graphics mode for Windows.

Used by: USER.EXE
Support: 3.0, 3.1
See also: Death, DisableOEMLayer, EnableOEMLayer

RGNOBJ

RSin   GDI.178

```
int FAR PASCAL RSin(int, int)
int nRadius;              /* hypotenuse */
int n10thDegrees;         /* angle in 10th degrees */
```

This is an integral sine function with scaling.

This function uses a lookup table and integer-only math to provide a very useful, very fast trigonometric drawing aid $[r * sin(a)]$.

The code is not exported, and does not appear to exist in 3.1.

Support:3.0
Return: The integer result of nRadius * sin(n10thDegrees/10)
See also: RCos
Example: See RCos example

SaveDC   GDI.30

Note that the SDK documentation for the SaveDC function in version 3.0 states that the return value 'specifies the saved device context.' We can determine that there is something wrong there from the fact that the return type is defined as int, not HDC. In fact the return is the value of the wDCSaveLevel field before it is incremented (see the entry for the GetDCState function earlier in the chapter).

See also: GetDCState

SaveVisRgn   GDI.129

```
HRGN FAR PASCAL SaveVisRgn(HDC)
HDC hDC;           /* Save the visible region of this DC */
```

This function allocates memory for a copy of the current VisRgn of the specified DC, copies the VisRgn region structure, and stores the resultant HRGN at the head of a linked list of HRGNs leading from the hVisRgn field of the DC structure. The first field in the region structure is used to store a pointer to the next region in the stack.

The complementary function, RestoreVisRgn, frees the current hVisRgn handle in the DC structure, and replaces it with the head of the stack, or list, of saved HRGNs.

See SelectVisRgn for a discussion of visible regions.

Return: HRGN of the newly created, saved, copy of the VisRgn for the DC
Used by: USER.EXE
Support: 3.0, 3.1

See also: InquireVisRgn, SelectVisRgn, OffsetVisRgn, RestoreVisRgn, IntersectVisRect, DC Structure

---

ScaleExt   GDI.140

```
DWORD FAR PASCAL ScaleExt(HDC, int, int, int, int)
HDC hDC;
int Xnum;
int Xdenom;
int Ynum;
int Ydenom;
/* BX, CX and DX contain offsets into DC appropriate to either window or
viewport scaling. */
```

This function is the engine behind the documented ScaleWindowExt and
ScaleViewportExt functions. Those functions set offsets into the DC structure corresponding to the start of the window or viewport data fields respectively into BX; set a
value in CX that is not currently understood; place in DX the offset of an internal near
function to perform the setting of the scaled values into the DC structure. They then
jump to this function.

   This function is included for completeness only and should never need to be called
directly.

Return: The previous extents for the window or viewport in logical units. The high
word of the return contains the y extent, and the low word contains the x extent.
Support: 3.0, 3.1

SelectBitmap   GDI.195

```
HBITMAP FAR PASCAL SelectBitmap(HDC, HBITMAP)
HDC hDC;             /* device context */
HBITMAP hBitmap;     /* bitmap to select into device context */
```

This function provides almost exactly the same functionality as the documented
SelectObject function when that function is used to select a bitmap.

   It is a little unclear why this function exists. It was introduced in version 3.1 but is
not referenced by any of the components of retail Windows.

   Because it is undocumented and provides no additional functionality over
SelectObject, it is not advisable to use this function.

Return: The handle of the previously selected bitmap or NULL if an error was
encountered
Support: 3.1

SelectVisRgn   GDI.105

```
int FAR PASCAL SelectVisRgn(HDC, HRGN)
HDC hDC;           /* device context */
HRGN hRgn;         /* region to select into device context */
```

This function sets a visible region handle into the device context. The hRgn parameter contains the handle to a region that describes that part of a window that is not overlayed by any other windows or by the bounds of the screen (that is, it describes that part of a window that is visible to the user).

Another way of looking at the VisRgn is as a special type of clipping region. This is actually how it is used, in conjunction with clipping at two other levels. The first is at the application level, implemented in documented calls such as SelectClipRgn, which allows drawing and painting operations to be clipped according to application logical requirements. At a second level, shared between the application and the window manager (USER) is the update region, managed by USER and application calls to Invalidate/ValidateRect/Rgn. This represents that region of the device context for the window that has been modified by output operations, without any consideration for whether that region is partially or entirely visible.

The Windows display manager (built into the USER window management routines) uses the VisRgn as a third-level clipping region to ensure that display output operations directed to a particular window DC do not overwrite other application windows that overlay the target window. Note that the role that many Windows developers attribute to the ClipRgn, actually belongs to the VisRgn.

In order to appear on the screen then, a painting operation will be clipped through the intersection of the three regions described above. In practice, the update region and VisRgn are intersected at Validate/InvalidateRect/Rgn time, and the resultant region is stored in the hVisRgn field of the DC. The clip region, selected using the documented SelectClipRgn function, defines the clipping region to be used by storing the supplied HRGN in the hrgnClip field of the DC. The intersection of the VisRgn and the clip region is performed by an internal GDI function called UpdateRaoRgn. This function is named after Rao Remala, an engineer at Microsoft, on whose insistence the hRaoRgn field was introduced into the DC structure. This field, in which the final intersected region is stored, was introduced to overcome the performance problems associated with the previous functionality, whereby the intersection of VisRgn and ClipRgn was performed at DC update time.

Visible regions are by no means a Windows invention. The mechanism and even the name (VisRgn) are used and described thoroughly in the Apple Macintosh operating system and its documentation. See *Inside Macintosh* for further details on grafPort->visRgn.

Return: One of the documented constants COMPLEXREGION, NULLREGION, SIMPLEREGION, or ERROR
Used by: USER.EXE

Support: 3.0, 3.1
See also: InquireVisRgn, OffsetVisRgn, SaveVisRgn, RestoreVisRgn, IntersectVisRect, DC structure

---

SetDCHook   GDI.190

```
BOOL FAR PASCAL SetDCHook(HDC, FARPROC, DWORD)
HDC hDC;                    /* Set DC hook for this DC */
FARPROC lpHookProc;         /* Callback function address */
DWORD data;                 /* Additional data */
```

SetDCHook() is not documented, but a function prototype and some #defines do appear in the version of WINDOWS.H included with the 3.1 DDK. The function installs a hook function for the specified DC. The hook function is a callback that is notified whenever the DC is updated or destroyed.

USER calls this function to install the undocumented DCHook() function (see chapter 6) as the callback for each of the five DCs that it allocates at startup (see the DC structure entry in this chapter), and although it is not known what DCHook's purpose is, the function does use the opportunity to change the visible region of the DC using the undocumented SelectVisRgn() function described earlier in this chapter.

SetDCHook() places the hook procedure's address in the lpfnNotify field of the DC, and the additional data in the dwHookData field. The hook procedure must have a prototype of:

```
WORD HookProc(HDC hDC, WORD code, DWORD data, DWORD lParam);
```

The two callback codes are:

```
#define DCHC_INVALIDVISRGN  0x0001
#define DCHC_DELETEDC       0x0002
```

No validity checking is done on the supplied HDC other than to check that it is nonzero. Passing an invalid HDC will therefore corrupt GDI's default data segment.

Return: TRUE if the callback function was successfully installed; FALSE if the specified HDC was zero.
Used by: USER.EXE
Support: 3.1
See also: GetDCHook, SetHookFlags, DC structure, DCHook (chapter 6)

SetDCOrg   GDI.117

```
DWORD FAR PASCAL SetDCOrg(HDC, WORD, WORD)
HDC hDC;                    /* Set DC Origin for this DC */
```

```
WORD wOrgX;          /* New X coordinate */
WORD wOrgY;          /* New Y coordinate */
```

This function sets the origin coordinates of the specified DC. It returns the previous x and y coordinates in effect. The function complements GetDCOrg(), which is documented.

It operates on the wDCOrgX and wDCOrgY fields of the DC structure. Note that as a result of the DC origin's setting, the Rao region, or the intersection of the clip and VisRgn regions is recalculated. For more information on the relationship between visible and clip regions, see the SelectVisRgn entry earlier in this chapter.

Return: A DWORD containing the x- and y-origin coordinates previously in effect for the DC in the low and high words, respectively
Used by: USER.EXE
Support: 3.0, 3.1
See also: SelectVisRgn, DC structure
Note: No validity checking is done on the supplied HDC other than to check that it is nonzero. Passing an invalid HDC will therefore corrupt GDI's default heap segment.

SetDCState   GDI.180

```
void FAR PASCAL SetDCState(HDC, HDCS)
HDC hDC;          /* device context */
HANDLE hDCSave;   /* handle to DCSAVE structure from prev GetDCState */
```

This function restores the state of the specified device context from the HDCS created by a previous call to GetDCState.

The hDCSave is the handle to a DCSAVE structure maintained in the GDI near heap, and described in the DCSAVE structure entry earlier in this chapter.

This function is similar to the documented RestoreDC function. Both SetDCState and RestoreDC call an unexported internal function, RestoreDCState, to restore the state of the given DC. However, RestoreDC "pops" the HDCS from the top of the linked list of DCSAVE structures attached to the hNext field of the GDI object header of the specified DC, and decrements the wDCSaveLevel field of the DC. SetDCState, however, allows the DCSAVE to be used to specified as a parameter to the function, and is effectively an exported cover over the RestoreDCState function. Thus, SaveDC and RestoreDC act on a stack of DCSAVEs associated with the specified DC. GetDCState and SetDCState, by contrast, allows a DC to be restored from a DCSAVE structure saved from a different DC, or even built from scratch.

Used by: USER.EXE
Support: 3.0, 3.1
See also: GetDCState, DC and DCSAVE structures

SetDCStatus   GDI.170

```
BOOL FAR PASCAL SetDCStatus(HDC, BOOL, LPRECT)
HDC hDC;          /* Set status for this DC */
BOOL bSetDirty;   /* lpRect contains update rectangle of display */
LPRECT lpRect;    /* pointer to RECT specifying update rectangle */
```

This function allows the "dirty" (that is, update) rectangle of the device context to be defined. If bSetDirty is TRUE, the rectLVB field of the DC is overwritten by the contents of the RECT pointed at by the lpRect parameter, and bit 0x0002 of the wDCGlobFlags field of the DC is set, to signify that the DC is dirty, that is, needs updating.

If bSetDirty is TRUE, but the lpRect parameter is NULL, the DC is set dirty, but the previous rectLVB is left in effect.

If the bSetDirty parameter is FALSE, the DC is set clean, (not in need of update) by resetting bit 0x0002 of the wDCGlobFlags field, and the rectLVB field is set to an invalid rectangle.

Return: TRUE if DC was dirty upon entry, FALSE if not. If the hDC parameter is NULL, the return is -1.
Used by: USER.EXE
Support: 3.0, 3.1
Note: There is no GetDCStatus; the nearest equivalent is IsDCDirty, but since that function itself calls SetDCStatus, there appears to be no way to determine nondestructively if the DC is dirty. In an API function set that is most consistent across undocumented and undocumented calls in providing matching Get/Set pairs, the DC status calls are an interesting aberration.
See also: IsDCDirty, DC Structure

SetHookFlags   GDI.192

```
WORD FAR PASCAL SetHookFlags(HDC, WORD)
HDC hDC;          /* device context */
WORD flags;       /* hook flags */
```

SetHookFlags() is not documented, but a function prototype and some #defines do appear in the version of WINDOWS.H included with the 3.1 DDK. The function provides a means for modifying a DC flag:

```
#define DCHF_INVALIDATEVISRGN 0x0001
#define DCHF_VALIDATEVISRGN   0x0002
```

If flags is 1, bit 2 of the DC byFlags field is set; if flags is 0, the byFlags field is cleared. This flag deteremines whether the VisRgn for the DC has been changed, and whether the RaoRgn needs to be recomputed (see SelectVisRgn for more information on visible regions). This function is used by the undocumented DCHook() function in USER (see chapter 6).

Return: Previous state of the flag
Support: 3.1
See also: GetDCHook, SetDCHook, SelectVisRgn, DCHook (chapter 6)

SetObjectOwner   GDI.461

```
HANDLE FAR PASCAL SetObjectOwner(HANDLE, HANDLE)
HANDLE hObject;            /* handle of GDI object */
HANDLE hTask;             /* hTask of new owner */
```

This function allows the owner of a GDI object, such as a brush, a pen, or a bitmap, to be set or changed when the debug version of Windows is running. The code for the retail version of this function consists only of normal compiler prolog and epilog.

In the normal course of events, an application that creates an object must delete it before terminating. This function provides a means for the debug version to track whether a GDI object has been destroyed when an application terminates, or whether it is being deleted by an application other than the one that created it.

The supplied task handle is placed into the owner field of the debug version of the GDI object header at offset 0Ah, and the previous value of that field is returned.

Return: In the debug version, the return is the task handle of the previous owner of the object or NULL if either handle is invalid. In the retail version, the return is undefined.
Support: 3.1
See also: MakeObjectPrivate, IsGdiObject, GDI Object Header

SetRelAbs   GDI.5

```
int FAR PASCAL SetRelAbs(HDC, int)
HDC hDC;                  /* set location mode for this DC */
int nRelAbs;             /* ABSOLUTE or RELATIVE */
```

This function sets the coordinate mode for the specified device context and returns the mode previously in effect. The nRelAbs parameter should be one of the documented WINDOWS.H constants, ABSOLUTE or RELATIVE.

This function operates on the wRelAbs field of the DC structure. The complementary undocumented GetRelAbs function returns the contents of the field.

Return: The coordinate mode previously in effect for the DC unless the DC is NULL, in which case it returns NULL

Support: 3.0, 3.1

Note: This function was documented in 2.1. The documentation of the return value states that it is NULL *if the DC is invalid.* The code for the function in 3.0 actually checks only for a zero hDC parameter. In version 3.1 a more rigorous test is applied.

See also: GetRelAbs, DC structure

SetWinViewExt   GDI.139

```
DWORD FAR PASCAL SetWinViewExt(HDC, int, int)
HDC hDC;                /* device context */
int x;                  /* x extent */
int y;                  /* y extent */
// BX contains offset into DC structure
```

This function is the engine behind the documented SetWindowExt and SetViewportExt functions. The window and viewport extents are held in the DC structure for the window. The documented functions are entry points that set into BX the offset of the appropriate extent fields (WndExtX and VportExtX respectively) in the DC structure and then jump through to this function.

This function is similar to the more generalized WordSet function described later in this chapter, but updates two adjacent word length fields rather than the one handled by WordSet.

It should never be necessary to call this function directly, and it is included here for completeness only.

Return: The previous extents at the specified offset, unless the DC is invalid, in which case the return is 0.

Support:3.0

See also: WordSet, DC Structure

ShrinkGdiHeap   GDI.354

```
void FAR ShrinkGdiHeap(void);
```

This function does pretty much what its name suggests. It shrinks GDI's local heap to a minimum of 4K. In addition, the function ensures that there is 1K of free space in the heap.

It is aided in this by the undocumented KERNEL functions LocalCountFree, LocalHeapSize, and the documented LocalShrink function.

The function is referenced, but never called, from within the code that services the documented GetMessage and PeekMessage functions in USER, in version 3.0.

SetWinViewExt

It does not appear to be called from any of the primary Windows modules in version 3.1.

Support: 3.0, 3.1
See also: LocalCountFree and LocalHeapSize (both in Chapter 5)

StuffInRegion   GDI.186

```
BOOL FAR PASCAL StuffInRegion(HRGN, LPRECT)
HRGN hRgn;                 /* region */
LPRECT lpRect;             /* rectangle/point */
/* CX contains point/rectangle flag */
```

This function provides the functionality behind the documented RectInRegion function.

It is unclear why it warrants its own entrypoint, although it may have been designed to serve not only RectInRegion, but a nonexistent PointInRegion function as well. The code continues to exist in version 3.1, but the entrypoint is no longer exported.

If CX contains zero, the function only checks that the first two coordinates in the RECT buffer are within the specified region. If CX is nonzero, all four coordinates are checked.

Return: TRUE (1) if the coordinates are within the specified region, FALSE (0) if not.
Support: 3.0
See also: StuffVisible

StuffVisible   GDI.185

```
BOOL FAR PASCAL StuffVisible(HDC, LPRECT)
HDC hDC;                   /* device context */
LPRECT lpRect;             /* rectangle */
/* CX contains point/rectangle flag */
```

This function provides the functionality behind the documented RectVisible function.

It is unclear why it warrants its own entrypoint, although it may have been designed to serve not only RectVisible, but a nonexistent PointVisible function as well; in any case, neither the entrypoint nor the code itself is present in version 3.1.

If CX contains zero, the function only checks that the first two coordinates in the RECT buffer are visible. If CX is nonzero, all four coordinates are checked.

There should never be any need to call this function directly, and it is included here for completeness only.

Return: TRUE (1) if the coordinates are within the clipping region, FALSE (0) if not
Support: 3.0

UnicodeToAnsi   GDI.467

```
int FAR PASCAL UnicodeToAnsi(LPSTR, LPSTR)
LPSTR lpUnicodeStr;      /* input unicode string */
LPSTR lpAnsiBuff;        /* buffer to receive translated string */
```

This function translates from the Unicode character set into the ANSI character set.

UnicodeToAnsi provides similar functionality to the documented OemToAnsi function, except that its source is a string of 2-byte Unicode characters and the source buffer may not exceed 64K in length.

The function performs the translations against a static lookup table within the GDI default data segment.

Return: The length, including the terminating null, of the resultant ANSI string
Support: 3.1

WordSet   GDI.141

```
WORD FAR PASCAL WordSet(HDC, WORD)
HDC hDC;                    /* device context */
WORD wNewValue;            /* new value for DC field */
// DL contains the offset into the DC of the affected field.
```

WordSet is a general-purpose function used by many documented and undocumented GDI functions to set a word value into an offset within a DC and return the previous value at that offset. It is the back end to the documented SetROP2, SetPolyFillMode, SetTextAlign, SetMapMode, SetBkMode, SetStretchBltMode functions and the undocumented SetRelAbs function.

The above functions set the offset of the appropriate word length field in the DC structure into DL, and a value whose purpose is not currently understood into DX, and then jump to this function.

The code continues to exist in 3.1, but the function is only exported in version 3.0. WORDSET appears to complement the GSV function described earlier in the chapter, but does not use that function's exotic "fall through" technique.

Return: The previous value at the offset in DL
Support: 3.0
See also: GSV

CHAPTER ■ 9

SYSTEM

Although most of the device drivers that come with Microsoft Windows are documented in the Windows Device Driver Kit (DDK) and, in fact, have their *source code* included with the DDK, SYSTEM.DRV is not documented in the Windows 3.x DDK. It was documented in the Windows 2.x DDK, which was available only under a nondisclosure agreement; in contrast, the Windows 3.x DDK can be freely purchased through normal retail channels. The functions in SYSTEM.DRV today are apparently documented in the Microsoft Windows Binary Adaptation Kit (BAK), but the BAK is distributed only to a handful of hardware original equipment manufacturers (OEMs).

SYSTEM.DRV provides functions to manage asynchronous timers and to manage the 80x87 coprocessor state; it also provides redundant functionality for querying drive types.

System Timers

EnableSystemTimers   KillSystemTimer
DisableSystemTimers   GetSystemMsecCount
CreateSystemTimer

80x87 State

Get80x87SaveSize   Restore80x87State
Save80x87State

Miscellaneous

A20_Proc   InquireSystem

The CreateSystemTimer() and KillSystemTimer() functions are potentially useful, as they allow *asynchronous* (INT 8) timer callback functions to be installed. In contrast, the documented SetTimer() and KillTimer() functions manage *synchronous* timers, with which your callback function is called only after your program has polled its message queue. In other words, system timers bypass the Windows message facility and are much closer to the INT 8 handlers one would install in DOS. System timers appear to be used, for example, by Microsoft Excel; they are also used by the Windows COMM driver. The documented timer functions in USER are implemented using SYSTEM timers.

There are currently two versions of the SYSTEM driver shipped with Windows: SYSTEM.DRV and HPSYSTEM.DRV. HPSYSTEM.DRV is installed on Hewlett-Packard Vectra computers by placing the statement SYSTEM.DRV=HPSYSTEM.DRV in the Windows SYSTEM.INI file; SYSTEM.DRV is installed on all others.

An additional version, ATMSYS.DRV, ships with Adobe Type Manager (ATM). However, ATMSYS.DRV is not a substitute for SYSTEM.DRV; it passes all function calls through to the original SYSTEM.DRV. Instead, ATM uses the alternative SYS-TEM.DRV solely because, in Windows 3.0 and 3.1, SYSTEM happens to get loaded early in the Windows boot process, before GDI and USER. Believe it or not, ATM patches into the KERNEL LoadModule() function, watches for the call that loads GDI, and then goes in and patches GDI calls. When you're running with ATM, you effectively have a slightly different version of GDI.

The SYSTEM initialization routine uses INT 11h (the BIOS Get Equipment List service) to determine the number of floppy drives on the system and whether an 80x87 math coprocessor is present (if INT 11h reports that one is, it is initialized with the FNINIT instruction). HPSYSTEM.DRV uses INT 16h AX=6F00h to ensure it is running on HP hardware; this function returns BX=4850h ('HP') if the extended HP functions are available. HPSYSTEM makes additional INT 16h AH=6Fh and INT 6Fh calls to manage HP EX-BIOS drivers, such as HPHIL (Hardware Interface Level).

The SYSTEM module is also briefly discussed in Dan Norton's *Writing Windows Device Drivers*, pp. 271-273; the system timer functions are briefly mentioned in a *Microsoft Systems Journal* (July 1991) article by Jerry Jongerius, "Accurately Timing Windows Events Without Timer Reprogramming," pp. 75-79.

A20_Proc   SYSTEM.20

This function simply returns the value 2 in both SYSTEM.DRV and HPSYSTEM.DRV. This is identical to the A20Proc function in KERNEL.

CreateSystemTimer   SYSTEM.2

```
WORD CreateSystemTimer(wRate, fpCallback)
WORD wRate;            /* rate in milliseconds at which function should be
                          called (1000 = once every second) */
FARPROC fpCallback;    /* far pointer to callback function; must be
                          located in FIXED segment */
```

CreateSystemTimer() is used to install a timer callback function. The INT 8 handler inside SYSTEM (see the entry for EnableSystemTimers()) calls the installed timer callback function *asynchronously*, in contrast to the documented SetTimer() and KillTimer() functions, which manage *synchronous* timers, with which a callback function is only called after a program has polled its message queue. In other words, system timers bypass the Windows message facility and are much closer to the INT 8 handlers one would install in DOS.

CreateSystemTimer() returns a timer handle or 0 if no more system timers are available. In present implementations of SYSTEM, only eight system timers are available.

The callback function installed with CreateSystemTimer will be called directly by the SYSTEM INT 8 handler, based on the millisecond rate specified. For example, if wRate is 1000, the function is called once every second. However, granularity is limited; in present implementations of SYSTEM, the function will never be called more than 18.2 times per second, corresponding to a wRate of about 55.

However, there are two situations in which the callback will *not* be invoked: in Standard mode (or Windows 3.0 Real mode) when a DOS box is active and in Enhanced mode when a full-screen DOS box is active and the user is idle (i.e., not hitting keys). The Enhanced mode behavior may be changeable via Virtual Timer Device (VTD) settings such as IdleVMWakeupTime= and TrapTimerPorts= in SYSTEM.INI.

Even though the callback function is not an interrupt handler (it does *not* return with an IRET, for example), it must in other ways be treated essentially as interrupt code because it is invoked directly from an interrupt handler. In particular, the callback function *must* be located in a *fixed* (nonmovable, nondiscardable) segment. Furthermore, because registers other than CS:IP are unknown when the function is called, to access any data it must load DS. MakeProcInstance() takes care of this.

In current implementations of SYSTEM, when the system timer function is called, AX happens to hold the timer handle (i.e., same number returned by CreateSystemTimer()).

Calling most Windows API functions inside the system timer appears to have no effect. This is not surprising because the system timer is essentially interrupt code. However, simple functions (such as MessageBeep() in the following example) can be called. One useful simple function is GetCurrentTask(). Also, Microsoft garantees that PostMessage() can be called from inside an interrupt handler. In any case, generally the timer will instead be used to set a variable whose value can be checked inside tight loops.

In current implementations, the returned timer handle happens to be an offset into a hard-wired table of eight system timers in SYSTEM:

```
typedef struct {
    WORD wInUse;      // initialized to FFFFh = not in use
    WORD wRate;       // or FFFFh = end of table
    FARPROC fpCallback;
    } SYSTEMTIMER;
```

Each time it is invoked, about 18.2 times per second, the INT 8 handler in SYS-TEM (installed by EnableSystemTimers; see the entry later in this chapter) loops over the table, calling the installed functions. Similarly, CreateSystemTimer() itself walks through the table, looking for an unused entry.

Support: Windows 3.0, 3.1
Used by: KERNEL (LDBOOT), USER; Microsoft Excel; Windows COMM driver (see source code in DDK\COMM\IBMSETUP.ASM and \COMM\IBMINT.ASM)
Example: The following program, SYSTIMER.C, creates an asynchronous timer and then goes into a loop. Normally, it is a tight loop that shows that the timer is indeed asynchronous. A command-line argument can be used instead to go into a loop that will yield whenever the async timer is invoked. Command-line arguments can also be used to change the duration of the loop and the system-timer rate. If the rate is low (twice per second or less), the system timer calls MessageBeep(). This helps demonstrate the behavior of system timers when a DOS session is running: in Stand-ard mode, running a DOS box causes the system timer to grind to a halt (you don't hear any beeps); in Enhanced mode, a full-screen DOS box in which the user is idle (i.e., not hitting keys) also brings system timers to a halt.

```
/*
SYSTIMER.C -- demonstrate CreateSystemTimer and KillSystemTimer

usage:
systimer [loops] [rate] [any third arg disables tight loop]
*/

#include <windows.h>
#include "winio.h"
#include "wmhandlr.h"

#define LOOPS   200
#define RATE    100

#define INQSYS_TIMERRES     0

WORD FAR volatile gTicks = 0;
WORD FAR volatile gGotTick = 0;
WORD FAR giRate;

/*
    NOTE:  Because it will be called directly, at interrupt time,
    from SYSTEM's INT 8 handler, the callback function installed
    with CreateSystemTimer() *MUST* be located in a FIXED segment.
    For this example program, we've made the entire code segment
    fixed by changing the .DEF file statement from the normal
    CODE PRELOAD MOVEABLE DISCARDABLE to simply CODE PRELOAD (i.e.,
    non-moveable, non-discardable). In a genuine application, the
```

```
    callback should be located in its own fixed segment. On the
    other hand, the callback does *NOT* have to be located in a
    DLL, even though Microsoft's documentation suggests that this is
    necessary for Windows interrupt handlers.
*/
void FAR _export TimerFunc(void)
{
    gTicks++;
    gGotTick = 1;
    if (giRate >= 500)
        MessageBeep(0);  // this just happens to work
    // PostMessage is guaranteed to work at interrupt time
    // other simple functions:  GetCurrentTask, etc.
}

static WORD hTimer = 0;
static FARPROC fpTimerProc = 0;
static WORD FAR PASCAL (*KillSystemTimer)(WORD hTimer);

void cleanup(void)
{
    if (hTimer)
    {
        if (KillSystemTimer(hTimer) != 0)    // 0 = success
            fail("Couldn't kill timer");
        hTimer = 0;
    }
    if (fpTimerProc)
    {
        FreeProcInstance(fpTimerProc);
        fpTimerProc = 0;
    }
}

// just in case they close window while system timer is installed
void on_close(HWND hwnd) { cleanup(); }

int main(int argc, char *argv[])
{
    WORD FAR PASCAL (*CreateSystemTimer)(WORD wRate, FARPROC fpCallback);
    DWORD FAR PASCAL (*InquireSystem)(WORD wFlag, WORD wOption);
    DWORD dwTimerRes;
    DWORD t1, t2;
    WORD hSystem;
    BOOL bTightLoop;
    int iLoopMax;
    int iLoop, iLoopLoop;

    iLoopMax = (argc < 2) ? LOOPS : atoi(argv[1]);
    giRate = (argc < 3) ? RATE : atoi(argv[2]);
    bTightLoop = (argc < 4) ? 1 : 0;

    /* dynamically link to undocumented SYSTEM functions */
    hSystem = GetModuleHandle("SYSTEM");
    CreateSystemTimer = GetProcAddress(hSystem, "CREATESYSTEMTIMER");
```

CreateSystemTimer

```
KillSystemTimer = GetProcAddress(hSystem, "KILLSYSTEMTIMER");
InquireSystem = GetProcAddress(hSystem, "INQUIRESYSTEM");

if (CreateSystemTimer && KillSystemTimer && InquireSystem)
    puts("Installing asynchronous timer with CreateSystemTimer...");
else
    fail("Can't find CreateSystemTimer and KillSystemTimer");

dwTimerRes = InquireSystem(INQSYS_TIMERRES, 0);
if (giRate < (dwTimerRes / 1000))
    printf("Warning: Lowest rate is %u\n", dwTimerRes / 1000);

gTicks = 0;

/* install the asynchronous timer handler */
fpTimerProc = MakeProcInstance((FARPROC) TimerFunc, __hInst);
if ((hTimer = CreateSystemTimer(giRate, fpTimerProc)) == 0)
    fail("CreateSystemTimer failed");

winio_onclose(__hMainWnd, on_close);

t1 = GetCurrentTime();

if (bTightLoop)
{
    /*
        NOTE!  The following is a tight loop, with no calls to
        GetMessage or PeekMessage. If our TimerFunc gets called,
        it means system timers really are asynchronous.
    */

    for (iLoop = 0; iLoop < iLoopMax; iLoop++)
        for (iLoopLoop = 0; iLoopLoop != -1; iLoopLoop++)
                ;
}
else
{
    /* If we weren't trying to show that the timer function is
       called asynchronously, we would probably use system timers
       in the following way */

    for (iLoop = 0; iLoop < iLoopMax; iLoop++)
        for (iLoopLoop = 0; iLoopLoop != -1; iLoopLoop++)
            if (gGotTick != 0)  // check volatile variable
            {
                printf("%u\n", gTicks); // printf will yield
                gGotTick = 0;
            }
}

t2 = GetCurrentTime();

cleanup();

printf("System timer handle: %04xh\n", hTimer);
```

CreateSystemTimer

```
    printf("SetSystemTimer rate: %u\n", giRate);
    printf("GetCurrentTime elapsed: %lu\n", t2 - t1);
    printf("Calls to handler: %u\n", gTicks);
    if (gTicks != 0)
        printf("Actual rate: %lu\n", (t2 - t1) / gTicks);

    return 0;
}
```

DisableSystemTimers   SYSTEM.5

`void DisableSystemTimers(void);`

This function restores the previous INT 8 handler that was saved by
EnableSystemTimers (see below). Normally, it should only be called by Windows at
termination (DisableSystemTimers() is called by ExitKernel()). Even though there is
probably no good reason to call this function, a perverse application *can* call it. After
calling DisableSystemTimers(), functions such as GetSystemMsecCount() and
GetCurrentTime() continue to return the same value; in programs such as Clock, time
stands still. To reenable time, call EnableSystemTimer(); programs such as Clock catch
up properly.

EnableSystemTimers   SYSTEM.4

`void EnableSystemTimers(void);`

This function installs the INT 8 (BIOS IRQ0 timer interrupt) handler for Windows;
functions such as CreateSystemTimer (see above), and consequently all time-related
functions in Windows (with the exception of VTD-related functionality in Enhanced
mode) are based on this INT 8 handler.

EnableSystemTimers() calls INT 21h AX=3508h to save the previous INT 8 handler; this can later be restored with DisableSystemTimers (see above). The function
then calls INT 21h AX=2508h to install the SYSTEM INT 8 handler.

This function should only be called by Windows at initialization time. However, a
perverse program that calls DisableSystemTimers() would later call EnableSystem-
Timers() to resume the march of time.

Interestingly, in current implementations of SYSTEM the EnableSystemTimers()
function does *not* access the 8253 programmable interval timer. The standard timer
resolution of 0D68Dh (18.2 timer interrupts per second) is hard-wired into the SYSTEM
module. (However, the Enhanced mode Virtual Timer Device (VTD) and the Windows 3.1 multimedia driver TIMER.DRV both reprogram the 8253.)

Get80x87SaveSize   SYSTEM.7

```
WORD Get80x87SaveSize(void);
```

This function returns the number of bytes that need to be allocated for the buffer whose address is passed to the Save80x87State() and Restore80x87State() functions (see later in this chapter). The return value will be zero if an 80x87 math coprocessor is not present. Otherwise, in present versions of Windows, the value returned is 94 bytes.

See also: WIN87EM functions Win87EmSaveArea() and Win87EmInfo()

GetSystemMsecCount   SYSTEM.6

```
DWORD GetSystemMsecCount(void);
```

This function returns the number of milliseconds Windows has been running. Because the documented GetCurrentTime() function in USER simply JMPs to this function and, therefore, produces identical results, there should be no reason to call GetSystemMsecCount().

It is important to note that the time returned by GetSystemMsecCount() and GetCurrentTime() is not necessary genuine (i.e., wristwatch or wall-clock) time. The number merely reflects how many times the INT 8 handler in SYSTEM has been called; each time it is called, the INT 8 handler adds 54 milliseconds to the SYSTEM msec count. As explained earlier in the entry for CreateSystemTimer(), this INT 8 handler is *not* invoked when a DOS box is running in Standard mode (or in Windows 3.0 Real mode), and in some circumstances it is will not invoked when a full-screen DOS box is running in Enhanced mode, so the values returned by GetCurrentTime() and GetSystemMsecCount() may be quite skewed.

InquireSystem   SYSTEM.1

```
DWORD InquireSystem(wFlag, wDriveNumber, bOptionalEnable)
WORD wFlag;              /* one of the INQSYS flags indicated below */
WORD wDriveNumber;       /* a zero-based drive number (i.e., 0 = A:, 1 =
B:) */
BOOL bOptionalEnable;    /* an optional parameter; see below */
```

InquireSystem() is a hodge-podge function that can return the SYSTEM timer resolution, determine whether a drive exists, or enable/disable single-drive logic:

```
#define INQSYS_TIMERRES    0        /* get timer resolution */
#define INQSYS_DRIVEEXIST  1        /* does drive exist? */
#define INQSYS_ONEDRIVE    2        /* enable/disable one-drive logic */
InquireSystem(INQSYS_TIMERRES, 0) ==> timer resolution
```

This returns the hard-wired value 0D68Dh, or 54925 decimal, for the Windows SYSTEM timer resolution. (Note that 1 divided by 54925 is .0000182066, giving the familiar 18.2 timer interrupts per second.) This number, divided by 1000, gives the smallest number that can reasonably be passed to Windows timer-handler functions such as SetTimer() and CreateSystemTimer(). The same value is returned by the undocumented GetTimerResolution() function in USER. For an example, see SYSTIMER.C in the entry for CreateSystemTimer().

```
InquireSystem(INQSYS_DRIVEEXIST, wDriveNumber) ==> drive information
```

Like the documented GetDriveType() function, this form of InquireSystem() reports on whether a drive *physically* exists and whether it is removable or fixed:

```
#define DRIVE_NOTEXIST      0
#define DRIVE_REMOVEABLE    2
#define DRIVE_FIXED         3
#define DRIVE_REMOTE        4
```

Note that if the drive does not physically exist (e.g., drive B: on most systems), the HIWORD of the return value (AX) is 0, and the LOWORD (DX) indicates the status of the corresponding mappable drive. For instance, on most systems InquireSystem(1, 1) returns 0x20000L, indicating that drive B: is not physically present, but that the drive to which it corresponds is removable. Thus, the return value from Inquire-System(INQSYS_DRIVEEXIST) should *not* be tested against DRIVE_NOTEXIST; instead, test the HIWORD of the return value:

```
DWORD dwStatus = InquireSystem(INQSYS_DRIVEEXIST, 1);
if (HIWORD(dwStatus) == DRIVE_NOTEXIST)
    return LOWORD(dwStatus);
```

There is little reason to use this because GetDriveType() is documented. In fact, GetDriveType() in KERNEL is simply a wrapper around InquireSystem(INQSYS _DRIVEEXIST); KERNEL uses GetProcAddress() to link to InquireSystem().

```
InquireSystem(INQSYS_ONEDRIVE, wDriveNumber, bEnable)
```

In this operation, InquireSystem() is used not to inquire a value, but to change it. Setting the bEnable flag to FALSE (0) disables single-drive logic; setting it to TRUE (nonzero) enables it. Most Windows applications seem not to recognize any such change in the status of drive B:, however, thus limiting the usefulness of this function.

InquireSystem() uses the undocumented NoHookDOSCall() function in KERNEL to call the following DOS functions: Get Current Drive (INT 21h AH=19h), Set Default Drive (INT 21h AH=0Eh), Removable Media Check (INT 21h AX=4408h), Is Drive Remote (INT 21h AX=4409h), Get Logical Drive Map (INT 21h AX=440Eh), and Get Network Assign-List Entry (INT 21h AX=5F02h).

InquireSystem

KillSystemTimer   SYSTEM.3

```
WORD KillSystemTimer(hTimer);
WORD hTimer;    /* timer handle returned by CreateSystemTimer */
```

KillSystemTimer() deallocates a system timer allocated with CreateSystemTimer(). It returns zero for success; on error, it returns whatever number was passed in.

Example: See SYSTIMER.C in the entry for CreateSystemTimer()

Restore80x87State   SYSTEM.9

```
void Restore80x87State(fpState)
BYTE far *fpState;  /* Far pointer to 94-byte buffer */
```

This function restores the 80x87 math coprocessor state (floating-point stack, exception pointers, control words, etc.) from the specified buffer; the function is equivalent to the 80x87 FRSTOR instruction. The buffer will have previously been set with a call to Save80x87State() (see below).

See also: WIN87EM Win87EmRestore()

Save80x87State   SYSTEM.8

```
void Save80x87State(fpState);
BYTE far *fpState;  /* Far pointer to 94-byte buffer */
```

This function saves away the 80x87 math coprocessor state (floating-point stack, exception pointers, control words, etc.) to the specified buffer; the function is equivalent to the 80x87 FSAVE instruction. The buffer can later be restored by calling Save80x87State(). The size of the buffer to allocate can be verified with Get80x87-SaveSize().

See also: WIN87EM Win87EmSave()

CHAPTER 10

ToolHelp: A Partial
Replacement for Undocumented Windows

TOOLHELP.DLL is a dynamic link library provided by Microsoft that allows programmers to obtain information about the state of Windows internals that was previously unobtainable by documented means. In addition, it provides a higher level interface to several portions of the Windows operating system functionality. Another design goal of ToolHelp is to insulate the programmer from having to worry about changes to the internal data structures from version to version of Windows: TOOLHELP.DLL is shipped with Windows 3.1 but will also work with the somewhat different internal data structures of Windows 3.0. Lastly, Microsoft intends for ToolHelp to eventually replace WINDEBUG.DLL as the operating system interface for debuggers. On the other hand, it appears as though ToolHelp will not be part of the Win32 API; the current Win32 specification includes debugging functions, but they are different from what's in ToolHelp.

ToolHelp does not "give" you the actual data structures used internally by Windows. However, it does give you data in a consistent, documented form. The idea is to provide a stable interface layer to operating system information, while still allowing Microsoft to change the internals of Windows as needed. In other words, ToolHelp functions return what Microsoft wants you to see from its internal data structures. The functions copy selected information from the actual data structures into "idealized" and "sanatized" images of the structures. Often, not having the actual structure is just fine.

Additionally, ToolHelp provides the functionality necessary to implement a GUI debugger. GUI debuggers are distinct from text mode debuggers in that they use the windowing system to display themselves, rather than using a character mode interface. Multiscope and Quick C for Windows are GUI debuggers; TDW and CVW are text mode debuggers. There is some confusion on this last point. TDW and CVW are Windows programs and have WinMain functions. The key difference between them and "normal" Windows applications is that they use a text mode display to show their output. This is done by using the predefined KERNEL selectors __B000H and __B800H to access the text mode video memory.

Creating a GUI debugger requires much more control over the tasking and messaging mechanisms than is possible with WINDEBUG.DLL. Programs that use WINDEBUG have a much simpler, higher level interface to debugging functionality than they would with ToolHelp, but they are more constrained in how they can handle their output. A ToolHelp-based debugger has to operate closer to the Windows kernel, is lower level, and must duplicate much of the code and algorithms that are enscapsulated in WINDEBUG.DLL, but the benefit is that it leaves the display options much more open.

Lastly, ToolHelp provides the capability to implement post-mortem debugging tools such as Dr. Watson and WinSpector. In the CORONER sample program at the end of this chapter we'll see exactly how this is done.

What Undocumented Functionality Can ToolHelp Replace?

As this book demonstrates, it is not always a simple task to do something that requires information maintained by Windows (for instance, obtaining a list of all window classes registered with the system, or making a list of all the tasks). Because internal data structures such as the format of a task database may need to change, Microsoft chose not to publish their formats. However, you might need to know this information. For example, how do you find out the instance handle associated with a given task handle?

Using undocumented Windows, getting an instance handle from a task handle looks like this excerpt from HANDLES.H in the introduction to chapter 5:

```
/* Turn hTask into hInstance: use WORD at TDB offset 1Ch */
#define HINSTANCE_FROM_HTASK(hTask) \
    *((WORD far *) MK_FP(hTask, 0x1C))
```

This is trivially simple, but obviously open to any changes Microsoft might make in future versions of the Task Database (TDB).

Using ToolHelp, the code might look like this:

```
#include "toolhelp.h"

HANDLE HINSTANCE_FROM_HTASK(HANDLE hTask)
{
    TASKENTRY te;
    te.dwSize = sizeof(te);
    if (TaskFindHandle(&te, hTask))
        return te.hInst;
    else
        return 0;
}
```

Notice that the ToolHelp version is checking for invalid tasks, which our simple undocumented Windows macro isn't doing. To truly duplicate the effect of the ToolHelp function, the undocumented Windows macro would also need to call the IsTask() function in Windows 3.1, or use the IsValidTask() function from HANDLES.C in chapter 5.

In other words, ToolHelp can vastly simplify a lot of code that used to require undocumented Windows.

Microsoft has packaged up some previously undocumented knowledge in ToolHelp. Specifically, ToolHelp knows

- The format of the Standard and Enhanced mode Global heaps
- The format of a Local heap (USER and GDI have normal Local heaps)
- The format of a Module database (associated with a Module handle)
- The format of a Task database (associated with a Task handle)
- The register contents for "System notifications"

For example, programs often need to show the amount of free system resources (the magic number that appears in Program Manager's Help | About box). As explained in chapter 5, an undocumented function in Windows 3.0 (GetHeapSpaces()) will give you information for calculating that number. However, in Windows 3.1 a different function gives you similar information. But to have a program that runs under either Windows version requires code to determine what version of Windows you're under, as well as to calculate the value two different ways.

ToolHelp can eliminate this problem because it has a function (SystemHeapInfo()) that returns the same information regardless of which version of Windows you're running. Thus, there is no need to play with undocumented functions simply to get the free system resources magic number.

The downside to this is that any program using the more portable SystemHeapInfo() function does require that TOOLHELP.DLL itself be available when the program runs, which might not be the case under Windows 3.0. You can ship TOOLHELP.DLL with your application, but this might be overkill just to display one free system resources number. In this situation, you might want to use LoadLibrary() and GetProcAddress(), so that if TOOLHELP.DLL isn't already present on a Windows 3.0 user's hard disk, the situation can be handled gracefully by your program, rather than gracelessly by Windows.

Another example: Prior to ToolHelp, walking the global heap would require using an undocumented function (GlobalMasterHandle()), as well as having code specific to the mode Windows was running in. Windows 3.0 HEAPWALK does just this. You could not write your own version of HEAPWALK without using undocumented information. The Windows 3.1 version of HEAPWALK, however, instead uses ToolHelp to walk the system heaps. The closest thing to an abstract interface to the heaps in Windows 3.0 was WINDEBUG.DLL, which is not documented by Microsoft and which is overkill if you only want to know how many selectors are in use.

Later in this chapter, more details are provided on precisely what undocumented functionality each ToolHelp function replaces, plus what undocumented functionality the ToolHelp function itself uses. (Because ToolHelp partially removes the need to use undocumented functions and structures, it must itself use these functions and structure.)

There is no contradiction between using ToolHelp and using undocumented Windows functions and data structures. As shown by sample programs in other parts of this book (ATOMWALK in chapter 5, USERWALK in chapter 6, and GDIWALK in chapter 8), you can use ToolHelp to simplify all your basic access to Windows internals and then, when ToolHelp gives out, switch over to using undocumented functions and data structures. For example, ToolHelp doesn't know anything about the structure of an atom table, so an atom-table browser like ATOMWALK can't rely totally on ToolHelp. However, ToolHelp does supply the basic mechanics of walking the global heap, so ATOMWALK uses this to locate atom tables:

```
GLOBALENTRY ge;
BOOL ok;
ge.dwSize = sizeof(ge);
ok = GlobalFirst(&ge, GLOBAL_ALL);
while (ok)
{
    // TOOLHELP can't help us with this part: figure out
    // if ge.hBlock contains an atom table, and, if it
    // does, display its contents

    ok = GlobalNext(&ge, GLOBAL_ALL);
}
```

Assorted ToolHelp Programming Considerations

To use ToolHelp, you must include TOOLHELP.H (which contains function prototypes and structure definitions for the library), and link with the import library TOOLHELP.LIB. As noted earlier, TOOLHELP.DLL must be available when the program runs.

With a few exceptions, ToolHelp is a read-only API: You can obtain information contained in Windows internal data structures, but you cannot modify them. Information can be retrieved with the XXXFirst/XXXNext functions, but there is no provision to *change* the contents. To do that requires the use of the risky and highly version-specific undocumented information presented in chapter 5.

For the most part, ToolHelp functions return a BOOL, indicating success or failure. ToolHelp is strict about what it will accept and will fail a function call with invalid parameters. In other words, it's a good idea to always check return values from ToolHelp functions.

All the heap and information functions take a FAR pointer to a data structure and return BOOL. Each structure has a dwSize field; a common mistake made with

ToolHelp is forgetting to initialize the dwSize field. The C sizeof( ) operator provides an easy way to initialize the structure. For example:

```
#include "toolhelp.h"
// ...
GLOBALENTRY myGlobalEntry;
myGlobalEntry.dwSize = sizeof(GLOBALENTRY);
```

The standard prolog inside each ToolHelp function does the following:

- Checks a global variable set in ToolHelp's LibMain to see if ToolHelp is initialized properly; the function returns FALSE if not.
- Returns FALSE if the structure pointer passed in is NULL.
- Verifies that the dwSize field in the structure agrees with what ToolHelp thinks the structure size should be. Doing this allows for backward compatibility. For example, if a future ToolHelp adds information to a data structure, but you run a program written for an older ToolHelp, then ToolHelp can choose to fill in only the fields that the older ToolHelp knows about. Alternatively, if a program written for a newer ToolHelp is used with an older ToolHelp, the call will be failed if the sizes don't match.

Several groups of calls are of the form xxxFirst/xxxNext. These are similar to the DOS FindFirst/FindNext calls that are used to iterate through all the files in a directory. The simplest way to use these functions is expressed in the following pseudocode:

```
BOOL not_finished;
STRUCT info_struct;

info_struct.dwSize = sizeof(STRUCT);

not_finished = xxxFirst(&info_struct);

while ( not_finished )
{
    Display/process info in info_struct

    not_finished = xxxNext(&info_struct);
}
```

There is one crucial point about this basic ToolHelp heap-walking loop: the code "Display/process info in info_struct" must not yield control to other applications or do anything else that might change the state of the list that you're walking. For example, if you are using GlobalFirst/GlobalNext, it would be a mistake to call GlobalAlloc( ) inside the loop, because this would change the Windows global heap right out from under you.

ToolHelp does not care too much about the difference between a memory handle and its associated selector. Almost all ToolHelp functions that expect a handle of some sort call an internal function that returns a selector. If the parameter passed to this function is a handle, it is converted to a selector. If the parameter is a selector value, it's returned unchanged. This internal function has code specifically for Windows 3.0 vs. 3.1, due to the change in processor ring level from Ring 1 in Windows 3.0 to Ring 3 in Windows 3.1. The bottom line is that you can call ToolHelp functions with either a handle or a selector.

There are a few pitfalls to be aware of when debugging programs that use ToolHelp. Certain key portions of ToolHelp overlap functionality in WINDEBUG.DLL. Since WINDEBUG was written before ToolHelp, WINDEBUG assumes that it's the only user of certain Windows operating system facilities. To attempt to alleviate this potential conflict between ToolHelp and WINDEBUG, the NotifyRegister() function in ToolHelp will return FALSE under Windows 3.0 if the module WINDEBUG.DLL is currently loaded. This means that if you're running a debugger that uses WINDEBUG.DLL (TDW, CVW, or Multiscope), you can't debug programs that use NotifyRegister(). Conversely, when ToolHelp is loaded before WINDEBUG.DLL, you'll find that your notification callback function is no longer called back. ToolHelp under Windows 3.1 does not have these problems, as it uses ToolHelpHook (see chapter 5) to provide a "parallel" set of services to the RegisterPtrace function (again, see chapter 5) used in Windows 3.0.

A related situation occurs with interrupts and exceptions. Both WINDEBUG and ToolHelp install handlers for the commonly encountered interrupt/exceptions. If your program uses InterruptRegister(), it is important that you chain on any interrupt that you don't handle yourself. Also, loading and unloading ToolHelp and WINDEBUG "out of sequence" can cause problems. This is similar to the problem of multiple TSRs hooking the same interrupt and then being removed in the incorrect order.

There is one additional warning for programmers who are concerned about running their code under Real mode in Windows 3.0, but who want to use ToolHelp: Get with the program, dudes! Real mode is dead; ToolHelp will not load in Windows 3.0 Real mode.

Using ToolHelp in Your Product

ToolHelp comes with Windows 3.1, but it was designed to provide a consistent interface, regardless of Windows version. It runs under Windows 3.0 as well as 3.1.

Microsoft ships ToolHelp with Windows 3.1, but you can redistribute a copy of it with your program and install it on the user's machine if your application requires it to run under Windows 3.0. A very important warning: There were several different beta versions of ToolHelp floating about before Windows 3.1 became available. Thus, you may run into an old version on the user's disk. Some really old versions of ToolHelp actually have different ordinal numbers and functions from the ToolHelp shipped with

Windows 3.1. If your program encounters one of these old versions of ToolHelp while running under Windows 3.0, problems will occur, especially if the debug version of Windows is running. With Windows 3.1, Microsoft introduced VER.DLL, which assists installation programs in identifying different versions of a DLL and installing the correct one (that is, installing a DLL only if it is not already there, or if it is *newer* than the one already installed). Because the versioning facilities provided by this DLL are compatible with Window 3.0, it's a good idea to use them. See chapter 11 ("File Installation Library") of Volume 1 (Overview) of the Windows 3.1 SDK *Programmer's Reference*.

The ToolHelp Functions

The following is a list of ToolHelp functions, grouped by functionality. *It is not intended to replace the ToolHelp documentation* (see chapter 8 of Volume 1 of the 3.1 *Programmer's Reference*). Instead, the aim is to show how the functions might be used, as well as what undocumented functionality they replace and what undocumented functionality in Windows they themselves use.

The Heap Functions

The ToolHelp global heap functions are really just shells around a small set of core, internal routines. There are different internal routines for KRNL286 (Standard mode) and KRNL386 (Enhanced mode, and 3.1 Standard mode on a 386) because the format of the heap is different in the two modes. Each function gets the address of the header block that precedes each actual heap block. From that point on, a fairly standard sequence of internal routines is called to transfer the information from the header block into the GLOBALEENTRY structure that was passed in.

In KRNL386, the GlobalMasterHandle is a selector for a 32-bit segment, which contains a table matching selectors to their linear address. A simple table lookup provides the offset of the header for the block. (See Selector Table in chapter 5.)

In KRNL286, two selectors are used for each memory block. One selector is used for the actual data block; the other selector points to a header that is 10h bytes in length and immediately precedes the data block in the linear address space. (If the header information was stored in the data block itself, it would be impossible for a program to allocate a full 64K segment.)

DPMI services are used to find the linear address of the data block, then 10h bytes are subtracted from the address. DPMI is then used again to create a selector with this new address. The resultant selector is used to access the block header.

These functions are used in the WinWalk sample program, presented later in this chapter.

SystemHeapInfo

```
BOOL FAR PASCAL SystemHeapInfo
    (SYSHEAPINFO FAR* lpSysHeap);

typedef struct {
    DWORD dwSize;
    WORD wUserFreePercent;
    WORD wGDIFreePercent;
    HANDLE hUserSegment;
    HANDLE hGDISegment;
    } SYSHEAPINFO;
```

SystemHeapInfo() is the simplest way to obtain the free system resources referred to in the Program Manager About box. To obtain this number, simply take the lower value of the wUserFreePercent and wGDIFreePercent fields in the SYSHEAPINFO structure.

The other two fields in the SYSHEAPINFO structure are actually more useful than you might expect. hUserSegment corresponds to the DGROUP (default data segment) of USER, and hGDISegment corresponds to the DGROUP of GDI. To walk the default USER and GDI heaps, you can pass hUserSegment or hGDISegment as the second parameter to LocalFirst(). (In 3.1 remember that USER and GDI may have *multiple* local heaps.)

Without this function, there are several methods to obtain the DGROUP of USER and GDI. One way is to obtain the DLL's module handle (via GetModuleHandle), and then look up the DGROUP value in the segment/selector table (see chapter 5 on KERNEL). As explained in chapter 6, to get USER's DGROUP you might also use

```
GetWindowWord(GetDesktopWindow(), GWW_INSTANCE);
```

To determine the DGROUPs, ToolHelp itself uses the module table lookup method described earlier. If running under Windows 3.0, it calculates the percentage free by looking at values stored in the local heap's memory. If running under Windows 3.1, it calls GetFreeSystemResources() to obtain the percentages directly.

GlobalEntryHandle

```
BOOL FAR PASCAL GlobalEntryHandle
    (GLOBALENTRY FAR *lpGlobal,
    HANDLE hItem);

typedef struct {
    DWORD dwSize;
    DWORD dwAddress;
    DWORD dwBlockSize;
```

```
    HANDLE hBlock;
    WORD wcLock;
    WORD wcPageLock;
    WORD wFlags;
    BOOL wHeapPresent;
    HANDLE hOwner;
    WORD wType;
    WORD wData;
    DWORD dwNext;
    DWORD dwNextAlt;
    } GLOBALENTRY;
```

Initially, GlobalEntryHandle() doesn't stand out as one of the key functions in ToolHelp. It is. A multitude of functions return or deal with memory handles (hMems); GlobalEntryHandle is the quick and easy way to find out more about an arbitrary memory block.

One common use for GlobalEntryHandle() is to determine who owns a particular memory block. By calling GlobalEntryHandle, you can obtain the module handle of the block owner. The handle will be in the "hOwner" field of the GLOBALENTRY structure and can be passed to ModuleFindHandle() to obtain the name of the owning module.

This function does not have the overhead one might expect. It does *not* walk the global heap until it stumbles across a block whose handle matches the one passed in to the function. Instead, it uses an internal routine with knowledge of the heap to quickly find the block header.

GlobalEntryModule

```
BOOL FAR PASCAL GlobalEntryModule
    (GLOBALENTRY FAR *lpGlobal,
    HANDLE hModule, WORD wSeg);
```

GlobalEntryModule, like its sister function GlobalEntryHandle, is really just a function for looking up something in the global heap. It's not quite as useful as GlobalEntryHandle and is used only by programs that deal with logical addresses, rather then selector offsets.

A logical address is given by specifying a module, a segment number within the module, and an offset within the segment. For instance, "USER 4:01234" means "offset 01234h in the 4th segment in USER's segment table." A debugger uses logical addresses. Because the selectors assigned to each segment of a program are not known until run-time, the debug information is specified in terms of logical addresses. A debugger would use this function to "convert" the logical address to an actual address.

This conversion of logical to actual address can also be obtained through an undocumented use of GetCodeHandle(). GetCodeHandle is documented as taking an lpProc. However, as explained in chapter 5, if you pass it MK_FP(ModuleHandle, SegNumber), it will return a DWORD, with the high word containing the segment selector and the low word containing the corresponding handle. DPMI functions or the GetSelectorXXX functions can then be used to obtain information about the length and linear address of the block. One caveat: calling GetCodeHandle in this way will force the segment into memory if it's not already there. This may or may not be what you want.

Alternatively, without ToolHelp, you could find the selector for a given segment number by looking it up in the segment table inside the module table. This has the advantage (or disadvantage) of returning 0 for the selector if it's not loaded.

The ToolHelp implementation first verifies that you've passed in a valid module handle (by checking for the NE signature). Then it verifies that the wSeg parameter passed in is within range of the segments specified in the module table. Once it goes through those checks, it executes essentially the same code as GlobalEntryHandle.

GlobalFirst
GlobalNext

```
BOOL FAR PASCAL GlobalFirst
    (GLOBALENTRY FAR *lpGlobal, WORD wFlags);

BOOL FAR PASCAL GlobalNext
    (GLOBALENTRY FAR *lpGlobal, WORD wFlags);
```

These two functions are the core of any global heap walking program. GlobalFirst calls an internal routine that uses GlobalMasterHandle to return the address of the first block header. Then the standard set of internal functions is used to fill in the GLOBALENTRY structure.

GlobalNext simply obtains the address of the next block from the dwNext or dwNextAlt fields of the passed in GLOBALENTRY structure. It then calls the standard set of internal functions to fill in the GLOBALENTRY.

One interesting aspect of GlobalNext is that it can start walking the heap anywhere, as long as a GLOBALENTRY structure that has previously been used is passed in.

GlobalInfo

```
BOOL FAR PASCAL GlobalInfo
    (GLOBALINFO FAR *lpGlobalInfo);

typedef struct {
    DWORD dwSize;
    WORD wcItems;
    WORD wcItemsFree;
    WORD wcItemsLRU;
    } GLOBALINFO;
```

This function will return values that are useful if you wish to walk the global heap. GlobalInfo() tells you how many items you'll encounter during a global heap walk, so you can allocate space for an array of structures beforehand. This is much easier than having to create a new node for a linked list every time you encounter another heap block. If you are going to allocate global memory after calling this function, however, beware that the act of allocating global memory may invalidate the results you get back from GlobalInfo!

This function is extremely fast, as it simply extracts values from heap data structures pointed to by the GlobalMasterHandle. As noted in chapter 5, this information is at different offsets in the GlobalMasterHandle segment, depending on whether you're running under KRNL286 or KRNL386.

LocalFirst
LocalNext

```
BOOL FAR PASCAL LocalFirst
    (LOCALENTRY FAR *lpLocal, HANDLE hHeap);

BOOL FAR PASCAL LocalNext
    (LOCALENTRY FAR *lpLocal);

typedef struct {
    DWORD     dwSize;
    HANDLE    hHandle;
    WORD      wAddress;
    WORD      wSize;
    WORD      wFlags;
    WORD      wcLock;
    WORD      wType;
    WORD      hHeap;
    WORD      wHeapType;
    WORD      wNext;
    } LOCALENTRY;
```

These functions are the equivalent of GlobalFirst/GlobalNext except that they work on a specific local heap. Windows has only one global heap, but almost every instance has its own local heap. Programs can call LocalInit() to create additional local heaps. In contrast to the global heap functions, you must specify which local heap you want to walk.

The documentation is somewhat incomplete, as it tells you to pass LocalFirst a "heap handle," without explaining what this is. A heap handle is really just the DGROUP segment of the instance in question, assuming that you're using only the single local heap already set for you in the data segment at startup. If you are managing multiple local heaps created by LocalInit(), then you can pass LocalFirst() the selector value that you used when you created the heap.

LocalFirst

The Windows SDK HEAPWALK utility lets you select a segment and pop up another window that displays the contents of the local heap within the block, if there is one. The format of the local heap structures was not documented, thereby making programmers dependent on HEAPWALK. With LocalFirst/LocalNext (or information on local heaps in chapter 5), you can now do this yourself. This functionality is especially useful for the USER and GDI heaps. With the ability to examine these heaps, programmers can write tools to check for unreleased resources and other problem-causing conditions.

These functions are relatively robust, as they perform sanity checking to eliminate the possibility of a bogus heap segment being passed in. In both Standard and Enhanced mode, offset 6 in a heap segment is a near pointer to the start of the heap. One of the first things done internally by ToolHelp is to verify that the near pointer falls within the limit of the selector passed in.

Additionally, in KRNL286 the signature bytes 'LH' (484Ch) will be found 22h bytes past the start of the local heap. In KRNL386 the same signature can be found 28h bytes past the local heap start. Naturally, ToolHelp shields you from having to know these details.

LocalNext relies on the wHeap field of the LOCALENTRY structure. Thus, it's important to preserve the value in the LOCALENTRY structure from the previous call to LocalFirst or LocalNext.

When walking the USER heap under Windows 3.0, be aware that you will always get back zeros for the heap block type. Internally, ToolHelp checks the hHeap field in the LOCALENTRY structure, and takes special action if the value is either USER's or GDI's heap handle. When the hHeap corresponds to USER's heap, it calls the undocumented function GetUserLocalObjType(), which was introduced in Windows 3.1 and is available only in the debugging version of Windows (see chapter 6). If the hHeap belongs to GDI, the wType value is extracted from the data block itself.

See the USERWALK program in chapter 6, and the GDIWALK program in chapter 8. These use ToolHelp for their basic heap walking and then, where ToolHelp falls short, they use undocumented Windows.

LocalInfo

```
BOOL FAR PASCAL LocalInfo
    (LOCALINFO FAR *lpLocal, HANDLE hHeap);

typedef struct {
    DWORD dwSize;
    WORD wcItems;
    } LOCALINFO;
```

This function is the local heap equivalent of GlobalInfo. It allows you to find out how many items you're going to encounter in the local heap before you walk it using

LocalFirst/LocalNext. The same cautions about influencing the heap by allocating from it apply here also.

LocalInfo goes through the same sanity checks for a valid heap as GlobalInfo does. It then finds the beginning of the local heap (described in the preceeding page) and places the WORD from offset 4 into the wcItems field.

The Windows Data Structure Walking Functions

ClassFirst
ClassNext

```
BOOL FAR PASCAL ClassFirst
    (CLASSENTRY FAR *lpClass);

BOOL FAR PASCAL ClassNext
    (CLASSENTRY FAR *lpClass);

typedef struct {
    DWORD dwSize;
    HANDLE hInst;
    char szClassName[MAX_CLASSNAME + 1];
    WORD wNext;
    } CLASSENTRY;
```

These functions allow you to traverse the linked list of window classes maintained in the USER heap.

The class structure (see chapter 6 on USER) members that ToolHelp uses are as follows:

00H	WORD	offset of next class in USER default local heap
04H	ATOM	atom handle of class name (note: DS must be set to USER's DS)
14h	WORD	instance handle of registering application

Internally, ClassFirst has to find the address of the first class in different ways, depending on which version of Windows is running. If running under Windows 3.0 non-debug version, offset 01B8h in the USER heap is a near pointer to a near pointer (near * near *) to the first class entry. If running under the 3.0 debug version, offset 01CCh is used instead. If using Windows 3.1, UserSeeUserDo(0x0500, 0x0000) is called to return the offset. (See chapter 6.) It's readily apparent that it's easier to let ToolHelp do the hard work than to try to do this yourself.

Incidentally, the "hInst" field in the CLASSNTRY structure is in fact a *module* handle, not an instance handle. Since other Windows class functions expect an hInstance, Microsoft felt it was less confusing to refer to the value as an hInst. Clear enough?

ClassFirst

ModuleFindHandle

```
HANDLE FAR PASCAL ModuleFindHandle
    (MODULEENTRY FAR *lpModule, HANDLE hModule);

typedef struct {
    DWORD dwSize;
    char szModule[MAX_MODULE_NAME + 1];
    HANDLE hModule;
    WORD wcUsage;
    char szExePath[MAX_PATH + 1];
    WORD wNext;
    } MODULEENTRY;
```

One of the most interesting and useful undocumented data structures in Windows is the module table. This table contains all sorts of information that Windows must maintain for every program and DLL that's loaded. A module handle is a handle to a global memory block that contains the module table (see chapter 5).

ModuleFindHandle returns what Microsoft wants you to see in the module table. Given a module handle, this function will copy select information from the module table into a MODULEENTRY structure. The most likely reason for calling this function is to get the module name (corresponding to the "Name" or "Library" field in the .DEF file).

Unfortunately, there are many more items present in a module table than you'll get from this function. For instance, the number of segments for a module, the segment number of the module's DGROUP, the initial stack size, and more can all be found if you know the module table format (again, see chapter 5). In fact, the ModuleXXX functions in ToolHelp don't really give you anything that you couldn't get with documented functions. The main benefit is that all the documented information about a module is collected in one place.

ModuleFindName

```
HANDLE FAR PASCAL ModuleFindName
    (MODULEENTRY FAR *lpModule, LPSTR lpstrName);
```

This function, like its sister function ModuleFindHandle, is basically useful only for obtaining the path name of the .EXE or .DLL for the module. If you know the module name and want the module file name, you could as easily call GetModuleFileName (GetModuleHandle (lpModName), lpstrName, len).

Internally, ModuleFindName verifies that the two pointers passed in are not NULL. Then it just calls ModuleFirst/ModuleNext and uses lstrcmp to compare the returned "szModule" field against the string that was passed in. In other words, this function is case-sensitive.

ModuleFirst
ModuleNext

```
BOOL FAR PASCAL ModuleFirst
    (MODULEENTRY FAR *lpModule);

BOOL FAR PASCAL ModuleNext
    (MODULEENTRY FAR *lpModule);
```

These functions are what you'd use to create a complete list of modules currently loaded in Windows. Like the other ModuleXXX functions, they just take a module handle, extract a portion of the data from the table, and put it into the MODULE-ENTRY structure.

TaskFindHandle

```
BOOL FAR PASCAL TaskFindHandle
    (TASKENTRY FAR *lpTask, HANDLE hTask);

typedef struct {
    DWORD dwSize;
    HANDLE hTask;
    HANDLE hTaskParent;
    HANDLE hInst;
    HANDLE hModule;
    WORD wSS;
    WORD wSP;
    WORD wStackTop;
    WORD wStackMinimum;
    WORD wStackBottom;
    WORD wcEvents;
    HANDLE hQueue;
    char szModule[MAX_MODULE_NAME + 1];
    WORD wPSPOffset;
    HANDLE hNext;
    } TASKENTRY;
```

Another useful, undocumented data structure in Windows is the Task Database (see chapter 5). There is a task database for every instance of a running program. There are no task databases for DLLs, which are just program code that wasn't linked until run time. A task handle is a global memory block handle. By obtaining the selector for the handle, we can access the task database.

Like ModuleFindHandle, TaskFindHandle is really just a copier of information. It first verifies that the hTask passed in is a valid task handle by looking for the 4454h ('TD') signature at offset 0FAh in the task database. It then copies information from the undocumented Task database structure to the passed-in TASKENTRY structure.

There is one minor excursion outside the task database segment. In order to fill the wStackTop, wStackMinimum, and wStackBottom fields, the values are retrieved from the base of the task's stack segment (see Instance Data, in chapter 5).

TaskFirst
TaskNext

```
BOOL FAR PASCAL TaskFirst
    (TASKENTRY FAR *lpTask);

BOOL FAR PASCAL TaskNext
    (TASKENTRY FAR *lpTask);
```

With these functions, you can walk the list of task databases that Windows maintains in the global heap.

One obscure use for the task walking functions is to obtain the DGROUP of a TASK that is the second instance of a program. For example, let's say that you want to obtain the DGROUP of the second instance of Solitaire that you're playing. If you look in the module table for Solitaire, the DGROUP value that you obtain will be for the first instance. By walking the task list, you can look for a task whose module handle is that of Solitaire but whose DGROUP (hInst) is different from the one you already have.

Debugger and Miscellaneous Functions

GlobalHandleToSel

```
WORD FAR PASCAL GlobalHandleToSel
    (HANDLE hMem);
```

Despite Microsoft's warnings not to use bit twiddling to obtain selector values from handles, the practice is alive and well in ToolHelp.

GlobalHandleToSel() is just a wrapper function around an internal routine that's used heavily elsewhere in ToolHelp. The wrapper function twiddles bits in the passed-in handle and does not verify that the handle is actually for an allocated, valid selector.

Because Microsoft changed the ring-level that user code runs in between versions 3.0 and 3.1, there is version-specific code in the internal functions. Windows 3.0 runs programs at Ring 1. Windows 3.1 runs programs at Ring 3. This affects the possible values that a selector can have.

If running under Windows 3.0 protected mode, selectors are always numbered either xxx5h or xxxDh. Their handles are just the selector value, incremented by 1 (if not a FIXED segment). In this internal function, a check is made to see if the bottom-most bit is on (indicating an odd value, hence the selector). If so, then it returns the value, unchanged. If the bottom bit is off, it subtracts 1 from the value and returns the result.

Under Windows 3.1, selectors are numbered xxx7h and xxxFh. Their non-FIXED handles are the selector values minus 1. Thus, to turn a handle into a selector, the bottom bit must be turned on. This is just what ToolHelp does, with an OR instruction. See the HandleToSel() function in the WINMOD.C sample program for the Module Table in chapter 5.

In both cases, either a selector or its handle can be passed in. It always returns the selector. As mentioned earlier, ToolHelp doesn't really care about handles verses selectors.

InterruptRegister
InterruptUnRegister

```
BOOL FAR PASCAL InterruptRegister
    (HANDLE hTask,
    Farproc lpfnIntCallback);

BOOL FAR PASCAL InterruptUnRegister
    (HANDLE hTask);
```

The InterruptRegister function is one of two functions in ToolHelp that make it much more than just an information provider. InterruptRegister is at the heart of any debugger based on ToolHelp. For the purposes of this discussion, the term "interrupt" will be used to mean interrupt or exception.

Interrupt handling under Windows can be tricky. Fortunately, ToolHelp makes it much less tricky by calling your program in a nice, consistent manner. Without ToolHelp, you'd have to have special code for Standard vs. Enhanced modes because the information on the stack of an interrupt/exception handler differs between the two Windows modes. In addition, some handlers would be installed using INT 21h, while others are set up using DPMI services. ToolHelp has quite a bit of internal code that "cooks" the interrupts and sends them to you in an easily digestible form.

On top of this, ToolHelp multiplexes the interrupts. Previously, a program that took over an interrupt was the only one to receive it; it was entirely responsible for chaining to previous owners of the interrupt. Now, with ToolHelp, many programs can hook into the interrupt chain and not interfere with each other.

Behind the scenes, there are many more interrupts and exceptions going on than you'll see with a ToolHelp interrupt handler. Windows uses GP faults as a "hacky" method of doing ring transitions that aren't allowable with legal 80x86 instructions. The virtual memory system of Enhanced mode is implemented via the page fault. Luckily, these interrupts are handled behind the scenes, and ToolHelp never sees those faults that are part of Windows normal operation. Thus, the installed interrupt handlers do not have to concern themselves with whether the GP or page fault it received should be ignored.

When a program calls InterruptRegister, it provides a callback address. ToolHelp maintains a list of tasks that have called InterruptRegister, and their callback addresses. When InterruptRegister is called for the first time, ToolHelp uses a combination of DPMI calls and DOS Set Vector (INT 21h Function 25h) calls to install a set of interrupt handlers to its own internal routine. When an interrupt occurs, ToolHelp first "processes" the data to create a consistent "view" of what's on the stack. It then iterates through the list of installed handlers, calling the registered callback function. If none of the callback functions process the interrupt themselves, it is chained on to the original handler that existed before ToolHelp installed its own.

Your callback function is almost always written in assembly language. It is responsible for maintaining the state of all registers. It can do one of four things:

1. Handle the interrupt itself and then adjust the stack pointer so that the ToolHelp-pushed items are no longer on the stack. It can then IRET back to the task, as if nothing had happened.
2. Not handle the interrupt. It can simply do a far return (RETF), and ToolHelp will then call the next installed handler.
3. Terminate the task by calling TerminateApp. This is essentially committing suicide, as you're killing your own task (see below).
4. Do a non-local goto using the Catch/Throw functions (the Windows versions of setjmp/longjmp). If you do this, you must verify that the stack you're calling Throw() is the same one that you did the original Catch() on.

When an interrupt occurs, all of the code executed in ToolHelp, and all of the code in the callback functions, is considered by Windows to be running as the task that had the interrupt. In other words, if you were to call GetCurrentTask inside of your interrupt handler, it would return the task handle of the faulting program and not the task handle of the program that contains the callback function. Another way to think of it is that the interrupt is processed while running on the stack of the faulting task. The callback function has magically become part of the faulting task's code!

ToolHelp gives you access to the following interrupts and exceptions:

00 (Divide by 0)
- Hooked by DPMI (INT 31h AH=0203h)
- Chained on in Windows 3.1 if fTrapping0() callback function available (see the entry on fTrapping0 in chapter 8)

01 (Single step instruction)
- Hooked by INT 21h AH=25h
- Used almost exclusively by debuggers

02 (Non Maskable Interrupt) (NMI)
- Hooked by DPMI
- Rarely encountered
- The Windows 3.1 documentation claims that INT 2 is hookable by ToolHelp. However, this does not appear to be true.

03 (Breakpoint)
- Hooked by INT 21h AH=25h
- Used almost exclusively by debuggers

06 (Undefined Opcode)
- Hooked by DPMI

0Ch (Stack fault)
- Hooked by DPMI
- Rarely encountered
- Has different internal handler for Standard and Enhanced modes

0Dh (General protection fault)
- Hooked by DPMI
- Most UAEs are GP faults
- Has different internal handler for Standard and Enhanced modes
- Windows internally generates almost constant GP faults to do ring transitions between application and system code, but these Windows-driven GP faults are not seen when you use ToolHelp to hook GP faults.

0Eh (Page fault)
- Hooked by DPMI
- Rarely encountered (There are constant page faults in Windows Enhanced mode—this is how virtual memory works—but you never see these "expected exceptions" via ToolHelp.)
- Has different internal handler for Standard and Enhanced modes

100h (Not a real interrupt)
- When ToolHelp receives a Control-Alt-SysReq notification via RegisterPtrace (see chapter 5), it sets a temporary breakpoint and resumes. When the breakpoint is hit, it removes it and calls the callback function as if it were a normal interrupt.

InterruptRegister

There are a few things to keep in mind if you wish to do serious work with InterruptRegister:

1. Pass on any interrupts that you don't care about. For instance, the CORONER sample application later in this chapter does not handle INT 1 or INT 3. This allows it to be used at the same time as a debugger.

2. The AX register on entry to the callback function does not contain the AX register value at the time of the interrupt. That value is placed on the stack and should be retrieved from there if you're going to use it.

3. It is generally a very good idea to have your assembler callback function save all the registers on entry, set up a standard stack frame, set the DS to the DS of your application, and call a high-level language function that does the real work. The CORONER sample application shows how to do this.

4. ToolHelp only allows one callback function to be installed per task. You can pass in the hTask of your application, or zero. If you pass in zero, ToolHelp does a GetCurrentTask() and uses that value.

5. The list of callback functions is stored as a linked list. Each new callback function that's registered is put at the end of the list. This means that the first task to call InterruptRegister will get first crack at the interrupts.

6. When InterruptUnregister is called for the last remaining callback function, ToolHelp uninstalls its internal interrupt handlers.

7. Due to a bug in the Windows 3.0 DPMI implementation, a debugger that single steps an instruction that GP faults will find itself receiving an INT 1, with a CS:IP inside of the ToolHelp GP fault handler. This behavior also manifests itself in WINDEBUG.DLL.

MemManInfo

```
BOOL FAR PASCAL MemManInfo
    (MEMMANINFO FAR *lpEnhMode);

typedef struct {
    DWORD dwSize;
    DWORD dwLargestFreeBlock;
    DWORD dwMaxPagesAvailable;
    DWORD dwMaxPagesLockable;
    DWORD dwTotalLinearSpace;
    DWORD dwTotalUnlockedPages;
    DWORD dwFreePages;
    DWORD dwTotalPages;
    DWORD dwFreeLinearSpace;
    DWORD dwSwapFilePages;
    WORD wPageSize;
    } MEMMANINFO;
```

MemManInfo

This function is basically just a shell around DPMI function 0500h (Get Free Memory Information). Every field in the MEMMANINFO structure is copied verbatim from the information returned by the DPMI call, with one exception. The wPageSize field is hard coded to always return 01000h. A note of caution here: the values returned by the DPMI server are sometimes suspect, especially with regard to the amount of linear memory.

Much of the information returned by this call relates to paging, which is not implemented in Standard mode. Because no check is made to see if you're under Standard mode, this function will merrily return TRUE. However, the returned information is useless in this case.

MemoryRead
MemoryWrite

```
DWORD FAR PASCAL MemoryRead
    (WORD wSel, DWORD dwOffset, LPSTR lpBuffer, DWORD dwcb);

DWORD FAR PASCAL MemoryWrite
    (WORD wSel, DWORD dwOffset, LPSTR lpBuffer, DWORD dwcb);
```

MemoryRead and MemoryWrite add a nice touch to ToolHelp. They let you attempt to read and write any selector:offset address without having to worry about GP faulting with an invalid address. Additionally, they allow reading and writing across tiled selectors without having to worry about when to bump the selector value. Lastly, they let you read from 32-bit selectors (note that the offset is a DWORD), without requiring 386-specific code in your program.

Internally, the functions do a series of sanity checks, including using the protected-mode LAR and LSL instructions. If the read/write causes a GP fault, due to an invalid selector or going past the segment limit, the function returns FALSE.

When calling MemoryRead/MemoryWrite, it is a good idea to save the SI and DI registers before the function call and restore them afterwards. Some versions of ToolHelp have a habit of trashing these registers, which can wreak havoc with your register variables.

These functions are well-suited to a debugger, which does a great deal of accessing the debuggee's memory. By providing a nice, safe function to access memory, it relieves the debugger of having paranoid code all over the place.

Additionally, in most robust operating systems, the address space of the debugger is separate from the address space of the debuggee. A special operating system call is required to read from the debuggee's memory space (see, for example, the READ_I_SPACE and READ_D_SPACE options in OS/2's DosPTrace() debugging function). While this is not required under Windows 3.0 and 3.1, it does provide a nice abstraction to the debugger; we hope it will be required in future versions of Windows.

MemoryRead

Interestingly, ToolHelp itself does not use MemoryRead to access the internal data structures of Windows. It relies on a smaller routine to verify that it can read the end of the data structure it's working with; if the routine returns TRUE, ToolHelp directly accesses the memory, instead of copying the data into a buffer.

NotifyRegister
NotifyUnRegister

```
BOOL FAR PASCAL NotifyRegister
    (HANDLE hTask, LPFNNOTIFYCALLBACK lpfn,
    WORD wFlags);

BOOL FAR PASCAL NotifyUnRegister
    (HANDLE hTask);

typedef BOOL (FAR PASCAL *LPFNNOTIFYCALLBACK)(WORD wID, DWORD dwData);
```

The NotifyRegister function is the other major piece of functionality, besides InterruptRegister, required to implement a debugger with ToolHelp.

Like InterruptRegister, this function packages information coming from the Windows kernel into a consistent interface. It will multiplex this information among a list of programs that wish to receive notifications of events such as the loading of a segment, the start of a task or DLL, Windows RIP ("rest in peace" or FatalExit), and so on.

Internally, the code for NotifyRegister, and for dealing with notifications, is very similar to InterruptRegister. Instead of installing an interrupt handle, though, it installs a "notification" handler. When an event occurs, it packages it and then iterates through the list of installed callback functions, calling each in turn. If a callback function indicates that it handled the notification, then the iteration stops. If the callback did not handle the notification, the next installed handler in the list is called.

NotifyRegister installs the notification handler by calling the undocumented RegisterPtrace function (described in chapter 5). In Windows 3.1, it uses the ToolHelpHook function (also described in chapter 5), but the two functions are essentially identical in actual use. WINDEBUG.DLL also uses RegisterPtrace and informs you of a subset of the notifications that you would receive with NotifyRegister. The downside to NotifyRegister is that you're interfacing to the operating system at a lower level, but it's still a far sight better than trying to install your own RegisterPtrace handler.

When the internal notification hook is called, the information is stored in the general-purpose registers. If the information for a given notification is small enough to fit into a DWORD, it's passed as a parameter to the callback function. If there's more than a DWORD of information, it's stored in a static buffer, and a far pointer to the buffer is passed as a parameter to the callback function. Based upon which notification came in, the callback can decide how to interpret the DWORD parameter.

The notifications from RegisterPtrace/ToolhelpHook are documented in the entry for RegisterPtrace() in chapter 5. Here's some of the more interesting ones, as they appear through ToolHelp:

NFY_LOADSEG Of primary interest to debuggers. Windows discards code segments and reloads them from disk. If a debugger has written a breakpoint into a code segment, it will be lost if the segment is discarded. The NFY_LOADSEG gives the debugger an opportunity to reinsert any breakpoints that may have been lost.

NFY_STARTDLL Called before the startup code for a DLL is called. If a debugger wishes to debug the startup code, it can set a breakpoint at the address specified by the wCS and wIP fields of the NFYSTARTDLL structure.

NFY_STARTTASK Called before the first instruction in the program is executed. Debuggers can use this notification to set a breakpoint to gain control at the first instruction of the program.

NFY_EXITTASK Calls GetCurrentTask() to determine which task is terminating.

NFY_DELMODULE Called when a DLL or the last instance of an EXE is being removed from the module list. **Warning:** When this function is called, you may be on an extremely small stack. It is a good idea to do nothing that requires stack space in the callback function when processing this notification. For instance, having any significant amount of local variables or calling Windows functions other than PostMessage() can cause the operating system to become unstable. PostMessage is what Microsoft recommends using, as it uses little stack space. It also is reentrant, allowing its use in other low-level Windows code.

NFY_RIP Called when FatalExit has been called, either by the debugging version of Windows or by the program itself. It will usually be followed by a series of NFY_OUTSTR notifications and then by an NFY_INCHAR.

NFY_OUTSTR When a notification handler is installed, Windows sends its information output via this notification. When there is no installed handler, Windows sends it to the AUX device. (In Win 3.1, there's an option to have Windows send these messages to any DOS file you specify.) The actual string is sent in one call, and the associated carriage-return/linefeed in the next.

NFY_INCHAR Sent when Windows needs to know how to proceed in response to the NFY_RIP notification. If 0 is returned, the ToolHelp will return "i" (ignore) to the Windows kernel. For this notification, the callback function return type is not BOOL; the ASCII value for the character should be returned. For instance, to select abort, you could return "a" from your function.

Here are some points to remember when working with NotifyRegister (note the similarity to the recommendations for working with InterruptRegister):

1. Under Windows 3.0, there can be conflicts between TOOLHELP.DLL and WINDEBUG.DLL (the .DLL used by TDW, CVW, and Multiscope).

NotifyRegister

The undocumented RegisterPtrace function is expecting to be used by only one caller. Since both ToolHelp and WINDEBUG will attempt to use RegisterPtrace under Windows 3.0, ToolHelp attempts to sidestep the problem by determining if the WINDEBUG module is loaded in the system. If so, NotifyRegister will return failure. The end result is that it's not an easy task to debug ToolHelp applications that use NotifyRegister under Windows 3.0. Under Windows 3.1, these problems do not exist, because the TOOLHELPHOOK function in KERNEL provides an alternate, parallel set of services to the RegisterPtrace function.

2. Pass on any Notifications that you don't care about (return 0).

3. ToolHelp only allows one callback function to be installed per task. You can pass in the hTask of your application or 0. If you pass in 0, ToolHelp does a GetCurrentTask() and uses that value.

4. The list of callback functions is a linked list. Each new callback function that's registered is put at the end of the list. This means that the first task to call NotifyRegister will get first crack at the notifications.

5. When InterruptUnregister is called for the last remaining callback function, ToolHelp uninstalls its RegisterPtrace/ToolhelpHook handler.

StackTraceFirst

StackTraceCSIPFirst

StackTraceNext

```
BOOL FAR PASCAL StackTraceFirst
    (STACKTRACEENTRY FAR *lpStackTrace,
    HANDLE hTask);

BOOL FAR PASCAL StackTraceCSIPFirst
    (STACKTRACEENTRY FAR *lpStackTrace,
    WORD wSS, WORD wCS, WORD wIP, WORD wBP);

BOOL FAR PASCAL StackTraceNext
    (STACKTRACEENTRY FAR *lpStackTrace);

typedef struct {
    DWORD dwSize;
    HANDLE hTask;
    WORD wSS;
    WORD wBP;
    WORD wCS;
    WORD wIP;
    HANDLE hModule;
    WORD wSegment;
    WORD wFlags;
    } STACKTRACEENTRY;
```

StackTraceFirst

The StackTraceXXX functions do just what their name implies. StackTraceFirst will get the first stack trace entry for any stack other than your own. StackTraceCSIPFirst is for the case where you wish to walk your own stack (such as in an InterruptRegister call-back function). StackTraceNext has the dirty job of interpreting what's on the stack to find the previous frame.

StackTraceFirst verifies that the hTask passed in corresponds to a valid task database. It then extracts the SS:SP from the field at offset 2 in the Task Database (see chapter 5). It then assumes that SS:SP is pointing to a far stack frame that would have been set up like this:

```
PUSH BP
MOV BP, SP
SUB SP, 10h
```

The WORD at (SP+10h) is AND'ed with 0xFE to zero out the bottom bit, in case it was set to indicate a far stack frame. It is then assigned to the wBP field of the STACKTRACEENTRY structure. The WORDS at (SP+12h) and (SP+14h) are assigned to wIP and wCS, respectively. It is most likely that this is the stack frame that exists for a task whenever the Windows scheduler switches away from it. Essentially, all tasks, other than the current task, are "parked" with this stack frame.

After filling in the CS:IP and SS:BP fields of the STACKTRACEENTRY structure, another internal routine is called to fill in the hModule and wSegment fields. The routine uses the passed-in hTask to find the module table handle. It then looks up the CS in the module table to find the logical segment number to put in the wSegment field. Before all this is done, the CS value is first verified to be in the global heap by making a call to GlobalEntryHandle.

To use StackTraceCSIPFirst, you need to pass a valid SS:BP and CS:IP. These values are just copied into the appropriate fields, and then the same internal routine is called to fill in the hModule and wSegment fields.

StackTraceNext has a tough job to perform. It not only has to find the previous frame on the stack, it also has to somehow figure out whether the stack frame is from a near or a far call.

In a typical stack frame, the WORD at [BP+0] is the value of the BP in the previous frame. ToolHelp makes the following checks to determine if it looks valid:

1. Is the frame for the previous BP within the limit of the SS segment?
2. Is [BP+0] not equal to 0?
3. Is the previous BP greater than the current BP?
4. Is the previous BP within the SP limits in the task database?

The next job is to determine if the new stack frame is from a near CALL or a far CALL. In Windows 3.0, far stack frames were indicated by an odd value at [BP+0]; near stack frames were indicated by an even value. It was essential for this convention to be followed by Real-mode Windows, which had to crawl the stack to search for

StackTraceFirst

code segments that had been discarded. In Windows 3.1, Real mode is no more, so the Windows kernel no longer needs to walk the stack. Thus the odd-BP convention can be disposed of, resulting in savings of space and size.

This gives rise to a new problem, namely how to determine if a stack frame is a near frame or a far frame. StackFrameNext attempts to deal with this situation. If it sees an odd BP value on the stack, it automatically assumes that it's a far frame. If it's an even value, it first assumes that it's a far stack frame and then goes through the following sanity checks on the potential new CS:IP at [BP+2]:

1. Are the ring-level bits in the potential CS equal to the ring-level bits of ToolHelp's code segment?
2. Use LAR on the potential CS. Is the 0x0800 bit on, indicating a code segment?
3. Is the potential IP within the segment limit of the potential CS?

If any of these tests fail, then ToolHelp treats the frame as a near stack frame. It is readily obvious that the above method is not foolproof. It's quite possible that a near frame could slide through the sanity checks, creating a bogus CS:IP in the STACKTRACEENTRY structure. The moral of the story is that it's a good idea to use the "Odd-BP" stack frame convention, at least during the debugging stage. At the time of this writing, most compilers always use the odd-BP convention in their code generation. As Windows 3.1 becomes more prevalent, though, the option to dispose of the odd-BP code generation is sure to become a popular one, making life harder for StackTraceNext, and making its results a little less reliable.

TaskGetCSIP
TaskSetCSIP

```
DWORD FAR PASCAL TaskGetCSIP
    (HANDLE hTask);

DWORD FAR PASCAL TaskSetCSIP
    (HANDLE hTask, WORD wCS, WORD wIP);
```

These functions let you obtain and modify the CS:IP for any task in the system, except the one currently running.

TaskGetCSIP is an extremely simple function. It compares the hTask passed in to the current task (returned by GetCurrentTask). If they're the same, it returns failure, as it should (after all, if you really want to move your own program's CS:IP, there are easier ways to do it!). It then gets the current SS:SP from the task database and obtains the CS:IP values from the stack frame, discussed previously in the StackTraceFirst description.

TaskSetCSIP is almost identical to TaskGetCSIP, except that it *changes* the CS:IP values in the stack frame instead of reading them. This is one of the few functions that is not "read-only" in ToolHelp. When the task is scheduled to run, it will start at the CS:IP that you set with this function. Note: No sanity checking is done on the CS:IP that you pass in, so be careful.

TaskSwitch

```
BOOL FAR PASCAL TaskSwitch
    (HANDLE hTask, DWORD dwNewCSIP);
```

TaskSwitch enables you to execute some arbitrary section of code, while running as some arbitrary task. Effectively, it provides a SetCurrentTask( ) function for Windows.

For instance, let's say you have a DLL that's in use by multiple tasks. You want the DLL to perform file I/O. The problem is that the file handles opened by one task are not available to another task: Windows uses the PSP to keep a separate file handle table for each task, just as in plain-vanilla DOS (the per-task PSP is kept, of course, in the Task Database; see chapter 5).

With TaskSwitch, you can switch to the task that opened the files before doing the file I/O and then switch back to the original task.

The sequence of events when using TaskSwitch should look something like this:

1. Use TaskGetCSIP to save the address of the switched-to task in a global variable that will be accessible when running as the new task.
2. Use TaskSwitch to switch to the desired address and task.
3. When done with your work in the desired task, use a JMP instruction to continue execution at the address saved away in step 1. Eventually, the original task will be scheduled again, and control will pick up after the call to TaskSwitch.

How does TaskSwitch work? A good question. It's a nifty excursion into the bowels of undocumented Windows. First, TaskSwitch ensures that you're not asking it to switch to the current task. Then it verifies that the hTask passed in is a valid task handle (by looking for the 'TD' signature in the Task Database). Next, it does a TaskSetCSIP, using the address of an internal routine. It then stores the passed-in CS:IP into two global variables. It then bumps up the event counter field at offset 6 in the hTask's database to ensure that the Windows scheduler will run it. Finally, it does a DirectedYield(hTask). We now close our eyes, tap our heels together three times, and we magically appear at the start of the internal routine, running as the new task.

Now what happens? First, four bytes are subtracted from SP, and then a standard stack frame is set up with PUSH BP /MOV BP,SP. What are the four bytes for? Well, it seems that the saved away CS:IP is put in those four bytes. The end result is that it now looks like a stack frame for a far CALL! The next thing done is to decrement the

TaskSwitch

event count in the current task database. This restores the event count to what it was before the DirectedYield. Last, the stack frame is removed and a RETF is executed. It is the RETF, in conjunction with the tweaked return address, that actually starts execution at the CS:IP that was passed to the TaskSwitch function.

TerminateApp

```
void FAR PASCAL TerminateApp
    (HANDLE hTask, WORD wFlags);
```

TerminateApp is useful primarily to debuggers and post-mortem tools. A debugger would call TerminateApp and pass it the NO_UAE_BOX flag. By doing so, it makes it look like a graceful termination. It's not. Internally, TerminateApp uses quite a few undocumented functions and has Windows version-specific code.

First, TerminateApp checks to see if the hTask passed in is either 0 or the current task, as returned by GetCurrentTask. If it's not, it uses TaskSwitch to force itself to be running as the hTask that was passed in. If TaskSwitch was used, it then zeros out the DWORD at offset 54 in the Task Queue, but only if it's running under Windows 3.0.

Next, the wFlags parameter is checked for the NO_UAE_BOX flag. If it's set, then the word at offset 18h in the Task Database is OR'ed with 02h. This sets a flag which tells Windows not to put up a UAE box in the event of this task generating a UAE.

With that done, the app is terminated with a call to FatalAppExit(0,0).

If for some reason you return from the call to FatalAppExit (see the SDK documentation for details), then an undocumented flag in the wFlags parameter is inspected. The flag is the high bit (0x8000), and if it's set, it tells ToolHelp to not call the task signal proc (see the entry for SetTaskSignalProc in chapter 5). Otherwise, the task signal proc is called, and, finally, DOS Exit (INT 21h AH=4Ch) is called with an exit code of 0FFh in the AL register.

There is a problem with calling TerminateApp for a task under Windows 3.0, if InitApp has not been called yet in the task's startup code. InitApp creates a message queue for a task. Under Windows 3.0, TerminateApp always tries to write to offset 54h in the message queue (see chapter 5). But if the massage queue doesn't exist because InitApp hasn't been called yet, this will cause a UAE. This is a problem for debuggers that are stepping through startup code. In 3.1, the documented GetSystemDebugState() function can return the value SDS_NOTASKQUEUE.

TimerCount

```
BOOL FAR PASCAL TimerCount
    (TIMERINFO FAR *lpTimer);

typedef struct {
```

```
DWORD dwSize;
DWORD dwmsSinceStart;
DWORD dwmsThisVM;
} TIMERINFO;
```

TimerCount, as its name implies, will be most often used by programs that need to time events. TimerCount tries to get more accurate timings than available via SYSTEM timers, which don't reprogram the 8253 (see chapter 9).

Internally, it's relatively simple. If Windows is running in Enhanced mode, a call is made to INT 2Fh, with AX = 1684h and BX=5. This returns the address of the VTD (Virtual Timer Device) entry point. It then calls the VTD entry point with AX=0101h and stores the return value in the "dwmsSinceStart" field of the TIMERINFO structure. A second call is made, this time with AX=0102h, and the result is stored in the "dwmsThisVM" field.

In Standard mode, a check is first made to see if the timeGetTime() function in MMSYSTEM.DLL was successfully found via GetProcAddress(). If so, then TimerCount() calls timeGetTime(), and stores the information in the TIMERINFO structure. If timeGetTime() isn't found, a call is made to GetTickCount. The DWORD returned is stored in dwmsSinceStart. Then a series of port I/O instructions is made to determine the number of milliseconds that have transpired since the last timer tick. This value is added to dwmsSinceStart. Last, the dwmsSinceStart is copied into dwmsThisVM.

Sample Program: WinWalk

The WinWalk program demonstrates use of the Windows data structure functions in ToolHelp. It displays the module list, the task list, the window class list, and the global heap. The USER and GDI local heaps are not included, as they are handled in the separate USERWALK and GDIWALK examples in chapters 6 and 8.

WinWalk uses the WINIO library (described in chapter 4); it makes particularly heavy use of the WINIO clickable-lines facility. It is written in Borland C++ 3.0 small model.

Running WinWalk WinWalk uses the WINIO library to create a menu of available reports in the main window. By selecting items from the main menu, you can display secondary windows that walk the appropriate data structures via ToolHelp.

Global Heap, Hex Dump, and Local Walk
The WinWalk Global Heap window looks like this:

```
(Double-click to dump first 1k of a block)
HANDLE   SIZE   OWNER     TYPE
0000        0             SENTINEL
011F     A940   KERNEL    CODE SEG 01h
0796       40   GDI       TASK MEM ALLOCATION
```

```
1577        480    MMSYSTEM    CODE SEG 01h
1537         20    MMSYSTEM    DATA
1517        140    TIMER       CODE SEG 02h
1507        240    TIMER       DGROUP
1527         20    WINFILE     TASK MEM ALLOCATION
14AF        200    WINOLDAP    TASK DATABASE
1497        120    USER        TASK MEM ALLOCATION
147E         40    WINOLDAP    CODE SEG 03h
136F        200    SH          TASK DATABASE
... etc. ...
```

Double clicking on any of the items displays an additional window with a hex dump of the first 1K bytes. For example, if you double click on a Task Database, you can see its current directory (\SICE in the example below), the instance thunk array signature ('PT'), the module name (DRWATSON in this example), the 'TD' signature, and the PSP (note the bytes CD 20 on the last line, corresponding to an INT 20h instruction at the start of a PSP):

```
12F7        200    DRWATSON    TASK DATABASE

0000: 07 08 92 2A CF 12 00 00 00 00 00 00 F7 12 00 00    ...*............
0010: 00 00 00 00 00 00 00 00 00 00 00 03 CE 12 7F 13    ................
0020: DF 12 07 08 00 00 25 61 1F 01 C5 16 B7 12 00 00    ......%a........
0030: 00 00 17 1D 77 03 04 00 3B 00 08 00 3B 00 0C 00    ....w...;...;...
0040: 3B 00 0E 00 3B 00 7C 00 3B 00 EA 00 3B 00 00 00    ;...;.|.;...;...
0050: 00 00 00 00 00 00 00 00 00 00 00 00 00 00 00 00    ................
0060: EF 12 80 00 EF 12 82 5C 53 49 43 45 00 00 00 00    .......\SICE....
0070: 00 00 00 00 00 00 00 00 00 00 00 00 00 00 00 00    ................
0080: 00 00 00 00 00 00 00 00 00 00 00 00 00 00 00 00    ................
0090: 00 00 00 00 00 00 00 00 00 00 00 00 00 00 00 00    ................
00A0: 00 00 00 00 00 00 00 00 36 00 00 00 00 00 00 00    ........6.......
00B0: E7 12 00 00 50 54 00 00 C0 00 00 00 00 00 00 00    ....PT..........
00C0: C8 00 00 00 00 00 00 00 D0 00 00 00 00 00 00 00    ................
00D0: D8 00 00 00 00 00 00 00 E0 00 00 00 00 00 00 00    ................
00E0: E8 00 00 00 00 00 00 00 F0 00 00 00 00 00 00 00    ................
00F0: 00 00 44 52 57 41 54 53 4F 4E 54 44 00 00 00 00    ..DRWATSONTD....
0100: CD 20 EF 13 00 9A F0 FE 1D F0 9B 18 44 18 A0 0B    . ..........D...
... etc. ...
```

If the item you click on contains a local heap, WinWalk will also display a Local Walk window. For example:

```
12AF        340    ToolHelp    DGROUP

HANDLE    ADDR    SIZE    TYPE
0144      0144    0008    FIXED
0150      0150    002C    FIXED
0180      0180    000C    FIXED
0190      0190    000C    FIXED
01A0      01A0    0008    FIXED
0000      01AC    0188    FREE
```

Walks of the USER and GDI local heaps are performed by the USERWALK and GDIWALK programs, elsewhere in this book.

Task List

The WinWalk Task List window shows each task on the system. For each task, Win-Walk displays the module name, task handle, module handle, instance handle (DGROUP), and the module name of its parent:

```
Task list:
NAME        HTASK   HMOD   HINST   PARENT
SH          136F    14B7   1346    WINFILE
DRWATSON    12F7    137F   12CE    WINFILE
WINOLDAP    14AF    14C7   146E    WINFILE
WINFILE     0807    0547   17AE
WINWALK     11FF    1217   122E    SH
```

Module List

The WinWalk Module List window shows the modules on the system. The handle, the filename, the module name (which is not necessarily the same as the filename; see the example below), and the reference count are shown:

```
Module list:
NAME        HMOD    COUNT   FILENAME
KERNEL      0117    20      C:\WIN31\SYSTEM\KRNL386.EXE
SYSTEM      0147    13      C:\WIN31\SYSTEM\SYSTEM.DRV
KEYBOARD    014F    13      C:\WIN31\SYSTEM\KEYBOARD.DRV
MOUSE       0167    11      C:\WIN31\SYSTEM\MOUSE.DRV
DISPLAY     01C7    12      C:\WIN31\SYSTEM\VGAMONO.DRV
SOUND       01DF    11      C:\WIN31\SYSTEM\MMSOUND.DRV
COMM        022F    11      C:\WIN31\SYSTEM\COMM.DRV
FONTS       032F    2       C:\WIN31\SYSTEM\VGASYS.FON
OEMFONTS    035F    2       C:\WIN31\SYSTEM\VGAOEM.FON
GDI         036F    11      C:\WIN31\SYSTEM\GDI.EXE
FIXFONTS    0357    1       C:\WIN31\SYSTEM\VGAFIX.FON
USER        037F    10      C:\WIN31\SYSTEM\USER.EXE
... etc. ...
```

Class List

Finally, the WinWalk Class List window shows all the window classes on the system. For example

```
Class list:
OWNER       INST    NAME
WINWALK     11D7    winio_wcmain
SH          14B7    winio_wcmain
WINOLDAP    14C7    WOAFontPreview
WINOLDAP    14C7    WOAWinPreview
WINOLDAP    14C7    tty
MMSYSTEM    0817    #42
... etc. ...
```

```
USER       037F    #32772
USER       037F    #32771
USER       037F    #32769
USER       037F    MDIClient
USER       037F    ComboBox
USER       037F    ComboLBox
USER       037F    ScrollBar
USER       037F    ListBox
USER       037F    Edit
USER       037F    #32770
USER       037F    Static
USER       037F    Button
USER       037F    #32768
```

The WinWalk Code   The main() function in WinWalk creates strings for each option on the main menu and calls AppendMenu() to add them. At the same time, it installs a handler function for each selection. Because so much code for setting up each secondary window display is common, the menu handlers all point to the same function.

The names of each item on the main menu are obtained by iterating through WalkFunctionArray[]. WalkFunctionArray[] is an array of WALKFUNCTION structures. Each structure contains information specific to a report. In addition to the name of the report, the structure also contains a pointer to the appropriate "walking" function. Each structure also contains a reasonable value for the maximum buffer size necessary to display all the information in the report.

In the menu-handling function, MenuHandler() (great name, huh?), the appropriate report to display is determined via the menuID parameter, which contains a unique value for each different report. In all cases, a new window is created, and the title and buffer size are set according to the values in WalkFunctionArray[]. Next, window refreshes are turned off in the new window in order to make output go as quickly as possible and, more important, to make sure that the state of Windows doesn't change while ToolHelp is walking some structure. Then a call is made through the function pointer stored in the WalkFunctionArray[]. After the report function finishes, window refreshes are turned back on.

The heap/list walking functions themselves are very simple. They each initialize the "dwSize" field of their specific ToolHelp structure, and then go through the classic find-first/find-next loop. After obtaining each new list element, selected fields are displayed. To do the walk, the following ToolHelp services are used:

Global Heap walk	GLOBALENTRY	GlobalFirst	GlobalNext
Local Heap walk	LOCALENTRY	LocalFirst	LocalNext
Task walk	TASKENTRY	TaskFirst	TaskNext
Module walk	MODULEENTRY	ModuleFirst	ModuleNext
Class walk	CLASSENTRY	ClassFirst	ClassNext

ToolHelp certainly has a lot more order and symmetry than the underlying undocumented data structures!

In the Global Heap display, a double-click handler is installed to provide additional useful information on a selected block. The handler uses sscanf() to retrieve the handle value and block length from the clicked-on line. Next, the handle value is converted to a selector using the ToolHelp GlobalHandleToSel() function. Following that, the selector value is tested to see if it is still a "legal" selector. This is necessary, because a program may have terminated, or deallocated a global memory block, without the block being removed from the Global Heap window display. After verifying that the selector value is good, the MemDump function is called to display up to the first 1024 bytes of the block in a new window. If the block contains a valid local heap, LocalHeapWalk() is called to create an additional window that walks the local heap of the selected block.

The GetModuleNameFromHandle() function is a "helper" function that's used in a variety of contexts. Given a handle to the owner of a block, it returns the module name of the program that it's owned by. Memory blocks that are shared by all instances of a program (such as code segments) will have the module handle as their owner. For this case, a call to ModuleFindHandle() will return success, and we have the module name. On the other hand, blocks that were allocated by a task (via GlobalAlloc(), for instance), will have a task handle as their owner. If ModuleFindHandle() returns failure, them the handle might be a task handle, so TaskFindHandle() is tried. If it succeeds, the module name is extracted from the TASKENTRY structure.

```
//=================================
//  WinWalk, by Matt Pietrek, 1992
//  File: WINWALK.C
//  With changes/suggestions by
//  David Maxey & Andrew Schulman
//=================================

#include <windows.h>
#include <stdio.h>
#include <string.h>
#include <dos.h>
#include <ctype.h>
#include "toolhelp.h"
#include "winio.h"

typedef struct _WALKFUNCTION {
    char *  description;          // Description of function
    void    (*display_func)(void); // Pointer to display function
    WORD    displayBuffSize;      // Size in bytes of display buffer
} WALKFUNCTION;

void ModuleWalk(void);
void TaskWalk(void);
void ClassWalk(void);
void GlobalHeapWalk(void);

void GlobalHeapDoubleClickHandler(HWND, LPSTR, int);
void MemDump(LPSTR, WORD, LPSTR, LPSTR);
void LocalHeapWalk(WORD sel, LPSTR);
```

```
char szModuleList[] = "Modules";
char szTaskList[]   = "Tasks";
char szClassList[]  = "Classes";
char szGlobalHeap[] = "Global Heap";

// Create an array of WALKFUNCTIONs

WALKFUNCTION     WalkFunctionArray[] = {
    { szModuleList, ModuleWalk,    2048     },
    { szTaskList,   TaskWalk,      2048     },
    { szClassList,  ClassWalk,     2048     },
    { szGlobalHeap, GlobalHeapWalk, 65535L  }
};

#define WALKFUNCTIONCOUNT \
    (sizeof(WalkFunctionArray) / sizeof(WALKFUNCTION))

char UnknownString[] = "<UNKNOWN>";

char *GlobalEntry_Resources[] = {
"User defined",     // 0
"Cursor",           // 1
"Bitmap",           // 2
"Icon Component",   // 3
"Menu",             // 4
"Dialog",           // 5
"String table",     // 6
"Font directory",   // 7
"Font",             // 8
"Accelerators",     // 9
"RC data",          // 10
"Error table",      // 11
"Group cursor",     // 12
UnknownString,      // 13
"Group icon",       // 14
"Name table"        // 15
};

char HelpText[] =
"WinWalk is a simple demonstration of the ToolHelp API\n"
"\n"
"By clicking on the options on the main menu, it can show you:\n"
"- The list of EXE/DLL modules in the system\n"
"- The list of running tasks\n"
"- The list of registered windows classes in the USER heap\n"
"- The contents of the global heap\n"
"\n"
"Additionally, up to the first 1K of memory in each global\n"
"memory block can be viewed by double clicking on the\n"
"appropriate line in the global heap window. If the block\n"
"selected has a local heap, an additional window is popped\n"
"up to display the local heap\n"
"\n"
"The USER and GDI heaps are not shown in detail here, as\n"
"they are shown in more detail in a separate sample program\n";
```

```
//------------------------------------------------
// Given a "owner" handle, return back the
// name of the module. Use ToolHelp functions
// To avoid undocumented methods
//------------------------------------------------
char *GetModuleNameFromHandle(HANDLE handle)
{
    MODULEENTRY me;
    TASKENTRY   te;
    static char name[40];

    me.dwSize = sizeof(me);
    if ( ModuleFindHandle(&me, handle) )
    {
        strcpy(name, me.szModule);
        return name;
    }

    te.dwSize = sizeof(te);
    if ( TaskFindHandle(&te, handle) )
    {
        strcpy(name, te.szModule);
        return name;
    }

    name[0] = 0;
    return name;
}

char *ResourceName(WORD handle)
{
    if ( handle > GD_MAX_RESOURCE )
        return UnknownString;
    return GlobalEntry_Resources[handle];
}

char *GetGlobalBlockType(WORD type, WORD wData)
{
    static char description[40];

    switch ( type )
    {
        case GT_UNKNOWN : strcpy(description, "TASK MEM ALLOCATION");
                          break;
        case GT_DGROUP  : strcpy(description, "DGROUP"); break;
        case GT_DATA    : strcpy(description, "DATA"); break;
        case GT_CODE    : sprintf(description,"CODE SEG %02Xh", wData);
                          break;
        case GT_TASK    : strcpy(description, "TASK DATABASE"); break;
        case GT_RESOURCE: sprintf(description,"RESOURCE %s",
                          ResourceName(wData) ); break;
        case GT_MODULE  : strcpy(description, "MODULE TABLE"); break;
        case GT_FREE    : strcpy(description, "FREE"); break;
        case GT_INTERNAL: strcpy(description, "INTERNAL"); break;
```

```
            case GT_SENTINEL: strcpy(description, "SENTINEL"); break;
            case GT_BURGERMASTER : strcpy(description, "BURGERMASTER"); break;
            default          : strcpy(description, UnknownString);
    }

    return description;
}

void GlobalHeapWalk(void)
{
    GLOBALENTRY ge;
    BOOL ok;

    printf("Global heap:\n"
    "(Double-click to dump block)\n"
    "HANDLE   SIZE  OWNER     TYPE\n");

    ge.dwSize = sizeof(ge);
    ok = GlobalFirst(&ge, GLOBAL_ALL);
    while ( ok )
    {
        printf("%04X    %5lX  %-8s  %s\n",
            ge.hBlock, ge.dwBlockSize,
            GetModuleNameFromHandle(ge.hOwner),
            GetGlobalBlockType(ge.wType, ge.wData));

        ok = GlobalNext(&ge, GLOBAL_ALL);
    }

    winio_setlinefn(winio_current(), GlobalHeapDoubleClickHandler);
}

void ClassWalk(void)
{
    CLASSENTRY ce;
    BOOL ok;

    printf("Class list:\n");
    printf("OWNER     INST  NAME\n");

    ce.dwSize = sizeof(ce);
    ok = ClassFirst(&ce);
    while ( ok )
    {
        printf("%-8s  %04X  %s\n",
            GetModuleNameFromHandle(ce.hInst),
            ce.hInst, ce.szClassName);

        ok = ClassNext(&ce);
    }
}

void TaskWalk(void)
{
    TASKENTRY te;
```

```
    BOOL ok;

    printf("Task list:\n");
    printf("NAME       HTASK  HMOD  HINST  PARENT\n");

    te.dwSize = sizeof(te);
    ok = TaskFirst(&te);
    while ( ok )
    {
        printf("%-8s  %04X   %04X  %04X   %s\n",
            te.szModule, te.hTask, te.hModule, te.hInst,
            GetModuleNameFromHandle(te.hTaskParent));

        ok = TaskNext(&te);
    }
}

void ModuleWalk(void)
{
    MODULEENTRY me;
    BOOL ok;

    printf("Module list:\n");
    printf("NAME       HMOD   COUNT FILENAME\n");

    me.dwSize = sizeof(me);
    ok = ModuleFirst(&me);
    while ( ok )
    {
        printf("%-8s  %04X   %2u     %s\n",
            me.szModule, me.hModule, me.wcUsage, me.szExePath);

        ok = ModuleNext(&me);
    }
}

// Returns whether a global memory block contains
// a local heap. It does this by trying to
// initiate a local walk of the passed in block
BOOL ContainsLocalHeap(WORD seg)
{
    LOCALENTRY le;
    le.dwSize = sizeof(le);
    return LocalFirst(&le, seg);
}

void LocalHeapWalk(WORD sel, LPSTR description)
{
    GLOBALENTRY ge;
    LOCALENTRY le;
    HWND hWndNew, hWndSav;
    char buffer[120];
    char * szFlags;
    BOOL ok;
```

```
        // Call GlobalEntryHandle() to get the "owning" block
        ge.dwSize = sizeof(ge);
        ok = GlobalEntryHandle(&ge, sel);

        // Create a title for the window, create a new window,
        // and save away the old current window
        sprintf(buffer, "Local heap: %04X  %s",
            sel, GetModuleNameFromHandle(ge.hOwner) );

        hWndNew = winio_window(buffer, 32768L, WW_HASMENU);

        if (!hWndNew)
            MessageBox(NULL, "Not Enough Memory", "Error",
                MB_OK | MB_ICONEXCLAMATION);

        hWndSav = winio_setcurrent(hWndNew);
        winio_setpaint(hWndNew, FALSE);

        // Print the header information
        printf("%s\n\n", description);

        printf("HANDLE  ADDR  SIZE  TYPE\n");

        // Walk the local heap
        le.dwSize = sizeof(le);
        ok = LocalFirst(&le, sel);
        while ( ok )
        {
            switch ( le.wFlags )
            {
                case LF_FIXED:    szFlags = "FIXED"; break;
                case LF_FREE:     szFlags = "FREE"; break;
                case LF_MOVEABLE: szFlags = "MOVEABLE"; break;
                default:          szFlags = "";
            }

            printf("%04X    %04X  %04X  %s\n",
                le.hHandle, le.wAddress, le.wSize, szFlags);

            ok = LocalNext(&le);
        }

        // Turn painting back on, and put things back
        // into a sensible state of affairs
        winio_setpaint(hWndNew, TRUE);
        winio_home(hWndNew);
        winio_setcurrent(hWndSav);
}

// Define how wide the memory dump will be
#define WIDTH 16

void MemDump(LPSTR fp, WORD bytes, LPSTR addr, LPSTR description)
{
    HWND hWndNew, hWndSav;
```

```
        LPSTR p;
        WORD i, j, c;
        char buffer[120];

        // Create a title for the window, create a new window,
        // and save away the old current window
        sprintf(buffer, "Dump: %Fp - %04X bytes", fp, bytes);
        hWndNew = winio_window(buffer, bytes * 5, WW_HASMENU);

        if (!hWndNew)
            MessageBox(NULL, "Not Enough Memory", "Error",
                MB_OK | MB_ICONEXCLAMATION);

        hWndSav = winio_setcurrent(hWndNew);
        winio_setpaint(hWndNew, FALSE);
        printf("%s\n\n", description);

        // Dense code to actually do the memory dumping
        for (i=0; i<bytes; i += WIDTH)
        {
            c = ((bytes-i) > WIDTH) ? WIDTH : bytes-i;
            printf("%04X: ", addr+i);
            for (j=c, p=fp+i; j--; p++)
                printf("%02X ", (unsigned char) *p);
            for (j=WIDTH-c; j--; )  // pad out on last line
                printf("   ");
            putchar(' ');
            for (j=c, p=fp+i; j--; p++)
                putchar( isprint(*p) ? *p : '.' );
            putchar('\n');
        }

        // Turn painting back on, and put things back
        // into a sensible state of affairs
        winio_setpaint(hWndNew, TRUE);
        winio_home(hWndNew);
        winio_setcurrent(hWndSav);
}

void GlobalHeapDoubleClickHandler(HWND hwnd, LPSTR line, int lineNum)
{
        WORD wSel;
        DWORD blockSize=0;
        WORD dumpSize;
        char buffer[80];
        int retVal;

        // Make a local copy of the line as it appears in the global
        // heap window. sscanf() in the handle and block size
        lstrcpy(buffer, line);
        retVal = sscanf(buffer, "%04X    %5lX ", &wSel, &blockSize);
        dumpSize = min(blockSize, 1024L);

        // Verify that we got sensible values from the line
        if ( (retVal != 2) || ( dumpSize == 0 ) )
```

```
    {
        MessageBox(NULL, "Not a valid line", "Error",
                MB_OK | MB_ICONEXCLAMATION);
        return;
    }

    // Convert the handle to a selector we can use
    wSel = GlobalHandleToSel(wSel);

    // Determine if the selector is O.K. Display an error
    // message and get out if not
    asm     lar     ax, wSel
    asm     jz      Selector_OK

    MessageBox(NULL, "Selector not valid", "Error",
                MB_OK | MB_ICONEXCLAMATION);
    return;

    // We get here if the selector is O.K. Call MemDump
    // to create a new window and display the memory.
    // If there is a local heap in the block, display
    // it in a local heap window as well
Selector_OK:

    MemDump(MK_FP(wSel, 0), dumpSize, MK_FP(wSel,0), line);

    if ( ContainsLocalHeap(wSel) )
        LocalHeapWalk(wSel, line);
}

void MenuHandler(HWND hwnd, WORD menuID)
{
    HWND newWindow;
    WORD selected;
    char buffer[80];

    selected = menuID-1;

    // Create an appropriate title for the new window,
    // then create a new window with an appropriately
    // sized buffer.
    sprintf(buffer, "WinWalk: %s",
        WalkFunctionArray[selected].description);
    newWindow = winio_window(buffer,
        WalkFunctionArray[selected].displayBuffSize,
        WW_HASMENU);
    winio_setcurrent(newWindow);

    // Turn off repaints
    winio_setbusy();
    winio_setpaint(winio_current(), FALSE);

    // Call the appropriate display function
    WalkFunctionArray[selected].display_func();
```

```
        // Turn repaints back on, and position at the top of the info
        winio_setpaint(winio_current(), TRUE);
        winio_resetbusy();
        winio_home(newWindow);
}

int main(int argc, char *argv[] )
{
        char buffer[40];
        unsigned i;

        buffer[0] = '&';

        winio_defwindowsize(MAKELONG(55, 10));

        // Create the main menu, and assign selection handlers
        for ( i=0; i < WALKFUNCTIONCOUNT; i++)
        {
            // make a string with an '&', then a description of
            // the display that it will trigger
            strcpy(&buffer[1], WalkFunctionArray[i].description);

            AppendMenu(winio_hmenumain(__hMainWnd), MF_STRING,
                i+1, buffer);

            winio_setmenufunc(__hMainWnd, i + 1, (MENU_FUNC) MenuHandler);
        }

        DrawMenuBar(__hMainWnd);
        printf(HelpText);
        return 0;
}
```

Suggestions for Enhancements With some user-interface work, WinWalk could become the basis of a full-blown HEAPWALK program.

A simple way to do this would be to install "clickable-line" handlers for all the various heap and list windows. For the local heaps, if you select an item, it might pop up a child window with information (or a display) about the item. For the global heap, if you select a task database, it might pop up a window that displays the information in a more readable form than just a simple memory dump. It could include undocumented information that ToolHelp doesn't give you, but that is described elsewhere in this book. Complete heapwalk-type programs will need to supplement a basic core of ToolHelp with some selected use of undocumented Windows; the two complement each other nicely.

Another nifty utility would be a "heap-diff" program. The Microsoft SDK says that you can check for resource "leaks" by using HEAPWALK to compare the GDI heaps before and after your application runs. But there's no need to do this by hand, when your computer can do the hard work. For example, the user could select a "start" button in this heap-diff program before running the application. The heap-diff application could walk the GDI heap and store away the block handles. After the user terminates the app, they could select a "stop" button. The heap-diff would then walk the heap again. Any blocks that aren't in the original walk can be considered "left-over." The same idea applies to the USER local heap.

The Windows Task Manager is really just a list of top level windows. With the Task list functions, you could write a real "Task Manager." To kill a task in the list, use TerminateApp() from ToolHelp. To give a better idea of exactly which program is running, display the full pathname of the .EXE file for each task. You can do this by calling ModuleFindHandle, using the hModule that's in the TASKENTRY structure. To get the top-level windows for a task, you can use EnumTaskWindows().

Sample Program: Coroner

The Coroner program shows the use of InterruptNotify, the stack trace functions, and the module and task walking functions. Conceptually, it is similar to Dr. Watson and WinSpector. When an exception occurs, it writes out information about the faulting program to a disk file. The disk file can then be examined for clues about where the problem occurred and why. The Coroner is written in Borland C++ 3.0 small model.

Running Coroner

To use the Coroner, simply invoke it while running under Windows. It will immediately iconize itself. If you double click on its icon, it will bring up a small copyright dialog box. That's all it does ordinarily. It comes alive when a UAE occurs. Before you see the UAE box, the Coroner has been called and it has written its information out to its log file. After you remove the UAE box, you'll see another dialog box, which informs you that there was an exception and what the faulting application's module name is. You can then go look at the CORONER.LOG file, which is in the Windows directory (usually C:\WINDOWS). You can cross reference the logical addresses in the stack trace section with your .MAP file and see where in the code the exception occurred.

A typical CORONER.LOG file (with some detail removed) looks like the following. In this example, a program called CALLFUNC made an illegal Windows KERNEL call:

```
Coroner exception report - 1/09/1992 13:19:41
Exception 13 at KERNEL 0117:2D6C (0001:2D6C) (TASK=CALLFUNC)
Stack Trace:
0  KERNEL     CS:IP 0117:2D6C (0001:2D6C)  SS:BP 1297:25A8
1  CALLFUNC   CS:IP 129F:065B (0001:065B)  SS:BP 1297:25CE
2  CALLFUNC   CS:IP 129F:0938 (0001:0938)  SS:BP 1297:2708
3  CALLFUNC   CS:IP 129F:0AD0 (0001:0AD0)  SS:BP 1297:2816
4  CALLFUNC   CS:IP 129F:00A3 (0001:00A3)  SS:BP 1297:2824
Registers:
AX   000B
BX   D88E
CX   0000
DX   0739
SI   D888
```

```
DI  25A0
SP  2594
BP  25A8
IP  2D6C
FL  0286
CS  0117   Limit: B15F   execute/read
DS  00E7   Limit: 1FFF   read/write
ES  1297   Limit: 383F   read/write
SS  1297   Limit: 383F   read/write
Tasks:
C:\WIN31.B2\SYSTEM\WINOA386.MOD
     Module: WINOLDAP  hModule: 1437   hTask: 141F   hInstance: 13DE
C:\UNDOCWIN\TOOLHELP\CORONER.EXE
     Module: CORONER   hModule: 12C7   hTask: 123F   hInstance: 1216
C:\WIN31.B2\WINFILE.EXE
     Module: WINFILE   hModule: 053F   hTask: 179F   hInstance: 16EE
C:\WINSERV\CALLFUNC.EXE
     Module: CALLFUNC  hModule: 12CF   hTask: 12BF   hInstance: 1296
Modules:
C:\WIN31.B2\SYSTEM\KRNL386.EXE
     Module: KERNEL    hModule: 010F   reference count: 19
C:\WIN31.B2\SYSTEM\SYSTEM.DRV
     Module: SYSTEM    hModule: 013F   reference count: 11
........
Heaps:
USER  Free  93%
GDI   Free  85%
System info:
Running in enhanced mode under Windows 3.10 debug version
CPU: 80386
Largest Free memory block: 14036992 bytes
Total linear memory space: 15728 K
Free linear memory space : 13708 K
Swap file Pages: 4c3 (4876 K)
```

Note: ToolHelp does not get called when a DOS box crashes (the "stop-box" dialog). This means that the Coroner, like Dr. Watson, cannot trap exceptions in the DOS box. This requires a debugger, such as NuMega's Soft-ICE for Windows, or a virtual device driver, such as WINX, written by Brett Salter of Periscope.

The Coroner Code

The Coroner code is split into several files. The file CORONER.C contains the WinMain and the user interface code.

```
//==================================
// Coroner, by Matt Pietrek, 1992
// File: CORONER.C
//==================================

#include <windows.h>
#include <stdio.h>
#include <string.h>
```

```
#include "coroner.h"

char AppName[]       = "CORONER";

char LogFileName[MAX_PATH_LENGTH];
char ExceptionTaskName[14];

HANDLE HInstance;
HANDLE HCoronerWnd;
char ERROR_CAPTION[] = "Problem!!!";

long FAR PASCAL _export CoronerDialogProc(HWND hDlg, WORD message,
    WORD wParam, DWORD lParam)
{
    char buffer[128];

    switch ( message )
    {
        case WM_COMMAND:
            if ( wParam == IDOK )
            {
                CloseWindow(hDlg);
                return TRUE;
            }
            break;

        case WM_CORONER_FILEOPEN_ERROR :
            MessageBox
            (
                hDlg,
                "CORONER could not open a .LOG file",
                ERROR_CAPTION,
                MB_OK
            );
            break;

        case WM_CORONER_EXCEPTION :
            sprintf(buffer, "Exception %u in %s", wParam,
                ExceptionTaskName);
            MessageBox(hDlg, buffer, AppName, MB_OK);
            break;

        case WM_DESTROY:
            PostQuitMessage(0);
            return 0;
    }

    return DefWindowProc(hDlg, message, wParam, lParam);
}

void GetProgramVariables(void)
{
    char WindowsDirectory[MAX_PATH_LENGTH];
    int i;
```

```
        GetWindowsDirectory(WindowsDirectory, MAX_PATH_LENGTH);

        i = strlen(WindowsDirectory);

        if ( WindowsDirectory[i-1] != '\\' )
        {   // Tack on a '\' if there isn't one
            WindowsDirectory[i] = '\\';
            WindowsDirectory[i+1] = 0;
        }

        strcpy(LogFileName, WindowsDirectory);
        strcat(LogFileName, "CORONER.LOG");
}

int RegisterCoronerWindowClass(void)
{
        WNDCLASS wndclass;
        wndclass.style = CS_HREDRAW | CS_VREDRAW;
        (FARPROC)wndclass.lpfnWndProc = (FARPROC)CoronerDialogProc;
        wndclass.cbClsExtra = 0;
        wndclass.cbWndExtra = DLGWINDOWEXTRA;
        wndclass.hInstance = HInstance;
        wndclass.hIcon = LoadIcon(HInstance,"CORONERICON");
        wndclass.hCursor = LoadCursor(NULL, IDC_ARROW);
        wndclass.hbrBackground = GetStockObject(WHITE_BRUSH);
        wndclass.lpszMenuName = NULL;
        wndclass.lpszClassName = AppName;

        return RegisterClass(&wndclass);
}

int CoronerError(char *msg)
{
        char buffer[128];
        sprintf(buffer, "CORONER %s", msg);
        MessageBox(NULL, buffer, ERROR_CAPTION, MB_OK);
        return 0;
}

#pragma argsused

int PASCAL WinMain( HANDLE hInstance,  HANDLE hPrevInstance,
                    LPSTR lpszCmdLine, int nCmdShow)
{
        HWND hWnd;
        MSG msg;

        HInstance = hInstance;
        if ( hPrevInstance )
            return CoronerError("can only be run once");
        if ( RegisterCoronerWindowClass() == 0)
            return CoronerError("can't create its window class");
        HCoronerWnd = hWnd = CreateDialog( HInstance, "CORONER", NULL, NULL);
        if ( hWnd == 0 )
            return CoronerError("can't create its window");
```

```
    ShowWindow(hWnd, SW_MINIMIZE);

    GetProgramVariables();

    if ( SetupInterruptHandler() == FALSE )
        return CoronerError("can't install a fault handler");

    while ( GetMessage(&msg, NULL, 0, 0) )
    {
        TranslateMessage(&msg);
        DispatchMessage(&msg);
    }

    ShutdownInterruptHandler();

    return 0;
}
```

Coroner's user interface is very simple and is based the classic modeless dialog box made popular by Charles Petzold's HEXCALC program.

The meat of the Coroner application is in XCPTREPT.C, which contains the code for setting up exception handlers, handling the exception, and writing out the information about the exception:

```
//=================================
// Coroner, by Matt Pietrek, 1992
// File: XCPTREPT.C
//=================================

#include <windows.h>
#include <stdarg.h>
#include <string.h>
#include <stdio.h>
#include <alloc.h>
#include <time.h>
#include <dos.h>

#include "toolhelp.h"
#include "coroner.h"

unsigned int Output(char *format, ... );
void DoReportLineFeed(void);
void GetDateTimeString(char *s);

extern HANDLE HCoronerWnd;
extern char LogFileName[];
extern char ExceptionTaskName[];

int   HReportFile=-1;
char pszNull[] = "NULL";

WORD   Exception_AX, Exception_BX, Exception_CX, Exception_DX;
WORD   Exception_SI, Exception_DI;
```

```
WORD     Exception_SP, Exception_BP, Exception_IP, Exception_FLAGS;
WORD     Exception_CS, Exception_DS, Exception_ES, Exception_SS;

char *DescriptorTypes[] =
{
    "read-only",                "read/write",
    "read-only, expand-down",   "read/write, expand-down",
    "execute-only",             "execute/read",
    "execute-only, conforming", "execute/read-only, conforming"
};

int GetLogicalSegmentFromSelector(WORD selector, char *name, WORD *lseg)
{
    GLOBALENTRY ge;
    MODULEENTRY me;

    name[0] = 0;
    *lseg = 0;
    ge.dwSize = sizeof(ge);

    if ( GlobalEntryHandle(&ge, (HANDLE)selector) == 0 )
        return 0;
    if ( ge.wType != GT_CODE )  // Logical segments are only valid for
        return 0;               // code segments
    me.dwSize = sizeof(me);
    if ( ModuleFindHandle(&me, ge.hOwner) == 0 )
        return 0;
    strcpy(name, me.szModule);
    *lseg = ge.wData;
    return 1;
}

void DoWhatHappenedReport(int wNumber)
{
    char moduleName[13];
    WORD lseg;
    TASKENTRY te;

    if ( GetLogicalSegmentFromSelector(Exception_CS, moduleName, &lseg) == 0 )
    {
        Output("Exception %u at unknown address\r\n", wNumber);
    }
    else
    {
        Output
        (
            "Exception %u at %s %04X:%04X (%04X:%04X)",
            wNumber, moduleName, Exception_CS, Exception_IP,
            lseg, Exception_IP
        );
    }

    te.dwSize = sizeof(te);
    if ( TaskFindHandle(&te, GetCurrentTask()) )
    {
```

```
            Output("  (TASK=%s)", te.szModule);
            strcpy(ExceptionTaskName, te.szModule);
    }

    DoReportLineFeed();
    DoReportLineFeed();
}

void DoStackTraceReport(void)
{
    char moduleName[13];
    WORD lseg;
    STACKTRACEENTRY ste;
    BOOL ok;
    WORD stackframe_id = 0; // Keeps track of the current frame in the trace

    Output("Stack Trace:\r\n");
    ste.dwSize = sizeof(ste);
    ok = StackTraceCSIPFirst
        (
            &ste,
            Exception_SS, Exception_CS,
            Exception_IP, Exception_BP
        );

    while ( ok )
    {
        GetLogicalSegmentFromSelector(ste.wCS, moduleName, &lseg);

        Output
        (
            "%-2u %-8s  CS:IP %04X:%04X (%04X:%04X)  SS:BP %04X:%04X\r\n",
            stackframe_id++, moduleName, ste.wCS, ste.wIP, lseg, ste.wIP,
            ste.wSS, ste.wBP
        );

        ok = StackTraceNext(&ste);
    }

    DoReportLineFeed();
}

void DoRegisterReport(void)
{
    WORD CSlimit, DSlimit, ESlimit, SSlimit;
    WORD CSrights, DSrights, ESrights, SSrights;
    Output("Registers:\r\n");

    Output("AX  %04X\r\n", Exception_AX);
    Output("BX  %04X\r\n", Exception_BX);
    Output("CX  %04X\r\n", Exception_CX);
    Output("DX  %04X\r\n", Exception_DX);
    Output("SI  %04X\r\n", Exception_SI);
    Output("DI  %04X\r\n", Exception_DI);
    Output("SP  %04X\r\n", Exception_SP);
```

```
        Output("BP   %04X\r\n", Exception_BP);
        Output("IP   %04X\r\n", Exception_IP);
        Output("FL   %04X\r\n", Exception_FLAGS);

        asm {
                xor     ax, ax
                lsl     ax, word ptr (Exception_CS)
                mov     CSlimit, ax
                lar     ax, word ptr (Exception_CS);
                shr     ax, 9    // Put the type field, minus the "accessed" bit
                and     al, 07h  // in the low bits of AX, and mask them off.
                mov     CSrights, ax

                xor     ax, ax
                lsl     ax, word ptr (Exception_DS)
                mov     DSlimit, ax
                lar     ax, word ptr (Exception_DS);
                shr     ax, 9
                and     al, 07h
                mov     DSrights, ax

                xor     ax, ax
                lsl     ax, word ptr (Exception_ES)
                mov     ESlimit, ax
                lar     ax, word ptr (Exception_ES);
                shr     ax, 9
                and     al, 07h
                mov     ESrights, ax

                xor     ax, ax
                lsl     ax, word ptr (Exception_SS)
                mov     SSlimit, ax
                lar     ax, word ptr (Exception_SS);
                shr     ax, 9
                and     al, 07h
                mov     SSrights, ax
        }

    Output("CS   %04X   Limit: %04X   %s\r\n",
            Exception_CS, CSlimit, DescriptorTypes[CSrights] );
    Output("DS   %04X   Limit: %04X   %s\r\n",
            Exception_DS, DSlimit,
            Exception_DS ? DescriptorTypes[DSrights] : pszNull );
    Output("ES   %04X   Limit: %04X   %s\r\n",
            Exception_ES, ESlimit,
            Exception_ES ? DescriptorTypes[ESrights] : pszNull );
    Output("SS   %04X   Limit: %04X   %s\r\n",
            Exception_SS, SSlimit, DescriptorTypes[SSrights] );

    DoReportLineFeed();
}

void DoTaskReport(void)
{
    char fileName[MAX_PATH_LENGTH];
```

```
    TASKENTRY te;
    BOOL ok;

    Output("Tasks:\r\n");

    te.dwSize = sizeof(te);
    ok = TaskFirst(&te);

    while ( ok )
    {
        GetModuleFileName(te.hModule, fileName, sizeof(fileName));
        Output("%s\r\n", fileName);
        Output(
            "    Module: %-8s  hModule: %04X  "
            "hTask: %04X  hInstance: %04X\r\n",
            te.szModule, te.hModule, te.hTask, te.hInst );
        ok = TaskNext(&te);
    }
    DoReportLineFeed();
}

void DoModuleReport(void)
{
    MODULEENTRY me;
    BOOL ok;

    Output("Modules:\r\n");
    me.dwSize = sizeof(me);
    ok = ModuleFirst(&me);

    while ( ok )
    {
        Output("%s\r\n", me.szExePath );
        Output
        (
            "    Module: %-8s  hModule: %04X  reference count: %u\r\n",
            me.szModule, me.hModule, me.wcUsage
        );
        ok = ModuleNext(&me);
    }

    DoReportLineFeed();
}

void DoHeapsInfoReport(void)
{
    SYSHEAPINFO sysHeapInfo;
    BOOL ok;
    Output("Heaps:\r\n");
    sysHeapInfo.dwSize = sizeof(sysHeapInfo);

    if (! (ok = SystemHeapInfo(&sysHeapInfo)))
        return;

    Output("USER  Free %3u%%\r\n", sysHeapInfo.wUserFreePercent );
```

```
    Output("GDI   Free %3u%%\r\n", sysHeapInfo.wGDIFreePercent );

    DoReportLineFeed();
}

void DoWindowsInfoReport(void)
{
    DWORD winFlags;
    WORD  version;
    MEMMANINFO mmi;
    BOOL ok;
    char *cpuName;

    winFlags = GetWinFlags();
    version = GetVersion();
    Output("System info:\r\n");
    Output("Running in %s mode under Windows %d.%d %s version\r\n",
        (winFlags & WF_STANDARD) ? "Standard" : "Enhanced",
        LOBYTE(version), HIBYTE(version),
        GetSystemMetrics(SM_DEBUG) ? "Debug" : "Retail" );

    if ( winFlags & WF_CPU486 )
        cpuName = "80486";
    else if ( winFlags & WF_CPU386 )
        cpuName = "80386";
    else if ( winFlags & WF_CPU286 )
        cpuName = "80286";
    else
        cpuName = "Unknown";
    Output("CPU: %s\r\n", cpuName);

    if ( winFlags & WF_STANDARD )  // MemManInfo is useless for Standard mode
        return;

    mmi.dwSize = sizeof(mmi);
    if (! (ok = MemManInfo(&mmi)))
        return;

    // Output select fields from the MEMMANINFO structure
    Output("Largest Free memory block: %lu bytes\r\n",
            mmi.dwLargestFreeBlock);

    Output("Total linear memory space: %-5lu K\r\n",
            mmi.dwTotalLinearSpace * (mmi.wPageSize/1024) );

    Output("Free linear memory space : %-5lu K\r\n",
            mmi.dwFreeLinearSpace * (mmi.wPageSize/1024) );

    Output("Swap file Pages: %lx (%lu K)\r\n",
            mmi.dwSwapFilePages, mmi.dwSwapFilePages * (mmi.wPageSize/1024) );
}

void GetDateTimeString(char *s)
{
    struct date mydate;
```

```
    struct time mytime;
    getdate(&mydate);
    gettime(&mytime);
    sprintf(s, "%u/%02u/%u   %02u:%02u:%02u",
            mydate.da_mon, mydate.da_day, mydate.da_year,
            mytime.ti_hour, mytime.ti_min, mytime.ti_sec
            );
}

unsigned int Output(char *format, ... )
{
    static char mybuff[512];
    va_list argptr;
    unsigned len;

    if ( HReportFile == -1 )
        return 0;

    va_start( argptr, format );      /* Open the output list format  */
    len = vsprintf(mybuff, format, argptr);
    va_end( argptr );                /* Close the output list     */

    if ( len == 0)
        return 0;
    len = _lwrite(HReportFile, mybuff, len);
    return len;
}

int OpenReportFile(void)
{
    HReportFile = _lopen(LogFileName, OF_WRITE);
    if ( HReportFile != -1 )
    {
        _llseek(HReportFile, 0, 2);
        return HReportFile;
    }

    // We couldn't open the file. It may not exist. Try creating it.
    HReportFile = _lcreat(LogFileName, 0);

    if ( HReportFile == -1 )
        return 0;

    return 1;
}

void CloseReportFile(void)
{
    if ( HReportFile != -1 )
    {
        _lclose(HReportFile);
        HReportFile = -1;
    }
}
```

```c
void DoReportLineFeed(void)
{
    Output("\r\n");
}

void DoReportHeader(void)
{
    char buffer[80];
    Output("\r\n\r\n\r\n");
    GetDateTimeString(buffer);
    Output("Coroner exception report - %s\r\n", buffer );
}

int PrepareForReport(void)
{
    int ok;
    ExceptionTaskName[0] = 0;   // Null out the task name string
    ok = OpenReportFile();
    if ( ok )
        return 1;

    // If we get here, we couldn't open the report file. Maybe there wasn't
    // an available file handle in the task that blew up. Remember, we're
    // not running as the CORONER. So, let's try closing STDPRN to try to
    // free up file handles, and then try again.
    _lclose(4);
    ok = OpenReportFile();
    return ok;
}

void DoExceptionReport(int wNumber)
{
    if ( !PrepareForReport() )
    {
        PostMessage(HCoronerWnd, WM_CORONER_FILEOPEN_ERROR, 0, 0);
        return;
    }

    DoReportHeader();
    DoWhatHappenedReport( wNumber);
    DoStackTraceReport();
    DoRegisterReport();
    DoTaskReport();
    DoModuleReport();
    DoHeapsInfoReport();
    DoWindowsInfoReport();
    CloseReportFile();

    // Post a message to the CORONER window, so it can display the
    // exception message.
    PostMessage(HCoronerWnd, WM_CORONER_EXCEPTION, wNumber, 0);
}

char *tempstack;          // Pointer to temporary working stack
WORD tempstack_end;       // offset of the end of the temporary stack
```

```
WORD old_ss;                   // A place to save the SS:SP that we came in on.
WORD old_sp;
WORD exception_number;

void C_ExceptionHandler(
    WORD wES,
    WORD wDS,
    WORD wDI,
    WORD wSI,
    WORD wBP,
    WORD wSP,
    WORD wBX,
    WORD wDX,
    WORD wCX,
    WORD wAX,
    WORD wOldBP,
    WORD wRetIP,
    WORD wRetCS,
    WORD wRealAX,
    WORD wNumber,
    WORD wHandle,
    WORD wIP,
    WORD wCS,
    WORD wFlags)
{
    // Flag tells if we're already processing an interrupt/exception
    static WORD inHandler = 0;

    // Pass on the debugger interrupts. We don't care about them.
    if ( (wNumber == 1) || (wNumber == 3) )
        return;

    /* See if we're already here. If so, chain on */
    if (inHandler)
        return;
    else
        inHandler = 1;

    // Save off all of the parameters that we care about. We're going to
    // be switching stacks, so they won't be available.
    exception_number = wNumber;
    Exception_AX = wRealAX;
    Exception_BX = wBX;
    Exception_CX = wCX;
    Exception_DX = wDX;
    Exception_SI = wSI;
    Exception_DI = wDI;
    Exception_BP = wOldBP;
    Exception_IP = wIP;
    Exception_FLAGS = wFlags;
    Exception_CS = wCS;
    Exception_DS = wDS;
    Exception_ES = wES;

    asm     mov     [Exception_SS],ss
```

```
    asm     lea     ax, [wES + 26h]      // calculate SP at time of exception
    asm     mov     [Exception_SP],ax

    // We're now going to switch the stack over to the temporary 4K stack
    // we allocated before we called InterruptRegister
    asm {
            mov     [old_ss], ss
            mov     [old_sp], sp

            mov     ax, ds
            mov     ss, ax
            mov     sp, [tempstack_end]
        }

    DoExceptionReport(exception_number);

    // Switch the stack back to the original stack
    asm {
            mov     ss, [old_ss]
            mov     sp, [old_sp]
        }

    inHandler = 0;

    // Return to .ASM handler, which will chain on to the other installed
    // handlers. If none of them handle it, Windows will kill the task for us.
    return;
}

#define TEMPSTACK_SIZE  4096

BOOL SetupInterruptHandler(void)
{
    tempstack = malloc(TEMPSTACK_SIZE);
    if ( !tempstack )
        return 0;
        tempstack_end = (WORD)((tempstack + TEMPSTACK_SIZE) - 2);
    return InterruptRegister(NULL, (LPFNINTCALLBACK)EXCEPTIONHANDLER);
}

void ShutdownInterruptHandler(void)
{
    InterruptUnRegister(NULL);
    if ( tempstack )
        free(tempstack);
}
```

To enable the Coroner to receive exceptions, the SetupInterruptHandler function allocates a stack that will be switched to while writing out the exception report. It then calls InterruptRegister, passing the address of the EXCEPTIONHANDLER function (from TH_ASM.ASM; see below). We'll come back to the EXCEPTION-HANDLER function in a moment.

The key function in XCPTREPT.C is C_ExceptionHandler. At the beginning of the function, checks are made to see if we want to write out a report for this particular invocation. We don't want to do anything with INT 1 or INT 3, since they're used by debuggers and are quite normal. We also don't want to be in the middle of writing a report and have another exception come in. To prevent this, the "inHandler" flag is set to make the function a "critical section."

Because this code is running on the stack of the faulting task, it is desirable to get on to a "safe stack" as soon as possible. Before that can be done, though, the parameters that were passed on the stack need to be copied to variables that can be accessed with the DS register. Once this is complete, the old SS:SP is saved off, and the stack is switched to the safe stack allocated when InterruptRegister was called.

At this point, it is now safe to write information about the exception to the log file. This is accomplished by DoExceptionReport. When DoExceptionReport is finished, the stack is switched back to the original stack, and the exception is chained to the next handler. If there are no other programs that have called InterruptRegister and that actually dealt with the exception, Windows will kill the application and display the UAE box.

The DoExceptionReport function is responsible for opening the log file, writing the various report sections, closing the log file, and then informing the user. Because Windows is in a potentially unstable state at the time of the exception, the report is written out before the user is informed. By doing it this way, even if Windows crashes while bringing up the exception dialog, the report is still safely on the disk. As a side note, if you're experiencing severe system crashes it's a good idea to turn off write caching in your disk cache. If you don't, the system may crash before the cache has a chance to be flushed.

The code that opens the log file is a bit unusual. Because Windows considers the exception handler to be part of the faulting application, it will use the faulting application's file handle table when opening a file. In some cases, there may not be any available file handles. If the first call to _lopen fails, the file opening code tries to free up a file handle by closing the handle in use by STD PRN. Another attempt is then made to open the file. If the file still can't be opened, the Coroner gives up and chains on to the next handler.

The functions that display the information for various sections of the log file are reasonably straightforward. For the most part, they just call the appropriate ToolHelp functions and display selected information from the returned structures.

The function GetLogicalSegmentFromSelector is a helper function that is called by both DoWhatHappenedReport and DoStackTraceReport. It takes a selector (which should be a code segment selector) and returns the module that it belongs to and its segment number in the module table. First, it looks up the selector by using GlobalEntryHandle. This gives the module handle of the owning module and lets us verify that the selector really is a code segment. Then the module handle is converted to a module name by calling ModuleFindHandle.

TH_ASM.ASM, just an assembly language extension to XCPTREPT.C, contains the callback function that is registered via InterruptRegister.

```
;=================================
; Coroner, by Matt Pietrek, 1992
; File: TH_ASM.ASM
;=================================

.model small .286

PUBLIC EXCEPTIONHANDLER ; Make EXCEPTIONHANDLER public

extrn _C_ExceptionHandler: NEAR
.code

; The EXCEPTIONHANDLER proc is called directly from ToolHelp. It
; sets up a stackframe, and calls the 'C' function C_ExceptionHandler.
; On entry, the stack looks like this:

;        ------------
;BP---->|  Old BP   | [BP + 00h]
;       |  Ret IP   | [BP + 02h]
;       |  Ret CS   | [BP + 04h]
;       |    AX     | [BP + 06h]
;       |Exception#| [BP + 08h]
;       |  Handle   | [BP + 0Ah]
;       |    IP     | [BP + 0Ch]
;       |    CS     | [BP + 0Eh]
;       |   Flags   | [BP + 10h]
;        ------------

EXCEPTIONHANDLER proc far

        push    bp          ;Make a stack frame
        mov     bp,sp
        pusha               ;Save all registers
        push    ds
        push    es

        mov     ax, @data ; There's only one instance of the CORONER running, so
        mov     ds, ax    ; we save work by loading DS directly, like a DLL does.

        call    _C_ExceptionHandler

        pop     es          ;Chain on to next fault handler
        pop     ds
        popa
        pop     bp
        retf

EXCEPTIONHANDLER endp

END
```

This function is in assembly language because when it's called, the register values (with the exception of AX) are what they were at the time of the exception. The function exists to save the registers on the stack, set up the DS to point to Coroner's DS, and then call C_ExceptionHandler.

The DS is set up similarly to a DLL entry point. By putting in the code to load the DS with an explicit value @data, we restrict ourselves to running only one instance. The benefit is that we do not have to use MakeProcInstance and pass the instance thunk to InterruptRegister.

Finally, there's CORONER.H (yawn):

```
//==================================
// Coroner, by Matt Pietrek, 1992
// File: CORONER.H
//==================================

#define    MAX_PATH_LENGTH              144
#define    WM_CORONER_FILEOPEN_ERROR    WM_USER + 0x200
#define    WM_CORONER_EXCEPTION         WM_USER + 0X201

// The .ASM InterruptRegister handler in TH_ASM.ASM
void FAR PASCAL EXCEPTIONHANDLER(void);

// From XCPTREPT.C
BOOL SetupInterruptHandler(void);
void ShutdownInterruptHandler(void);
```

Suggested Enhancements

The Coroner is a good starting point for writing a post-mortem debugging tool. Obvious improvements include letting the user set options such as the output file name and whether the log file should be appended vs. overwritten, among others. Some users have second monitors or terminals to which a small summary report could be written. A private profile file is a good way to save and read these options.

A time-consuming but helpful addition is to add a disassembler. The faulting instruction could be disassembled, as well as a few instructions before and after to save the user from having to load the program into a debugger to see which instruction blew up. Given this information and the registers section of the log file, it is almost always trivial to determine exactly why the exception was generated.

Another useful feature would be to use the logical addresses in the stack trace to look up and display symbolic names. This is what the debugging version of Windows does when it RIPs. The Windows SDK comes with .SYM files that contain symbolic names and their corresponding logical addresses. You can create .SYM files for your own programs also by using TMAPSYM (Borland style .MAP files) and MAPSYM (Microsoft style .MAP files).

It is also possible to write a utility (similar to the DFA utility that comes with Borland's WinSpector) that post-processes the CORONER.LOG file and cross references the stack trace information with Turbo Debugger or CodeView debug information. Trying to do this in the Coroner code is a bad idea because it takes significantly more memory to process a full-blown debug information file than it does to process a

.SYM file. Allocating large amounts of memory in the exception handler may cause memory movement and system instability.

A really ambitious implementation would involve saving a copy of the stack memory and using debug information to display the parameters and local variables for each stack frame. Additionally, the data segments of the application could be saved in a file, so that the post-processor could display the global variables also.

In Windows 3.1, Microsoft added parameter validation. To use it effectively, you need to know where in the code your program used an invalid parameter. The Coroner code that walks the stack for an exception is also useful for finding where an erroneous parameter was passed. To add this capability, you'll need to use NotifyRegister to install a callback function for notifications.

WINIO Library Reference

WINIO, the library of functions used to build the sample programs in this book, supports a subset of the C stdio library under protected-mode Windows 3.0 and higher, plus a set of extensions for event handling, window manipulation, menus, clickable lines, and so on. WINIO works with Borland C++ 2.0 and 3.0 small and medium models, and Microsoft C 6.0 and C/C++ 7.0 small and medium models. It has been ported to MetaWare's 32-bit Windows ADK, using MetaWare High C 1.7, but this version isn't fully supported at this time.

An overview of WINIO, with several example programs, appears in chapter 4. The following is a reference to each function and variable in the WINIO library.

To use WINIO, #include "windows.h" and "winio.h." If you are calling any wmhandler_ functions, #include "wmhandlr.h" as well:

```
/* hello.c */
#include "windows.h"
#include "winio.h"

main(int argc, char *argv[])
{
    int i;
    winio_settitle(winio_current(),
        "Hello from WINIO; Wish You Were Here");
    for (i=0; i<argc; i++)
        printf("%d\t%s\n", i, argv[i]);
    return 0;
}
```

Each WINIO function begins with main() rather than with WinMain(). The standard argc, argv parameters are supported. When main() is called, a window has already been created, with a buffer size of 32K, a window title holding the program's executable file name and command-line, and a default File... menu with the options Save Buffer... and Exit. See the graphic on the following page.

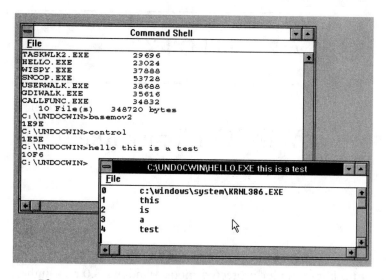

If more output appears than can fit within the window, the user can scroll through the window using the mouse or the arrow, Pg, or Home and End keys. Unfortunately, cut and paste are not currently supported.

The program can use the following stdio functions:

fgetchar	fputchar	getchar	gets	kbhit
printf	putchar	puts	ungets	vprintf

Except for ungets (see later discussion), these functions are similar to what the C standard library provides. However, WINIO programs should #include "winio.h" rather than <stdio.h> because some of these functions are implemented as macros. If every stdio function used by your program appears as a function prototype (not a macro #define) in <stdio.h>, and if you are not using any winio_ or wmhandler_ extension functions, you can simply relink your DOS program's .OBJ file with SWINDOS.LIB or MWINDOS.LIB to create a Windows version of the program.

Your program can call any Windows API function. Use winio_current() or the _h Main Wnd global variable (described later in this appendix) to find your HWND. For graphics, see the winio_onpaintentry() function. To handle WM_ messages, see the wmhandler_ functions.

It is convenient having the program begin with main() rather than WinMain(), but you may also want to access the WinMain() parameters hInstance, hPrevInstance, lpCmdLine, and nCmdShow. WINIO saves these values, plus a few others, in global variables you can use:

```
HANDLE __hInst;          HANDLE __hPrevInst;      LPSTR __lpCmdLine;
int __nCmdShow;          HWND __hMainWnd;         char szModule[];
```

Link with either the Borland or Microsoft version of SWINDOS.LIB (small model) or MWINDOS.LIB (medium model). If you want your program to have the standard WINIO "Windows meets stdio" handshake icon, use WINDOS.RC. For example, with Borland C++:

```
bcc -WS -DWINIO hello.c swindos.lib
rc windos.rc hello.exe
```

With Microsoft C (including Microsoft C/C++ 7.0), you need a linker .DEF file:

```
; WINDOS.DEF - generic DEF file for programs built with WINDOS
DESCRIPTION       'WINDOS Windows program'
EXETYPE           WINDOWS
STUB              'WINSTUB.EXE'
CODE              PRELOAD MOVEABLE DISCARDABLE
DATA              PRELOAD MOVEABLE MULTIPLE
HEAPSIZE          4096
STACKSIZE         8192
EXPORTS           WMHANDLER_WNDPROC
```

A sample Microsoft C command line is:

```
cl -G2w -c hello.c
link /nod hello,,, swindos slibcew libw, windos.def
rc windos.res hello.exe
```

WINIO Differences from Stdio

The printf() and vprintf() functions have an internal limitation of 4K bytes. That is, you cannot display more than 4K bytes per call to printf() or format more than 4K bytes per call to vprintf().

All output to stdio, and all input from stdio, must go through the functions indicated above. For example, printf() and puts() both work with WINIO, but fprintf(stdout, ...) and fputs(stdout, ...) do not. Likewise, you can use getchar() or fgetchar(), but not fgetc(stdin). Also, stderr is not supported. The scanf() function is not supported, but you can instead use sscanf() together with gets():

```
HWND hwnd;
char buf[80];
gets(buf);
sscanf(buf, "%04X", &hwnd);
```

In WINIO, getchar() by default behaves differently than it does under DOS. The following C construct

```
int c;
while ((c = getchar()) != EOF)
    putchar(c);
```

does not have the desired effect under WINIO because characters input via getchar() are by default echoed to the screen. The putchar() included in the above loop causes each character to be echoed a second time. The call to putchar can be removed, or the echo can be suppressed by calling winio_setecho(FALSE).

In addition, the test for EOF is often inappropriate because the user can always double click the window's close box. Thus, the standard C echo loop can be recoded for WINIO most simply as

```
for (;;)
    getchar();
```

DOS displays the ASCII codes 1 through 26 using the strings ^A through ^Z, except for 8 (Backspace), 9 (Tab), 10 (Line feed), 11 (VT), 16 (Toggle print), and 19 (Stop output), which are interpreted and not displayed. WINIO does not print anything below ASCII code 32, which is the space character. With the exception of ^P and ^S, WINIO does interpret the same characters that DOS does in much the same way, including reporting ASCII 26 as EOF.

WINIO Functions

The following is an alphabetical list of the extension functions provided by WINIO; all functions appear in "winio.h," with the exception of the wmhandler_ functions, which appear in "wmhandlr.h."

void fail(static char *fmt, ...);

This function displays a message box and exits the program. The function takes a format string and a variable number of arguments, just like printf.

char *ungets(char *string);

This function is like the stdio ungetc() function (which WINIO does not support), except that it allows an entire string, rather than just one character, to be pushed back onto the input queue. Calling this function is equivalent to sending the current window a WM_CHAR message for each character in the string.

void winio_about(char *string);

The text of the About box, which is the only choice by default on the Help popup menu, may be changed using this function. The string passed to this function will make up part of the About box text. The string may include newline characters, which will be honored, and will be truncated if greater than 128 characters in length.

WORD winio_bufsize(HWND hwnd);

This function returns the size of the output buffer allocated for the specified window. See the winio_setbufsize() function for more information on the buffer.

void winio_clear(HWND hwnd);

This function clears the output buffer for the specified window, effectively reinitializing the window. The window will also be redisplayed, blank.

void winio_close(HWND hwnd);

Provided only for symmetry, this function simply calls the Windows API function DestroyWindow().

void winio_closeall(void);

This function closes all WINIO windows for the application. It does this simply by closing the main window of the application, the one created in WinMain( ) before main( ) is called.

HWND winio_current(void);

This function returns the handle of the WINIO window that is current. This is the window to which stdio output functions write and from which stdio input functions obtain user input. See winio_setcurrent( ) for information on how to change the current window. Given the HWND, you can manipulate the WINIO window with any Windows API function.

DWORD winio_defwindowsize(DWORD);

This function sets the default window size for all subsequent winio_window( ) calls. The window size is specified in characters, not pixels, with the height in the HIWORD and the width in the LOWORD. The function returns the previous size in effect.

void winio_end(void);

This function enters a message loop until the user has closed all application windows. It simply calls the wmhandler_yield( ) function repeatedly until the count of windows is 0.

void winio_getinfo(HWND hwnd, PWINIOINFO pwinfo);

This function returns various pieces of information about the WINIO window and its associated buffer into a WINIOINFO structure:

```
typedef struct {
    POINT dimChar;      // dimensions of a character cell
    POINT posCurr;      // curr pos from top of buffer in chars.
    RECT rectView;      // part of buffer in view in chars/lines.
    long cDiscarded;    // lines discarded from buffer so far
    }   WINIOINFO, * PWINIOINFO, FAR * LPWINIOINFO;
```

The dimChar member will vary depending on what font is in effect for the window; see the winio_setfont( ) function. The posCurr member indicates where the logical text cursor is. The x and y values of the point contain the character and line (not pixel) offsets from the start of the buffer. The rectView member is a RECT describing, relative to the top left of the buffer, what is currently in the window. The left and right fields of the RECT contain the left and right character columns, and the top and bottom fields contain the top and bottom line numbers of what is visible. Finally, cDiscarded indicates how many display lines have been discarded from the buffer to make room for later output. This allows a line-handler function, for example, to account for the "shifting up" of lines in the display buffer over time.

HMENU winio_hmenufile(HWND hwnd);

If a window was created with the WW_HASMENU flag, this function will return the menu handle of the "File" popup menu that initially contains the "Save buffer..." and "Exit" selections. It allows the menu to be extended or modified: see winio_setmenufunc( ) for how to register menu-selection handlers.

This function returns the handle of the &Help popup menu in the main menu bar, if the window was created with the winio_window() WW_HASMENU flag; otherwise it returns NULL. The Help popup menu by default has one choice on it for the &About dialog. Using the handle returned by this function with InsertMenu, additionalchoices may be inserted into the Help menu. In order for an application to gain control when any additional items are selected from the menu, their IDs must be registered together with a handler function using winio_setmenufunc().

HMENU winio_hmenumain(HWND hwnd);

If a window was created with the WW_HASMENU flag, this function will return the menu handle of the main menu bar (that initially contains the "File" selection). It allows the menu to be extended or modified: see the winio_setmenufunc().

void winio_home(HWND hwnd);

This function simulates the user pressing the Home function key. It is useful, for example, if an informational window is created to hold text that might not fit into the window. Once the text has been output, perhaps wrapped in calls to winio_setpaint(), this function leaves the window positioned at the start of the buffer.

BOOL winio_init(void);

This function is used internally by WINIO; it registers the WINIO class ("winio_wcmain") and initializes some global variables.

void winio_onclose(HWND hwnd, DESTROY_FUNC exitfunc);

In most applications, especially those that rely on some form of character-based input, there must be a means for providing notification that the user has closed the window from which input was expected! This function could be simulated using:

```
prev_wmdestroy = wmhandler_set(hwnd, WM_DESTROY, my_wmdestroy);
```

However, the winio_onclose() mechanism not only is more convenient, but it also guarantees that WINIO's own WM_DESTROY handler is called, without depending on the application to chain. The DESTROY_FUNC callback function should have a prototype that matches:

```
void callback(HWND hwnd);
```

Note that because the onclose mechanism comes into operation when the window receives the WM_DESTROY mechanism, it is too late to ask the users if they really want to close the window. If that functionality is wanted, a WMHANDLER should be established for the WM_CLOSE message. If exitfunc is NULL, the current callback function is disabled.

PAINT_FUNC winio_onpaintentry(HWND hwnd, PAINT_FUNC paintfunc);

This function gives WINIO program access to GDI. For example, the sample program in chapter 8 for the undocumented Windows RSin() and RCos() functions in 3.0 draws a star on the window. It is a persistent star that scales to fit the window and that responds to the window being scrolled. So that text and graphics can be integrated, and so that the application has an easy-to-use way of influencing the painting process, WINIO provides hooks within the processing of a WM_PAINTmessage.

The first hook, as supplied through this function, allows the application to gain control after WINIO has obtained a DC, but before the internal winio_wmpaint() function has actually started painting text into the window. The callback function has the opportunity to perform whatever painting or DC modification it wants, and then it returns TRUE or FALSE to indicate whether WINIO should go ahead with, or bypass, its regular display update. Returning FALSE will cause WINIO not to update the window, leaving it empty of buffer text.

The callback function type is PAINT_FUNC and should have a prototype that matches

```
BOOL callback(HWND hwnd, HDC hdc, PAINTSTRUCT *pps, PWINIOINFO pwi);
```

where hwnd is the window being updated, hdc is the display context returned by the BeginPaint function, pps is a pointer to the PAINTSTRUCT filled in by the BeginPaint call, and pwi is a pointer to a WINIOINFO structure, as described for the winio_getinfo() call.

If paintfunc is NULL, the current callback function is disabled.

PAINT_FUNC winio_onpaintexit(HWND hwnd, PAINT_FUNC paintfunc);

As its name suggests, this function provides the hook into the end of the update process. It operates in exactly the same way as the winio_onpaintentry() function, except that a function registered using this call will be invoked just before WINIO calls EndPaint() to release the display context. Unless a function has been registered using winio_onpaintentry(), and it returned FALSE, this will be invoked after the window has been updated with text from the window's buffer.

The callback function type is again PAINT_FUNC, but note that the BOOL return code is ignored at paint exit. If paintfunc is NULL, the current callback function is disabled.

int winio_openwindows(void);

This function returns the number of WINIO windows that are currently open.

void winio_resetbusy(void);

This function returns the WINIO cursor to the previous shape and releases the capture. See the winio_setbusy() function below.

WORD winio_setbufsize(HWND hwnd, WORD wBufSize, BOOL bClear);

This function resizes the output buffer for the specified window. If bClear is FALSE, the buffer cannot made smaller than the amount currently in use. If bClear is TRUE, the buffer will be cleared, and the new size can be anything over 4K bytes. The return value is the new actual buffer size. The default buffer size for a WINIO program's main window is 32K; for secondary windows, the default buffer size is 8K.

void winio_setbusy(void);

This function provides a simple mechanism for indicating that some operation is in progress that may not be interrupted. It changes the cursor into the stock hourglass "busy" cursor and captures the cursor, effectively blocking user input. The cursor is returned to its previous state and the capture is released through a call to winio_resetbusy( ). Second and subsequent calls to winio_setbusy( ) without an intervening call to winio_resetbusy( ) simply increment a counter. winio_resetbusy( ) only restores the cursor if the counter is zero; otherwise it decrements it.

HWND winio_setcurrent(HWND hwnd);

As described in the text, WINIO stdio functions operate on the current window. This function allows the current window to be changed. It returns the handle of the previously current window.

BOOL winio_setecho(HWND hwnd, BOOL bEcho);

This function controls echoing of stdin. The default behavior of the WINIO version of the input function getchar( ) is that characters input are automatically echoed to stdout. This function allows the behavior to be modified. Specifying a bEcho parameter of FALSE disables echoing of stdin; specifying TRUE reenables it. The function returns the previous value in effect.

WORD winio_setfont(HWND hwnd, WORD wFont)

Although only stock fonts are currently supported, it is possible to change the font in effect for a particular window using this function. The function accepts the WINDOWS.H stock object constants ANSI_FIXED_FONT, OEM_FIXED_FONT, and SYSTEM_FIXED_FONT only. It returns the font previously in effect.

LINEHANDLER winio_setlinefn(HWND hwnd, LINEHANDLER linefunc);

This function installs a handler to be invoked when the user double clicks on a line of text in the window, as discussed earlier. The callback function is of type LINEHANDLER and should have a prototype that matches

```
void callback(HWND hwnd, LPSTR lpstrLine, int nLineNo);
```

where lpstrLine will be a pointer to the line of text in the buffer that the user double clicked on, and nLineNo is the line number from the top of the buffer. Note that when text is lost from the top of the buffer, the line number for a particular line will decrease over time. However, the cDiscarded field of the WINIOINFO structure supplied by the winio_getinfo( ) function can be used to derive an absolute line number for the line.

MENU_FUNC winio_setmenufunc(HWND hwnd, int nID, MENU_FUNC menufunc);

If menu items are added to either the main or file menus, a handler function should be installed to process user selection of a new item. Note that if a particular menu item id for a particular window's menu hierarchy is not registered with a handler in WINIO, there is no way for the application to know that the menu option has been picked. The callback function is of type MENU_FUNC and should have a prototype that matches:

```
void callback(HWND hwnd, int nID);
```

BOOL winio_setpaint(HWND hwnd, BOOL bPaint);

This function allows the painting of text added to the window buffer to be deferred. If bPaint is FALSE, the window is not updated with new text added using the stdio functions. When a subsequent call to the function is made with a bPaint parameter of TRUE, the window is then updated.

Use of this function around a block of code that makes many puts() or printf() avoids jerkiness. Equally important, WINIO does not yield control to other applications between a winio_setpaint(FALSE) and a winio_setpaint(TRUE). If a WINIO program is walking a data structure that could be changed by another application (e.g., the Windows task list or the global heap), it should call winio_setpaint(FALSE) before starting the walk and winio_setpaint(TRUE) when the walk is complete. This will keep the structure's state from being changed underneath you by other applications.

void winio_settitle(HWND hwnd, char *strTitle);

The default window caption for WINIO windows is the module name (together with, in the case of the main window, any command line arguments to the program). This function is really only a cover over the documented SetWindowText() function and is included only to round out the WINIO API.

BOOL winio_warn(BOOL bConfirm, char *strCaption, static char *fmt, ...);

The documented MessageBox() function is a useful tool, and this function further simplifies its use by treating it with a printf style format string and variable arguments. It also has two operational flavors. If the bConfirm parameter is FALSE, the message box is displayed with just an OK button, and the return value will always be TRUE. If the bConfirm parameter is TRUE, both OK and Cancel buttons will be included, and the return value will be FALSE if the user cancels; otherwise it will be TRUE.

HWND winio_window(LPSTR lpstrTitle, WORD wBufSize, WORD wFlags);

This function allows additional windows to be created by the application. The lpstrTitle parameter specifies the caption for the new window; the wBufSize parameter specifies the size of the buffer to be allocated for the window. This buffer is allocated from global memory and determines the amount of display history that will be kept with the window. If the value is 0, a default size of 8K is used; otherwise if the specified value is lower than 4K it is rounded up. The wFlags parameter is a combination of any (or none) of the following flags ORed together:

`WW_HASMENU (0x0001)`

The new window will have the default WINIO menu, which can be modified as described in winio_setmenufunc() above.

`WW_EXITALLOWED (0x0002)`

The Exit option on the File popup menu of the window will be enabled. If this flag is used, the application may be exited from any window. If the WW_HASMENU flag is not used, this flag is ignored.

WW_STAYSONTOP (0x0004)

By default, WINIO windows are owned popups, not child windows. In this case, when the main WINIO window is active, it may cover part or all of the new window. Further, if the main window is minimized, the new window will not automatically be minimized as well. If the WW_STAYSONTOP flag is used, the new window is created as a child window and will never be overlayed by the main WINIO window. Also, minimizing the main window will cause this window to be minimized automatically.

WMHANDLER Functions

The following functions have prototypes in wmhandlr.h. Although it is usually used together with WINIO, it is possible to have a WMHANDLER application that does not use WINIO (see wmhandler_hwnd() below). A WINIO application will probably only use wmhandler_set() and wmhandler_yield(); the other functions are most likely to be used by non-WINIO programs.

WMTAB wmhandler_create(void);

Pointers to the functions registered to handle messages for a window are stored in several arrays. This function allocates the memory for those arrays, initializes them, and returns a pointer to the memory. The pointer returned by this function should be stored in the CREATEPARAMS structure wmTab field (see wmhandler_wndproc()). The wmhandler_wndproc() function retrieves this pointer together with an application-supplied 32-bit value (usually a far pointer) when the WM_CREATE message for the window is received and places them in the extra-data area associated with the window. Thereafter, wmhandler_wndproc() uses the WMTAB pointer to locate a handler for all messages received for the window.

void wmhandler_destroy(HWND hwnd);

This is the complementary function to wmhandler_create(). It retrieves the WMTAB pointer from the specified window and frees the associated allocation.

WMHANDLER wmhandler_get(HWND hwnd, WORD wMsg);

This function returns a pointer to the function that is currently handling the specified message for the specified WINIO window. The returned value is never NULL, since any messages for which handlers have not been installed using wmhandler_set() are handled by a WMHANDLER internal handler that passes them on to DefWindowProc(). See wmhandler_set() for more information and for a description of the WMHANDLER type.

HWND wmhandler_hwnd(char *strTitle);

This function creates an invisible window with an associated handler table. The returned window can be used as a message recipient, and its handle used in calls to wmhandler_set(). This facility parallels the concept of an "object window" in OS/2 Presentation Manager. It can be used when you want event handling without a user interface.

WMHANDLER wmhandler_set(HWND hwnd, WORD message, WMHANDLER wmhandler);

This function allows a function to be installed to handle messages of the specified type that arrive at the specified window. The message number can be any number you want, including numbers greater than WM_USER (400h), and including message numbers returned from the Windows RegisterWindowMessage() function. However, there is one restriction: your program can install no more than 16 handlers for message numbers greater than WM_USER (400h). Most applications don't install 16 handlers, period, so this should not present a problem.

The WMHANDLER callback function should have a prototype that matches:

```
long wmhandler(HWND hwnd, WORD message, WORD wParam, DWORD lParam);
```

The callback function should return whatever is appropriate to the WM_ message type it is handling.

If the wmhandler parameter to wmhandler_set() is NULL, the message handler for the function becomes an internal default handler that passes the message on to DefWindowProc.

wmhandler_set() returns the previous handler in effect. The callback function can chain onto this. If your program takes over one of the WM_ messages also handled by WINIO, your callback function *must* chain; these messages are listed earlier in this appendix.

Generally, wmhandler_set() will be used in a WINIO program. If used in a non-WINIO program, your window must use wmhandler_wndproc() as its window procedure and must have a WMTAB pointer as the first four bytes of associated user data (see wmhandler_create()). Again, this is only a concern for non-WINIO windows that use the WMHANDLER package.

DWORD FAR PASCAL wmhandler_wndproc(HWND hwnd, WORD wMsg,

  WORD wParam, DWORD lParam);

This is a generic window procedure that implements the message switching on which WMHANDLER is based. It may be attached to any window for which WMHANDLER-style message handling is required, so long as the following pieces of the puzzle are in place (all of this is taken care of automatically if you use WINIO):

- The lpfnWndProc field of the WNDCLASS structure for the window class referenced in the CreateWindow() call is set to wmhandler_wndproc.
- The cbWndExtra field of the WNDCLASS structure for the window class is set to at least 8.
- The lpParam parameter of the CreateWindow() call used to create the window is pointed to a CREATEPARAMS structure:

```
typedef struct {
    WMTAB wmTab;
    LPSTR lpData;
    } CREATEPARAMS, FAR *LPCREATEPARAMS;
```

where the lpData can be any 32-bit value of use to the application and will usually point to data to be stored with the window.

As described in the wmhandler_create( ) entry, these pointers are transferred to the 8-byte user data area set aside for our use. WINIO uses lpData to point to additional window state information. lpData may be retrieved from within a message handler using:

`LPMYSTRUCT lpMyStruct = (LPMYSTRUCT)GetWindowLong(hwnd, 4);`

void wmhandler_yield(void);

This function is the means by which WINIO releases the processor to allow for messages of its own and other applications to be processed.

APPENDIX ▪ B

Annotated Bibliography

Timothy Adams, "Intercepting DLL Function Calls," *Windows/DOS Developer's Journal*, June 1992
Windows is missing a SetProcAddress() function—hey, the Mac has SetTrapAddress() and DOS has the Set Vector call—but API calls can be intercepted; you just have think like a debugger and set breakpoints.

Rakesh K. Agarwal, *80x86 Architecture and Programming*, Volume II (Architecture Reference), Englewood Cliffs NJ: Prentice-Hall, 1991, 627 pp., ISBN 0-13-245432-7
Windows is a protected-mode DOS extender, and it is often necessary for Windows programmers to understand how protected mode works. This is by far the best book available on the Intel 80x86 protected-mode architecture, with detailed pseudocode for each instruction. (Volume I isn't written yet!)

Alfred V. Aho, Brian W. Kernighan, and Peter J. Weinberg, *The AWK Programming Language*, Reading MA: Addison-Wesley, 1988, 210 pp., ISBN 0-201-07981-X
Several of the utilities in Chapter 2 of Undocumented Windows were written in AWK. The book by A-K-W is the place to go if you want to learn more about this wonderful pattern-matching, text-processing language.

Robert Arnson, Daniel Rosen, Mitchell Waite, and Jonathan Zuck, *Visual Basic How-To*, Mill Valley CA: Waite Group Press, 1992, 546 pp., ISBN 1-878739-09-3
Chapter 6 (Environment and System) shows how to make Windows API calls, including undocumented ones like GetHeapSpaces(), from Visual Basic.

Paul Bonneau, "3.1's Internal Window Structure," *Windows/DOS Developer's Journal*, June 1992
Describes the WND structure in Windows 3.1, very close to what we show in Chapter 6. This is a continuation from the author's excellent "Windows Q&A" column in the December 1991 issue. Bonneau's "Windows Q&A" is essential reading for serious Windows programmers.

Borland Languages Open Architecture Handbook, 1991, Borland Part No. 14MN-RCH01-10
Chapter 3 documents the Turbo Debugger (TD) symbol table format.

Ralf Brown and Jim Kyle, *PC Interrupts: A Programmer's Reference to BIOS, DOS, and Third-Party Calls*, Reading MA: Addison-Wesley, 1991, ISBN 0-201-57797-6
Chapter 14 covers some of the INT 2Fh calls supported in Windows; Chapter 11 covers DPMI, and Chapter 12 covers the Virtual DMA Specification (VDS) services (INT 4Bh) provided by Windows.

Geoff Chappell, *Inside DOS 5*, Reading MA: Addison-Wesley, 1992 (forthcoming)
An in-depth dissection of HIMEM and EMM386, showing how DOS 5 (and Windows) make use of extended memory.

Paul Chui, "Undocumented DOS from Protected-Mode Windows 3," *Dr. Dobb's Journal*, February 1992
One of several articles now available on how to use DPMI to call undocumented DOS functions from a protected-mode Windows application.

Bob Chiverton, "Shed Some Light on Your Windows Application's Default Data Segment with HeapPeep," *Microsoft Systems Journal*, January-February 1992
A good description of the NULL segment, or Instance Data, area (for some reason called a "Task Header" by Microsoft). Both TOOLHELP and non-TOOLHELP techniques are used.

Alan Cobb, *Reverse Engineering Windows and OS/2 Software*, February 1991. Available from the author (CIS 73170,3543)
Discusses legalities and ethics of reverse engineering, plus tools, file formats, disassembly with SYMDEB, and import/export analysis. Contains tons of good advice; for example: "It is desirable that programs to be reverse engineered be purchased through large well-known national outlets such as Egghead. The objective is to highlight the fact that it was a mass market purchase, since as we have seen previously, license agreements prohibiting reverse engineering and patching are weaker when they are attached to high volume, mass market software."

Ralph Davis, *The Windows Programmer's Guide to Networking*, Reading MA: Addison-Wesley, 1992 (forthcoming)
A detailed explanation of the WNet functions, and of using DPMI to access real-mode TSRs and drivers.

Harvey M. Deitel and Michael S. Kogan, *The Design of OS/2*, Reading MA: Addison-Wesley, 1992, 389 pp., ISBN 0-201-54889-5
Chapters 1 (Historical Background), 5 (Multitasking, especially 5.5 on Kernel Architecture), 6 (Memory Management), and 10 (Compatibility) are quite useful.

Paul DiLascia, *Windows++: Writing Reusable Windows Code in C++*, Reading MA: Addison-Wesley, 1992, 608 pp., ISBN 0-201-60891-X
The nitty-gritty details of how Windows applications frameworks are implemented, and of how Windows programs can hide the Windows API, get rid of WinMain, get rid of switch statements, and generally make Windows code more readable, modular, and reusable. This is a brilliant book!

DOS Protected Mode Interface (DPMI) Specification, Version 0.9 (May 15, 1990), Intel Order No. 240763-001
There is also the DPMI 1.0 specification (March 12, 1991), Intel Order No. 240977-001, but the 0.9 spec is what Windows implements, so the 1.0 spec leads a largely Platonic existence at present. On the other hand, a number of vendors such as Phar Lap and even Microsoft itself have extended the 0.9 spec, using VxDs to provide parts of the 1.0 spec (particularly debug and floating-point coprocessor support), so maybe Windows really supports 0.95 now. Anyhow, the 0.9 spec is the one you want.

Ray Duncan, *Advanced OS/2 Programming*, Redmond WA: Microsoft Press, 1989, 782 pp., ISBN 1-55615-045-8
Windows has a lot in common with OS/2 1.x, including the NE executable file format. Appendix D ("OS/2 Load Module Format") of Ray's book thus serves as an excellent (and still largely accurate) discussion of the Windows executable file format.

Ray Duncan et al., *Extending DOS: A Programmer's Guide to Protected-Mode DOS*, Reading MA: Addison-Wesley, 1992, 538 pp., ISBN 0-201-56798-9
Chapter 9 (DPMI) contains a detailed look at the DPMI interface provided by Windows. Other chapters provide good background to protected-mode programming in general. Once you remember that Windows is just a graphical DOS extender, much of the material in here will suddenly be relevant to your Windows programming.

James D. Foley, Andries van Dam, Steven K. Feiner, and John F. Hughes, *Computer Graphics: Principles and Practice*, Second Edition, Reading MA: Addison-Wesley, 1990, 1174 pp., ISBN 0-201-12110-7
The standard work on computer graphics. Chapter 10 is on window-management systems; Chapter 19 includes BitBlt.

Robert L. Hummel, *PC Magazine Programmer's Technical Reference: The Processor and Coprocessor*, Emeryville CA: Ziff-Davis Press, 1992, 761 pp., ISBN 1-56276-016-5
Because protected mode until recently has not been as well-exercised as real mode, even on 386 and 486 machines, there tend to be bugs in some of the more obscure protected mode-specific instructions, including ones used heavily in Undocumented Windows, *like LAR, LSL, VERR, and VERW. Hummel discusses these chip bugs ("errata"), so you know what to watch out for and stay away from.*

Jerry Jongerius, "Accurately Timing Windows Events without Timer Reprogramming," *Microsoft Systems Journal*, July 1991
A good discussion of timers under Windows, including the undocumented CreateSystemTimer() and KillSystemTimer() functions.

Mike Klein, "Subclassing Applications," *Dr. Dobb's Journal*, Windows Supplement, December 1991
"Subclassing: A legal means by which a programmer can appropriate and use code and objects developed by others."

Scott Knaster, *Macintosh Programming Secrets*, Second Edition, Reading MA: Addison-Wesley, 1992, 536 pp., ISBN 0-201-58134-5
Few Windows programmers seem familiar with the Macintosh. Knaster's books (this one, and How to Write Macintosh Software, Third Edition*) provide wonderful overviews of how the Mac works. Would that Windows programming books were this good!*

Donald Knuth, *The Art of Computer Programming*, Volume I (Fundamental Algorithms) and Volume III (Sorting and Searching), Reading MA: Addison-Wesley, 1973
Volume I, 2.5 (Dynamic Storage Allocation) and Volume III, 6.4 (Hashing) are particularly relevant here.

Woody Leonhard, *Windows 3.1 Programming for Mere Mortals*, Reading MA: Addison-Wesley, 1992, 537 pp., ISBN 0-201-60832-4
Windows programming in Visual Basic and WordBasic. Woody's excellent (and extremely odd!) book shows how to make Windows API calls from Basic. Chapter 6 on DDE is sheer brilliance.

Gordon Letwin, *Inside OS/2*, Redmond WA: Microsoft Press, 1988, 289 pp., ISBN 0-55615-117-9
Much (though by no means all) of this book is relevant to Windows. In particular, see Chapters 2 (Goals and Compatibility Issues), 7 (Dynamic Linking), and 9 (Memory Management).

Brian Livingston, *Windows 3.1 Secrets*, San Mateo CA: IDG Books, 1992, 990 pp., ISBN 1-878058-43-6
While "secrets" is used somewhat loosely here (much of this material is available in the widely-distributed Microsoft Windows Resource Kit), there is also useful material here. Chapter 3 on TrueType is quite good, as are the chapters on hardware compatibility. Somehow using WIN /S to force Windows into Standard mode doesn't strike us as an "undocumented way to start Windows," but if you want to know how to get the "gang screens" (Easter eggs) in Windows and in various Windows apps, and want to actually see Bear, check out pp. 141-143.

Microsoft C Developer's Toolkit Reference, 1990, 115 pp., Microsoft Document No. LN18161-0990.
Contains the CodeView (CV) symbol format, and the IMPDEF and EXPDEF object file extensions. The CV format used in MSC/C++ 7.0 is different, and so far only seems to have been documented as part of Open Tools (if you need CV format for C7, try sending email to isv@microsoft.com).

Microsoft Developer Network Technical Library, CompuServe forum (GO MSDNLIB)
A newly-formed Microsoft library. Includes Bob Gunderson's article on modules, tasks, and instances (MTI.ZIP), articles on subclassing (SUBCLS.ZIP), hooks (HOOKS.ZIP and HOOKSC.ZIP), DOS TSR interfacing to Windows (GMEM.ZIP and TMEM.ZIP), 3.1 File Manager extensions (XTEN.ZIP), and so on.

Microsoft Developer Relations Forum, CompuServe forum (GO MSDR)
Along with Microsoft job postings (i.e., offerings of large pay cuts in exchange for stock options), there are some useful files here, such as the TrueType specification (SPEC1.ZIP, SPEC2.ZIP, SPEC3.ZIP), and TrueType sample code (TTNAME.ZIP, TTDUMP.ZIP).

Microsoft KnowledgeBase, CompuServe forum (GO MSKB); also Microsoft Developer KnowledgeBase (GO MDKB)
The MSKB and MDKB are probably the best resources available if there's something about Windows that you can't find in the SDK, DDK, or Undocumented Windows. There is a huge amount of information here, and the ability to quickly search for words or phrases occurring anywhere in documents makes it all easy to find. You can also do complicated searches, such as "(pcode eq winsdk)" and "(doctype eq buglist)" to find all documented bugs in the SDK! Here is a small sampling of the articles available:
"Accessing Physical Memory Using Kernel Exported Selectors"
"Calling PostMessage() from a Virtual Device Driver (VxD)"
"Communicating Between Windows Virtual Machines with DDE"
"DeferWindowPos() Documented Incorrectly"
"Errors in the VDS API in Enhanced Mode Windows"
"File Manager's Mechanism for Sensing File System Changes"
"Full-Screen DOS Apps Slow Timer Messages in Enhanced Mode"
"GetCodeInfo() Documented Incorrectly"
"GlobalReAlloc() Fails in Enhanced Mode"
"Hook_Device_PM_API & Hook_Device_V86_API Flawed "
"How to Determine When Another Application Has Finished"
"How to Transparently Intercept Procedure Calls in Windows"
"How to Use PeekMessage Correctly"
"Idle Interrupt (INT 28h) Under Windows 3.0"
"Overcoming the 64 Kilobyte Limit for List Box Data"
"Performance Differences Between LineTo() and Polyline()"

"'Power Friendly'" Applications
"Reset A20 Bit Set During DPMI Simulate Interrupt Crash "
"UAE Caused from Releasing Aliased Selector"
"Use of GetInputState( ) Is Faster Than Using PeekMessage( )"
"Using Memory Below 1 Megabyte"
"VKD_API_Force_Key Can Cause Windows Crash"

Microsoft Win32 Application Programming Interface, 2 volumes, Redmond WA:
    Microsoft Press, 1992, ISBN 1-55615-497-6 and 1-55615-498-4
Some functions and messages that are present but undocumented in 16-bit Windows have been documented in Win32.

Microsoft Windows Device Driver Kit, Version 3.1, 1992, Microsoft Part No. 29132
The DDK is a wonderful product that should be important to a much wider group of programmers than just those few who write device drivers. The DDK is essentially the "Windows internals" kit. The two manuals that come with the DDK are pretty poor, but the DDK disks are an invaluable resource: they contain header files that aren't with the SDK, such as TDB.INC and WINKERN.INC, a version of WINDOWS.H that contains things not in the SDK version, but more important, the DDK comes with disk after disk of source for most of the device drivers that come with Windows: display drivers, printer drivers, the Enhanced mode page swapper, the 3.1 FastDisk devices, and so on.

Microsoft Windows Software Development Kit, Version 3.1, 1992, Microsoft Part
    No. 30211
The SDK has improved a lot since 3.0. Many of the example programs are now genuinely useful. The manuals, while still woefully incomplete (Windows is a huge system, and documenting it properly will require something like Apple's Inside Macintosh*), do now contain a lot of material that was not documented in 3.0. The Programmer's Reference is now split into four volumes:*

Volume 1 (Overview) includes chapters on Windows startup code, protected-mode prolog and epilog code, self-loading Windows applications, and other subjects. Some of the chapters are even accurate (not the one on DPMI though, which starts by asserting that Windows supports DPMI 1.0 and goes downhill from there).

Volume 2 (Functions) is 1,000 pages of API function descriptions. Many documented functions are missing (they're scattered through the overview articles in Chapter 1, or they're in the DDK).

Volume 3 (Messages, Structures, and Macros). It's a pain not having the structures in the same place as the functions.

Volume 4 (Resources) is a handy guide to Windows file formats. The new-executable (NE) format is here, as are resource formats, .OBJ module extensions such as IMPDEF and EXPDEF, and so on.

The Guide to Programming, Chapters 14 (C and Assembly Language), 15 (Memory Management), and 16 (More Memory Management) contain material that's missing from the Programmer's Reference. Chapter 18 provides a good overview of fonts.

Microsoft Windows Resource Kit, 1992, 538 pp., Microsoft Document No. 0030-31645
Who says Microsoft doesn't produce good doc? Forget the User's Guide that comes with 3.1, and get the Windows Resource Kit (WRK) instead. This inexpensive book/disk set has excellent explanations of the files that come with Windows, all those weird *.INI file settings, troubleshooting, network configuration issues, etc. Most of the third-party power-user books on Windows are just cribbed from the WRK.

Raymond T. Nimmer, *The Law of Computer Technology*, Boston MA: Warren, Gorham, & Lamont, 1985, ISBN 0-88712-355-4. Also, *The Law of Computer Technology, 1991 Cumulative Supplement No. 1*, ISBN 0-7913-0898-7
Contains excellent discussions of reverse engineering, trade secrets, disassembly, shrinkwrap license agreements, and so on. See Chapter 3 ("Trade Secrets and Confidentiality"), particularly 3.05[b] (Sale of a Product: Reverse Engineering) and 3.07 (End Users: Reverse Engineering).

Daniel A. Norton, *Writing Windows Device Drivers*, Reading MA: Addison-Wesley, 1992, 434 pp., ISBN 0-201-57795-X
If you want an overview of the Windows device layer (both 16-bit, such as display and printer drivers, and 32-bit VxDs), before buying the DDK, this is place to go. Dan also covers some undocumented Windows functions.

Peter Norton and Paul Yao, *Borland C++ Programming for Windows*, New York: Bantam Books, 1992, 746 pp., ISBN 0-553-35143-5
Chapters 17-19 of Yao's book have good "conceptual" overviews of Kernel objects. The individual details are sometimes wrong, and the whole thing is (like most Windows programming books by long-time Windows developers) too rooted in Windows real mode, but this is an excellent starting point for thinking about how KERNEL does what it does. The book has a good glossary.

Nu-Mega Technologies, *Soft-ICE/W Reference Guide*, Nashua NH, 1991
Chapter 3 of the Soft-ICE/Windows manual has a nice section on "Exploring Windows Internals with Soft-ICE/W."

Thomas W. Olsen, "Making Windows and DOS Programs Talk," *Windows/DOS Developer's Journal*, May 1992
A good introduction to Virtual Device Driver (VxD) programming.

Walter Oney, "Parlez-vous Windows?," *Windows Tech Journal*, April 1992
As you can no doubt tell from the title, this article describes how to make WinExec(), which behaves like spawn(P_NOWAIT), into ExecWait(), using the ToolHelp NotifyRegister() function.

Tim Paterson and Steve Flenniken, "Managing Multiple Data Segments Under Microsoft Windows," *Dr. Dobb's Journal*, February 1990 (Part 1) and March 1990 (Part 2).
The definitive statement on real-mode Windows segment tables.

Charles Petzold, *Programming Windows*, Second Edition, Redmond WA: Microsoft
  Press, 1990, 944 pp., ISBN 1-55615-264-7
*The standard book on programming Windows; accept no substitutes! Petzold makes no
attempt to write modular or reusable code, so all the sample programs look essentially the
same, but this is a beautifully written book, with many gems scattered throughout. Sit
down and read this cover-to-cover. There's not much here on Windows internals, but it
does have a nice discussion of SYSTEM.DRV and timers.*

Phar Lap 386|DOS-Extender Programmer's Guide to DPMI and Windows, Cam-
  bridge MA, July 1991
*How Windows looks from the DOS extender's perspective; discusses DPMI, and accessing
Windows from the DOS box. Some of the writing style in this manual is shockingly similar
to that found in* Undocumented Windows.

Matt Pietrek, "Inside the Windows Scheduler," *Dr. Dobb's Journal*, forthcoming
  (August 1992?)
A detailed look, with pseudocode, of the internal Reschedule() function in KERNEL.

Matt Pietrek, "Writing a Windows Debugger," *Windows/DOS Developer's Journal*,
  June 1992
*Discusses a host of issues related to building a Windows debugger: how to load the
debuggee, how to terminate it, how to run it, how to single-step, how to set breakpoints, how
to map logical debug symbol addresses to actual run-time memory addresses, and so on.*

Matt Pietrek, "A Windows assert() with Symbolic Stack Trace," *Windows/DOS Developer's Journal*, forthcoming (July 1992)

Eric Raymond, *The New Hacker's Dictionary*, Cambridge MA: MIT Press, 1991, 433
  pp., ISBN 0-262-68069-6
*Along with many other excellent definitions (bagbiter, cargo cult programming, foo, Eas-
ter Egg, green bytes, magic, UTSL, You are not expected to understand this, and hundreds
of others), here is where you will find the true meaning of "thunk."*

Jeffrey M. Richter, "Drop Everything: How to Make Your Application Accept and
  Source Drag-and-Drop Files," *Microsoft Systems Journal*, May-June 1992
*How to be a drag-and-drop client and server in 3.1. Jeff describes the 3.1-type drag and
drop protocol. This is a good complement to our own description, in Chapter 6, of the 3.0-
type protocol, which continues to work under 3.1 as well.*

Jeffrey M. Richter, *Windows 3: A Developer's Guide*, Redwood City CA: M&T Books,
  1991, 671 pp., ISBN 1-55851-164-4
*Chapters 1 (Anatomy of a Window), 2 (Subclassing and Superclassing Windows), and 6
(Tasks, Queues, and Hooks) are brilliant. There will be a Second Edition out soon.*

Neil J. Rubenking, *Turbo Pascal for Windows Techniques and Utilities*, Emeryville CA: Ziff-Davis Press, 1992, 1100 pp., ISBN 1-56276-035-1
If you're wondering how to apply the C code in Undocumented Windows *to TPW, get Neil's book. If you're doing anything at all in TPW, get Neil's book. Chapter 14 ("Access to Real Mode") shows how to access undocumented DOS data structures from protected-mode Windows, using DPMI and some (at the time) undocumented Wincalls.*

Richard Sadowsky, "It's a Real Jungle Out There," *Windows Tech Journal*, January 1992
You wouldn't know it from the title (these Windows Tech Journal *articles always have cute titles), but this is another article explaining how to use DPMI to call real-mode code from a protected-mode Windows application.*

Tom Sato and Lin F. Shaw, "Bringing Windows To the Expanding Japanese Market," *Microsoft Systems Journal*, March 1988
Explains WM_CONVERTREQUEST, WM_CONVERTRESULT, KKLIB, and other aspects of Kanji Windows.

Andrew Schulman, "Porting DOS Programs to Protected-Mode Windows with the WINDOS Library," *Microsoft Systems Journal*, September-October 1991
Another version of the WINIO library, using LocalXXX calls to implement a Windows version of Microsoft C based-pointer functions.

Andrew Schulman, "The Programming Challenge of Windows Protected Mode," *PC Magazine*, June 25, 1991
Using DPMI and undocumented Windows calls to make undocumented DOS calls. The sort of excruciatingly detailed, long-winded, and tiresome discussion one expects from this author.

Andrew Schulman, "Windows 3.0: All That Memory, All Those Modes," *PC Magazine*, June 11, 1991
A detailed discussion of the amount of memory available under the (then) three modes of Windows.

Andrew Schulman and David Maxey, "Call Standard I/O Functions from Your Windows Code Using the WINIO Library," *Microsoft Systems Journal*, July 1991
Source code for an early version of the WINIO library, with a detailed explanation of how WINIO works.

Andrew Schulman et al., *Undocumented DOS: A Programmer's Guide to Reserved MS-DOS Functions and Data Structures*, Reading MA: Addison-Wesley, 1990, 694 pp., ISBN 0-201-57064-5
Windows sits on top of DOS, and it is often important for Windows programmers to know about DOS internals. It would be self-serving to say anything more about this fine book.

Andrew Schulman, David Maxey, and Matt Pietrek, *Undocumented Windows*, Reading
    MA: Addison-Wesley, 1992
A jumble of material on undocumented functions and internal data structures in KER-
NEL, USER, and GDI. Apparently a second book is planned to cover Windows DLLs such
as SHELL, 16-bit device drivers, 32-bit VxDs, DPMI, interrupts, and other lower-level
aspects of Windows. Contains an extensive bibliography, with only one recursive self-refer-
ence, which one of the coauthors uses just to talk about different books and articles he likes:
some of them don't even have anything to do with Windows!

Andrew Tanenbaum, *Modern Operating Systems*, Englewood Cliffs NJ: Prentice Hall,
    1992, 728 pp., ISBN 0-13-588187-0
An excellent operating-systems textbook, covering both traditional OSs (such as Unix and
MS-DOS) and distributed OSs (such as Mach). There are few explicit mentions of Win-
dows here, but Chapters 2 (Processes) and 3 (Memory Management) are useful back-
ground to KERNEL, and the entirety of Part 2 (Chapters 9-15) are crucial for an
understanding of NT (even though NT is never directly mentioned).

David Thielen, "Behind the Curtain," *Windows Tech Journal*, March 1992, April
    1992, May 1992, June 1992
A continuing series on virtual device drivers (VxDs) and the Virtual Machine Manager
(VMM), by an engineer, and writer from Microsoft. "The opinions expressed in this article
are those of the author and not necessarily (in some cases definitely not) those of Microsoft."

V Communications, *Windows Source Disassembly Pre-Processor*, San Jose CA, April
    1992
The manual contains tutorials on disassembling Windows; the manual's style at times
seems vaguely reminiscent of the writing in Undocumented Windows.

Al Williams, *DOS 5: A Developer's Guide*, Redwood City CA: M&T Books, 1991, 914
    pp., ISBN 1-55851-177-6
Part III (Protected-Mode Techniques) provides a good overview of Virtual-86 (V86)
mode, which Enhanced mode Windows uses. No direct mentions of Windows here, but most
of the material is still relevant.

Al Williams, *Protected-Mode Programming in C*, Reading MA: Addison-Wesley, 1992
    (forthcoming)
Accessing real-mode code, protected-mode interrupt handling, virtual memory, perfor-
mance issues, working with DPMI servers, and so on, both for conventional DOS extenders
and for Windows.

Paul Yao, "Explore Previously Uncharted Areas of Windows Using the ToolHelp
    Library," *Microsoft Systems Journal*, May-June 1992
Contains good conceptual overviews of how tasks, modules, and segments interrelate.

INDEX

X

Y

Z

Attention 5$\frac{1}{4}$" disk drive users:

The disk to accompany *Undocumented Windows* is also available in a 5$\frac{1}{4}$" high density format. Please return the coupon below with a check for $10.00 payable to Addison-Wesley to:

Addison-Wesley Publishing Company
Order Department
1 Jacob Way
Reading, MA 01867-9984

- -

Please send me the 5$\frac{1}{4}$" disk (ISBN 0-201-63286-1) to accompany *Undocumented Windows* by Andrew Schulman, David Maxey, and Matt Pietrek. I am enclosing a check for $10.00.

Name _____

Address _____

City _____ State _____ Zip _____